DEDICATION

To Amit and Amrita, for their love and support.

— Gunnit S. Khurana and Balbir S. Khurana

Message from the
Publisher

WELCOME TO OUR NERVOUS SYSTEM

Some people say that the World Wide Web is a graphical extension of the information superhighway, just a network of humans and machines sending each other long lists of the equivalent of digital junk mail.

I think it is much more than that. To me, the Web is nothing less than the nervous system of the entire planet—not just a collection of computer brains connected together, but more like a billion silicon neurons entangled and recirculating electro-chemical signals of information and data, each contributing to the birth of another CPU and another Web site.

Think of each person's hard disk connected at once to every other hard disk on earth, driven by human navigators searching like Columbus for the New World. Seen this way the Web is more of a super entity, a growing, living thing, controlled by the universal human will to expand, to be more. Yet, unlike a purposeful business plan with rigid rules, the Web expands in a nonlinear, unpredictable, creative way that echoes natural evolution.

We created our Web site not just to extend the reach of our computer book products but to be part of this synaptic neural network, to experience, like a nerve in the body, the flow of ideas and then to pass those ideas up the food chain of the mind. Your mind. Even more, we wanted to pump some of our own creative juices into this rich wine of technology.

TASTE OUR DIGITAL WINE

And so we ask you to taste our wine by visiting the body of our business. Begin by understanding the metaphor we have created for our Web site—a universal learning center, situated in outer space in the form of a space station. A place where you can journey to study any topic from the convenience of your own screen. Right now we are focusing on computer topics, but the stars are the limit on the Web.

If you are interested in discussing this Web site or finding out more about the Waite Group, please send me e-mail with your comments, and I will be happy to respond. Being a programmer myself, I love to talk about technology and find out what our readers are looking for.

Sincerely,

Mitchell Waite

Mitchell Waite, C.E.O. and Publisher

200 Tamal Plaza
Corte Madera, CA 94925
415-924-2575
415-924-2576 fax

Website:
http://www.waite.com/waite

CREATING THE HIGHEST QUALITY COMPUTER BOOKS IN THE INDUSTRY

Waite Group Press

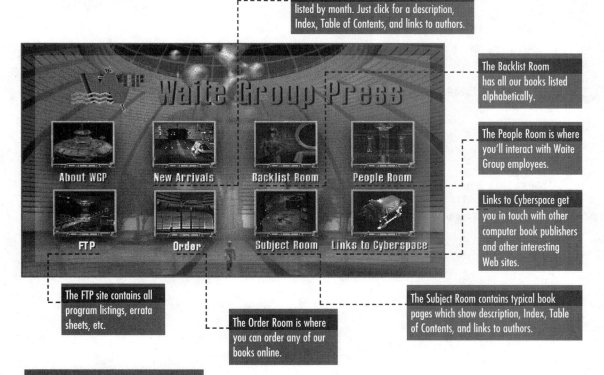

About the Authors

Gunnit S. Khurana has an M.S. in Computer Science from the University of Nebraska, Lincoln. He has been involved with publishing databases on the Web since the standardization of Common Gateway Interface (CGI). He initially worked with World Wide Web servers and CGI programs in the UNIX environment but quickly realized that it was not the easiest way to develop database-oriented Web sites. Being an expert Microsoft Access programmer, he sees great benefits in Windows- and Windows NT-based World Wide Web servers that support Windows CGI, and has employed that combination to rapidly develop various database publishing applications for the Web.

Balbir S. Khurana is a professor in the School of Computer and System Sciences at Jawaharlal Nehru University, New Delhi. He received his B.S. from the University of Roorkee, his M.S. from the University of Rajasthan, and his Ph.D. from the University of Tokyo. During his twenty years of teaching, and ten years of industrial experience, he has developed many teaching aids and construction kits to augment his lectures, mastered the intricacies of the most difficult technical concepts, and developed them in a clear and simple manner. He enjoys exploring the Web and imagining new and creative ways of utilizing this powerful technology.

TABLE OF CONTENTS

CONTENTS

ACKNOWLEDGMENTS

We wish to thank Joanne Miller for initiating this project and Laura Brown for overseeing it to its successful completion. We are grateful to Keith Allison for the book's technical review and for keeping us abreast of the latest technology and software-related developments. We also wish to extend our sincere appreciation to Scott Rhoades for pointing out the grammatical "kinks" in the initial drafts and for helping us enhance the readability of the manuscript. Finally, many thanks to Navtej Pal, Arshdeep, and Raman for assisting in the graphic layout and the HTML coding of the Web applications described in the book.

1

INTRODUCTION

1

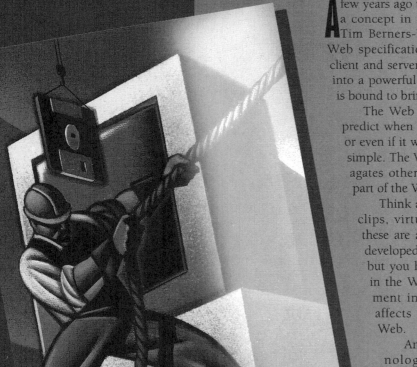

A few years ago the World Wide Web was just a concept in the minds of visionaries like Tim Berners-Lee (who defined the initial Web specifications and wrote the first Web client and server software). Now it has turned into a powerful communication interface that is bound to bring the world closer together.

The Web is still evolving. Nobody can predict when its concept will finally mature or even if it will mature at all. The reason is simple. The Web is a technology that propagates other technologies that become a part of the Web itself.

Think about it! Sound, images, video clips, virtual reality, and databases—these are all examples of independently developed and researched disciplines—but you hear them mentioned together in the Web domain. So, any advancement in any of these areas directly affects the user's perception of the Web.

Among these Web-related technologies, database storage and management is the oldest and currently the most utilized technology. In spite of all its powerful features, database storage and management achieves a new level of applicability when given a Web interface.

Imagine being able to make your databases available to remote places without having to worry about expensive long-distance communication charges or variations in the computer platforms. The Web-database combination has proven that this wish list can be turned into a practical reality.

If you look at the Web-database picture from the other side, you will see that not only the database technology benefits from the Web's universal appeal, but the regular sites on the Web can also utilize a database back-end to automate their information maintenance and presentation tasks.

For example, let's say you are planning to publish a movie catalog through your Web site, and you want to list movies by their theme as well as present an alphabetical index of their titles. If you decide to store your movie catalog as flat HTML-formatted text files, then whenever a new movie is added to your catalog, you have to create a link for that movie on both the theme and the index pages. This link-maintenance task becomes an even greater challenge if you further decide to arrange the movies by their actors, by their release dates, and even by their ratings.

However, by organizing the movie catalog in a database and then dynamically linking that database with your Web site, you can reduce the challenge to a simple matter of adding the new movie and its related attributes to the database only once. Granted, this sounds like a great option, but it requires you to venture into the database territory and learn the Web-database linking techniques.

Wondering how to proceed? Worry no more. In this book, we not only explore the database territory, but also show you how to conquer it. We present one of the easiest approaches to creating the Web-database link you can learn and show you how to apply the information in this book to develop your own practical Web-based database applications.

WHAT THIS BOOK IS ABOUT

This book is about integrating two complementary technologies, the Web and the relational database management system (RDMS), using a glue called the *Windows Common Gateway Interface*. As the title of this book suggests, we explain this integration process through a step-by-step construction kit approach.

Overall, this book is written to explain the following:

- How to create and query a relational database

- The elements of the Web and how they function together

- How data is transferred between a Web site and a Web user

- How the Windows Common Gateway Interface works

- How to link a database with the Web

- How to design commercial-grade Web-based database applications

Underlying all these objectives, we maintain another important objective: *keep it simple*. To do this, we have based the book on three software packages that have acquired high honors for being both powerful and user friendly.

We used O'Reilly & Associates' WebSite™ 1.1 as our Web server (the book includes its evaluation copy on the accompanying CD-ROM and is also available from http://website.ora.com), Microsoft Access 95 as our relational database management system, and Microsoft Visual Basic 4.0 (32-bit Professional version) as our CGI programming language.

Although we have selected these popular packages for our construction kit, the concepts we describe are general in nature and can be applied using other software packages with similar capabilities. For example, most sample applications discussed in this book will run on Netscape, Alibaba, Purveyor, or any other Windows CGI–compatible Web server.

WHO THIS BOOK IS FOR

This book is for you if any of the following thoughts have crossed your mind:

- How do I create HTML pages on-the-fly and send them through my Web site?

- I wish there were an easier way of managing the information than manually updating the HTML pages.

- I don't want to learn Perl or C programming to create CGI applications.

- How can I publish my database over the World Wide Web?

- How do I provide a general-purpose guest book for my Web site?

- How do I conduct a survey through the World Wide Web?

- How do other Web sites provide such fast and flexible search functionality?

- How do I create a Web-based virtual store and an on-line ordering system?

Do not get anxious if you have never dealt with a database management system or created a CGI program before. In both cases, this book works from the ground up. We do assume, though, that you know how to explore the Web and are familiar with at least one programming language, preferably a recent version of Visual Basic.

WHAT YOU GAIN FROM THIS BOOK

Besides acquiring a wealth of Web- and database-related information, you will learn how to design feature-rich Web applications. You will learn concepts, approaches, tricks, and popular techniques used for creating and integrating Microsoft Access databases with the WebSite server.

The sample applications discussed in this book (and provided on the accompanying CD) will give you hands-on experience experimenting with fully functional Web software that utilizes a database back-end. To top all this, you will have access to a powerful Visual Basic utility library (designed by the authors) to help you expedite the process of designing your own Web applications.

HOW THIS BOOK IS ORGANIZED

This book is divided into 18 chapters and two appendixes. Most chapters follow a lesson-oriented format, where each lesson not only describes the concepts, but also presents step-by-step instructions to implement those concepts. Review questions and exercises are provided at the end of each chapter to help you recapitulate the key concepts and mold them toward other situations and practical applications.

Chapter 2, Getting Started, shows how to install the evaluation copy of the WebSite 1.1 Web server software and all the sample Web applications provided on the CD accompanying this book. It then reviews the features and configuration parameters of the WebSite server and finally walks you through two elementary Web applications— GuestBook and On-Line Questionnaire.

Chapter 3, Dissecting a Job Listing System, examines a more advanced Web-based database application called the Job Listing System. This application is an example of how you can connect job seekers and potential employers over the Web.

Chapters 4, 5, and 6 describe the use of Microsoft Access as a relational database management system. Chapter 4, Building a Database with Microsoft Access, shows how to create tables in a Microsoft Access database and deals with important concepts like the primary key, normalization, and referential integrity.

Chapter 5, Building Microsoft Access Queries, introduces the powerful and user-friendly query design interface of Microsoft Access and shows how easily you can create criteria-based queries to search for database information.

Chapter 6, Designing Advanced Queries, illustrates that an Access database is not just useful for searching information, but also for analyzing it. The chapter then describes the various ways of analyzing data through the use of total queries and nested queries. Finally, this chapter shows how to create parameter-based queries, which are heavily used for designing the advanced Web applications described in the book.

The focus of the book changes with Chapter 7, Elements of the World Wide Web, where we cover the details of the Hypertext Transfer Protocol (HTTP) and Hypertext Markup Language (HTML). HTTP is the communication protocol used to transfer data between the Web client and the Web server, whereas HTML is the language that the document writer (one who designs the HTML page) uses to communicate with the document reader (the Web user).

Chapter 8, Creating HTML Forms, explains the use of HTML forms for gathering user data and passing it to the Web server. It covers the different types of input controls you can provide on an HTML form, describing their syntax, function, and applicability.

Chapters 9 and 10 deal with the Windows Common Gateway Interface, by which a Web user can request the services of an external program. The knowledge of the HTTP format discussed in Chapter 7 helps considerably when reading through these chapters.

Chapter 9, Windows Common Gateway Interface, describes how the WebSite server passes user data to an external program. Chapter 10, Windows CGI Output Standard, discusses the various ways an external program can generate a response, and the role of the Web server in sending that response back to the requesting Web user.

All the main concepts examined in the previous chapters are integrated for the first time in Chapter 11, Designing a Windows CGI Application, where you learn how to create an operational but noninteractive Web application.

Chapter 12, Designing a Windows CGI Application to Process Form Data, shows how to add interactivity to a Web application. As a practical example, it describes a step-by-step construction process for designing a guest book application that can manage multiple guest books.

Chapter 13, Utilizing an Access Database in a CGI Application, uncovers the mystery of linking an Access database with a Web application, and describes the Visual Basic objects that allow your Web application to search and retrieve data directly from an Access database.

After reading Chapter 13, you may feel that you can lose some flexibility by creating Web applications through the Windows CGI approach, especially when you have to modify the format of a CGI response. Chapter 14, Processing Template Files with a CGI Application, and Chapter 15, Processing Database Records Through Template Files, highlight the technique of using template files to eliminate this "inflexibility" and describe how you can easily generate CGI responses based on external template files.

Chapters 16, 17, and 18 discuss a feature-rich Web application that simulates a virtual bookstore with the capability of accepting orders and payments on-line. Chapter 16, Creating an On-Line Bookstore, highlights the factors that dictated the application's objectives and explains the implementation of a "Catch of the Day" concept that adds freshness to this virtual bookstore.

Chapter 17, Enhancing the On-Line Bookstore, continues with the discussion of the bookstore application and covers its powerful keyword and concept search feature, which uses the word-indexing technique to achieve speed and flexibility.

Chapter 18, Setting Up an On-Line Ordering System, concentrates on the issues involved with creating a Web-based ordering system and shows how the on-line bookstore application follows a shopping-basket approach to allow Web users to order books while they are browsing through the virtual bookstore.

Appendix A, Organization of Files on the CD, describes how the shareware programs, book examples, and sample Web applications are stored on the CD.

Appendix B, Source Code of the UTILS.BAS Library, lists the documented source code of the Visual Basic utility library developed by the authors and used heavily in this book.

A FINAL NOTE

As mentioned earlier, to keep things simple, we chose a Web-database solution that relies on an approach known as Windows Common Gateway Interface (Windows CGI). Compared with alternative approaches such as standard CGI or Web server application programming interface (Server API), Windows CGI has been criticized as falling short on performance-related issues.

However, it has been our experience that unless performance is your only concern, the rapid application development and the ease of debugging made possible by Windows CGI (details explained in Chapter 9) stand out as important factors in today's information age, where the time required for implementing a product is as critical as the overall efficiency of that product.

Furthermore, if your server machine is equipped with adequate RAM (32MB for Windows 95 and 64MB for Windows NT), the performance shortcoming of Windows CGI tends to become negligible when weighed against the overall performance of a Web application. As a result, in this book, we mainly concentrate on concepts and techniques that use the powerful information storage and retrieval capabilities of a database engine to design practical and efficient Web applications.

We hope you enjoy reading this book as much as we enjoyed writing it!

2
GETTING STARTED

2

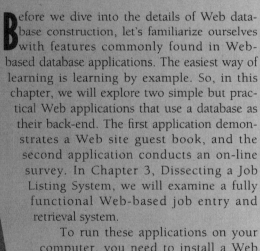

Before we dive into the details of Web database construction, let's familiarize ourselves with features commonly found in Web-based database applications. The easiest way of learning is learning by example. So, in this chapter, we will explore two simple but practical Web applications that use a database as their back-end. The first application demonstrates a Web site guest book, and the second application conducts an on-line survey. In Chapter 3, Dissecting a Job Listing System, we will examine a fully functional Web-based job entry and retrieval system.

To run these applications on your computer, you need to install a Web server that supports a special standard called *Windows CGI*. Chapter 9, Windows Common Gateway Interface, describes this standard in detail. WebSite™ from O'Reilly & Associates is one such popular Web server that completely supports Windows CGI. It even provides a Visual Basic library module and various debugging options for designing applications that use Windows CGI.

All Web applications described in this book are based on the WebSite server and utilize its Visual Basic library. The CD-ROM accompanying this book contains an evaluation copy of the WebSite server.

This chapter begins by reviewing the features of the WebSite server. It then shows how to install its evaluation copy from the accompanying CD-ROM and describes its configuration parameters that prove useful when designing Web applications. Later, this chapter shows how to set up the programs and libraries discussed in this book and walks you through two Web applications: GuestBook and On-Line Questionnaire.

NOTE: We recommend that you first follow the examples in this book with the evaluation version of the WebSite server supplied with this book. After you are comfortable with the concepts, you can then port the examples and the sample applications to run with another Web server, such as Alibaba, also included on the book's CD-ROM. You will find that porting these applications to other Windows CGI–compatible Web servers is a relatively easy task and in most cases does not require any other step except moving the files to a different directory.

FEATURES OF THE WEBSITE WWW SERVER

The WebSite WWW server is a 32-bit multithreaded server designed to run on Windows 95 and Windows NT systems. This server extends the fame of its Windows 3.1-based predecessor, WIN-HTTPD, which brought the ability of World Wide Web publishing to PC users without compromising any powerful features traditionally found in its UNIX counterparts. The evaluation copy of the WebSite server package supplied on the CD (version 1.1e) includes the following additional tools and programs:

- Map This! imagemap editor

- Server Admin configuration utility for the WebSite server (listed as "Server Properties" in the WebSite's program group)

- WebView Web site management program

- WebIndex and WebFind full text indexing and searching tools

WebSite is a robust and efficient server capable of delivering over 100,000 transactions per hour on a single CPU Pentium over a full T-1 connection. Its developer, Robert Denny, is known for his prompt technical support over the Usenet newsgroup *comp.infosystems.www.servers.ms-windows* as well as over a dedicated mailing list whose subscription information is available at *http://www.ora.com/archives/website-talk/*. Some highlights of the WebSite server included in this demo package are described next.

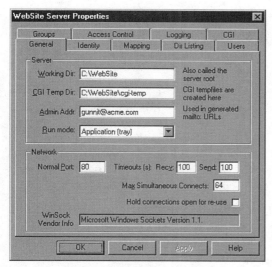

Figure 2-1 WebSite Server Admin utility

Easy To Configure

All configuration parameters of the WebSite server can be set through the *Server Admin utility* that groups these parameters into appropriate categories and provides a user-friendly graphical interface to display and configure those parameters. Figure 2-1 shows how the Server Admin utility appears when launched. The "Administering WebSite" section later in this chapter describes the important configuration settings and how to use the Server Admin utility.

Running External Programs

The WebSite server allows you to execute external programs and make them part of your Web site. For this, it supports three Common Gateway Interface (CGI) standards to run a Windows-, DOS-, or a script-based application. Through these external programs, you can provide search facilities and process forms. Design of these external programs using the Windows CGI standard is one of the main topics covered in this book. The two applications presented at the end of this chapter demonstrate how you can add interactivity to your Web site through the use of Windows CGI programs.

Mapping Support

WebSite supports the following main types of mappings to help you easily manage your documents and extend the capabilities of your server.

 Document mapping lets you map a *URL (universal resource locator)* path to a physical directory location of your computer. A URL path defines the logical Web location of a file or information resource. The "Document Mapping" section of this chapter covers this mapping in more detail.

 Redirect mapping lets you redirect one URL to another URL, generally on another server. See the "Redirect Mapping" section for further information on how to define and use this mapping.

 CGI mapping performs document mapping and lets you associate a URL to a specific type of executable program (Windows-, DOS-, or script-based). The section "CGI Mapping" describes the three types of CGI mappings in more detail.

 Content type mapping allows you to describe your documents in the standard MIME (Multipurpose Internet Mail Extensions) format. The Web browser uses the document's MIME type to appropriately display the document. The section "Content Type Mapping" provides more explanation on this mapping.

Multiple Web Identity Support

You can assign multiple *Web identities* (also known as *virtual servers*) to the WebSite server. For example, with the appropriate configuration parameters, one running copy of WebSite can serve separate home pages for the *http://www.acme.com* and the *http://www.foo.com* Web addresses. The only requirement is that each Web address must have its own distinct IP address.

The explanation of how to configure the WebSite server to support multiple Web identities is beyond the scope of this book. You can consult the on-line help provided with the Server Admin configuration utility (described later in Lesson 2, Administering WebSite) for more information on this topic.

Access and Error Logs

The WebSite server automatically records every request it tried to serve into an *access log file* (or separate log files if the server is configured with multiple Web identities) that follows the common log format established by the NCSA (National Center for Supercomputing Applications) and CERN (Conseil Europeen pour la Recherche Nucleaire). If an error is generated while it is processing a request, the server makes an entry in a separate error log.

You can analyze the access log to gather information on which sites got connected to your server, what type of documents were being requested, how busy your server was, and so on. Figure 2-2 shows a few entries from the access log created by WebSite.

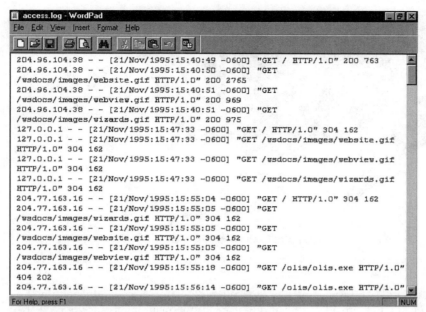

Figure 2–2 A sample of WebSite's access log

Each entry in the access log contains the following information:

- Internet address of the user requesting the document

- Date, time, and type of the request

- Document being requested

- Server's response to that request

- Amount of data transferred in response to a request

The "Logging Section Parameters" section describes how to set the file paths for the various log files. The discussion of the exact syntax of the access log entry format and how to analyze that information is beyond the scope of this book.

Built-In Imagemap Processing

The WebSite server has the capability to internally process imagemaps. An imagemap is a region-sensitive image that makes your server perform different actions based on which part of that image a user clicks on.

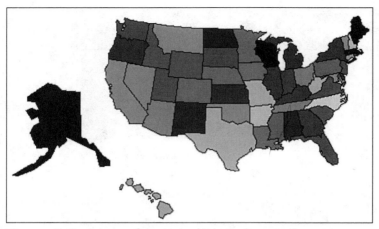

Figure 2-3 A map of the United States showing the state boundaries

Imagemaps are a powerful way of presenting location-based information. For example, if you want to provide a directory service for the main home page of each state of the United States, you can convert a U.S. map with state boundaries, similar to the one shown in Figure 2-3, into an imagemap where clicking on any state takes the user to the home page of that state.

Some more uses of imagemaps are as follows:

Creating attractive menus to provide selection choices

Simulating a zoom facility to present portions of an image in more detail, such as when describing various organs of a human body or components of a machine

WebSite comes with an imagemap editor through which you can quickly overlap transparent rectangles, ellipses, or polygons on your image and associate an action with each region. This book does not cover the details of how to use the imagemap editor to create imagemaps. You can consult the on-line help provided with the imagemap editor for more information.

Automatic Directory Indexes

The WebSite server can automatically create an index of a directory requested by a Web browser if that directory does not contain a default home page. Figure 2-4 shows a sample directory index returned by the WebSite server.

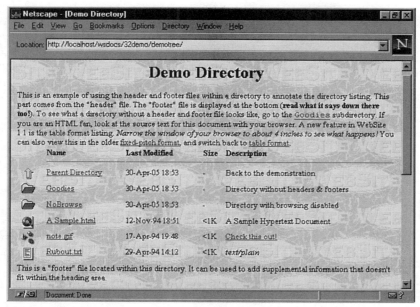

Figure 2–4 Directory index created by the WebSite server

As evident from this figure, the files can also have descriptions and icons associated to them.

You can use the directory index feature of the WebSite server to allow users to easily fetch files from your computer through their Web browsers. This book does not cover the process of creating directory indexes. The Mapping category of the Server Admin utility contains all the parameters for configuring directory indexes, and the on-line help provided with the Server Admin utility gives a detailed explanation of these parameters.

Site Security

There is tremendous flexibility offered by the WebSite server to help secure your documents. You can control access to any part of your Web site in the following ways:

- By user
- By group of users
- By Web client's Internet name
- By Web client's Internet address
- Any combination of the preceding

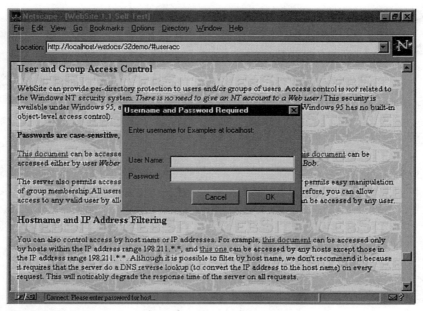

Figure 2-5 Browser asking for user authentication

As an example, if you restrict a document or a directory containing that document to a specific set of users, then the WebSite server prompts the browser to ask for a user name and password anytime a user tries to access that document as shown in Figure 2-5.

To add access control to your Web site, the Server Admin utility provides three sections: Users, Groups, and Access Control. The discussion of these sections is beyond the scope of this book. The book that accompanies the commercial version of WebSite, *Building Your Own WebSite,* dedicates a chapter to this topic. You can also use the on-line help of the Server Admin utility to guide you through the process of establishing access control.

Server-Side Includes

WebSite supports the powerful Server-Side Include (SSI) feature that allows you to dynamically insert data from various sources into an HTML document. Using the built-in SSI directives, you can easily add access counters, current date and time, and the contents of other files to your HTML page. You can even insert CGI variables (described in Chapter 9, Windows Common Gateway Interface) and the output of external CGI programs with the SSI feature.

Although the explanation of the Server-Side Include feature is beyond the scope of this book, Chapter 14, Processing Template Files with a CGI Application, carries a brief discussion on the SSI feature's CGI-related capabilities.

LESSON 1: INSTALLING THE EVALUATION VERSION OF WEBSITE

Follow the steps described in this lesson to install and test the evaluation copy of the WebSite server supplied with the CD-ROM accompanying this book. After evaluating this product, you may purchase the commercial version of WebSite (or any other Web server supporting Windows CGI).

STEP 1: Complete the Prerequisites

The following requirements must be met to install and run the WebSite server.

Hardware

The hardware requirements are as follows:

- 80486 or higher microprocessor; Pentium recommended
- 16MB RAM; 32MB recommended
- 10MB free hard disk space
- CD-ROM drive (local or accessible through your local area network)

Software and Connectivity

The software and connectivity requirements are as follows:

- Windows 95 or Windows NT 3.51 with long file names enabled
- TCP/IP protocol stack installed and running (even if your PC is not connected to any TCP/IP network)

Tools and Utilities

To follow the examples and exercises described in this book, you also need the following application development tools and programs:

- A WWW client that supports HTML tables and other HTML 3 extensions, such as Netscape or Internet Explorer
- Visual Basic 4.0 development environment (32-bit Professional version)
- Microsoft Access 95 (version 7.0)

STEP 2: Setting Up WebSite

To run WebSite's Setup program residing in the directory \SHAREWAR\WEBSITE\ of the accompanying CD-ROM:

1. Insert the CD provided with this book in your CD-ROM drive, here assumed to be your D drive.

2. Start the WebSite Setup Wizard by running the following program:

```
D:\SHARWARE\WEBSITE\WEBSITE.EXE
```

3. The Setup program asks if you want to install the WebSite server.

4. Press Yes to confirm the installation process.

5. The program starts the InstallShield Wizard and displays the Welcome screen as shown in Figure 2-6.

6. Click on the Next button to proceed with the installation.

7. The Setup program displays the license agreement.

8. Read through the agreement and click on the Yes button to proceed with the rest of the setup. The Setup program then asks for the location of the installation directory. It shows C:\WEBSITE as the default directory.

9. Click on the Next button to select the default value for the installation directory.

Figure 2–6 First screen of WebSite Setup Wizard

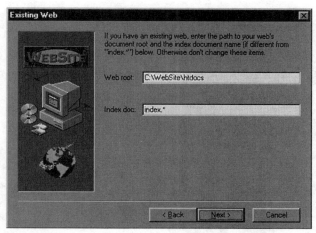

Figure 2-7 Setup program asking for Web root and index document information

NOTE: For simplicity, some Web applications described in this book assume that WebSite is installed in the C:\WEBSITE directory. Hence, we strongly recommend that you keep C:\WEBSITE as the installation directory.

10. The Setup program then asks for the path of the document root directory and the file-name pattern of the index documents as shown in Figure 2-7. It gives C:\WEBSITE\HTDOCS and INDEX.* as the default values for these fields. Select the default options by clicking on the Next button.

11. A document *root directory* is the directory that is mapped to the first slash of a URL path. So, when the Web server gets a request for the following URL:

`http://YourServerName/`

it tries to deliver the index document located in the document root directory. If you chose the default values for the document root directory and the index document, then the server will try to deliver the first file matching the file path C:\WEBSITE\HTDOCS\INDEX.* to the requesting client.

12. If the index document is missing, then the server returns a directory index of the document root directory (unless the directory index option is turned off for this directory).

13. In the next screen, the Setup program asks if you want to start the server manually or automatically. Since you will need to run the server to follow this book, we recommend you select the Automatic option and then click on the Next button.

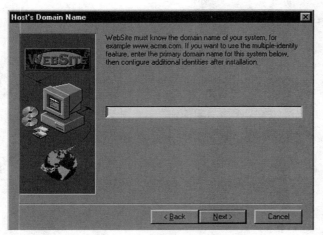

Figure 2–8 Setup program asking for the Internet name

14. The Setup program then asks for your machine's Internet name as shown in Figure 2-8.

15. Specify the fully qualified domain name of your machine for the Internet name field, and click on the Next button. A *fully qualified domain name* is a unique name that identifies your computer on the Internet. It is listed in the format *hostname.domainname*. If your PC does not have a fully qualified domain name yet, then specify *localhost* for the Internet name in the setup. You can always change this setting later from the Server Admin utility, as explained in the section "General Section Parameters" of the next lesson.

16. As the last installation option, Setup asks for your e-mail address as shown in Figure 2-9. Specify your Internet e-mail address in the e-mail address field, and click on the Next button.

17. The setup then installs the WebSite server (HTTPD32.EXE) and all related files and subdirectories in the C:\WEBSITE directory. After the installation is complete, it gives you an option of displaying the Readme file and automatically launching your Web server. We recommend that you go through the contents of the Readme file and launch the server at this point by clicking on the Finish button.

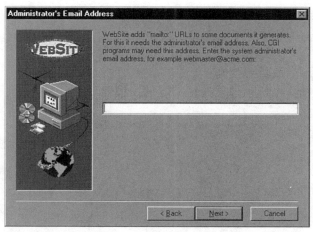

Figure 2–9 Setup program asking for the administrator's e-mail address

NOTE: The Setup program creates a program group named "WebSite 1.1," which contains icons that you can click on to launch the WebSite server, Server Admin utility (labeled "Server Properties"), and other programs that are included in the WebSite evaluation package.

STEP 3: Testing the WebSite Server

To test whether the server is functioning correctly, start the WebSite server on your PC (if it is not already running) and specify the following location on your Web client:

```
http://Your_PCs_Internet_Name/
```

NOTE: You can use *localhost* for the Internet name if your PC does not have an assigned Internet name.

If everything is installed correctly, you should see the home page (C:\WEBSITE\HTDOCS\INDEX.HTML-SSI) returned by your WebSite server as shown in Figure 2-10.

Figure 2–10 Initial home page of your WebSite server

If you do not see a home page, try the following:

1. Check whether the TCP/IP stack is installed on your computer by viewing the Network settings from your control panel.

NOTE: If you are able to connect to other servers through your Web client, then your TCP/IP stack is configured properly.

2. Check whether the Web server is running. Press <ALT>-<TAB> to display the icons of each running program, and then tab through each icon to locate the Web server. If the Web server is not running, try restarting it from the WebSite 1.1 demo group.

3. View the file C:\WEBSITE\LOGS\ERROR.LOG by using the Notepad application. It may give some hints on why the server may not be starting.

4. Reinstall WebSite by repeating the instructions listed in the previous section, "Setting Up WebSite."

5. Post an article on the Internet in the Usenet newsgroup:

```
comp.infosystems.www.servers.ms-windows
```

Hopefully, some kind soul will help you bring up your home page.

6. Purchase the commercial version from *http://website.ora.com* and get technical support.

STEP 4: Demonstrating the Server Features

From the home page shown in Figure 2-10, click on the Server Self-Test And Demonstration link. Your browser now displays a document (see Figure 2-11) that demonstrates various features of the WebSite server described earlier in this chapter. You can go through the links on this page and familiarize yourself with the server's features at this point.

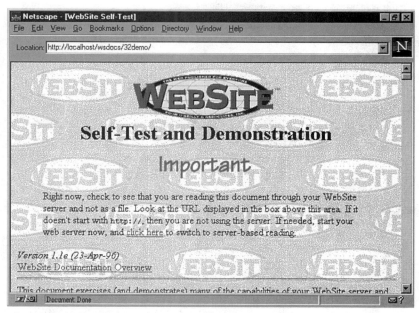

Figure 2–11 WebSite server's self-test page

Finally, if your computer is connected to the Internet, you can also check the link pointing to WebSite Central (*http://website.ora.com/*) for the latest news, technical support, and other related information about WebSite.

LESSON 2: ADMINISTERING WEBSITE

The Server Admin utility included with the WebSite server contains nine sections that can be configured for administering the server. Table 2-1 lists these sections and their purpose.

Table 2-1 List of sections in the Server Admin utility

Section	Purpose
General	Setting the basic information about the WebSite server
Identity	Configuring multiple Web identities
Mapping	Establishing document, CGI, and other mappings
Dir Listings	Configuring automatic directory indexes and defining default docs
Users	Adding user names, passwords, and assigning users to groups
Groups	Creating user groups
Access Control	Securing a URL path by users, groups, IP addresses, and host names
Logging	Specifying the path and name of log files and setting server tracing options
CGI	Fine-tuning the CGI process

Here we review only those sections and parameters of the Server Admin utility that are important in creating database applications for your Web site. You can refer to the on-line help provided with the Server Admin utility for details on the configuration settings not discussed in this section.

At this point, you can double-click on the Server Properties icon in the WebSite 1.1 program group to launch the Server Admin utility. It should display the parameters in the general section. (See Figure 2-1 in the section "Features of the WebSite WWW Server.")

General Section Parameters

The general section parameters will be discussed next.

Working Dir

The *working directory* is the directory relative to which all other file and directory paths in the Server Admin utility can be defined. It is also called the *server root directory*. By default, the working directory is the same as the WebSite's installation directory (C:\WEBSITE\).

CGI Temp Dir

The WebSite server uses the *CGI TEMP directory* to store all the temporary files created during a Windows CGI session. The role of this directory is discussed in Chapter 9, Windows Common Gateway Interface.

Admin Addr

This field holds the e-mail address of the WebSite server administrator. This e-mail address is automatically shown by the server to a Web user if the server encounters any error in processing that user's request.

Run Mode

This option is enabled if WebSite is running on a Windows NT platform. It has three choices:

- Desktop application
- System service with icon
- System service without icon

Normal Port

This option makes the WebSite server listen on the TCP port shown in this field. The default value is set to *80,* which is the port used by a client when no port number is specifically listed in the requested URL. If you want to specify any other value besides 80 for the TCP port, then we recommend you use a value greater than 1024. The port numbers below 1024 are used for other standard Internet services such as FTP, Gopher, and Telnet.

   One reason for using a different TCP port number is to prevent general-public access to your server, since most outside users will not know which port number your server is listening on. This does not prevent any user from connecting to your server, it just reduces the chances of a random Web user accessing your Web site. For complete security, you will need to use the WebSite server's access control feature.

Recv and Send Timeouts

Again, these are standard settings that generally should be left as they are. You may increase the timeouts to 60 seconds if your server is running on a slow PPP/SLIP connection.

Maximum Simultaneous Connects

This parameter limits the number of simultaneous connections that the server will accept. You use this to guarantee a minimum speed for each active connection. This is most important for slower lines (56K and below). You can click on this section's Help button to list the recommended values for different line speeds.

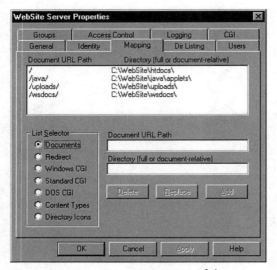

Figure 2-12 Mapping section of the Server Admin utility

Hold Connections Open For Re-use

This parameter instructs the server to keep a connection alive so that a Web browser can request multiple documents in the same connection.

Winsock Vendor Info

This option shows all the Winsock-compliant TCP/IP stacks detected on your computer. This setting is for information only and cannot be changed.

Mapping Section Parameters

Click on the Mapping tab in the Server Admin utility to display its mapping section. (See Figure 2-12.)

The mapping section lets you specify seven types of mappings using the following elements of the section:

A List Selector box that lets you select the mapping you want to work with

A rectangular window called the *mapping window* that displays the object pairs participating in the currently selected mapping

Two input fields through which you specify the objects that need to be mapped

Command buttons to add, change, or remove a mapping between objects

Next, we discuss the purpose of each type of mapping except Directory Icon mapping (it is not relevant to the subject of this book) and show how to associate objects through them.

Document Mapping

A *document mapping* is created between a URL path (or a portion of a URL path) and a physical directory location on your system.

A *URL path* is the information specified after the server name (or IP address) in a URL. For example, a URL path for the URL

```
http://Your_Server_Name/server/support/logcycle.txt
```

is

```
/server/support/logcycle.txt
```

As a rule, your server considers a URL path to be the file path relative to the document root directory (C:\WEBSITE\HTDOCS). So, for the URL in the previous example, your WebSite server will try to fetch the file

```
C:\WEBSITE\HTDOCS\SERVER\SUPPORT\LOGCYCLE.TXT
```

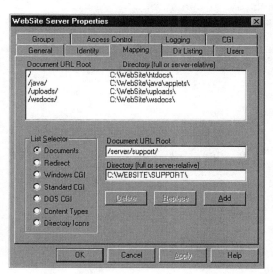

Figure 2–13 Creating a document mapping

The document mapping lets you overwrite this default URL path to directory path association with your own mapping. Let's say you want the server to return the icon file C:\WEBSITE\SUPPORT\LOGCYCLE.TXT for the URL listed in the previous example. You can tell the WebSite server to start from the directory C:\WEBSITE\SUPPORT\ anytime it encounters a URL path beginning with "/server/support/" by creating a document mapping. Refer to Figure 2-13 and follow these steps to create this document mapping:

1. Click on the Documents option in the List Selector box if that option is not already selected.

2. Click on the Document URL Root input field, and type */server/support/* in the field.

3. Click on the Directory (Full Or Server-Relative) input field, and type *C:\WEBSITE\SUPPORT* in the field.

4. Click on the Add button to add this document mapping.

5. Click on the OK button to close the Server Admin utility.

NOTE: If your Web server was running when you closed the Server Admin utility, it will beep after a few seconds, indicating that it has accepted the new configuration settings. You do not need to shut down the server and restart it.

To test whether the document mapping you added is correct and active:

1. Start the WebSite server if it is not already running.

2. From your Web client, specify the following URL:

```
http://localhost/server/support/logcycle.txt
```

3. Your browser should display the contents of the LOGCYCLE.TXT file residing in the C:\WEBSITE\SUPPORT\ directory.

Absolute and Relative Directory Paths

In a document mapping, you can specify an *absolute* path for the directory location or a path *relative* to the server working directory (C:\WEBSITE\). If you refer to Figure 2-13, you will see that the URL path / is mapped to C:\WEBSITE\HTDOCS\, which indicates an absolute directory path. You can achieve the same result by mapping the URL path / to HTDOCS\ (and not \HTDOCS\). The absence of the first backslash tells the server that it is a relative path.

How the Server Determines Which Mapping to Apply

If there are many mappings that may match a URL path, the server uses the mapping matching the longest portion of the URL path. For example, if you have the following two document mappings:

```
/users/ <==> C:\USERS\
/users/bob <==> C:\USERS\ROBERT\
```

and you specify the URL path *lusers/bob/picture.gif*, the server will try to retrieve the file C:\USERS\ROBERT\PICTURE.GIF.

Changing the Document Root Directory

You can assign a different directory as the document root directory by changing the mapping for the URL path / as described next:

1. Click on the mapping of / in the mapping window.

2. Specify the new document directory (in a relative or absolute path) in the Directory field.

3. Click on the Replace button and then the OK button.

Serving Documents Residing on Many Computers

You can use document mapping to serve documents residing on other computers through one URL hierarchy. For example, if your colleagues want to serve their home pages through your server but enjoy the flexibility of maintaining the pages from their computer, you can share their home page directories from your computer and map them to a URL path hierarchy as shown in the following example:

```
/home/jim/ <==> \\JIMMY\C\WWW\
/home/mary/ <==> \\MARRY_PC\C\WEBDOCS\
```

Redirect Mapping

Redirect mapping lets you reassign a URL to another URL (possibly leading to another Web server). When your WebSite server receives a request for a redirected URL, it tells the browser to go to the new URL. The user generally is unaware that this redirection has taken place.

You can use redirection mapping if some of your documents become inaccessible due to a network-connection or hard-disk failure, and you want to temporarily redirect the URLs leading to those documents to a URL that explains the current problem. By default, WebSite does not carry any redirect mappings.

CGI Mapping

WebSite allows three types of CGI mappings: Windows, Standard, and DOS. These CGI mappings let you map a URL path to the location of a CGI directory. A *CGI directory* contains programs and scripts that the server should execute if it encounters a URL containing the CGI-mapped URL path.

Purpose of CGI Mapping

The normal role of the WebSite server is to deliver document files (whether text or images) to the Web browser. However, your server is also capable of executing external programs and delivering their output to the Web client using the CGI.

To distinguish between executable programs and regular document files, the server requires that these programs be present in their own directories. By default, the following subdirectories of the working directory are assigned for the three types of executable programs:

- CGI-WIN for Windows programs, assigned to URL path /cgi-win/

- CGI-BIN for scripts based on a scripting language such as PERL, assigned to URL paths /cgi-bin/ and /cgi-shl

- CGI-DOS for DOS programs, assigned to URL path /cgi-dos/

As an example, if your server receives the following URL request:

```
http://Your_Server_Name/cgi-win/cgitest.exe
```

it executes the Windows program C:\WEBSITE\CGI-WIN\CGITEST.EXE and returns the output of this program to the browser. On the other hand, if the CGITEST.EXE program file resides in the C:\WEBSITE\CGI-WIN\HTDOCS directory and the following URL is requested:

```
http://Your_Server_Name/cgitest.exe
```

the server simply delivers the executable code of this program to the Web client.

NOTE: You can apply a special content type mapping, as explained in the section "Content Type Mapping" later in this chapter, to make the server execute the CGITEST.EXE file even when it is residing in the HTDOCS directory.

Creating a CGI Mapping

To create a CGI mapping:

1. Select the CGI mapping type from the List Selector box.

2. Follow the steps described in the "Document Mapping" section to associate a URL path to a CGI directory location.

CGI Mapping and Subdirectories... When you mark a directory as a CGI-type directory, the server automatically considers its subdirectories as part of that CGI-type mapping.

Content Type Mapping

A content type mapping associates a file extension to a content type. A *content type* classifies a document and is defined using the MIME (Multipurpose Internet Mail Extensions) format. A MIME format contains a main type and a subtype, separated by a forward slash (/). For example, a plain text document generally has a MIME content type of *text/plain,* whereas an HTML document is classified with a MIME content type of *text/html.*

You can refer to the Resource Center section at *http://website.ora.com/* for a comprehensive list of accepted MIME types.

Purpose of Content Types

When a Web client requests a document from your WebSite server, the server not only sends that document file, but also passes the content type of that document. The server is able to determine the content type based on that document's file extension and the content type mappings. The Web client uses the content type supplied by the server to appropriately display that document.

If the Web client is not programmed to handle a particular content type by itself, it checks its configuration settings to see if the user has configured an external application for that content type. If no application is configured to handle that content type, then the Web client takes some default action, such as giving the user an option to save that file.

NOTE: If the server cannot match a file extension of a document to any content type mapping, it does not send any content type information with that document. It is up to the Web client as to how it should handle a document with no attached content type information.

Also, if a server is sending the output of a CGI program, then it is the responsibility of that program to provide the content type of the output.

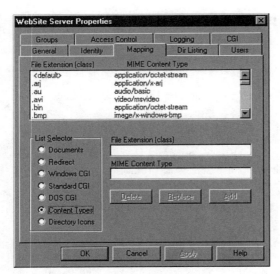

Figure 2-14 Content type mappings

Adding a New Content Type

By default, the WebSite server includes the content type mappings for almost 50 types of file extensions. Figure 2-14 shows some of the predefined content type mappings.

Even though the default mappings are sufficient to classify most types of documents served over the Web, there are times when you may have to add a new content type mapping. Let's say your friend brings you a number of *.DAT files, claiming that they are HTML-formatted data files, and wants you to publish them through your Web site. The easiest way to correctly present these files to Web clients is if you map the .DAT extension to the content type *text/html* as follows:

1. Run the Server Admin utility, and click on the Mapping tab.

2. Click on the Content Types option in the List Selector box.

3. Click on the File Extension (Class) input field, and type *.dat* in the field.

4. Click on the MIME Content Type input field, and type *text/html* in the field.

5. Click on the Add button to add this content type mapping.

6. Click on the OK button to close the Server Admin utility and apply the new settings.

CGI Programs and Content Types

As described earlier in the "CGI Mappings" section, the WebSite server determines whether a file is a CGI program by checking if that file resides in a CGI directory. This also means that if you place a regular document file in a CGI directory, the server assumes that file to be a CGI program. To keep CGI programs and regular documents in the same directory and maintain their proper identities, the WebSite server provides three special content types:

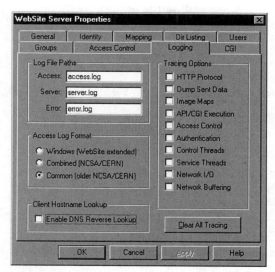

wwwserver/wincgi for Windows CGI programs

wwwserver/shellcgi for standard shell scripts

wwwserver/doscgi for DOS-based CGI programs

You can map special file extensions to these content types and keep the CGI programs with those file extensions in a non-CGI directory. For example, if you create a content type mapping between .WIN and *wwwserver/wincgi* and design a Windows CGI application named TEST.WIN, the server always tries to run this application regardless of which directory this file resides under.

Figure 2-15 Logging section of the Web Server Admin utility

Logging Section Parameters

The parameters in the logging section control the type of information you want the server to log during its operation. These parameters are further consolidated into subsections in the Server Admin utility. To display the logging section of the Server Admin utility as shown in Figure 2-15:

1. Run the Server Admin utility.

2. Using the navigation buttons next to the tabs, scroll to the Logging tab.

3. Click on the Logging tab to display the Logging section.

The subsections of the Logging section are described next.

Log File Paths

This section lets you specify the file paths of the three logs maintained by the server:

 Access log, which records the completed requests made to the server and their corresponding response codes, is by default kept in the file ACCESS.LOG.

 Server log, which traces the information generated by the options marked in the Tracing Options subsection, is by default kept in the file SERVER.LOG.

 Error log, which logs the errors that occurred while processing requests, is by default maintained in the file ERROR.LOG.

If you do not specify a directory path for these log files, the WebSite server stores them in the C:\WEBSITE\LOGS\ directory. If you delete a log file, the server automatically creates a new log file the next time it is started. The server also clears the server log each time it starts.

Cycling Logs... By changing the log file directories at the beginning of every month, you can create a month-to-month history of access logs. The WebSite server also recognizes special URL paths, */~cycle-acc*, */~cycle-err*, and */~cycle-both*, to start a new log in the same logging directory and gives the previous logs a numbered file extension, as in ACCESS.001, and so on. Refer to the URL *http://localhost/wsdocs/32demo/#admin* for more details on how to use these special URL paths.

Client Hostname Lookup

By default, the WebSite server records the IP address of the requesting clients in its access log. If you check the Enable DNS Reverse Lookup option, the server tries to determine the fully qualified domain name of the client and stores that name instead of the client's IP address. Be careful when setting this option as the reverse lookup can decrease the server performance.

Tracing Options

The tracing options dictate what information the server provides in the server log. You can enable the appropriate tracing options to troubleshoot your server if it appears to function incorrectly. Brief descriptions of the tracing options are provided next:

🌱 HTTP Protocol—The server traces incoming requests, translation of URL to file paths, and the request action. The HTTP protocol is described in Chapter 7, Elements of the World Wide Web.

🌱 Dump Sent Data—This option produces a hex/ASCII dump of all data sent by the server to the client. This and the HTTP protocol option together can help detect the cause of any problem between a client and your server.

🌱 Image Maps—This option traces the operation of the imagemapping process, including the location coordinates sent by the client when the user clicked an imagemap, and the result returned by the server.

🌱 API/CGI Execution—This option records the server's handling of all CGI programs, including the command line used to launch the program, and the server's processing of the results that come back from the CGI program. Chapter 12, Designing a Windows CGI Application to Process Form Data, shows how to use this tracing option for debugging Windows CGI applications.

🌱 Access Control—This option traces the actions taken by the server for access control, showing access control path searching, user authentication requirements, IP address filtering, and host name filtering.

🌱 Authentication—This option traces all attempts at user name and password validation.

🌱 Control Threads, Service Threads, Network I/O, and Network Buffering—These options provide traces of threads and network input/output. These options are mainly used by the technical support staff for diagnosing server performance and other operational and network-related problems.

LESSON 3: INSTALLING THE SAMPLE APPLICATIONS

The accompanying CD-ROM also contains the sample applications discussed in this chapter and the rest of the book. To set up these sample applications from the CD-ROM (assumed to be your D drive) on your C drive:

1. Go to an MS-DOS prompt.

2. Copy the directory D:\CGIAPPS\HTDOCS\BOOK\ and all its subdirectories and files to the directory C:\WEBSITE\HTDOCS\ by issuing the following MS-DOS command:

```
xcopy d:\cgiapps\htdocs\*.* c:\website\htdocs /s
```

3. Copy the directory D:\CGIAPPS\CGI-WIN\BOOK\ and all its subdirectories and files to the directory C:\WEBSITE\CGI-WIN\ by issuing the following MS-DOS command:

```
xcopy d:\cgiapps\cgi-win\*.* c:\website\cgi-win /s
```

4. Copy the files under the directory D:\LIB\ to the directory C:\WEBSITE\LIB\ by issuing the following MS-DOS command:

```
xcopy d:\lib\*.* c:\website\lib\*.* /s
```

NOTE: We recommend you use the XCOPY command instead of the Windows 95 Explorer (or File Manager in the case of Windows NT) to copy all the files from the CD as shown in these steps. The use of the XCOPY command ensures that all files have read/write permission after they get copied. Whenever you use Explorer or File Manager to copy files from a CD, all files are copied as read-only.

5. Start your WebSite server if it is not already running.

6. To test if the sample applications are working, start your Web client and enter the following location:

```
http://localhost/book/chap2/chap2.htm
```

7. Your Web client should display a page with links to the guest book and questionnaire applications as shown in Figure 2-16.

The GuestBook Application

The guest book is a favorite feature among Web sites. It acts as an interactive medium for finding out more about their visitors and for getting their feedback. However, it is up to each Web site how it saves the information provided by its visitors. Many just append the new information to an ASCII file and provide a link to view that file.

The GuestBook application we look at here keeps the same basic guest book functionality, except it uses a database to store all the information. You will find out in the next three lessons how the use of the database helps the application monitor and maintain the guest book.

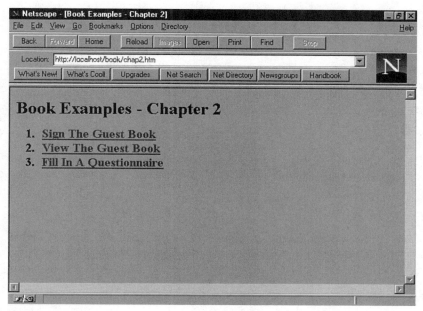

Figure 2–16 Main menu of the applications discussed in this chapter

The On-Line Questionnaire

An on-line questionnaire is another popular Web application that takes advantage of input forms and the CGI capability of the Web server. The Internet, being a large community of diverse individuals, is an ideal place for collecting information. In fact, there are many Web sites, such as *www.survey.net*, devoted to gathering demographics and opinions on various issues through on-line questionnaires.

Questionnaires generally involve questions that can be answered with a yes or a no (as in *Are you currently employed?*) or an answer may be picked from a given list of options (for example, *What income range do you fall under?*). Fortunately, there are special form controls for Web applications that can facilitate responses to such types of questions.

In addition to accepting user feedback, most on-line Web-based survey applications also provide a way to view an analysis of that feedback. While some Web applications require manual intervention or present an interval-based analysis (one that is generated at regular intervals), the advanced Web applications can provide the most up-to-date analysis that includes the data from the most recent feedback.

The sample On-Line Questionnaire application we demonstrate in Lesson 7 is an example of such an advanced Web application. Like the GuestBook application, this application stores the user feedback in a database and uses the query feature of the database management system to dynamically generate the feedback analysis.

LESSON 4: SIGNING THE GUEST BOOK

This lesson assumes that you have installed the sample applications in your WebSite directory as explained in Lesson 3. Here, we describe how to add a guest book entry by use of the GuestBook application.

1. Ensure that your WebSite server is running.

2. Start your Web client and display the main menu of Chapter 2 applications as shown in Figure 2-16 by entering the following location:

`http://localhost/book/chap2/chap2.htm`

3. Click on the Sign The Guest Book link.

4. You will see a screen asking for your personal information and some remarks for the guest book. (See Figure 2-17.)

5. This screen is different from a typical page you see on the Web; instead of displaying information, it is asking for information. This type of screen is also called a *form*.

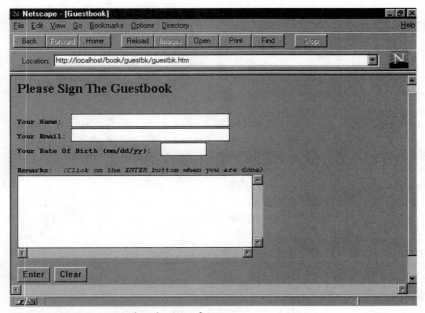

Figure 2–17 Guest book entry form

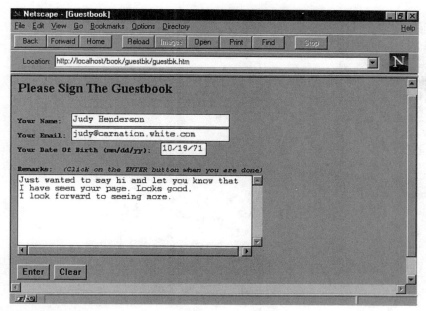

Figure 2-18 A sample guest book entry

6. Click in the Your Name text box, and type in your full name.

7. In the same fashion, specify your e-mail address (if any), your date of birth, and your remarks in the appropriate text boxes.

8. A sample guest book entry is shown in Figure 2-18.

9. Click on the Enter button.

10. In seconds, you see a response thanking you for signing the guest book. (See Figure 2-19.) The response also lists the day you were born.

You may wonder how the browser returned with the day of birth. The date you entered in the Your Date Of Birth field was used to pass a page with the correct day to the browser. Welcome to the world of the mysterious back-end CGI processing!

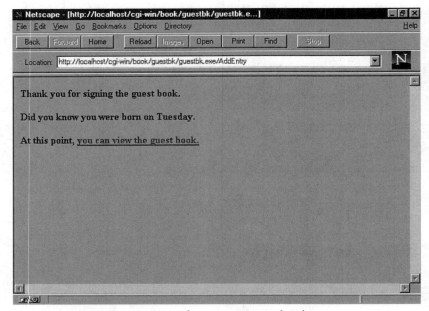

Figure 2-19 Response on submitting a guest book entry

LESSON 5: VIEWING THE GUEST BOOK

Like any regular guest book, this on-line guest book should save your entry and also allow you to see all other entries. And so it does. To view the guest book:

1. Ensure that the WebSite server is running.

2. If you have been following the previous lesson and reached the screen similar to the one shown in Figure 2-19, then just click on the You Can View The Guest Book link. Otherwise, enter the following location from your browser:

   ```
   http://localhost/cgi-win/book/guestbk/guestbk.exe/ViewGuestBook
   ```

3. A list of everyone's entry in the on-line guest book is displayed. (See Figure 2-20.)

At this point, you may use the Back button of your browser and have someone else sign the guest book. Tell them it is a great way of finding their day of birth. Play with the GuestBook application till you become comfortable with its functionality.

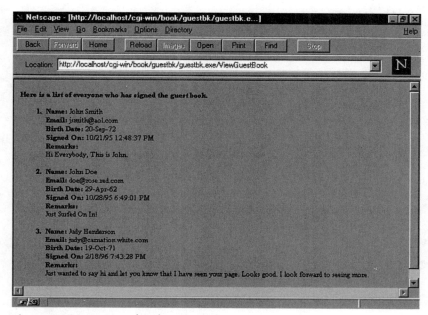

Figure 2-20 Guest book entries

LESSON 6: DISPLAYING RECENT ENTRIES OF THE GUEST BOOK

If your Web site is popular, you may find your guest book list expanding rapidly. In that situation, it can become cumbersome to see a long list every time you view the on-line guest book. Chances are you only want to see the entries of the visitors who have recently signed the guest book. This is where storing the entries in a database helps.

Your guest book application can search the database for information entered after a certain date using a simple *structured query language (SQL)*. SQL is supported by most relational database management systems including Microsoft Access. In this lesson, you will learn how to use that feature of the GuestBook application by following these steps:

1. Ensure that the WebSite server is running.

2. Bring up this location from your browser:

```
http://localhost/book/guestbk/view.htm
```

3. You will see a form asking you for a starting date.

4. Enter a valid starting date in the Enter Starting Date field, and then click on the View button. (See Figure 2-21.)

5. Any entries in the guest book made on or after the specified starting date are displayed as shown in Figure 2-22.

In your guest book, notice that a Signed On date is listed with every entry. This date is used to determine the selection of each entry. When the entries are submitted through the guest book Entry form, the Signed On date is also tracked with each entry.

Since you can specify any starting date on the View form, the list returned must be generated *dynamically* based on that starting date. The GUESTBOOK.EXE Windows CGI program executed by your server when the user submits this form accomplishes this task with the help of a Microsoft Access guest book database named GUESTBK.MDB. Both the program and the database are stored in the Windows CGI directory C:\WEBSITE\CGI-WIN\BOOK\GUESTBK\.

Chapter 11, Designing a Windows CGI Application, Chapter 12, Designing a Windows CGI Application to Process Form Data, and Chapter 13, Utilizing an Access Database in a CGI Application, describe how an enhanced version of this GuestBook application is constructed.

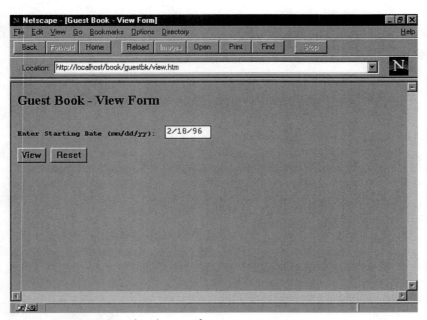

Figure 2–21 Guest book View form

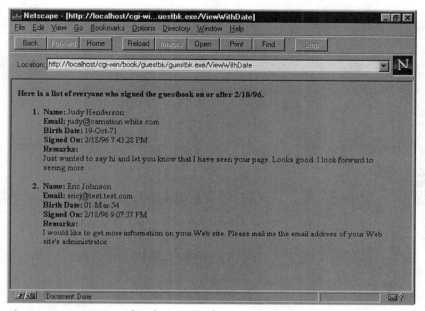

Figure 2-22 Guest book entries after a specified starting date

LESSON 7: DEMONSTRATING THE ON-LINE QUESTIONNAIRE APPLICATION

In this lesson, we will demonstrate the functionality of our sample On-Line Questionnaire application. Let's bring up its starting page.

1. Start your WebSite server if it is not already running.

2. Display the main menu of this chapter's applications by typing the following location on your Web browser:

```
http://localhost/book/chap2/chap2.htm
```

3. Click on the Fill In A Questionnaire link.

4. You should see a Reader Survey form as shown in Figure 2-23.

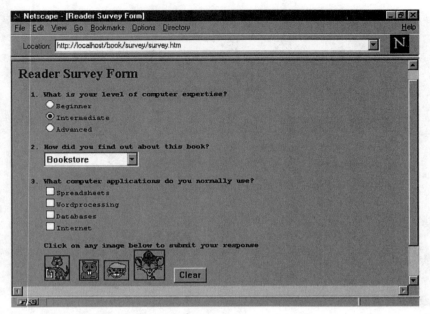

Figure 2–23 Reader Survey form

The Reader Survey form lists some questions about your skills and readership interests. It also displays different types of controls on the form. Answer the questions as described next to see such smart form controls in action.

1. For the first question, click on one of the circles that most appropriately describes your level of computer expertise.

2. Initially, the circle next to the Intermediate option is marked as the default answer for this question. If you click on a circle next to either of the other two options, you will notice that the Intermediate option is automatically deselected. These circles are called *radio controls* (or *radio buttons*) and are normally used to allow the selection of only one of many available options.

3. For the second question, click on the arrow next to the text box displaying "Bookstore" to drop down a list of choices, and then click on the appropriate choice.

4. This question shows another way of selecting one out of a given list of choices by use of a drop-down or pop-up menu. Notice that in either the first or the second question, your browser only allows you to select an existing option. You cannot add an option of your own. This helps the questionnaire developer to control the content of the information that the readers provide.

5. The third question is about the type of computer applications you regularly use. Again, a list of choices is provided with a check box next to each choice. Unlike the previous two questions, here you can select more than one choice. So, click on the check box next to all the applicable choices. If you select a check box by mistake, simply click on it again to deselect it.

6. Finally, click on any of the four gopher icons to submit your response.

A link to view the analysis of all the submitted questionnaire responses is returned as shown in Figure 2-24.

7. Click on the link for viewing the questionnaire analysis.

8. A survey result similar to the one shown in Figure 2-25 is displayed. The result also shows which icon is most liked by the readers.

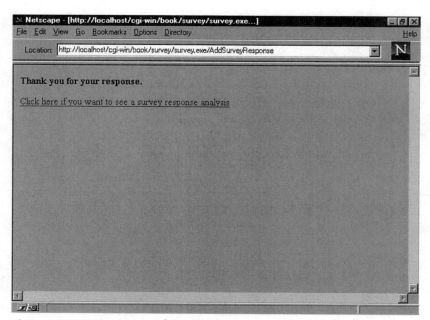

Figure 2–24 Response of the Reader Survey form

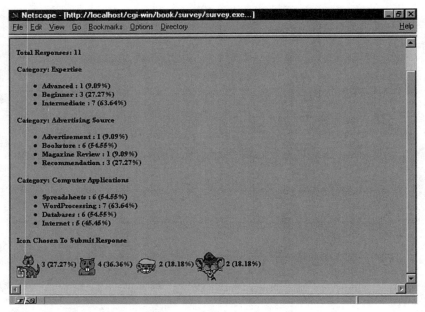

Figure 2–25 Questionnaire analysis

The information you provide on the questionnaire form is passed to a Windows CGI application called SURVEY.EXE, which stores it in an Access database named SURVEY.MDB. Both files reside in the directory C:\WEBSITE\CGI-WIN\BOOK\SURVEY\. You will understand the design of the Questionnaire application after you go through Chapter 11, Designing a Windows CGI Application; Chapter 12, Designing a Windows CGI Application to Process Form Data; and Chapter 13, Utilizing an Access Database in a CGI Application.

Are the Sample Applications Giving a Slow Response? The GuestBook, the On-Line Questionnaire, and the other sample Web-database applications described in this book utilize the CGI-WIN interface. This interface, while easy to work with, involves additional communications overhead, which we will explain in Chapter 9, Windows Common Gateway Interface. In addition, these Web applications use Visual Basic programs as their back-end, and these programs require the Visual Basic runtime DLL to be loaded every time they are launched. The CGI-WIN overhead and the DLL loading can significantly affect the response time if your Web server is running on a machine with minimum RAM requirements (less than 32MB). So, if you get a slow response from these applications, try increasing the server machine's RAM to 32MB or higher.

REVIEW QUESTIONS

1. What is WebSite? Who developed it?

2. What is the main function of a Web server?

3. List some advanced features supported by powerful Web servers like WebSite.

4. How do you configure the WebSite server?

5. Why does WebSite support three types of CGIs?

6. How does document mapping help you in serving documents residing on the other computers of your network?

7. When would you use redirect mapping?

8. Which directory is by default mapped through the Windows CGI mapping?

9. How does the server use the content type mapping?

10. In what situations does an imagemap prove useful? Can you think of any disadvantage of using an imagemap?

11. What types of logs are maintained by the WebSite server?

12. What is an automatic directory index?

13. In how many ways does the WebSite server allow you to control access to your Web documents?

14. What is the utility of a guest book application to a Web site?

15. What is a form?

16. How does the GuestBook application search for recent entries?

17. What are radio buttons?

18. What form controls are typically used to allow selection of multiple options?

19. What is the role of the four icons on the Questionnaire form?

EXERCISES

1. Create a new subdirectory called TEST.HTM under the C:\WEBSITE\HTDOCS directory. Start your WebSite server. Then run your Web browser and enter the following location:

```
http://localhost/test.htm
```

2. What does your browser display? Can you explain why?

3. Configure your server so that you can view the LOGCYCLE.TXT file residing in the C:\WEBSITE\SUPPORT\ directory by specifying the following URL:

```
http://localhost/support/logcycle.txt
```

4. Configure your Web server so that when you specify the URL given in the previous exercise from your browser, the browser gives you an option to save the LOGCYCLE.TXT file instead of displaying its contents. Hint: Apply content mapping.

5. Display the guest book Entry form and click on the Submit button without filling the form. What happens? Can you determine what fields must be filled in before the GuestBook application accepts an entry?

6. Bring up the survey Entry form of the On-Line Questionnaire application, fill in a response, and then click on any icon to submit your response. Now, using the Back button of your browser, return to the Questionnaire form and click on any icon again. Repeat this a few times, and then view the survey response analysis. What happens? Can you list other potential difficulties encountered by such Web applications?

3
DISSECTING A JOB LISTING SYSTEM

3

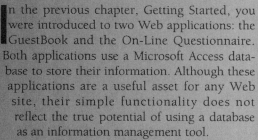

In the previous chapter, Getting Started, you were introduced to two Web applications: the GuestBook and the On-Line Questionnaire. Both applications use a Microsoft Access database to store their information. Although these applications are a useful asset for any Web site, their simple functionality does not reflect the true potential of using a database as an information management tool.

Here, we examine a more advanced Web application that depends on the efficient storage and retrieval capability of a database management system such as Microsoft Access. This application, called the Job Listing System, attempts to connect the job seekers and potential employers across the vast reaches of the World Wide Web. It lets employers advertise their jobs through this system and allows Web users to locate jobs of interest by using various search mechanisms. Some highlights of this system are as follows:

- More than one job for a company can be listed.

- The company information needs to be entered only once for all its jobs.

- Jobs can be searched by matching keywords in the job title, company name, city, state, or any combination of the above.

- The job search can be limited, for example, to estimated salary.

- Jobs can be searched by use of a drill-down method.

- Company information can be displayed for each job.

- Advanced users can design their own SQL criteria for a customized job search.

Even though this Job Listing System is not fine-tuned for a commercial operation, it lays out the groundwork for any Web application geared toward handling large amounts of information.

The initial lessons of this chapter orient you to the features of the Job Listing System. Later lessons of the chapter present an overview of the components and processes involved in the dynamics of this system. You will see where the Web browser, the Web server, the CGI program, and the database fit in the big picture.

LESSON 1: ADDING A NEW COMPANY IN THE JOB LISTING SYSTEM

The Job Listing System requires that every job must be associated with a company. The term "company" refers to the organization listing the job. A company could be a large corporation, a recruiting agency, or an individual employer who is willing to provide the name, address, and some other relevant information. This company information is automatically associated with all the jobs of that company as shown later in Lesson 3, Finding Jobs Using Keyword Search.

In this lesson, you will add a new dummy company called "Webs 'R Us" located in Austin, Texas, to the Job Listing System. Follow these steps:

1. Ensure that your WebSite server is running and all the sample applications included with this book have been installed as described in Chapter 2, Getting Started.

2. From your Web browser, specify the following URL:

```
http://localhost/book/joblist/joblist.htm
```

3. Your browser displays the main menu of the Job Listing System as shown in Figure 3-1.

4. Click on the Add A New Company link.

5. Your browser displays the Company Add form, which asks for information about the new company as shown in Figure 3-2.

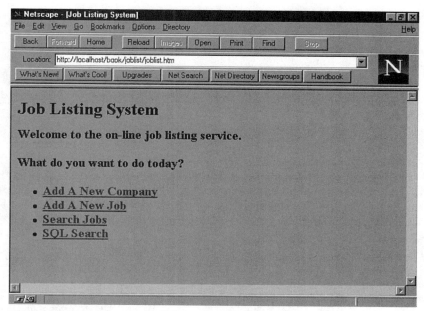

Figure 3-1 Main menu of the Job Listing System

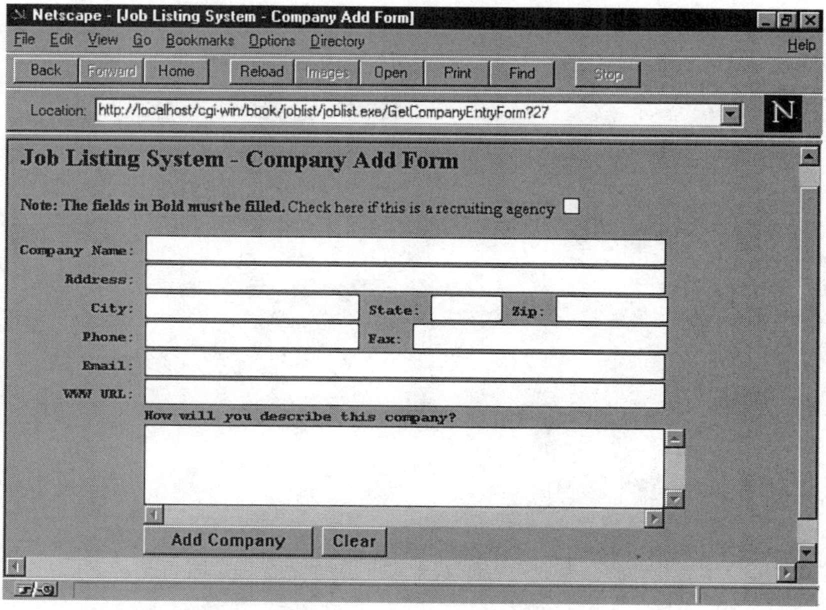

Figure 3-2 Company Add form

6. Fill in the Company Add form with the following information:

```
Company Name: Webs 'R Us
     Address: 123 Web Street
        City: Austin
       State: TX
         Zip: 54321-6789
       Phone: 800-WEB-SITE
         Fax: 512-302-0101 ext 1221
       Email: hire@websrus.com
     WWW URL: http://www.websrus.com/index.html
 Description: An expanding company that deals with all aspects
              of a Web site. Our main areas are:
              <B>Design of HTML documents</B>
              <B>Publishing databases over the Web</B>
```

7. Notice that the description field has some special codes such as *<B>* and *</B>* embedded in the regular text. These are HTML tags used for adding special effects to your text. Chapter 7, Elements of the World Wide Web, explains the various HTML tags in more detail.

8. Click on the Add Company button when you are done entering all the information on this form. The browser sends your information to the Job Listing System, which responds with a message indicating that the company has been added successfully. (See Figure 3-3.) The message also has a link attached to the company name.

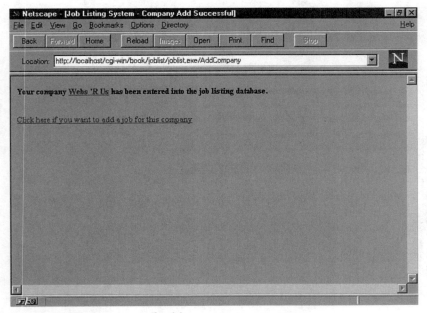

Figure 3–3 Response of adding a new company

9. Click on the link attached to the company name. The browser shows the company information returned by the Job Listing System. (See Figure 3-4.) Notice that a portion of the company description is shown in boldface, indicating that the HTML tags are effective.

The company information page also shows a numeric value listed as the CompanyID. The CompanyID value is a unique number automatically assigned by the Job Listing System to each company added to the system. Chapter 4, Building a Database with Microsoft Access, and Chapter 5, Building Microsoft Access Queries, explain how this CompanyID value is used by the Job Listing System to associate the company information with the jobs.

LESSON 2: ADDING JOBS IN THE JOB LISTING SYSTEM

Let's say the Webs 'R Us company you added in the previous lesson has two job openings, one for an HTML developer and the other for a CGI programmer. This lesson shows how to list both jobs with the Job Listing System.

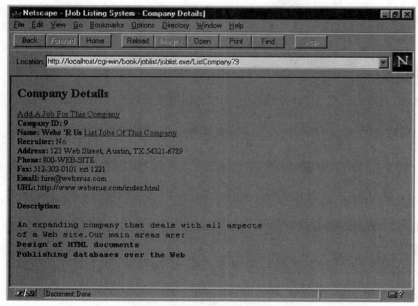

Figure 3-4 Company information shown by the Job Listing System

Listing the First Job

To add the first job for an HTML developer:

1. Ensure that your WebSite server is running.

2. Bring up the main menu of the Job Listing System from your Web browser by specifying the following URL:

```
http://localhost/book/joblist/joblist.htm
```

3. Click on the Add A New Job link.

4. A Job Add form is displayed as shown in Figure 3-5.

5. The Job Add form has fields for the company name, job title, contact name, and other job-related information.

6. Click on the arrow of the drop-down menu list showing the company names and select "Webs 'R Us." If you do not see this name listed, then follow the steps in the previous lesson to add this company to the Job Listing System.

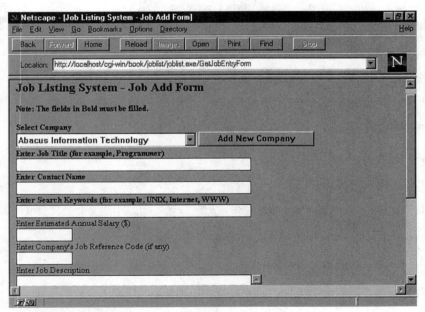

Figure 3–5 Job Add form

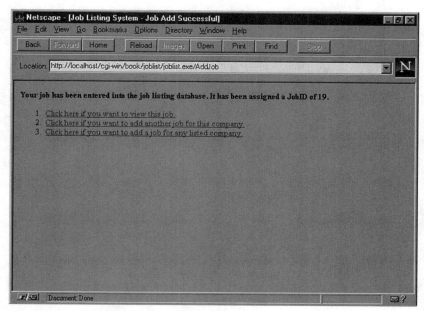

Figure 3–6 Response to submitting a job

7. Fill in the rest of the Job Add form with the following information:

```
         Job Title: HTML Developer
      Contact Name: Aseem Chandra
   Search Keywords: HTML,Web,WWW,Page,Publishing
   Estimated Salary: 32000
 Job Reference Code: HTML-B
   Job Description: Develop creative Web pages using HTML 3.
                   Design attractive backgrounds and appealing
                   images for the customers.
  Job Requirements: Must have at least one year experience with
                   HTML development. Must be a people person.
```

8. Click on the Add Job button (not visible in Figure 3-5) after you are done entering all the information. Figure 3-6 displays the response of submitting this job. The response includes the Job ID of this job.

The response also provides links to view this job, add another job for the same company, and add another job for some other company. You will use the second link to add the other job for Webs 'R Us as described in the following section.

Listing the Second Job

To list the second job for Webs 'R Us:

1. Click on the link that says "Click here if you want to add another job for this company."

2. Again, the Job Add form is returned, but this time only the company name "Webs 'R Us" is present in the drop-down list. (See Figure 3-7.)

3. Enter the following information in this form:

```
        Job Title: CGI Programmer
     Contact Name: Ron Smith
  Search Keywords: HTML,Web,WWW,CGI,Programmer
 Estimated Salary: 43000
Job Reference Code: PGMR-A
  Job Description: Design Web applications using Windows CGI.
                  Develop HTML forms, Visual Basic programs.
                  Convert Microsoft Access, FoxPro, and Paradox
                  database applications for the Web.
 Job Requirements: Must be proficient with Windows CGI. Minimum
                  one year Visual Basic and Microsoft Access
                  experience required.
```

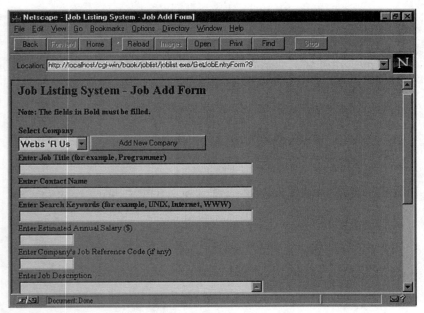

Figure 3-7 Job Add form for a specific company

4. Click on the Add Job button when done entering all the information.

5. Again, a response similar to Figure 3-6 is displayed indicating the JobID of this job.

At this point, you can add more jobs for this company or any other existing company.

Points to Note on Adding Jobs

Although it is fairly intuitive to add a new job in the Job Listing System, let's highlight a few points of this job adding process, which may not be evident right away.

Mandatory and Optional Fields

The Job Listing System rejects a job entry if the Company Name, Job Title, Contact Name, and Search Keywords fields are not filled in. This requirement ensures that all the jobs in the Job Listing System adhere to a minimum standard and can be located in some way. The Job Add form clearly states this requirement and marks the names of these fields in bold.

The other fields, such as Estimated Salary and Job Description, are optional. The next lesson shows how you can miss a job when you perform a job search using a criterion based on an optional field.

Complete Company Information Not Required

The Job Add form does not ask for any other company information except the name of the company. Based on this company name, the Job Listing System automatically links the company's existing information with the new job. You will see the evidence of this automatic link in the next lesson.

Search Keywords Field

While describing a job, think also from the perspective of Web users who will be searching this job. How will they find this job? What search keywords will they use if they are interested in this job? The Search Keywords field is provided on the Job Add form so that words or phrases that can help locate the job can be listed with this job.

At this point, the Job Listing System does not impose any format for specifying the search keywords, except that the Search Keywords field must not exceed 100 characters. The next two chapters will analyze the performance factors involved with using a free format Search Keywords field and propose other ways of handling search keywords.

Button to Add a New Company

Sometimes, new users may not realize that they have to first add a company before they can add a job for that company. They may go directly to the Job Add form just to find that the drop-down menu list does not contain their company name, which is required for the Job Listing System to accept a job entry.

The button next to the Add New Company drop-down menu serves as a visual cue on what a user needs to do to add a new company.

This is how it works:

1. The user checks on the Add New Company button on the Job Add form.

2. An empty Company Add form is returned.

3. The user supplies the necessary data and submits the form.

4. The new company is added, and the user is given a link to add a job for that company. (See Figure 3-3.)

5. The user clicks on this link, and a Job Add form with the new company name listed in the drop-down menu is returned to the user.

NOTE: If, after adding the company, the user clicks on the Back button of the browser to return to the old Job Add form, the new company name does not appear in the drop-down list. This is because the Web forms work similarly to paper forms. Once a copy of a Web form is requested, it does not change. Another request must be made to get a similar form with updated information. Chapter 8, Creating HTML Forms, details how the form interaction works over the Web.

Big Advantage of a Shortcut... The main menu of the Job Listing System already contains a link for adding a new company. But it is the shortcut buttons such as "Add New Company" on other forms that make a system intuitive and user friendly.

JobID for Each Job

When you add a job, the system assigns a unique number to this job called its *JobID*. This number is not to be confused with the CompanyID value assigned to each company. A CompanyID uniquely identifies a company and a JobID uniquely identifies a job existing in the Job Listing System. Lesson 6 of this chapter describes how you can quickly retrieve a job from the Job Listing System using the JobID.

LESSON 3: FINDING JOBS USING KEYWORD SEARCH

The Job Listing System supports three search mechanisms to help Web users find jobs of interest. They are as follows:

- *Keyword search* locates jobs based on keywords appearing in different fields.

- *Drill-down search* narrows the job search in a hierarchical manner, like finding the leaves of a tree by following the branches.

- *SQL search* finds jobs by specifying any valid SQL criteria.

The examples in this lesson demonstrate the keyword search feature. The next two lessons explore the drill-down search and SQL search features of the Job Listing System.

Keyword Search Example I

Let's begin by searching for all Programmer jobs with a salary of $40,000 or higher from the Job Listing System:

1. Ensure that your WebSite server is running.

2. Bring up the main menu of the Job Listing System from your Web browser by specifying the following URL:

   http://localhost/book/joblist/joblist.htm

3. Click on the Search Jobs link. (See Figure 3-1.)

4. A Search form is displayed as shown in Figure 3-8.

5. Type *Programmer* in the Job Title input box.

6. Specify the value *40000* in the Annual Salary Above input box.

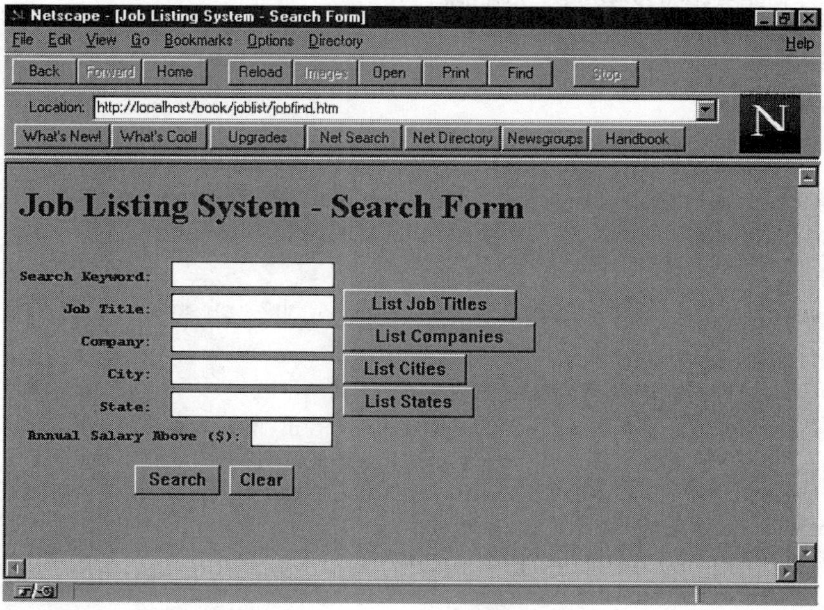

Figure 3–8 Search form

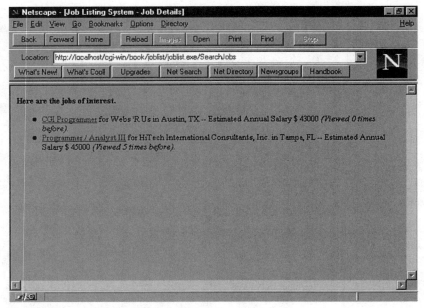

Figure 3-9 Result of keyword search example 1

7. Click on the Search button.

8. A page listing a brief description of selected jobs is returned as shown in Figure 3-9. Notice that all jobs have the word "Programmer" in their job title and have an estimated salary of $40,000 or above. Also, there is a link attached to each job title.

9. Click on the link attached to the job title "CGI Programmer."

10. The browser displays the complete description of this job as presented by the Job Listing System. (See Figure 3-10.)

NOTE: There is a link attached to the Webs 'R Us company name in the job information. If you click on this link, the Job Listing System gives the details of this company as shown in Figure 3-4. The presence of this link confirms that the Job Listing System can associate the complete company information with a job, based on the company name selected while adding that job.

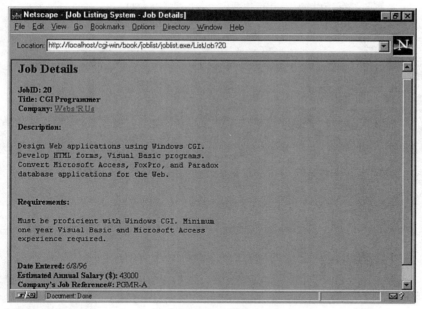

Figure 3-10 Description of the selected job

Keyword Search Example 2

Let's remove the salary criterion from the previous search and see how many additional Programmer jobs are in the system:

Bring up the Search form by specifying the following URL from your browser:

```
http://localhost/book/joblist/jobfind.htm
```

1. Type *Programmer* in the Job Title input box, and click on the Search button.

2. This time, your browser displays a list of all the Programmer jobs. (See Figure 3-11.) This list includes the jobs shown during the previous search. The other jobs in this list that were not selected during the previous search either had an estimated salary specified below $40,000 or not specified at all.

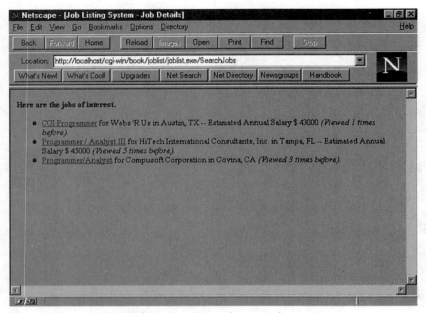

Figure 3–11 Result of keyword search example 2

NOTE: The two preceding examples show that if you specify a criterion based on an optional field through this keyword search, the Job Listing System excludes the jobs that do not have a value for the optional field from the search result.

Keyword Search Example 3

For this example, let's say you want to locate all jobs in Texas that have something to do with the World Wide Web. Since you are not sure what job titles may have been used for Web-related jobs, your best option is to specify the keyword "Web" for the Search Keywords field:

1. Bring up the Search form by specifying the following URL from your browser:

```
http://localhost/book/joblist/jobfind.htm
```

2. Type *Web* in the Search Keywords input box.

3. Type *Texas* in the State input box, and click on the Search button.

Your browser will probably return a "No jobs meet the search criteria..." message. But in Lessons 1 and 2, you added two Web-related jobs for the Webs 'R Us company, which is located in Texas. What happened? Look at the value for the State field for this company (see Lesson 1). You entered the two-letter state code for Texas, "TX." The Job Listing System could not match "Texas" with "TX" in the State field and therefore did not include these jobs.

To provide the correct keyword for the State field:

4. Go back to the job Search form using the Back button of your browser.

5. Click on the Clear button to empty all the fields.

6. Type *Web* in the Search Keywords field.

7. Type *TX* in the State field and click the Search button.

8. This time, the browser returns the jobs you were looking for as shown in Figure 3-12.

Keyword Search Example 4

In the previous example, you saw that it can make a big difference in the search result if you specify an incorrect representation of a particular keyword. To search for jobs in Texas, you had to type in "TX" and not "Texas" in the State field to find the matching jobs. Imagine how a typical user would figure out that Texas-based jobs need to be searched by use of the keyword "TX."

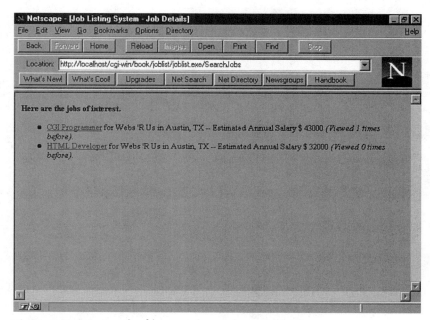

Figure 3–12 Result of keyword search example 3

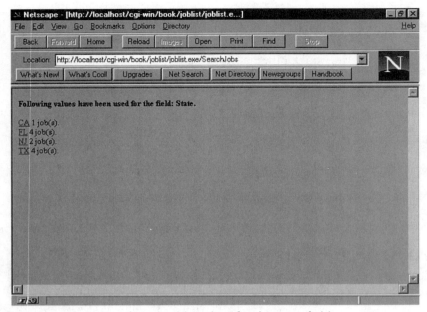

Figure 3-13 List of applicable values for the State field

Not knowing the proper keyword is a common difficulty faced by users when performing a keyword search. Often it is easier if the system presents a list of keywords you can choose from—or better still, lets you start from a good keyword and drill down from there. The Job Listing System provides you with both options. The next lesson demonstrates the drill-down feature of this system. To get the list of applicable keywords for the State field when searching for Web-related jobs in Texas:

1. Bring up the Search form by specifying the following URL from your browser:

```
http://localhost/book/joblist/jobfind.htm
```

2. Type *Web* in the Search Keywords input box.

3. Click on the List States button to display a list of all the values used for the State field as shown in Figure 3-13. The figure shows that Texas is specified as "TX" in the Job Listing System.

4. Use the Back button of your browser to return to the Search form, and type in the keyword *TX* in the State field. Click on the Search button to perform the search.

LESSON 4: FINDING JOBS USING DRILL-DOWN SEARCH

The Job Listing System provides a simple two-level drill-down facility that can be used in place of the keyword search. To drill down to all the jobs in Texas:

1. Bring up the Search form by specifying the following URL from your browser:

    http://localhost/book/joblist/jobfind.htm

2. Click on the List States button to display a list of all the values used for the State field as shown in Figure 3-13.

3. Click on the TX link.

4. The browser displays a list of all the jobs in Texas as shown in Figure 3-14.

From here, you can click on any job to get more information about that job and its associated company.

In general, the drill-down search method is mostly effective when:

You are not sure what you are looking for.

You want to find out what type of information is available.

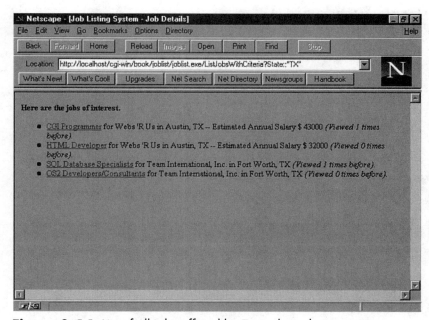

Figure 3–14 List of all jobs offered by Texas-based companies

The keyword search is producing few or no results.
Some disadvantages of the drill-down search are as follows:

It is generally more time-consuming.

It is difficult to perform if the drill-down levels are too deep or too broad.

LESSON 5: PERFORMING SQL-BASED SEARCHES

The keyword and drill-down search features of the Job Listing System are adequate for handling common types of search criteria. However, these features only allow searches on a limited number of fields. What if you want to retrieve jobs entered after a certain date? Or maybe you are interested in jobs listed by companies that do not claim to be recruiting agencies. It is hard to anticipate all possible user queries and come up with a general-purpose keyword search form that can handle all types of search criteria.

The Job Listing System provides a general-purpose search facility by letting users specify criteria using SQL expressions. The only disadvantage of an SQL-based search is that the users are expected to know SQL syntax. The details of how to construct SQL criteria expressions are covered in Chapter 5, Building Microsoft Access Queries. Here, we demonstrate the use of simple SQL criteria expressions with the Job Listing System to perform customized searches that cannot be handled by the regular keyword Search form.

SQL Search Example I

To use the SQL search interface of the Job Listing System to locate jobs added after a certain date:

1. Ensure that your WebSite server is running.

2. From your Web browser, bring up the main menu of the Job Listing System by specifying the following URL:

   `http://localhost/book/joblist/joblist.htm`

3. Click on the SQL Search link to display the SQL Search form as shown in Figure 3-15.

The SQL Search form has one input text box for specifying the criteria. It also lists the names of fields that can be used in the SQL expression and gives some examples of valid SQL expressions.

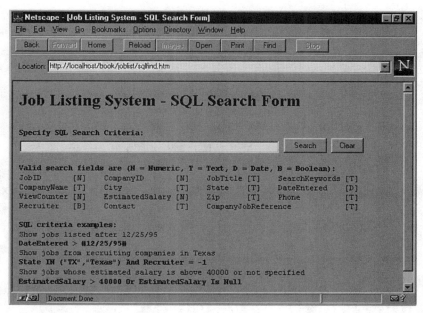

Figure 3-15 SQL Search form

4. Enter the following criterion in the input text box and click on the Search button:

```
DateEntered > #1/1/96#
```

5. The search result will list all jobs added after January 1, 1996.

SQL Search Example 2

This example shows how to locate jobs whose details have never been viewed. Here, an SQL criterion is specified on the ViewCounter field of a job. The Job Listing System automatically increments the value of a job's ViewCounter field anytime a user requests the complete details of that job.

1. Bring up the SQL Search form as explained in the previous example.

2. Enter the following criterion in the input text box, and click on the Search button:

```
ViewCounter = 0
```

SQL Search Example 3

This example shows another way of finding Web-related jobs listed by Texas-based companies. It shows how you can deal with the state name dilemma by searching for both "TX" and "Texas" for the State field as shown in the following steps:

1. Bring up the SQL Search form as explained in the previous example.

2. Enter the following criteria in the input text box, and click on the Search button:

```
SearchKeywords Like "*Web*" And State IN ("TX","Texas")
```

DYNAMICS OF THE JOB LISTING SYSTEM

The previous lessons of this chapter presented a functional overview of the Job Listing System application. By now, you are probably aware that some interaction takes place between a Web client and your Web server. Why is this interaction necessary? What other components are part of the Job Listing System? The following lessons take you one step further to help you get an idea of how the Job Listing System works.

LESSON 6: UNDERSTANDING THE ROLE OF THE WEB BROWSER

We have been designating the Job Listing System as a Web application. This signifies that any user who can connect to your computer using any standard Web client such as Netscape or Mosaic can work with this application. Essentially, a *Web browser* (also referred to as a *Web client*) is software with three main roles:

- To pass a user's request to the Web server
- To pass any user data related to the user's request to the Web server
- To show the results returned by the Web server in a manner that the user can easily understand

Passing User Requests

A user request refers to an information resource residing on the Web server. This information resource can be a document file or a program capable of generating the information. The location of an information resource is specified through a standard notation known as *Universal Resource Locator (URL)*. URL notation is covered in Chapter 7, Elements of the World Wide Web.

Usually, the Web browser passes a user request for an information resource when a user performs any of the following actions:

🦃 Enters a URL in the Location window of the Web browser

🦃 Clicks on a link attached to a text or an image

🦃 Submits a form

For example, when you type the URL *http://localhost/book/joblist/joblist.htm* in your Web browser's Location window, your Web browser passes the URL path describing the information resource (/book/joblist/joblist.htm) as a request to the WebSite server running on your computer.

Passing User Data

A Web browser can also pass user-specified data to the Web server along with the request for an information resource. This data is generally used by the program specified as the information resource in the user request. A user can specify this data by submitting a form or part of the URL itself.

Lessons 1 and 2, where you supply the company and job information, are examples of passing data by use of a form. Let's see an example where you pass data attached with the URL itself. Here, you will retrieve the information of the job with JobID 1 from the Job Listing System by supplying the JobID value as part of the URL:

1. Ensure that the Web server is running.

2. Type the following URL from your Web browser:

```
http://localhost/cgi-win/book/joblist/joblist.exe/ListJob?1
```

3. The Job Listing System returns the information of the job associated to JobID 1 as shown in Figure 3-16.

In this example, the information resource being requested by your browser is a program on your computer whose URL path is */cgi-win/book/joblist/joblist.exe*. The data passed to the WebSite server is "/Listjob?1." Your Web browser does not know that data including a JobID needs to be provided with the preceding URL. It simply delivered your request (as specified) to the Web server. How this request is processed between your server and the requested program is described in the next two lessons.

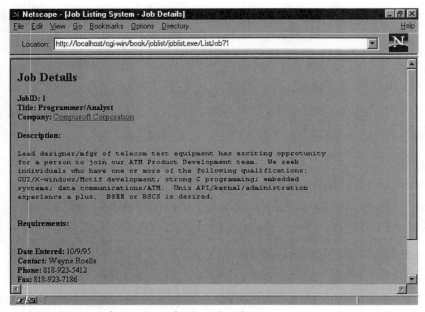

Figure 3-16 Information of job with JobID 1

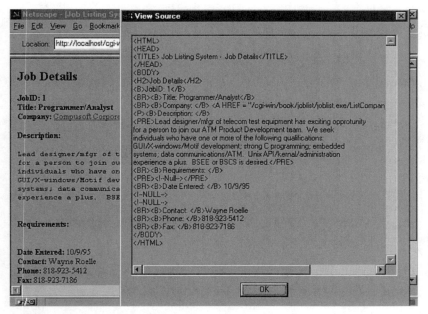

Figure 3-17 Response of a Web server

Showing Server Response

As mentioned earlier, the Web client makes a request without knowing what that request is for. All it expects is a response from the Web server after it delivers the request. It then tries to display that response in a manner most suitable for the user. Figure 3-17 shows the actual HTML response returned by the Web server when you requested the job with JobID 1 in the previous example.

LESSON 7: UNDERSTANDING THE ROLE OF THE WEB SERVER

The *Web server* is software that listens and responds to the requests made by Web browsers. That is why you were asked to ensure that your Web server is running when exploring the Job Listing System application. Let's see what happens if your Web server is not running and you make a request directed to your server:

1. Close your Web server if it is running.

2. Close your Web browser and then rerun it. This clears any document history your Web browser may be keeping in memory.

3. Specify the following URL from your Web browser:

`http://localhost/book/joblist/jobfind.htm`

4. Your Web browser sends the request and waits for a response. It probably shows an hourglass to indicate that it is in wait mode. Depending on which Web browser you are using, the browser may stay in wait mode indefinitely or stop after a specific time-out period.

5. While your Web browser is in wait mode, restart your WebSite server, and then return to your Web browser's window.

6. Your Web browser displays the Search form, indicating that the request has been responded to by the server.

Chapter 7, Elements of the World Wide Web, describes the HTTP standard followed by a Web client and a Web server when interacting with each other.

Primary Function of a Web Server

By itself, a Web server is capable of delivering a document file residing on its computer to a requesting client. It is not responsible for creating a document or updating it. When you request the URL *http://localhost/book/joblist/jobfind.htm,* the server delivers the file C:\WEBSITE\HTDOCS\BOOK\JOBLIST\JOBFIND.HTM.

What happens if this file is missing from the JOBLIST directory? To find out:

1. Rename the JOBFIND.HTM file residing in the C:\WEBSITE\HTDOCS\ BOOK\JOBLIST\ directory to *JOBFIND.OLD*.

2. Ensure that your WebSite server is running.

3. Close your Web browser and then rerun it.

4. Specify the following URL from your Web browser:

   `http://localhost/book/joblist/jobfind.htm`

5. Your Web browser displays a "404 Not Found" message similar to the one shown in Figure 3-18. The "404" refers to a status code that is explained in Chapter 7, Elements of the World Wide Web.

6. Again, this response is returned by the Web server and not generated by the Web browser.

7. Rename the JOBFIND.OLD file back to its original name, *JOBFIND.HTM,* so that your Job Listing System works correctly.

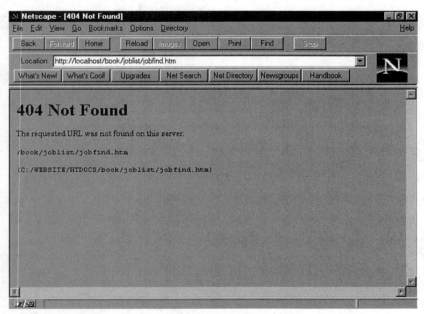

Figure 3–18 Response indicating file not found

Running External Programs

A Web server such as WebSite can also act as a gateway to external programs when it gets a request for an information resource pointing to an executable program or script. This interaction between the Web server and the external program occurs using a standard called the Common Gateway Interface (CGI).

In the previous lesson, you specified the following URL to request the information about the job with JobID 1:

```
http://localhost/cgi-win/book/joblist/joblist.exe/ListJob?1
```

Let's see how the WebSite server handled this request:

1. The WebSite server recognizes the reference to the "/cgi-win" element in the URL path and determines that the request is for a Windows executable program based on the Windows CGI mapping configuration. See the CGI Mapping section in Chapter 2, Getting Started, for more information about CGI mapping configuration.

2. The server then uses the complete URL path and maps it to the file JOBLIST.EXE in the C:\WEBSITE\CGI-WIN\BOOK\JOBLIST\ directory.

3. The server executes the JOBLIST.EXE program, passes the user data "/ListJob?1" according to the Windows CGI standard, and waits till this program terminates. The details of the Windows Common Gateway Interface and how data is passed between the server and the external Windows-based programs are described in Chapter 9, Windows Common Gateway Interface.

4. When the JOBLIST.EXE program terminates, the server simply delivers the output of this program as a response to the client's request.

Let's look at another example to verify that the server is passing the response generated by the JOBLIST.EXE program when a request is made for that program:

1. Ensure that your WebSite server is running.

2. Enter the following URL from your Web client:

```
http://localhost/cgi-win/book/joblist/joblist.exe/Test
```

3. The Web browser should display the test message generated by the JOBLIST.EXE program as shown in Figure 3-19.

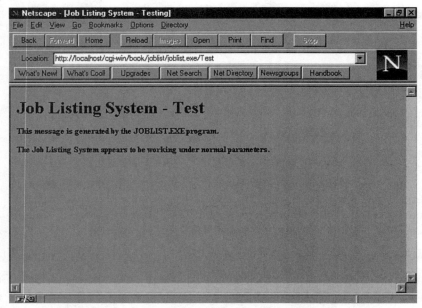

Figure 3-19 Test message returned by the JOBLIST.EXE program

LESSON 8: UNDERSTANDING THE ROLE OF THE CGI PROGRAM

The JOBLIST.EXE file is a Windows CGI program. It is designed mainly to interact with your Web server by use of the Windows CGI standard. Unlike your Web server, this program does not keep running on your computer. It is executed by the server every time the server receives a request to run this program.

Note: If the server receives two concurrent requests for executing this program, then it will run two copies of this program at the same time. This generally works well due to the multitasking capabilities of Windows 95 and Windows NT, but this concurrence factor should be considered by the person designing the CGI program.

Performing Multiple Functions

The JOBLIST.EXE program handles all the main functions of the Job Listing System, whether you are adding a company, adding a job, or performing a job search through this system. It uses part of the user data supplied with the URL to decide which action to carry out in response to the user request. This part of the data is the *extra path information*.

For example, when you request the job details of JobID 1 using the following URL:

```
http://localhost/cgi-win/book/joblist/joblist.exe/ListJob?1
```

the Web server breaks the data "/ListJob?1" into an extra path portion ("/ListJob") and a query string portion ("1") according to the Windows CGI standard and passes these portions to the JOBLIST.EXE program. The JOBLIST.EXE program is designed to consider the data in the extra path portion as the task selector.

In this example, the JOBLIST.EXE program knows that you want the information on a job based on the extra path data "/ListJob." After the task has been determined, the JOBLIST.EXE program looks at the other parameter(s) needed to complete the task, which in this case is the JobID value.

NOTE: The person who develops the CGI program decides how the user should supply the data. For example, the JOBLIST.EXE program expects the JobID to be passed as a numeric value after a question mark. If you try to pass the JobID value using a form or in a different format such as "?JobID=1," you will not get the desired result.

The JOBLIST.EXE program only recognizes a few keywords in the extra path information such as "ListJob," "ListCompany," "/GetCompanyAddForm," "/GetJobAddForm," "Test," and so on. Let's see how the JOBLIST.EXE program responds when it encounters an unknown keyword in the extra path information:

1. Ensure that your Web server is running.

2. Enter the following URL from your Web client:

`http://localhost/cgi-win/book/joblist/joblist.exe/xyz`

3. The JOBLIST.EXE program responds by indicating that it is not programmed to handle the "xyz" action.

Processing Template Files

There is one disadvantage when you use an external program for generating a response. It is hard to change the format of the response unless you have the source code of that program.

For example, when you specified the following URL:

`http://localhost/cgi-win/book/joblist/joblist.exe/Test`

the Job Listing System responded with the fixed format message as shown in Figure 3-19 of the previous lesson. What if you want to change this message or change the way the jobs are listed as a result of a job search?

You are probably thinking that you will have to go into the source code of the JOBLIST.EXE program and figure out where to make the format changes. Fortunately, this program is designed to use external template files that dictate the format of most of its responses. Figure 3-20 shows the template file TEST.TXT processed by the JOBLIST.EXE program in response to the "Test" action. All the template files reside in the same directory that contains the JOBLIST.EXE file and have a .TXT extension.

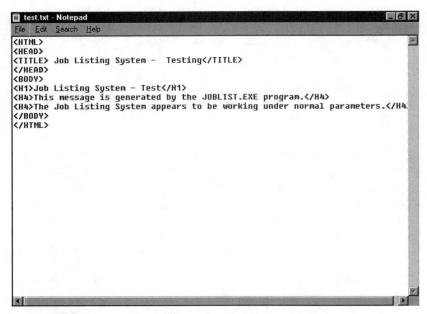

Figure 3–20 The TEST.TXT template file

The template files can contain embedded variables and even simple looping instructions that make them versatile enough to handle most common types of responses. The details of how to construct and apply these template files in a CGI program are explained in Chapter 14, Processing Template Files with a CGI Application. Here, let's just modify the TEST.TXT template file to see how it affects the result:

1. Open the file C:\WEBSITE\CGI-WIN\BOOK\JOBLIST\TEST.TXT in your text editor. (See Figure 3-20.)

2. Insert the following line before the line that says "</BODY>" so that the TEST.TXT file looks like the one shown in Figure 3-21:

```
<H4>The extra path information is: `[C:LogicalPath]` </H4>
```

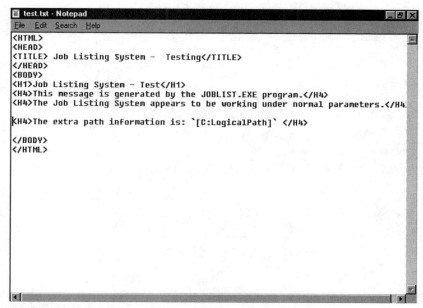

Figure 3–21 The modified TEST.TXT template file

3. Make sure that the text "[C:LogicalPath]" in the above line is bracketed by back-quote (`) characters. On a regular keyboard, a backquote character normally appears with the key that has the tilde (~) character.

4. Save the modified TEST.TXT file by selecting the Save option from the File menu of your text editor.

5. Ensure that your Web server is running.

6. Enter the following URL from your Web browser:

```
http://localhost/cgi-win/book/joblist/joblist.exe/Test
```

7. The Web browser should display the extra path information with the rest of the test message as shown in Figure 3-22. The JOBLIST.EXE replaces the variable `[C:LogicalPath]` with the value "/Test."

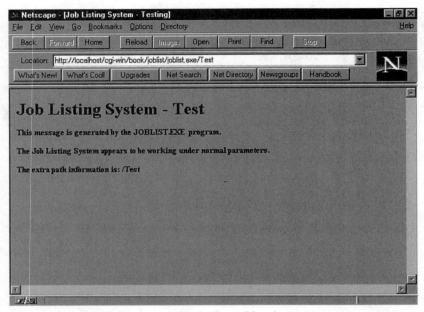

Figure 3-22 New test message returned by the JOBLIST.EXE program

LESSON 9: UNDERSTANDING THE ROLE OF THE ACCESS DATABASE

The Job Listing System is mainly about adding and retrieving job-related information. The JOBLIST.EXE program uses a Microsoft Access database named JOBLIST.MDB for these critical functions. This database file also resides in the same directory that contains the JOBLIST.EXE program file.

Utilizing a database for managing information not only helps improve the runtime performance, but also reduces programming effort. The JOBLIST.EXE program is designed in Visual Basic 4.0 (Professional version) and uses the built-in functions of Visual Basic to link to the Access database. Chapter 13, Utilizing an Access Database in a CGI Application, describes how this link is established.

Directly Viewing the Information in Microsoft Access

The JOBLIST.MDB database has been created by use of Microsoft Access (version 7.0). Chapter 4, Building a Database with Microsoft Access, describes the complete process of creating this database.

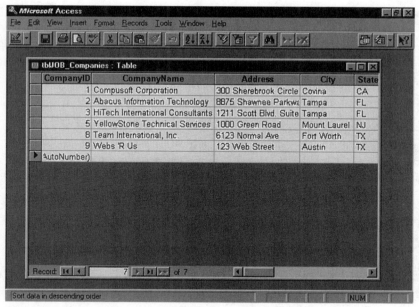

Figure 3-23 Using Microsoft Access to access the company information

As demonstrated in Lessons 1 and 2 of this chapter, a Web user can add companies and jobs through the Job Listing System. However, since this system is operating on your computer, you can directly access all its information by opening the JOBLIST.MDB file in Microsoft Access as shown in Figure 3-23.

Managing Information Through Microsoft Access

Once a job has been added to the Job Listing System, how do you remove it? What if a company wants to modify the requirements of a job already listed in the Job Listing System? The version of the Job Listing System described in this chapter is not designed to handle such tasks of data deletion or data updates. Later chapters in this book will address these issues. Currently, the only way of updating the JOBLIST.MDB database is through Microsoft Access.

Microsoft Access not only lets you manipulate your data, but also maintains the integrity of your data. As mentioned in Lessons 1 and 2, the Job Listing System does not allow you to enter a job unless that job's company information already exists in the system. The JOBLIST.MDB is designed in such a way that Microsoft Access automatically enforces this "company first" rule. The section on Referential Integrity in Chapter 4, Building a Database with Microsoft Access, discusses how this design is accomplished.

Searching for Information

By far, the biggest advantage to using an Access database over using a flat file is its powerful data searching capability. All search methods provided by the Job Listing System take advantage of this capability. Lesson 5 in this chapter previewed the SQL search facility of this system. Implementing this feature in the Job Listing System or any other similar application is a breeze, thanks to the comprehensive SQL support in Visual Basic and Microsoft Access.

Chapter 5, Building Microsoft Access Queries, and Chapter 6, Designing Advanced Queries, show how easy it is to design SQL queries using the query design interface of Microsoft Access. Chapter 13, Utilizing an Access Database in a CGI Application, describes various ways of using SQL queries in a CGI program to retrieve the information from an associated Access database.

REVIEW QUESTIONS

1. What are some of the features of the Job Listing System?

2. Why does the Job Listing System provide a separate form for the company information?

3. What does the Job Listing System do to uniquely identify a company?

4. How does the Job Listing System associate the company information with a job?

5. What fields are mandatory for submitting a job? Why does the Job Listing System require these fields to be filled in before it accepts a job entry?

6. What is the purpose of the Add New Company button on the Job Add form?

7. What is a keyword search? Which fields are provided for keyword search in the Job Listing System?

8. Is the keyword search case-sensitive?

9. What is the main difficulty encountered by users when performing a keyword search? What are the two ways by which the Job Listing System helps users overcome this difficulty?

10. What is a drill-down search? When is a drill-down search useful?

11. How does the Job Listing System support the drill-down search?

12. What is an SQL search? When is this search helpful?

13. List all the ways by which you can find all the jobs offered by Texas-based companies in the Job Listing System.

14. What is a Web client? What are its main functions?

15. What is the primary role of a Web server? What does it do when it is unable to fulfill this role?

16. How does a Web server act as a gateway to external programs?

17. What is the main purpose of a CGI program? When is it executed?

18. How does the JOBLIST.EXE determine which function to perform when it is executed?

19. Why is it difficult to change the response generated by a CGI program? How does the JOBLIST.EXE program resolve this difficulty?

20. How does the JOBLIST.EXE program take advantage of a Microsoft Access database?

21. In what ways can you use Microsoft Access with the Job Listing System?

EXERCISES

1. Add some more jobs and companies in the Job Listing System.

2. Find the networking jobs in the Job Listing System using the keyword Search form.

3. Using Yahoo or any other Web search site, find the Web sites that operate an application similar to the Job Listing System. For these sites:

 Identify the common features found in their implementation of the this system.

List the features that make the system of a particular site more useful than others.

4. Analyze the limitations of the Job Listing System discussed here. List the features that can make this system a commercial-grade application.

5. Determine the mapping between the template files and the responses generated by the Job Listing System. The template files are the *.TXT files residing in the C:\WEBSITE\CGI-WIN\BOOK\JOBLIST\ directory.

TIP: Make a small change to one template file, and then check which response was affected.

4

BUILDING A DATABASE WITH MICROSOFT ACCESS

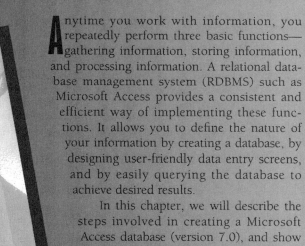

Anytime you work with information, you repeatedly perform three basic functions—gathering information, storing information, and processing information. A relational database management system (RDBMS) such as Microsoft Access provides a consistent and efficient way of implementing these functions. It allows you to define the nature of your information by creating a database, by designing user-friendly data entry screens, and by easily querying the database to achieve desired results.

In this chapter, we will describe the steps involved in creating a Microsoft Access database (version 7.0), and show how you can directly store and manipulate the database information using Microsoft Access' user-friendly interface. As a practical example, we will construct a database similar to the one utilized by our Web-based Job Listing System application. We assume that you have already gone through Chapter 3, Dissecting a Job Listing System, and are familiar with the basic functionality of this application.

LESSON 1: CREATING A NEW DATABASE

A Microsoft Access database is a collection of data and objects related to a particular topic or purpose. While the *data* represents the information stored in the database, the *objects* help you define the structure of that information and automate the data manipulating tasks. The neat part is that Access lets you keep these objects and the data as one file, which generally carries an .MDB file extension.

Microsoft Access supports the following basic object types from which all the database objects are created:

🦅 *Table* is used to define the data structure for different related topics.

🦅 *Query* lets you select or change data stored in one or more table type objects.

🦅 *Form* lets you create user-interface screens for entering, displaying, and editing data.

🦅 *Report* lets you present information, formatted and organized according to your specifications.

🦅 *Macro* lets you specify one or more actions to automate tasks.

🦅 *Module* acts as a repository of declarations and procedures that you can write to design advanced Microsoft Access applications.

In this book, we will mainly be concentrating on the Table- and Query-type database objects, since these are the only two database components that we use for our Web-based database applications. If you want to learn more about the other four database object types, you can refer to the Microsoft Access user manual or to its on-line help.

With this brief introduction about the overall philosophy of a Microsoft Access database, let's create a new database that we can use to store the job- and company-related information:

1. Create a JOBLIST2 subdirectory under the C:\WEBSITE\CGI-WIN\BOOK\ directory.

2. Launch Microsoft Access (version 7.0).

3. Access presents you with an option of creating a new database or opening an existing database as shown in Figure 4-1.

4. Select the Create A New Database Using Blank Database option, and then click on the OK button.

5. Access then presents a File dialog box asking you for the location and name of the new database file.

6. Select the C:\WEBSITE\CGI-WIN\BOOK\JOBLIST2\ directory, and type *JOBLIST2.MDB* in the File Name text box as shown in Figure 4-2. Then click on the Create button.

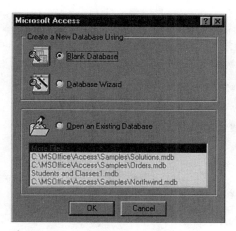

Figure 4-1 Creating a new Microsoft Access database

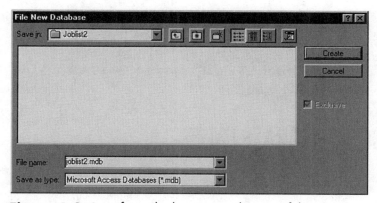

Figure 4-2 Specifying the location and name of the new database

7. Access quickly creates a blank database named JOBLIST2.MDB and displays its database container as shown in Figure 4-3.

The database container holds six tabs representing the six types of objects you can create in this database. The Tables tab is selected by default. Since we have not yet defined any Table-type objects for this database, the database container displays an empty window.

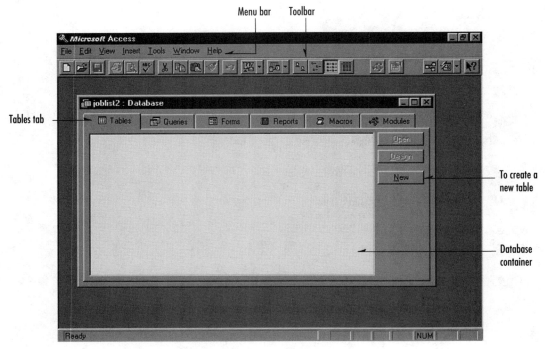

Figure 4-3 The Access database container

LESSON 2: CREATING A DATABASE TABLE

Now that you have created a blank JOBLIST2.MDB database, the first thing to do is define one or more database tables. As mentioned earlier, a database table represents the information pertaining to a specific topic. Usually, a topic consists of many related pieces of data. For example, if you are planning to keep detailed data about each listed job, you may want to store the company name, the job requirements, and the estimated salary along with the job title for each job.

In Microsoft Access, these pieces of information are called *fields,* and a collection of all the fields for a job comprises a *record.* All job records are held together in a database table. Figure 4-4 shows these table elements.

From the figure, note that the table fields represent different types of job-related data. The JobTitle and JobDescription fields hold text data; the JobID and the EstimatedSalary fields contain numeric data. Associating a field with an appropriate data type is one of the main tasks when you define a database table.

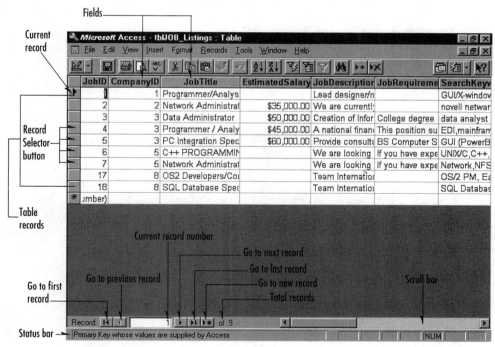

Figure 4-4 Datasheet view of a table

Data Types Supported by Access

Access supports a comprehensive set of data types that you can use to represent almost any type of data value. Here, we list these data types and provide a brief description of the type of data they can represent.

Text

This data type can hold alphanumeric characters and is useful for storing names, addresses, phone numbers, postal codes, and other nondescriptive text attributes. This is one of the most versatile and commonly used data types, with one limitation—you can store only up to 255 characters in a Text field.

Memo

This data type eliminates the 255-character limit of the Text data type by allowing you to store up to 64,000 characters, but you cannot sort or index a Memo field. You use this data type for notes, remarks, explanations, and other descriptive fields.

Number

This is a generic data type used to store numeric values with field size of Byte, Integer, Long Integer, Single, or Double. You can use the fields of this data type in mathematical calculations.

Currency

This data type is used for storing numbers involving money. It represents a scaled integer that can handle large monetary values with great precision. Accuracy is maintained up to four decimal places.

Date/Time

This data type allows you to represent fields that signify a date and time value. Sorting on this type of field produces a chronological order of the records. Access also provides several built-in functions that can be applied to Date/Time-type field values, many of which are described in the next chapter.

AutoNumber

This data type is equivalent to a long integer, except Access automatically provides unique numbers (usually in a numeric sequence) for each record. You cannot edit a value in the AutoNumber field.

Yes/No

This data type is used for fields that hold logical values such as Yes/No, True/False, and so on.

OLE Object

This data type is used for fields that hold pictures, graphs, sound, video, or other program objects, which can be linked or embedded in Access.

Field Properties Supported by Access

In addition to specifying the data type, you can also characterize the nature and appearance of the field data through the field properties, some of which are described next.

Field Size

For Number and Text fields, the Field Size property describes the maximum range (for numeric) or the maximum length (for text) of data values.

Format

This property specifies how Access should display the field data. For example, a MediumDate format on a date value of 7/1/96 will force Access to show the date as "1-Jul-96."

Caption

This property specifies how Access displays the field heading when you view the table records in its datasheet view as shown in Figure 4-4. If you do not specify a value for the field's Caption property, then Access uses the field name as the default caption for that field.

Required

This property tells Access to ensure that a data value is always specified for that field before it stores the record in the table.

Validation Rule

The Validation Rule property allows you to add constraints on the field data values by requiring the data to follow specific rules. You can test for individual values, data ranges, or even multiple conditions.

For example, if you want to allow only positive values for a currency field such as EstimatedSalary, you can enter *>0 OR Is Null* as a validation rule. Note that the *Is Null* condition is needed to permit a null value in this field in case EstimatedSalary is defined as a nonrequired field.

Validation Text

The Validation Text property holds the message that you want Access to display if the user-entered data does not meet the validation rule. For instance, you can specify the Validation Text for the EstimatedSalary field as *Please enter a positive salary*. Then anytime you try to enter a negative number for EstimatedSalary, Access will pop up a message box with this validation text.

Default Value

This property holds the value (or an expression) that you want Access to automatically fill in for that field when a new record is entered. For example, if you want today's date to automatically come up in a date field, you can set its default value to the *=date( )* expression.

Indexed

The Indexed property tells Access to index the field for faster data retrieval and searches based on that field. For example, if you plan to frequently search jobs in the job table based on the job title, you can set the Indexed property for the JobTitle field.

Concept of a Primary Key

A *primary key* acts as a unique tag for addressing a record. It not only helps in quickly searching a particular record, but also plays an important role in linking two related tables, as explained later in this chapter. You can specify one or more table fields during the table design phase to act as the table's primary key. Access then automatically prevents you from entering duplicate values in the primary key of that field.

The selection of fields to act as the primary key is sometimes not easy. For example, when creating a jobs table, you may consider the job reference number provided by the company listing that job as a candidate for the primary key. But what if two companies happen to use the same job reference number for their jobs? This may be unlikely, but it is certainly possible. When this happens, Access will not allow you to store the second job, since the uniqueness requirement of a primary key would be violated.

In such situations where the choice of one or more fields for a primary key is not obvious, you can add a new field (for example, JobID) to your table that serves as a unique ID for each record. Setting this new field to an AutoNumber data type generally works well, since Access automatically assigns a unique number to this field for each record you add to the table. Note that the AutoNumber data type does impose some editing restrictions as explained in Lesson 4 of this chapter.

Recommended Practice... Although Access does not require you to set a primary key for a table, it is a good practice to establish a primary key for every database table.

Defining the Jobs Table

Since our objective in this chapter is to design the JOBLIST2.MDB database for storing job- and company-related information (similar to the original JOBLIST.MDB database of the Job Listing System), let's define a table to store the job-related information based on the concepts we have studied so far.

We will start by setting a meaningful name for this jobs table, such as tblJOB_Listings. In this name, the "tbl" prefix reflects the Table object type, "JOB" identifies a base theme indicating that this is a job-related table, and the suffix "Listings" represents the actual topic this table is dealing with, which is the list of jobs. To create the tblJB_ JOBS table:

1. Open the C:\WEBSITE\CGI-WIN\BOOK\JOBLIST2\JOBLIST2.MDB database file in Microsoft Access if it is not already open.

2. Ensure that the Tables tab of the database container is highlighted, and then click on the New button.

3. Access presents several options for creating a new table as shown in Figure 4-5.

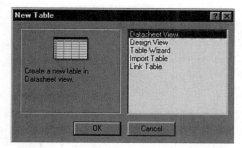

Figure 4–5 Options for creating a new table

4. For this exercise, select the Design View option, and then click the OK button.

5. Access now displays a new table in its design view as shown in Figure 4-6. It gives this table a default name of Table1.

6. Move the cursor into the Field Name column of the first row, and type *JobID* in that column.

7. Press <TAB> to move the cursor to the Data Type column of the first row.

8. Access automatically defaults the Data Type as Text for the JobID field. However, we want the JobID to be an AutoNumber type field.

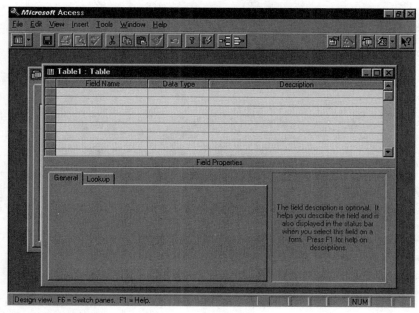

Figure 4–6 Design view of a new table

9. Click on the arrow displayed in the Data Type column, and select the AutoNumber data type from the drop-down list as shown in Figure 4-7.

10. Note from Figure 4-7 that Access automatically shows the field properties that you can customize for the current field. It also adds the most common values as defaults for many properties. For example, it sets the field size property of the JobID field as Long Integer, which is the standard size for a field with an AutoNumber data type.

11. For the JobID field, you do not need to change its properties. However, we do want to set it as a primary key of this table. So while the cursor is in the row of the JobID field, click on the Edit menu and select the Primary Key option.

12. Access responds by displaying a key-shaped icon beside the JobID field.

13. At this point, you can define the rest of the fields and their properties as listed in Table 4-1. Notice that the Default Value property is not specified for many fields of this table. This means that you should leave this property blank when defining the field. Also, Access automatically hides certain properties (such as Field Size and Indexed) for data types (such as Memo) where these properties are inapplicable.

14. Save the table as *tblJOB_Listings* by selecting the Save option from the File menu.

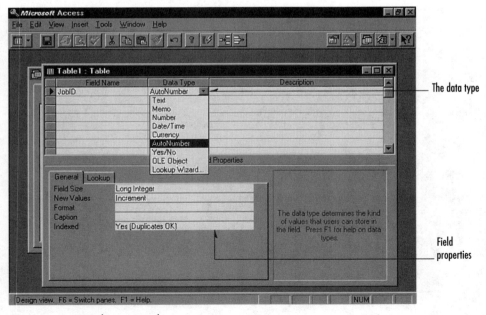

Figure 4–7 Selecting a data type

NOTE: If you do not want to carry out this last tedious step, you can close Microsoft Access and then overwrite the current JOBLIST2.MDB database file residing in the C:\WEBSITE\CGI-WIN\BOOK\JOBLIST2\ directory with the following file:

```
C:\WEBSITE\HTDOCS\BOOK\CHAP4\LESSON2\JOBLIST2.MDB
```

Table 4–1 Initial design of the tblJOB_Listings table

Field Name	Data Type	Field Size	Default Value	Indexed
JobID	AutoNumber	Long Integer	Primary Key	
JobTitle	Text	50	No	
EstimatedSalary	Currency			No
JobDescription	Memo			
JobRequirement	Memo			
SearchKeywords	Text	255	Yes (duplicates OK)	
ViewCounter	Number	Long Integer	0	No
DateEntered	Date/Time	Date()	Yes (duplicates OK)	
Contact	Text	255	No	
CompanyJobReference	Text	255	No	
CompanyName	Text	50	No	
Address	Text	50	No	
City	Text	50	No	
State	Text	15	No	
Zip	Text	20	No	
Phone	Text	50	No	
Fax	Text	50	No	
Email	Text	255	No	
ReferenceURL	Text	255	No	
CompanyInformation	Memo			
Recruiter	Yes/No		No	

Things to Consider When Designing a Table

While Access' table design interface makes it extremely simple to define the fields of any table, there are many additional factors you should consider when designing your table structure.

Using On-Line Help

You can search for "Tables" and "Creating Tables" under Microsoft Access Help Topics for more detailed information. You can also use the Microsoft Access Answer Wizard (from the Help menu) to guide you through the table design process. You can seek help on any field property by putting the cursor on that property and pressing <F1>. You can also look at the design of existing tables in sample databases that come with Microsoft Access.

Field Size Versus Actual Storage Space

For Text fields, the Field Size property indicates the maximum length allowed for the field. If you enter text shorter than the field size, Access only takes up storage space for the text entered.

Range of Data Values

When deciding on a field's data type, think of what kind of values that field should accept. For example, if a field name such as "Apartment#" can contain alphanumeric characters, it needs to be set as a Text data type.

Also, consider the storage capacity and the data range of each field. If you are designing a field to hold a person's age in years, a Number field of a *byte* size, which only accepts integer values from 1 to 255 is sufficient. If you want to store decimal information (for example, 5.25 years), a byte will not work. You will have to select a *single* size numeric field.

Record Level Validation

You can also specify a validation rule for the table itself. This validation rule is applied before the record is saved. To set a table validation rule, choose the Properties option from the View menu while the table is opened in its design view.

Microsoft Access Table Specifications

Table 4-2 lists the specifications related to Access tables.

Table 4–2 Access table specifications

Attribute	Maximum
Number of characters in a table name	64
Number of characters in a field name	64
Number of fields in a table	255
Table size	1 gigabyte
Size of an OLE Object field	1 gigabyte
Number of indexes in a table	32
Number of fields in an index	10
Number of characters in a validation message	255

Attribute	Maximum
Number of characters in a validation rule	2,048
Number of characters in a field description	255
Number of characters in a record (excluding Memo and OLE Object fields)	2,000
Number of characters in a field property setting	255

LESSON 3: POPULATING A DATABASE TABLE

The straightforward way of populating records in an Access table is through a table's datasheet view, which presents the table in a grid format, with rows acting as the records, and the columns acting as the table fields. The following steps show how you can display the datasheet view of the tblJOB_Listings table that you created in the previous lesson and add a few sample job records to this table:

1. Open the C:\WEBSITE\CGI-WIN\BOOK\JOBLIST2\JOBLIST2.MDB database file in Microsoft Access if it is not already open.

2. If you successfully completed the previous lesson, then Access should list the tblJOB_Listings table in the database container as shown in Figure 4-8.

3. While the tblJOB_Listings table object is highlighted, click on the Open button at the right end of the database container.

4. Access displays the tblJOB_Listings table in its datasheet view as shown in Figure 4-9. Note that due to the limited screen size, the datasheet view only shows a few table fields at a time. You can use the horizontal scrollbar to scroll to the other fields of this table.

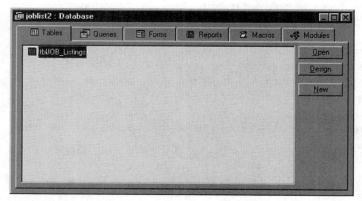

Figure 4-8 Database container showing the tblJOB_Listings table

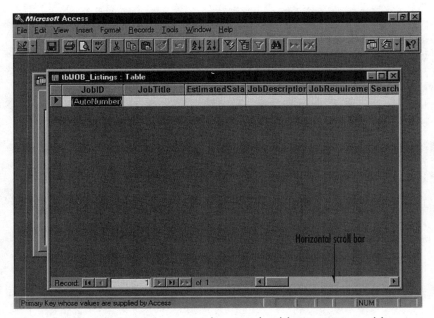

Figure 4–9 Database container showing the tblJOB_Listings table

5. Click on the JobTitle field, and type *Programmer/Analyst* in that field. Access automatically enters a numeric value for the JobID field.

6. Next, press <TAB> twice to skip the EstimatedSalary field and move the cursor to the JobDescription field. We will assume that the salary information is not available for this job.

NOTE: When you do not specify data for a particular field, Access automatically inserts a Null value for that field.

7. While the cursor is in the JobDescription field, press <SHIFT> <F2> to display this field in a zoom window. Type the information in that zoom window as shown in Figure 4-10, and press <ENTER> when you are done.

NOTE: You need to press <CTRL> <ENTER> if you want to insert a new line when entering data in a field.

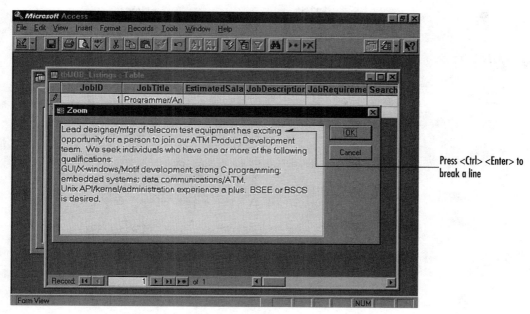

Figure 4–10 Displaying the field data through a zoom window

8. Now enter the following values for the rest of the table fields that do not have a default value:

```
      JobRequirement: BS Computer Science/Business
      SearchKeywords: GUI,X-windows,Motif,C
             Contact: Dayle Williamson
 CompanyJobReference: PGR-1
         CompanyName: XYZ Systems
             Address: 123 Park Street
                City: XYZ City
               State: NE
                 Zip: 12345
               Phone: (111) 111-1111
                 Fax: (111) 111-1112
               Email: dayle@xyz.com
        ReferenceURL: http://www.xyz.com/jobs
 CompanyInformation: XYZ Systems has been a leader in the Information
                     Technology Industry for the past 20 years. XYZ
                     is a national firm with offices in 28 cities. We
                     offer competitive salaries and excellent
                     benefits. Our benefits include medical/dental,
                     vacation and holidays, 401K, relocation
                     assistance, tuition reimbursement, and training.
```

9. After entering the data for all the table fields, press <SHIFT> <ENTER> to save the current record.

10. Now go to the next blank row, and add another job record for XYZ Systems as follows:

```
           JobTitle: Software Engineer
     EstimatedSalary: 53000
     JobDescription: Lead designer/mfgr of telecom test equipment has
                      exciting opportunity for a person to join our
                      ATM Product Development team. We seek an
                      individual who has one or more of the following
                      qualifications:
                      GUI/X-windows/Motif development; proven project
                      management skills; embedded systems; data
                      communications/ATM.
     JobRequirement: MS Computer Science/3 Year software development
                      experience
     SearchKeywords: GUI,X-windows,ATM,Leadership
            Contact: Dayle Williamson
  CompanyJobReference: PGR-5
        CompanyName: XYZ Systems
            Address: 123 Park Street
               City: XYZ City
              State: NE
                Zip: 12345
              Phone: (111) 111-1111
                Fax: (111) 111-1112
              Email: dayle@xyz.com
       ReferenceURL: http://www.xyz.com/jobs
 CompanyInformation: XYZ Systems has been a leader in the Information
                      Technology Industry for the past 20 years. XYZ
                      is a national firm with offices in 28 cities. We
                      offer competitive salaries and excellent
                      benefits. Our benefits include medical/dental,
                      vacation and holidays, 401K, relocation
                      assistance, tuition reimbursement, and training.
```

Now you can add some more sample jobs for this company as well as for other companies.

NOTE: The following version of the JOBLIST2.MDB database contains the two records listed in this lesson:

```
C:\WEBSITE\HTDOCS\BOOK\CHAP4\LESSON3\JOBLIST2.MDB
```

LESSON 4: MANIPULATING EXISTING RECORDS

Besides adding records, you can also edit or delete existing table records from the table's datasheet view.

Editing Records

The process of editing a record is similar to adding a new record. Let's say the XYZ Systems company changed its fax number from (111) 111-1112 to (111) 111-1113. The following steps show how you can reflect that fax number change in the two job records you entered for this company in the previous lesson:

1. Open the tblJOB_Listings table in the datasheet view.

2. Move the cursor to the Fax field of the first job record.

3. Press <F2> to highlight the current phone number in the Fax field.

4. Type *(111) 111-1113* in the Fax field. Access overwrites the previous number with the new number.

5. Press <SHIFT><ENTER> to save the modified record.

6. Repeat these steps for updating the Fax field of the second record.

Deleting a Record

You can also delete an existing record:

1. Select the record by clicking on the Record Selector button (see Figure 4-4) next to the record you want to delete. Access will highlight that record.

2. Press <DEL>. Access will ask for your confirmation before deleting that record.

Things to Consider During Data Editing

Here are some additional tips that you may find useful when editing data through Microsoft Access tables:

Access supports a Multi Document Interface, allowing you to open and edit multiple tables at a time.

You can copy the data from one field and paste it into another field. To make a duplicate of an existing record, select a record, and then choose the Copy command from the Edit menu. Then go to a new record, choose the Paste command from the Edit menu, and save the pasted record.

If you make a mistake while editing and have not saved the record yet, press <ESC> once to undo the changes made in the current field. Pressing <ESC> twice will undo all the changes made to the current record. If you have already saved the record, select the Undo Saved Record command from the Edit menu to undo any changes.

Two users on different machines can open the same database file and edit the records of the same table concurrently, provided neither user opens the database in the *exclusive* mode. Refer to the on-line help of Access for more information on multiuser data editing.

Editing Characteristic of an AutoNumber Type Field

As mentioned in Lesson 1, Access does not allow you to edit the data value of an AutoNumber type field. For example, if you move your cursor to the JobID field of any job record in the tblJOB_Listings table and then try to change its value, Access signals an error message in its status bar. Besides the editing restriction, there is another aspect of an AutoNumber type field that may be of concern if you are hoping for a regular numeric sequence for your AutoNumber type field. This aspect can best be explained by the following experiment:

1. Open the tblJOB_Listings table in its datasheet view.

2. Go to the new record, and type *Programmer* in the JobTitle field. As expected, Access automatically fills in a unique value for the JobID field.

3. Press <ESC> twice to cancel the addition of this new record.

4. Now, again type *Programmer* in the JobTitle field of this new record. This time, Access fills in the one number higher for the JobID field. If you keep repeating this process, you will notice that it is relatively easy to create a gap in the numeric sequence of an AutoNumber type field.

This possibility of a gap should not be a concern if you are mainly interested in the uniqueness aspect of an ID field when designing your table. However, if you want to ensure a regular numeric sequence for your ID field, then an AutoNumber data type may not be a good choice. Instead, you can define your ID field as a Numeric type, and design your own autonumbering method to add values to that field. We implement one such method for our virtual bookstore application, which is described in Chapter 16, Creating an On-Line Bookstore.

LESSON 5: NORMALIZING TABLES

In the previous lesson, you had to update two job records to make a small change in the fax number of XYZ Systems. Imagine how tedious it could get if XYZ Systems had several job records in the tblJOB_Listings table. While data maintenance is one difficulty with the way the tblJOB_Listings table currently stores the job and the company data, the other issues such as data inconsistency and data repetition also arise from its current design.

As you have already seen, you have to add the same company information with every job of that company. This wastes disk space. Furthermore, suppose two managers of a company called Compusoft Corporation want to list a job opening in their section, and one manager lists the company name as "Compusoft Corporation," while the other just specifies "Compusoft Corp." for the company name, resulting in the discrepancy of data.

The preceding issues can be resolved by a process called *table normalization,* where you break a table into two or more tables that are linked only through their key fields. This way the information is stored at only one place, and the necessity of data duplication is eliminated.

Our tblJOB_Listings table is a prime candidate for this normalization process, since we would prefer not to repeat the same company information with each job record of that company. The following procedure outlines what tasks are involved in normalizing the tblJOB_Listings table:

Move all the company-related fields from the tblJOB_Listings table to a new table named tblJOB_Companies.

Add a new AutoNumber type field named CompanyID to the tblJOB_Companies table to act as this table's *primary* key.

Add a CompanyID field in the tblJOB_Listings table to act as the linking field between this table and the tblJOB_Companies table. This CompanyID field is also referred to as the *foreign* key.

Add one record for each company in the tblJOB_Companies table.

Set the CompanyID field of each job record in the tblJOB_Listings table to the CompanyID value of the company offering that job.
To accomplish the preceding tasks:

1. Using the method described in Lesson 2, create a new table named *tblJOB_Companies* in the JOBLIST2.MDB database with the fields listed in Table 4-3.

NOTE: None of these fields need any value set for their Default Value property.

Table 4-3 Design of the tblJOB_Companies table

Field Name	Data Type	Field Size	Default Value	Indexed
CompanyID	AutoNumber	Long Integer		Primary Key
CompanyName	Text	50	No	
Address	Text	50	No	
City	Text	50	No	
State	Text	15	No	
Zip	Text	20	No	
Phone	Text	50	No	

continued on next page

continued from previous page

Field Name	Data Type	Field Size	Default Value	Indexed
Fax	Text	50	No	
Email	Text	255	No	
ReferenceURL	Text	255	No	
CompanyInformation	Memo			
Recruiter	Yes/No		No	

2. Open the existing tblJOB_Listings table in the design view.

3. Click on the JobTitle field.

4. Click on the Insert menu, and then select the Field option.

5. Access inserts a blank row between the JobID field and the JobTitle field, as shown in Figure 4-11.

6. Add a Number type field named CompanyID with the following properties in this blank row:

```
      FieldSize: Long Integer
  DefaultValue: Null
       Indexed: Yes (Duplicates OK)
```

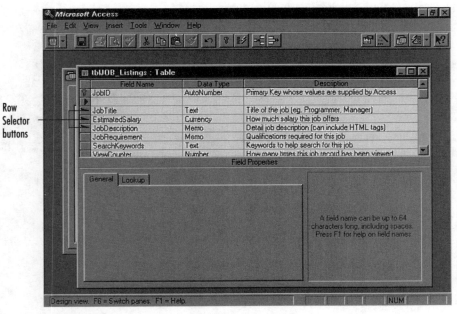

Figure 4-11 Inserting a new field in a table

7. Click on the Row Selector button next to the CompanyName field and press <DEL>.

8. Access asks if you want to permanently delete the CompanyName field from the tblJOB_Listings table.

9. Select Yes to confirm the deletion of the CompanyName field.

10. In the same manner, delete the following company fields from the tblJOB_Listings table:

```
Address
City
State
Zip
Phone
Fax
Email
ReferenceURL
CompanyInformation
Recruiter
```

11. Save the modified design of the tblJOB_Listings table.

12. Open the tblJOB_Companies table in its datasheet view, and add the XYZ System's company record.

13. Access automatically assigns a CompanyID value of 1 to this company record.

14. Next, add a record for all other companies whose jobs you entered at the end of Lesson 3.

15. Now open the tblJOB_Listings table, and set the CompanyID field to *1* for all the jobs belonging to XYZ Systems.

16. In the same manner, set the CompanyID field of all other jobs to their company's CompanyID value.

As you can see, we have successfully separated the original tblJOB_Listings table into two tables through the normalization process. The tblJOB_Listings table now contains only the job-specific information, while the tblJOB_Companies table contains all the company-specific information.

Observe that one company record in the tblJOB_Companies table can be linked to any number of job records in the tblJOB_Listings table through the CompanyID field. In other words, there is a *one-to-many* relationship that exists between the tblJOB_Companies table and the tblJOB_Listings table.

Under the database terminology, the tblJOB_Companies table (the "one" side of this relationship) is referred to as the *parent* table, and the tblJOB_Listings table (the "many" side of this relationship) is referred to as the *child* table.

One task that we still have not addressed is how to reconnect the information between the tblJOB_Companies and the tblJOB_Listings tables so that we can view the complete company information with each job. The answer lies in building Access queries, which is our topic for the next two chapters.

NOTE: The following version of the JOBLIST2.MDB database contains the result of this lesson:

`C:\WEBSITE\HTDOCS\BOOK\CHAP4\LESSON5\JOBLIST2.MDB`

LESSON 6: ESTABLISHING TABLE RELATIONSHIP AND REFERENTIAL INTEGRITY

While the objective of the normalization process is to store information efficiently and sensibly by identifying how the data fields are related, you can benefit from this process only if you correctly maintain the linking fields. For example, if you change the CompanyID field of a job belonging to XYZ Systems from *1* to say, *100,* that job immediately gets associated to the company with CompanyID 100 in the tblJOB_Companies table. Furthermore, if the tblJOB_Companies table does not have a company record with CompanyID 100, that job record then becomes an *orphan* record (a child record that does not have any parent record).

Although it may not be your intention to create orphan job records, a small typing error in the CompanyID field of the tblJOB_Listings table can easily be responsible for such a data mismatch. Fortunately, you can have Access warn you of such an occurrence right at the time of data entry if you specifically set a relationship between the two tables and establish the appropriate referential integrity rules as explained in the following:

1. Open the C:\WEBSITE\CGI-WIN\BOOK\JOBLIST2\JOBLIST2.MDB database in Microsoft Access if it is not already open.

2. Click on the Tables tab of the database container.

3. Select Relationships from the Tools menu.

4. Access displays the Relationships window and pops up a list of database tables as shown in Figure 4-12.

5. Click on the Add button to add the currently selected tblJOB_Companies table to the Relationships window.

6. Select the tblJOB_Listings table, and again click on the Add button. Then click on the Close button to close the pop-up table list.

7. Access adds the tblJOB_Listings table to the Relationships window as shown in Figure 4-13.

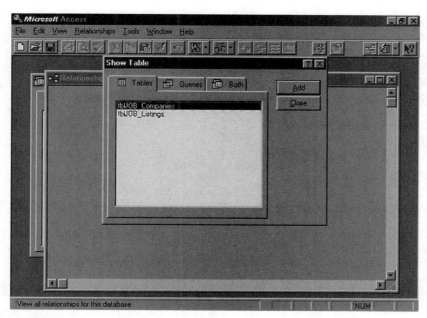

Figure 4–12 List of database tables

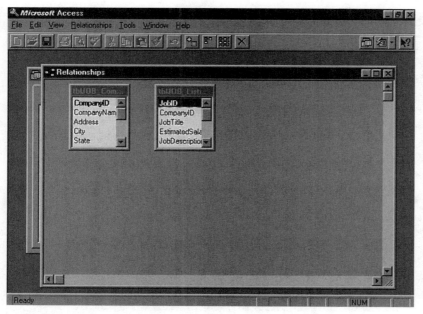

Figure 4–13 Adding tables to the Relationships window

8. Click on the CompanyID field in the tblJOB_Companies table, and while keeping your left mouse button pressed, drag that field over to the CompanyID field listed in the tblJOB_Listings table.

9. In response, Access pops up another dialog box that lists the linking fields of the two tables, as shown in Figure 4-14. This dialog box also gives you an option to enforce the referential integrity between the two tables.

10. Select the Enforce Referential Integrity check box.

11. Access highlights the two available referential integrity options.

12. Select the Cascade Update Related Fields option, and then click on the Create button to set the one-to-many relationship between the two tables.

13. Access now indicates the existence of that relationship by displaying a line between the linking fields of the two tables in the Relationships window as shown in Figure 4-15.

In the previous step, you saw that there are two referential integrity options you can have Access enforce between related tables. These options prevent the records of the child table from getting orphaned.

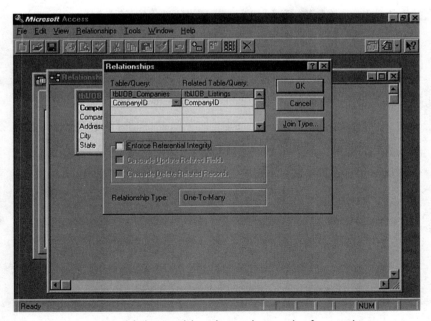

Figure 4-14 Establishing table relationship and referential integrity

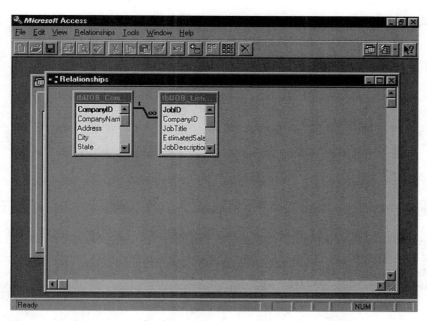

Figure 4-15 Access displaying a one-to-many relationship between two tables

Cascade Update Option

By selecting the Cascade Update Related Fields option, you tell Access that if a user changes the value of the CompanyID field in a company record, then it should automatically change the value of the CompanyID field in all the related job records. If you do not select this option, then Access will not allow you to change the value of the CompanyID field of a company record if any related jobs exist in the tblJOB_Listings table.

Note that in our case, the Cascade Update Related Fields option does not help much—you cannot change the CompanyID field of a company record anyway, since this field is set to an AutoNumber data type.

Cascade Delete Option

By selecting the Cascade Delete Related Records option, you tell Access that if a user deletes a company record, then it should automatically delete all the related job records. If you do not select this option, then Access will not allow you to delete the company record if any related job records exist in the tblJOB_Listings table.

Testing Referential Integrity Rules

As an example of referential integrity enforcement, let's see how Access responds when you try to delete the company record of XYZ Systems:

1. Close the Relationships window by selecting the Close option from the File menu.

2. Open the tblJOB_Companies table in the datasheet view.

3. Select the record of XYZ Systems and then press <DEL>.

4. Access signals an error message as shown in Figure 4-16, instead of deleting the record.

5. Click on the OK button to close the message box displaying the error.

NOTE: The following version of the JOBLIST2.MDB database contains the result of this lesson:

```
C:\WEBSITE\HTDOCS\BOOK\CHAP4\LESSON6\JOBLIST2.MDB
```

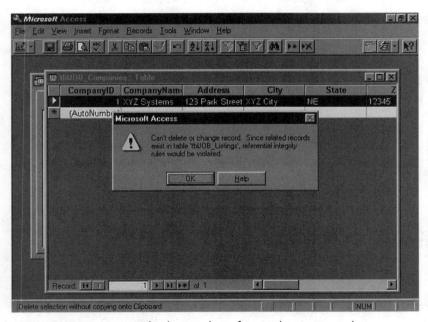

Figure 4–16 Access displaying the referential integrity violation error

114

REVIEW QUESTIONS

1. What is a field? How is it related to a record?

2. Which data types can you use to represent a phone number? Which one do you prefer? Why?

3. What does the default value field property do?

4. Define the role of a primary key in a table design.

5. When is an AutoNumber field useful? What are its main limitations?

6. Can you store a blank record in Access (where all fields are null)?

7. What is the objective of a Normalization process? How do you normalize a table?

8. How does referential integrity prevent the creation of orphan records?

9. What referential integrity options are available in Access and how do they work?

EXERCISES

1. Explore the topics discussed in this chapter on the on-line help system of Microsoft Access. Once you start using Access on a regular basis, you will quickly realize the tremendous potential of the wealth of information contained in this on-line help facility.

2. The On-Line Questionnaire application demonstrated in Chapter 2, Getting Started, uses the following database for storing user feedback:

```
C:\WEBSITE\CGI-WIN\BOOK\SURVEY\SURVEY.MDB
```

3. Open this database in Microsoft Access and examine its table structure.

4. When you try to create a new database, Access gives you an option to create 22 commonly used databases through its built-in Database Wizard. Create a few databases from this list, and analyze the design of the tables (and their associated relationships) in those databases.

5. Create a database for a video store. The database should store basic information about the movie (title, actors, duration, theme, and so on) as well as each actor's profile. Add some sample records into the database. Remember to normalize your database. Hint: Since one movie can have many actors and one actor can act in many movies, you will need to create a *many-to-many* relationship between the movies table and the actors table. This is accomplished with the help of a junction table that holds only the primary key of each table. Search for the *many-to-many* keyword in the Answer Wizard for details on creating a many-to-many relationship among tables. Chapter 16, Creating an On-Line Bookstore, also throws more light on this topic.

5

BUILDING MICROSOFT ACCESS QUERIES

5

In Chapter 4, Building a Database with Microsoft Access, you learned how to store data in an Access database by creating and using tables. You can look at your stored data anytime by opening the table in the datasheet view. When your table is populated with few records (say, less than 50), you can comfortably glance at all the records and find the information you want. However, if your table grows to hold thousands of records, browsing the table datasheet is not a viable option every time you want to look for some information. This is where Access queries come to the rescue. By designing queries, you can probe your tables to view, filter, analyze, and even manipulate data in various ways.

In this chapter, we will show how to create queries in Access using its powerful query design window. For our examples, we will use a copy of the JOBLIST2.MDB database constructed in the previous chapter. This copy is stored as JOBLIST3.MDB in the

C:\WEBSITE\HTDOCS\BOOK\CHAP5\ directory and is prepopulated with some good data that we will use in analyzing the results of the queries we design in this chapter.

NOTE: For a handy reference, all the queries created in this chapter are stored in the C:\WEBSITE\HTDOCS\BOOK\CHAP5\RESULT\JOBLIST3.MDB database file.

LESSON 1: CREATING A SINGLE TABLE QUERY

Let's say you are interested in locating jobs that offer a salary of $40,000 or above. To quickly accomplish this task, you design a query that extracts those jobs from the job listing table:

Open the C:\WEBSITE\HTDOCS\BOOK\CHAP5\JOBLIST3.MDB database file in Microsoft Access.

1. Click on the Queries tab of the database container.

2. Click on the New button to design a new query.

3. Access gives you an option of using either the four available query wizards or going directly into the query design view as shown in Figure 5-1.

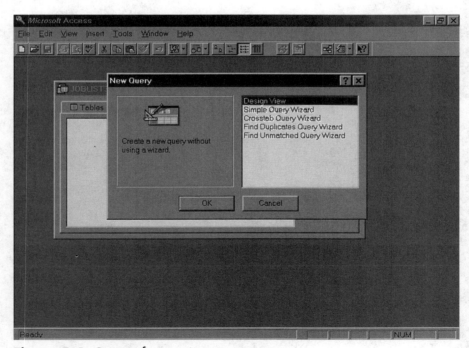

Figure 5–1 Options for creating a new query

Query design window

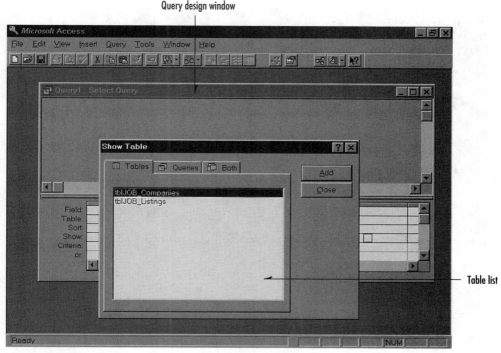

Table list

Figure 5-2 Adding a table in a query design window

For this lesson, select the Design View option.

Access brings up the query design window and displays a list of tables present in the current database as shown in Figure 5-2.

NOTE: For most types of queries, the query wizards can give you a good head start. Eventually, each query wizard takes you to the query design window with major portions of the query predesigned (based on the choices you made while using the wizard). However, it is ultimately through the query design window that you are able to exploit the tremendous power of Access queries.

4. Select the tblJOB_Listings table from the displayed table list, and click on the Add button. Click on the Close button to hide the table list.

Access adds the tblJOB_Listings table to the query design window as shown in Figure 5-3.

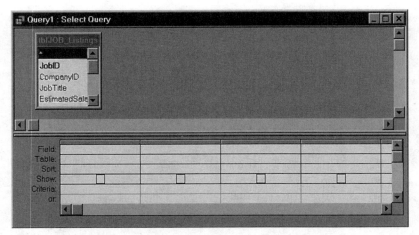

Figure 5-3 Query design window displaying the fields of the selected table

5. Double-click on the asterisk (*) symbol present in the tblJOB_Listings table.

Access adds that asterisk symbol in the first cell of the Field row as shown in Figure 5-4. It also lists the table name in the first cell of the Table row and automatically selects the first Show check box.

6. Now, double-click on the EstimatedSalary field displayed in the tblJOB_Listings table.

Access adds the EstimatedSalary field to the second cell of the Field row and also selects its Show check box by default as shown in Figure 5-5.

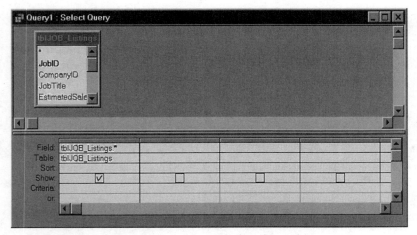

Figure 5-4 Adding the asterisk symbol to the Field row

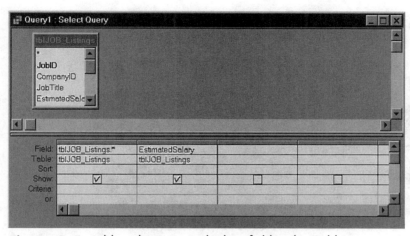

Figure 5-5 Adding the EstimatedSalary field to the Field row

7. Deselect the Show check box associated with the EstimatedSalary field, and then type in the criterion >=40000 in its Criteria cell as shown in Figure 5-6.

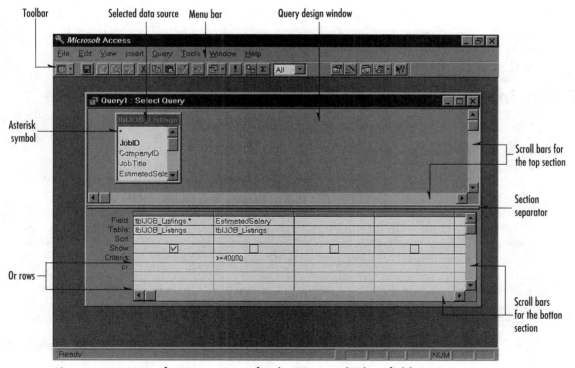

Figure 5-6 Specifying a criterion for the EstimatedSalary field

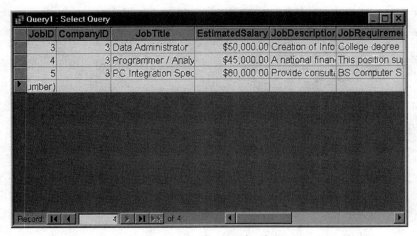

Figure 5-7 Jobs matching the estimated salary criterion

8. Finally, select the Run option from the Query menu.

Access executes your query and returns a list of jobs with an estimated salary of $40,000 or higher as shown in Figure 5-7.

Note that Access presents the query result in a form similar to the datasheet view of a table. We will explain the reason behind this similarity later in the lesson. Let's first examine how this query is designed.

Examining the Query Design

As you can see from Figure 5-6, the query design window contains two main sections. The top section holds a rectangular list box, representing your selected table, which acts as the data source of your query. The asterisk (*) symbol in the rectangular list box acts as a special field that stands for "All Table Fields." We use this special field whenever we want the query to display the data from all the table fields in its result.

The bottom section of the query design appears as a grid of rows and columns. You use this grid to specify the goal of your query. You list the table fields you want to work with in the Field row. The Table row indicates which table each field listed in the Field row belongs to and is particularly helpful when you include multiple tables in your query, as you will see in Lesson 7, "Creating a Two-Table Query."

The Sort row (described further in the next lesson) is provided to generate the query result in a particular sort order by specifying the two available sort options (Ascending or Descending) against one or more fields listed in the Sort row. Note that you cannot specify a sort option for the asterisk field.

The check boxes in the Show row let you select which fields you want to include in the query result. In our current example, we deselected the Show check box for the EstimatedSalary field, since it was already represented by the asterisk field.

The Criteria row of the query design grid allows you to define the limiting criteria against any field listed in the Field row. Access applies the criteria to filter the records from the source table. The subsequent Or rows act as an extension of the Criteria row and are used to combine multiple criteria through the logical OR operator as explained in Lesson 7, "Creating a Two-Table Query."

Saving the Query Design

You can store your query design as a database object. This way, you can run the query anytime in the future without having to redesign the query. The result of the query is always based on the current data. To save your current query as qryJOB_HighSalaries:

1. Select the Save option from the File menu.

Access prompts you for a query name and displays "Query1" as the default name.

2. Type *qryJOB_HighSalaries* for the query name, and click on the OK button.

Access saves the query design as a query object named qryJOB_HighSalaries.

3. Select the Close option from the File menu.

Access closes the query result window and displays the stored query object in the database container as shown in Figure 5-8.

4. Click on the Open button in the database container.

Access redisplays the filtered job records.

Figure 5-8 Saving the query design

Examining the Query Result

Refer to the query result shown in Figure 5-7. As you can see, the query result contains the subset of job records that meet the specified estimated salary criterion. By presenting this result in the form of a table datasheet, Access provides a familiar interface for browsing through the filtered information. Furthermore, you can even edit the data listed in this query result just like you edit data in a table. Any changes made to this query result are reflected back in the tblJOB_Listings table itself, as demonstrated by the following:

1. Open the qryJOB_HighSalaries query (if it is not already open) to display the query result shown in Figure 5-7.

2. Click in the JobTitle field of the job record with JobID 3, and change the data from "Data Administrator" to *Database Administrator* in that field.

3. Press (SHIFT)-(ENTER) to save the record.

4. Close the query result window.

5. Select the Tables tab of the database container, and open the tblJOB_Listings table in the datasheet view.

The JobTitle field of the job record with JobID 3 now contains the value "Database Administrator" as shown in Figure 5-9.

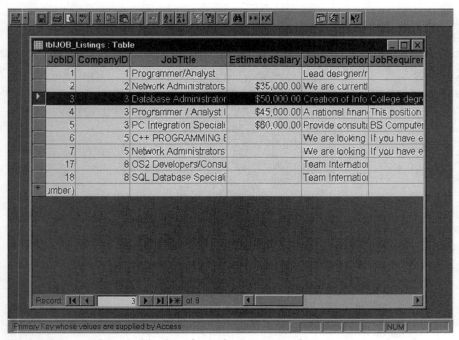

Figure 5–9 Editing table data from the query result

🔩 **NOTE:** The preceding steps also illustrate how you can use this powerful feature of Access queries for *selective editing,* where you first filter your records of interest and then make changes to them. You can even add new jobs. Access enforces all the field properties such as default values and validation rules defined in the table design during this data editing process.

An Experiment... Change the estimated salary of any job returned by this query to *$30,000* and save the record. What do you notice? Access does not automatically remove that job record from the query result, even though the job does not meet the *[EstimatedSalary]>=40000* criterion anymore. Now, close the query result window and reopen the query. This time that job is not included in the result.

LESSON 2: SORTING RECORDS

Normally, Access shows the table records in the primary key order whether you are viewing them from the table datasheet or as part of the query result. For example, in the query result of the previous lesson, Access displayed all the job records in the ascending order of their JobID.

Oftentimes though, there is a need to view the records in a different sort order. Say you want to show all the high salary jobs selected by the qryJOB_HighSalaries query with the highest salaried job listed first. You can easily accomplish this task by making a small change in the design of the qryJOB_HighSalaries:

1. Select the qryJOB_HighSalaries query from the database container, and click on the Design button.

2. Access displays the design of the qryJOB_HighSalaries query in the query design window.

3. Type *Descending* in the Sort cell of the EstimatedSalary field as shown in Figure 5-10.

4. Select the Run option from the Query menu to run the modified query.

    Access displays the selected job records in the descending order of their estimated salaries as shown in Figure 5-11.

5. Save this query as qryJOB_HighSalaries_Sorted using the Save As option from the File menu.

Note that if you want to further sort your jobs in the reverse chronological order of their listing date, you can specify an additional Descending sort option on the DateEntered field as shown in Figure 5-12.

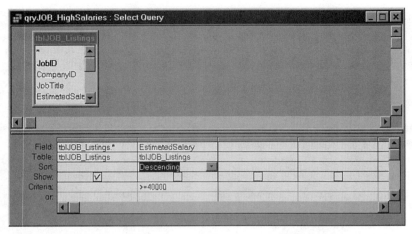

Figure 5-10 Specifying a sort option in a query

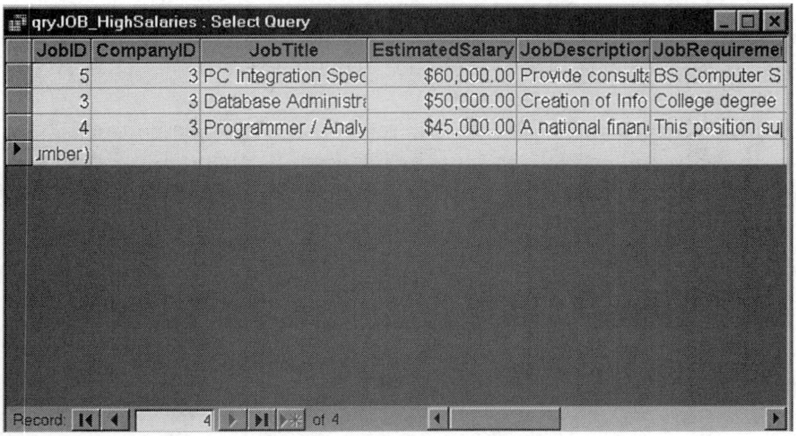

Figure 5-11 Result of specifying a sort option in a query

When sorting on multiple fields, the order in which you place these fields on the Field row decides which field is sorted on first. The leftmost sort field becomes the primary sort field, and so on. Search on the keyword "Field" in the Answer Wizard to learn how to insert and rearrange fields in the design grid of the query window. Remember, if you frequently sort on a field, it is a good idea to set the indexed property of that field to speed up the sort process.

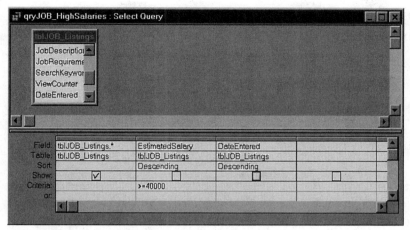

Figure 5-12 Sorting on multiple fields

Sort Alert... The way data is sorted depends on the data type of the Sort field. Text fields are sorted in alphabetical order, Number and Currency fields in numeric order, and Date fields in chronological order. So, if you sort on a Text type field such as Apartment# that contains numeric values, then *1* will be followed by *10* and not *2*. Also, you cannot sort on a Memo- or OLE-type field.

LESSON 3: EXAMPLES OF DIFFERENT CRITERIA

Here we explore some common situations to illustrate the syntax and functionality of different query criteria. You can use them in similar situations or combine them to create multiple-criteria queries.

Filtering a Date Range

Suppose you want to design your query to return the jobs listed during the month of November 1995. This requires a limiting criterion on the job listing table's DateEntered field, which stores each job record's listing date. The month of November can be described as any date falling between 11/1/95 and 11/30/95. In a query, you specify this date range criterion using the *Between...And* operator as follows:

```
Between #11/1/95# AND #11/30/95#
```

Observe that the date values are bracketed by the pound (#) sign. The surrounding pound signs are required when you specify a date value in your criterion.

NOTE: You can also describe the same date range criterion as follows:

`>=#11/1/95# AND <=#11/30/95#`

To create a query named *qryJOB_Listings_November_95* that returns all the jobs listed in November 1995:

1. From the database container of the JOBLIST3.MDB database, open a new query in the query design window.

2. Add the tblJOB_Listings table to this query.

3. Add the asterisk field and the DateEntered field to the Field row.

4. Deselect the Show check box of the DateEntered field.

5. Specify the *Between...And* criterion in the Criteria cell of the DateEntered field as shown in Figure 5-13.

6. Save the query under the name *qryJOB_Listings_November_95* by selecting the Save option from the File menu.

7. Run the query.

Access displays all the jobs listed in November 1995 as shown in Figure 5-14.

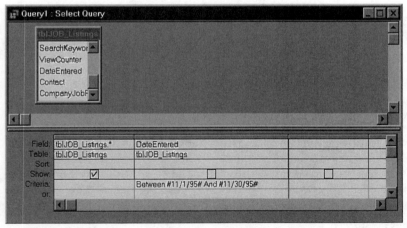

Figure 5–13 Specifying a date range criterion

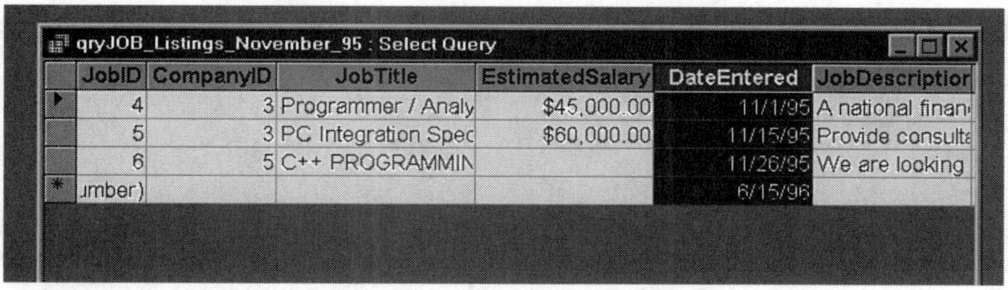

Figure 5-14 Result of specifying a date range criterion

NOTE: In our query result, we moved the DateEntered column next to the EstimatedSalary column so that it shows up in Figure 5-14. You can examine the date values in this column to verify the accuracy of the query result. For more information on how to rearrange columns in a query result, search for the topic "Moving columns in Datasheet view" from Access's on-line help.

Using Criteria Against a Calculated Field

What if you wanted to see all jobs entered in the month of November, irrespective of the year? You somehow need to retrieve the month information from the DateEntered field and compare it against the number *11*. To help you with this task, Access provides a *Month* function, which takes a date expression as a parameter and returns its month as a number between 1 and 12. To display the jobs listed in November:

1. Open a new query in the query design window with tblJOB_Listings table as its data source.

2. Click on the first column of the Field row and type the following text:

   ```
   MonthEntered: Month([DateEntered])
   ```

3. Add the asterisk field to the second column of the Field row.

4. Type *11* in the Criteria cell of the first column as shown in Figure 5-15.

5. Save this query as qryJOB_Listings_November.

6. Run the query.

   Access displays all the November jobs in the query result as shown in Figure 5-16.

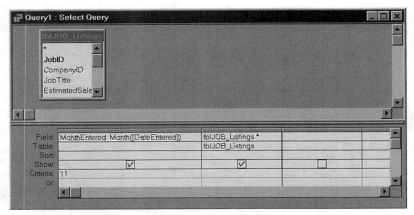

Figure 5-15 Specifying a criterion on a calculated field

MonthEntered	JobID	CompanyID	JobTitle	EstimatedSalary	DateEntered
11	4	3	Programmer / Analy	$45,000.00	11/1/95
11	5	3	PC Integration Spec	$60,000.00	11/15/95
11	6	5	C++ PROGRAMMIN		11/26/95
11	7	5	Network Administrat		11/3/96
11	17	8	OS2 Developers/Co		11/21/96
11	18	8	SQL Database Spec		11/21/96
	umber)				6/15/96

Figure 5-16 Result of specifying a criterion on a calculated field

NOTE: You can also use the *Year*, *Day*, and many other built-in date functions described in the next lesson to extract other date-related information from a date expression.

Calculated Fields... When you compose an expression on a table field by applying a function or an operator, you create a *calculated field*, which for most purposes can be treated like any other regular field. Calculated fields can be created only through a query by use of the syntax *FieldName:FieldExpression* (for example, MonthEntered: Month([DateEntered]). Note that the DateEntered field is surrounded by square brackets ([ ]).

Filtering Records on Discrete Values with the *IN* Operator

Sometimes it is not easy to define a range using the *Between...And* operator to filter a record against a list of values. For instance, if you want to search all U.S. companies from tblJOB_Companies table residing along the southern border of the United States, you have to check the State field for California (CA), Arizona (AZ), New Mexico (NM), Texas (TX), Mississippi (MS), Louisiana (LA), Alabama (AL), and Florida (FL). To specify the criterion for such a situation, you use the IN operator as follows:

1. Open a new query in the query design window.

2. Add the tblJOB_Companies table to this query.

3. List the asterisk field of the tblJOB_Companies table in the first column of the Field row.

4. Add the State field to the second column of the Field row.

5. Deselect the Show check box under the State field.

6. Insert the following criterion in the Criteria cell of the State field as shown in Figure 5-17.

```
In ("CA","AZ","NM","TX","MS","LA","AL","FL")
```

7. Save the query as qryJOB_Companies_Southern_US_States.

8. Run the query.

9. Access shows all the southern U.S. companies in its query result as shown in Figure 5-18.

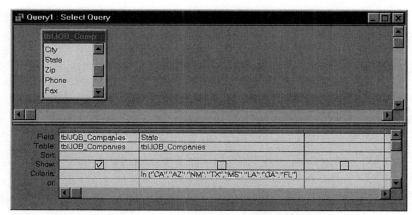

Figure 5-17 Specifying a criterion using the IN operator

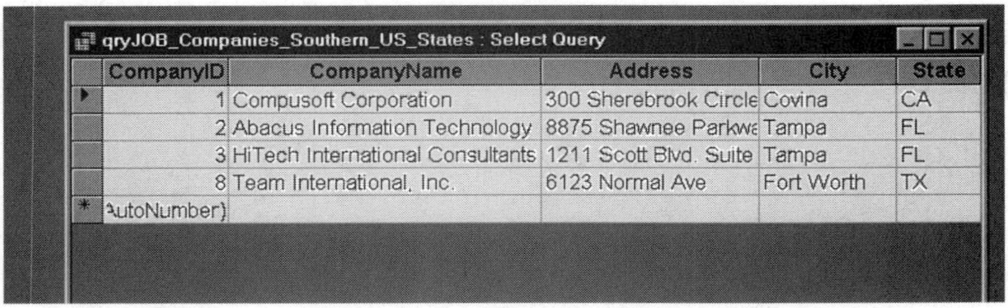
qryJOB_Companies_Southern_US_States : Select Query

CompanyID	CompanyName	Address	City	State
1	Compusoft Corporation	300 Sherebrook Circle	Covina	CA
2	Abacus Information Technology	8875 Shawnee Parkwa	Tampa	FL
3	HiTech International Consultants	1211 Scott Blvd. Suite	Tampa	FL
8	Team International, Inc.	6123 Normal Ave	Fort Worth	TX
AutoNumber)				

Figure 5-18 Result of specifying a criterion using the IN operator

NOTE: If you want to select all the states *except* those, you can append a NOT operator before the IN operator as follows:

```
NOT In ("CA","AZ","NM","TX","MS","LA","AL","FL")
```

In general you can use the NOT operator before any criterion to reverse your condition. Also, Access is not case-sensitive when it comes to text comparison. For example, specifying *tx* instead of *TX* in the above criterion will produce the same query result.

LESSON 4: USING EXPRESSIONS IN CRITERIA

Not only can you use expressions to create calculated fields, but you can also make them part of your criteria. For example, if you want to see those jobs that were entered in the past seven days, you can type the expression *>=Date()-7* as a criterion for the DateEntered field. Whenever you run the query, Access first gets the current system date through the *Date()* function, subtracts 7 (days) from that date, and compares all the jobs against that resulting date.

Following is a list of many built-in Access functions you can use when creating an expression. You can seek on-line help on any function for its exact syntax, parameters, and purpose.

- *Abs*—This function returns the absolute value of a number.
- *Date*—This function returns the current system date.
- *DateAdd*—This function adds a time interval (positive or negative) to a given date and returns the resulting date.
- *DateDiff*—This function returns the number of time intervals between two specified dates.
- *DatePart*—This function returns a specified part of a given date. It can be used in place of the *Day*, *Month*, or *Year* functions.

🍄 *DateSerial*—This function returns a Date in Access's native date format (a double precision number) for a specified year, month, and day.

🍄 *Format*—This function formats an expression according to instructions contained in a format expression.

The *Format* function is an extremely powerful function that helps you display your data in various ways. Some examples of this function follow:

```
Format("m",#1/1/96#) returns "1"
Format("mm",#1/1/96#) returns "01"
Format("mmm",#1/1/96#) returns "Jan"
Format("mmmm",#1/1/96#) returns "January"
```

See help on "Format" for all the available formatting options.

🍄 *IIf*—This function returns one of two parts based on the given expression.

For example, *IIF([A]>[B],[A],[B])* returns the value of field [A] if it is greater than the value of field [B]; otherwise, it returns the value of field [B].

🍄 *InStr*—This function returns the position of the first occurrence of one string within another.

🍄 *IsNull*—This function determines if an expression results in a Null value.

For example, *IsNull([EstimatedSalary])* returns True (-1) if no value has been specified for the EstimatedSalary. Note that you cannot use = *Null* in the Criteria row to check for Null values in a field. You must use *Is Null* instead, or pass that field through the *IsNull* function and then test the resulting calculated field against a True (or -1) value.

🍄 *Mid*—This function returns a specified number of characters from a string.

🍄 *Now*—This function returns the current date and time according to the setting of your computer's system date and time.

Note that the *Date* function only returns the current date (with time always set to 00:00 or 12:00 A.M.).

🍄 *Val*—This function returns the numbers contained in a string.

LESSON 5: MATCHING PATTERNS WITH WILDCARDS AND THE *LIKE* OPERATOR

When you compare a Text field against a string value using the = operator (for example, [STATE] = "CA"), Access performs an exact match. Access will not select a record with the value of "CALIFORNIA" in the State field. If you want to include the phrase *Starting With,* *Ending With,* or *Any Part Of* in your search statement, then you need to apply the following wildcard characters along with the LIKE operator:

- * stands for any number of alphanumeric characters.

- ? represents any single character.

- # represents any single digit.

As an example, if you want to search all jobs that have the word "Programmer" anywhere in the JobTitle field, you can specify the following criterion for the JobTitle field:

```
Like "*PROGRAMMER*"
```

This selects jobs with job titles such as "Programmer," "Programmer/Analyst," "Computer Programmer," and so on. (No, it will not select Software Engineer!) Similarly, the criterion *Like "PROGRAMMER*"* represents *Starting with the word "Programmer,"* and the criterion *Like "*PROGRAMMER"* represents *Ending with the word "Programmer."*

While the LIKE operator adds a lot of flexibility in specifying the search criteria, these pattern matching searches do not occur as fast as the searches made through an exact match using the = operator. In fact, only the *Like "PROGRAMMER*"* criterion can take advantage of any indexing done on the JobTitle field.

Another Way of Finding Jobs Listed In November 1995... Specify the criterion *Like "11/*/95"* for the DateEntered field to search jobs listed in November 1995. Note that this search is not as efficient as the search made using the *Between...And* operator.

LESSON 6: SPECIFYING CRITERIA ON MULTIPLE FIELDS

Often, there is a need to filter records based on more than one field of a table. You can combine the criterion expression for each field into one query to make a complex query. (Actually, it is not that complex.)

For example, if you want to see the job description and job requirements for all the high paying programming jobs listed within the past seven days in the reverse chronological order, you need to design a query as shown in Figure 5-19.

When the query criteria are listed side by side on the same Criteria row, Access finds records that match all the specified criteria. On the other hand, if you want to create a query that matches one or more of these criteria, you use the Or rows of the query design grid to list the individual query criteria. To create a query to list either the Programmer or the high paying jobs:

1. Open a new query in the query design window, and list the tblJOB_Listings table as its data source.

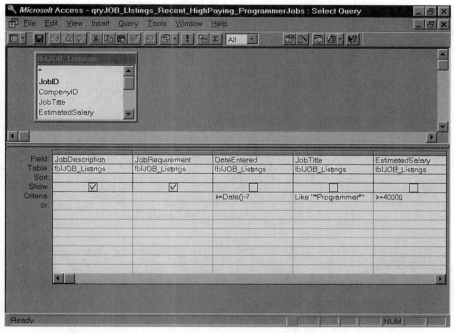

Figure 5–19 Specifying criteria on multiple fields with the AND combination

2. Add the asterisk (*), JobTitle, and the EstimatedSalary fields, respectively, to the first, second, and third columns of the Field row.

3. Deselect the Show check box for the JobTitle and the EstimatedSalary fields.

4. Add the following criterion in the Criteria cell of the JobTitle field:

```
Like "*Programmer*"
```

5. Add the following criterion in the Or cell of the EstimatedSalary field. (See Figure 5-20.)

```
>=40000
```

6. Save your query as qryJOB_Listings_Programmer_Or_HighPaying.

7. Run your query.

Access displays the query result as shown in Figure 5-21.

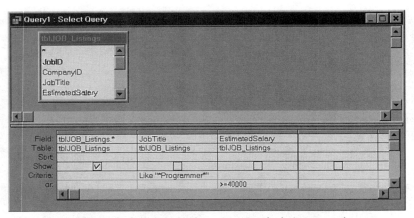

Figure 5–20 Specifying multiple criteria with the OR combination

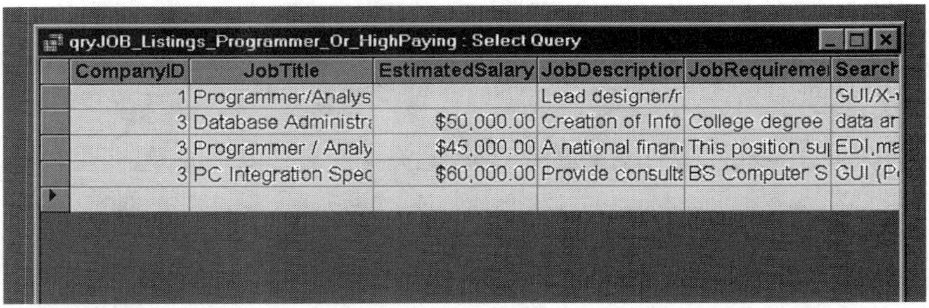

Figure 5–21 Result of specifying multiple criteria with the OR combination

LESSON 7: CREATING A TWO-TABLE QUERY

In Lesson 5, "Normalizing Tables," of Chapter 4, Building a Database with Microsoft Access, we showed how separating job- and company-specific information into two related tables through the normalization process helps in preventing data duplication and data inconsistencies.

However, this normalization approach proves advantageous only if you have an easy way of combining the two tables and seeing all the information together. Moreover, you must be able to query your records using criteria based on the fields of both tables. An example of such a case would be to list all high paying jobs in Florida with their company names. Fortunately, achieving this result is not only possible in Access, but also is relatively easy to do through the query design window:

1. Open a new query in the query design window.

Access presents you with the table list to select the data source for the query. The name of the tblJOB_Companies table is highlighted by default.

2. Click on the Add button to add the tblJOB_Companies table to the query. Now highlight the tblJOB_Listings table, and click on the Add button again. Then click on the Close button to hide the table list.

Access not only adds the tblJOB_Listings table to the query, but also displays a line connecting this table to the tblJOB_Companies table as shown in Figure 5-22.

3. Double-click on the CompanyName field of the tblJOB_Companies table.

Access adds this field to the first cell of the Field row.

4. Double-click on the asterisk (*) field of the tblJOB_Listings table.

Access adds the asterisk field to the second cell of the Field row. Observe how the Table row clarifies which table each field on the Field row belongs to.

5. In the same manner, add the State field from the tblJOB_Companies table and the EstimatedSalary field from the tblJOB_Listings table to the Field row, and deselect their Show check boxes.

6. Specify the *Like "FL*"* criterion for the State field and the *>=40000* criterion for the EstimatedSalary field as shown in Figure 5-23.

7. Save the query as qryJOB_Listings_Florida_HighPaying.

8. Run the query.

Access shows all the high-paying Florida-based jobs with their company names as shown in Figure 5-24.

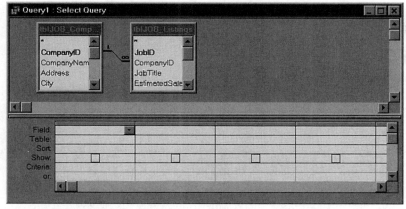

Figure 5–22 Adding two tables to a query

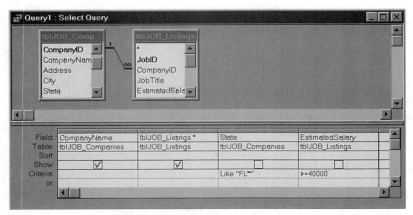

Figure 5–23 Specifying criteria against the fields of two tables

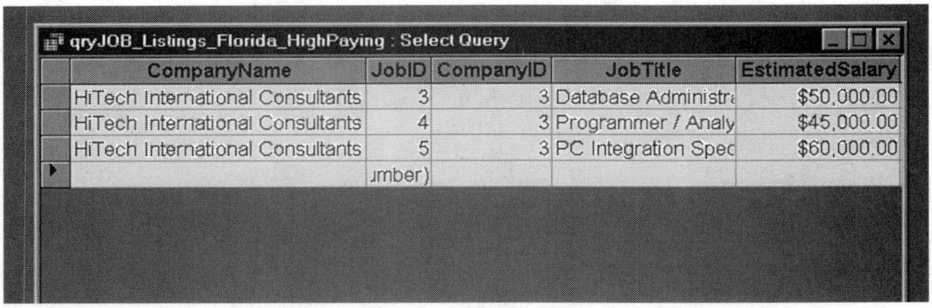

Figure 5–24 Specifying criteria against the fields of two tables

NOTE: As with the single-table queries, Access allows you to edit the query result of a two-table query. Changes are updated directly to the underlying tables. Try modifying the company name of one of the job records in your query result and save that record. You will see that this change is immediately reflected in the company name field of all other jobs belonging to this company. If you open the tblJOB_Companies table and view the record of this company, you will see the changed company name.

LESSON 8: WORKING WITH INNER AND OUTER JOINS

In the previous lesson, you saw that Access connected the tblJOB_Companies and the tblJOB_Listings tables in your two-table query. This connection tells Access that the two tables are related by use of their CompanyID fields. When you run the query, Access combines the fields of the tblJOB_Listings table with the fields of the tblJOB_Companies table. In database terminology, this type of connection is called an *inner join* (or sometimes, an *equi-join*).

Understanding How the Inner Join Works

The most important aspect of an inner join is that it causes Access to combine only those records where the values of the joining fields match in *both* the tables. The following demonstration clarifies this aspect:

1. Open a new query in the query design window.

2. Add the tblJOB_Companies table and the tblJOB_Listings table to this query as shown in Figure 5-22 of the previous lesson.

3. Add the CompanyName field from the tblJOB_Companies table and the asterisk (*) field from the tblJOB_Listings table.

4. Run the query.

    Access displays the names of all the companies with their associated job records as shown in Figure 5-25.

5. Save this query as qryJOB_Companies_Listings_InnerJoin.

6. Close the query design window.

7. Open the tblJOB_Companies table, and add a record of a new company named DataTech Corporation. For this demonstration, you do not need to fill in any other field except the CompanyName for this new record.

CompanyName	JobID	CompanyID	JobTitle	EstimatedSalary
Compusoft Corporation	1	1	Programmer/Analys	
Abacus Information Technology	2	2	Network Administrat	$35,000.00
HiTech International Consultants	3	3	Database Administra	$50,000.00
HiTech International Consultants	4	3	Programmer / Analy	$45,000.00
HiTech International Consultants	5	3	PC Integration Spec	$60,000.00
YellowStone Technical Services	6	5	C++ PROGRAMMIN	
YellowStone Technical Services	7	5	Network Administrat	
Team International, Inc.	17	8	OS2 Developers/Co	
Team International, Inc.	18	8	SQL Database Spec	

Figure 5–25 Result of an inner join between the company and the job table

WEB DATABASE CONSTRUCTION KIT

8. Close the tblJOB_Companies table, and reopen the qryJOB_Companies_Listings_InnerJoin query once again.

You will notice that Access does not include the name of the newly added company in its query result. This is because the new company does not have any associated job record in the tblJOB_Listings table.

Creating an Outer Join

If you want Access to list this new company along with the other companies in the query result, even though this company does not have any jobs yet, you have to connect the tblJOB_Companies table and the tblJOB_Listings table using a different link known as the *outer join*. To create this link:

1. Open the qryJOB_Companies_Listings_InnerJoin query in the query design window.

2. Double-click on the link representing the inner join between the two tables.

Access displays the join properties as shown in Figure 5-26.

4. Select the option (2) that says "Include ALL records from 'tblJOB_Companies' and only those records from 'tblJOB_Listings' where the joined fields are equal," and then click on the OK button.

Access now displays the link as a directed line pointing from the tblJOB_Companies table to the tblJOB_Listings table as shown in Figure 5-27.

Click here to display join properties

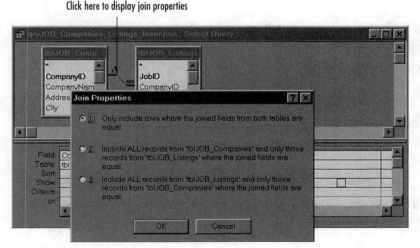

Figure 5-26 Displaying the join properties

142

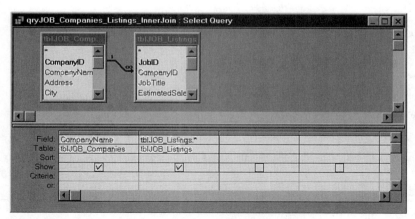

Figure 5-27 Creating an outer join between tables

5. Save the query as qryJOB_Companies_Listings_OuterJoin.

6. Run the query. This time Access lists the name of the new company in the query result as shown in Figure 5-28.

   Note that all the job fields associated with this company are Null in this query result.

Creating a Subtract Query

A *Subtract query* of two tables returns all those records from one table that do not have any related records in the other table. This query comes in handy if you are looking for child-less records in a parent table or orphan records in a child table.

CompanyName	JobID	CompanyID	JobTitle	EstimatedSalary
Compusoft Corporation	1	1	Programmer/Analys	
Abacus Information Technology	2	2	Network Administrat	$35,000.00
HiTech International Consultants	3	3	Database Administra	$50,000.00
HiTech International Consultants	4	3	Programmer / Analy	$45,000.00
HiTech International Consultants	5	3	PC Integration Spec	$60,000.00
YellowStone Technical Services	6	5	C++ PROGRAMMIN	
YellowStone Technical Services	7	5	Network Administrat	
Team International, Inc.	17	8	OS2 Developers/Co	
Team International, Inc.	18	8	SQL Database Spec	
Datatech Corporation				
	umber)			

Figure 5-28 Result of creating an outer join between tables

As an example, if you want Access to list companies with no associated job records, you can create a Subtract query between the company and the job listing table as follows:

1. Create a new query in the query design window.

2. Add tblJOB_Companies and tblJOB_Listings to this query.

3. Establish an outer join from tblJOB_Companies to tblJOB_Listings as explained in the previous section.

4. Add the CompanyName field from the tblJOB_Companies table to the first column of the Field row.

5. Add the JobID field (the job table's primary key) from the tblJOB_Listings table to the second column of the Field row.

6. Type *Is Null* in the Criteria cell of the JobID field as shown in Figure 5-29.

7. Save the query as qryJOB_Companies_NoListings.

   Run the query.

   Access returns only Datatech Corporation in the query result as shown in Figure 5-30.

THINGS TO CONSIDER WHEN DESIGNING A QUERY

Like most major database management systems, Access uses structured query language (SQL) to query its databases. You generally do not have to worry about writing these SQL statements, because Access creates them behind the scenes when you design your queries through the query design window.

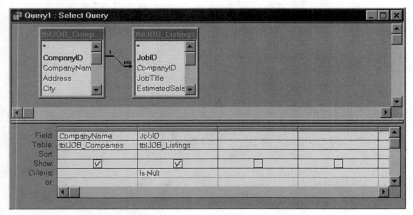

Figure 5–29 Designing a Subtract query

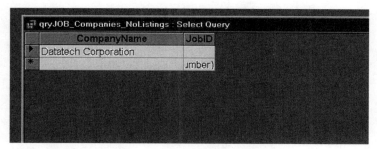

Figure 5–30 Result of a Subtract query

Viewing the SQL Statement Behind Your Query

Those who are familiar with SQL and want to double-check their design can easily view the associated SQL statements by selecting the SQL option from the View menu of the query design window. Figure 5-31 shows the SQL statement constructed by Access for the subtract query (qryJOB_Companies_NoListings) we constructed in the previous lesson.

Another advantage of viewing SQL statements constructed by Access is that if you do not know SQL, then this is an excellent way of learning it. In addition, there are some types of queries (for example, Union queries) that cannot be created through the query design screen and have to be typed through the SQL window.

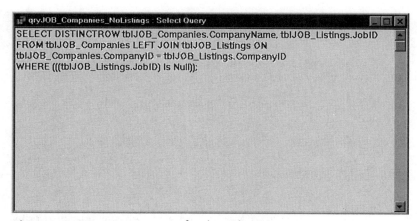

Figure 5–31 SQL statement for the Subtract query

SQL Tip... If you are used to writing SQL statements for your query design, you can directly type or modify the SQL statement in the SQL view of the query. When you run your query, Access will interpret your SQL statement and run the query or notify you of any errors if it is unable to run the query. Although Access closely follows the ANSI SQL standard, there are some subtle differences that you should familiarize yourself with by reading the "Programming and Language Reference" section of the Answer Wizard when you search on the word "SQL."

Criteria and Field Data Types

It is important that the data values you list in your criteria match the data type of the field. Although Access is sometimes forgiving if you put incorrect syntax (for example, if you forget the quotes) and tries to make the best guess, we recommend that you follow proper syntax to guarantee the accuracy of your query, as described next:

🔑 For a Date field, your date value must be surrounded by a pair of pound (#) characters (for example, >=#11/1/95#).

🔑 For a Text field, your text values must be bracketed by either a pair of single quotes (for example, 'NE'), or a pair of double quotes (for example, "NE").

Note that if you have a quote as part of your text data value, then you should replace that quote with two quotes (for example, "5"" long") before specifying that data value in your criterion. Another way of getting around this situation is to use the other quote character around the data value (for example, '5" long').

🔑 For a Yes/No field, your criterion value must result in a True (-1) or a False (0) value.

🔑 Numeric values (for example, 11) for a Number, Currency, or AutoNumber type field do not need any special surrounding characters.

🔑 In the case of a calculated field, you should try to evaluate the data type of the final field expression and then apply the appropriate syntax for your criterion.

For example, Month([DateEntered]) must be set against a numeric criterion, whereas DateAdd("d",1,[DateEntered]), which adds one day to each job's DateEntered field, must be set against a date criterion.

🔑 **NOTE:** Even though you cannot sort on a Memo field, you can still specify a criterion against it (for example, the Like "*Computer Science*" condition for the JobRequirement memo field).

Cartesian Product of Two Tables

If you delete the join line between two tables and display the fields from both tables in your query design, Access returns every combination of records (or *Cartesian product*) between the tables. So, if one table has 8 records and the other table has 5 records, then 40 records will be produced by the query.

TABLE-QUERY RELATIONSHIP

The kind of queries you have learned in this chapter are known as Select queries, because they let you select the data of interest from the database tables, and because they generate a SELECT SQL statement. But how is the result of a query related to the underlying table? Does Access create a temporary table in virtual memory to hold the result and somehow maintain its link with the original table? The correct answer is, "Not exactly!"

When you run a query, Access generates a list of pointers called a *recordset*. (See Figure 5-32.)

Each pointer in this recordset points to a record in the underlying table(s). That is why when you edit data from the query result, the change is dynamically reflected in the table itself. The concept of recordsets is one of the many features that has made Access popular and is discussed further in Chapter 13, Utilizing an Access Database in a CGI Application.

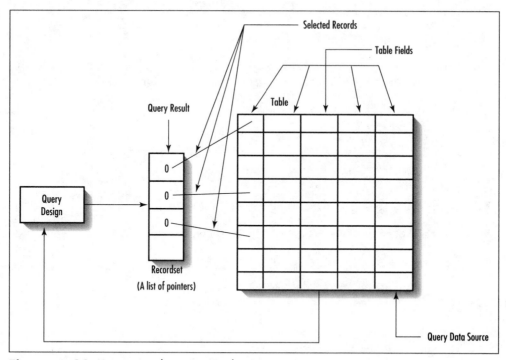

Figure 5-32 Query result as a recordset

REVIEW QUESTIONS

1. Why do you need Access queries?

2. Can you think of the advantages of using the asterisk (*) field over adding all the table fields in the Field row of a query? Hint: Think what happens when you add a new field to the table in the future.

3. What happens to the underlying table if you edit the data in a query datasheet? How is selective editing useful?

4. What is stored in the database when you save a query? Why is saving a query helpful?

5. Is it possible to sort a table on multiple fields? If so, how does Access know about the primary sort field?

6. Where does a text sort differ from a numeric sort?

7. In how many ways can you specify a range criterion?

8. What is a calculated field? How is it created?

9. How can you apply the *Format* function to show all the jobs listed in January irrespective of their year? How would you do it using the *IIf* function?

10. When does an IN operator come in handy?

11. What does the search criterion *LIKE* "*" imply? When are searches using a wildcard needed? What type of wildcard searches can take advantage of a field index?

12. How do you combine the records from two related tables into one record?

13. What is an inner join? How is it different from an outer join?

14. What is the use of a Subtract query? How do you create it?

15. What is a recordset?

EXERCISES

1. Design a query to show all jobs listed in 1995.

2. Design a query to show all jobs that have the word "UNIX" in their SearchKeywords field.

3. Design a query that shows the JobTitle, CompanyName, and the EstimatedSalary. If no estimated salary is available, then your query should show the phrase "Not specified" instead of an empty field.

4. Create a query to display all the Florida- and Texas-based companies that do not claim to be a recruiter in alphabetical order of their company name.

5. Design a query to show the jobs of the companies selected in Exercise 3.

6

DESIGNING ADVANCED QUERIES

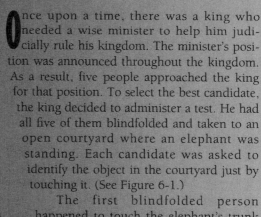

Once upon a time, there was a king who needed a wise minister to help him judicially rule his kingdom. The minister's position was announced throughout the kingdom. As a result, five people approached the king for that position. To select the best candidate, the king decided to administer a test. He had all five of them blindfolded and taken to an open courtyard where an elephant was standing. Each candidate was asked to identify the object in the courtyard just by touching it. (See Figure 6-1.)

The first blindfolded person happened to touch the elephant's trunk and immediately declared it to be a python. The second person felt around the elephant's leg with both hands, noticed the cylindrical shape, and identified it as a pillar. The third person, who was holding the elephant's tail, said that it must be a rope. The fourth person, who touched the flat surface of the elephant, identified it as a wall. The king then turned toward the fifth person, who was curiously standing still and had not touched the object at all.

Figure 6–1 Five blindfolded men and an elephant

After a momentary pause, that person proclaimed the object to be an elephant. The king, amazed by the reply, offered him the position and asked how he came to that conclusion without touching the object. The candidate smiled and answered, "I formed my decision by listening to the observations made by the other four candidates."

In this information age, this story makes a lot of sense. Different people view the same information and come up with different opinions about that information based on how they look at it. It is all a matter of perspective. It is generally true that the more ways you can analyze information, the more accurate and dependable an opinion you can form about that information. This chapter deals with this macroscopic view of information. It explains how you can design advanced queries in Microsoft Access to examine the information from various standpoints.

As you saw in Chapter 4, Building a Database with Microsoft Access, Access allows you to view any stored data by looking at the table datasheet. You can even find selective information by creating a single or multiple table query. For example, in Chapter 5, Building Microsoft Access Queries, you learned how to display each company and its job in one datasheet.

Now, you might want to get a bigger picture of your job database. For example, you might be curious about the average salary of a programmer, or which company has the highest number of jobs listed, or you might just want a job count and average salary by each state. All this and much more is possible in Access through Total queries, which is one of the main topics of this chapter.

As with the previous chapter, we will use a version of the JOBLIST.MDB database residing in the C:\WEBSITE\HTDOCS\BOOK\CHAP6\ directory for the data analysis queries discussed in this chapter. This version is named JOBLIST4.MDB. The resulting queries are stored in the JOBLIST4.MDB database file residing in the C:\WEBSITE\HTDOCS\BOOK\CHAP6\RESULTS\ directory.

LESSON 1: CREATING A TOTAL QUERY

As our first step in the data analysis of the job listing database, let's find out how many jobs are listed by each company. To generate this information, we design a Total query in Access. *Total queries* allow you to calculate a sum, average, count, or other total on a set of records.

1. Open the C:\WEBSITE\HTDOCS\BOOK\CHAP6\JOBLIST4.MDB database file in Microsoft Access.

2. Select the Query tab of the database container, and click on the New button to open a new query in the query design window.

Access prompts you to select the data source for this query.

3. Add tblJOB_Companies and tblJOB_Listings to the query.

Access automatically links the two tables with an inner join.

4. Add the CompanyName field of the tblJOB_Companies table and the JobID field of the tblJOB_Listings table to the Field row.

5. Select the Totals option from the View menu.

Access adds a new row labeled "Total:" to the query design grid as shown in Figure 6-2.

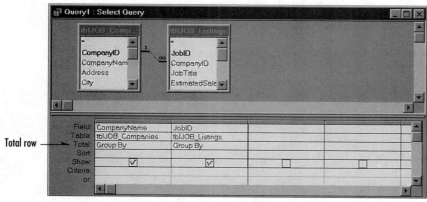

Figure 6-2 Adding the Total row to the query design grid

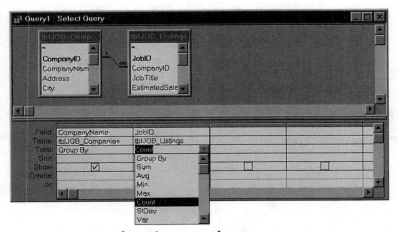

Figure 6-3 Specifying the **Count** function

This Total row shows the *Group By* function by default under the two selected fields.

6. Change the *Group By* function to the *Count* function for the JobID field as shown in Figure 6-3.

7. Select the Save option from the File menu, and save this query as *qryJOB_Companies_JobCount*.

8. Run the query.

The query result consists of two fields as shown in Figure 6-4.

The CompanyName field shows the name of each company, and the CountOfJobID field shows a count of all the jobs associated with each company. In plain text, the query we just constructed can be described as: *Group* all the jobs *by* their CompanyName and return a *count* of JobIDs for each group.

Also notice that the records are shown in alphabetical order by company name.

9. Now, select the Query Design option from the View menu to return to the query design window.

10. Specify a *Descending* sort option for the JobID field.

11. Select the Save As option from the File menu, and save this modified query as *qryJOB_Companies_JobCount_Sorted*.

12. Run the query again.

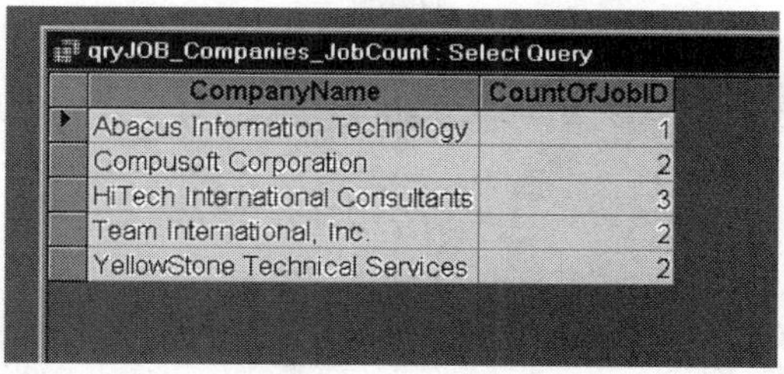

qryJOB_Companies_JobCount : Select Query

CompanyName	CountOfJobID
Abacus Information Technology	1
Compusoft Corporation	2
HiTech International Consultants	3
Team International, Inc.	2
YellowStone Technical Services	2

Figure 6–4 Result of the Count query

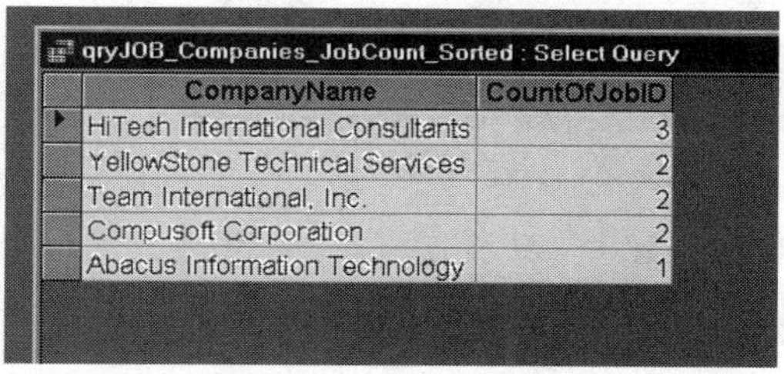

qryJOB_Companies_JobCount_Sorted : Select Query

CompanyName	CountOfJobID
HiTech International Consultants	3
YellowStone Technical Services	2
Team International, Inc.	2
Compusoft Corporation	2
Abacus Information Technology	1

Figure 6–5 Query result listing the companies in the order of their job count

How did the result change? The company with the highest job count is now listed first, as shown in Figure 6-5. There you have it! An easy way of not only producing the job count by each company, but also finding out which company has listed the most jobs in the database.

The *Group By* Function

As you can see from the design of the qryJOB_Companies_JobCount query, the *Group By* function indicates the field you want to group in when performing calculations such as count, sum, and average. You can also group in multiple fields by specifying the *Group By* function for all those fields. In that case, the leftmost Group By field becomes the primary grouping field, and so on.

It turns out that, in our JOBLIST4.MDB database, the tblJOB_Companies table has two records with the same company name (representing two branches of Compusoft Corporation), as shown in Figure 6-6. Moreover, each branch has one job record listed in the tblJOB_Listings table.

However, observe from Figure 6-5 that the qryJOB_Companies_JobCount query returns only one record for Compusoft Corporation. The associated CountOfJobID indicates the total number of jobs listed by both branches of this company. This is because you are grouping on the company name and not on the company ID (which is different for the two branches).

If you want to ensure that you get a separate job count for each branch, you have to group on the CompanyID field and then on the CompanyName field, as shown in Figure 6-7.

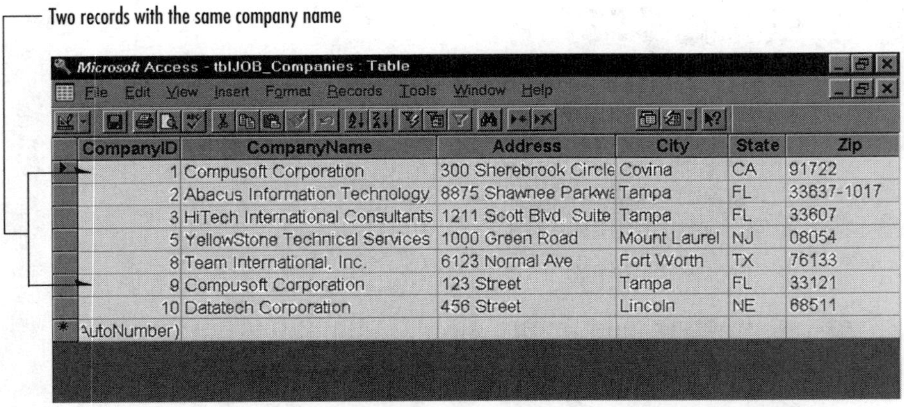

Two records with the same company name

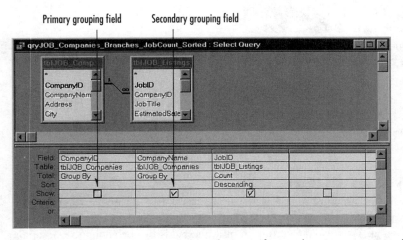

Figure 6–6 Company table containing two records with the same company name

Figure 6–7 Query to return the job count for each company record

Note that in this query, the Show option for the CompanyID field is deselected so that the query result still contains only the company names and the job counts. Figure 6-8 shows the query result.

Finding Unique Values... You can list unique values of any table field (except Memo and OLE fields) by adding only that field to the Field row and then applying a *Group By* function to it.

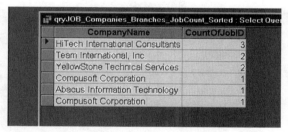

Figure 6-8 Job count for each company record

Aggregate Functions

The kind of analysis carried out by a Total query depends on the aggregate functions specified in its Total row. These functions aggregate data within the grouping specified by the *Group By* function. In the query shown in Figure 6-5, the *Count* function counts the number of job IDs for each CompanyName group.

If you remove the CompanyName field from the Field row, then the query result returns a total count of the jobs listed by all companies. Would this query return the same result if you were to apply the *Count* function to the EstimatedSalary field instead of the JobID field? Not necessarily.

The *Count* and other aggregate functions only consider records where the aggregated field is not Null. If you perform your count on the EstimatedSalary field, the job count might return lower numbers (and might give you a wrong picture), since some job records might have a Null value for their estimated salary field. So, if you want to consider all your records for counting purposes, it is important to choose a field that is not Null in any record. The JobID field, being the primary key, is the ideal candidate.

Table 6-1 lists all the aggregate functions available for the Total row.

Table 6-1 Aggregate functions for a Total query

Function	Purpose	Applicable Data Types
Sum	Total of the values in a field	Number, Date/Time, Currency, AutoNumber
Avg	Average of the values in a field	Number, Date/Time, Currency, AutoNumber
Min	Lowest value in a field	Text, Number, Date/Time, Currency, AutoNumber
Max	Highest value in a field	Text, Number, Date/Time, Currency, AutoNumber
Count	Number of non-Null values	All data types

continued on next page

continued from previous page

Function	Purpose	Applicable Data Types
StDev	Standard deviation	Number, Date/Time, Currency, AutoNumber
Var	Variance of the values in a field	Number, Date/Time, Currency, AutoNumber

LESSON 2: USING MULTIPLE AGGREGATE FUNCTIONS

In many cases, you can apply several aggregate functions at a time in a single Total query. As an example, let's examine the job database from a state perspective and identify how many jobs are available in each state, out of that how many jobs belong to recruiting companies, and finally, what the average and maximum salary per state are.

The following steps illustrate how you can design one query to get all the answers.

Step 1: Deciding the Grouping Field(s)

Our current data analysis task can be broken into four questions:

- How many jobs are available in each state?

- How many jobs belong to the recruiting companies in each state?

- For each state, what is the average salary?

- What is the maximum salary of a job offered in each state?

Observe the universal element among these questions. The reason it is possible to respond to all these questions with just one query is because they are all asking information by state. Thus the State field becomes the common grouping field. We use this observation to start the design of our query as follows:

1. Open a new query in the query design window.

2. Add tblJOB_Companies and tblJOB_Listings to the query.

3. Select the Total option from the Query menu.

4. Add the State field from the company table to the Field row.

   Access automatically sets the *Group By* function for this field and selects its Show check box.

Step 2: Performing the Job Count by State

Now we can calculate the job count by state in a manner similar to the job count we calculated for each company in the previous lesson:

1. Add the JobID field from the tblJOB_Listings table to the Field row.

2. Set the *Count* function for this field in the Total row.

Step 3: Finding the Jobs from Recruiting Companies

For each state, how will you find the number of jobs that belong to the recruiting companies? You cannot use the *Count* function on the Recruiter field of the company table, because it will return the same result as the job count. Remember, the *Count* function simply counts the number of records with a non-Null value in the specified field; it does not distinguish between the values. The way to handle this question is to employ the *Sum* function as shown next:

1. Create a calculated field in the query's Field row as follows:

```
RecruiterCount: IIf([Recruiter],1,0)
```

This calculated field returns a *1* if the Recruiter field of the company record is True (or Yes); otherwise, it returns *0*.

2. Set the Total row for this calculated field to the Sum function as shown in Figure 6-9.

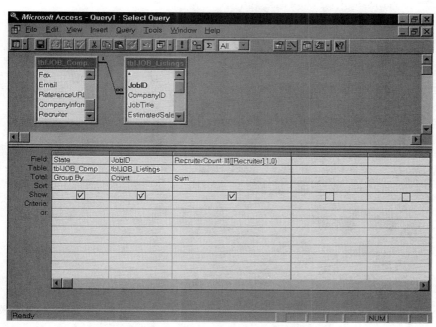

Figure 6-9 Calculating jobs from recruiting companies

The *Sum* function adds all the 1s and returns an accurate reflection of total jobs listed by recruiting companies by each state.

NOTE: Even though the Recruiter field belongs to the company table, it can be considered as a field of every job record due to the inner join between the company table and the job listing table. That is why performing a sum on the calculated version of the Recruiter field represents a count of recruiter-based jobs.

Step 4: Finding Average and Maximum Salary

To find the average and the maximum salary for each state:

1. Double-click on the EstimatedSalary field of the tblJOB_Listings table.

Access adds it to the Field row.

2. Set the Total cell for this field to *Avg*.

3. Double-click on the EstimatedSalary field of the tblJOB_Listings table once again.

Access adds another copy of this field to the Field row.

4. Set the Total cell for this copy to *Max*, as shown in Figure 6-10.

5. Save the query as *qryJOB_Analysis_ByState*.

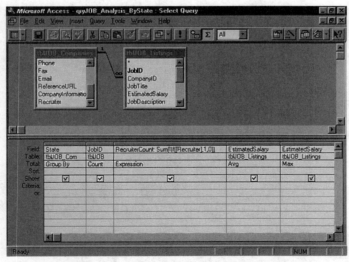

Figure 6–10 Calculating average and maximum salary

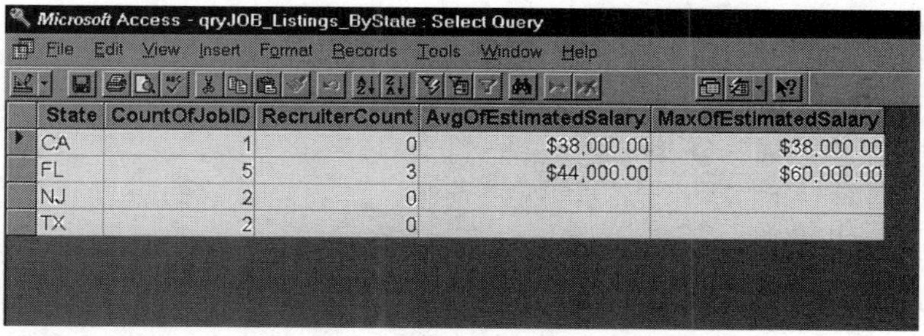

Figure 6–11 Result of the qryJOB_Listings_ByState query

Step 5: Testing Your Query

You should never consider your query design complete until you have tested the query and verified the result at least at an intuitive level. Figure 6-11 shows the output of the query being discussed.

The query result contains one record per state. The records are sorted in the alphabetical (ascending) order of the state code, since no particular sort order was forced in the query design. The CountOfJobID field shows the number of jobs listed in each state. Notice that this number is larger than the corresponding RecruiterCount value, which makes sense, because only some companies have the recruiter status.

How did the recruiter count field get the name "RecruiterCount?" Look at Figure 6-9 again, and notice the expression *RecruiterCount: IIf([Recruiter],1,0)* used to construct this field. The label before the colon becomes the name of the resulting field. Similarly, if you do not like the name CountOfJobID and want to change it to "TotalJobCount," just add the label *TotalJobCount:* before the JobID field in the query design.

Why are the average and maximum salaries not listed for some states? It happens that none of the jobs in these states have a value specified for their EstimatedSalary field. Once your database grows and more job records are added, you should expect this situation to go away. But if it does not or you see that only one state shows up with no available average salary even after your database is decently populated, it is worth spending the time to find out what's so unique about the companies in that state who are listing those jobs.

Total Queries Cannot Be Updated... Although Total queries show their result in a datasheet view similar to other Select queries, you cannot edit the data in their resulting recordset.

LESSON 3: APPLYING CRITERIA IN TOTAL QUERIES

In Total queries, you can specify two types of criteria: those that are applied before the records are aggregated (*precriteria*), and those that are applied after the records are aggregated (*postcriteria*). Which type of criteria you use depends on the objective of your query. Consider the following three data analysis tasks:

- Show all companies that have listed only one job.

- Show a job count of all companies for the year 1995.

- Show all companies that have listed only one job in 1995.

Specifying a PostCriterion in a Total Query

To accomplish the first task, you design a query that asks for all the companies with a job count of 1, as follows:

1. Construct the job count query as described in Lesson 1.

2. Add the criterion =1 in the Criteria cell of the JobID field as shown in Figure 6-12.

3. Save the query as *qryJOB_Companies_WithOnlyOneJob*.

4. Run the query.

Access first counts the jobs for each company and then applies the *=1* criterion to the resulting job count, thereby returning those companies with only one job in the database.

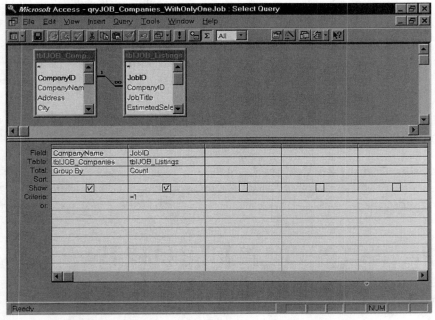

Figure 6-12 Query for listing companies with only one job

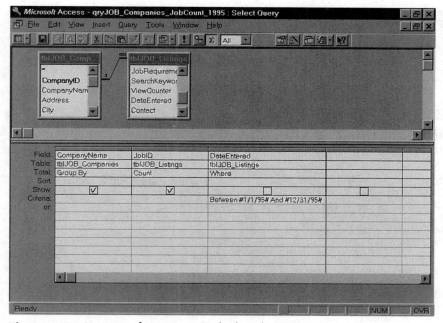

Figure 6-13 Query for counting jobs listed in 1995

To handle the second task, you make your job count query consider only jobs listed in 1995. In other words, you have it count those jobs whose DateEntered field is between 1/1/95 and 12/31/95.

1. Construct the job count query as described in Lesson 1.

2. Add the DateEntered field of the tblJOB_Listings table to the Field row.

3. Set the Where option for the Total cell of this field.

The Where option indicates to Access that you want to apply the criterion before it starts counting the jobs.

4. Specify the date range criterion to its Criteria cell as shown in Figure 6-13.

5. Save the query as *qryJOB_Companies_JobCount_1995*.

6. Run the query.

Access displays the job count of all the jobs listed in 1995 by company name as shown in Figure 6-14.

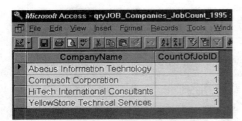

Figure 6–14 Job count of all the jobs listed in 1995 by company name

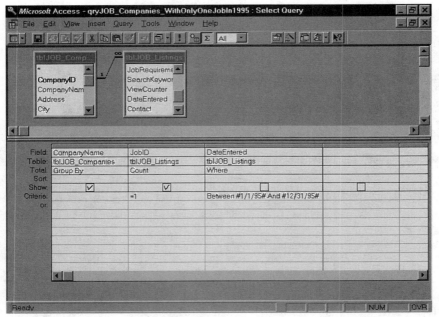

Figure 6–15 Using both a precriterion and a postcriterion in a Total query

The third task is just a combination of the first two tasks. You can design its query by specifying both types of criteria in the job count query as shown in Figure 6-15.

Finding Duplicate Values in a Field... To identify which values appear more than once in a table field, add two copies of that field to the Field row of a Total query. Apply a *Group By* function to the first copy and the *Count* function to the second copy. Then set a postcriterion of *>1* against the *Count* function.

LESSON 4: TOTAL QUERIES AND TABLE JOINS

Refer again to the job count query design of Figure 6-3 in Lesson 1. Notice that the two tables are linked with an inner join. How does this affect the job count query? The inner join causes the selection of only those companies that have at least one related job in the job listing table. Therefore, the CountOfJobID field in the query result can never be 0. If you change the link to an outer join directed from tblJOB_Companies to tblJOB_Listings, the query result will include those companies with no listed jobs, and for those companies the CountOfJobID field will be 0. (See Lesson 8 of Chapter 5, Building Microsoft Access Queries, for a detailed explanation of an outer join.)

As an example of a Total query based on an outer join, say you want to do a company status report showing the entry date of the most recent job listed by each company. Moreover, you want to include all the companies in the company table for this status report, and if a company does not have any associated job in the job table, then a "No Job" message should show against that company as shown in Figure 6-16.

For this query, the company and the job listing table should be linked with an outer join to include the "No Job" companies. The last entry date can be easily computed by applying the *Max* aggregate function on the DateEntered field. The tricky thing is how to embed the "No Job" message instead of the last entry date for the companies with no jobs in the database. The answer is to apply the *Max* function on a calculated field instead of directly on the DateEntered field as follows:

1. Open a new query in the query design window.

2. Add tblJOB_Companies and tblJOB_Listings to this query.

3. Change the link between these two tables to an outer join directed from tblJOB_Companies to tblJOB_Listings. (See Lesson 8 of Chapter 5, Building Microsoft Access Queries, on how to create an outer join.)

4. Select the Total option from the View menu.

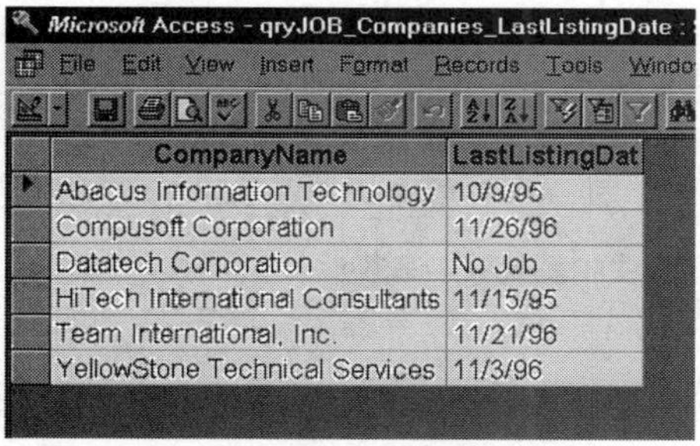

Figure 6–16 Showing the last job listing date by company name

5. Add the CompanyName field from tblJOB_Companies to the first cell of the Field row.

6. Add the following calculated field to the second cell of the Field row:

```
LastListingDate: IIf(IsNull([DateEntered]),"No Job",[DateEntered])
```

This calculated field, labeled "LastListingDate," returns the DateEntered field value if that value is not Null, otherwise it returns the string "No Job."

7. Select the *Max* aggregate function in the Total cell of this calculated field as shown in Figure 6-17.

8. Save the query as *qryJOB_Companies_LastListingDate*.

9. Run the query.

Access returns the query result of Figure 6-16.

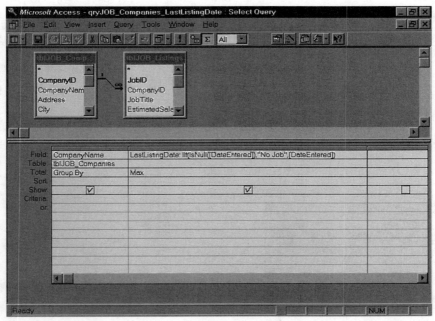

Figure 6–17 Query that shows the last job listing date by company name

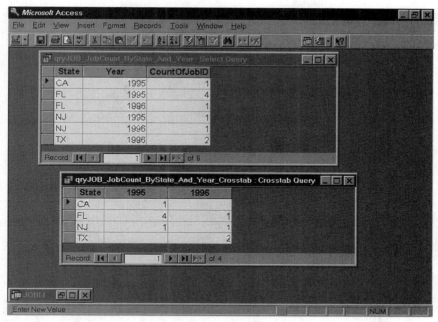

Figure 6-18 Result of a Total query and its equivalent Crosstab query

LESSON 5: USING A CROSSTAB QUERY

A *Crosstab* query is a specialized type of Total query through which you aggregate data that is grouped by two types of information: one down the left side of the datasheet and another across the top. Figure 6-18 shows you datasheets of the following two queries that both show a count of jobs grouped by state and year:

A Total query named *qryJOB_JobCount_ByState_And_Year*.

A Crosstab query named qryJOB_JobCount_ByState_And_Year_Crosstab.

As you can see, the Crosstab query compacts the result and makes it more readable. Figure 6-19 shows these two queries in their design view. The design of the *qryJOB_JobCount_ByState_And_Year* query shows a grouping on the State field and the calculated field labeled "Year," and a *Count* function applied to the JobID field. The Year field is a calculated field that extracts the year from the DateEntered field and is based on the following expression:

```
Year: Year([DateEntered])
```

The Crosstab query is essentially a derivative of the Total query with an extra Crosstab row in its design grid. You design this Crosstab query as follows:

1. Design a Total query similar to the *qryJOB_JobCount_ByState_And_Year* query.

2. Display the Crosstab row on the query design grid by selecting the Crosstab option from the Query menu.

3. Select the Row Heading option for the Crosstab cell under the State field.

4. Select the Column Heading option for the Crosstab cell under the Year field.

5. Select the Value option for the Crosstab cell under the JobID field.

6. Save the query as *qryJOB_JobCount_ByState_And_Year_Crosstab*.

7. Run the query to verify the results.

The Crosstab row defines which field becomes the row heading, which field's values act as the column heading, and which field's values to aggregate. You can specify a group of multiple fields for your row heading, but only one field as your column heading and one field for your Value option.

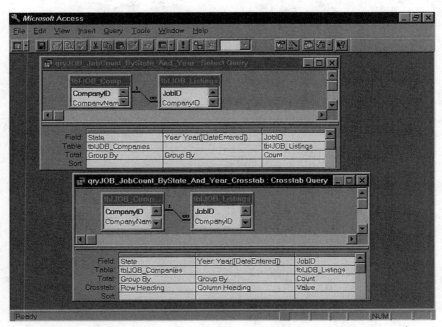

Figure 6-19 Design view of a Total query and its equivalent Crosstab query

You can add criteria to your Crosstab query just like you add criteria to a Total query, except you cannot specify a precriterion directly on the Value field. If you have to specify a precriterion against the Value field:

1. Add another copy of the Value field to the Field row.

2. Select the *Where* function for its Total cell, and keep its Crosstab cell empty.

3. Set your criterion against this copy.

This criterion will be applied before the totals are computed.

NOTE: The easiest way to define a Crosstab query is to use the Crosstab Wizard option provided by Access when you start to design a new query. For complete details on creating and using Crosstab queries, search "Crosstab" from the on-line Answer Wizard provided by Access.

LESSON 6: PARAMETER QUERIES

Until now, the only way we've discussed to change the query criteria is from the query design grid. If you find yourself repeatedly using the same query but with different values in your criteria, you can save time by creating a Parameter query. As the name implies, a *Parameter query* is one in which you add parameters (or variables) to your query. By supplying different values to the parameters at the time of executing the query, you can dynamically change the target of the query.

Parameter queries are the closest you can come to creating general-purpose queries in Access. They prove extremely useful for World Wide Web–based database searches and data publishing, as you will see in later chapters of this book. Let's create a parameter query that allows you to list the jobs of any company whose name you specify at the time you run the query. Follow the steps given next.

Step 1: Create a Regular Criteria Query

First, create an ordinary query containing the company and job tables and add a specific criteria against the company name as described here:

1. Create a new query in the query design window.

2. Add tblJOB_Companies and tblJOB_Listings to this query.

3. Add the CompanyName field from the company table and the asterisk (*) entry from the job listing table to the Field row.

4. Specify the following criterion in the Criteria cell of the CompanyName field:

   `"Compusoft Corporation"`

5. Run the query.

   The query returns the job records associated with Compusoft Corporation.

Step 2: Replace the Criterion Value with a Parameter

1. Return to the query design window.

2. Change the string *"Compusoft Corporation"* by substituting the following parameter as shown in Figure 6-20:

   `[Enter Company Name]`

3. Save the query as *qryJOB_Listings_Select_Company*.

4. Run the query again.

   Access now prompts you to specify a company name as shown in Figure 6-21.

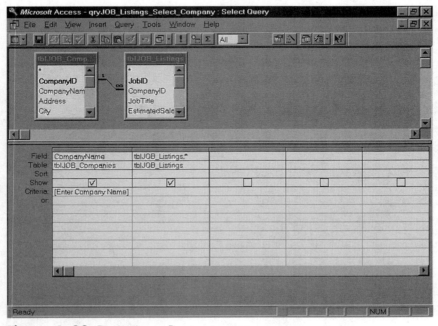

Figure 6-20 Designing a Parameter query

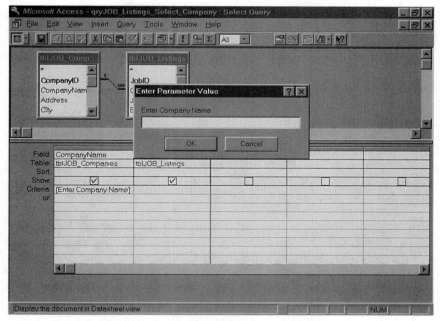

Figure 6-21 Running a Parameter query

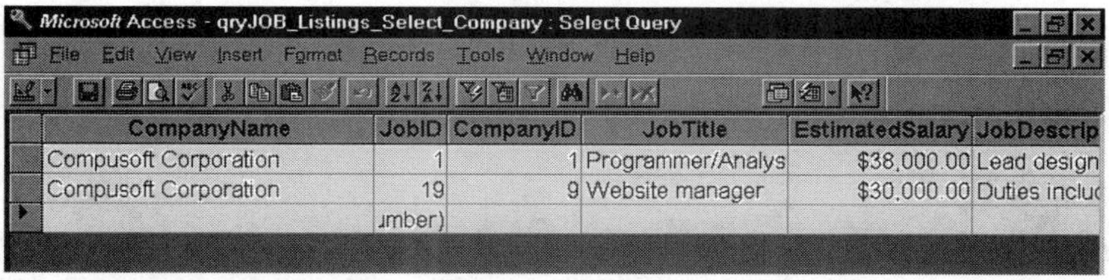

CompanyName	JobID	CompanyID	JobTitle	EstimatedSalary	JobDescrip
Compusoft Corporation	1	1	Programmer/Analys	$38,000.00	Lead design
Compusoft Corporation	19	9	Website manager	$30,000.00	Duties includ
	umber)				

Figure 6-22 Result of a Parameter query

5. Enter *Compusoft Corporation* (no quotes) in the input text box, and click on the OK button.

Access again displays the Compusoft Corporation's job records as shown in Figure 6-22.

6. Now, close the query result window.

7. Run the *qryJOB_Listings_Select_Company* query directly from the database container.

Access again prompts you for the company name.

8. This time, specify *Abacus Information Technology* in the input text box, and click on the OK button.

Access returns the records for that company. Dynamic, isn't it?

If you get tired of typing the full company name for your parameter and just want to specify the first few characters of the company name, change the query criterion to:

```
Like [Company Name Starts With] & "*"
```

The *&* "*" in this criterion concatenates a wildcard character * to whatever you type for the company name parameter. So, if you specify *Compusoft* as a value for the parameter, Access executes the query with the criterion *Like "Compusoft*"* and returns the jobs for all companies whose names start with "Compusoft."

> **NOTE:** If you want to display the jobs for all companies with names starting with *A, B,* or *C,* you can specify the value *[A-C]* for your Company Name Starts With parameter. Here the square brackets surrounding the A-C text are part of the parameter value, and the criterion expression becomes *Like "[A-C]*"* when Access runs the query.

Syntax of Query Parameters

You place a parameter in a query by enclosing an alphanumeric prompt within square brackets ([]). The prompt can include spaces, and it becomes the name of the parameter. The parameter name must not match any field name of the underlying tables (that confuses Access!).

Specifying Multiple Parameters

You can add more than one parameter to the same query by specifying different parameter names at different places in the query. When you run the query with multiple parameters, Access first prompts for the value of the first parameter by showing its name in the input box, then the second parameter, and so on. After substituting the values for each parameter, Access runs the query. The following example demonstrates a query that uses two parameters to display the jobs listed within a specified date range:

1. Open a new query in the query design window.

2. Add tblJOB_Listings as its data source.

3. Add the asterisk field to the first cell and the DateEntered field to the second cell of the Field row.

4. Deselect the Show check box for the DateEntered field.

5. Add the following parameter-based criterion to the Criteria cell of the DateEntered field:

```
Between [Enter Starting Date] And [Enter Ending Date]
```

6. Save the query as *qryJOB_Listings_Select_DateRange*.

7. Run the query.

Access prompts you for the starting date.

8. Enter *11/1/95* and click on the OK button. (Do not use any surrounding pound [#] characters.)

Access now prompts you for the ending date.

9. Enter *11/30/95* and click on the OK button.

Access displays all the job records listed in November 1995.

Specifying Multiple Occurrences of the Same Parameter

You can also repeat the same parameter name at different places in a query. When you run the query, Access recognizes that there are multiple occurrences of the same parameter and prompts for its value only once. It then faithfully substitutes that value wherever that parameter name appears in the query.

For example, say you want to design a Parameter query that prompts for a search keyword and finds all jobs that have that search keyword in either the JobDescription field or the SearchKeywords field. You can use two occurrences of the search parameter in this query as follows:

1. Open a new query in the query design window.

2. List tblJOB_Listings as its data source.

3. Add the asterisk field, the JobDescription field, and the SearchKeywords field to the Field row.

4. Deselect the Show check boxes of the JobDescription and the SearchKeywords fields.

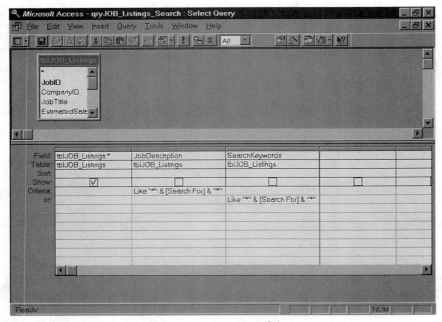

Figure 6-23 Query with two occurrences of the same parameter

5. Type the following criterion in the Criteria cell of the JobDescription field and the Or cell of the SearchKeywords field as shown in Figure 6-23:

```
Like "*" & [Search For] & "*"
```

6. Save the query as *qryJOB_Listings_Search.*

7. Run the query.

   Access prompts for the search word.

8. Enter *HTML* and click on the OK button.

   Access returns all the job records with "HTML" in either the JobDescription or the SearchKeywords field. Note that Access asked for the search parameter only once.

Specifying Parameters in Calculated Fields

Parameters are not just for specifying variable criteria values. You can also make parameters part of your calculated fields. For example, if you want to design a query that displays the jobs with the Estimated Salary converted to the currency of your choice (like British pounds or Australian dollars), you can create a calculated field labeled "ConvertedCurrency" that uses a parameter for the current exchange rate as follows:

1. Create a new query with tblJOB_Listings as its data source.

2. Add the asterisk field in the first cell and the following calculated field in the second cell of the Field row:

```
ConvertedSalary: [EstimatedSalary] * [Specify Exchange Rate]
```

3. Save the query as *qryJOB_Listings_ConvertedSalary*.

4. Run the query.

Access prompts for the exchange rate.

5. Enter a numeric exchange rate, and click on the OK button.

Access displays the job records with their U.S. salaries as well as the converted salaries.

Specifying the Data Type of a Query Parameter

Access tries to intelligently guess the data type of a parameter value by its context. That is why you do not need to add quotes around text value parameters or pound (#) signs around date value parameters. However, sometimes Access guesses wrong, and you end up with incorrect results or even an error message. Take the following case, for example, in which you want to filter job records based on the recruiter status of the listing companies:

1. Open a new query in the query design window.

2. Add tblJOB_Companies and tblJOB_Listings to this query.

3. Add the CompanyName and the Recruiter fields from the tblJOB_Companies table, and the asterisk field from the tblJOB_Listings table to the Field row.

4. Specify the following criterion for the Recruiter field as shown in Figure 6-24.

```
=[Recruiting Companies?]
```

5. Save the query as *qryJOB_Listings_Select_RecruiterStatus*.

6. Run the query.

Access asks if you want to see jobs listed by recruiting companies.

7. Type *Yes* and click on the OK button.

8. Instead of a query result, Access returns a "Can't Evaluate Expression" error message.

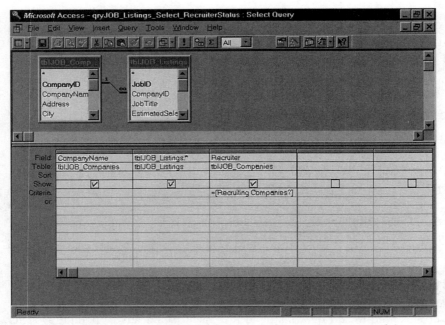

Figure 6-24 Query to select jobs based on the recruiter status of the companies

What went wrong? The problem was that Access mistook the Yes parameter value as a text data type ("Yes") and tried to evaluate the Yes/No type Recruiter field against that value. Since the Yes/No data type is incompatible with a Text data type, you got that error message. To resolve that error, you have two options:

Specify a numeric value (-1 for Yes and 0 for No) when Access prompts for a value for the Recruiting Companies parameter.

or

Force Access to always consider the value supplied for the Recruiting Companies parameter as a Yes/No data type.

The first option is not appealing, especially if this query is to be executed by you as well as other users who may not know what kind of values to specify. The second option makes Access recognize the Yes and No values for the parameter and correctly respond to the query. Let's go with this second option:

1. Select Parameters from the Query menu.

Access displays the Query Parameters dialog box.

2. Type the exact parameter name *[Recruiting Companies?]* with its Yes/No data type as shown in Figure 6-25.

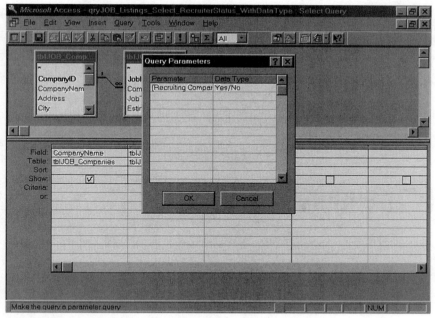

Figure 6-25 Specifying the data type of a query parameter

3. Click on the OK button to hide the query parameter window.

4. Save the query as *qryJOB_Listings_Select_RecruiterStatus_WithDataType*.

5. Run the query and enter *Yes* for the Recruiting Companies prompt.

This time, Access accepts the Yes value and returns the appropriate job records.

NOTE: Once you specify the parameters in the Query Parameters dialog box, Access always prompts for a value of those parameters when you run that query, even though you may eliminate some of the parameters in your query design. Also, in a parameter-based Crosstab query, Access requires you to specify the data type of its parameters.

Other Considerations About Parameters

Parameters cannot be used to substitute as functions or any query options. For example, you cannot specify a parameter for a sort order. You can certainly specify a parameter to act as an argument of a function. For example:

```
ListingDate: Format([DateEntered],[Specify Format?])
```

Once you specify a parameter in the query design, Access always considers that parameter. For example, you cannot make Access ignore the parameter in a parameter-based criterion. If you do not specify a value for a parameter at the query execution time, Access assigns a Null value to that parameter and handles the query accordingly. So, if you do not enter any value for the *[Enter Company Name]* parameter query designed earlier in this lesson (see Figure 6-20), Access returns an empty query result.

NOTE: If you want a Null parameter to mean all records, you can change the criterion for the CompanyName field to:

```
=[Enter Company Name] OR [Enter Company Name] Is Null
```

LESSON 7: NESTED QUERIES

Just when you may be thinking that you have covered some major query concepts, here is another power punch from Access: Nested queries. *Nested queries* are queries based on other queries (or a combination of queries and tables). Nested queries prove useful in the following situations:

- Simplifying the query design through query reuse
- Easily propagating changes
- Performing advanced data analysis

Simplify Query Design Through Query Reuse

If you find yourself designing different queries that have a lot in common, you can first design a query that computes the common part, and then base other queries on that query. Once the common query is working correctly, then you can concentrate on the extra requirements of the final query.

Many examples in the previous lessons have used queries where the company table and the job listing table are linked with an inner join. Every time you design these queries, you have to add tblJOB_Companies and tblJOB_Listings to your query design window, then click on the CompanyName field from the company table and the asterisk (*) field from the job listing table. It is not a hard thing to do, but if you have to do it again and again, you might as well use the strength of Nested queries as described next:

1. Create a common query whose only purpose is to link the company and job listing tables with an inner join, and add the asterisk field of both the tables to the Field row as shown in Figure 6-26.

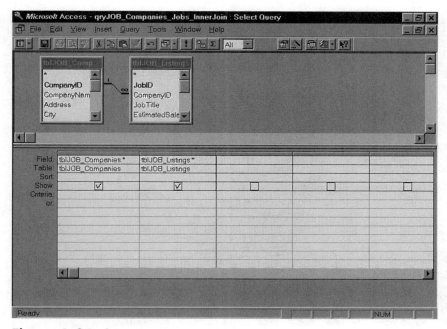

Figure 6–26 Creating a common query

2. Save this query as *qryJOB_Companies_Jobs_InnerJoin*.

3. Run the query.

Access displays a datasheet showing the fields from both tables. Only the CompanyID field comes up twice, and to distinguish between them, Access appends the table names to them.

4. Close the query result window.

Now, say you want to design a Total query to count jobs by companies using this common query:

1. Open a new query in the query design window.

Access displays the Show Table dialog box prompting you to add tables for the query data source.

2. Click on the Queries tab of this dialog box.

Access now shows the list of stored queries as shown in Figure 6-27.

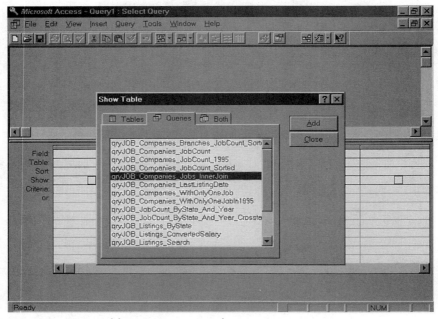

Figure 6–27 Adding a query as a data source

3. Select the *qryJOB_CompaniesJobs_InnerJoin* query from this list, and click on the Add button.

Access adds this query to the query design window and shows its field list, which includes the fields from both the company and the job listing tables.

4. Add the CompanyName and the JobID fields from this field list to the Field row.

5. Display the Total row and do a *Group By* on the CompanyName and a *Count* on the JobID field as shown in Figure 6-28.

6. Save the query as *qryJOB_Companies_JobCount_UsingNestedQuery*.

7. Run the query.

Access displays the job count by company name.

Tip on Creating Common Queries... The reason you displayed all fields from both tables in the design of your common query is because it is hard to predict what fields would be needed by the queries that use this query. When designing queries that may be used by other queries, try to make them as general purpose as you can.

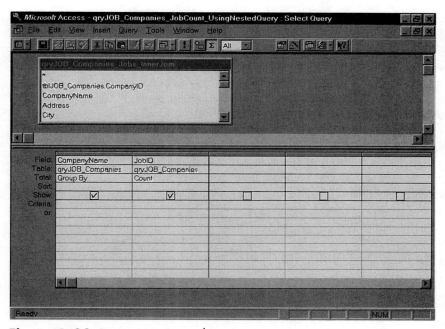

Figure 6-28 Designing a nested query

Propagate Changes

Nested queries also help in propagating changes common among different queries. If many queries are based on one common query, any change you make to the common query is automatically reflected in all those dependent queries. How does this help?

Take the case of the *qryJOB_Companies_Jobs_InnerJoin* query you designed to act as a common query in the previous example. It contains an inner join between the company and the job listing tables. All queries based on this query will exclude companies with no listed jobs from their analysis. Say your boss notices this and wants you to consider all the companies in the company table in the result of each query. You make an unhappy face, but grin inside because all you have to do is change the inner join to an outer join in that common query as described next:

1. Open the *qryJOB_Companies_Jobs_InnerJoin* query in the query design window.

2. Double-click on the link between the company and job listing tables, and change that link to an outer join.

3. Save the query and close its query design window.

4. Run the *qryJOB_Companies_JobCount_UsingNestedQuery* query.

Access now includes the names of those companies that do not have any job records in its query result.

NOTE: There is one limitation to the change propagation procedure though. You cannot change the name of the common query and expect it to be propagated among dependent queries. In our example, if you change the name of the common query from *qryJOB_Companies_Jobs_InnerJoin* to *qryJOB_CompaniesJobs _OuterJoin* and try to run the dependent queries, you will get an error. So, as a rule of thumb, give general-purpose names (for example, *qryJOB_Companies_Jobs*) when you initially design your common queries.

The change propagation concept also helps in query optimization. Say you had a common parameter query with the criterion *Like "*" & [Search For?] & "*"* for the JobTitle field (show jobs whose job title field contains your supplied keyword). Based on this common query, you designed a job count query, a date range criterion query, and some other dependent queries.

Later on, your job table gets populated with thousands of records, and you realize that these queries take considerable time to process. To improve their performance, you simply have to optimize the common query as follows:

1. Set an index on the JobTitle field.

2. Change the criterion for the JobTitle field to *Like [Search For?] & "*"*

As mentioned in Lesson 5, Matching Patterns with Wildcards and the LIKE Operator, of Chapter 5, Building Microsoft Access Queries, Access can take advantage of the index while evaluating the preceding LIKE criterion. You will notice performance improvement in all the dependent queries as well (of course, at the cost of limited pattern matching).

Parameters and Nested Queries... Any parameters of a common query automatically become the parameters of dependent queries.

Perform Advance Data Analysis

There are certain types of data analysis questions that cannot be answered with just one query. You have to use nested queries in those cases. Consider a simple situation where you want to show the most recent job listed by each company.

Instinctively, you might create a Total query which performs a *Group By* operation on the CompanyName field and applies the *Max* function to the DateEntered field. But then you try to figure out how to list the job associated with the maximum value of the DateEntered field. You can't. This example is sufficient to make you realize that Total queries tend to lose the details when they produce their results.

You might try another approach and say that you can sort on the DateEntered field in the descending order and somehow filter out the most recent jobs for each company. Do not be surprised if you get stuck on that "somehow."

To handle this apparently simple situation, you need to use Nested queries:

1. Create a new Total query as shown in Figure 6-29.

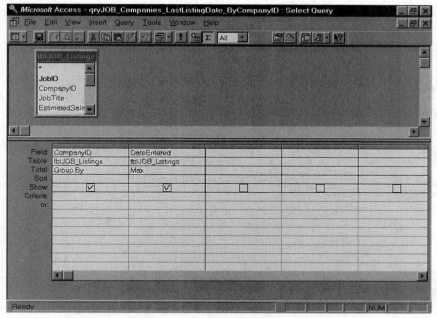

Figure 6–29 Query that shows last job listing date by CompanyID

2. Save this query as *qryJOB_Companies_LastListingDate_ByCompanyID*.

3. Close its query design window.

4. Open a new query in the query design window.

5. Add tblJOB_Companies and tblJOB_Listings from the table list of the Show Table dialog box.

6. Select the Queries tab of the Show Table dialog box, and add the *qryJOB_Companies_LastListingDate_ByCompanyID* query to the query design window.

7. Click on the OK button to close the Show Table dialog box.

Access shows the inner join between tblJOB_Companies and tblJOB_Listings as usual, but it also automatically links *tblJOB_Companies* and *qryJOB_LastListingDate_ByCompanyID* on the CompanyID field as shown in Figure 6-30. For this example, you do not want that link.

Click here to select link

Figure 6-30 Automatic links created by Access between the data sources

8. So, click on the link between tblJOB_Companies and the Nested query to select it, and press <DEL> to delete it.

9. Drag the CompanyID field from tblJOB_Listings to the CompanyID field of the Nested query to create an inner join between these two data sources.

10. Next, drag the DateEntered field from tblJOB_Listings to the MaxOfDateEntered field of the Nested query.

   Access creates a multi-field link between the tblJOB_Listings table and the Nested query as shown in Figure 6-31.

11. Add the CompanyName field from tblJOB_Companies, the MaxOfDateEntered field from the Nested query, and the asterisk (*) field from tblJOB_Listings to the Field row of the query design grid as shown in Figure 6-32.

12. Save the query as *qryJOB_Companies_MostRecentJob*.

13. Run the query.

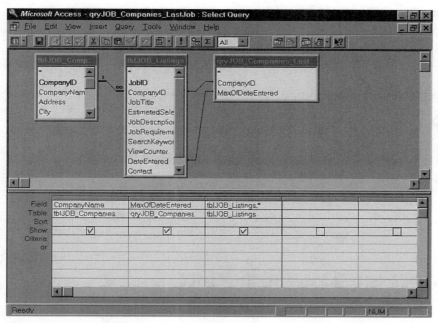

Figure 6-31 Establishing a multi-field link between the job table and the nested query

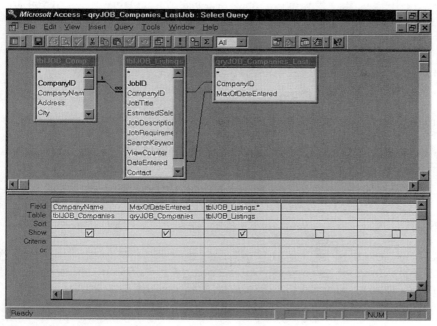

Figure 6-32 Query for displaying the most recent job of each company

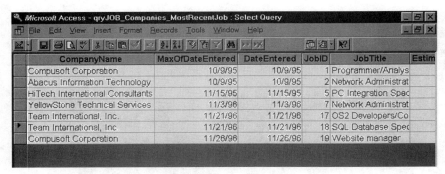

Figure 6-33 Most recent job of each company

Access shows the most recent job listed by each company as shown in Figure 6-33. You can verify the result by comparing the DateEntered field of each job with the MaxOfDateEntered field.

OPTIMIZING PERFORMANCE OF QUERIES

Although Access is capable of employing state-of-the-art techniques for optimizing queries, a lot rests on your shoulders to help it exploit these techniques. Here is a list of pointers to make your queries execute faster:

- Choose the smallest data type appropriate for a field during table design. If you are not particular about the precision of a numeric field, set the size of that field to Single instead of Double.

- Index fields on both sides of a join, or better still, create a relationship between these fields. Access then automatically indexes them. Try to use the joins between fields that have the same data type and size.

- When creating a query, add only the fields you need. Clear the Show check box of fields you used only to set criteria. This point may clash with the design of Nested queries, where you were recommended to add as many fields as possible in the common query. It is up to you to decide what kind of balance you want to achieve between the two recommendations.

- Avoid restrictive query criteria on calculated and nonindexed columns whenever possible. The Rushmore technology that Access uses for fast index-based searches cannot work on such types of criteria.

NOTE: For more information on Rushmore technology and when it can be applied, search for the keyword "Rushmore" from the Answer Wizard.

As an example, if you want to select jobs listed in the year 1995, use the *Between #1/1/95# And #12/31/95#* criterion directly on the DateEntered field instead of first computing the year from the DateEntered field using the *Year* function and then setting the criterion *=1995* on that calculated field.

When creating Nested queries, do not put the calculated fields as part of your common query. Put them in your main queries.

Index the fields that you use for sorting.

Use the Performance Analyzer tool to have Access analyze your queries for potential improvements. It is available under the Tools, Analyze Performance menu option.

REVIEW QUESTIONS

1. What is the advantage of analyzing information from different perspectives?

2. What is the function of a Total query?

3. Define the role of the *Group By* function in a Total query?

4. When does the *Sum* function prove more useful for counting than the *Count* function?

5. Will Null values in the EstimatedSalary of some records affect the Average estimated salary computed by the *Avg* function?

6. Give an example in which you might need to group on multiple fields.

7. Under what circumstances can you use multiple aggregate functions in the same query?

8. What type of criteria can you use with a Total query? How do you specify each type of criterion?

9. How is a Crosstab query different from a Total query? When is a Crosstab query useful?

10. How do you specify parameters in a Parameter query? When do you need Parameter queries?

11. Under what circumstances should you consider designing Nested queries?

12. What type of criteria cannot take advantage of Rushmore query optimization?

EXERCISES

1. Design a query to compute the average salary of a programmer's job (all jobs containing "Programmer" in the JobTitle field).

2. Design a query that produces a count of companies for each state.

3. Create a Parameter query that allows you to find all companies whose code's first three digits match the first three digits of your supplied parameter. Hint: Use the *Mid* function on the parameter in your query criterion to extract the first three digits.

4. Design a query that shows the ratio of recruiting companies to nonrecruiting companies for each state. Hint: You may have to use nested queries.

5. Create a Crosstab query that shows the job count grouped by city (row heading) and month listed (column heading) for the year 1995.

6. Design a query that shows the job title of the highest salaried job for each company. If a company has no estimated salary specified for any job, or has no job listed at all in the job table, then a "NO DATA" message should appear in the job title field for that company. Hint: Try nested queries and outer joins.

7

ELEMENTS OF THE WORLD WIDE WEB

The tremendous popularity of the World Wide Web proves that it is possible to place advanced technology in the hands of the masses. The key is the Web's simplicity and clarity. The simplicity arises from its intuitive concepts, its concealment of technical details from the end user, and its use of a special text-based language called *HTML,* whose basics can be learned in less than an hour. The clarity arises from its commitment to open standards and a completely defined role for each Web component.

As a Web user, you may not be concerned about the details of the Web architecture. But as a Web site developer, you can harness the Web's enormous power if you understand the functionality of its elements and the communication that goes on between them. Essentially, the Web is comprised of two main elements: the *Web server* and the *Web client.* These elements are not limited by any computer platform, operating system, or distance. A Windows-based Web client from the home of a school kid could easily display the weather pictures made available by a Web server running on a supercomputer in the space station orbiting the Earth. In the case of the World Wide Web, even the sky is not the limit.

The interaction within the Web takes place using three protocols (or communication standards): TCP/IP, HTTP, and HTML. Each protocol operates in its own level. *TCP/IP (Transmission Control Protocol/Internet Protocol),* the oldest of them all, existed even before the Web was conceived. It is the protocol followed by all computers connected to the Internet and is responsible for transporting data accurately between any two computers on the Internet.

HTTP (Hypertext Transfer Protocol) is the language that the Web server understands. That is why a Web server is often called an HTTP server. The Web client talks to a Web server by sending it HTTP messages through the TCP/IP transport mechanism. The main purpose of these messages is to request a specific document residing on the server. However, the client can also send user-specified information to the server through an HTTP message.

HTML (Hypertext Markup Language) is a standard followed by the document author to provide information that can be presented by the Web client in a manner most suitable to the reader. The author of the document can be you, someone else, or even a computer program. In the same way, the reader could be a person or the input queue of another program. Figure 7-1 shows how these protocols work together to form the basis of the gigantic World Wide Web.

CLIENT-SERVER INTERACTION THROUGH HTTP

HTTP is a message-based, open-ended protocol that can be efficiently implemented to support a distributed communication medium such as the World Wide Web. This protocol was designed to fulfill the need for quick retrieval of information resources located at different remote sites and provide venues for advanced functions like document searching, front-end update, and annotation.

The TCP/IP-based file retrieval and upload protocols that existed before HTTP (for example, FTP) were slow and could serve only a limited number of clients at a time. Their

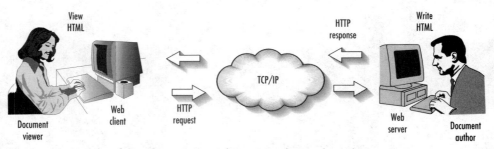

Figure 7-1 Role of TCP/IP, HTTP, and HTML in the Web architecture

inefficiency was due to their inherent assumption that a client needs to establish a complete session with a server and may transfer more than one document (possibly located in different directories on the server) during a session. The connection between the client and the server was kept alive till the client closed the session (except in the case of inactivity time out). Further, the server had to allocate memory to remember the current state of each open session. The other protocols (like Gopher), although superior in speed, carried an oversimplified model of document retrieval (such as directory-based menus) and were insensitive to the needs of high-end graphical-document publishing.

HTTP takes a different approach to client/server interaction. By utilizing the concept of a standard document addressing method called the universal resource locator (URL), it concentrates on minimal transaction between the server and the client. See the next section for more information on the syntax of URLs.

In HTTP, the Web client initiates the connection and sends one *precomposed* request message in a precise format to the server. The message contains the nature of the request (request method), the URL of the document requested, and any necessary data needed by the server to fulfill the request.

The Web server listens to that request and responds with a status code summarizing the action taken on the request. Further, if the request is valid, the server also sends the requested document using the MIME (Multipurpose Internet Mail Extensions) format, thereby making it possible to serve various types of documents.

The main features that characterize HTTP are as follows:

- In one connection, a client can request only a certain number of documents from the server. This maximum limit is generally a configurable parameter of the Web server as well as the Web client.

- The connection can be closed by either party. While the server automatically closes the connection after the request is completed, the client has the option to terminate the connection anytime during the document transfer.

- It is a stateless protocol. Every transaction between the client and the server is assumed to be independent of other transactions.

- It is a message-based protocol that follows the object-oriented model. In this model, the list of messages can be easily extended for newer versions of HTTP or to design customized information-retrieval systems based on this protocol.

- The MIME format of data representation allows client/server systems to be built independently of the data being transferred.

The "HTTP Request" and the "HTTP Response" sections in this chapter cover the communication aspects of HTTP in more detail.

UNIFORM RESOURCE LOCATOR

The uniform resource locator (URL) is a text string that uniquely identifies an information resource. In other words, it defines the address of a document and is constructed by use of the following syntax:

```
protocol://host[:port]/absolute_path
```

An example of a URL is *http://www.waite.com/waite*. The *protocol* entry (HTTP) defines the communication method needed to access the document. The *host* entry (www.waite.com) specifies a legal Internet host domain name or IP address in dotted-decimal form. The *port* entry identifies the port of that host on which the Web server is listening for requests. This entry is optional if the Web server is listening for client requests on TCP port 80. The *absolute_path* entry (/waite/) specifies the location of the requested document on the host server. The server uses its standard set of rules to determine the physical location of the information resource from this *absolute_path* entry.

As a basic rule, most Web servers are designed to consider the *absolute_path* entry as a directory path leading to the file containing the requested information. You can change this default behavior by specifying a mapping of all or a portion of the URL path to a different location in the server's configuration. See Lesson 2, "Administering WebSite," in Chapter 2, Getting Started, for more information on how to establish this URL-to-document mapping on the WebSite Web server.

URL for HTTP Specifications... You can retrieve specifications on the latest version of HTTP through the URL `http://www.w3.org/pub/WWW/Protocols/`.

HTTP REQUEST

An HTTP request is sent by the client to the server. It can be a simple message like "GET *URL*" terminated by a newline (NL), or it can be a complete request of the form:

```
Method URL_Absolute_Path ProtocolVersion NL [Header][NL Data]
```

Method specifies the type of request being sent to the server. *URL_Absolute_Path* indicates the location of the requested resource. *ProtocolVersion* is supplied so that the server knows how to handle this request. In many cases, the request can also include *header fields* and *user-entered data* that the server or the requested information resource may need to complete the request.

HTTP Request Method

As mentioned earlier, the *request method* indicates the type of request and acts as a command to be performed on the object referred to by the URL. There are three methods currently supported by most HTTP servers:

🦐 GET

🦐 HEADER

🦐 POST

GET Method

GET is the simplest and the fastest method for retrieving information identified by the *URL_AbsolutePath* request parameter. Note that if *URL_AbsolutePath* refers to an executable program, then the GET method expects the result of that program from the server. As an example, the following GET request returns the home page of Waite Group Press once you connect to the host *www.waite.com* on TCP port 80:

```
GET /waite/ HTTP/1.0 <ENTER>
```

In the response to this GET request, the server returns an HTTP response containing some header information describing the outcome of the request as well as the requested document. The format of the HTTP response is discussed in the next section.

Conditional GET

The GET method supports an enhancement called conditional GET, intended for reducing network usage. With the conditional GET, the request message also includes an If-Modified-Since header field with a date value. The server returns the requested document only if that document has been modified since the date given by the If-Modified-Since header. The conditional GET feature allows a client to store documents locally when they are retrieved for the first time and reload them only if they have changed, a concept known as *document caching*.

HEAD Method

The HEAD method is identical to the GET method, except that the server only returns the header information. The actual document is not transferred. The HEAD method is useful for a client to test the validity and availability of an information resource.

POST Method

The POST method allows a client to supply supplemental data with the HTTP request to the server. This data is generally used by the requested document, which is normally an executable program. It is up to the server and the executable program to work out the details of accessing that data after it is transferred to the server. The Common Gateway Interface (CGI) is one prominent standard supported by most Web servers for making the data available to the executable script or program.

The client can utilize the POST method to annotate existing resources residing at the server, provide keywords to search databases, post messages to newsgroups or mailing lists, and even supply data for remotely adding or updating database records.

HTTP Request Header

An HTTP request can contain optional header fields to supply additional information about the request or about the client itself. Table 7-1 lists some common header fields that appear in an HTTP request.

Table 7-1 HTTP request header fields

Field	Used To
Accept: *range of media-types*	Indicate the set of MIME types the client can accept. For example: Accept: text/*; image/jpeg
Authorization: *credentials*	Allow a client to authenticate itself by supplying the username and password information if the server asks for an authentication before returning the requested document.
Host: *host [: port]*	Specify the Internet host and port number of the resource being requested, as obtained from the original URL given by the user or referring resource.
If-Modified-Since: *HTTP-Date*	Perform a conditional GET request where the server returns the document only if the document has been modified after the given date. The date must be in the format similar to Friday, 26-Jan-96 02:12:28 GMT.
Referer: *URL*	Specify the address (URL) of the object from which the Request-URL was obtained.
User-Agent: *product or comment*	Identify the name of the client sending the request as well as any other comments that the client may want to pass to the server.
Date: *HTTP-Date*	Represent the date and time at which the message was originated.
Content-Encoding: *MIME encoding*	Indicate how the body message has been encoded.
Content-Length: *number*	Specify the size in bytes of the data being transferred with the request.
Content-Type: *media-type*	Specify the MIME type of data being transferred with the request.

HTTP Request Data

The data optionally supplied with an HTTP request can be any MIME-conforming message. The size and type of the data is indicated in the Content-Length and Content-Type header fields, respectively. If the Content-Type field is absent in the header, then the data should be assumed to be specified in "plain/text" format using "8-bit" (or ASCII) encoding.

HTTP Response

The server generates an HTTP response to every HTTP request using the following syntax:

```
ProtocolVersion StatusCode Reason NL [Header][NL Data]
```

The protocol version identifies the Hypertext Transfer Protocol version being used by the server (for example, *HTTP/1.1*).

HTTP Status Code

The status code following the protocol version is a three-digit integer describing the result of the request. The reason string is a more detailed description of the returned status code. The first digit of the status code characterizes the type of status being returned as follows:

- Informational (type 1xx)
- Successful (type 2xx)
- Redirection (type 3xx)
- Client error (type 4xx)
- Server error (type 5xx)

Informational Status Codes (Type 1xx)

This class of status codes is used to indicate a provisional response, which consists only of the Status-Line and optional headers, and is terminated by a blank line. They were included only with version 1.1 of HTTP. For more information on the standardized informational status codes, refer to the HTTP/1.1 specifications available from the following location:

```
http://www.w3.org/pub/WWW/Protocols/
```

Successful Status Codes (Type 2xx)

This class of status code indicates that the client's request was successfully received, understood, and accepted. Table 7-2 lists some commonly used status codes in the 2xx category.

Table 7–2 Type 2xx status codes, indicating success

Status Code and Reason	Explanation
200 OK	The request has been fulfilled successfully.
201 Created	The POST request has resulted in the creation of a new resource whose URL is being returned in the body of the response.
202 Accepted	The request has been accepted, but there is no guarantee that it has been processed.
203 Provisional Information	When received in response to a GET command, this indicates that the result includes information associated with the document, such as its annotation information.
204 No Content	The server has fulfilled the request, but does not have any information to send back. The client should stay in the same document view.

Redirection Status Codes (Type 3xx)

This class of status code indicates that further action needs to be taken by the client in order to fulfill the request. The client may carry out the action without requiring any user interaction if and only if the method used in the second request is a GET or a HEAD. Table 7-3 lists the commonly used status codes in the 3xx category.

NOTE: Some Web servers (including WebSite) intelligently detect a *local redirection* (redirection to another resource on the server machine) and automatically send the redirected resource to the client, thereby eliminating the extra communication overhead generally involved in carrying out the redirection process.

Table 7–3 Type 3xx status codes, indicating redirection

Status Code and Reason	Explanation
301 Moved Permanently	The requested resource has been assigned a new permanent URL specified in the Location header field (see Table 7-6). Any future reference to this resource should be done by use of that URL.
302 Moved Temporarily	The requested resource resides temporarily under a different URL. However, the client should continue to use the original URL for future requests.
304 Not Modified	The requested document has not been modified since the date specified in the If-Modified-Since field of the conditional GET request. Date, Server, and Expires are the header fields passed with this response (see Table 7-6).

Client Error Status Codes (Type 4xx)

A 4xx status code means that the client has made an erroneous request. The error could be caused by either a programming bug in the client, a bad network connection, or some other unknown factor. In any case, the client is expected to cease any data transfer the moment it receives this type of response, to reset its connections, and possibly to try to send the request again. Table 7-4 lists the commonly used status codes in the 4xx category.

Table 7–4 Type 4xx status codes, indicating client error

Status Code and Reason	Explanation
400 Bad Request	The request had bad syntax or was inherently impossible to satisfy.
401 Unauthorized	The request requires user authentication.
403 Forbidden	The server understood the request, but is refusing to fulfill it. Authorization will not help and the request should not be repeated.
404 Not Found	The server has not found anything matching the Request-URL.

Status Code and Reason	Explanation
405 Method Not Allowed	The method specified in the Request-Line is not allowed for the resource identified by the Request-URL.
406 Not Acceptable	The resource identified by the request is only capable of generating response entities which have content characteristics not acceptable according to the accept headers sent in the request.
408 Request Timeout	The client did not produce a request within the time that the server was prepared to wait.
409 Conflict	The request could not be completed due to a conflict with the current state of the resource.
410 Gone	The requested resource is no longer available at the server, and no forwarding address is known.

Server Error Status Codes (Type 5xx)

Response status codes beginning with the digit "5" indicate cases in which the server is aware that it has erred or is incapable of performing the request. Table 7-5 lists the commonly used status codes in the 5xx category.

Table 7–5 Type 5xx status codes, indicating server error

Status Code and Reason	Explanation
500 Internal Server Error	The server was unable to fulfill a request due to an unexpected reason, such as an abnormal termination of an executable program.
501 Not Implemented	The server does not support the functionality required to fulfill the request. For example, the server may send this status code if it is unable to recognize the request method used in an HTTP request.
502 Bad Gateway	The server needs to pass the request to another program or server that is not responding.
503 Service Unavailable	The server is temporarily overloaded and unable to handle the request. This can occur if the server receives too many requests a time.
504 Gateway Timeout	The server, while acting as a gateway or proxy, did not receive a timely response from the upstream server it accessed in attempting to complete the request.
505 Version Not Supported	The server does not support, or refuses to support, the HTTP protocol version that was used in the request message.

HTTP Response Header

The response header fields allow the server to pass additional information that cannot be covered in the status code. Table 7-6 lists the header fields that commonly accompany an HTTP response.

Table 7–6 HTTP response header fields

Field	Used To
Location: *AbsoluteURL*	Define the exact location of the resource that was identified by the Request-URL. For redirection type (3xx) responses, the location indicates the server's preferred URL for automatic redirection to the resource.
Server: *product or comment*	Contains information about the software used by the server to handle the request.
WWW-Authenticate: *challenge*	Specifies the authentication scheme(s) and parameters applicable to the Request-URL. Used with the 401 (unauthorized) response messages to gather the necessary authentication information.
Last-Modified: *HTTP-Date*	Indicate the date and time at which the sender believes the resource was last modified.
Expires: *HTTP-Date*	Give the date and time after which the information should be considered stale by the client.
Date: *HTTP-Date*	Represent the date and time at which the message was originated.
Content-Encoding: *MIME encoding*	Indicate how the body message has been encoded.
Content-Length: *number*	Specify the size in bytes of the data being transferred with the request.
Content-Type: *media-type*	Specify the MIME type of data being transferred with the request.

Common Header Fields... Certain header fields like Content-Encoding, Content-Type, Content-Length, and Date can be used by the HTTP request as well as the HTTP response.

AN OVERVIEW OF HTML

Web clients designed to act as *users-agents* (to be used by human readers) support text documents written in HTML (Hypertext Markup Language) for displaying text, pictures, and hyperlinks on the same page. HTML is currently an evolving standard; each new version adds more features and text-formatting capabilities.

HTML is called a *markup language* because the HTML instructions are embedded in the text itself. These instructions are specified through HTML tags which are keywords enclosed within the <> characters. The HTML tags that format a block of text come in pairs. For example, to emphasize a complete paragraph text, you surround that paragraph with the <EM> and </EM> tag pair.

Certain HTML tags stand alone and cause a formatting effect independent of the text involved. And certain tags can have additional attributes besides the keyword. For example, an <HR> tag causes the client to add a horizontal line in the document view. There is no </HR> counterpart for this tag. <FONT SIZE=2> has a size attribute defining the font size. The tag keywords are not case-sensitive. (<HR> is the same as <hr>.)

HTML supports the following features (some of which were added in HTML 3):

- Document structure definition

- Text formatting, including logical and physical styles, headings, paragraphs or line breaks, font sizing, alignments, and use of special characters

- Bulleted, numbered, or definition style lists

- Tables to show data in rows and columns

- Inline images and image/text alignment

- Hypertext anchors, both external and within the same document

- Point-and-click imagemaps

- E-mail

- Forms to send user data to the server

In the following lessons, we cover commonly used HTML tags and document formatting techniques. For a complete reference on HTML and the syntax of all tag elements not covered in this chapter, refer to the following publications from Waite Group Press:

- *HTML Web Publisher's Construction Kit with HTML 3.2* by David Fox and Troy Downing

- *HTML 3 Interactive Course* by Kent Cearly

- *HTML 3 How-To* by David Kerven, Jeff Foust, and John Zakour

NOTE: When designing HTML documents, it is important to realize that not all users may possess the latest upgrade of the client software that can handle the most recent version of HTML. Consequently, content providers make available different versions (for example, a text-only version and a table-based version) of their Web pages to accommodate all types of Web clients. In addition, many providers also provide a link to the public domain versions of those Web clients that support the needed HTML enhancements.

LESSON 1: DEFINING THE DOCUMENT STRUCTURE IN HTML

All HTML documents should contain the following three document structure tag pairs:

- <HTML>…</HTML>

- <HEAD>…</HEAD>

- <BODY>…</BODY>

The <HTML>…</HTML> Tag Pair

This tag pair identifies the enclosed text as an HTML-formatted document. The <HTML> tag is placed at the beginning of the text, and the </HTML> tag is placed at the end of the text.

The <HEAD>…</HEAD> Tag Pair

This tag pair identifies the document header and encloses information about the document itself. Table 7-7 lists the HTML tags that can be included in the document header. The tags relevant to the objectives of this book are described in further detail.

Table 7-7 Tags used in the header section of an HTML document

HTML Tag	Used To
<BASE>	Specify base address of the HTML document
<ISINDEX>	Allow keyword searching of the document
<LINK>	Indicate relationship between documents
<NEXTID>	Create unique document identifiers
<TITLE>…</TITLE>	Specify the document title
<META>	Supply server- or client-specific information

The <BASE> Tag

This tag allows the URL of the document itself to be recorded in situations in which the document may be read out of context. URLs within the document may be in a *partial* form relative to this base address. In documents, where the base address is not specified, the browser uses the URL it used to access the document to resolve any relative URLs. The <BASE> tag has one attribute, HREF, which identifies the URL. For example:

```
<BASE HREF="http://www.acme.com/abc/">
```

specifies *http://www.acme.com/abc/* to be the base from which all relative URLs should be determined.

The <ISINDEX> Tag

This tag indicates that the browser should allow the user to search an index by giving a text keyword input field. When a user enters a set of one or more keywords in this field, the browser requests a URL constructed by appending "?" and the keywords to the base URL. The keywords are escaped according to the URL encoding scheme (described in Lesson 2 of the next chapter, Creating HTML Forms). For example, if a document contains

```
<BASE HREF="http://www.acme.com/index">
<ISINDEX>
```

and the user provides the keywords "world" and "web," then the browser sends the following URL request:

```
http://www.acme.com/index?world+web
```

The <TITLE>...</TITLE> Tag Pair

This tag pair is used to identify the contents of the document in a global context. The enclosed text generally appears in the title bar of a browser's window as well as in its history list.

The <META> Tag

This tag is used to embed document meta-information not defined by other HTML elements. Such information can be extracted by servers/clients for identifying, indexing, and cataloguing specialized document-related information.

One typical use of this tag is to send custom header fields in an HTTP response. When you specify the HTTP-EQUIV attribute for this tag, the Web server reads the data in the CONTENT to generate a corresponding HTTP header field. As an example, if the document contains the following <META> in the header section:

```
<META HTTP-EQUIV="Refresh" CONTENT="5;URL=http://acme.com/last.htm">
```

then the HTTP corresponding response header generated would be

```
Refresh: 5;URL=http://acme.com/last.htm
```

which will cause the browser to automatically load the URL *http://acme.com/last.htm* after five seconds, a feature known as *Client-Pull*.

The <BODY>...</BODY> Tag Pair

This tag pair defines the *body* of an HTML document, which contains all the text and images that make up the page, together with all the HTML control and formatting tags. For Netscape and other HTML 3.0–compatible browsers, you can also include either the BACKGROUND or the BGCOLOR attribute with the BODY tag.

The BACKGROUND attribute identifies a URL pointing to an image that acts as the background tile for the document. The BGCOLOR attribute allows you to change the background color without having to specify any image file and is listed as a hexadecimal triplet (xxyyzz) representing the intensity of the red (xx), green (yy), and blue (zz) colors.

To create a simple HTML page with a white background by use of the BGCOLOR attribute:

1. Using a text editor, create a text file with the following contents:

```
<HTML>
<TITLE>Chapter 7 Lesson 1 Example</TITLE>
<BODY BGCOLOR="FFFFFF">
This is an HTML page with a white background.
</BODY>
</HTML>
```

2. Save this file as *LESSON1.HTM* in the C:\WEBSITE\HTDOCS\BOOK\CHAP7\ directory.

3. Start your WebSite server if it is not already running.

4. Specify the following URL from your Web browser:

```
http://localhost/book/chap7/lesson1.htm
```

If your browser supports HTML 3 extensions, then it should display a page with a white background as shown in Figure 7-2.

NOTE: A copy of LESSON1.HTM and all other *.HTM files created in this chapter resides in the C:\WEBSITE\HTDOCS\BOOK\CHAP7\RESULTS\ directory.

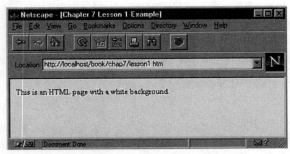

Figure 7-2 A basic HTML document with a white background

LESSON 2: FORMATTING TEXT USING HTML

HTML supports two levels of text formatting:

🛰 Block level, to format a block of text

🛰 Character level, to format a text sequence without causing a paragraph break

Block-Level Formatting

Block-level formatting is normally used when you want to format complete sections of text. Each block formatting tag causes a paragraph break to occur at the end of the formatted section. Table 7-8 lists the HTML tags related to block-level formatting.

Table 7–8 HTML tags used for block-level formatting

HTML Tag	Used To
<ADDRESS>...</ADDRESS>	Format an address section
<BLOCKQUOTE>...</BLOCKQUOTE>	Show text as a quotation
<BR CLEAR=Left|Right|Both>	Force a line break
<CENTER>...</CENTER>	Center sections
<DFN>...</DFN>	Format text section as a definition
<Hn>...</Hn>	Format six levels of heading (n = level number)
<HR SIZE=n>	Add a sizable horizontal line (n = thickness in pixels) on the page
<NOBR>	Indicate that words are not to be broken
<P ALIGN=Left|Center|Right>...</P>	Specify a paragraph boundary and text alignment
<PRE>...</PRE>	Display text as originally formatted
<WBR>	Specify that a word can be broken if necessary

To experiment with some frequently used block-level formatting tags, create a file named *LESSON2A.HTM* in the C:\WEBSITE\HTDOCS\BOOK\CHAP7\ directory with the following contents, and display it through your browser as explained in Lesson 1:

```
<HTML>
<TITLE>Chapter 7 Lesson 2a Example</TITLE>
<BODY BGCOLOR="FFFFFF">
<H1>Level 2 Heading</H1>
<H2>Level 3 Heading</H2>
<P ALIGN=Left>This is a left indented paragraph.
All text within the paragraph will be aligned to
the left side of the page layout.</P>
<P ALIGN=Center>This is a centered paragraph.</P>
<PRE>
```

```
State        State Code
_____        _____
Nebraska     NE
Iowa         IA
</PRE>
The following is a block quote:
<BLOCKQUOTE>
This paragraph appears in a block quote. The browser
might display it with a left and right indent and
add some space above and below the quote.
</BLOCKQUOTE>
<HR>
<ADDRESS>
XYZ Corporation, 123 Street, Lincoln, NE 12321
</ADDRESS>
</BODY>
</HTML>
```

Figure 7-3 shows the LESSON2A.HTM file displayed under the Netscape 2.0 browser.

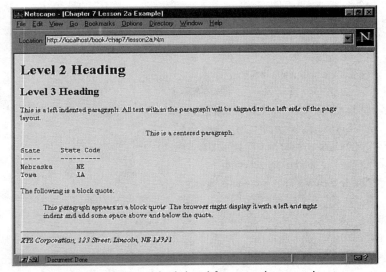

Figure 7–3 Displaying block-level formatted text under Netscape

Character-Level Formatting

Character-level formatting deals with changing the display attributes of one or more text characters without causing a paragraph break. It can be specified by use of either logical style HTML tags or physical style HTML tags.

Logical Style HTML Tags

Logical style HTML tags indicate text semantics (or meaning). It is up to the Web browser (and the user who configures it) as to how it displays the text formatted by use of logical tags. Some common logical tags are listed in Table 7-9.

Table 7–9 Logical style tag pairs

Logical Style Tag Pairs	Used For
<CITE>...</CITE>	Citation (usually italics)
<CODE>...</CODE>	Program code (usually fixed-width font)
<EM>...</EM>	Emphasizing text (usually italics)
<KBD>...</KBD>	Keyboard input (usually fixed-width font)
<STRONG>...</STRONG>	Strong emphasis (usually bold)
<VAR>...</VAR>	Listing a variable name (usually fixed-width font)

To experiment with logical style tags, create a file named *LESSON2B.HTM* in the C:\WEBSITE\HTDOCS\BOOK\CHAP7\ directory with the following contents, and display it through your browser:

```
<HTML>
<TITLE>Chapter 7 Lesson 2b Example</TITLE>
<BODY BGCOLOR="FFFFFF">
<P ALIGN=Left>This is a left indented paragraph with
logical style HTML tags for
<CITE>citation</CITE>,
<CODE>code: i=i+1</CODE>,
<EM>emphasized text</EM>,
<KBD>keyboard input</KBD>,
<STRONG>strong text</STRONG>,
and listing a variable name such as
<VAR>szFilePath</VAR>.
</P>
<P>Note that the logical style tags do not cause a
paragraph break.
</P>
</BODY>
</HTML>
```

Figure 7-4 shows the LESSON2B.HTM file displayed under the Netscape 2.0 browser.

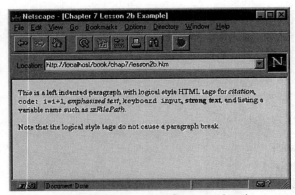

Figure 7-4 Displaying text formatted with logical style HTML tags

Physical Style HTML Tags

Physical style tags directly define the font attribute of the marked text and are listed in Table 7-10.

Table 7-10 Physical style tag pairs

Physical Style Tag Pairs	Attribute
<B>...</B>	Boldface
<I>...</I>	Italics
<TT>...</TT>	Nonproportional typewriter type font
^{...}	Superscript (HTML 3 only)
_{...}	Subscript (HTML 3 only)
<STRIKE>...</STRIKE>	Strike-through (HTML 3 only)
<BLINK>...</BLINK>	Blinking text (HTML 3 only)
<BASEFONT ...>	Default font size of the document
<FONT ...> ... </FONT>	Current font size

To experiment with physical style tags, create a file named *LESSON2C.HTM* in the C:\WEBSITE\HTDOCS\BOOK\CHAP7\ directory with the following contents, and display it through your browser:

```
<HTML>
<TITLE>Chapter 7 Lesson 2c Example</TITLE>
<BODY BGCOLOR="FFFFFF">
<B>Bold text</B>,
<I>Italicized text</I>,
<U>Non-proportional text</U>,
<SUP>Superscript</SUP>,
```

```
<SUB>Subscript</SUB>,
<STRIKE>Strike through</STRIKE>, and
<BLINK>Blinking text</BLINK>
<BASEFONT SIZE=5> This is font size 5
<FONT SIZE=3> This is font size 3 </FONT>
<FONT SIZE=+1> This is one size larger than the base font </FONT>
</BODY>
</HTML>
```

Figure 7-5 shows the LESSON2C.HTM file displayed under the Netscape 2.0 browser.

NOTE: Whitespace and tabs between words or paragraphs are usually considered a single space in an HTML document. If you want to show the spaces (say, for aligning or indenting text) as originally formatted, you need to use the <PRE>...</PRE> tag.

LESSON 3: CREATING LISTS IN HTML

You can create three types of lists in HTML:

- Ordered (or numbered)

- Unordered (or bulleted)

- Definition

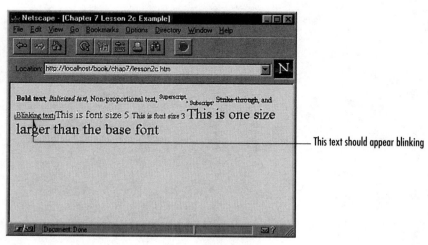

This text should appear blinking

Figure 7–5 Displaying text formatted with physical style HTML tags

Ordered List

The *ordered* list is used to present a numbered list of items, sorted by sequence or order of importance. You specify the <OL> tag to begin an ordered list, and then precede each list item with the <LI> tag. You terminate the ordered list with the </OL> tag.

Unordered List

An *unordered* list is used to present a list of items which are typically separated by white-space and/or marked by bullets. You begin an unordered list with the </UL> tag, and then precede each list item with the <LI> tag. You terminate the unordered list with the </OL> tag.

Definition List

A *definition* list is used to list terms and their corresponding definitions. The term being defined generally is flush-left, and the definition is formatted as an indented paragraph. You use the <DL>...</DL> tag pair to specify a definition list. The terms are preceded by the <DT> tag, and their corresponding definitions are preceded by the <DD> tag.

Experimenting with HTML Lists

Not only can you include different types of lists in the same document, you can also put one list within another to create nested lists. The following HTML text serves as an example of individual and nested lists. Create a file named *LESSON3.HTM* containing this text, and display it through your browser:

```
<HTML>
<TITLE>Chapter 7 Lesson 3 Example</TITLE>
<BODY BGCOLOR="FFFFFF">
<B>Ordered List</B>
<OL>
  <LI>First Item.
  <LI>Second Item.
</OL>
<B>Unordered List</B>
<UL>
  <LI>First Item.
  <LI>Second Item.
</UL>
<B>Definition List</B>
<DL>
  <DT>HTTP
  <DD>Hypertext Transfer Protocol
  <DT>HTML
  <DD>Hypertext Markup Language
</DL>
<B>Nested Lists</B>
```

```
<OL>
  <LI>List A Item 1
      <UL>
          <LI>List B Item 1
          <LI>List B Item 2
      </UL>
  <LI>List A Item 2
</OL>
</BODY>
</HTML>
```

Figure 7-6 shows the LESSON3.HTM file displayed under the Netscape 2.0 browser.

NOTE: HTML lists contain many optional attributes to give you more control on how the browsers should present these lists. For more information on these attributes, consult the HTML references listed earlier in the HTML overview section.

LESSON 4: CREATING COMMENTS AND META CHARACTERS

You can specify comments in an HTML document by enclosing them within the <!-- and --> tag pair. The client does not display these comments in the document view. Also, if you need to display characters such as "<" and ">," which have special meaning in HTML in their original appearance, you need to use character sequences as listed in Table 7-11.

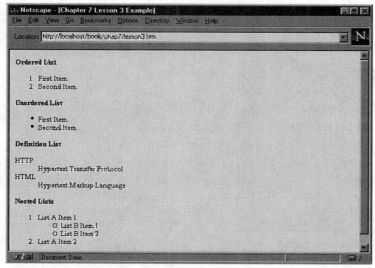

Figure 7-6 Displaying HTML lists

Table 7–11 Character sequences for special characters

Character Sequence	Character Displayed
&lt	<
&gt	>
&amp	&
&quot	"

The following text serves as an example of including comments and displaying special characters in an HTML document. Create a file named *LESSON4.HTM* containing this text, and display it through your browser:

```
<HTML>
<TITLE>Chapter 7 Lesson 4 Example</TITLE>
<BODY BGCOLOR="FFFFFF">
<!-- <B>Text inside the comment.</B>-->
<B>Text outside the comment.</B>
<BR>
<UL>
  <LI>Less than sign: &lt
  <LI>Greater that sign: &gt
  <LI>Ampersand sign: &amp
  <LI>Double quote sign: &quot
</UL>
</BODY>
</HTML>
```

Figure 7-7 shows the LESSON4.HTM file displayed under the Netscape 2.0 browser.

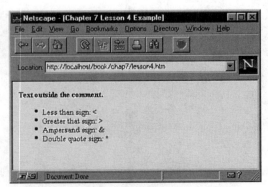

Figure 7-7 Including comments and special characters in an HTML document

LESSON 5: CREATING TABLES

The table feature allows you to format data in rows and columns. This feature was added as part of the HTML 3 specification and is thus not supported by all browsers. Table 7-12 lists the various HTML tags associated with the table feature.

Table 7-12 HTML tags related to the table feature

Tag Pairs	Used to Define a Table...
<TABLE ...>...</TABLE>	Delimiter
<TR ...>...</TR>	Row
<TD ...>...</TD>	Cell
<TH ...>...</TH>	Header cell
<CAPTION>...</CAPTION>	Caption

In a nutshell, the <TABLE>...</TABLE> tags identify the beginning and the end of a table. The <TR>...</TR> tag pair marks each new table row. Within each table row, the <TD>...</TD> tag pair marks the data cell. The <TH>...</TH> tags are used to specify the column headings. You may use the <CAPTION>...</CAPTION> tag pair to define the table caption.

The <TABLE>...</TABLE> Tag Pair

All table-related HTML tags have an effect only if they are included within the <TABLE>...</TABLE> tag pair. The <TABLE> tag can accept the following optional attributes:

BORDER=<value>, to specify the size of a table border.

NOTE: The absence of this attribute creates a default space around the table cells to reflect an invisible border. To eliminate this default space, set the value of the BORDER attribute to 0.

CELLSPACING=<value>, to specify the amount of space inserted between individual cells in a table.

CELLPADDING=<value>, to specify the amount of space between the border of the cell and the contents of the cell.

215

- WIDTH=<*value_or_percent*>, to describe the desired width of the table, either as an absolute width in pixels, or a percentage of document width.

  Ordinarily, the browser tries to automatically size the table so that it looks presentable. However, by setting the <WIDTH> attribute, you can force the browser to display the table within the specified width.

- HEIGHT=<*value_or_percent*>, to describe the desired height of the table.

- ALIGN=<Left|Right>, to align the table to the left or to the right of a page, allowing text to flow around it.

The <TR>...</TR> Tag Pair

The number of rows in a table is exactly specified by how many <TR>...</TR> tag pairs it contains. The <TR> tag of a table row can take the following two alignment attributes, which if specified, become the default alignments for all cells in that row:

- ALIGN=<Left|Center|Right>, to control horizontal alignment of the data within a table cell.

- VALIGN=<Top|Middle|Bottom|Baseline>, to control vertical alignment of the data within a table cell.

The <TD>...</TD> Tag Pair

This tag pair defines a table cell within a table row. A cell can contain any of the HTML tags normally present in the body of an HTML document. By default, the browser displays the cell data using left horizontal alignment and middle vertical alignment. These alignments can be overridden by any alignments specified in the associated <TR> element, and those alignments in turn can be overridden by any ALIGN or VALIGN attributes explicitly specified with the <TD> tag. Altogether, the <TD> tag can accept the following attributes:

- ALIGN=<Left|Center|Right>, to control horizontal alignment of the data within a table cell.

- VALIGN=<Top|Middle|Bottom|Baseline>, to control vertical alignment of the data within a table cell.

- WIDTH=<*value_or_percent*>, to describe the desired width of the cell, either as an absolute width in pixels, or a percentage of table width.

- HEIGHT=<*value_or_percent*>, to describe the desired height of the cell, either as an absolute height in pixels, or a percentage of table height.

- NOWRAP, to indicate to the browser that it should not break the lines to fit the width of the cell.

COLSPAN, to specify how many columns of the table this cell should span. The default COLSPAN for any cell is 1.

ROWSPAN, to specify how many rows of the table this cell should span. The default ROWSPAN for any cell is 1.

The <TH>...</TH> Tag Pair

This tag pair stands for table header. *Header* cells are identical to data cells in all respects, with the exception that the data in the header cells appears as boldfaced and centered within the cell. All attributes of the <TD> tag are also applicable with the <TH> tag.

The <CAPTION>...</CAPTION> Tag Pair

This tag pair represents the caption of a table. It should appear inside the <TABLE>...</TABLE> tags but not inside the table rows or table cells. Captions are always horizontally centered with respect to the table, and they may have their lines broken to fit within the width of the table. The <CAPTION> tag accepts the ALIGN attribute, which can be set to either Top or Bottom, to control whether the caption appears above or below the table.

Experimenting with Tables

The following HTML text displays two tables that essentially rely on the default values of most tag attributes. Create a file named *LESSON5A.HTM* containing the following text, and display it through your browser:

```
<HTML>
<HEAD>
<TITLE>HTML Tables</TITLE>
</HEAD>
<BODY BGCOLOR="FFFFFF">
<TABLE>
<CAPTION>Table with no border</CAPTION>
<TH ALIGN=CENTER>Column 1 </TH> <TH ALIGN=CENTER>Column 2</TH>
<TR ALIGN=CENTER> <TD>Item 1</TD> <TD>Item 2</TD> </TR>
<TR ALIGN=CENTER> <TD>Item 3</TD> <TD>Item 4</TD> </TR>
</TABLE>
<P>

<TABLE BORDER>
<CAPTION>Table with border</CAPTION>
<TH>Column 1 </TH> <TH>Column 2</TH>
<TR> <TD>item1</TD> <TD>item2</TD> </TR>
<TR> <TD>item3</TD> <TD>item4</TD> </TR>
</TABLE>
</BODY>
</HTML>
```

Figure 7-8 shows the LESSON5A.HTM file displayed under the Netscape 2.0 browser.

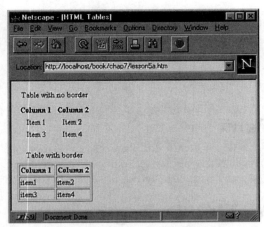

Figure 7-8 Displaying basic tables

The following HTML text displays two tables that use COLSPAN, ROWSPAN, and specific tag attributes. Create a file named *LESSON5B.HTM* containing the following text, and display it through your browser:

```
<HTML>
<HEAD>
<TITLE>HTML Tables</TITLE>
</HEAD>
<BODY BGCOLOR="FFFFFF">
<TABLE BORDER=5 CELLSPACING=10 CELLPADDING=5>
<CAPTION ALIGN=BOTTOM>
<B>Table with COLSPAN, ROWSPAN, and other attributes</B>
</CAPTION>
<TH>Column 1</TH>
<TH>Column 2</TH>
<TH>Column 3</TH>
<TR ALIGN=LEFT VALIGN=BOTTOM>
<TD>Item 1 Line 1<BR>Item 1 Line 2</TD>
<TD ALIGN=CENTER>Item 2</TD>
<TD ALIGN=RIGHT VALIGN=MIDDLE ROWSPAN=2>Item 3</TD>
</TR>
<TR> <TD>Item 4</TD> <TD>Item 5</TD></TR>
<TR><TD ALIGN=CENTER COLSPAN=3>Item 6</TD></TR>
</TABLE>
</BODY>
</HTML>
```

Figure 7-9 shows the LESSON5B.HTM file displayed under the Netscape 2.0 browser.

218

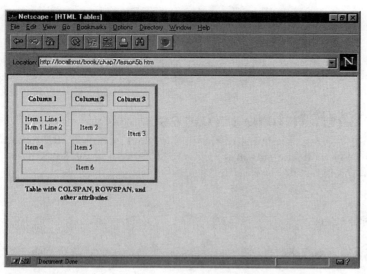

Figure 7-9 Table containing ROWSPAN, COLSPAN, and other tag attributes

LESSON 6: ADDING INLINE IMAGES

Inline images are images that appear as part of the document. They are usually encoded in GIF or JPEG format and are stored in a separate file. HTML's support for inline images has played a substantial role in increasing the popularity of the World Wide Web. You use the <IMG> tag with the following attributes (most of which are optional) to include an inline image:

- SRC (required attribute), to specify the URL that references the image file.

- ALIGN=<Left|Right|Top|Middle|AbsMiddle|Bottom>, to specify how the following text floats around the image.

- ALT=<*text*>, to specify an optional text that nongraphical browsers can display in place of the image.

- ISMAP, to identify the image as an imagemap.

- WIDTH=<*value*>, to specify the width of the image in pixels.

- HEIGHT=<*value*>, to specify the height of the image in pixels.

- BORDER=<*value*>, to control the thickness of the border around the displayed image.

◗ HSPACE=<*value*>, to specify the amount of horizontal space between the image and the floating text.

◗ VSPACE=<*value*>, to specify the amount of vertical space between the image and the floating text.

Experimenting with Inline Images

To experiment with the various attributes of the inline image, create a file named *LESSON6.HTM* with the following contents in the C:\WEBSITE\HTDOCS\BOOK\CHAP7 directory, and display it through your browser:

```
<HTML>
<HEAD>
<TITLE>Inline Images</TITLE>
</HEAD>
<BODY BGCOLOR="FFFFFF">
<IMG SRC="/book/survey/goph1.gif" ALIGN=LEFT ALT="Gopher 1"
WIDTH=36 HEIGHT=37>
This image is defined as left aligned so this text floats
around it. It also contains the width and height attributes indicating
the size of the image.
<BR CLEAR=Both>
<HR SIZE=2>
<IMG SRC="/book/survey/goph1.gif" ALIGN=RIGHT ALT="Gopher 1"
WIDTH=36 HEIGHT=37 HSPACE=10>
This image is defined as right aligned with some horizontal
space between the image and the floating text.
<BR CLEAR=Both>
<HR SIZE=2>
<IMG SRC="/book/survey/goph1.gif">
<IMG SRC="/book/survey/goph2.gif" BORDER=1>
<IMG SRC="/book/survey/goph3.gif" HSPACE=3 BORDER=2>
<IMG SRC="/book/survey/goph4.gif" BORDER=4>
You can also display images side-by-side and add borders of varying
dimensions around them.
<BR CLEAR=Both>
<HR SIZE=2>
<TABLE>
<TR ALIGN=CENTER>
<TD><IMG SRC="/book/survey/goph1.gif"></TD>
<TD ALIGN=LEFT>
Sometimes, the easiest way to get the desired alignment effect
among images and text is by using HTML tables.
</TD>
<TD><IMG SRC="/book/survey/goph4.gif"></TD>
<TR>
</TABLE>
<BR CLEAR=Both>
<HR SIZE=2>
</BODY>
</HTML>
```

Figure 7-10 shows the LESSON6.HTM file displayed under the Netscape 2.0 browser.

Things to Consider When Adding Inline Images to Your Document

Although an appropriate use of inline images can dramatically increase the appeal of your Web site, its misuse can be a big turn-off for visitors who are coming in through a slow Internet connection. It is important that you consider the following factors when including inline images in your HTML document:

- While the GIF image format is supported by every graphical browser, the GIF images tend be much larger than their equivalent JPEG-formatted counterparts.

- The JPEG format gradually is being supported in the newer versions of most browsers.

- The JPEG format creates smaller images at the expense of some image-quality.

- The GIF format has two versions: GIF 87a and GIF 89a. GIF 89a format allows you to create animated images as well as images with transparent backgrounds.

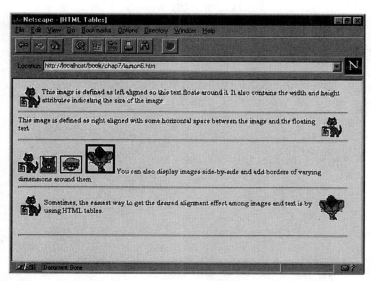

Figure 7-10 Experimenting with inline images

You can insert a <BR CLEAR=Both> tag to stop the text from floating around a left-, middle-, or right-aligned image.

The WIDTH and HEIGHT attributes help a browser to allocate the necessary page space for the image and proceed with the display of the rest of the document. This has a net effect of speeding up the document display at the client end.

LESSON 7: CREATING HYPERTEXT AND HYPERGRAPHICS

Hypertext and *hypergraphics* are features that let you click on text or an image and be taken to a different section of the same document or another document potentially residing on a different host. You use the <A>...</A> anchor tags to create a hyperlink using the following syntax:

```
<A HREF="URL">Text_to_be_anchored</A> (for Hypertext links)
<A HREF="URL"><IMG SRC="Image URL"></A> (for Hypergraphics)
```

The URL is the destination where a client takes you if you click anywhere on the *Text_to_be_anchored* or the inline image (in case of the second option). Links within the same document are specified by use of the #BookmarkName value for the HREF attribute as in:

```
<A HREF="#Tables">Click here to learn about HTML tables</A>
```

In addition, you must mark the bookmark's destination within the same document using the NAME attribute of the anchor tag as in:

```
<A NAME="Tables">LESSON #5: CREATING TABLES</A>
```

You can also use the *mailto* function in your anchor destination to allow users to send mail to a given address directly from their client application. An example of the *mailto* function follows:

```
<A HREF="mailto:abc@xyz.com">Comments to Webmaster</A>
```

To experiment with the hyperlinking feature of HTML:

1. Create a file named *LESSON8.HTM* with the following contents:

```
<HTML>
<HEAD>
<TITLE>Hypertext Links</TITLE>
</HEAD>
<BODY BGCOLOR="FFFFFF">
<A NAME="Lesson7"><H1>Lesson 7 Example</H1></A>
<UL>
<A HREF="/book/chap7/lesson1.htm">
<LI>Lesson 1: Defining Document Structure</A>
<A HREF="/book/chap7/lesson2a.htm">
<LI>Lesson 2a: Block Level Formatting</A>
<A HREF="/book/chap7/lesson2b.htm">
```

```
<LI>Lesson 2b: Logical Style Tags</A>
<A HREF="/book/chap7/lesson2c.htm">
<LI>Lesson 2c: Physical Style Tags</A>
<A HREF="/book/chap7/lesson3.htm">
<LI>Lesson 3: HTML Lists</A>
<A HREF="/book/chap7/lesson4.htm">
<LI>Lesson 4: Comments and Meta Characters</A>
<A HREF="/book/chap7/lesson5a.htm">
<LI>Lesson 5a: Basic HTML Tables</A>
<A HREF="/book/chap7/lesson5b.htm">
<LI>Lesson 5a: Advanced HTML Tables</A><BR>
<A HREF="/book/chap7/lesson6.htm">
<LI><IMG SRC="/book/chap7/results/lesson6.jpg"></A>
<A HREF="#Lesson7">
<LI>Lesson 7: Hypertext and Hypergraphics</A>
</UL>
</BODY>
</HTML>
```

2. Display LESSON8.HTM through your browser as shown in Figure 7-11.

3. Click on each link to verify its destination.

REVIEW QUESTIONS

1. What are the main reasons for the popularity of the World Wide Web?

2. Can a computer be both a Web server and a Web client?

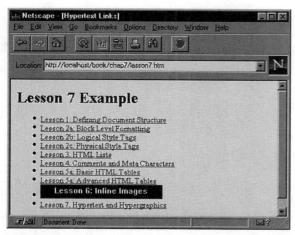

Figure 7-11 Experimenting with hypertext and hypergraphics

3. List the names of some popular Web servers and Web clients.

4. How is the data transferred within the World Wide Web?

5. Why is a Web server called an HTTP server?

6. What factors make HTTP superior to other document-retrieval protocols?

7. How does HTTP support the object-oriented model?

8. What does "URL" stand for? What is its function?

9. What methods can be used in an HTTP request? How do they differ?

10. How can a Web client take advantage of the conditional GET method?

11. What is the role of header fields in an HTTP request and in an HTTP response?

12. What are the four main classes of HTTP status codes?

13. Why is HTML called a hypertext markup language?

14. What is an HTML tag?

15. How do you specify headings in HTML?

16. What is the difference between physical styles and logical styles?

17. What kind of lists are supported in HTML?

18. What can be an alternative way for designing tables (besides using the <TABLE> tag)?

19. How is an inline image added in an HTML document?

20. How do you create a hypertext link in HTML?

EXERCISES

1. Using your Web client, experiment with URLs to return as many status codes as possible from the servers on the World Wide Web. Which is the most common status code you encounter that does not fall in the 2xx category? Hint: If you ran the job list application discussed in Chapter 2, try the URL: *http://localhost/cgi-win/book/joblist/joblist.mdb,* and see what status code is generated by your local Web server.

2. Create an HTML document that incorporates all the common features of HTML presented in this chapter.

8

CREATING HTML FORMS

8

If it weren't for HTML forms, the Web would be shaping the information superhighway into a one-way street where the information passes from the Web server to the Web client. HTML forms allow a user to specify information that a Web client sends back to the Web server. Incidentally, HTML forms closely resemble paper forms, not just in their appearance, but also in their operation.

Take the case of a credit card application. The paper application form has fields for your name, date of birth, and other pertinent information. You supply all the required information and mail the application to the bank. After receiving your application, the bank verifies information on each field for its accuracy and completeness, evaluates your credit history, and notifies you about the acceptance or rejection of your application.

Now, suppose the same bank ran a Web-based, automated, credit card issuing service. To apply for a credit card through this service, you request an application form from the bank's Web server. The server sends you an HTML document that your Web client interprets to generate an application form on your computer screen. Using your keyboard and mouse, you fill in that form and click on a special Submit button. The client then delivers that information to the bank's Web server and waits for the server's response.

Depending on the functionality and efficiency of the automated service, you may get a decision within seconds, or the server might just notify you that your application has been filed for further review. It could even give you the location of another HTML form that you can fill in and submit to check the current status of your application.

The following list summarizes the similarities between HTML forms and paper forms:

- You can fill them in at your own time, place, and convenience.

- You can specify text, select from a list, check multiple options, and even provide comments.

- They are designed to organize your data. They accept any information (even invalid data). They are not interactive (which might change in HTML forms once JavaScript becomes popular). You only get feedback after you submit your form to the server or data processing agency.

- They have a capacity to adapt to their environment. Just as there can be translations of a paper form in many languages, HTML forms can be displayed on various hardware platforms.

LESSON 1: CREATING A SIMPLE HTML FORM

In Chapter 2, Getting Started, you were introduced to a guest book application which allowed any user to supply a name, e-mail address, date of birth, and remarks over the Web using the entry form shown in Figure 8-1.

This guest book entry form contains an instructional heading, four white rectangular input fields with attached labels indicating what type of information is expected in each field, an *Enter* button that submits the data, and a *Clear* button that empties each input field so that you can start all over again. This form is indeed an HTML document.

The only difference between this form and a regular HTML page is the presence of input fields, special buttons, and the fact that the supplied information is added into the guest book database when the Enter button is clicked on. HTML supports all these form features through the following additional tags:

- <FORM ...>...</FORM>

- <INPUT ...>

- <TEXTAREA ...> ... </TEXTAREA>

- <SELECT ...> ... </SELECT>

- <OPTION ...>

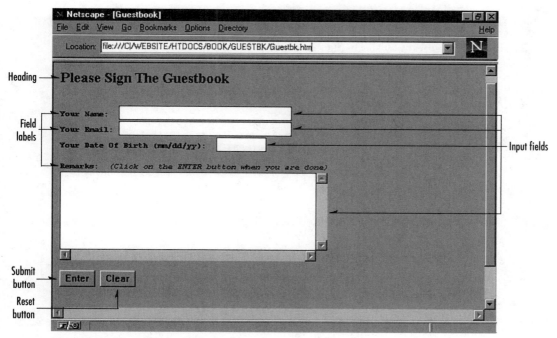

Figure 8-1 Guest book entry form

In a nutshell, the <FORM>...</FORM> tag pair defines the scope of the form. The <INPUT> tag allows you to create various types of input controls such as single-line text boxes, radio buttons, check boxes, and submit buttons. The <TEXTAREA> tag represents a multiline text box. The combination of the <SELECT> and <OPTION> tags allows you to create various forms of selection lists.

Before we examine these form-related tags in detail, let's see what it takes to create the guest book entry form shown in Figure 8-1. Follow these steps:

1. Create a new file in your text editor, and enter the following HTML text to specify the text representing the title of the form:

```
<HTML>
<HEAD>
<TITLE>Guestbook</TITLE>
</HEAD>
<BODY>
<H1>Please Sign The Guestbook</H1><P>
```

2. Specify the instruction for the beginning of preformatted text by adding the following tag:

```
<PRE>
```

The only role of this <PRE> tag in this example is to help align the form fields.

3. Initialize your form by specifying the <FORM> tag as follows:

```
<FORM METHOD=POST ACTION=/cgi-win/book/guestbk/guestbk.exe/AddEntry>
```

4. Add the form input fields along with their labels as follows:

```
<B>Your Name:  </B><INPUT NAME="Name" MAXLENGTH=50 SIZE=30>
<B>Your Email: </B><INPUT NAME="Email" MAXLENGTH=50 SIZE=30>
<B>Your Date Of Birth (mm/dd/yy): </B><INPUT NAME="BirthDate" SIZE=8>

<B>Remarks:  </B><I>(Click on the ENTER button when you are done)</I>
<TEXTAREA NAME="Remarks" ROWS=6 COLS=45></TEXTAREA>
```

5. Cancel the current preformatted mode by adding the following tag:

```
</PRE>
```

6. Create a submit button by adding the following line:

```
<INPUT NAME="Submit" TYPE="SUBMIT" VALUE="Enter">
```

7. Add a reset button by adding the following line:

```
<INPUT NAME="Reset" TYPE="RESET" VALUE="Clear">
```

8. Define the closing boundary of the form and the HTML document as follows:

```
</FORM>
</BODY>
</HTML>
```

9. Save the text file as *LESSON1.HTM* in the C:\WEBSITE\HTDOCS\BOOK\CHAP8\ directory.

10. Start your WebSite server if it is not already running.

11. Specify the following URL from your Web browser:

```
http://localhost/book/chap8/lesson1.htm
```

Your browser should display the guest book entry form as shown in Figure 8-1.

NOTE: For a handy reference, a copy of each example file created in this chapter is stored in the C:\WEBSITE\HTDOCS\BOOK\CHAP8\RESULTS\ directory.

LESSON 2: EXAMINING THE <FORM> TAG

A single HTML document is capable of supporting multiple forms where the data from each form can potentially go to different Web servers. The <FORM>...</FORM> tag pair defines a form's boundary. All form fields listed within this boundary automatically get associated to that form. A submit button (created through the <INPUT> tag) must be present on every form to allow a user to individually send each form's data to its specified destination. The form's destination and how the data should be sent to the server are indicated through the following attributes of the FORM tag:

➤ ACTION=<*URL*>

➤ METHOD=<*Request_Method*>

➤ ENCTYPE=<Data_Encoding_Type>

Note that you cannot nest a form within another form. Also, you cannot have a universal submit button that will send the data from all forms to their respective destinations at one time.

The ACTION Attribute

The ACTION attribute points to the URL of the resource that should receive the form data. The resource, which is generally a script or an executable program on the Web server, is responsible for processing that form data. This script or program is also expected to generate a response that the Web server returns to the Web client. If this program resides on the same server from which the form is retrieved, then the URL of that program can be specified in terms of the relative path.

The guest book entry form we created in the previous lesson is set to send the field data to the GUESTBK.EXE program residing in the C:\WEBSITE\CGI-WIN\BOOK\GUESTBK\ directory, because the ACTION attribute of its <FORM> tag points to the following (relative) URL:

```
/cgi-win/book/guestbk/guestbk.exe/AddEntry
```

Note that the "AddEntry" text at the end of this URL acts as the extra path parameter, which is also sent to the GUESTBK.EXE program along with the form data. The next chapter covers the role of this extra path parameter in more detail.

Redirecting the Form Data

If you want to redirect your form data to a different destination, you just need to change the value of the ACTION attribute. Often, this idea is used to test the design and functionality of the form independent of the actual program that processes the form data. For example, the following steps show how you can use the CGITEST32.EXE utility present in the C:\WEBSITE\CGI-WIN\ directory to verify the data sent through the guest book entry form when its submit button is clicked on:

1. Open the C:\WEBSITE\HTDOCS\BOOK\CHAP8\LESSON1.HTM file in your text editor.

2. Change the <FORM> line as follows:

```
<FORM METHOD=POST ACTION=/cgi-win/cgitest32.exe/Form>
```

3. Save the file as *LESSON2A.HTM* in the same directory.

4. Ensure that your WebSite server is running.

5. Specify the following location from your Web browser:

```
http://localhost/book/chap8/lesson2a.htm
```

The browser displays the guest book entry form, which looks identical to the form we created in the previous lesson.

6. Enter the data for the form fields as follows:

```
        Name: John Smith
       Email: smith@xyz.com
Date Of Birth: 09/20/72
     Remarks: Testing how the field data is sent through this form.
```

7. Click on the Enter button.

8. The CGITEST32.EXE utility returns a report of the field names and the data it received from the form as shown in Figure 8-2.

The METHOD and the ENCTYPE Attributes

The METHOD attribute tells the Web client what request method to use when submitting the form data. As explained in the "HTTP Request" section of Chapter 7, Elements of the World Wide Web, there are two common request methods, GET and POST, through which a request is sent to a Web server. The main difference between these two request methods is how they transport the form data.

The GET method appends the form data to the URL with a question mark as follows:

```
GET URL_Path?Encoded_data HTTP/1.x
[NewLine]
Header Fields
[NewLine]
```

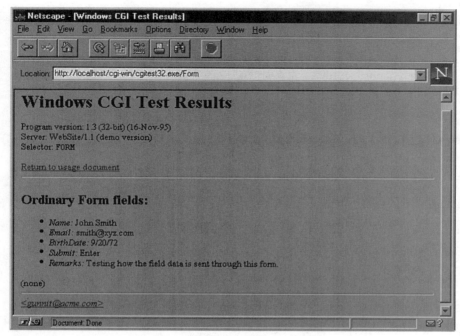

Figure 8-2 Using the CGITEST32.EXE utility to verify a form

whereas the POST method passes the form data in the body of the request as follows:

```
POST URL_Path HTTP/1.x
[NewLine]
Header Fields
[NewLine]
Encoded_data
[NewLine]
```

In either case, the client sends the form data using an encoding scheme specified by the ENCTYPE attribute. Today, the most commonly used encoding scheme for sending form data is called *URL encoding*, which is specified as follows:

```
ENCTYPE="application/x-www-form-urlencoded"
```

Note that the ENCTYPE attribute is an optional attribute, and if you do not include this attribute in the <FORM> tag, the browser automatically applies the URL encoding scheme to send the data.

URL Encoding Scheme

The URL encoding scheme packages data from all the fields into a single text string using the following *name=value* pair format:

```
name1=value1&name2=value2&name3=value3...
```

The *name* parameters refer to the name of the input form fields specified through their NAME attribute. The *value* parameters associated with each field name enumerate the data entered for that field. During the URL encoding process, the spaces (in either the field name or the data) are converted into plus signs (+). The plus sign and other special symbols—such as ampersand (&), equal sign (=), quote ("), percent sign (%), and the newline characters (carriage return and line feed)—are translated as %*xx*, where *xx* denotes the hexadecimal representation of their ASCII code.

Viewing URL Encoded Data

For your convenience, we have provided a CGI utility called FORMINP.EXE residing in the C:\WEBSITE\BOOK\FORMAPPS\ directory that returns the URL encoded version of any form's data. To use this utility to view the URL encoded data sent by the browser when you submit the guest book entry form:

1. Change the <FORM> tag of the C:\WEBSITE\HTDOCS\BOOK\LESSON1.HTM file as follows:

```
<FORM METHOD=POST ACTION=/cgi-win/book/formapps/forminp.exe>
```

2. Save this modified file as *LESSON2B.HTM* in the same directory.

3. Ensure that your Web browser is running.

4. Specify the following URL from your browser:

```
http://localhost/book/chap8/lesson2b.htm
```

The browser displays the guest book entry form.

5. Type the data from the previous example in the form fields, and click on the Enter button.

The FORMINP.EXE utility returns the URL encoded data as shown in Figure 8-3.

Notice how the spaces have been replaced by the plus sign, and certain symbols have been translated to their hex ASCII codes preceded by a percent sign. If you scroll through the complete encoded string and count the Name=Value pairs in it, you will find that it contains five pairs. Even the Enter button, which was named *Submit* in this form's HTML code, is passed as a Submit=Enter pair to the server. Later on, you will see how you can use the information of this additional pair to your advantage.

Multipart Encoding Scheme

Recently, a new encoding scheme known as *Multipart Encoding* has been added to the HTML specifications for sending form data. It is specified as follows:

```
ENCTYPE="multipart/form-data"
```

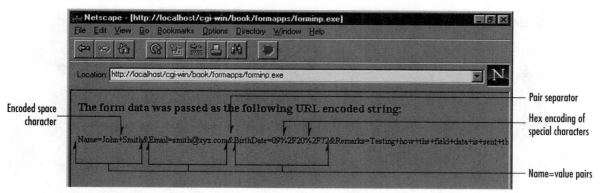

Figure 8-3 URL encoded string of the guest book entry form data

The main reason for introducing this scheme was to allow file uploads through HTML forms. Under this scheme, a boundary string is selected that does not occur in any of the data. (This boundary string selection is sometimes done using random-text-generation algorithms.) Each field of the form is sent, in the order in which it occurs in the form, as a part of the multipart stream. Each part identifies the field name and is labeled with an appropriate content type if the media type of the data is known (for example, inferred from the file extension or operating system typing information). If the media type cannot be established, then a default content type of "application/octet-stream" is sent with the data section.

The detailed coverage of this encoding scheme is beyond the scope of this book. For more information on this scheme and how you can implement the file upload process, please refer to the following URL:

```
http://www.ics.uci.edu/pub/ietf/html/rfc1867.txt
```

LESSON 3: EXAMINING THE <INPUT> TAG

You can select from a choice of input controls for a data entry field. An input control is a *graphical user interface (GUI)* element that directs the user on the size and type of data required for a field. A single-line text box is the most widely used control because it accepts any character input from the user without taking too much physical space on the form. The other controls, such as radio buttons and check boxes, limit the user to certain data values. It is up to the form designer to decide what type of control to use for a data entry field.

A control is assigned to a data entry field through the <INPUT> tag, which supports the following attributes:

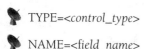 TYPE=<control_type>

NAME=<field_name>

- VALUE=<*default_value*>

- SIZE=<*value*>

- MAXLENGTH=<*value*>

- CHECKED

- SRC=<*URL*>

Next, we describe the purpose of each attribute, and then we will construct sample forms to demonstrate their functionality.

The TYPE Attribute

The TYPE attribute allows you to select one of the following control types for a data entry field:

- TEXT—This is a single-line text box that can accept any type of characters (default value for the TYPE attribute).

- PASSWORD—This is a single-line text box where the characters are displayed as asterisks.

- CHECKBOX—This is a small square box that can be checked or unchecked.

- RADIO—This is a small circle normally combined with other radio controls to allow the selection of one choice from a given set of choices.

- SUBMIT—This is a special button that, when selected, sends the form data to the action URL.

- RESET—This is a special button that sets the fields to their default values.

- IMAGE—This displays a user-specified image that can be clicked on to submit the form data.

- HIDDEN—This is an invisible control whose value is sent along with the rest of the form data.

- FILE—This is a control for specifying an existing file on the local computer.

The NAME Attribute

Each input field is referred to by the name specified in the NAME attribute of that field. This attribute is passed to the server and used by the executable program on the server to distinguish the data of one field from the other. It is a mandatory attribute.

The NAME attribute is not displayed on the form except in the case of submit (TYPE=SUBMIT) or reset (TYPE=RESET) buttons when their VALUE attribute (described next) is absent from the <INPUT> tag. That is why you have to use regular HTML text to label an input field on the form.

Note that the value of the NAME attribute does not have to be unique for each field. As a matter of fact, radio controls require the same name for their NAME attribute in order to work together, as you will see in Lesson 4. If there are two text controls on the form named "Test," both are passed to the server in the URL encoded string as follows:

```
Test=Value_Of_First_Test_Control&Test=Value_Of_Second_Test_Control
```

It is up to the executable program to figure out how it wants to process the data of each Test control.

The VALUE Attribute

You can supply a default value for each text box control through the VALUE attribute. When a user retrieves the form from the Web server or clicks on a RESET type button, the client automatically fills in the default value for each text input field. If the user does not overwrite that default value, then that value is sent to the server as the data for that field. If this attribute is missing, then the default value of "" is assumed by the client.

The VALUE attribute, when specified for a check box or radio control, defines the value of that check box or radio control. When that check box or radio control is selected, the data specified in its VALUE attribute is returned to the server. Also, for hidden fields, the use of this attribute is the only way to set their value.

The SIZE and MAXLENGTH Attributes

The SIZE attribute specifies the visible width of the text box on the form, whereas the MAXLENGTH attribute specifies the number of characters accepted by that text box. The value of the MAXLENGTH attribute can be greater than the value of the SIZE attribute, in which case the field will scroll appropriately. If the MAXLENGTH attribute is absent from a field's <INPUT> tag, then you can enter any number of characters in that field.

The CHECKED Attribute

The CHECKED attribute is used to indicate to the browser that it should select a check box or radio button by default. As you will see in the next two lessons, the unselected check boxes and radio buttons do not return *name=value* pairs when the form is submitted.

The SRC Attribute

The SRC attribute accepts an URL of an image. It is used only when the TYPE attribute of the <INPUT> tag is set to IMAGE. Lesson 6 demonstrates the use of this attribute.

Example: Creating a Text Box and a Password Field

Let's say you want to create a login form that asks users for their username (15 characters maximum) and a password (10 characters maximum):

1. Using your text editor, create a new file named *LESSON3A.HTM* in the C:\WEBSITE\HTDOCS\BOOK\CHAP8\ directory with the following contents:

```
<HTML>
<HEAD>
<TITLE>Login Form</TITLE>
</HEAD>
<BODY>
<CENTER>
<H1>Please Identify Yourself</H1><P>
<FORM METHOD=POST ACTION=/cgi-win/book/formapps/forminp.exe>
<B>Username:   </B>
<INPUT NAME="UserName" MAXLENGTH=15 SIZE=10><BR>
<B>Password: </B>
<INPUT NAME="UserName" TYPE="PASSWORD" MAXLENGTH=10 SIZE=10>
<BR><BR>
<INPUT NAME="Login" TYPE="SUBMIT" VALUE="Login">
<INPUT NAME="Reset" TYPE="RESET" VALUE="Clear">
</FORM>
</CENTER>
</BODY>
</HTML>
```

2. Ensure that your WebSite server is running.

3. Specify the following URL from your browser.

   `http://localhost/book/chap8/lesson3a.htm`

   The browser displays a login form as shown in Figure 8-4.

4. Enter *John* for the Username field.

5. Type *qwerty* for the Password field. Note that the browser displays an asterisk for every character you type.

6. Click on the Login button to submit the form.

   Your form data is received by the FORMINP.EXE utility, which returns the associated URL encoded string as shown in Figure 8-5.

238

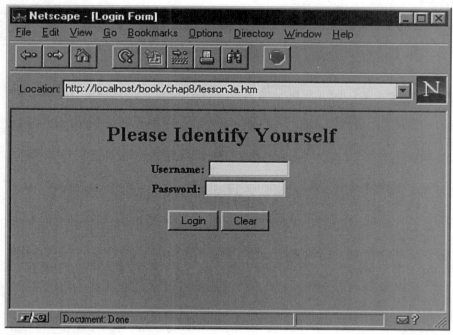

Figure 8–4 Creating a login form

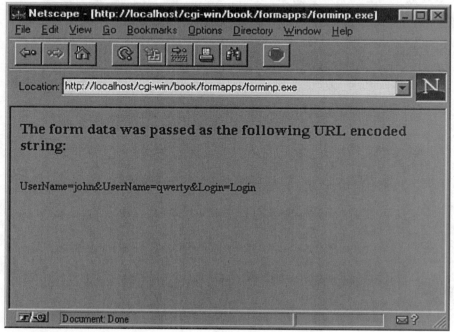

Figure 8–5 URL encoded string of the login form data

NOTE: The browser itself does not perform any checks on the username or the password value. It is the responsibility of the executable program receiving the data to ensure that the user entered a valid name and password.

Empty Text Box... If the text box or password control is initially empty and the user does not provide any information for that control before submitting the form, the client still passes that control along with other fields in this format: *TextBoxName=&Name2=Value2&Name3=Value3...*

LESSON 4: CREATING RADIO CONTROLS

In Chapter 2, Getting Started, we introduced a Web application called the On-Line Questionnaire that allows you to conduct an electronic survey. This application contains a reader survey form, shown in Figure 8-6, which is used for accepting user feedback. This and the next three lessons discuss the choice and the construction of the input controls used for the questions on this form.

The first question on this form asks for the reader's level of computer expertise. If the response to this question had been sought through a text box control, then different readers might use different words to describe their expertise levels (high, fair, novice, low,

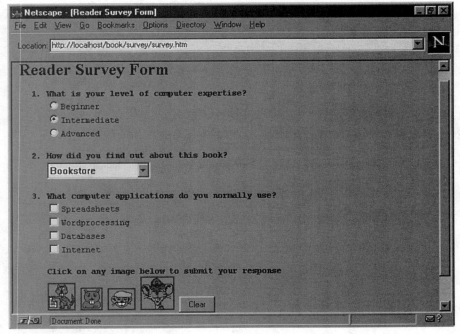

Figure 8–6 Reader survey form

and so on). Since you are conducting a survey, such responses can make your analysis difficult (and even biased). Different words are hard to categorize and can introduce ambiguity. For example, does "fair" mean intermediate or advanced?

Radio controls requiring a user to select one of the given options are the most suitable interface for such situations. They not only limit the number of options, but also help the user by providing a list of acceptable responses. Furthermore, the user just has to click on one option instead of typing in the answer. Even though users may not find any of the provided options as an exact match to their natural response, they are forced to select the closest match. However, this does relieve your analysis headaches.

The following steps explain how the radio controls representing the three options of the first question of this survey form are designed and how the browser sends the selected option when the form is submitted:

1. Create a file named *LESSON4.HTM* with the following text:

```
<HTML>
<HEAD>
<TITLE>Reader Survey Form</TITLE>
</HEAD>
<BODY>
<H1>Reader Survey Form</H1><P>
<FORM METHOD=POST ACTION="/cgi-win/book/formapps/forminp.exe">
<OL>
<STRONG><LI>What is your level of computer expertise?</STRONG><BR>
<INPUT NAME="Expertise" TYPE="RADIO" VALUE="Beginner">Beginner<BR>
<INPUT NAME="Expertise" TYPE="RADIO" VALUE="Intermediate" ⇐
CHECKED>Intermediate<BR>
<INPUT NAME="Expertise" TYPE="RADIO" VALUE="Advanced">Advanced<BR>
</OL>
<INPUT NAME="SUBMIT" TYPE="SUBMIT" VALUE="SUBMIT">
<INPUT NAME="DEFAULT" TYPE="RESET" VALUE="DEFAULT">
</FORM>
</BODY>
</HTML>
```

2. While your WebSite is running, specify the following URL from your browser:

```
http://localhost/book/chap8/lesson4.htm
```

Your browser displays the first survey question with the default response set to the Intermediate option as shown in Figure 8-7.

3. Select the Advanced option. Notice that the Intermediate option automatically gets deselected.

4. Click on the Submit button.

The response displays the URL encoded string representing the submitted data as shown in Figure 8-8.

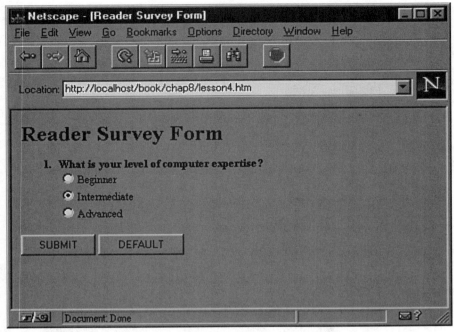

Figure 8–7 The first question on the reader survey form

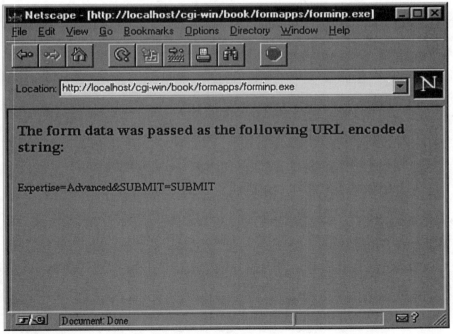

Figure 8–8 URL encoded string representing the selected radio option

Now, let's examine the construction of these radio controls in detail. The three radio controls are constructed by specifying TYPE="RADIO" for the three INPUT tags. They all have the same name ("Expertise"). This tells the client that these radio controls are different options of the same field. Note that it does not matter where you place these radio controls on the form. As long as they have the same name, they become part of one logical option group.

The CHECKED attribute in the second radio control (labeled "Intermediate") makes that control the default selection when the form is retrieved from the server. The user can change the selection by clicking on one of the other two radio controls. But at all times, one option always stays checked.

The string specified in the VALUE attribute of the selected radio control is passed to the server. So when you selected the radio control labeled "Advanced," the browser sent the following URL encoded string to the server:

```
Expertise=Advanced
```

You can specify the same VALUE for more than one radio control. For example, to add another radio control called "Unknown" that is grouped with the Beginner's category, you can specify the following HTML code:

```
<INPUT NAME="Expertise" TYPE="RADIO" VALUE="Beginner">Beginner<BR>
<INPUT NAME="Expertise" TYPE="RADIO" VALUE="Intermediate" CHECKED>Intermediate<BR>
<INPUT NAME="Expertise" TYPE="RADIO" VALUE="Advanced">Advanced<BR>
<INPUT NAME="Expertise" TYPE="RADIO" VALUE=" Beginner ">Unknown<BR>
```

The client will always pass the value "Beginner" if the user selects the radio control labeled "Beginner" or "Unknown." If you do not specify the VALUE attribute for a radio control, then the client passes the value "on" to the Web server if that control is selected.

Forcing a Valid Selection... Setting the CHECKED attribute of one radio control is a way to ensure that a valid option in that option group is always passed back to the server. On the other hand, if no radio control is initially checked and the user does not select an option, the client will not include that field in the final URL encoded string.

LESSON 5: CREATING CHECK BOXES

A check box control provides a natural way for seeking a Yes/No type answer. It is constructed just like a radio control, except that the TYPE is set to "CHECKBOX."

The main difference between a check box and a radio control is that the check boxes do not form a logical group as the radio controls do, even if they have the same name. Every check box is an independent toggle control whose value (specified through its VALUE attribute) is passed to the server if that check box is checked. If the VALUE attribute is missing, then the default value of "on" is returned. If the check box is left unchecked, then it is not included in the URL encoded string. To select the check box by default, you add the CHECKED attribute to its INPUT tag.

The third question on the reader survey form (see Figure 8-6 in the previous lesson) makes use of multiple check box controls to simulate a "select as many as applicable" type response. The following steps show you how to construct this question and how the browser handles the selected check boxes when the form is submitted:

1. Create a file named *LESSON5.HTM* with the following text:

```
<HTML>
<HEAD>
<TITLE>Reader Survey Form</TITLE>
</HEAD>
<BODY>
<H1>Reader Survey Form</H1><P>
<FORM METHOD=POST ACTION="/cgi-win/book/formapps/forminp.exe">
<OL>
<STRONG><LI>What computer applications do you normally use?</STRONG><BR>
<INPUT NAME="OtherApplication" TYPE="CHECKBOX" ⇐
VALUE="Spreadsheets">Spreadsheets<BR>
<INPUT NAME="OtherApplication" TYPE="CHECKBOX" VALUE="Wordprocessing">Word ⇐
processing<BR>
<INPUT NAME="OtherApplication" TYPE="CHECKBOX" VALUE="Databases">Databases<BR>
<INPUT NAME="OtherApplication" TYPE="CHECKBOX" ⇐
VALUE="Internet">Internet<BR></OL>
<INPUT NAME="SUBMIT" TYPE="SUBMIT" VALUE="SUBMIT">
<INPUT NAME="DEFAULT" TYPE="RESET" VALUE="DEFAULT">
</FORM>
</BODY>
</HTML>
```

2. While your WebSite server is running, specify the following URL from your browser:

```
http://localhost/book/chap8/lesson5.htm
```

Your browser displays the third survey question with no default selections as shown in Figure 8-9.

3. Click on the check boxes labeled "Spreadsheets" and "Databases," and then click on the Submit button.

The response displays the URL encoded string representing the submitted data as shown in Figure 8-10.

As you can see, the user can select one or all of the check boxes in response to this question. A *name=value* pair is added to the URL encoded string for each check box that is selected. We reiterate that these check boxes having the same name has no special purpose in this example. It is just for the convenience of the executable program (SURVEY.EXE) designed for the On-Line Questionnaire application to process these responses.

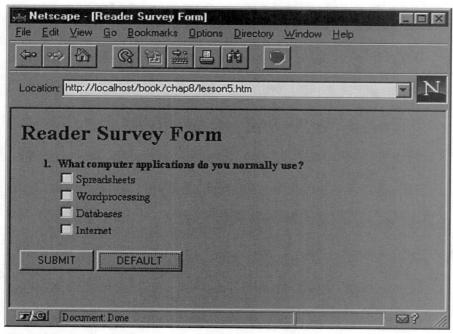

Figure 8–9 The third question on the reader survey form

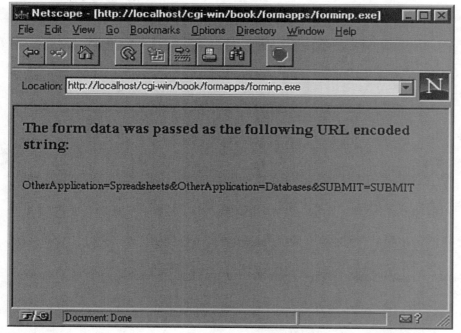

Figure 8–10 URL encoded string representing the selected check boxes

LESSON 6: CREATING MULTIPLE SUBMIT BUTTONS

A form without a submit button is like an envelope with no postage. You can add as much information to it as you want, but it is not going anywhere. If you observe the content of any URL encoded string resulting from a form submission, you will see that the submit button is always passed as a *name=value* pair. For example, the submit button defined with the following code:

```
<INPUT TYPE="SUBMIT" NAME="Urgency" VALUE="Hurry">
```

is included in the URL encoded string as follows when selected:

```
Urgency=Hurry
```

You can also use an image to create a submit button with the following code:

```
<INPUT TYPE="IMAGE" NAME="Send" SRC="Image_URL">
```

In this case, the browser passes two *name=value* pairs in the URL encoded string representing the image as follows:

```
Send.x=value&Send.y=value
```

The first pair indicates the horizontal coordinate, and the second pair indicates the vertical coordinate of the point on which the user clicked the image. These coordinates are measured relative to the image (0,0 being the top left corner).

What makes the situation interesting is that you can have multiple submit buttons (standard or image type) on the same form, each potentially with a different VALUE attribute. A user needs to click on only one submit button to send the form data to the server, but you can tell which submit button was clicked on in your executable program and probably take different actions on the form data.

As an example, let's say you want to create a notification form that allows users to send you messages with different priority levels. You can use multiple submit buttons for designing this form as follows:

1. Create a file named *LESSON6.HTM* with the following text:

```
<HTML>
<HEAD>
<TITLE>Notification Form</TITLE>
</HEAD>
<BODY>
<CENTER>
<H1>Notification Form</H1><P>
<FORM METHOD=POST ACTION="/cgi-win/book/formapps/forminp.exe">
<B>Message</B><BR>
<TEXTAREA NAME="Message" ROWS=5 COLS=40></TEXTAREA><BR><BR>
<INPUT NAME="SUBMIT" TYPE="SUBMIT" VALUE="Urgent">
<INPUT NAME="SUBMIT" TYPE="SUBMIT" VALUE="High Priority">
<INPUT NAME="SUBMIT" TYPE="SUBMIT" VALUE="Low Priority">
</FORM>
</BODY>
</HTML>
```

2. While your WebSite is running, specify the following URL from your browser:

`http://localhost/book/chap8/lesson6.htm`

Your browser displays the notification form as shown in Figure 8-11.

3. Type *Testing* in the message box, and click on the High Priority button.

The response displays the URL encoded string representing the submitted data as shown in Figure 8-12.

As another example, you can create the four gopher images used as submit buttons for the reader survey form shown in Figure 8-6 (see Lesson 4) as follows:

```
<STRONG>Click on any image below to submit your response</STRONG><INPUT NAME="goph1"⇐
TYPE="IMAGE" SRC="/book/survey/goph1.gif>
<INPUT NAME="goph2" TYPE="IMAGE" SRC="/book/survey/goph2.gif>
<INPUT NAME="goph3" TYPE="IMAGE" SRC="/book/survey/goph3.gif>
<INPUT NAME="goph4" TYPE="IMAGE" SRC="/book/survey/goph4.gif>
```

If the user clicks on the second image, then the following two *name=value* pairs are passed to the server:

```
goph2.x=relative_x_coordinate&goph2.y=relative_y_coordinate
```

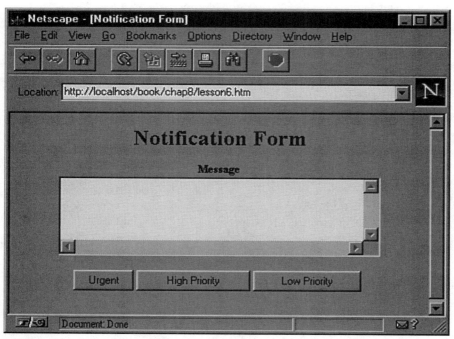

Figure 8–11 Notification form containing multiple submit buttons

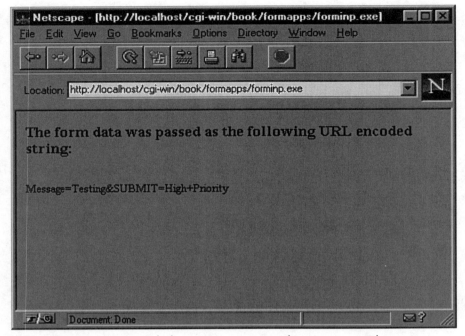

Figure 8–12 URL encoded string representing the message and its priority

Note that the idea behind using images as submit buttons for the survey application was that while the users may not give much thought to which image they click on when they submit their response, you may still keep track of this information to decide which gopher icon was the most clicked (and probably the most popular among the readers).

LESSON 7: CREATING SELECTION LISTS

A selection list can show a list of choices for an input field either as a drop-down list, or as a scrollable window where a subset of choices at a time is displayed. You can design a selection list to allow one selection (similar to radio controls) or accept multiple selections (similar to check boxes with the same name).

The advantage of using a selection list over a group of radio controls is that a selection list requires less space to present the choices on the form. You can easily add more choices to an existing selection list without increasing the physical size of your form.

To create any selection list, you use the combination of the following two form-related tags:

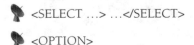 <SELECT ...> ...</SELECT>

 <OPTION>

The <SELECT>...</SELECT> Tags

A selection list is defined through the <SELECT>...</SELECT> tag pair. The <SELECT> tag supports the following attributes:

- NAME=<*field_name*>
- SIZE=<*value*>
- MULTIPLE

The NAME attribute of the <SELECT> tag describes the name of the input field represented by the selection list. The SIZE attribute specifies how many items are visible in the selection list at a time. It is an optional attribute, and in its absence, a default size of 1 is assumed. The presence of the MULTIPLE attribute allows a user to select many items at once from a selection list.

The <OPTION> Tag

The <OPTION> tag delineates each item in the selection list and is specified as follows:

```
<OPTION [VALUE="ReturnValue"] [SELECTED]>Item description
```

The item description that follows the <OPTION> tag is shown in the selection list, whereas the value specified in the VALUE attribute is returned to the server if that item is selected. In the absence of the VALUE attribute, the item's description is returned to the server.

The SELECTED attribute, if present for an option, informs the browser to preselect that item when it displays the form. You can set the SELECTED attribute on more than one item in a multiple-selection list.

Passing Item Codes to the Server... It is often convenient to design scripts that process item codes instead of the item descriptions that appear in a selection list. For instance, you may have a selection list showing complete names of all the states, but you want to pass the state codes (such as "CA" for California) to the server script. This can be achieved by assigning the appropriate code to the VALUE attribute of each option.

Example 1: Creating a Drop-Down List

The simplest way to create a drop-down selection list is to remove the SIZE and MULTIPLE attributes from the SELECT tag. Initially, the drop-down list shows the default selected item (or the first item if the SELECTED attribute is not specified for any item in the list). A user can click on the down arrow to open the list and select a different item. The selected item then appears in the selection list text box.

As an example, let's construct the drop-down list displayed on the reader survey form shown in Figure 8-6 (see Lesson 4):

1. Create a file named *LESSON7A.HTM* with the following text:

```
<HTML>
<HEAD>
<TITLE>Reader Survey Form</TITLE>
</HEAD>
<BODY>
<H1>Reader Survey Form</H1><P>
<FORM METHOD=POST ACTION="/cgi-win/book/formapps/forminp.exe">
<OL>
<STRONG><LI>How did you find out about this book?</STRONG><SELECT ⇐
NAME="AdvertisingSource">  <OPTION>Bookstore  <OPTION>Recommendation ⇐
<OPTION>Magazine Review  <OPTION>Mailing  <OPTION>Advertisement  <OPTION>World ⇐
Wide Web</SELECT></OL>
<INPUT NAME="SUBMIT" TYPE="SUBMIT" VALUE="SUBMIT">
<INPUT NAME="DEFAULT" TYPE="RESET" VALUE="DEFAULT">
</FORM>
</BODY>
</HTML>
```

2. While your WebSite is running, specify the following URL from your browser:

```
http://localhost/book/chap8/lesson7a.htm
```

Your browser displays the drop-down list as shown in Figure 8-13.

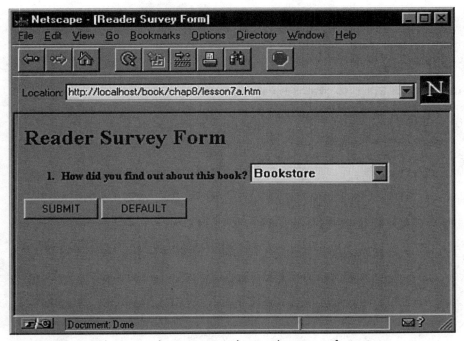

Figure 8-13 The second question on the reader survey form

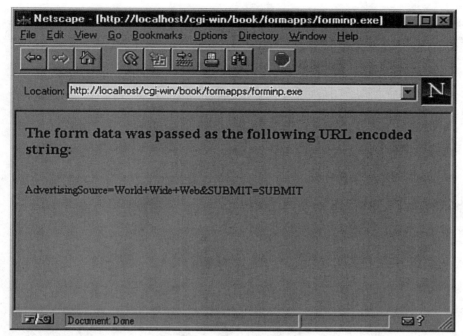

Figure 8-14 Second question on the reader survey form

3. Select "World Wide Web" from the list, and click on the Submit button.

The response displays the URL encoded string representing the submitted data as shown in Figure 8-14.

Example 2: Creating a Multiple-Selection List

In Lesson 5, we showed how you can use check box controls to accept a "select as many as applicable" type response. In this example, we show how you can use a multiple selection list to achieve the same result.

1. Create a file named *LESSON7B.HTM* with the following text:

```
<HTML>
<HEAD>
<TITLE>Reader Survey Form</TITLE>
</HEAD>
<BODY>
<H1>Reader Survey Form</H1><P>
<FORM METHOD=POST ACTION="/cgi-win/book/formapps/forminp.exe">
```

continued on next page

continued from previous page

```
<OL>
<LI><B>What computer applications do you normally use?</B><BR>
(Press CTRL+LEFT mouse button to select multiple items)<BR>
<SELECT NAME="OtherApplication" SIZE=4 MULTIPLE>
  <OPTION VALUE="Spreadsheets">Spreadsheets
  <OPTION VALUE="Wordprocessing">Word processing
  <OPTION VALUE="Databases">Databases
  <OPTION VALUE="Internet">Internet
</SELECT>
</OL>
<INPUT NAME="SUBMIT" TYPE="SUBMIT" VALUE="SUBMIT">
<INPUT NAME="DEFAULT" TYPE="RESET" VALUE="DEFAULT">
</FORM>
</BODY>
</HTML>
```

2. While your WebSite is running, specify the following URL from your browser:

`http://localhost/book/chap8/lesson7b.htm`

Your browser displays the multiple selection list as shown in Figure 8-15.

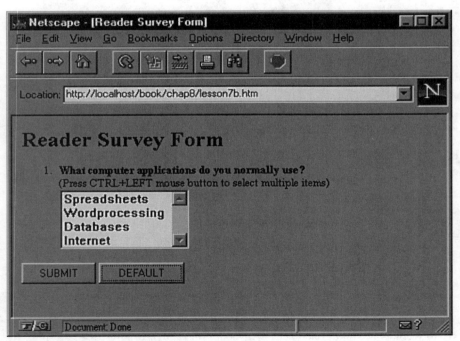

Figure 8-15 Creating a multiple selection list

3. Click on the Spreadsheets list item.

The browser highlights it, indicating that the item has been selected.

4. Press (CTRL) and then click on the item labeled "Internet" using the left mouse button.

The browser now highlights the Spreadsheets as well as the Internet option.

5. Click on the Submit button.

The response displays the URL encoded string representing the two selected options as shown in Figure 8-16.

Note that when a user submits a form containing a multiple selection list, the value specified in the VALUE attribute of all items is included in the resulting URL encoded string. No pair is included for this selection list if none of the items are selected when the form is submitted.

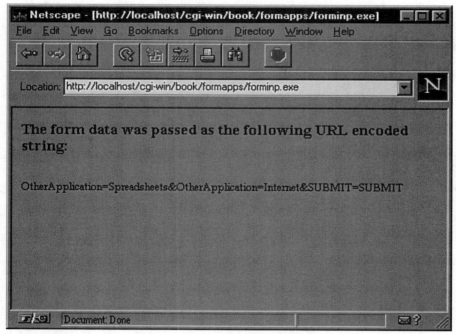

Figure 8–16 URL encoded string representing the selected list items

LESSON 8: USING HIDDEN FIELDS

A hidden field is created by using the INPUT tag as follows:

```
<INPUT TYPE="HIDDEN" NAME="Hidden_Field_Name" VALUE="Hidden_Value"
```

A hidden field is not displayed on the form and thus cannot be used to input user data. Its value is generally set by the form developer. A hidden field can be anywhere between the <FORM>...</FORM> block. When a user submits a form, the hidden field is also included in the URL encoded string as follows:

```
Hidden_Field_Name=Hidden_Value
```

Hidden fields help serve three main purposes:

- Define script functionality

- Specify script parameters

- Embed state information within a form

Defining Script Functionality

Often, the script or executable program designed to process the form data can also perform other functions. For example, the GUESTBK.EXE program (designed for the guest book application) can add a guest book entry to the database if used from the guest book entry form as shown in Figure 8-2 (see Lesson 1), or it can list guest book entries input after a date specified in the guest book view form shown in Figure 8-17.

The GUESTBK.EXE program is currently programmed to identify the submitted form through the extra path information specified in the ACTION attribute of each form, *AddEntry* in the case of a guest book entry form, and *ViewWithDate* in the case of a guest book view form. If you decide to use the extra path parameter for a different purpose (for example, to specify the location of the guest book database), you can specify the desired task through a hidden field as follows:

1. Open the file named LESSON2B.HTM residing in the C:\WEBSITE\HTDOCS\BOOK\CHAP8\ directory in your text editor.

2. Add the following line before the </FORM> tag:

```
<INPUT TYPE="HIDDEN" NAME="Task" VALUE="AddEntry">
```

3. Save this modified file as *LESSON8.HTM*.

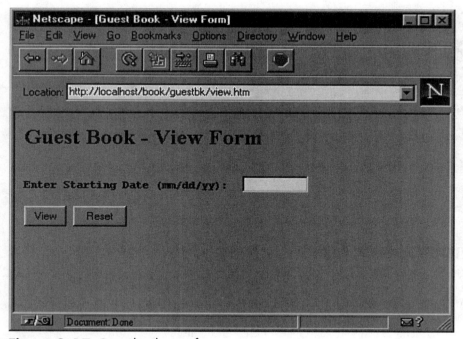

Figure 8-17 Guest book view form

4. While your WebSite server is running, specify the following URL from your Web browser:

```
http://localhost/book/chap8/lesson8.htm
```

The browser displays the guest book entry form with no indication of any change from the original guest book entry form. This is because the Task field is hidden.

5. Enter the following data for the guest book entry, and click on the Enter button.

```
          Name: Amit
         Email: amit@abc.com
 Date Of Birth: 3/10/71
       Remarks: Testing.
```

As you can see from Figure 8-18, the browser appends the hidden field as another *name=value* pair to the URL encoded string, which the receiving GUESTBK.EXE program can eventually use to identify the task being requested.

Figure 8-18 Sending a hidden field to specify script functionality

Specifying Script Parameters

From another perspective, you can take advantage of hidden fields to pass script parameters. Let's say you want the message sent through the notification form you created in Lesson 6 to be e-mailed to a list of people. Furthermore, this e-mail list could change periodically. The easiest way to handle this situation is to pass the e-mail addresses of all the message recipients through hidden fields present in the notification form as follows:

```
<INPUT TYPE="HIDDEN" NAME="MailTo" VALUE="Email_Address1">
<INPUT TYPE="HIDDEN" NAME="MailTo" VALUE="Email_Address2"> ...
```

This way, to change the e-mail list, you just have to add, modify, or remove a MailTo hidden field from this form. The destination program that you refer to in the ACTION attribute of this form can then compose a file based on the form data and e-mail that file to the address specified for each MailTo field listed in this form.

Embedding State Information

Hidden fields can also be used to pass information between forms, effectively creating a session between the client and the server. You order an item from an on-line catalog using their order entry form, and in response to your order, you receive another form asking for the color and size of that item. If you view the HTML source of the second form, you will probably find a hidden field with information that helps the catalog company link the two forms.

Many on-line stores also use this state tracking feature for accepting orders over the Web. When a user connects to their Web site, the server assigns them a unique Session ID and places this ID as a hidden field every time it serves a form to the user. Any time a user orders a product during that session, this Session ID is also passed to the server as a hidden field, and the server can use that ID to group all the products into one order. Chapter 18, Setting Up an On-Line Ordering System, shows a practical application of this technique.

REVIEW QUESTIONS

1. How is an HTML form similar to a paper form?

2. What elements are commonly present in an HTML form?

3. How does the client know where to submit the form data?

4. Why is the POST method preferred for submitting the form data?

5. What attribute must be specified for all input fields of a form?

6. How do you attach a label to a form field?

7. What is the role of the reset button on a form? How is it constructed?

8. How do you specify a default value for a text box field?

9. How is a password field constructed?

10. How do you create an option group using radio controls?

11. What is the difference between a check box and a radio control?

12. In how many ways can you submit the form data to the server?

13. How can you use multiple submit buttons to your advantage?

14. What is an URL encoding scheme?

15. What are the advantages of using a selection list in place of radio controls and check boxes?

16. When is a selection list presented as a drop-down list?

17. How do you design a multiple selection list?

18. What are the two ways of passing script parameters from a form?

19. How do hidden fields help to create a session between the user and the server?

EXERCISES

1. There is an excellent tutorial on HTML forms from NCSA (the makers of the popular Mosaic Web browser). Connect to their tutorial at the following location and work through their examples:

`http://www.ncsa.uiuc.edu/SDG/Software/Mosaic/Docs/fill-out-forms/overview.html`

257

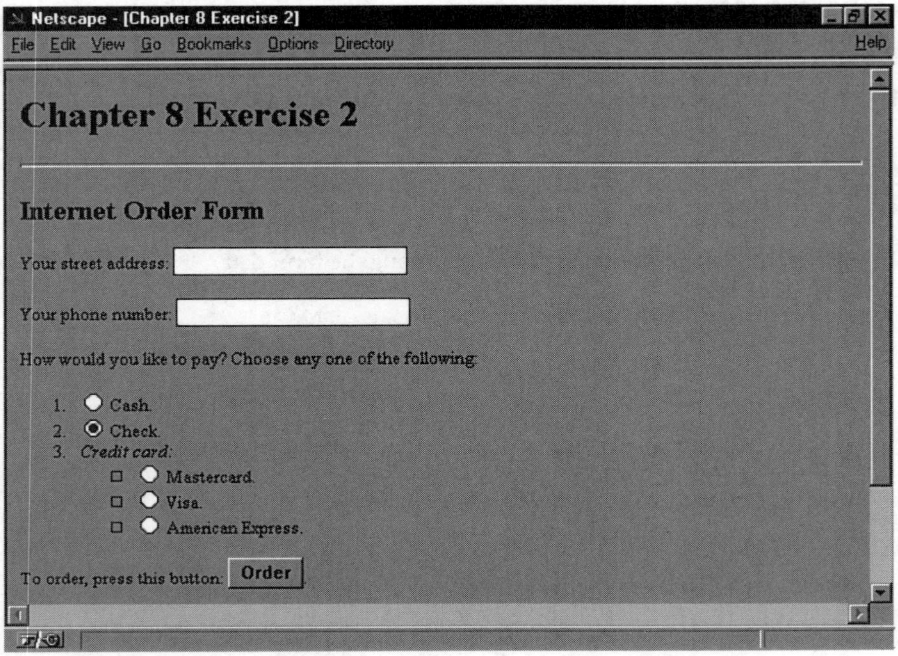

Figure 8–19 An order form

You can also refer to the following publications from Waite Group Press:

🛰 *HTML Web Publisher's Construction Kit* by David Fox and Troy Downing

🛰 *HTML 3 Interactive Course* by Kent Cearly

🛰 *HTML 3 How To* by David Kerven, Jeff Foust, and John Zakour

2. Design an order form similar to the one shown in Figure 8-19. A user should be able to select only one payment option. The Check option should be selected as the default.

3. Create a recipe entry form whose data is submitted to the following URL:

```
http://localhost/cgi-win/cgitest32.exe
```

The form should have the following elements:

- Two submit buttons (named *Eastern* and *Western*) and one reset button (named *Clear*)

- A text field named *RecipeName*

- A yes/no check box named *Vegetarian*

- A radio control group named *MealType* listing these options: *Appetizer, Main Dish,* and *Dessert*

- A drop-down list named *PrepTime* listing the options *Less than 10 minutes, Under 30 minutes,* and *One to two hours*

- A six-line text box named *Ingredients*

- A six-line text box named *Cooking Instructions*

- A multiple-selection list named *Attributes* listing the choices *Spicy, Sweet, Fast, Low Fat, Fried, Baked, Juicy,* and *Creamy*

- A hidden field named *Action* with the value *AddRecipe*

9

WINDOWS COMMON GATEWAY INTERFACE

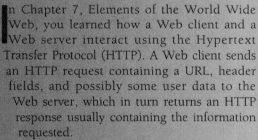

In Chapter 7, Elements of the World Wide Web, you learned how a Web client and a Web server interact using the Hypertext Transfer Protocol (HTTP). A Web client sends an HTTP request containing a URL, header fields, and possibly some user data to the Web server, which in turn returns an HTTP response usually containing the information requested.

When the client's request requires the services of an external program or an executable script residing on the server's machine, the Web server positions itself as a gateway between the Web client and the external program. In its role as a gateway, the Web server passes information attached to the HTTP request to the external program and then delivers the response from that program to the requesting client.

A Common Gateway Interface (CGI) defines how a Web server and the external program (also called a CGI program) communicate with each other. Specifically, this interface provides answers to the following five questions:

1. How is the information transferred between the Web server and a CGI program?

2. What information is supplied by the Web server to a CGI program?

3. What format is used by the Web server to supply the information?

4. What information can be returned by a CGI program?

5. What format is used by a CGI program to return the information?

The WebSite server you installed in Chapter 2, Getting Started, supports three Common Gateway Interfaces: DOS, Standard, and Windows. The difference between these CGIs is in how they answer the above five questions.

If you look into the history of the World Wide Web, the first Web servers arriving on the Web were developed for UNIX platforms. They supported one CGI that allowed communication between a Web server and UNIX-based scripts or programs to occur in an efficient manner. However, when Web servers were ported for Windows-based platforms, the communication method defined by the existing CGI specification could not be applied to pass data between the Web server and a Windows program.

Consequently, developers of Windows Web servers provided their own methods for hooking up Windows programs with their Web servers. One such method, known as *Windows CGI*, gained quick acceptance among CGI programmers and is now supported by many Windows Web servers. The popularity of Windows CGI can be attributed to various factors. Windows CGI:

- Is simple to understand and easy to work with

- Provides user data in decoded form

- Allows easy debugging of Windows CGI programs

- Includes most of the features of the original CGI

This chapter describes the Windows CGI specifications that relate to the first three questions listed earlier in this section. The first lesson of this chapter reviews the communication model used under Windows CGI. The rest of the lessons deal with the type and format of the information passed by the Web server to a Windows CGI program. Chapter 10, Windows CGI Output Standard, discusses the types of results a Windows CGI program can return to the Web server.

LESSON 1: TRACING WINDOWS CGI COMMUNICATION

Under Windows CGI, the data is passed between the Web server and a Windows CGI program through temporary files. This data communication occurs in the following sequence:

1. The Web server receives a client's request for a response from a Windows CGI program. This request is also termed a *Windows CGI request.*

2. The server places the data to be passed to the Windows CGI program in a primary input file termed the *CGI profile* file. In certain cases (described later in Lesson 4), the server may create secondary input files for storing additional data. In such cases, the CGI profile file includes the file paths of all the secondary input files.

   The CGI profile file also contains the name and path of the file where the server expects the Windows CGI program to write its result. This file is termed the *CGI output* file.

3. The Web server then executes the Windows CGI program, passing the location of the CGI profile file as its first command-line argument.

4. After executing the Windows CGI program, the server waits for the CGI program to terminate. While waiting, the server may process other regular or CGI requests.

5. The Windows CGI program reads the profile file whose location is specified in its first command-line argument and performs the necessary actions. The program may use the data included in the CGI profile file and any other associated secondary input files.

6. Before terminating, the CGI program writes its response to the CGI output file whose location is listed in the profile file.

7. On getting the termination signal, the Web server reads the CGI output file, determines if the output data needs any packaging, and sends the final data to the requesting client.

8. The Web server then deletes all the temporary files created during the processing of this request unless the server's *API/CGI Execution* tracing option in the Logging section of the Server Admin utility is enabled.

Identifying the Temporary CGI Files

Let's locate the temporary files that get created during a Windows CGI operation. We will then take a peek at what kind of data these files contain. Follow these steps:

1. Launch the Server Admin utility by double-clicking on the Server Properties icon in the WebSite 1.1 program group.

2. Using the navigation buttons next to the tabs, scroll to the Logging tab.

3. Click on the Logging tab to display the Logging section. (See Figure 9-1.)

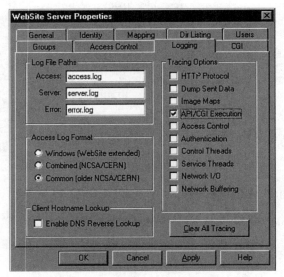

Figure 9–1 Logging section of the Server Admin utility

4. Select the tracing option labeled "API/CGI Execution," and click on the OK button to close the Server Admin utility. Wait a few seconds for this configuration change to take effect.

5. Start your WebSite server if not already running.

6. Run your Web browser and enter the following URL in its Location window:

   ```
   http://localhost/cgi-win/book/joblist/joblist.exe
   ```

   This URL causes the WebSite server to execute the JOBLIST.EXE Windows CGI program.

7. After the browser shows the response to the preceding CGI request, go to an MS-DOS window, and list the files matching the pattern *WS.* in the C:\WEBSITE\CGI-TEMP\ directory by typing the following commands:

   ```
   CD C:\WEBSITE\CGI-TEMP <ENTER>
   DIR <ENTER>
   ```

   The directory listing produces three files with the same first name but different file extensions as shown in Figure 9-2. Note that you may see a different set of file names than the ones shown in the figure. This is because WebSite auto-increments the file name to ensure it is unique.

Figure 9-2 Temporary files created by the WebSite server

The files with the .INI and .OUT extensions are respectively the CGI profile file and the CGI output file created during this CGI interaction between the server and the JOBLIST.EXE program.

The directory listing also shows a file with an .INP extension. This is called the *CGI content* file, and it holds any data attached with a request. Lesson 4 describes the format of the data contained in this file.

Keeping a Permanent Temp Directory... By default, the WebSite server keeps all the Windows CGI files in the C:\WEBSITE\CGI-TEMP directory, although you can change this location from the General section of the Server Admin utility. Furthermore, if you have problems running Windows CGI applications, make sure that the directory used for holding these temporary files exists on your computer.

The CGI Profile File

Open the CGI profile (.INI) file identified in the previous section in your text editor. (See Figure 9-3.)

The CGI profile file is a text file that mimics the structure of a regular Windows .INI file. It contains data organized under different sections. The name of each section appears on its own line and is enclosed within square brackets ([]). The data appears as a *key=value* pair, and each pair is listed on a separate line. The remaining lessons of this chapter discuss each section of a CGI profile file.

Figure 9-3 Notepad displaying the contents of a CGI profile file

The CGI Output File

Display the contents of the CGI output (.OUT) file identified in this lesson through your text editor. You will notice that this CGI output file contains the following text:

`Location: /book/joblist/joblist.htm`

This line is an instruction for the WebSite server to redirect the Web client to a different location specified by the relative URL path *\/book\/joblist\/joblist.htm*. The next chapter explains how the WebSite server performs this redirection.

Limitations Of the Windows CGI Communication Model

File-based communication is old, but it's the most general-purpose way of passing data between applications. However, it involves an overhead of creating and deleting files on physical disk media. This potentially makes Windows CGI less efficient than the other CGI methods that use environment variables created in the computer's memory to pass the information.

Another disadvantage of the Windows CGI communication model is that you cannot send the result of the CGI program while the result is being generated. So, if a user requests the services of a Windows CGI program designed to perform a search function, the server returns the search results only when the program completes the search and terminates. Until then, the user is left waiting. This same reason also prevents you from creating animations on a Web page (using the Server Push feature, not described in this book but you can read about this feature at *http://home.netscape.com/assist/net_sites/push-pull.html*) through Windows CGI applications.

Luckily, most practical Web applications do not require page animation. Chapter 17, Enhancing the On-Line Bookstore, shows how you can design your Windows CGI application to reduce a user's waiting period by designing the program to present a limited amount of information at a time.

NOTE: The performance of the Windows CGI significantly improves if you increase the RAM of your computer to 32MB for Windows 95 and 64MB for Windows NT platform.

LESSON 2: LISTING THE CGI VARIABLES

Whenever a Web server executes a Windows CGI program, the server passes a number of CGI variables as required by the Windows CGI specification. These CGI variables contain information about the user request, the Web client, and the server itself.

The CGI variables are included in the CGI section of a CGI profile file. As explained in the previous lesson, you can enable the WebSite server's *API/CGI Execution* configuration option and then display the contents of the CGI profile file to find out the value of these variables passed by the server to the Windows CGI program.

As an alternative, there is a Windows CGI utility program called *CGITEST32.EXE* provided with the WebSite server, which lists the information contained in each CGI variable as part of its response. In this lesson, we will use this CGITEST32.EXE to view the values of these CGI variables. Follow these steps:

1. Ensure that your WebSite server is running.

2. Enter the following URL from your browser:

```
http://localhost/cgi-win/cgitest32.exe/CGI?Value=1
```

The CGITEST32.EXE program returns the values of the CGI variables passed by the WebSite server to the program as shown in Figure 9-4.

The rest of this lesson describes the information contained in these CGI variables.

CGI Version

This variable describes the version of the Windows CGI that the Web server is using to interact with the Windows CGI program. Since Windows CGI is an evolving standard, this information can be helpful when you design a Windows CGI program that may be used with different Web servers or different versions of the same Web server.

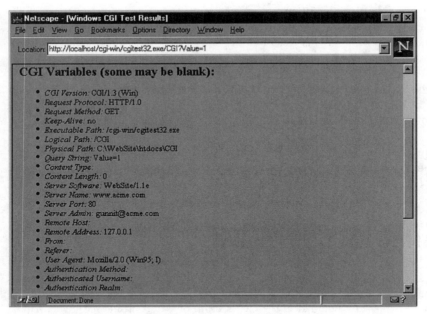

Figure 9–4 Values of CGI variables returned by the CGITEST32.EXE
program

Request Protocol

This variable indicates the name and version of the information protocol used by the Web
client to make the Windows CGI request. The information in this variable is listed in the
format *protocol/version*. It generally contains the value of the form "HTTP/*x.x*," since most
Web clients currently use HTTP to interact with the Web servers.

Request Method

This variable lists the method with which the Windows CGI request was made. It
normally refers to the HTTP request methods such as GET, POST, and HEAD, which are
described in Chapter 7. As explained in Lesson 4, this variable helps in determining if the
request was made as a result of submitting a form and how the user data is passed with
the request.

Keep-Alive

This variable indicates if the Web client requested reuse of the connection for future
requests.

Executable Path

This variable refers to the URL path leading to the CGI program being executed. For example, when you entered the URL path */cgi-win/cgitest32.exe/CGI?Value=1* to execute the CGITEST32.EXE program, the WebSite server passed the URL path */cgi-win/cgitest32.exe* in the Executable Path CGI variable. (See Figure 9-4.) Lesson 3 illustrates a typical use of this CGI variable.

Logical Path

This variable holds the additional information provided between the name of the CGI program and the question mark symbol. As Figure 9-4 shows, the Logical Path CGI variable contains the value "/CGI," which is the extra information supplied between the *http://localhost/cgi-win/cgitest32.exe* and the *?value=1* portions of the URL requested in this lesson. Lesson 3 describes the different ways a Windows CGI program can make use of this CGI variable.

Physical Path

This variable contains a physical path that the Web server generates based on the information listed in the Logical Path CGI variable. As depicted in Figure 9-4, the server maps the */cgi* value in the Logical Path variable to a physical path: C:\WEBSITE\HTDOCS\CGI.

The Web server derives the physical path assuming that the information in the Logical Path variable refers to a URL path. The server does not check the validity of the resulting physical path. It is up to the CGI program to correctly interpret the value of the Physical Path variable. See Lesson 3 for more details on this CGI variable.

Query String

This variable contains the data that follows the question mark symbol (?) in the URL passed with the Windows CGI request. The query string is one way user data can be supplied to a CGI program. Lesson 4 covers this variable in more detail.

Content Type

This variable holds the MIME content type of the data attached with the Windows CGI request. The attached data is generally a result of a user submitting a form. As described in Chapter 8, Creating HTML Forms, a Web client sends form data as a URL encoded string. Hence, the Content Type CGI variable usually contains the value *application/x-www-form-urlencoded,* indicating that the attached data is in URL encoded format.

Content Length

This variable indicates the length (in bytes) of the data attached with the request. The actual data is provided in the CGI content file, whose file length is the same as the value listed for this variable.

Server Software

This variable indicates the name and version of the Web server software executing the CGI program. The information is listed in the format *name/version*.

Server Name

This variable holds the fully qualified Internet domain name of the Web server. The WebSite server uses the host name configured in the General section of its Server Admin utility for this variable.

Server Port

This variable indicates the TCP port on which your Web server is listening for incoming requests. You can use the values of the Server Name and the Server Port CGI variables in your CGI program to compose a URL that points to an information resource residing on your server.

Server Admin

This variable holds the e-mail address of the server's administrator as listed in the Web server's configuration. You can use this address to construct a "mailto" URL addressed to the server's administrator from your CGI program.

Remote Host

This variable lists the fully qualified domain name of the computer on which the Web client that made the Windows CGI request is running. This information is not always available, since all computers connected to the Web do not have a fully qualified domain name. The WebSite server also does not supply this information if the DNS Reverse Lookup option in the Logging section of its Server Admin utility is disabled. See the Logging Section Parameters section in Chapter 2 for the function of the DNS Reverse Lookup configuration option.

Remote Address

This variable contains the network (IP) address of the computer on which the Web client that made the Windows CGI request is running. This is the only identity information that a Web client is currently required to provide to a Web server. You can use this information in your CGI program to distinguish one Web client from the other as explained in Chapter 18, Designing an On-Line Ordering System.

From

This variable lists the e-mail address of the Web user who made the request. Note that the value in this variable is almost never available, due to privacy concerns, and is kept for backward-compatibility reasons.

Referer

This variable holds the URL of the document that referred the user to the requested CGI program. The value in this variable cannot be relied upon, since all Web clients currently do not supply this information.

User Agent

This variable lists information on the requesting Web client. It generally contains the product code name, the version, and the operating platform for which the client software is designed.

Authentication Method, Authenticated Username, Authentication Realm

These three variables, whose details are not covered in this book, contain the authentication information supplied by the Web server based on which the Web server executes the Windows CGI program.

LESSON 3: INTERPRETING THE PATH INFORMATION

The Windows CGI specification includes three CGI variables that hold the path information about the various components of the requested URL. The Executable Path CGI variable contains the portion of the URL path that refers to the CGI program. For example, the Executable Path CGI variable contains the value */cgi-win/cgitest32.exe* for all the following URL requests:

```
http://localhost/cgi-win/cgitest32.exe
http://127.0.0.1/cgi-win/cgitest32.exe
http://localhost/cgi-win/cgitest32.exe?xxx
http://localhost/cgi-win/cgitest32.exe/CGI
http://localhost/cgi-win/cgitest32.exe/CGI?xxx
```

Application of the Executable Path CGI Variable

The Executable Path CGI variable proves useful when you need to include a link referring to your CGI program in your program's response. This situation occurs frequently with the Job Listing System described in Chapter 3, Dissecting a Job Listing System. Let's revisit the Job Listing System to list such a case:

1. Ensure that your WebSite server is running.

2. Specify the following URL from your browser:

```
http://localhost/cgi-win/book/joblist/joblist.exe/ListCompany?3
```

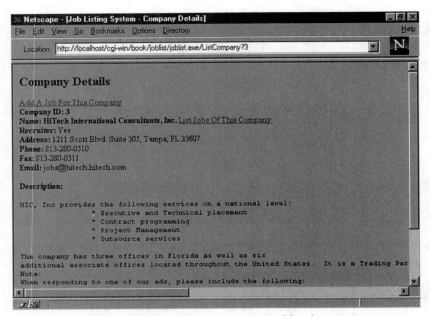

Figure 9-5 The company information returned by the JOBLIST.EXE program

The JOBLIST.EXE program responds by returning the company information of the company with CompanyID 3 as shown in Figure 9-5.

The company information includes two links to add a job or display existing jobs for that company. The link labeled "Add A Job For This Company" points to the following URL:

```
http://localhost/cgi-win/book/joblist/joblist.exe/GetJobEntryForm?3
```

The link labeled "List Jobs Of This Company" points to the following URL:

```
http://localhost/cgi-win/book/joblist/joblist.exe/ListJobsOfCompany?3
```

Both these links are supplied by the JOBLIST.EXE program and refer back to that program. The JOBLIST.EXE program uses the value of the Executable Path CGI variable to construct these links. This statement can be verified as follows:

1. Rename the JOBLIST.EXE program residing in the C:\WEBSITE\CGI-WIN\BOOK\JOBLIST\ directory to *JOBTEST.EXE*.

2. Ensure that your WebSite server is running.

3. Specify the following URL from your browser:

```
http://localhost/cgi-win/book/joblist/jobtest.exe/ListCompany?3
```

New file name automatically appearing in the URL path

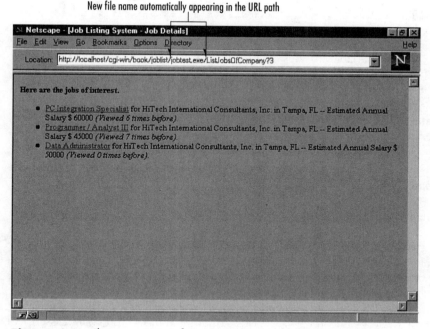

Figure 9–6 The company information returned by the JOBTEST.EXE program

The browser displays the same company information containing the two links as shown in Figure 9-5.

4. Click on the link that says "List Jobs Of This Company."

You see the jobs for this company as shown in Figure 9-6.

Observe that the URL listed in the Location window of the browser shows JOBTEST.EXE in its path, indicating that the Job Listing System was able to adapt to the file name change. It used the information supplied in the Executable Path CGI variable as you will see in Chapter 14, Processing Template Files with a CGI Application.

5. Rename JOBTEST.EXE back to *JOBLIST.EXE* to return the Job Listing System application to its original state.

Application of the Logical and Physical Path CGI Variables

The Logical Path CGI variable contains the extra information supplied after the executable path in a URL request. The Physical Path CGI variable is a translation of the logical path to a Windows file path performed according to the server's document mapping.

Tip To Determine The Physical Path... If you need to determine the physical path from a logical path, just imagine how the server would treat the logical path if it were the actual URL path of your request. For example, if the logical path is /CGI, then the physical path will be the physical location pointed to by the URL http://localhost/cgi.

The primary use of the Logical and Physical Path CGI variables is to specify the path for a resource that a CGI program may need to fulfill its request. For example, if you want to design a guest book application that can handle multiple guest books, you can supply the path of a particular guest book through these CGI variables. Chapter 13, Utilizing an Access Database in a CGI Application, shows how to implement this feature in a guest book application.

If the CGI application you are designing does not require additional path information, you can use the Logical Path variable as a task selector for your CGI program. Lesson 7 of Chapter 3 illustrates how the Job Listing System uses the Logical Path variable in this manner.

NOTE: It has been our experience that not all Web servers provide the expected value in the Physical Path variable. For example, the Alibaba server always returns the physical path of the Windows CGI executable program in this variable no matter what value the Logical Path variable contains.

LESSON 4: PASSING USER DATA

In Chapter 8, you learned how HTML forms allow users to supply the information passed with the URL request. The following steps describe what a Web client does with that information:

1. The Web client converts the user information into a URL encoded string. See Chapter 8 for information on how the client performs this encoding.

2. The client then looks at the request method listed in the ACTION attribute of the FORM tag to determine how the encoded string has to be passed with the HTTP request.

3. If the ACTION attribute specifies the GET method, the client adds a question mark (?) to the end of the URL path, and then appends the encoded string after that question mark.

4. If the ACTION attribute specifies the POST method, the Web client encloses the encoded string in the body of the request.

Let's find out how the Web server handles these two data-passing request methods under the Windows CGI specifications. Follow these steps:

1. Ensure that the API/CGI Execution tracing configuration option of the WebSite server is enabled. (See Lesson 1 of this chapter.)

2. Go to an MS-DOS prompt, and type the following commands to delete all the temporary CGI files currently existing in the C:\TEMP directory:

```
CD C:\WEBSITE\CGI-TEMP <ENTER>
DEL *.* <ENTER>
```

3. Start your WebSite server if not already running.

4. Specify the following URL from your browser:

```
http://localhost/book/chap9/cmpadd1.htm
```

The browser displays a company add form as shown in Figure 9-7.

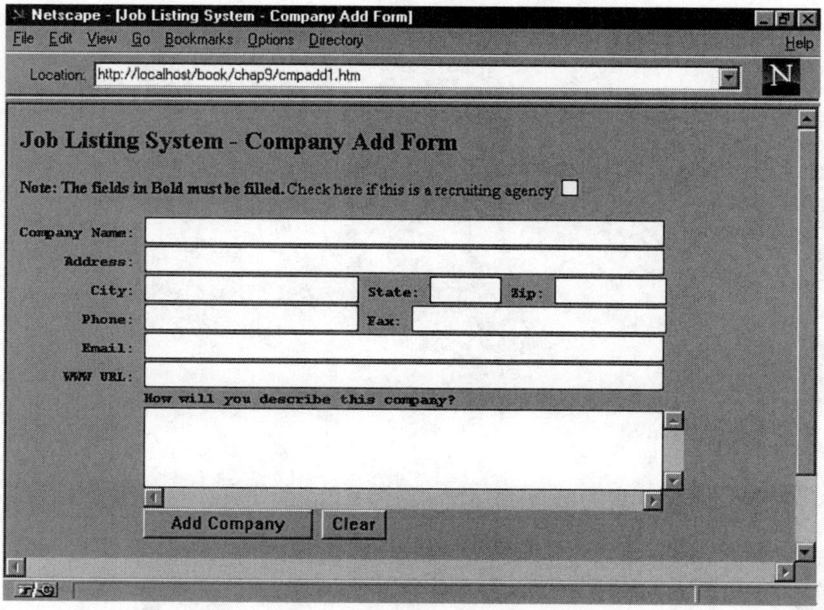

Figure 9-7 The company add form with the modified FORM tag

This entry form is similar to the company add form of the Job Listing System, except that the form data is submitted to the CGITEST32.EXE Windows CGI utility by use of the GET method instead of to the JOBLIST.EXE program. The FORM tag of this form is listed as follows:

```
<FORM METHOD="GET" ACTION="/cgi-win/cgitest32.exe/CGI">
```

5. Type *Test* in the Company Name field of this form, and click on the Add Company button.

6. The CGITEST32.EXE program responds by listing the values of the CGI variables passed by the WebSite server to this program as shown in Figure 9-8.

The response shows the Request Method CGI variable contains the value "GET," and the Query String variable contains the URL encoded string representing the data sent through the form.

7. Go to your MS-DOS prompt, and list the temporary files created during this request by entering the following DOS commands:

```
CD C:\WEBSITE\CGI-TEMP <ENTER>
DIR *.* <ENTER>
```

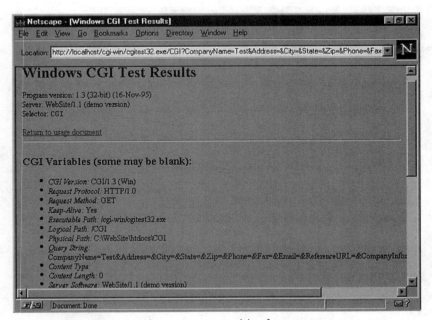

Figure 9-8 Response listing CGI variables for a GET request

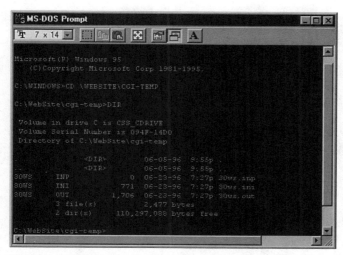

Figure 9–9 Files created while completing the Windows CGI GET request

Figure 9-9 shows the three temporary files created in the C:\WEBSITE\CGI-TEMP\ directory by the server and the CGITEST32.EXE program.

8. Return to your browser and enter the following URL in its Location window:

`http://localhost/book/chap9/cmpadd2.htm`

The browser again shows an empty company add form. This form is designed to pass data to the CGITEST32.EXE program by use of the POST method. Its FORM tag is listed as follows:

`<FORM METHOD="POST" ACTION="/cgi-win/cgitest32.exe/CGI">`

9. Type *Test* in the Company Name field of this form, and click on the Add Company button.

Figure 9-10 shows the CGI variables returned by the CGITEST32.EXE program in response to this POST request.

According to this response, the Request Method variable holds the value "POST," but the Query String variable does not contain any data. If you scroll through all the CGI variables listed in this response, you will see that no other CGI variable contains the data

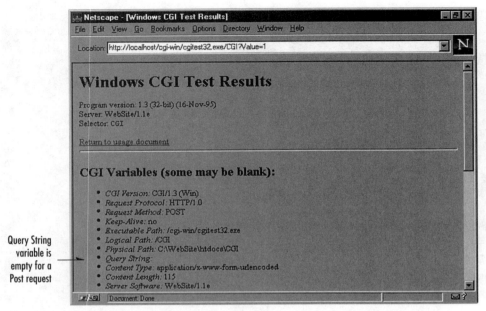

Query String
variable is
empty for a
Post request

Figure 9–10 Response listing CGI variables for a POST request

either. Where did the data go? As you will see through the following steps, the WebSite server stored the data in the CGI content file:

1. List the temporary CGI files by entering the following commands from your MS-DOS prompt:

```
CD C:\WEBSITE\CGI-TEMP <ENTER>
DIR *.* <ENTER>
```

Figure 9-11 shows the new set of CGI files created for the POST request along with the set of CGI files created for the previous GET request.

Notice that the CGI content (.INP) file included with the new set of CGI files has a file size that matches the value of the Content Length variable listed in Figure 9-10.

2. View the contents of the .INP file created with the new set through the Notepad application. You will see the URL encoded string representing your data in that file.

When a Web server receives a Windows CGI request, it passes any data appearing after the question mark symbol in the requested URL through the Query String CGI variable. The server creates a separate .INP CGI file for any data enclosed in the body of the HTTP request. In either case, the server delivers the URL encoded string passed by the Web client without any modification.

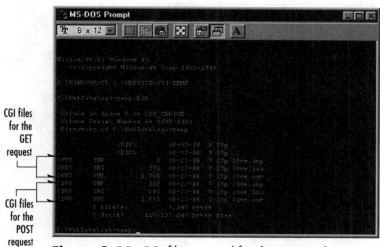

CGI files
for the
GET
request

CGI files
for the
POST
request

Figure 9-11 CGI files created for the GET and POST requests

Who is responsible for decoding the data in the URL encoded string into its original form? While other CGIs declare this to be the responsibility of their CGI programs, the Windows CGI specification goes one step further. It requires the Web server to decode the data (if passed as a URL encoded string using the POST method) and pass that decoded data to the Windows CGI program in addition to providing the raw data. The method used for decoding this data is explained in the next lesson.

LESSON 5: PASSING DECODED DATA

Under Windows CGI, the Web server decodes the data if it is passed as a URL encoded string by the Web client using the POST method by breaking the encoded string into separate fields. The following steps outline the method the Web server uses while decoding the data:

1. For each *key=value* pair occurring in the URL encoded string, the server decodes the value (replacing all the escape codes with the original characters as entered by the user) and lists each *key=(decoded) value* pair on a separate line under the [Form Literal] section of the CGI profile file.

2. If there are multiple pairs in the URL encoded string with the same key name (for example, when a user selects more than one option for a multiple-selection list), the server generates a regular *key=(decoded) value* line for the first pair. It appends an underscore (_) followed by a sequence number (starting with 1) to each subsequent occurrence of that key name.

3. If the decoded value string is more than 254 characters long and contains any control characters (for example, the sequence of line feed and carriage return characters that cause a new line in the data), the server puts the decoded value into an external temporary file. It then lists the key under the [Form External] section of the CGI profile file as:

```
key=pathname length
```

where *pathname* is the path and name of the temporary file containing the decoded value string, and *length* is the size in bytes of the decoded value.

4. If the raw value (before decoding) in a *key=value* pair is more than 65,535 bytes long, the server does no decoding. It marks the location and size of the value in the CGI content file and lists the key name with these parameters under the [Form Huge] section of the CGI profile file as:

```
key=offset length
```

where *offset* is the offset from the beginning of the CGI content file at which the raw value for this key appears, and *length* is the length in bytes of the raw value string.

Let's try to identify the server-decoded data in the CGI profile file when you submit the data in the company entry form that uses the POST method in its FORM tag:

1. Ensure that the API/CGI Execution tracing configuration option of the WebSite server is enabled. (See Lesson 1 of this chapter.)

2. Go to an MS-DOS prompt, and type the following commands to delete all the temporary CGI files currently existing in the C:\WEBSITE\CGI-TEMP directory:

```
CD C:\WEBSITE\CGI-TEMP <ENTER>
DEL *.* <ENTER>
```

3. Start your WebSite server if not already running.

4. Specify the following URL from your browser to bring up the company entry form:

```
http://localhost/book/chap9/cmpadd2.htm
```

5. Fill in the company entry form with the following information, and then click on the Add Company button:

```
Company Name: Webs 'R Us
     Address: 123 Web Street
        City: Austin
```

```
     State: TX
       Zip: 54321-6789
     Phone: 800-WEB-SITE
       Fax: 512-302-0101 ext 1221
     Email: hire@websrus.com
   WWW URL: http://www.websrus.com/index.html
Description: An expanding company that deals with all aspects
             of a Web site. Our main areas are:
             <B>Design of HTML documents</B>
             <B>Publishing databases over the Web</B>
```

6. List the contents of the CGI profile (.INI) file from the Notepad application or any text editor, and scroll to the "[Form Literal]" section as shown in Figure 9-12.

Note that the WebSite server placed each field with one line of data (the way you entered in the form) under the Form Literal section. Since the company description contains more than one line, the server placed the CompanyInformation field under the Form External section, associating it with the path and size of the temporary file holding the data for this field. You can view the contents of this secondary temporary file to ensure that it contains the data supplied for the CompanyInformation field. (See Figure 9-13.)

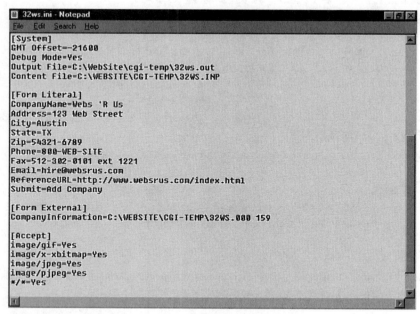

Figure 9-12 Displaying the server decoded data

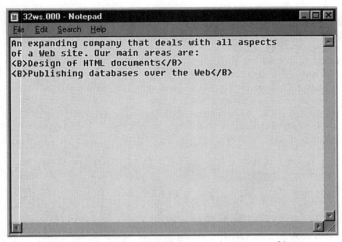

Figure 9–13 Contents of the secondary input file

LESSON 6: EXAMINING OTHER WINDOWS CGI INFORMATION

Aside from the CGI variables and the decoded user data, the WebSite server provides three additional sections of useful information in the CGI profile file. These sections are labeled as "[System]," "[Accept]," and "[Extra Headers]" in the CGI profile file. Figure 9-14 shows the typical information contained in these sections.

The [System] Section

The System section contains information for the parameters discussed next.

GMT Offset

This parameter specifies the number of seconds to be added to GMT time to reach local time. This number is useful for computing GMT times as shown in the next chapter.

Debug Mode

This parameter indicates whether the API/CGI Execution tracing option is enabled and is available to the Windows CGI programs for adding on-line debugging capabilities.

Output File

This parameter refers to the name and path of the CGI output file in which the server expects to receive the CGI program's results.

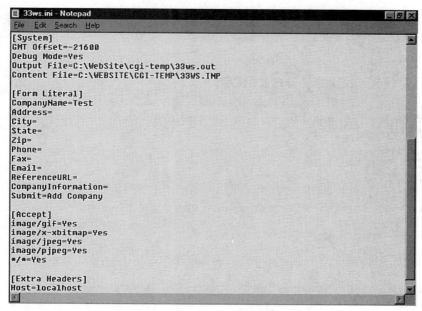

Figure 9–14 Other sections of a CGI profile file

Content File

This parameter refers to the name and path of the CGI content file that contains the user data passed in the body of the HTTP request.

The [Accept] Section

The [Accept] section lists the MIME content types acceptable to the requesting Web based on the information in the Accept header field passed with the HTTP request.

As mentioned in the "HTTP Request" section of Chapter 7, the Accept header field contains data about all the client's acceptable content types in the following format:

```
Accept: type/subtype {parameters}, type/subtype {parameters}
```

The server writes each content type appearing in the preceding list on a separate line in the [Accept] section. The type/subtype is listed as the key name, and the parameters are treated as the value for that key. If there are no parameters supplied with the content type, then the server assigns a "Yes" value to the key representing that content type.

As an example, if the following Accept header field is passed in an HTTP request:

```
Accept: */*, text/html, text/plain; q=0.5, image/gif
```

the Accept section will contain the following lines:

```
[Accept]
*/*=Yes
```

```
text/html=Yes
text/plain=q=0.5
image/gif=Yes
```

The [Extra Headers] Section

This section contains the HTTP request header fields that do not have a CGI variable associated with them. The Host header field listed in this section indicates the server's host name that the client used to connect to the server.

REVIEW QUESTIONS

1. What issues are covered by a Common Gateway Interface specification?

2. Why are different CGI specifications in existence?

3. What communication model is used under Windows CGI? How does it work?

4. What are the advantages and disadvantages of using Windows CGI for creating Web applications?

5. What is a CGI profile file? What type of file is it?

6. How do you trace the temporary CGI files created during a Windows CGI operation?

7. What are CGI variables? What kind of information do they contain?

8. How does a Web server pass the CGI variables to a Windows CGI program?

9. Which CGI variables contain information about the request made by a Web client?

10. Which CGI variables contain information about the Web server?

11. What kind of path information is available through CGI variables?

12. Which CGI variable defines a Web client's identity?

13. How does a Web server pass raw user data to a Windows CGI program?

14. How does a Web server provide decoded data to a Windows CGI program?

15. What information is contained in the [System] section of a CGI profile file?

16. What information does the [Accept] section of a CGI profile file contain?

17. What is the purpose of the [Extra Headers] section in a CGI profile file?

EXERCISES

1. Read the Windows CGI specifications provided with the on-line documentation of your WebSite server by specifying the following URL from your browser:

`http://localhost/wsdocs/32demo/windows-cgi.html`

2. Open the following URL from your browser:

`http://localhost/book/chap9/cmpadd3.htm`

The FORM tag of this form is specified as follows:

`<FORM METHOD="GET" ACTION="/cgi-win/cgitest32.exe/CGI?TestValue=1">`

This form uses the GET action, but also has the data "TestValue=1" listed in the query string portion of the URL. What happens to this data when you fill in this form and click on the Add Company button?

3. Open the following URL from your browser:

`http://localhost/book/chap9/cmpadd4.htm`

The FORM tag of this form is specified as follows:

`<FORM METHOD="POST" ACTION="/cgi-win/cgitest32.exe/CGI?TestValue=1">`

This form uses the POST action, but also has the data "TestValue=1" listed in the query string portion of the URL. What happens to this data when you fill in this form and click on the Add Company button?

10
WINDOWS CGI OUTPUT STANDARD

10

In Chapter 9, Windows Common Gateway Interface, you studied how a Web server passes information to a Windows CGI program through a CGI profile (.INI) file and some secondary input files. After furnishing the information and executing the program, the server expects a response from the CGI program in a CGI output file whose name and path is listed in the CGI profile file, so that it can pass that response to the Web client and complete the request.

This chapter looks into the types of responses a CGI program can generate and what role the Web server plays in returning these responses to the requesting Web client.

LESSON 1: UNDERSTANDING THE CGI OUTPUT FORMAT

The format of a CGI output file resembles the format of an HTTP response. It consists of two parts: a header and a body. The *header* is separated from the body by a blank line and indicates the type of response returned by the CGI program as follows:

```
CGI Response Header
...
[NewLine]
CGI Response Body
...
```

The *body* contains the data that the CGI program expects to be delivered to the requesting client.

A CGI program can generate a response in two ways: direct or indirect. A *direct* response allows the CGI program to bypass the server and directly interact with the Web client that made the request. The Web server is involved only as a data transporting agent. The server does not modify the response in any way and assumes that the output of the CGI program is in an HTTP response format. See Chapter 7, Elements of the World Wide Web, for a full description of the HTTP response format.

An *indirect* response from the CGI program requires additional processing from the server before it can be delivered to the Web client. Part of the processing is to package the output of the CGI program with additional header fields to make it a properly formed HTTP response.

A Web server inspects the first line of the CGI output file to determine the type of response being returned by a CGI program. If the first line starts with "HTTP/," the server considers the response to be a direct response. The server recognizes an indirect response if the first line starts with any of the following header lines:

```
Content-type: type/subtype
Location: absolute or relative URL
URI: <value>
Status: code description
```

Let's look at an example of a direct response generated by a Windows CGI program. For this example, you will use a Windows CGI utility program called *CGIOUT.EXE* whose only function is to send the contents of an external file as its output to the Web server. The CGI request to this program is made as follows:

```
http://localhost/cgi-win/book/cgiout/cgiout.exe/file?filename
```

where *filename* refers to the name of the external file. The CGIOUT.EXE program assumes that this external file resides in the C:\WEBSITE\BOOK\CGIOUT directory.

The C:\WEBSITE\BOOK\CGIOUT directory has a file called DIRRESP.OUT whose contents are shown in Figure 10-1. These contents represent an instance of a direct response.

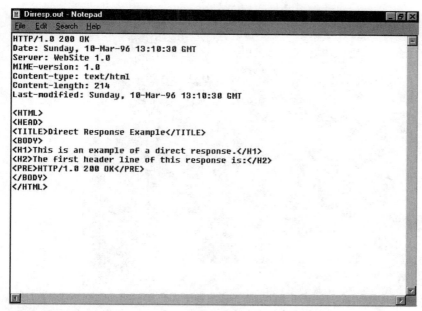

Figure 10–1 A direct response-type CGI output

You can see the effect of returning a direct response by making the CGIOUT.EXE return the contents of the DIRRESP.OUT file as its output:

1. Ensure that your WebSite server is running.

2. Enter the following Windows CGI request from your browser:

```
http://localhost/cgi-win/book/cgiout/cgiout.exe/file?dirresp.out
```

Figure 10-2 shows the response returned to the browser.

NOTE: The browser displays a direct response like any other regular response. It has no way of knowing what part of this response was created by the server and what part was created by the CGI program.

LESSON 2: RETURNING DATA THROUGH CGI OUTPUT

When sending a direct response, a Windows CGI program has to generate all the necessary HTTP header fields. If new HTTP standards evolve, the CGI program will have to be updated to accommodate any new changes deemed necessary for a smooth HTTP operation.

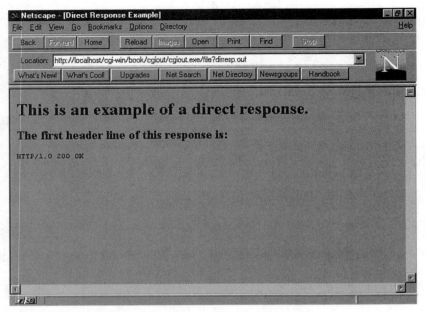

Figure 10–2 Browser showing a direct response

Also, CGI programs are usually designed to return information that is independent of the HTTP protocol being used to communicate that information. For these reasons, a CGI program is given the option to use an indirect response where the Web server takes care of most of the HTTP formalities.

One standard way of returning information through an indirect response is by listing a Content-type header line as the first line of the CGI output file. The syntax of this type of indirect response is as follows:

```
Content-type: type/subtype

<Data Starts from the third line>
```

where the *type/subtype* parameter in the Content-type header describes the MIME type of the data included in the output.

These steps demonstrate an example of an indirect response that uses a Content-type header line:

1. Ensure that your WebSite server is running.

2. Enter the following URL from your browser:

```
http://localhost/cgi-win/book/cgiout/cgiout.exe/file?ctypehtm.out
```

The CGIOUT.EXE program returns the contents of the file CTYPEHTM.OUT (shown in Figure 10-3) as its output.

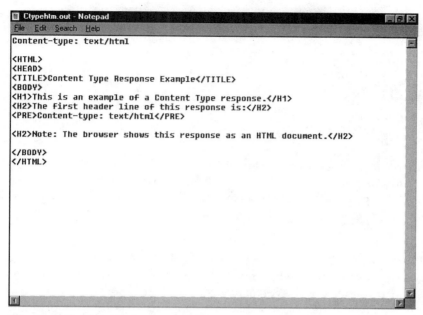

Figure 10–3 A Content-type CGI output

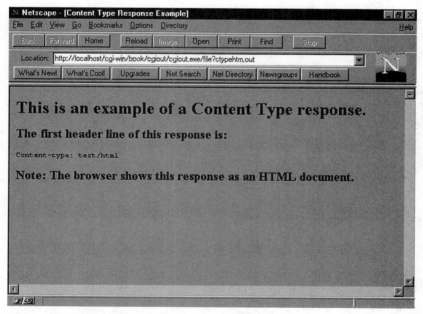

Figure 10–4 Browser showing a Content-type response

Figure 10-4 shows the browser displaying the information returned, indicating that the browser has appropriately treated this information as an HTML response.

Let's see what happens if the returned data is listed with a content type of *text/plain* instead of *text/html*. Enter the following URL from your browser:

```
http://localhost/cgi-win/book/cgiout/cgiout.exe/file?ctypetxt.out
```

The CTYPETXT.OUT file starts with the following header line:

```
Content-type: text/plain
```

As indicated in Figure 10-5, the browser in this case does not interpret the HTML codes while displaying the returned information.

NOTE: Some browsers such as the Internet Explorer assume that the beginning "<HTML>" in the response body is an indication of HTML-formatted data and ignore the Content-type header. Consequently, they interpret the HTML tags instead of listing them as shown in Figure 10-6.

Sending Binary Data... A CGI program can attach binary data instead of text data in the body of the output when the MIME type listed in the Content-type header refers to a binary object. For example, if a CGI program is sending a binary GIF image, the Content-type should list *image/gif*, and the binary data representing the GIF image should start from the third line of the CGI output file.

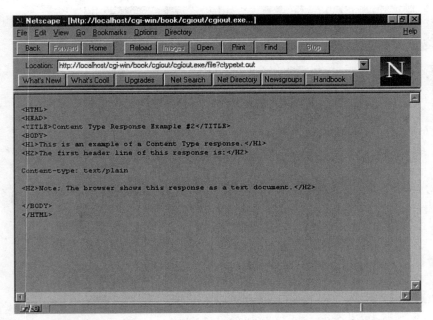

Figure 10-5 Browser showing a plain/text Content-type response

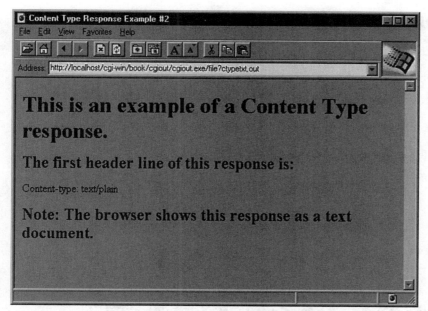

Figure 10–6 Internet Explorer ignoring the plain/text Content-type response

LESSON 3: REDIRECTING TO ANOTHER URL

Rather than generating the output itself, a CGI program can point to another information resource as its response by generating a Location or a URL header line as the first line of the CGI output. The syntax of these header lines is as follows:

```
Location: absolute or relative URL
URL: <absolute or relative URL>
```

When the Web server encounters either of the preceding header lines in the CGI output file, it returns a redirection status code with the specified URL to the client. The client then is responsible for fetching and displaying the contents of the new URL to the user.

NOTE: Some Web servers, including the WebSite server, examine the new URL to see if it points to a local or an external resource. If the URL refers to a local resource (a file or another CGI program residing on their machine), these servers automatically return the information from that local resource to the client, thereby eliminating a potential request-response cycle.

Redirection Example

The REDIRFIL.OUT file in the C:\WEBSITE\CGI-WIN\CGIOUT\ directory contains the following redirection line (followed by a blank line):

`Location: /book/survey/goph4.gif`

To test this Redirection-type response:

1. Ensure that your WebSite server is running.

2. Enter the following URL from your browser:

`http://localhost/cgi-win/book/cgiout/cgiout.exe/file?redirfil.out`

The browser shows the gopher image indicated by the relative URL */book/survey/goph.gif* as shown in Figure 10-7.

3. Now enter the following URL from your browser:

`http://localhost/cgi-win/book/cgiout/cgiout.exe/file?redircgi.out`

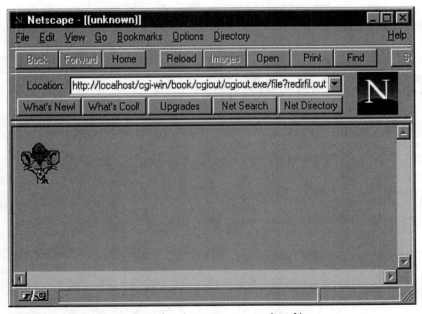

Figure 10-7 Response of redirecting to another file

The browser again displays the same gopher image, but this time the REDIRCGI.OUT file contains a Location header pointing to another CGI request:

```
Location: /cgi-win/book/cgiout/cgiout.exe/file?redirfil.out
```

In this case, the server performs double redirection before it fetches the final gopher image.

Advantages of Using Redirection as a CGI Response

A Redirection-type CGI response proves beneficial in the following cases:

- When the data to be returned does not have to be generated on-the-fly. For example, if a CGI program needs to return a static HTML form, it can redirect to an HTML file representing that form.

- When you are not sure about the data that needs to be returned while designing a CGI program. For example, if you want to return an error message from your CGI program, you can redirect to an external error file and later formulate the contents of that error file.

- When sending data created by another utility or program. For example, if you need to send a graph as your CGI program output, you may use a third-party library function or an external utility in your CGI program to create a temporary GIF image file of that graph. Your CGI program can then redirect to that GIF image file as its response.

LESSON 4: RETURNING A DIFFERENT STATUS CODE

When a Windows CGI program returns a Content-type or a Redirection-type response to the Web server, the server assumes that the CGI program has successfully handled the request. Hence, while delivering the response to the client, the server automatically sends a "200 OK" message for the HTTP status header field with the rest of the response.

However, if the CGI program needs to send a different status code, it may add a Status header line in its response using the following syntax:

```
Status: code description
```

where *code* and *description* represent the standard HTTP status code and reason phrase, respectively. For a complete list of HTTP status codes and their interpretation, refer to the "HTTP Response" section in Chapter 7, Elements of the World Wide Web.

Returning an Error Status

It is not uncommon for CGI programs to encounter an error while processing a user request. For example, a user may submit an invalid data value for a form field to a CGI program which may cause that program to flag an error and abort processing.

When an error condition occurs, it is a good practice to indicate that error not only to the user, but also to the Web client by sending an appropriate HTTP status code along with the HTML response explaining a possible cause of the error.

Consider the case where a CGI program cannot fulfill a request due to insufficient data supplied with the request. Chances are that the user did not provide all the information when submitting the request. But it is possible that the client may not have successfully delivered all the data. In either case, the CGI program can return a "400 Bad Request" status header with the error message as follows:

```
Status: 400 Bad Request
Content-type: text/html

<HTML>
<TITLE>Bad Request</TITLE>
<BODY>
<H1>400 Bad Request</H1>
<H4>The request cannot be fulfilled since all required data was not supplied.</H4>
</BODY>
</HTML>
```

This sample response is also included in the file named *stat400.out*. You can enter the following URL from your browser to see the effect of this response on your browser:

```
http://localhost/cgi-win/book/cgiout/cgiout.exe/file?stat400.out
```

Figure 10-8 shows how the Netscape browser displays this response.

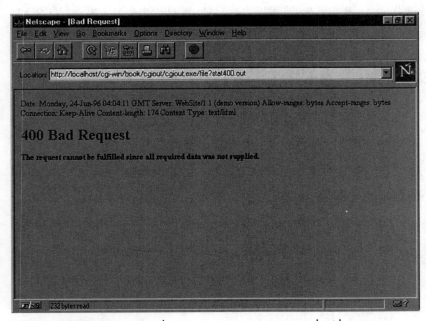

Figure 10-8 Netscape showing a response returned with a status code of 400

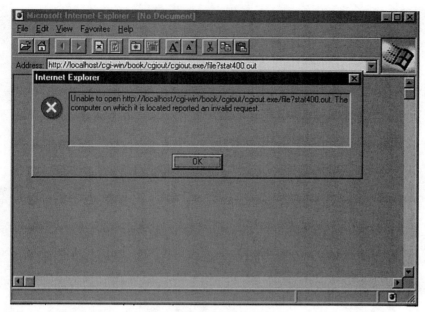

Figure 10–9 Internet Explorer displaying its own error message on receiving a response containing a status code of 400

NOTE: Different browsers take different approaches to handling error type status codes. For example, while Netscape simply displays the header fields and the HTML formatted body of the response returned by the server, Internet Explorer just displays its own error message as shown in Figure 10-9. The reason for such a discrepancy is because there are no HTTP specifications on how to handle these error status codes.

Returning a No Content Message

If a CGI program does not have any information to send back to the requesting client, it should send a "204 No Content" status message as its response to indicate that it has completed the request.

On receiving this status code, the browser stays in its current document view. You can enter the following URL from your browser to test if your browser correctly responds to a 204 status code:

```
http://localhost/cgi-win/book/cgiout/cgiout.exe/file?stat204.out
```

REVIEW QUESTIONS

1. What is the format of a CGI output file?

2. How does a CGI program create a direct response?

3. How does a Web server react to a direct response?

4. What are the advantages of an indirect response?

5. How do you send a response using the Content-type header?

6. How can a CGI program redirect to another URL?

7. When does a Redirection-type response prove useful?

8. In how many ways can you send binary data from a CGI program?

9. What default status code does a Web server send when packaging an indirect response? How can you overwrite this default?

10. What can you do if your CGI program does not have any information to return to the requesting client?

EXERCISES

1. Read the Windows CGI specifications provided with the on-line documentation of your WebSite server by specifying the following URL from your browser:

   `http://localhost/wsdocs/32demo/windows-cgi.html`

2. What happens if the output of a CGI program does not start with any of the expected header lines? To test this case, run your WebSite server, and enter the following URL from your browser:

   `http://localhost/cgi-win/book/cgiout/cgiout.exe/file?badhdr.out`

3. Test the case where a blank line is not present between the header and the body of a CGI output by entering the following URL from your browser:

   `http://localhost/cgi-win/book/cgiout/cgiout.exe/file?noblank.out`

4. Test the case where an extra header field is supplied with a Content-type response by entering the following URL from your browser:

   `http://localhost/cgi-win/book/cgiout/cgiout.exe/file?extrahdr.out`

11

DESIGNING A WINDOWS CGI APPLICATION

11

A Windows CGI application is based on a Windows executable (.EXE) program that is designed to run mainly in a noninteractive mode. The basic operation of a typical Windows CGI program can be described as follows:

1. Read data from the CGI content file and secondary input files.

2. Fulfill the CGI request based on the input data.

3. Generate CGI response in the designated output file.

The Web server passes the path and file name of the CGI content file as a command-line argument to the Windows CGI program. The type of data the server lists in the CGI content file is described in Chapter 9, Windows Common Gateway Interface.

A Windows CGI program is not required to read all the data listed in the CGI content file unless the functionality of the CGI program depends on that data. At the minimum, the CGI program needs to get the path and file name of the CGI output file from the CGI content file. The main objective of the Windows CGI program is to accomplish the desired task and produce a valid CGI response in the CGI output file. Chapter 10, Windows CGI Output Standard, describes what constitutes a valid CGI response.

You can use any programming language to design a Windows CGI program as long as the development environment for that language allows the creation of a Windows executable (.EXE) file from the source code. The following questions serve as a good measure to determine which programming environment best suits your needs for developing a Windows CGI program:

How easily can you pick up the language syntax?

How user-friendly is the development environment for that language?

What debugging facilities are available through the development environment?

Does the programming language provide support for accessing external databases?

Are there any libraries or tools available for the language environment to help in Windows CGI program development?

Visual Basic 4.0 (professional edition) earns high marks on the preceding factors and has been chosen as the development platform for the Windows CGI programs described in this book. This decision does not imply that other programming environments are any less suitable. They all have their strengths, and it may be possible to port the programming concepts discussed in this book to these environments.

This chapter describes how to create an elementary Windows CGI program with Visual Basic 4.0, utilizing a CGI library module which provides the basic framework for designing a Windows CGI program. This CGI library module, called CGI32.BAS, comes with the WebSite package and is written by Robert Denny, the developer of the WebSite server.

The Windows CGI program you will create in this chapter goes beyond the traditional "Hello World!" snippet. It is a greeting program that considers the possibility that the Web may one day extend its reach to other parts of the universe, and thus returns a "Hello Universe!" message. The following sequence outlines the tasks for creating this universal greeting program:

1. Set up a Visual Basic project for your Windows CGI program.

2. Write code to return the greeting as the CGI response.

3. Compile the project and create an executable program file.

4. Test your Windows CGI program.

LESSON 1: SETTING UP A VISUAL BASIC PROJECT

In Visual Basic (VB), you design a program by building a Visual Basic project. A *Visual Basic project* is a collection of files and configuration settings. The files represent the forms, custom controls, and library modules that you compile to create the executable program.

When you launch Visual Basic from Windows 95, VB automatically creates a new project containing a blank form and common custom controls. Visual Basic presets the environment options in this project with the assumption that you want to create a regular interactive application. However, these project settings do not work for a Windows CGI program, which is mainly a noninteractive application.

To create a project for the Windows CGI greeting program, you will use a template project file provided on the CD-ROM accompanying this book. This project file (NEWAPP.VBP) was copied to your local hard drive under the directory C:\WEBSITE\ CGI-WIN\BOOK\NEWAPP\ when you installed the sample Web applications in Chapter 2, Getting Started.

The NEWAPP.VBP project file includes two module files: CGI32.BAS and NEWAPP.BAS. The CGI32.BAS library file, which is located in the C:\WEBSITE\LIB\ directory, can be shared by other Windows CGI projects as well and thus is used as a read-only module. You write code specific to your CGI program in the NEWAPP.BAS module, which is unique to each project.

To set up the project for the Greeting program from the NEWAPP.VBP project template, use the following steps:

1. Go to an MS-DOS prompt.

2. Create a new directory called *C:\WEBSITE\CGI-WIN\BOOK\GREETING* by entering the following DOS commands:

    ```
    cd c:\website\cgi-win\book <ENTER>
    mkdir greeting <ENTER>
    ```

3. Copy the template project file to the GREETING directory as *GREETING.VBP* by entering the following command:

    ```
    copy newapp\newapp.vbp greeting\greeting.vbp <ENTER>
    ```

4. Copy the NEWAPP module file (NEWAPP.BAS) to the GREETINGS directory by entering the following command:

```
copy newapp\newapp.bas greeting <ENTER>
```

5. Verify that the CGI32.BAS file exists in the C:\WEBSITE\LIB directory by entering the following command:

```
dir c:\website\lib\*.bas
```

The directory listing should display the following two library files:

```
CGI32.BAS
UTILS.BAS
```

NOTE: If the directory listing did not display these files, follow the instructions given in Lesson 3 of Chapter 2, Getting Started, to reinstall these files from the CD-ROM accompanying this book.

If everything appears to be in order so far, you can open the GREETING.VBP project from Visual Basic as follows:

1. Launch Visual Basic 4.0 (32-bit professional version). VB opens a default project and a blank form.

2. Select the Open Project option from VB's File menu. VB pops up the standard file list dialog box showing the files and subdirectories under the Microsoft Visual Basic directory.

3. Using the directory selector in the file list dialog box, go to the C:\WEBSITE\CGI-WIN\BOOK\GREETING\ directory. The file list box displays the GREETING.VBP project file as shown in Figure 11-1.

4. Double-click on the GREETING.VBP file name to load this project file.

5. Select the Project option from VB's View menu to open the Project window. Figure 11-2 shows the Project window displaying the name and description of the CGI32.BAS and NEWAPP.BAS module files included with the GREETING.VBP project.

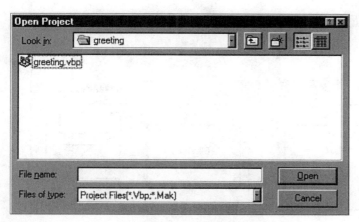

Figure 11-1 Opening the GREETING project file

Figure 11-2 The Project window

LESSON 2: WRITING CODE FOR YOUR CGI PROGRAM

The CGI32.BAS library module contains a procedure named Main which is set as the program's entry point in the GREETING.VBP project. The Main procedure initializes the CGI environment (see Lesson 5) and then calls another procedure named CGI_Main where you define the actual functionality of the Windows CGI program. Since the CGI_Main procedure contains code specific to your Windows CGI program, this procedure is kept in the NEWAPP.BAS module. Figure 11-3 illustrates the overall control structure of your project.

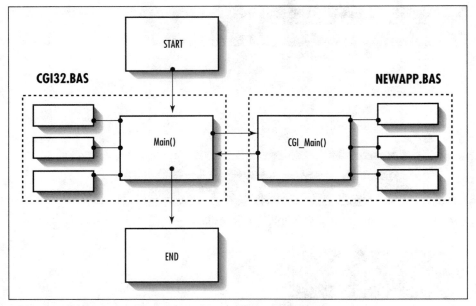

Figure 11-3 Control structure of a Windows CGI project

The NEWAPP.BAS module contains a skeleton of the CGI_Main procedure. To add your own code in the CGI_Main procedure for generating the greeting message:

1. Open the Project window if it is not already open.

2. Double-click on NEWAPP.BAS to open this module's Code window.

3. Select the CGI_Main procedure from the Code window's procedure selector. The Code window displays the skeleton of the CGI_Main procedure as shown in Figure 11-4.

NOTE: You can display the CGI_Main procedure in full screen by maximizing the Code window.

The CGI_Main procedure template has a comment section and the following procedure definition:

```
Sub CGI_Main()

  'Start your code here

End Sub
```

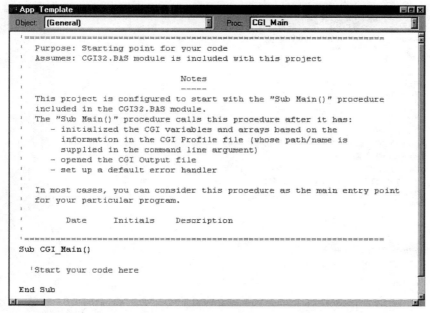

Figure 11-4 CGI_Main procedure template

The comment section lists the purpose, assumptions, and any notes related to the CGI_Main procedure. It also has a subsection for listing the revision history of this procedure. Although not required, it is a good practice to keep the information in the comment section up to date. In VB, all comments must start with an apostrophe symbol (') or the REM instruction.

Now you can add the code to this CGI_Main procedure to generate the greeting message:

1. Type the following VB code below the comment line that says "Start your code here":

```
Send ("Content-type: text/html")
Send ("")
Send ("<HTML>")
Send ("<HEAD>")
Send ("<TITLE>Greetings</TITLE>")
Send ("</HEAD>")
Send ("<BODY>")
Send ("<H1>Hello Universe!</H1>")
Send ("</BODY>")
Send ("</HTML>")
```

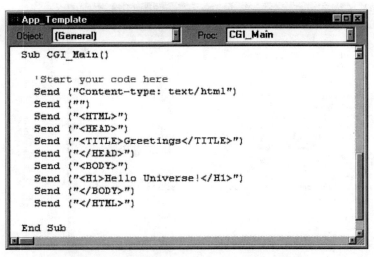

Figure 11–5 CGI_Main procedure with the code for the greeting message

Figure 11-5 shows the CGI_Main procedure after entering the preceding code. This code writes the HTML text for the greeting message to the CGI output file using the Send procedure provided in the CGI32.BAS module. The Send procedure is described further in Chapter 12, Designing a Windows CGI Application to Process Form Data.

1. Inspect your code again to ensure that there are no typing errors.

2. Save the NEWAPP.BAS module by selecting the Save File option from VB's File menu.

NOTE: You can also rename the NEWAPP.BAS module file to a more appropriate name such as *GREETING.BAS* as described in Lesson 4.

LESSON 3: COMPILING AND TESTING YOUR CGI PROGRAM

A Windows CGI program has to be an executable (.EXE) file. So you need to compile your Greeting project to create an executable file as follows:

1. Ensure that the GREETING.VBP project is currently loaded under VB.

2. Select the Make .EXE File option from VB's File menu.

Figure 11–6 Dialog box prompting for the name of the executable file

VB prompts for the name of the executable file as shown in Figure 11-6. It lists NEWAPP.EXE under the C:\WEBSITE\CGI-WIN\BOOK\GREETING directory as the default name.

3. Change NEWAPP.EXE to *GREETING.EXE*, and click on the OK button.

If your project is error-free, then VB creates the GREETING.EXE executable file; otherwise, it points to the first error found in your code. If you encounter an error, then return to your code, correct the error, and recompile your project.

Once you have created the GREETING.EXE file, you can place a CGI request to test your Greeting program as follows:

1. Start your WebSite server if it is not already running.

2. Specify the following URL from your Web browser:

```
http://localhost/cgi-win/book/greeting/greeting.exe
```

The browser should display the greeting message as shown in Figure 11-7.

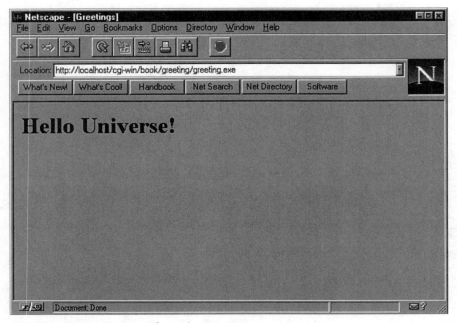

Figure 11-7 Response from the Greeting program

NOTE: If your browser displays a "File Not Found" error message instead of the greeting message, then verify that you saved the Greeting program as GREETING.EXE in the C:\WEBSITE\CGI-WIN\BOOK\GREETING directory and run this test again.

NOTE: For reference, the results of this lesson are available in the C:\WEBSITE\HTDOCS\BOOK\CHAP11\RESULTS\LESSON3\ directory.

LESSON 4: CUSTOMIZING THE PROJECT

This lesson describes how to rename the NEWAPP.BAS module to GREETING.BAS and looks into the project option where the Main procedure is preset as your program's entry point.

Renaming the NEWAPP.BAS Module

To rename the NEWAPP.BAS module to *GREETING.BAS*:

1. Load the GREETING.VBP project file under Visual Basic if it is not already loaded.

2. Open the Code window of the NEWAPP.BAS module.

3. Select the Save File As option from the File menu. VB pops up the standard file list box.

4. Specify *GREETING.BAS* as the new file name, and click on the Save button.

5. Select the Properties option from VB's View menu. VB pops up the Properties window showing "App_Template" as the module name, as shown in Figure 11-8.

6. Change the module name to *GREETING_APP* or any other suitable name (with no spaces) in the Properties window.

7. Save the new project settings by selecting the Save Project option from VB's File menu.

8. Delete the existing NEWAPP.BAS file from the C:\WEBSITE\CGI-WIN\ BOOK\GREETING directory.

Figure 11–8 Properties window showing module properties

The Program's Entry Point Setting

In Visual Basic, you can assign a form or a procedure as an entry point for your program. For all Windows CGI programs that utilize the CGI32.BAS library module, it is essential that the entry point of your program is set to the Sub Main procedure. You can verify the entry point setting as follows:

1. Load the GREETING.VBP project file under Visual Basic.

2. Select Options from VB's Tools menu, and then click on the Project tab to list the project configuration options as shown in Figure 11-9.

The option labeled "Startup Form" lists "Sub Main" as the program's entry point. This also implies that your program automatically terminates when the control reaches the end of the Main procedure.

NOTE: Next to the Startup Form option, there is another option labeled "Project Name," which is currently set as "Newapp." You can change this to *Greeting* or any other suitable name for your project.

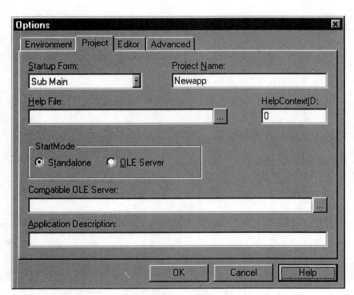

Figure 11-9 Project configuration options

LESSON 5: REVIEWING THE CGI32.BAS LIBRARY MODULE

The CGI32.BAS library module establishes a CGI framework for designing a Windows CGI program. By adding this module to your project, you are relieved from handling the details of parsing the CGI profile file and other input files. You can start writing code in the CGI_Main procedure and access all the CGI variables and the decoded form fields listed in the CGI profile file through the global VB variables declared in the CGI32.BAS module.

Altogether, the CGI32.BAS module helps you:

- Declare and assign global VB variables representing the data listed in the CGI profile file

- Open the CGI output file listed in the CGI profile file

- Set up a default error handler for trapping the runtime errors

- Provide utility procedures and functions related to CGI input and output operations

- Call the CGI_Main procedure if the CGI program is run noninteractively

- Call the Inter_Main procedure if the CGI program is run interactively

THE MAIN() PROCEDURE

As indicated earlier, the Main() procedure in the CGI32.BAS module acts as the entry point for your program. The code of this Main() procedure is given next:

```
Sub Main()
    On Error GoTo ErrorHandler

    If Trim$(Command$) = "" Then    ' Interactive start
        Inter_Main                   ' Call interactive main
        Exit Sub                     ' Exit the program
    End If

    InitializeCGI        ' Create the CGI environment

    '===========
    CGI_Main             ' Execute the actual "script"
    '===========

Cleanup:
    Close #CGI_OutputFN
    Exit Sub                         ' End the program
'------------
```

continued on next page

317

continued from previous page

```
ErrorHandler:
    Select Case Err                ' Decode our "user defined" errors
        Case ERR_NO_FIELD:
            ErrorString = "Unknown form field"
        Case Else:
            ErrorString = Error$    ' Must be VB error
    End Select

    ErrorString = ErrorString & " (error #" & Err & ")"
    On Error GoTo 0                ' Prevent recursion
    ErrorHandler (Err)             ' Generate HTTP error result
    Resume Cleanup
'------------
End Sub
```

The Main procedure works as follows:

1. Activate a default error handler.

2. Determine the program's run mode.

3. Initialize global variables and arrays.

4. Call the CGI_Main procedure and exit.

STEP 1: Activate a Default Error Handler

The On Error... line activates the error-handling routine to trap all runtime errors. If any error occurs during the execution of the program and there is no other error-handling routine set to preempt the error, then the control goes to the line labeled "ErrorHandler."

Activating a default error handler ensures that your program always terminates properly. The details of error handling are discussed in Chapter 12, Designing a Windows CGI Application to Process Form Data.

STEP 2: Determine the Program's Run Mode

Next, the Main procedure examines the program's command line to determine the run mode of the program. As explained in Lesson 1 of Chapter 9, Windows Common Gateway Interface, when the Web server executes a Windows CGI program, it always passes the path and file name of the CGI content file as the command-line argument. So, if the command line is empty, this procedure assumes that the program has been launched in the interactive mode and passes control to the procedure named Inter_Main.

The Inter_Main procedure, which resides in the GREETING.BAS (originally NEWAPP.BAS) module, contains the following code:

```
Sub Inter_Main()

  MsgBox "This is a Windows CGI program."

End Sub
```

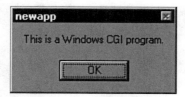

Figure 11-10 Running the
Greeting program directly
from Windows

So, if you run your Greeting program directly from Windows, you will get a message box as shown in Figure 11-10.

You can modify the Inter_Main procedure to have your program perform other tasks in the interactive mode.

STEP 3: Initialize Global Variables and Arrays

If the command line is not empty, the Main procedure assumes that the command-line argument contains a valid file path and file name of the CGI profile file. It then calls the InitializeCGI routine, which initializes the global variables and arrays based on the contents of the CGI profile file. The next lesson describes these global VB variables and arrays. The InitializeCGI routine also opens the designated CGI output file.

STEP 4: Call the CGI_Main Procedure and Exit

After successfully initializing the CGI environment, the Main procedure calls your CGI_Main procedure. All CGI global variables and arrays are directly accessible to the CGI_Main procedure. Upon completion of the CGI_Main procedure, the Main procedure closes the CGI Output file and exits, which also terminates the program.

LESSON 6: EXAMINING THE DECLARATIONS SECTION OF THE CGI32.BAS MODULE

The CGI32.BAS module declares global variables and arrays to hold the data listed in various sections of the CGI profile file. See Chapter 9, Windows Common Gateway Interface, for the structure of the CGI profile file. The names of these variables and arrays start with the *CGI_* prefix (see Figure 11-11), and being declared as Global, they are directly accessible from every procedure of your CGI program.

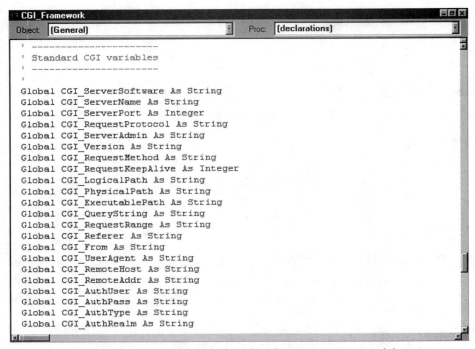

Figure 11-11 Global variables declared in the CGI32.BAS module

VB Variables Associated with the [CGI] Section

All CGI variables found in the [CGI] section of the CGI content file have an equivalent VB variable in the CGI32.BAS module. Tables 11-1 through 11-5 categorize these VB variables, listing their declared name, data type, and a brief description.

Table 11-1 Server-related CGI global variables

VB Variable Name	Type	Description
CGI_ServerSoftware	String	Name and version of the Web server
CGI_ServerAdmin	String	Server administrator's e-mail address (server configuration)
CGI_Version	String	The version of CGI used by the server

Table 11–2 Client-related VB global variables

VB Variable Name	Type	Description
CGI_RemoteHost	String	Client machine's network host name
CGI_RemoteAddr	String	Client machine's IP address
CGI_RequestProtocol	String	Name and revision of HTTP
CGI_Referer	String	URL of referring document
CGI_From	String	E-mail of client user (mostly comes in as blank)
CGI_UserAgent	String	Description (name/version) of the client
CGI_RequestKeepAlive	Integer	If the client requested connection reuse (Yes/No)

Table 11–3 Request-related VB global variables

VB Variable Name	Type	Description
CGI_RequestMethod	String	Method specified in the request (GET, POST, or HEAD)
CGI_ServerName	String	Server's network host name for this request
CGI_ServerPort	Integer	Server's network port number for this request
CGI_QueryString	String	Data following the "?" in the request URL
CGI_RequestRange	String	Byte-range specification received with the request
CGI_ContentType	String	MIME content type of the data supplied with the request
CGI_ContentLength	Long	Length (in bytes) of the data supplied with the request

Table 11–4 Path-related VB global variables

VB Variable Name	Type	Description
CGI_ExecutablePath	String	The URL path of the CGI executable program
CGI_LogicalPath	String	The extra path information provided with the request URL
CGI_PhysicalPath	String	Physical mapping of the logical path

Table 11–5 Access control-related VB global variables

VB Variable Name	Type	Description
CGI_AuthUser	String	Name of the user if present in the request
CGI_AuthPass	String	Password if present in the request
CGI_AuthType	String	Method used for authentication
CGI_AuthRealm	String	Realm of the authenticated user

VB Variables Associated with the [System] Section

Table 11-6 lists the global VB variables declared in the CGI32.BAS module which are associated with the [System] section of the CGI profile file.

Table 11–6 System-related VB global variables

VB Variable Name	Type	Description
CGI_GMTOffset	Long	Offset of local time zone from GMT, seconds
CGI_ContentFile	String	Path/name of the CGI content file
CGI_OutputFile	String	Path/name of the CGI output file
CGI_DebugMode	String	If server's CGI debug flag is set (Yes/No)

Global Arrays

The CGI32.BAS module uses one-dimensional arrays (see Figure 11-12) to hold the data provided in the Accept, Extra Headers, and all the form-related sections of the CGI profile file. The elements of these arrays are called *tuples* since each element is made up of multiple subelements.

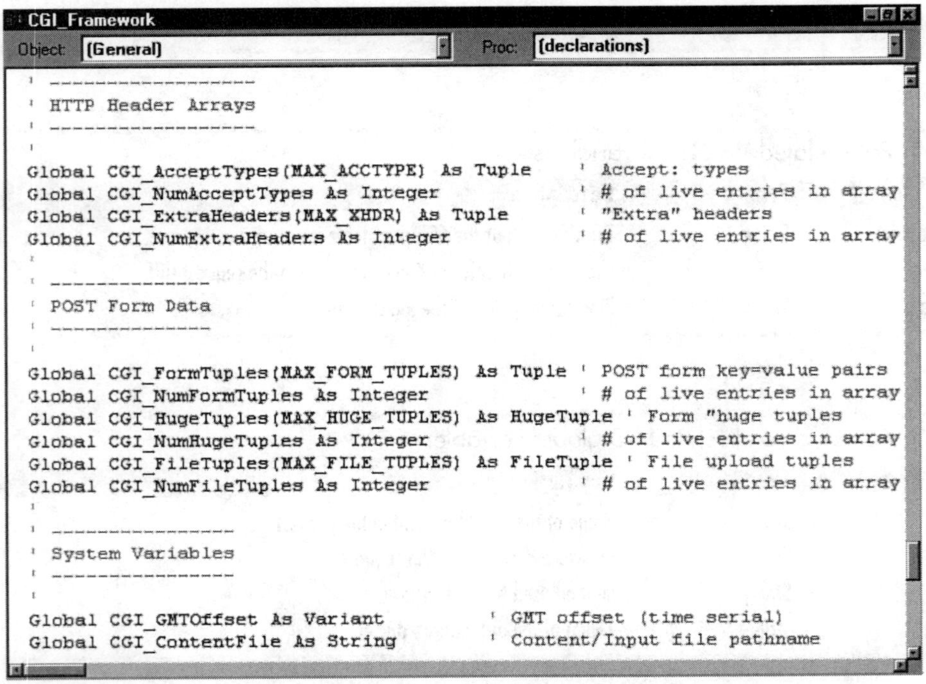

```
  CGI_Framework                                                    _ 回 X
Object:  [General]                        Proc:  [declarations]

'  --------------------
'  HTTP Header Arrays
'  --------------------
'
Global CGI_AcceptTypes(MAX_ACCTYPE) As Tuple     ' Accept: types
Global CGI_NumAcceptTypes As Integer             ' # of live entries in array
Global CGI_ExtraHeaders(MAX_XHDR) As Tuple       ' "Extra" headers
Global CGI_NumExtraHeaders As Integer            ' # of live entries in array
'
'  ----------------
'  POST Form Data
'  ----------------
'
Global CGI_FormTuples(MAX_FORM_TUPLES) As Tuple  ' POST form key=value pairs
Global CGI_NumFormTuples As Integer              ' # of live entries in array
Global CGI_HugeTuples(MAX_HUGE_TUPLES) As HugeTuple ' Form "huge tuples
Global CGI_NumHugeTuples As Integer              ' # of live entries in array
Global CGI_FileTuples(MAX_FILE_TUPLES) As FileTuple ' File upload tuples
Global CGI_NumFileTuples As Integer              ' # of live entries in array
'
'  ----------------
'  System Variables
'  ----------------
'
Global CGI_GMTOffset As Variant                  ' GMT offset (time serial)
Global CGI_ContentFile As String                 ' Content/Input file pathname
```

Figure 11–12 Global arrays declared in the CGI32.BAS module

Accept Types

The array that holds the data listed in the [Accept] section of the CGI Profile file is declared in the CGI32.BAS module as follows:

```
Global CGI_AcceptTypes(MAX_ACCTYPE) As Tuple
```

where the type Tuple has the following structure:

```
Type Tuple
    key As String
    value As String
End Type
```

Each line under the [Accept] section of the CGI profile file is stored as an element of this array. For example, if the CGI profile file contained the following lines under the [Accept] section:

```
[Accept]
image/gif=Yes
image/x-xbitmap=Yes
```

then, after the initialization routine of the Main procedure, the elements of the CGI_AcceptTypes array will appear as follows:

```
CGI_AcceptTypes(1).key   = "image/gif"
CGI_AcceptTypes(1).value = "Yes"
CGI_AcceptTypes(2).key   = "image/x-xbitmap"
CGI_AcceptTypes(2).value = "Yes"
```

The CGI32.BAS also declares an integer variable named CGI_NumAcceptTypes, which indicates the number of assigned elements in the CGI_AcceptTypes array.

The MAX_ACCTYPE is a constant which defines the maximum length of the CGI_AcceptTypes array. This constant generally corresponds with the maximum number of Accept types that the Web server provides in the CGI profile file.

Extra Headers

The array for extra headers is declared similar to the Accept Types array as shown next:

```
Global CGI_ExtraHeaders(MAX_XHDR) As Tuple
```

This CGI_ExtraHeaders array also has an associated integer variable named CGI_NumExtraHeaders which stores the count of the assigned elements.

Decoded Form Data

The Form data listed in the [Form Literal] and [Form External] section of the CGI profile file is stored in the CGI_FormTuples array, which is declared as follows:

```
Global CGI_FormTuples(MAX_FORM_TUPLES) As Tuple
```

The integer variable, CGI_NumFormTuples, keeps a total count of the active elements in this array.

Huge Form Data

The information listed in the [Form Huge] section of the CGI profile file is stored in the array named CGI_HugeTuples, which is declared as follows:

```
Global CGI_HugeTuples(MAX_HUGE_TUPLES) As HugeTuple
```

where the type HugeTuple has the following structure:

```
Type HugeTuple          ' Used for "huge" form fields
    key As String       ' Keyword (decoded)
    offset As Long      ' Byte offset into Content File of value
    length As Long      ' Length of value, bytes
End Type
```

The count of active elements in the CGI_HugeTuples array is stored in an integer variable named CGI_NumHugeTuples.

NOTE: The CGI_HugeTuples array elements contain not the field data but the information that points to the data associated with the field.

Uploaded Files

The information about the uploaded files listed in the [Form File] section of the CGI profile file is stored in an array named CGI_FileTuples, which is declared as follows:

```
Global CGI_FileTuples(MAX_FILE_TUPLES) As FileTuple
```

where the type FileTuple has the following structure:

```
Type FileTuple            ' Used for form-based file uploads
    key As String         ' Form field name
    file As String        ' Local tempfile containing uploaded file
    length As Long        ' Length in bytes of uploaded file
    type As String        ' Content type of uploaded file
    encoding As String    ' Content-transfer encoding of uploaded file
    name As String        ' Original name of uploaded file
End Type
```

The count of uploaded files referred to in the CGI_FileTuples array is stored in an integer variable named CGI_NumFileTuples.

LESSON 7: LISTING THE GLOBAL VARIABLES AND ARRAY ELEMENTS

Let's modify the CGI_Main procedure in the GREETING.VBP project to output the values of a few global variables and array elements made available by the CGI32.BAS library module:

1. Load the GREETING.VBP project file under Visual Basic.

2. Go to the CGI_Main procedure of the GREETING.BAS (originally NEWAPP.BAS) module.

3. Change the CGI_Main procedure so that it appears as follows:

```
Sub CGI_Main()

    'Start your code here
    Send ("Content-type: text/html")
    Send ("")
    Send ("<HTML>")
    Send ("<HEAD>")
    Send ("<TITLE>Greetings</TITLE>")
    Send ("</HEAD>")
    Send ("<BODY>")
    Send ("<H1>Hello Universe!</H1>")
    Send ("<B>Value of few global variables:</B>")
    Send ("<PRE>")
    Send ("<BR>CGI_ServerSoftware       : " & CGI_ServerSoftware)
    Send ("<BR>CGI_RemoteAddr           : " & CGI_RemoteAddr)
    Send ("<BR>CGI_ExecutablePath       : " & CGI_ExecutablePath)
    Send ("<BR>CGI_RequestMethod        : " & CGI_RequestMethod)
    Send ("<BR>CGI_NumAcceptTypes       : " & CGI_NumAcceptTypes)
    Send ("<BR>CGI_AcceptTypes(1).key   : " & CGI_AcceptTypes(1).key)
    Send ("<BR>CGI_AcceptTypes(1).value: " & CGI_AcceptTypes(1).value)
    Send ("</PRE>")
    Send ("</BODY>")
    Send ("</HTML>")

End Sub
```

4. Select Save File from VB's File menu to save the GREETING.BAS file.

5. Re-create the GREETING.EXE executable file by selecting the Make EXE File option from VB's File menu.

6. Start your WebSite server if it is not already running.

7. Enter the following URL from your Web browser:

```
http://localhost/cgi-win/book/greeting/greeting.exe
```

The browser displays the greeting message and the values of the listed VB variables as shown in Figure 11-13.

As you can see, it is not difficult to create a Windows CGI program to display the CGI variables passed by the server, thanks to the CGI32.BAS library. The CGITEST32.EXE utility that we used in the previous two chapters for testing the Windows Common Gateway Interface is designed with the same basic idea as the program we created here. The project file of this CGITEST32.EXE utility is stored as CGITST32.VBP in the C:\WEBSITE\CGI-SRC\VB4 SAMPLES\ directory. At this point, we recommend you open this project file in Visual Basic and familiarize yourself with the source code of the CGITEST32.EXE utility.

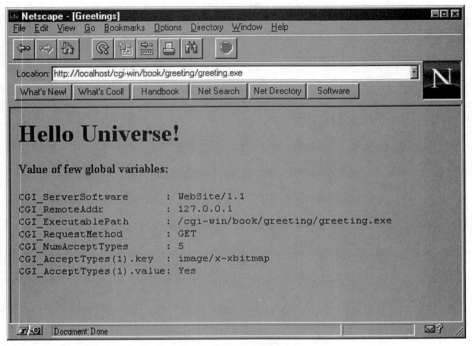

Figure 11-13 Displaying values of VB variables

NOTE: For reference, the results of this lesson are available in the C:\WEBSITE\HTDOCS\BOOK\CHAP11\RESULTS\LESSON7\ directory.

REVIEW QUESTIONS

1. List the basic operation of a Windows CGI program.

2. How does the Web server pass the path/name of the CGI content file to the Windows CGI program?

3. How does the Windows CGI program locate the path/name of the CGI output file?

4. What factors should be considered when selecting a programming environment for developing a Windows CGI program?

5. List the steps involved in creating a Windows CGI program using Visual Basic.

6. What is a Visual Basic project?

7. What is the advantage of using the NEWAPP.VBP project template file to create your Windows CGI project?

8. What is the relationship between the Main and the CGI_Main procedures?

9. How do you make an executable file from a Visual Basic project?

10. How do you test a Windows CGI program?

11. What is the utility of the CGI32.BAS module?

12. What is the advantage of setting a default error handler in the Main procedure?

13. How does the Main procedure decide the run mode of the Windows CGI program?

14. What is the purpose of the Inter_Main procedure?

15. List the global variables declared in the CGI32.BAS module.

16. What is a Tuple?

17. List the global arrays declared in the CGI32.BAS module.

EXERCISES

1. Read the description of the Windows CGI standard given in the declaration section of the CGI32.BAS module.

2. Open the C:\WEBSITE\CGI-SRC\VB4 SAMPLES\CGI32TST.VBP project in Visual Basic. Check out the settings of the project options, and go through the code contained in the CGI32TST.BAS module.

3. Modify the CGI_Main procedure in your GREETING.VBP project to list all the global variables and array elements initialized during the Main procedure of CGI32.BAS module.

12

DESIGNING A WINDOWS CGI APPLICATION TO PROCESS FORM DATA

12

The true capability of a CGI application lies in its ability to dynamically interact with Web users by processing their data and generating appropriate responses. Making a Web application interactive, however, brings in additional complexity, since now you not only have to design a CGI program, but you also need to decide on the HTML front-end that will drive your program.

Consider the GuestBook application examined in Chapter 2, Getting Started. To add a guest book entry, you had to use a guest book entry form as shown in Figure 12-1.

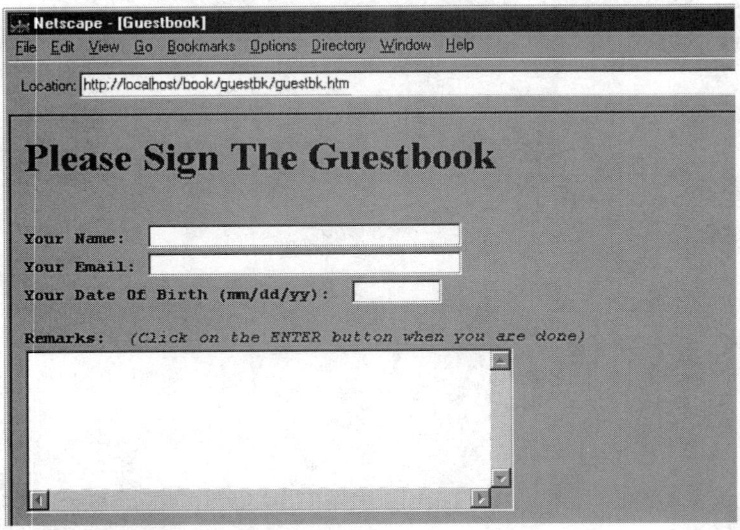

Figure 12–1 Guest book entry form

This HTML-formatted entry form is an integrated component of the GuestBook application. It serves as a data entry screen and establishes a proper interface for passing the data to the back-end Windows CGI program.

The interdependency between the HTML front-end and the CGI back-end must be resolved in the early stages of your CGI application development process. In effect, you need to address the following questions before you start implementing your CGI application:

1. What are the objectives of your CGI application?

2. What types of requests should your application handle?

3. How will the user make these requests?

4. How will you get data from the user for each type of request?

5. What minimum amount of data is needed to fulfill each request?

6. What does the user expect in response to a request?

7. What if the user supplies incorrect data?

8. What if the user provides insufficient data?

This chapter examines these issues in further detail by walking you through a step-by-step process of creating a general-purpose version of the GuestBook application. This application, called the Multi-Guestbook, essentially allows you to easily set up several guest books on your Web site. Through this application, you can assign a separate guest book to each client using your Web site.

NOTE: The files created in each lesson are available in the C:\WEBSITE\HTDOCS\BOOK\CHAP12\RESULTS\LESSON*x*\ directory, where *x* represents the lesson number. If you do not want to follow the steps that require you to type the text to create the files in this chapter, simply bypass those steps by copying the stored versions of the files in their indicated directories.

LESSON 1: DETERMINING THE OBJECTIVES OF YOUR WEB APPLICATION

Due to its interactive nature, the Multi-Guestbook application you are going to design requires both an HTML front-end and a CGI back-end, which must operate in harmony for the application to work smoothly. This creates an interesting dilemma: Which end should be designed first?

The instinctive approach may be to design the HTML documents and HTML forms first, and then create the back-end CGI routines to support the front-end. This approach, however, assumes that you have a clear perception of how the front-end interface would look, which requires ample foresight and is sometimes difficult to accomplish in the first try.

In practice, a Web application design process turns out to be an iterative cycle where you loop between the front-end and the back-end development until you meet all your goals.

The iterative development cycle does cost extra time and effort. However, you can minimize this cycle if you predefine the scope of your project by explicitly listing the main features and objectives of your application. As an example, for our guest book application, we will establish the following specifications:

1. The application should provide support for multiple but independent guest books.

2. Adding and removing a guest book should be relatively simple.

3. A user should be able to add entries to any guest book.

4. A user should be able to list existing entries added after a specified date from any guest book.

5. A guest book entry must include the name and e-mail address of the user. The entry can also optionally contain a user's phone number, comments, and date of birth.

6. The application should check for duplicate entries in a single guest book. This protects a user from accidentally clicking the Submit button twice.

7. You should be able to return a customized acknowledgment response when a user adds an entry to a guest book.

Note that these specifications do not get into any implementation details. They simply list the goals of the Multi-Guestbook application. You consider the implementation-related issues during the application's design phase as explained in the next lesson.

LESSON 2: CREATING AN IMPLEMENTATION DESIGN

After you know *what* you want from your application, you must decide on *how* you are going to achieve it. Now is the time to come up with an overall implementation strategy or a model that illustrates how the application will logically function to accomplish the set objectives.

You need to make decisions on how your front-end will interact with the back-end, what user data you need to process, and how you are going to store that data. For the Multi-Guestbook application, we will use the following design:

1. All guest books will be represented by Access database files named GBOOK.MDB that will be kept in separate directories.

2. A CGI request for a specific guest book will list the path of the guest book's directory in the extra logical path portion of the URL as follows:

   `http://localhost/CGI_Request_Path/DirectoryPath`

3. To add an entry to a guest book, a POST request will be made to a Windows CGI program named GBADD.EXE as follows:

   `http://localhost/cgi-win/book/multigb/gbadd.exe/DirectoryName`

   The body of this CGI request will include the necessary user data.

4. To list the entries from a guest book, a request will be made to a Windows CGI program named GBLIST.EXE as follows:

   `http://localhost/cgi-win/book/multigb/gblist.exe/DirectoryPath`

   The body of this CGI request will include the Starting Date parameter.

5. The GBADD.EXE program will use a hidden field listed in the guest book entry form to return a customized response.

The idea of using the extra logical path to specify the directory holding the guest book file is based on the capability of the Web server to return an equivalent physical path of the type C:\WEBSITE\HTDOCS*DirectoryPath* in the Physical Path CGI variable. This idea was fully explained in Lesson 3 of Chapter 9, Windows Common Gateway Interface.

NOTE: The use of the extra logical path for specifying the guest book's directory path is also the reason why you need two Windows CGI programs, GBADD.EXE and GBLIST.EXE, to handle the two tasks related to a guest book. If you want to design one program for both the tasks, your front-end will have to supply another parameter representing the desired action. You can pass this parameter through another hidden field in your HTML forms.

Often, it is difficult to come up with a clear demarcation between an application's objectives, its design, and its implementation. There is a natural tendency to describe the objectives in terms of the design or the actual implementation. While for small projects this tendency does not create any major difficulties, for large projects (especially those that involve a team of people), it is important that the project be broken into an objective-identification phase, a design phase, and a separate implementation phase.

The goal is to limit the scope of each phase to a certain level of abstraction. For example, in the *objective-identification* phase, you simply define the objectives of the application in layperson's terms. In the *design* phase, you add the technical touch to come up with a detailed picture of what components the application requires and how they will interact with each other. In the *implementation* phase, you actually perform the necessary tasks to bring these components to life. Of course, there is a testing and debugging phase that overlaps with the implementation phase to ensure that the final product meets the intended objectives.

LESSON 3: CREATING THE APPLICATION'S FRONT-END

The first aim you should keep in mind when creating the front-end is that you want to demonstrate the complete capabilities of your application. Your front-end does not have to be sophisticated or glamorous right away. You can always do that later as part of the revision cycle.

For the Multi-Guestbook application, you will design a simple but functional user interface consisting of the following items, which are sufficient to illustrate the main features of your application:

1. Two guest book entry forms providing the necessary input fields for submitting an entry. Each form will cause the entry to be added to its own guest book. These forms will also contain a hidden field whose value holds the custom response of the back-end.

2. Two guest book listing forms containing a starting date input field that allows you to list the entries from the two guest books entered after a specified starting date.

3. A main menu screen that provides links to the preceding forms.

To refer to the two guest books in this user interface, you will need to allocate two directories under your Web server's document root directory (C:\WEBSITE\HTDOCS) hierarchy. For this purpose, create two new directories, GBDIR1 and GBDIR2, under the C:\WEBSITE\HTDOCS\BOOK\ directory by typing the following DOS commands from an MS-DOS prompt:

```
cd c:\website\htdocs\book\
mkdir gbdir1
mkdir gbdir2
```

Setting Up the Two Guest Book Entry Forms

According to the Multi-Guestbook application's specifications, a guest book entry may contain the following fields:

🕯 Name (Required)

🕯 Email Address (Required)

🕯 Phone Number (Optional)

🕯 Comments (Optional)

🕯 Date Of Birth (Optional)

When you design the two guest book entry forms, you must use the same names for the HTML input controls that will represent these fields in both the forms. As you will see in the next lesson, the GBADD.EXE program identifies the data in the individual fields through these defined names.

The guest book entry forms can, however, differ in their layout and also reside in separate directories. You can even eliminate some optional fields from these forms. For example, if you do not want the date of birth information for your second guest book, then do not provide the input control for the date of birth field in the second guest book entry form. Of course, you will have to design the GBADD.EXE program to allow the absence of an optional field.

The following steps describe how you can create the two guest book entry forms for your front-end:

1. Using your text editor, create a new text file named *GBADD1.HTM* in the C:\WEBSITE\HTDOCS\BOOK\GBDIR1\ directory, and type the following HTML text:

```
<HTML>
<HEAD>
<TITLE>Guestbook (GBDIR1)</TITLE>
</HEAD>
<BODY>
<H1>Please Sign The Guestbook (GBDIR1)</H1><P>
<FORM METHOD=POST ACTION=/cgi-win/book/multigb/gbadd.exe/book/gbdir1>
<BR><B>Your Name:</B>
<INPUT NAME="Name" TYPE="TEXT" MAXLENGTH=50 SIZE=30>
<BR><B>Your Email Address:</B>
<INPUT NAME="Email Address" TYPE="TEXT" MAXLENGTH=50 SIZE=30>
<BR><B>Your Date Of Birth (mm/dd/yy):  </B>
<INPUT NAME="Date Of Birth" TYPE="TEXT" MAXLENGTH=8 SIZE=8>
<BR><B>Your Phone Number:  </B>
<INPUT NAME="Phone Number" TYPE="TEXT" MAXLENGTH=20 SIZE=20>
<BR><BR>
<B>Comments:</B><EM>(Click on the ENTER button when you are done)</EM>
<BR><TEXTAREA NAME="Comments"  ROWS=8 COLS=45></TEXTAREA>
```

```
<BR><BR>
<INPUT NAME="Response" TYPE="HIDDEN" VALUE="Entry added to GBDIR1.">
<INPUT NAME="Submit" TYPE="SUBMIT" VALUE="Enter">
<INPUT NAME="Reset" TYPE="RESET" VALUE="Clear">
</FORM>
</BODY>
</HTML>
```

2. Create another text file named *GBADD2.HTM* with the following HTML text in the
   C:\WEBSITE\HTDOCS\BOOK\GBDIR2\ directory:

```
<HTML>
<HEAD>
<TITLE>Guestbook (GBDIR2)</TITLE>
</HEAD>
<BODY>
<H1>Please Sign The Guestbook (GBDIR2)</H1><P>
<FORM METHOD=POST ACTION=/cgi-win/book/multigb/gbadd.exe/book/gbdir2>
<BR><B>Name:</B>
<INPUT NAME="Name" TYPE="TEXT" MAXLENGTH=50 SIZE=30>
<BR><B>Email:</B>
<INPUT NAME="Email Address" TYPE="TEXT" MAXLENGTH=50 SIZE=30>
<BR><BR>
<B>Remarks:</B><EM>(Click on the ENTER button when you are done)</EM>
<BR><TEXTAREA NAME="Comments"  ROWS=8 COLS=45></TEXTAREA>
<BR><BR>
<INPUT NAME="Response" TYPE="HIDDEN" VALUE="Entry added to GBDIR2.">
<INPUT NAME="Submit" TYPE="SUBMIT" VALUE="Enter">
<INPUT NAME="Reset" TYPE="RESET" VALUE="Clear">
</FORM>
</BODY>
</HTML>
```

Note that both entry forms include a hidden field named "Response." When you
design the GBADD.EXE program in the next lesson, you will return the value of this field
as the program's response.

Figure 12-2 shows the GBADD1.HTM file as displayed through a Web browser.

Figure 12-3 shows the GBADD2.HTM file as displayed through a Web browser.

Notice from these figures that the two forms have some layout differences, and the
second form does not include the date of birth and the phone number optional fields.

Setting Up the Two Listing Forms and the Main Menu Form

Just as with the guest book entry forms, you need two forms for listing the entries of the
two guest books. Each form will contain an input control for a starting date field, which
will allow a user to list the entries after a specified date. These two forms will mainly differ
in their ACTION argument and can be created as follows:

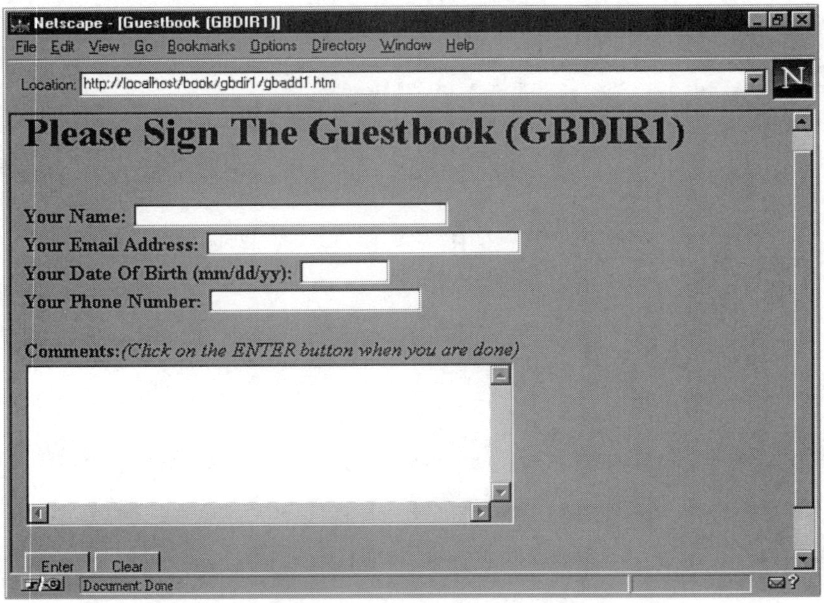

Figure 12–2 Web browser displaying the GBADD1.HTM form

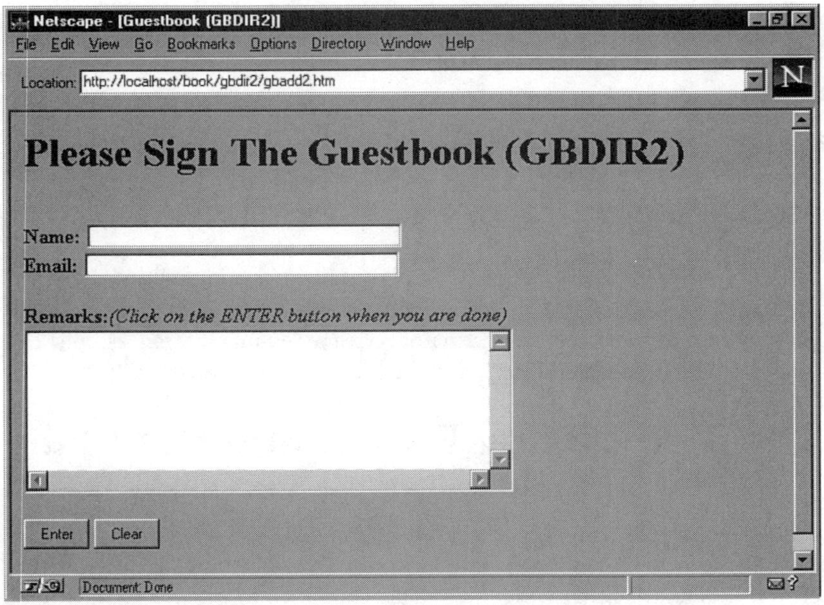

Figure 12–3 Web browser displaying the GBADD2.HTM form

1. Using the Notepad application, create a new text file named *GBLIST1.HTM* in the C:\WEBSITE\HTDOCS\BOOK\GBDIR1\ directory, and type the following HTML text:

```
<HTML>
<HEAD>
<TITLE>Guest Book - List Form (GBDIR1)</TITLE>
</HEAD>
<BODY>
<H1>Guest Book - List Form (GBDIR1)</H1><P>
<FORM METHOD=POST ACTION=/cgi-win/book/multigb/gblist.exe/book/gbdir1>
<B>Enter Starting Date (mm/dd/yy):  </B>
<INPUT NAME="StartingDate" TYPE="TEXT" MAXLENGTH=8 SIZE=8>
<BR>
<INPUT NAME="Submit" TYPE="SUBMIT" VALUE="View">
<INPUT NAME="Reset" TYPE="RESET">
</FORM>
</BODY>
</HTML>
```

2. Create another text file named *GBLIST2.HTM* with the following HTML text in the C:\WEBSITE\HTDOCS\BOOK\GBDIR2\ directory:

```
<HTML>
<HEAD>
<TITLE>Guest Book - List Form (GBDIR2)</TITLE>
</HEAD>
<BODY>
<H1>Guest Book - List Form (GBDIR2)</H1><P>
<FORM METHOD=POST ACTION=/cgi-win/book/multigb/gblist.exe/book/gbdir2>
<B>Enter Starting Date (mm/dd/yy):  </B>
<INPUT NAME="StartingDate" TYPE="TEXT" MAXLENGTH=8 SIZE=8>
<BR>
<INPUT NAME="Submit" TYPE="SUBMIT" VALUE="View">
<INPUT NAME="Reset" TYPE="RESET">
</FORM>
</BODY>
</HTML>
```

Figure 12-4 shows the GBLIST1.HTM form through a Web browser.

3. Finally, you can set up the main menu form which points to the two entry forms and the two listing forms. Create a text file named *GBMAIN.HTM* in the C:\WEBSITE\HTDOCS\BOOK\GBDIR1\ directory, and type the following text:

```
<TITLE>Guest Book Main Menu</TITLE>
</HEAD>
<BODY>
<H1>Guest Book Main Menu</H1><P>
<H2>
<OL>
<LI><A HREF="/book/gbdir1/gbadd1.htm">
```

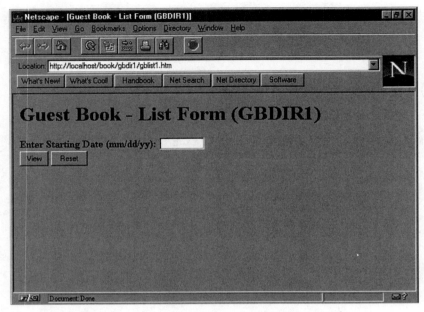

Figure 12–4 Web browser displaying the GBLIST1.HTM form

```
Add an entry to the first guest book</A>
<LI><A HREF="/book/gbdir2/gbadd2.htm">
Add an entry to the second guest book</A>
<LI><A HREF="/book/gbdir1/gblist1.htm">
List entries from the first guest book</A>
<LI><A HREF="/book/gbdir2/gblist2.htm">
List entries from the second guest book</A>
</OL>
</H2>
</BODY>
</HTML>
```

Figure 12-5 shows the main menu through a Web browser.

LESSON 4: DESIGNING THE APPLICATION'S BACK-END

After defining a functional front-end for the Multi-Guestbook application, you can concentrate on the two Windows CGI programs: GBADD.EXE and GBLIST.EXE. These two CGI programs closely resemble each other in their overall design structure, which can be described as follows:

1. Read necessary data provided by the front-end.

2. Check for data integrity and accuracy.

340

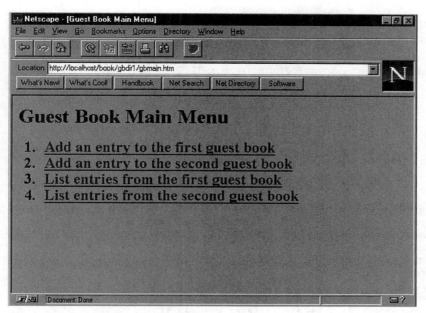

Figure 12–5 Web browser displaying the main menu

3. Hook to the specified GBOOK.MDB database to perform the desired action.

4. Generate an appropriate response.

5. Handle errors gracefully.

Also note that, according to the application's implementation design, these two programs are to be requested by use of the URL path */cgi-win/book/multigb/* and thus must reside in the C:\WEBSITE\CGI-WIN\BOOK\MULTIGB\ directory (unless you assign a different Windows CGI mapping for this URL path, as explained in the section, "CGI Mapping," of Chapter 2, Getting Started.)

Creating the **GBADD.EXE** Windows CGI Program

You can use the template project method described in the previous chapter to create the GBADD.EXE program as follows:

1. Create two new subdirectories, *MULTIGB* and *GBADD,* under the C:\WEBSITE\CGI-WIN\BOOK\ directory.

You will store the source files in the GBADD directory and the final GBADD.EXE file in the MULTIGB directory.

2. Copy the template project to the GBADD directory by issuing the following commands from an MS-DOS prompt:

```
cd c:\website\cgi-win\book <ENTER>
copy newapp\newapp.vbp gbadd\gbadd.vbp <ENTER>
copy newapp\newapp.bas gbadd <ENTER>
```

3. Launch Visual Basic and open the GBADD.VBP project file.

Open the Project window and double-click on NEWAPP.BAS to display this module's Code window.

4. Declare the following variables in the Declaration section of the NEWAPP.BAS module:

```
Dim Name As String            ' Guest book entry form field
Dim EmailAddress As String    '              "
Dim PhoneNumber As String     '              "
Dim Comments As String        '              "
Dim DateOfBirth As Variant    '              "
Dim Response As String        ' Guest book entry form's hidden field
Dim DataBaseFile As String    ' Path/Name of the guest book database
Dim ErrorMessage As String    ' Error message if any
```

NOTE: These variables automatically get a global scope within the NEWAPP.BAS module since they are defined in its Declaration section.

5. Using the Procedure selector of the NEWAPP.BAS module's Code window, go to the sample CGI_Main procedure and modify it as follows:

```
Sub CGI_Main()

    'Add Error Handler
    On Error Goto Err_CGI_Main

    'The overall steps
    ErrorMessage = ""         'Initially no error
    ReadFormData              'Read form data in the declared variables
    CheckDataValidity         'Check for required fields and valid data
    AddDataToGuestBook        'Add data to the guest book database
    GenerateResponse          'Send appropriate response

Exit_CGI_Main:
    Exit Sub                  'Exit this procedure

'Error Handling Section
Err_CGI_Main:
    HandleError               'Handle Error gracefully
    Resume Exit_CGI_Main      'Return to the Exit_CGI_Main section

End Sub
```

As you can see, this CGI_Main procedure follows the structured programming style by distributing the tasks among other procedures. It also sets its own error-trapping mechanism which not only helps in handling unexpected runtime errors, but also plays an important role in the logical flow of the program. The latter will become clear when you see the design of the CheckDataValidity procedure.

Reading Form Data

The first procedure that CGI_Main calls is ReadFormData. This procedure assigns the form field variables declared in the Declaration section with the appropriate data values. To create this new procedure in the NEWAPP.BAS module:

1. Ensure that the NEWAPP.BAS module's Code window is active.

2. Select the Procedure option from VB's Insert menu to create a new procedure.

VB asks for a new procedure name as shown in Figure 12-6.

3. Type *ReadFormData* in the Name field, and click on the OK button.

VB takes you to an empty ReadFormData procedure. (See Figure 12-7.)

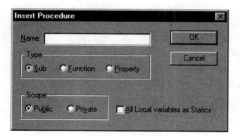

Figure 12–6 Inserting a new procedure in Visual Basic

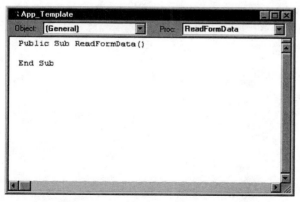

Figure 12–7 Empty ReadFormData procedure

343

4. Design the ReadFormData procedure as shown next:

```
'==================================================================
'  Purpose: Reads form data into the VB variables
'
'  Assumes: CGI32.BAS module is included with this project
'
'                              Notes
'                              -----
'  Tries to read all the expected form fields using the GetSmallField
'  function provided in the CGI32.BAS library module.
'
'==================================================================
Public Sub ReadFormData()

    Name = GetSmallField("Name")
    EmailAddress = GetSmallField("Email Address")
    PhoneNumber = GetSmallField("Phone Number")
    DateOfBirth = GetSmallField("Date Of Birth")
    Comments = GetSmallField("Comments")
    Response = GetSmallField("Response")

End Sub
```

As you can see, the ReadFormData procedure mainly uses the GetSmallField function provided in the CGI32.BAS library module to accomplish its task. To understand how this GetSmallField function works, let's recall how the CGI32.BAS library module stores the decoded form data.

As described in Lesson 6 of Chapter 11, Designing a Windows CGI Application, the CGI32.BAS library module reads the decoded form data from the CGI Profile file into a global array named CGI_FormTuples. The elements of CGI_FormTuples are made up of two components: Key and Value. For each element, the *Key* holds the name of the data field as specified in the HTML form, and the *Value* holds the data passed by the Web client for that field.

The GetSmallField function, which takes a string input parameter, simply scans the Key of each element in the CGI_FormTuples array until it finds a match for that input parameter, and then returns the Value associated with that key. In case the function cannot find a matching key, it generates a user-defined error. The code for the GetSmallField procedure is listed as follows:

```
'------------------------------------------------------------------
'
' Get the value of a "small" form field given the key
'
' Signals an error if field does not exist
'
'------------------------------------------------------------------
Function GetSmallField(key As String) As String
    Dim i As Integer

    For i = 0 To (CGI_NumFormTuples - 1)
        If CGI_FormTuples(i).key = key Then
```

```
            GetSmallField = Trim$(CGI_FormTuples(i).value)
            Exit Function           ' ** DONE **
        End If
    Next i
    '
    ' Field does not exist
    '
    Error ERR_NO_FIELD
End Function
```

NOTE: The GetSmallField procedure returns the data value after trimming the leading and trailing spaces.

Ensuring Data Validity

The ReadFormData procedure does not perform any checks for the integrity or accuracy of the data. It simply puts the necessary form data into appropriate VB variables. For example, if the user enters an invalid date such as 11/38/99 for the Date Of Birth field, ReadFormData will set the DateOfBirth variable to the "11/38/99" string. This is also the reason why the DateOfBirth variable is declared as a Variant type instead of VB's Date data type.

The CheckDataValidity procedure examines the assigned data more carefully. It essentially has two functions:

Check for the presence of required data.

Check for valid data.

The Name and Email Address fields fall under the category of the required data, whereas the date field needs to be verified for valid data. You can add the following CheckDataValidity procedure to the NEWAPP.BAS module using the steps described for the ReadFormData procedure:

```
'================================================================
'  Purpose: Checks for required and valid data
'
'                          Notes
'                          -----
'  Required Data: Name and Email Address fields
'  Valid Data Check: Date field
'
'================================================================
Public Sub CheckDataValidity()
  If Name = "" Then
    ErrorMessage = "The name must be specified."
    Error ERR_BAD_REQUEST
  End If
  If EmailAddress = "" Then
    ErrorMessage = "The email address must be specified."
```

continued on next page

continued from previous page

```
      Error ERR_BAD_REQUEST
  End If
If DateOfBirth <> "" And Not IsDate(DateOfBirth) Then
    ErrorMessage = "Please specify a valid date of birth."
    Error ERR_BAD_REQUEST
  End If

End Sub
```

The CheckDataValidity procedure generates an ERR_BAD_REQUEST error anytime it finds something wrong with the data. It also lists the reason in the ErrorMessage VB variable. The ERR_BAD_REQUEST is a global constant defined in the CGI32.BAS module.

The signaling of the error causes the flow control to immediately go to the Err_CGI_Main section of the CGI_Main procedure, where the HandleError procedure (described later in this lesson) notifies the user of the error. Observe that when such a situation occurs, the AddDataToGuestBook and the GenerateResponse procedures automatically get bypassed.

Processing Data

If the CheckDataValidity procedure does not flag any error, you can assume that the data meets the required guest book entry specifications, and you can process the entry by performing the following tasks:

1. Determine the path of the GBOOK.MDB database file.

2. Ensure that the supplied entry is not a duplicate.

3. Add the entry to the GBOOK.MDB database.

The next chapter describes how you will handle tasks 2 and 3. For now, you can just design the AddDataToGuestBook procedure where you only evaluate the path/name of the GBOOK.MDB file based on the CGI_PhysicalPath variable. So, insert the following AddDataToGuestBook procedure to your NEWAPP.BAS module:

```
Public Sub AddDataToGuestBook()

  DatabaseFile = CGI_PhysicalPath & "\GBOOK.MDB"  '& means join

  'Write code to add data to the guest book database

End Sub
```

Generating Output

Finally, you need to return a response in the CGI output file by designing the GenerateResponse procedure. This is where you will consider the Response field that accompanies the form data.

Moreover, since you are not actually adding the entry to the guest book yet, you can temporarily display the values of the guest book entry fields and other computed variables to indicate that your program's interface is working correctly.

You can thus insert the following GenerateResponse procedure in your NEWAPP.BAS module:

```
Public Sub GenerateResponse()

  Send ("Content-type: text/html")
  Send ("")
  Send ("<HTML>")
  Send ("<HEAD>")
  Send ("<TITLE>Guest Book Entry Added</TITLE>")
  Send ("</HEAD>")
  Send ("<BODY>")
  If Response = "" Then
    Send ("<H1>Thank you for signing the guest book!</H1>")
  Else
    Send (Response)
  End If
  Send ("<H3>Temporary Output</H3>")
  Send ("Name: " & Name)
  Send ("<BR>Email: " & EmailAddress)
  Send ("<BR>Phone#: " & PhoneNumber)
  Send ("<BR>BirthDate: " & DateOfBirth)
  Send ("<BR>Comments: " & Comments)
  Send ("<BR>Database File: " & DataBaseFile)
  Send ("</BODY>")
  Send ("</HTML>")

End Sub
```

Handling Errors

The HandleError procedure is similar to the GenerateResponse procedure, except it sends the error message instead of the normal output. You can design the HandleError procedure as shown next:

```
Public Sub HandleError()

  Send ("Content-type: text/html")
  Send ("")
  Send ("<HTML>")
  Send ("<HEAD>")
  Send ("<TITLE>Error</TITLE>")
  Send ("</HEAD>")
  Send ("<BODY>")
  If ErrorMessage = "" Then
    Send ("<H2>" & Error$ & "</H2>")          'Send VB's error message
  Else
    Send ("<H2>" & ErrorMessage & "</H2>") 'Send user-defined message
  End If
  Send ("</BODY>")
  Send ("</HTML>")

End Sub
```

Compiling Your Project

After you have created all the procedures, save the NEWAPP.BAS module file as well as the NEWAPP.VBP project itself. Then compile your project to create the GBADD.EXE executable file in the C:\WEBSITE\CGI-WIN\BOOK\MULTIGB directory (not the GBADD directory).

Creating the GBLIST.EXE Windows CGI Program

The main task of the GBLIST.EXE is to list the guest book entries entered after a specified date. As mentioned earlier, the basic design structure of the GBLIST.EXE program is similar to the structure of the GBADD.EXE program.

Again, you will design the actual code for retrieving the entries from the GBOOK.MDB file in the next chapter. Here, you will create only a functional prototype of the GBLIST.EXE program as follows:

1. Create a subdirectory named *GBLIST* under the C:\WEBSITE\CGI-WIN\BOOK\ directory.

2. Copy the template project to the GBLIST directory by issuing the following commands from an MS-DOS prompt:

```
cd c:\website\cgi-win\book <ENTER>
copy newapp\newapp.vbp gblist\gblist.vbp <ENTER>
copy newapp\newapp.bas gblist <ENTER>
```

3. Launch Visual Basic and open the GBLIST.VBP project file.

4. Declare the following variables in the Declaration section of the NEWAPP.BAS module:

```
Dim StartingDate As Variant   ' Form field
Dim DataBaseFile As String    ' Path/Name of the guest book database
Dim ErrorMessage As String    ' Error message if any
```

5. Design the CGI_Main procedure in the NEWAPP.BAS module as follows:

```
Sub CGI_Main()

    'Add Error Handler
    On Error Goto Err_CGI_Main

    'The overall steps
    ErrorMessage = ""         'Initially no error
    ReadFormData              'Read form data in the declared variables
    CheckDataValidity         'Check for required fields and valid data
    SelectDataFromGuestBook   'Select data from the guest book database
    GenerateResponse          'List selected data
```

```
Exit_CGI_Main:
  Exit Sub                      'Exit this procedure

'Error Handling Section
Err_CGI_Main:
  HandleError                   'Handle Error gracefully
  Resume Exit_CGI_Main          'Return to the Exit_CGI_Main section

End Sub
```

6. Insert the following five subprocedures in the NEWAPP.BAS module. Many of these procedures are conceptually similar to the ones we designed for the GBADD.EXE program:

```
Public Sub ReadFormData()

  StartingDate = GetSmallField("StartingDate ")

End Sub

Public Sub CheckDataValidity()

  If Not IsDate(StartingDate) Then
    ErrorMessage = "Please specify a valid starting date."
    Error ERR_BAD_REQUEST
  End If

End Sub

Public Sub SelectDataFromGuestBook()

  DatabaseFile = CGI_PhysicalPath & "\GBOOK.MDB"

  'Write code to select data from the guest book database

End Sub

Public Sub GenerateResponse()

  Send ("Content-type: text/html")
  Send ("")
  Send ("<HTML><HEAD><TITLE>")
  Send ("Guest Book Listing")
  Send ("</TITLE></HEAD><BODY>")
  Send ("<H2>Here are the guest book entries signed after ")
  Send (StartingDate & "</H2>")
  Send ("<H3>(Guest book entries will be listed here)</H3>")
  Send ("<H3>Temporary Output</H3>")
  Send ("Database File: " & DataBaseFile)
  Send ("</BODY></HTML>")

End Sub
```

continued on next page

continued from previous page

```
Public Sub HandleError()

    Send ("Content-type: text/html")
    Send ("")
    Send ("</TITLE></HEAD><BODY>")
    Send ("Error")
    Send ("</TITLE></HEAD><BODY>")
    If ErrorMessage = "" Then
       Send ("<H2>" & Error$ & "</H2>")        'Send VB's error message
    Else
       Send ("<H2>" & ErrorMessage & "</H2>") 'Send user-defined message
    End If
    Send ("</BODY></HTML>")

End Sub
```

7. Compile the GBLIST.VBP project to create the GBLIST.EXE executable file in the C:\WEBSITE\CGI-WIN\BOOK\MULTIGB\ directory.

LESSON 5: TESTING YOUR WEB APPLICATION

Even though you have not yet written the code for actually adding and listing the guest book entries, you can still test the interface between the front-end and the back-end to verify that the data is being handled as expected.

During your application's testing phase, you should try to check for as many types of data input cases as possible. You should start by testing your application with valid data inputs and gradually move into the domain of invalid data patterns to see how well your application works under the unexpected situations.

Testing with Valid Data in All Fields

To test your application against a normal case where you enter valid data in all the fields:

1. Start your Web server if it is not already running.

2. Display the main menu of your guest book application (see Figure 12-5) by specifying the following URL from your Web client:

`http://localhost/gbdir1/gbmain.htm`

3. Click on option 1, "Add an entry to the first guest book."

The browser takes you to your first guest book entry form. See Figure 12-2 in Lesson 3.

4. Fill in all the fields as shown in Figure 12-8, and click on the Enter button.

The back-end GBADD.EXE program returns the expected response as shown in Figure 12-9.

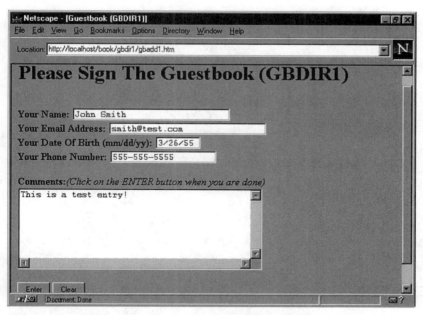

Figure 12–8 First guest book entry form filled in with valid data

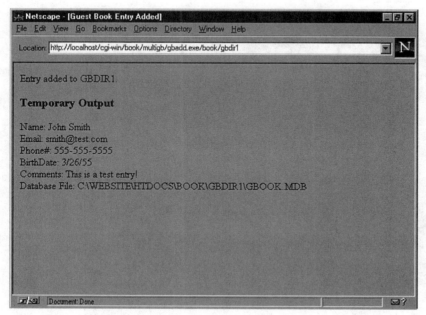

Figure 12–9 Response from the GBADD.EXE program to a valid input case

5. Now, return to the main menu and select option 3, "List entries from the first guest book."

   The browser displays the guest book listing form. Refer to Figure 12-4 in Lesson 3.

6. Specify a valid starting date such as *1/1/94,* and click on the View button.

   The GBLIST.EXE program also returns the expected response as shown in Figure 12-10.

Testing with Invalid Data

So far, things look good. Now let's see if these programs catch invalid cases:

1. Ensure that your Web server is running.

2. Select the first guest book entry form from your guest book application's main menu.

3. Fill in all the fields with the data shown in Figure 12-8 except the Email Address field, which you should leave blank. Then click on the Enter button.

   The GBADD.EXE program returns a message asking you to specify the e-mail address. (See Figure 12-11.)

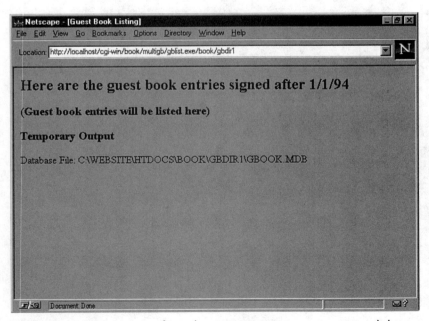

Figure 12-10 Response from the GBADD.EXE program to a valid input case

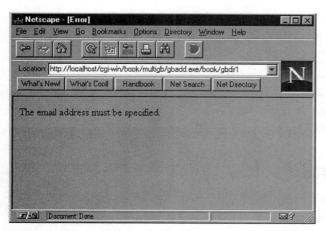

Figure 12–11 The GBADD.EXE program responding to insufficient input data

4. Now, using the Back button of your browser, return to the guest book entry form. Fill in the e-mail address field, but change the date of birth to, say, *13/26/55*. Then click on the Enter button.

This time the GBADD.EXE program responds by asking you to specify a valid date as shown in Figure 12-12.

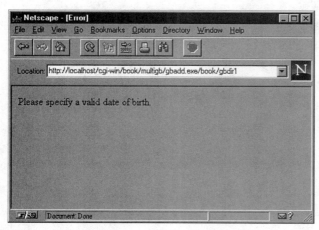

Figure 12–12 The GBADD.EXE program responding to an invalid date

5. Let's see how the GBADD.EXE program handles an invalid phone number. Return to the guest book entry form, and change the date of birth to *3/26/95.* Specify the value *999::????* for the phone number field, and click on the Enter button.

The GBADD.EXE accepts the spooky phone number with the rest of the data as shown by its response in Figure 12-13. This makes sense since the GBADD.EXE is currently not programmed to perform any special checks on the data associated with the phone number field.

Testing with Optional Fields

As noted in Lesson 3, there are two ways of looking at an optional field:

⚡ As a form field where a user is not required to fill any data

⚡ As a field that you can eliminate from the form itself

So, to test your application with respect to the optional fields, you need to consider both cases:

1. Ensure that your Web server is running.

2. Select the first guest book entry form (option 1) from your guest book application's main menu.

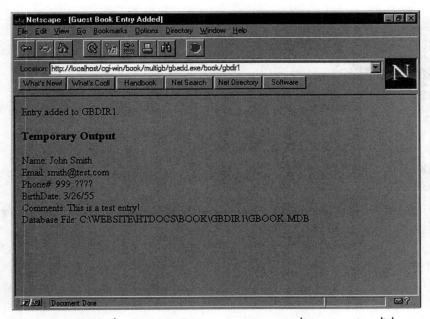

Figure 12–13 The GBADD.EXE program responding to an invalid phone number

3. Fill in all the fields with the data shown in Figure 12-8 except the phone number optional field, which you should leave blank. Then click on the Enter button.

The GBADD.EXE program returns a response indicating your entry with a blank phone number has been accepted. (See Figure 12-14.)

Now, let's test the GBADD.EXE program using the second guest book entry form (GBADD2.HTM), where some optional fields have been eliminated from the form itself:

1. Select the second guest book entry form (option 2) from your guest book application's main menu. (See Figure 12-3 in Lesson 3.)

2. Fill in all the fields as shown in Figure 12-15, and then click on the Enter button.

The browser displays an empty screen in response to your request as shown in Figure 12-16.

What happened? Did you get a response from the GBADD.EXE program at all? Observe the title of the browser's window. It says "Error." Now, display the HTML text behind this empty response by using your browser's document source viewing capability. (See Figure 12-17.)

As indicated by Figure 12-17, the GBADD.EXE program did return a response, but not the response expected. Furthermore, the Title tag in the response indicates that the response was generated by the HandleError procedure. Interestingly, no error message is listed in the body of the text.

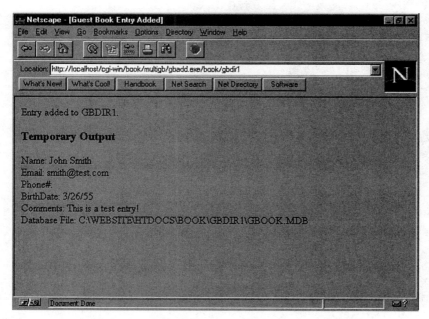

Figure 12–14 The GBADD.EXE program responding to a blank optional field

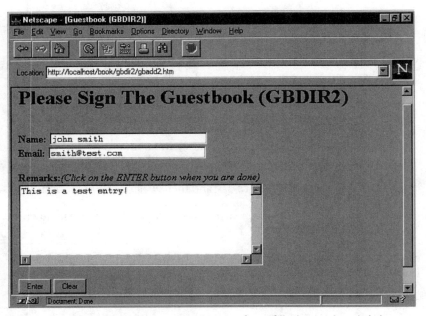

Figure 12–15 Second guest book entry form filled in with valid data

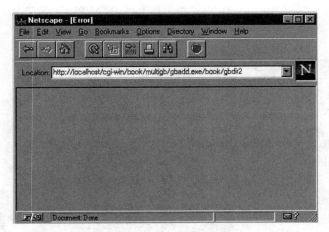

Figure 12–16 Response to submitting the second guest book entry form

Now the perplexing question is, "What is causing this unexpected behavior?" One way to answer this question is to go back to the GBADD.EXE program's source listing and carefully review the code. However, this is certainly not an easy way to locate the bug. It would be nice if you could trace through a live execution of the GBADD.EXE program for this CGI request and see why it generates this response.

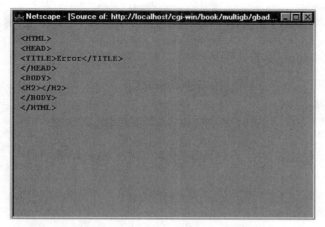

Figure 12–17 HTML text behind the response

Fortunately, the Windows CGI's file-based input/output model provides an ideal platform to perform such live debugging. In the next lesson you will see how you can take advantage of this file model along with the powerful debugging facilities of Visual Basic's integrated development environment to quickly track down the problem.

LESSON 6: DEBUGGING YOUR WEB APPLICATION

The process of debugging your Web application requires you to simulate the environment created by the Web server when it launches the CGI program. To enact this simulation:

1. Capture the CGI Profile file created by the Web server for the CGI request being debugged, and assign it a more distinct name such as *T.INI*.

2. Configure the environment options of your CGI program's project to specify the path and file name of the T.INI file as the command-line argument.

3. Trace the Windows CGI program within the development environment while monitoring the control flow and the values of the declared variables.

Capturing the CGI Profile File

You capture the CGI Profile file by enabling the CGI tracing configuration option of your WebSite server and reexecuting the CGI request that caused your Windows CGI program to return incorrect results. The following steps describe this procedure:

1. Launch the Server Admin utility of your WebSite server.

   The Server Admin utility displays the General section, which lists the path of the CGI-TEMP directory as shown in Figure 12-18.

2. Click on the Logging tab, and select the API/CGI Execution tracing option if it is not already selected. (See Figure 12-19.) Click on OK to close the Server Admin utility and to update the changes to the WebSite server.

3. Delete all the previous temporary files from the CGI-TEMP directory by executing the following MS-DOS commands:

   ```
   cd c:\website\cgi-temp
   del *.*
   ```

4. Ensure that your WebSite server is running.

5. Resubmit the second guest book entry form with all the fields filled in and wait for the blank response.

6. Using the MS-DOS prompt, list the new temporary CGI files created by the server as shown in Figure 12-20.

NOTE: Your temporary files may have different names.

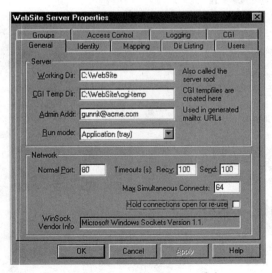

Figure 12–18 General section of the Server Admin utility

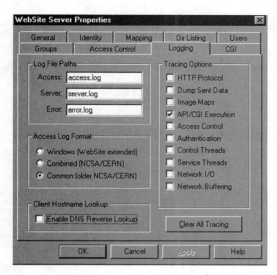

Figure 12–19 Logging section of the
Server Admin utility

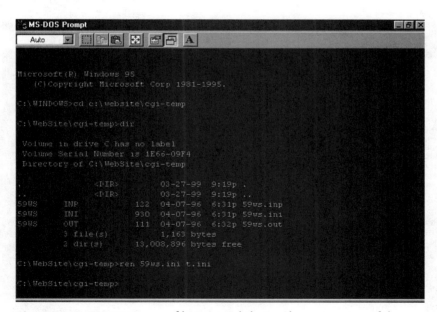

Figure 12–20 Temporary files created during the processing of the
CGI request

7. Rename the temporary .INI file to *T.INI*. Figure 12-21 shows a portion of the T.INI file. You can review the T.INI file to ensure that the front-end is passing data as expected.

Configuring the Environment Options of Your VB Project

Next, you need to tell Visual Basic what command-line argument to supply when you trace your program within VB's development environment. To configure this option in your VB project:

1. Load your C:\WEBSITE\CGI-WIN\BOOK\GBADD\GBADD.VBP project in Visual Basic.

2. Select Options from VB's Tools menu.

3. Click on the Advanced tab.

4. Type *c:\website\cgi-temp\t.ini* in the Command Line Arguments text box, and click on the OK button. (See Figure 12-22.)

```
t.ini - Notepad
File  Edit  Search  Help
Request Method=POST
Request Keep-Alive=Yes
Executable Path=/cgi-win/book/multigb/gbadd.exe
Logical Path=/book/gbdir2
Physical Path=C:\WEBSITE\HTDOCS\BOOK\GBDIR2
Server Software=WebSite/1.1 (demo version)
Server Name=localhost
Server Port=80
Server Admin=gunnit@nfinity.nfinity.com
CGI Version=CGI/1.3 (Win)
Remote Address=127.0.0.1
Referer=http://localhost/book/gbdir2/gbadd2.htm
User Agent=Mozilla/2.0 (Win95; I)
Content Type=application/x-www-form-urlencoded
Content Length=122

[System]
GMT Offset=-21600
Debug Mode=Yes
Output File=C:\WebSite\cgi-temp\59ws.out
Content File=C:\WEBSITE\CGI-TEMP\59WS.INP

[Form Literal]
Name=john smith
Email Address=smith@test.com
Comments=This is a test entry!
Response=Entry added to GBDIR2.
Submit=Enter
```

Figure 12-21 Contents of the T.INI file

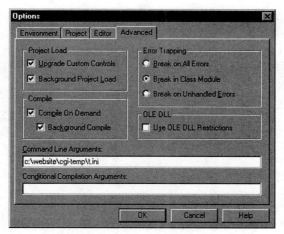

Figure 12–22 Specifying the command-line arguments in a VB project

Tracing the Windows CGI Program Execution

The Visual Basic development environment allows you to trace each step of your program's execution and monitor the values of the variables at each step. The following procedure describes how you can use these tracing features to debug your program:

1. Go to the CGI_Main procedure of the NEWAPP.BAS module, and place the cursor on the line that says "On Error Goto Err_CGI_Main."

2. Press F9 to insert a break point on this line. (See Figure 12-23.)

3. Press F5 to start executing your program.

VB starts with the Main procedure of the CGI32.BAS module and then stops at the break point inserted in the CGI_Main procedure. From here, you can single-step through the program to pinpoint the location of the error.

4. Press F8 to go to the next line. Keep pressing F8 until you enter the ReadFormData procedure as shown in Figure 12-24.

5. Press (SHIFT)-(F8) to step over the GetSmallField function so that you can move directly to the line that assigns the EmailAddress variable.

6. Press (SHIFT)-(F8) to move to the line that assigns the PhoneNumber variable.

7. Press (SHIFT)-(F8) again to step over this line.

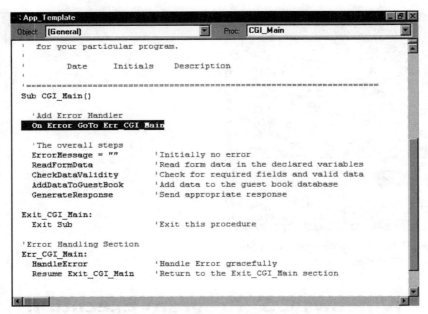

```
App_Template                                              _ 6 X
Object: [General]              ▼    Proc:  CGI_Main              ▼

'    for your particular program.
'
'         Date     Initials    Description
'
'==================================================================
Sub CGI_Main()

  'Add Error Handler
  On Error GoTo Err_CGI_Main

  'The overall steps
  ErrorMessage = ""              'Initially no error
  ReadFormData                   'Read form data in the declared variables
  CheckDataValidity              'Check for required fields and valid data
  AddDataToGuestBook             'Add data to the guest book database
  GenerateResponse               'Send appropriate response

Exit_CGI_Main:
  Exit Sub                       'Exit this procedure

'Error Handling Section
Err_CGI_Main:
  HandleError                    'Handle Error gracefully
  Resume Exit_CGI_Main           'Return to the Exit_CGI_Main section
```

Figure 12–23 Inserting a break point in the CGI_Main procedure

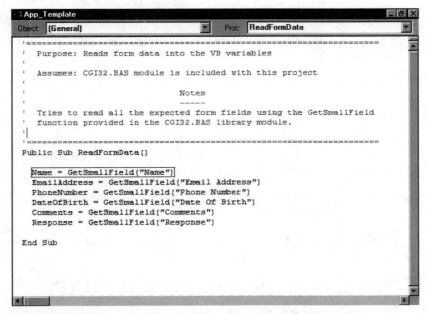

```
App_Template                                              _ 6 X
Object: [General]              ▼    Proc:  ReadFormData          ▼

'==================================================================
'  Purpose: Reads form data into the VB variables
'
'  Assumes: CGI32.BAS module is included with this project
'
'                        Notes
'                        -----
'  Tries to read all the expected form fields using the GetSmallField
'  function provided in the CGI32.BAS library module.
'|
'==================================================================
Public Sub ReadFormData()

  Name = GetSmallField("Name")
  EmailAddress = GetSmallField("Email Address")
  PhoneNumber = GetSmallField("Phone Number")
  DateOfBirth = GetSmallField("Date Of Birth")
  Comments = GetSmallField("Comments")
  Response = GetSmallField("Response")

End Sub
```

Figure 12–24 Tracing the ReadFormData procedure

You will notice that the execution control goes to the error-handling section of the CGI_Main procedure instead of moving to the next line of the ReadFormData procedure as shown in Figure 12-25.

The GetSmallField function generates an error when it is asked to return the value of the "Phone Number" field. This also coincides with the fact that the Phone Number field is absent from the second guest book entry form and is thus not passed with the CGI request.

If you review the code of the GetSmallField function listed in Lesson 4, you will observe that the GetSmallField function is designed to signal an error if it is unable to find a key matching the given parameter. As there is no Phone Number field accompanying the CGI request, the GetSmallField rightfully generates an ERR_NO_FIELD error.

Since we want to allow the absence of the optional fields just like they were fields with a blank data value, we need to properly handle the error generated by the GetSmallField function. The simplest option is to ignore this error in the ReadFormData procedure. You can accomplish this by adding an On Error Resume Next line in the beginning of the ReadFormData procedure as follows:

1. Press [F5] to complete the execution of your program.

2. Go to the ReadFormData procedure in the NEWAPP.BAS module, and add an On Error Resume Next line in the beginning of this procedure as shown in Figure 12-26.

Figure 12–25 Control going to the error-handling section

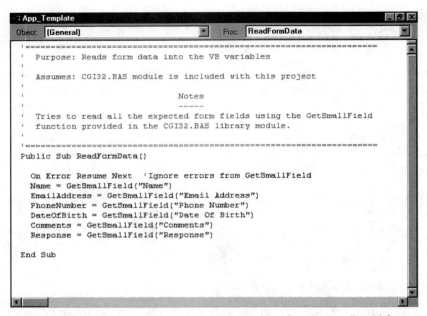

Figure 12-26 Ignoring the error generated by the GetSmallField function

3. Save and compile your project to re-create a new *GBADD.EXE* file in the C:\WEBSITE\CGI-WIN\BOOK\MULTIGB\ directory.

4. Resubmit the second guest book entry form to test the new GBADD.EXE program.

5. This time the GBADD.EXE program accepts the absence of optional fields as shown by Figure 12-27.

Note that while the ReadFormData procedure simply reads what it can, the CheckDataValidity procedure will still trap any missing required fields. Also, all the VB variables for which the GetSmallField function returns an error keep their original value, which in this case is an empty string ("").

REVIEW QUESTIONS

1. What are the two main components of an interactive Web application?

2. List the issues you need to address before implementing an interactive CGI application.

3. What are the advantages of defining the objectives of a Web application?

4. What is an implementation design phase? Why do you need it?

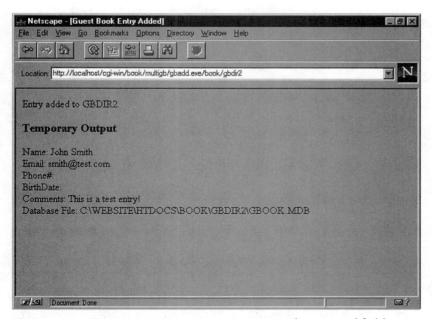

Figure 12–27 GBADD.EXE program accepting the optional fields

5. What is the first goal when creating a Web application's front-end?

6. Why should the two guest book entry forms have matching names for their input fields?

7. Which fields can you eliminate from a guest book entry form?

8. Why do the layout differences of the two guest book entry forms not affect the Multi-Guestbook application's back-end?

9. What is the main difference between the two guest book listing forms?

10. How does the front-end of the Multi-Guestbook application pass the guest book directory path to the back-end?

11. Why do the Windows CGI programs, GBADD.EXE and GBLIST.EXE, need to reside in the C:\WEBSITE\CGI-WIN\BOOK\MULTIGB\ directory?

12. What is the basic design structure of the GBADD.EXE and GBLIST.EXE programs?

13. How does the error-handling code of the CGI_Main procedure fit in the program's logical flow?

14. What is the role of the ReadFormData procedure in the GBADD.EXE program?

15. What is the role of the CheckDataValidity procedure in the GBADD.EXE program?

16. How is the data passed between the procedures of the NEWAPP.BAS module in the GBADD.EXE program?

17. Why is the StartingDate variable declared as a Variant type instead of the Date type?

18. What does the GetSmallField function do?

19. List the different types of cases that you can use to test your Web application.

20. What are the steps involved in debugging a CGI program?

EXERCISES

1. Change the GBADD.EXE program so that it only accepts valid phone numbers. For this exercise, a valid phone can be considered as any numeric string separated only by hyphens and a parenthesis pair.

2. Create another guest book directory named *GBDIR3* under the C:\WEBSITE\HTDOCS\BOOK directory. Design a new pair of guest book entry and listing forms, *GBADD3.HTM* and *GBLIST3.HTM,* in this directory which will act as a front-end interface for the guest book residing in this directory.

3. Change the GBLIST.EXE program so that it treats the starting date field as an optional field.

4. Redesign the Multi-Guestbook application so that it only uses one Windows CGI program for its back-end. (Hint: You can pass the Add or List action as another hidden field.)

13

UTILIZING AN ACCESS DATABASE IN A CGI APPLICATION

13

In the previous chapter, you studied how to create a working prototype of the Multi-Guestbook application. This prototype lays down the necessary groundwork for processing user requests, but does not actually add or list any guest book entries. For the add and list operations, the application's back-end Windows CGI programs, GBADD.EXE and GBLIST.EXE need to interact with the appropriate GBOOK.MDB Microsoft Access database file.

This chapter describes how to complete this missing portion of the Multi-Guestbook application. You will start by designing the structure of the GBOOK.MDB database. Then, you will modify the two CGI programs to utilize this GBOOK.MDB database for storing and retrieving the guest book entries.

LESSON 1: CREATING THE DATABASE FILE

The main factor to consider while designing the GBOOK.MDB database is that it needs to be a generic database file that you can simply copy to different directories for setting up multiple guest books. The structure of this generic database, hence, must be able to accommodate every guest book entry field listed in the application's specifications, even though some guest books may not use all the optional fields.

Furthermore, you also need to track the date when a guest book entry is submitted, as the GBLIST program will require this information to return the entries submitted after a given date. Table 13-1 lists the attributes of all the fields that need to be stored in the guest book database. It is easy to figure out that one database table is sufficient for defining these fields. We will name this table *tblGB_Entries*.

Table 13-1 Guest book fields that need to be stored in the database

FieldName	DataType	Field Value	Default Size	Field Type	Allow Zero Length
DateAdded	Date/Time		=Date()	Required	
Name	Text	50		Required	No
EmailAddress	Text	50		Required	No
PhoneNumber	Text	20		Optional	Yes
DateOfBirth	Date/Time			Optional	
Comments	Memo			Optional	Yes

Next, you need to determine a suitable primary key for the tblGB_Entries table. The rule for selecting a primary key is that it can only contain non-Null data values that must be unique for each record. This rules out all the optional fields. Moreover, no single required field can be assumed to hold unique values. This leaves you with two options:

🦞 Add a new AutoNumber field and assign it as a primary key.

🦞 Use a combination of required fields to act as a primary key.

To decide which option to select, consider the issue of preventing a user from submitting duplicate entries at this point. The principal reason for requiring a duplicate-entry check was to handle the situation where a user submits an entry and then accidentally (or even intentionally!) submits that entry again.

If we create a composite primary key using the DateAdded, Name, and EmailAddress fields, then the database will permit only one entry from the same user on any given day. This is a reasonable restriction, and as you will see in the next two lessons, it is not hard to find out through code that the same entry is being submitted more than once in one day.

To construct the GBOOK.MDB database file, you will use the design process outlined in Chapter 4, Building a Database with Microsoft Access. Follow these steps:

1. Launch Microsoft Access and pick the Create A New Database Using Blank Database option.

Microsoft Access pops up the Windows File dialog box, prompting you for the name of the new database file.

2. Select the C:\WEBSITE\CGI-WIN\BOOK\MULTIGB\ directory using the directory selector of this dialog box, and type *GBOOK.MDB* in the File Name field. Then, click on the Create button.

Microsoft Access creates a new GBOOK.MDB database and shows its empty database container. The Table tab is selected by default.

3. Click on the New button listed on the database container, and then select the Design View option.

Access opens the design view of a new table.

4. Define the table fields and their properties based on the information provided in Table 13-1.

5. Highlight the DateAdded, Name, and EmailAddress fields, and select the Primary Key option from the Edit menu to set a composite primary key, as shown in Figure 13-1.

6. Save the new table as *tblGB_Entries* by selecting the Save option from the File menu.

7. Close the GBOOK.MDB database and exit Microsoft Access.

8. Copy the GBOOK.MDB file from the C:\WEBSITE\CGI-WIN\BOOK\MULTIGB directory to the two experimental directories created in the previous chapter: C:\WEBSITE\HTDOCS\BOOK\GBDIR1 and C:\WEBSITE\HTDOCS\BOOK\GBDIR2.

NOTE: A copy of the GBOOD.MDB database created in this lesson resides in C:\WEBSITE\HTDOCS\BOOK\CHAP13\RESULTS\LESSON1\ directory.

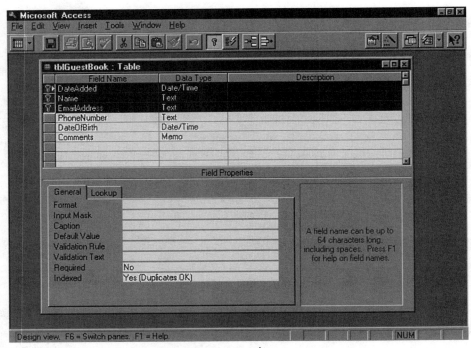

Figure 13–1 Setting a composite primary key

LESSON 2: ADDING A TABLE RECORD THROUGH VISUAL BASIC

Visual Basic provides a powerful object-oriented method for linking an Access database with your application. Essentially, all the data management operations that Microsoft Access allows you to carry out from its interactive interface you can programmatically accomplish through Visual Basic.

What makes Visual Basic's database access approach so powerful is its ability to represent database records as a *Recordset* object, which not only gives you access to virtually any data field, but also lets you work with individual records as if they were array elements. Through a Recordset object, you can add, update, and even quickly find records with minimal programming effort.

In this lesson, we will show you how to make the GBADD.EXE program add a valid guest book entry to the appropriate GBOOK.MDB database file with the help of a Recordset object. The following procedure summarizes the steps involved in accomplishing this task:

1. Declare variables for the data access Visual Basic objects.

2. Open the GBOOK.MDB database file.

3. Create a Recordset object representing the tblGuestBook table.

4. Add the new guest book entry to this recordset.

5. Trap any primary key violation error generated when adding the entry.

STEP I: Declaring Variables for the Data Access Objects

In Visual Basic, the data access objects follow a hierarchy that originates with a special object called the *DBEngine*. Figure 13-2 displays how some commonly used data access objects are related in this hierarchy.

The DBEngine object represents the Microsoft Jet database engine, which is responsible for handling all the database management operations. Microsoft Access is also built on this Jet engine.

Through the DBEngine object, you can create one or more Workspace objects. A *Workspace* object defines a session for a user. It is created by specifying a username and a password, which both define the security privileges used during the session.

When you start your application, a default Workspace object with the username *Admin* and a blank password is automatically assigned to your application. Microsoft Access also uses this default Workspace object (with the same username and password settings) when you create or open an unsecure database such as GBOOK.MDB.

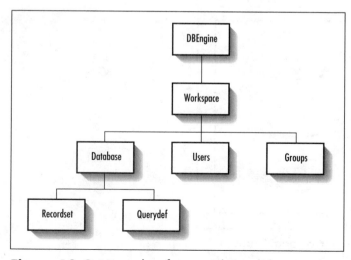

Figure 13-2 Hierarchy of commonly used data access objects

The Workspace object allows you to create multiple Database objects representing one or more database files. Each Database object can further generate other data access objects under its hierarchy, and so on.

To use these data access objects, you must first declare and associate variables with their object types as shown:

```
Dim ws As Workspace
Dim db As Database
Dim rs As Recordset
```

Note that by declaring these variables, you do not actually create the objects. These variables simply act as pointers to these objects, as shown in Figure 13-3.

STEP 2: Opening the Database File

After declaring the variables for the data access objects, you can open a Microsoft Access database file using the following statements:

```
Set ws = DBEngine.Workspaces(0)
Set db = ws.OpenDatabase(DatabaseFilePath)
```

where *DatabaseFilePath* refers to the physical location of the database file.

The first statement assigns the default workspace to the *ws* variable. The second statement calls the OpenDatabase method of the default Workspace object to return a Database object representing the specified database file. You can also merge these two statements into a single statement as follows:

```
Set db = DBEngine.Workspaces(0).OpenDatabase(DatabaseFilePath)
```

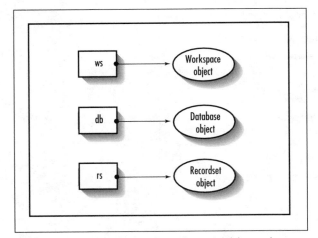

Figure 13-3 Relationship of a variable and a data access object

STEP 3: Creating a Recordset from a Database Object

As mentioned earlier, you use a Recordset object to access and manipulate database records. The Recordset object can be based on a table, a query, or an SQL statement that returns records. Depending on the nature of the record source and the sort of operations you want to perform, the Recordset object can be one of the following three types:

Table Recordset, where records are based on a single table. This is the most efficient way of accessing records.

Dynaset Recordset, where the record source is generally a query that returns updatable records. The query can be based on one or more tables.

Snapshot Recordset, which holds a static copy of the records. These records cannot be updated.

These different types of Recordset objects allow both flexibility and efficiency. For example, a Table Recordset takes minimum memory and can use user-specified indexes for quick searches. However, it lacks flexibility, since this Recordset can only be based on a single table of a database. On the other hand, the Dynaset Recordset can originate from queries involving multiple tables, but is not as efficient as the Table Recordset.

To create a Recordset object, you can use the Database object's OpenRecordset method, as follows:

```
Set rs = db.OpenRecordset(source[, type[, options]])
```

where *source* refers to a table name, a query name, or a valid SQL string; *type* can be set to any one of the three constants listed in Table 13-2; and *options* characterize the Recordset object (such as restrictions on other users' ability to edit and view the records while your recordset is active).

Table 13–2 Constants for defining a recordset type

Constant Name	Used to Open
dbOpenTable	Table Recordset
dbOpenDynaset	Dynaset Recordset
dbOpenSnapshot	Snapshot Recordset

Table 13-3 lists some important options that you may specify when creating a Recordset object. For a reference to all available recordset creation options, you can look up the keyword "OpenRecordset" in Visual Basic's on-line help.

Table 13-3 Some useful recordset options

Constant Name	Purpose
dbDenyWrite	To keep other users from modifying or adding records when the recordset is created
dbDenyRead	To keep other users from viewing records (Table Recordset only)
dbReadOnly	To allow you to only view records; other users can modify them
dbAppendOnly	To allow you only to append new records (Dynaset Recordset only)

NOTE: If you do not specify the *type* option in the OpenRecordset method, a Table Recordset is returned if the *source* is a single table. If the *source* is a query or an SQL string, the OpenRecordset method returns a Dynaset Recordset by default.

STEP 4: Adding a Record Through a Recordset Object

After you create a Recordset object, you can use its AddNew and Update methods to add a new record to the underlying record source as shown in the following code template:

```
rs.Add
rs!TableFieldName1 = DataValue1    'Assign data to the first field
rs!TableFieldName2 = DataValue2    'Assign data to the second field
. . .
rs.Update
```

Based on this code template, let's modify the source code of the GBADD.EXE program to add a guest book entry to the tblGuestBook table of the GBOOK.MDB database:

1. Open the GBADD.VBP project file residing in the C:\WEBSITE\CGI-WIN\BOOK\GBADD\ directory in Visual Basic.

2. Modify the AddDataToGuestBook procedure in the NEWAPP.BAS module as follows:

```
Public Sub AddDataToGuestBook()

    'Declare data access object variables
    Dim ws As Workspace
    Dim db As Database
    Dim rs As Recordset

    'Determine the path of the guest book database file
    DataBaseFile = CGI_PhysicalPath & "\GBOOK.MDB"

    'Open the database
    Set ws = DBEngine.Workspaces(0)
```

```
Set db = ws.OpenDatabase(DataBaseFile)

'Open the recordset representing tblGuestBook
Set rs = db.OpenRecordset("tblGB_Entries")

'Add a new record for the guest book entry
rs.AddNew
rs!Name = Name
rs!EmailAddress = EmailAddress
rs!PhoneNumber = PhoneNumber
rs!DateOfBirth = DateOfBirth
rs!Comments = Comments
rs.Update

End Sub
```

3. Select the References option from VB's Tools menu.

Visual Basic displays the list of available library references as shown in Figure 13-4.

4. Select the Microsoft DAO 3.0 Object Library option if it is not already selected, and then click on the OK button.

5. Save and recompile your project to create an updated *GBADD.EXE* file in the C:\WEBSITE\CGI-WIN\BOOK\ directory.

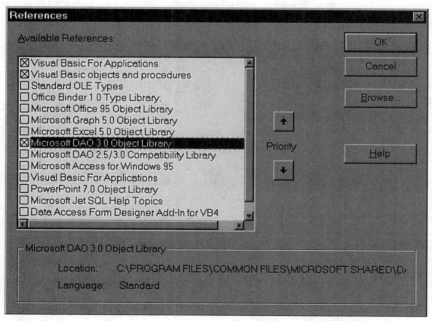

Figure 13–4 List of available library references in Visual Basic

At this point, you can test the updated GBADD.EXE program by submitting a new entry from the guest book entry form:

1. Start your WebSite server if it is not already started.

2. Ensure that a copy of the GBOOK.MDB file resides in the C:\WEBSITE\HTDOCS\BOOK\GBDIR1\ directory.

3. Open the first guest book entry form by specifying the following URL in your browser's location window:

```
http://localhost/book/gbdir1/gbadd1.htm
```

4. Submit the following test entry:

```
Name: John Smith
Email Address: smith@test.com
Phone Number: 555-555-5555
Date Of Birth: 3/26/55
Comments: This is a test entry!
```

The GBADD.EXE program should return a response indicating that the entry has been successfully added, as shown in Figure 13-5.

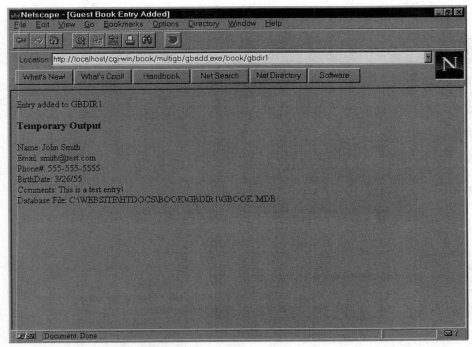

Figure 13–5 GBADD.EXE program responding with the entry added message

If, on the other hand, you receive an error response, then try the following options to fix the problem:

1. See if the error message displayed in the response leads to the source of the problem.

2. Close Microsoft Access if it is currently launched. This ensures that no exclusive lock is set on any GBOOK.MDB database file.

3. Use the debugging procedure described in Lesson 6, "Debugging Your Web Application," of Chapter 12, Designing a Windows CGI Application to Process Form Data, to see where the GBADD.EXE program fails.

Next, you need to verify whether the guest book entry actually got added to the correct GBOOK.MDB file:

1. Open the GBOOK.MDB database file residing in the C:\WEBSITE\HTDOCS\BOOK\GBDIR1 directory.

2. Open the *tblGB_Entries* table of this database.

3. The table should contain the data related to the submitted guest book entry, as shown in Figure 13-6.

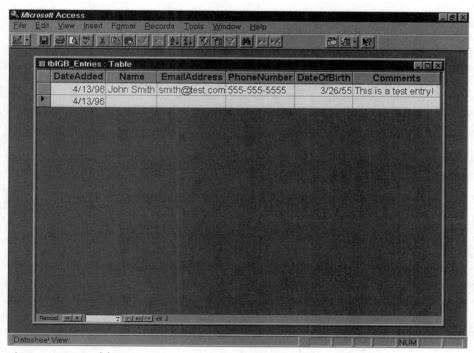

Figure 13–6 tblGB_Entries containing the submitted guest book entry

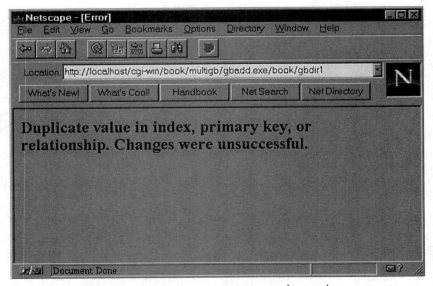

Figure 13-7 GBADD.EXE returning a primary key violation error

Let's see what happens if you try to resubmit the preceding entry. Using the Back button of your browser, return to the filled-in guest book entry form and click on the Enter button again. The GBADD.EXE program returns a primary key violation error as shown in Figure 13-7. If you reinspect the tblGB_Entries table of the GBOOK.MDB database, you will see that no new record was added in that table.

While it is evident that the uniqueness requirement of the primary key automatically prevents the GBADD.EXE program from adding a duplicate entry for the same date, the response it returns to indicate this occurrence is not very user-readable. The next lesson solves this problem by trapping this error and returning a more comprehensible error message.

NOTE: The results of this lesson are stored in the C:\WEBSITE\HTDOCS\BOOK\CHAP13\RESULTS\LESSON2\ directory.

LESSON 3: TRAPPING DATABASE-RELATED ERRORS

The first thing required for trapping the primary key violation error is to identify the Visual Basic error code associated with this error. When any trappable run-time error occurs, Visual Basic sets a global *Err* variable with that error code before passing control to the currently active error-handling routine.

You can examine the value of the Err variable in your error-handling routine when the primary key violation error occurs and later modify the error-handling procedure to appropriately deal with that error. The following steps describe this process:

1. Open the GBADD.VBP project file residing in the C:\WEBSITE\CGI-WIN\BOOK\GBADD\ directory in Visual Basic.

2. Output the value of the Err variable by adding the following highlighted line to the HandleError procedure residing in the NEWAPP.BAS module as shown:

```
Public Sub HandleError()

  Send ("Content-type: text/html")
  Send ("")
  Send ("<HTML>")
  Send ("<HEAD>")
  Send ("<TITLE>Error</TITLE>")
  Send ("</HEAD>")
  Send ("<BODY>")
  If ErrorMessage = "" Then
    Send ("<H2>" & Error$ & "</H2>") 'Send VB's error message
    Send ("<BR>Err = " & Err)          'Send VB's Err value
  Else
    Send ("<H2>" & ErrorMessage & "</H2>") 'Send user-defined message
  End If
  Send ("</BODY>")
  Send ("</HTML>")
End Sub
```

3. Save and recompile your project to create an updated *GBADD.EXE* file in the C:\WEBSITE\CGI-WIN\BOOK\MULTIGB\ directory.

4. Ensure that your WebSite server is running.

5. Resubmit the guest book entry added in the previous lesson through your browser.

This time the error response displays the 3022 error code value associated with the primary key violation error as shown in Figure 13-8.

6. Catch this error in the ErrorHandler procedure as shown:

```
Public Sub HandleError()

  Send ("Content-type: text/html")
  Send ("")
  Send ("<HTML>")
  Send ("<HEAD>")
  Send ("<TITLE>Error</TITLE>")
  Send ("</HEAD>")
  Send ("<BODY>")
  Select Case Err
    Case 3022                          'Duplicate value in primary key
      ErrorMessage = "<H2>Your entry has already been added " _
                     & "to the guest book.</H2>"
```

continued on next page

continued from previous page

```
                        'Trap any other possible errors here (as separate cases)
                        End Select
                        If ErrorMessage = "" Then
                           Send ("<H2>" & Error$ & "</H2>") 'Send VB's error message
                           Send ("<BR>Err = " & Err)         'Send VB's Err value
                        Else
                           Send (ErrorMessage)                'Send user-defined message
                        End If
                        Send ("</BODY>")
                        Send ("</HTML>")
                     End Sub
```

7. Re-create the GBADD.EXE file in the C:\WEBSITE\CGI-WIN\BOOK\MULTIGB\ directory by saving and recompiling your project.

8. Submit the original guest book entry again.

This time, the GBADD.EXE returns the proper message, as shown in Figure 13-9.

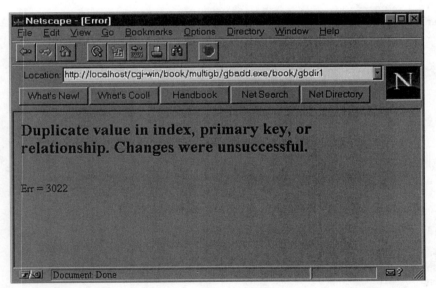

Figure 13–8 Displaying the Err value of the primary key violation error

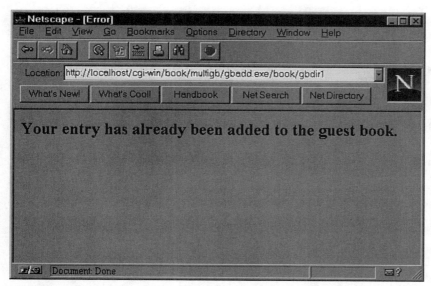

Figure 13–9 Returning a proper message for the primary key violation error

LESSON 4: LISTING EXISTING RECORDS

A recordset can be perceived as a virtual table consisting of records and fields with the capability to access and manipulate data one record at a time. Think of it as a book where you first must go to a specific page before you can read the contents of that page. Figure 13-10 shows a visual representation of a Recordset object.

Moving Between Records

When you create a Recordset object, the first record of the underlying record source is automatically set as the current record of the recordset. To set another record as the current record, you can use the following methods with your Recordset object:

```
rs.MoveFirst    'Set the current record to the first record
rs.MoveLast     'Set the current record to the last record
rs.MoveNext     'Make next record as the current record
rs.MovePrevious 'Make previous record as the current record
```

Field position:	0	1	2	3	4	5

	DateAdded	Name	EmailAddress	PhoneNumber	DateOfBirth	Comments
Current record → ▶	4/13/96	John Smith	smith@test.com	555-555-5555	3/26/55	This is a test entry!
	4/14/96	John Smith	smith@test.com	555-555-5555	3/26/55	This is a test entry!
	4/14/96	Sandy	sandy@test.com	111-111-1111		Test entry 2
	4/14/96	Joe	joe@test.com	222-2222	4/4/44	Test entry 3

Figure 13–10 A visual representation of a Recordset object

In addition, the Recordset object also supports a Move method, which allows you to move the current record a specific number of records up or down. The syntax of the Move method is as follows:

```
rs.Move rows[,start]
```

where the *rows* parameter specifies the number of rows to move (positive value for down, negative value for up), and the optional *start* parameter indicates the record relative to which the move should occur. If you do not specify the start parameter, then the move is made relative to the current record.

NOTE: The *start* parameter is defined in terms of a *bookmark,* which is a unique string assigned by the Jet engine to every record in the Recordset. To learn more about bookmarks, refer to Visual Basic's on-line help.

Accessing Record Fields

Once you set the record you want to work with as the current record, you can refer to any field of that record either by its field name or by its field position in the following ways:

- By directly specifying the field name using the syntax rs!*Fieldname,* where *Fieldname* refers to the name of a field as it appears in the underlying record source. If the field name contains one or more spaces, then you need to enclose that field name within square brackets, as in rs![*Fieldname*].

- By specifying a variable or string constant using the syntax rs(*FieldNameString*), where *FieldNameString* is a string constant or a string variable that refers to the name of the field.

- By specifying the numeric position using the syntax rs(*FieldPositionNumber*), where *FieldPositionNumber* identifies the numeric position of a field in the underlying source. The first field (leftmost) is considered to have a FieldPositionNumber of 0.

The following examples show how you can use the preceding methods to access the DateOfBirth field value of the current record of the recordset shown in Figure 13-10:

```
BirthDate = rs!DateOfBirth          'Direct reference to the field name
BirthDate = rs![DateOfBirth]        'Also, if field name has spaces
BirthDate = rs("DateOfBirth")       'Using a string constant
BirthDate = rs("DateOf" & "Birth")  'You can concatenate strings
BirthDate = rs(strBirthDate)        'Where strBirthDate = "DateOfBirth"
BirthDate = rs(4)                   'DateOfBirth is the fifth field
BirthDate = rs(intFieldPos)         'Where intFieldPos = 5
```

The BOF and EOF Properties

What happens if the recordset does not contain any records and you try to access a field, or if you execute the MovePrevious method from the first record of a nonempty recordset and then try to access a field value? In both cases, you will get a run-time error. To prevent you from getting into these situations, the Recordset object contains two properties, BOF and EOF, which help determine if the current record has moved beyond the limits of the recordset.

The BOF property is a Boolean value that indicates if the current record position is before the first record. The EOF property indicates if the current record position is after the last record. If the recordset contains no records, then both properties return a True value.

You can use these properties along with the Move methods to navigate through all the records of a non-empty recordset as illustrated by the following code templates:

```
'Move from first to last
rs!MoveFirst
Do Until rs.EOF
  'Process the current record
  rs.MoveNext
Loop

'Move from last to first
rs!MoveLast
Do Until rs.BOF
  'Process the current record
  rs.MovePrevious
Loop
```

Listing the Guest Book Entries

Let's apply the concepts discussed here to make the GBLIST.EXE program list all the guest book entries:

1. Open the GBLIST.VBP project file residing in the C:\WEBSITE\CGI-WIN\BOOK\GBLIST\ directory in Visual Basic.

2. Add the following variable declarations in the Declaration section of the NEWAPP.BAS module:

   ```
   Dim ws As Workspace
   Dim db As Database
   Dim rs As Recordset
   ```

   This gives these data access object variables a global scope within the NEWAPP.BAS module.

3. Create a Recordset object for the tblGB_Entries table by modifying the SelectDataFromGuestBook procedure in the NEWAPP.BAS module, as follows:

   ```
   Public Sub SelectDataFromGuestBook()

      'Determine the path of the guest book database file
   ```

continued on next page

continued from previous page

```
        DataBaseFile = CGI_PhysicalPath & "\GBOOK.MDB"

    'Open the database
    Set ws = DBEngine.Workspaces(0)
    Set db = ws.OpenDatabase(DataBaseFile)

    'Open the recordset representing tblGuestBook
    Set rs = db.OpenRecordset("tblGB_Entries")

End Sub
```

4. Modify the GenerateResponse procedure in the NEWAPP.BAS module to list all the guest book entries, as shown:

```
Public Sub GenerateResponse()

    Send ("Content-type: text/html")
    Send ("")
    Send ("<HTML><HEAD><TITLE>")
    Send ("Guest Book Listing")
    Send ("</TITLE></HEAD><BODY>")
    'List the guest book entries
    If rs.EOF Then   'Guest book is empty
      Send ("<H2>The guest book is currently empty.</H2>")
      Exit Sub
    End If
    Send ("<H2>The guest book has the following entries.</H2>")
    Send ("<OL>")
    Do Until rs.EOF
      Send ("<LI><B>Date Added: </B> " & rs!DateAdded)
      Send ("<BR><B>Name: </B> " & rs!name)
      Send ("<BR><B>Email: </B> " & rs!EmailAddress)
      'Display optional fields only if they have data
      If Not IsNull(rs!PhoneNumber) Then
        Send ("<BR><B>Phone: </B> " & rs!PhoneNumber)
      End If
      If Not IsNull(rs!DateOfBirth) Then
        Send ("<BR><B>BirthDate: </B> " & rs!DateOfBirth)
      End If
      If Not IsNull(rs!Comments) Then
        Send ("<BR><B>Comments: </B> " & rs!Comments)
      End If
      Send ("<P>")
      rs.MoveNext
    Loop
    Send ("</OL>")
    Send ("</BODY></HTML>")

End Sub
```

5. Select the References option from VB's Tools menu and enable the Microsoft DAO 3.0 Object Library option from the list of library references.

6. Save and recompile your project to create an updated *GBLIST.EXE* file in the C:\WEBSITE\CGI-WIN\BOOK\MULTIGB\ directory.

Testing the Program

You can use the GBLIST1.HTM guest book listing form to test the GBLIST.EXE program even though the current version of this program does not filter the guest book entries based on the starting date supplied through that form. Follow these steps:

1. Ensure that your WebSite server is running.

2. Open the first guest book listing form by specifying the following URL in your browser's location window:

```
http://localhost/book/gbdir1/gblist1.htm
```

3. List any valid date for the Starting Date field, and click on the View button.

4. The GBLIST.EXE lists the current contents of the guest book as shown in Figure 13-11.

At this point, you can add more entries to the guest book using the guest book entry form and then verify that the GBLIST.EXE lists all these entries.

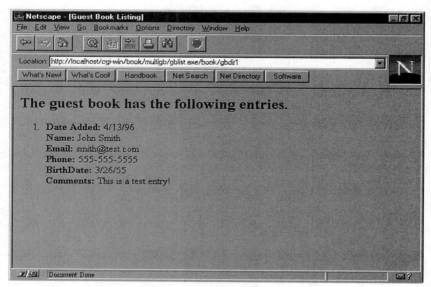

Figure 13–11 Listing all the guest book entries

LESSON 5: FINDING RECORDS MEETING A SPECIFIC CRITERIA

The GBLIST.EXE program you updated in the previous lesson currently lists all the records stored in the tblGB_Entries table of a guest book database. While this is not a bad start for displaying the entries of a guest book, you still have to meet the original objective of the GBLIST.EXE program, which is to list entries added after a given starting date. Specifically, the program needs to consider the value of each entry's DateAdded field to decide if that entry should be listed or not.

There are several ways of finding the guest book entries that meet the starting date criteria. Not surprisingly, they all are based on a Recordset object. The difference is in how you create the Recordset object and what object methods you use to access the appropriate entries.

Here, we describe different versions of the GBLIST.EXE program to illustrate how these techniques work. However, to verify that all these techniques return the same results, you need to set up some test entries in the C:\WEBSITE\ HTDOCS\BOOK\GBDIR1\GBOOK.MDB database. You may enter these sample entries directly through Microsoft Access. Ensure that there is a range of values for the DateAdded field in these entries.

Finally, use the GBLIST1.HTM guest book listing form to test the response of the GBLIST.EXE program in each case.

Performing a Sequential Search

In a sequential search, you simply navigate through the recordset representing all the table records and use Visual Basic code to determine if a particular record meets the required criteria. For example, you can add the following check in the GenerateResponse procedure described in the previous lesson to list the desired guest book entries:

```
Do Until rs.EOF
  'Check record to see if it meets the starting date criteria
  If rs!DateAdded >= StartingDate Then
    Send ("<LI><B>Date Added: </B> " & rs!DateAdded)
    Send ("<BR><B>Name: </B> " & rs!name)
    Send ("<BR><B>Email: </B> " & rs!EmailAddress)
    '... The rest of the send code ...
  End If
  rs.MoveNext
Loop
```

Using the Seek Method of a Table Recordset

As you may notice, the sequential search method is not very efficient since it always examines every record of the recordset to produce the selective output. To avoid this linear scanning, you can index the search fields and then use the Seek method to quickly locate specific records.

To apply the Seek method:

1. Set the Recordset object's Index property to the name of the table index you want to use with the Seek method using the following syntax:

```
rs.Index = "Index Name"
```

2. Execute the Seek method, giving it a relational operator and one or more search values. The relational operator could be one of the following, depending on how you want the Seek method to find the matching record:

- = First record whose key fields are equal to the search values

- < First record whose key fields are less than the search values

- > First record whose key fields are greater than the search values

- <= First record whose key fields are less than or equal to the search values

- >= First record whose key fields are greater than or equal to the search values

3. Test the Recordset's NoMatch property to determine if the Seek method found any record.

When you set a Recordset object's Index property, the records are re-sorted based on the fields participating in that index. For example, if you make the primary key of the tblGB_Entries table its recordset's index, then the records in that recordset will be arranged using the DateAdded, Name, and the EmailAddress fields as the sort fields. DateAdded, being the first field of the primary key, will be treated as the primary sort field.

Once the records are arranged in the desired order, you use the Seek method to search through the index to find the first record satisfying the specified criteria. Then, if you used a comparison operator other than =, you may move forward (for > and >= operators) or backward (for < and <= operators) from the current record to access all other records meeting your criteria.

The following code snippet illustrates how you can modify the GenerateResponse procedure of the GBLIST.EXE program to take advantage of the Seek method:

```
'List the guest book entries
If rs.EOF Then  'Guest book is empty
  Send ("<H2>The guest book is currently empty.</H2>")
  Exit Sub
End If
'Set recordset's Index property to the index named "Primary key"
'which is a combination of the DateEntered, Name, and EmailAddress
'fields
rs.Index = "PrimaryKey"
```

continued on next page

continued from previous page

```
'Perform seek operation based on just the DateEntered field
'Note: In this example, the other two fields are ignored
rs.Seek >= StartingDate   'StartingDate is a user-entered parameter
'Check if the seek operation found any record
If rs.NoMatch Then
  Send ("<H2>No entries added since " & StartingDate & ".</H2>")
  Exit Sub
End If
'List the found record and all the subsequent records
Send ("<H2>Here are the guest book entries signed on or after ")
Send (StartingDate & ".</H2>")
Send ("<OL>")
Do Until rs.EOF
  Send ("<LI><B>Date Added: </B> " & rs!DateAdded)
  Send ("<BR><B>Name: </B> " & rs!Name)
  Send ("<BR><B>Email: </B> " & rs!EmailAddress)
  '... The rest of the send code ...
  rs.MoveNext
Loop
Send ("</OL>")
```

NOTE: Although in this example you specified the search value for only the DateAdded field of the primary key, the Seek method does allow you to specify the search values for the other two fields participating in the primary key, as shown:

```
rs.Seek RelationalOperator, key1, key2, key3
```

For more details on the Seek method, refer to Visual Basic's on-line help.

Using the FindFirst Method of a Dynaset Recordset

Although the Seek method is the most efficient way of locating a record, it can be used only in limited cases where your recordset must have a single table as its record source (Table Recordset), and your search criteria must be based on a field participating in an index. Many times, it is not possible to satisfy these two conditions. For example, in database applications that use several related tables, accessing data from multiple tables with a Dynaset Recordset object is a common occurrence. You will see evidence of such cases in subsequent chapters.

Fortunately, the Dynaset and Snapshot Recordsets come with their own sets of Find methods which provide much greater flexibility than the Seek method. Their only drawback is that they do not match the efficiency of the Seek method. (They are still quite fast, though!) The Find methods are specified as follows:

```
rs.{FindFirst|FindPrevious|FindNext|FindLast} Criteria
```

where Criteria is an SQL criteria formed using the fields of the recordset.

To locate all the records matching the specified criteria from the beginning of a recordset, you first apply the FindFirst method to the Recordset object, and subsequently apply the FindNext method to the same criteria. Unlike the Seek method, the Find methods do not cause any rearrangement of the records in the recordset. They just let you move directly from one matching record to another matching record in the recordset.

Again, you can test the recordset's NoMatch property to determine if the last Find operation found any matching record. As an example, let's see how you can use the FindFirst and the FindNext methods in the GBLIST.EXE program to list the appropriate guest book entries:

1. Change the OpenRecordset statement in SelectDataFromGuestBook procedure of the GBLIST.EXE program as follows:

```
Set rs = db.OpenRecordset("tblGB_Entries", dbOpenDynaset)
```

The dbOpenDynaset option in the OpenRecordset method forces the Recordset object to be created as a Dynaset Recordset.

2. Modify the GenerateResponse procedure as shown:

```
Public Sub GenerateResponse()

  Dim Criteria As String

  Send ("Content-type: text/html")
  Send ("")
  Send ("<HTML><HEAD><TITLE>")
  Send ("Guest Book Listing")
  Send ("</TITLE></HEAD><BODY>")
  'List the guest book entries
  If rs.EOF Then   'Guest book is empty
    Send ("<H2>The guest book is currently empty.</H2>")
    Exit Sub
  End If
  Criteria = "DateAdded >= #" & StartingDate & "#"
  rs.FindFirst Criteria     'FindFirst to find the first record
  If rs.NoMatch Then        'NoMatch instead of EOF
    Send ("<H2>No entries added since " & StartingDate & ".</H2>")
    Exit Sub
  End If
  Send ("<H2>Here are the guest book entries signed on or after ")
  Send (StartingDate & ".</H2>")
  Send ("<OL>")
  Do Until rs.NoMatch       'NoMatch instead of EOF
    Send ("<LI><B>Date Added: </B> " & rs!DateAdded)
    Send ("<BR><B>Name: </B> " & rs!name)
    Send ("<BR><B>Email: </B> " & rs!EmailAddress)
    '... The rest of the send code ...
    rs.FindNext Criteria    'FindNext instead of MoveNext
```

continued on next page

continued from previous page

```
        Loop
        Send ("</OL>")
        Send ("</BODY></HTML>")

    End Sub
```

3. Compile and test the modified GBLIST.EXE program as explained in the beginning of this lesson.

NOTE: This version of the GBLIST.EXE program is stored in the C:\WEBSITE\HTDOCS\BOOK\CHAP13\RESULTS\LESSON5\ directory.

LESSON 6: ANALYZING AND FILTERING RECORDS

The Seek and Find methods discussed in the previous lesson help you search records after a recordset has been created. There is, however, another alternative for finding records that meet a specific criteria: Filter records right at the time of creating a recordset. Normally, you can accomplish this task by specifying a query or an SQL string as the source of the recordset in the OpenRecordset method.

However, if the source query contains one or more parameters in either the search criteria or a calculated field, you have to create the recordset through the Querydef data access object, which is explained in the next lesson. For more information on Parameter queries, refer to Chapter 6, Designing Advanced Queries.

This lesson describes how to create and use recordsets based on regular nonparameter queries or a direct SQL statement.

Using NonParameter Queries

Let's say you want the GBLIST.EXE program to return the statistics about all the guest book entries before listing the specific entries of the guest book. The statistics could include the following information:

- Total entries in the guest book

- Date of the oldest entry

- Date of the most recent entry

To add this new feature, you can create another recordset in the GBLIST.EXE program whose record source is a Total query that produces this information. You can use Microsoft Access to design and store this query as follows:

1. Launch Microsoft Access and open the GBOOK.MDB file residing in the C:\WEBSITE\HTDOCS\BOOK\GBDIR1\ directory.

2. Select the Queries tab from the Database window, and click on the New button to design a new query. Then select the Design View option to display the query design window.

3. Design your query as shown in Figure 13-12, and save it as *qryGB_List_Statistics*.

NOTE: To display the Total row on the query design grid, select Totals from the View menu.

4. Run the query to display the name of the fields returned by this query. (See Figure 13-13.)

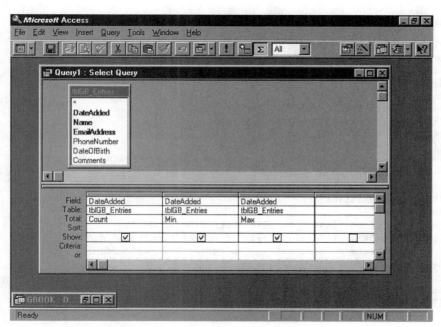

Figure 13–12 Design of qryGB_List_Statistics'

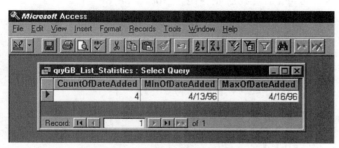

Figure 13–13 Result of qryGB_List_Statistics

Now that you have a stored query that returns the information you want, you can access this information from the GBLIST.EXE program as follows:

1. Open the GBLIST.VBP project in Visual Basic, and declare another Recordset variable named *rsStat* in the Declaration section of its NEWAPP.BAS module as shown:

```
Dim rsStat As Recordset
```

2. Add the following lines at the end of the SelectDataFromGuestBook procedure:

```
'Open the recordset representing qryGB_List_Statistics
Set rsStat = db.OpenRecordset("qryGB_List_Statistics")
```

3. Insert the following highlighted lines in the GenerateResponse procedure to display guest book statistics:

```
Public Sub GenerateResponse()

    Send ("Content-type: text/html")
    Send ("")
    Send ("<HTML><HEAD><TITLE>")
    Send ("Guest Book Listing")
    Send ("</TITLE></HEAD><BODY>")
    'List the guest book entries
    If rs.EOF Then   'Guest book is empty
      Send ("<H2>The guest book is currently empty.</H2>")
      Exit Sub
    End If
    'Display Statistics
    Send ("<H3>")
    Send ("Total entries: " & rsStat!CountOfDateAdded)
    Send ("<BR>Date of first entry: " & rsStat!MinOfDateAdded)
    Send ("<BR>Date of last entry: " & rsStat!MaxOfDateAdded)
    Send ("</H3>")
    Criteria = "DateAdded >= #" & StartingDate & "#"
    rs.FindFirst Criteria      'FindFirst to find the first record
    If rs.NoMatch Then         'NoMatch instead of EOF
      Send ("<H2>No entries added since " & StartingDate & ".</H2>")
      Exit Sub
    End If
    Send ("<H2>Here are the guest book entries signed on or after ")
    Send (StartingDate & ".</H2>")
    Send ("<OL>")
    Do Until rs.NoMatch        'NoMatch instead of EOF
      Send ("<LI><B>Date Added: </B> " & rs!DateAdded)
      Send ("<BR><B>Name: </B> " & rs!name)
      Send ("<BR><B>Email: </B> " & rs!EmailAddress)
      'Display optional fields only if they have data
      If Not IsNull(rs!PhoneNumber) Then
        Send ("<BR><B>Phone: </B> " & rs!PhoneNumber)
      End If
      If Not IsNull(rs!DateOfBirth) Then
        Send ("<BR><B>BirthDate: </B> " & rs!DateOfBirth)
```

```
      End If
      If Not IsNull(rs!Comments) Then
        Send ("<BR><B>Comments: </B> " & rs!Comments)
      End If
      Send ("<P>")
      rs.FindNext Criteria      'FindNext instead of MoveNext
   Loop
   Send ("</OL>")
   Send ("</BODY></HTML>")

  End Sub
```

Figure 13-14 shows a sample response from this version of the GBLIST.EXE program.

NOTE: A copy of this version of the GBLIST.EXE program is stored in the C:\WEBSITE\HTDOCS\BOOK\CHAP13\RESULTS\LESSON6\ directory.

Using an SQL Statement

Creating a recordset with an SQL statement comes in handy when you require maximum flexibility for specifying a record filtering criteria. For example, if you want to allow users to search the guest book using any valid SQL criteria, you can easily append that criteria to the Where clause of a base SQL statement, and then use that resulting SQL statement to produce a recordset representing the matching records.

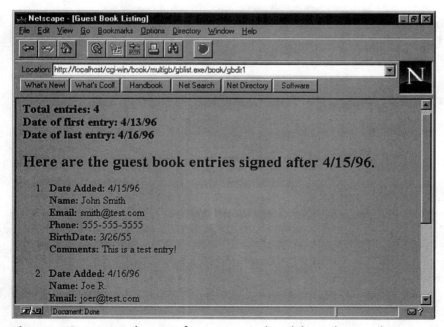

Figure 13–14 Displaying information produced through a Total query

One main hurdle of using an SQL statement is that you have to construct the statement through code, which requires a good working knowledge of the SQL syntax. Fortunately, there is an easy way to bypass this hurdle: Let Microsoft Access tackle the major portion of SQL composition.

The following steps show how you can apply this trick when using an SQL statement with the GBLIST.EXE program for listing entries after a given starting date:

1. Design a new query in the C:\WEBSITE\HTDOCS\GBDIR1\GBOOK.MDB database as shown in Figure 13-15.

2. Select the SQL option under the View menu to display the SQL statement that Access constructs for this query as shown in Figure 13-16.

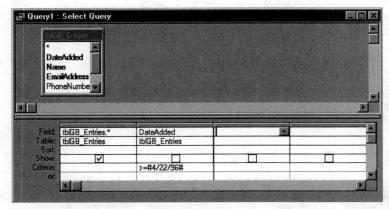

Figure 13–15 Designing an Access query to construct an SQL statement

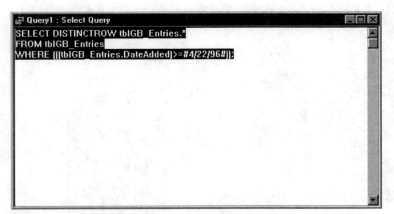

Figure 13–16 Displaying the SQL statement behind a query

Observe how the date criteria appears in the SQL statement.

3. While the SQL text is highlighted, press [CTRL]-[C] to copy the entire SQL statement to the Clipboard.

4. Go to the SelectDataFromGuestBook procedure of the GBLIST.EXE program, and declare a local string variable named SQL, as follows:

```
Dim SQL As String
```

5. Put your cursor on an empty line in this procedure, and press [CTRL]-[V] to paste the SQL text from the Clipboard into the procedure.

Visual Basic's editor will indicate a syntax error on these lines. Do not be concerned.

6. Assign this SQL statement to the SQL variable by editing the SQL text as shown in Figure 13-17.

7. Change the criteria of this SQL statement to use the given starting date by replacing the date value in the Where clause with the StartingDate variable as follows:

```
SQL = "SELECT DISTINCTROW tblGB_Entries.*, tblGB_Entries.DateAdded" _
        & "From tblGB_Entries" _
        & "WHERE (((tblGB_Entries.DateAdded)>#" & StartingDate _
        & "#));"
```

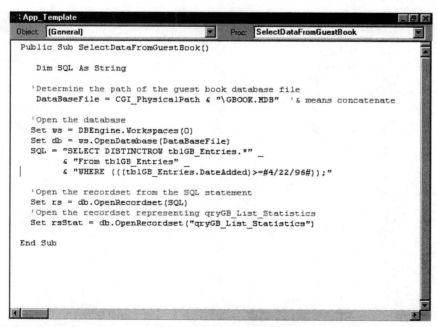

Figure 13–17 Assigning the SQL statement to the SQL variable

8. Specify the SQL statement as the record source of the *rs* recordset as shown:

```
Set rs = db.OpenRecordset(SQL)
```

9. Use the Move methods in the GenerateResponse procedure to navigate through the filtered records represented by the recordset as shown:

```
Public Sub GenerateResponse()

  Send ("Content-type: text/html")
  Send ("")
  Send ("<HTML><HEAD><TITLE>")
  Send ("Guest Book Listing")
  Send ("</TITLE></HEAD><BODY>")
  'List the guest book entries
  If rs.EOF Then  'Guest book is empty
    Send ("<H2>The guest book is currently empty.</H2>")
    Exit Sub
  End If
  'Display Statistics
  Send ("<H3>")
  Send ("Total entries: " & rsStat!CountOfDateAdded)
  Send ("<BR>Date of first entry: " & rsStat!MinOfDateAdded)
  Send ("<BR>Date of last entry: " & rsStat!MaxOfDateAdded)
  Send ("</H3>")

  Send ("<H2>Here are the guest book entries signed after ")
  Send (StartingDate & ".</H2>")
  Send ("<OL>")
  Do Until rs.EOF
    Send ("<LI><B>Date Added: </B> " & rs!DateAdded)
    Send ("<BR><B>Name: </B> " & rs!name)
    Send ("<BR><B>Email: </B> " & rs!EmailAddress)
    '... The rest of the send code ...
    rs.MoveNext
  Loop
  Send ("</OL>")
  Send ("</BODY></HTML>")

End Sub
```

10. Compile the GBLIST.EXE program and verify its results.

This version of the GBLIST.EXE program is also stored in the C:\WEBSITE\HTDOCS\BOOK\CHAP13\RESULTS\LESSON6\SQLBASED\ directory.

> **NOTE:** If your SQL criteria is based on a text field, such as *EmailAddress Like* "*.com", you will have to take special care in embedding the quote characters when you assign the SQL statement to the SQL variable. The simplest approach is to use a single quote for your text value, as shown:

```
SQL = "SELECT DISTINCTROW tblGB_Entries.*, tblGB_Entries.DateAdded" _
      & "From tblGB_Entries" _
      & "WHERE (((tblGB_Entries.EmailAddress) Like '*.com'));"
```

LESSON 7: FILTERING RECORDS THROUGH A PARAMETER QUERY

Parameter queries are perhaps the best option when filtering records based on a criteria that varies only in its condition values, as in the case of the starting date criteria of the GBLIST.EXE program. Parameter queries not only prevent you from going through the elaborate steps of constructing an SQL statement, but also give you the flexibility of modifying the query design without having to change the source code of your program. The only catch is that you have to use the Querydef data access object for creating a Parameter query-based recordset, as outlined next:

1. Declare a variable for a Querydef object as shown:

```
Declare qd As QueryDef
```

2. Set the *qd* variable to point to the definition of the Parameter query by using one of the following syntax:

```
Set qd = db.Querydefs![ParameterQueryName]
Set qd = db.Querydefs("ParameterQueryName")
```

3. Assign specific values to the parameters of the Parameter query by using one of the following methods:

```
qd![ParameterName] = ParameterValue
qd("ParameterName") = ParameterValue
```

4. Create the recordset based on the Parameter query by using the OpenRecordset method of the Parameter query as follows:

```
Set rs = qd.OpenRecordset()
```

To use this outline to create another version of the GBLIST.EXE program that employs a Parameter query for returning the matching guest book entries:

1. Open the C:\WEBSITE\HTDOCS\GBDIR1\GBOOK.MDB database in Microsoft Access.

2. Design a Parameter query containing the starting date parameter in its criteria as shown in Figure 13-18 and save it as *qryGB_List_StartDate*.

3. Modify the SelectDataFromGuestBook procedure of the GBLIST.EXE program as follows:

```
Public Sub SelectDataFromGuestBook()
  'Declare Querydef variable
  Dim qd As QueryDef

  'Determine the path of the guest book database file
   DataBaseFile = CGI_PhysicalPath & "\GBOOK.MDB"

  'Open the database and querdef objects
  Set ws = DBEngine.Workspaces(0)
  Set db = ws.OpenDatabase(DataBaseFile)
  Set qd = db.QueryDefs![qryGB_List_StartDate]
  qd![Starting Date] = StartingDate

  'Open the recordset from the querydef object
  Set rs = qd.OpenRecordset()
  'Open the recordset representing qryGB_List_Statistics
  Set rsStat = db.OpenRecordset("qryGB_List_Statistics")

  End Sub
```

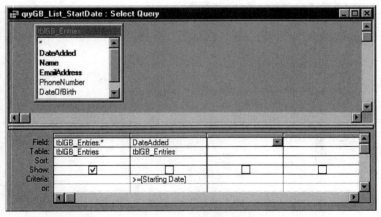

Figure 13-18 Designing the Parameter query

4. Compile this version of the GBLIST.EXE program and verify its results.

NOTE: This version of the GBLIST.EXE program is stored in the C:\WEBSITE\HTDOCS\BOOK\CHAP13\LESSON7\ directory.

To illustrate how Parameter queries provide the flexibility advantage, let's say that you want the guest book entries listed in reverse chronological order, that is, the most recent entry should be displayed first. All you need to do is slightly modify the design of your Parameter query using Microsoft Access (see Figure 13-19) and your job is done!

Editing and Deleting Records... You can also edit or delete any record of an "updatable" recordset using the *Edit* or the *Delete* method of a Recordset object. Note that the recordsets that are based on Total queries do not fall in this category. Refer to Visual Basic's on-line help on "Recordset Object" for more information.

REVIEW QUESTIONS

1. Why does the GBOOK.MDB have to be a generic database?

2. How does the composite primary key help in checking duplicate submissions?

3. What are data access objects?

4. What does the DBEngine object represent?

5. What is a workspace?

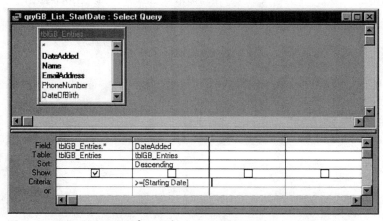

Figure 13-19 Specifying the sort order in the Parameter query

6. How do you open a Microsoft Access database?

7. What is the relationship between an object variable and the object it represents?

8. What is the difference between the three types of Recordset objects?

9. How do you add a record to a table?

10. How do you navigate between the records of a recordset?

11. What is the purpose of the BOF and EOF properties?

12. What is the main disadvantage of performing a sequential search to find selective records?

13. How do the Seek method and the Find method approaches differ?

14. What kinds of queries can you open with the OpenDatabase method of the database object?

15. What is an easy way to construct an SQL statement?

16. How do you access records produced by a Parameter query?

EXERCISES

1. Modify the Multi-Guestbook application to include the user's address and browser information.

2. Modify the GBADD.EXE and the GBLIST.EXE programs so that they return an appropriate message when they cannot open the GBOOK.MDB database file.

3. List the entries added after a given starting date in reverse chronological order by use of the Seek method.

4. Modify the GBLIST.EXE program so that it returns a count of guest book entries which have a *.com* in their e-mail address field.

14

PROCESSING TEMPLATE FILES WITH A CGI APPLICATION

14

From the previous two chapters, you can see that by creating back-end Windows CGI programs, you gain tremendous flexibility for interacting with Web clients. However, if you develop these programs for any large-scale Web application using Visual Basic and the CGI32.BAS library, you will quickly notice the following two limitations during the development process:

🎺 You have to use string expressions for sending any CGI output.

🎺 You have to change the program's source code and recompile your CGI program every time you change your CGI output.

The first limitation arises because Visual Basic handles all text processing through strings and string-related functions. For example, if you want to return information about your client's IP address, you have to say something like:

```
Send ("Your IP address is: " & CGI_RemoteAddr)
```

In addition, you have to take extra care in sending the double-quote (") character in your CGI response. For example, if you want to output the following text:

```
The rod length is 3".
```

you have the following two options:

🎺 Use two double-quote characters as shown:

```
Send ("The rod length is: 3""."")
```

🎺 Concatenate a quote character with the rest of the string as follows:

```
Send ("The rod length is: 3" & Chr$(34) & ".")
```

The second limitation, where you have to recompile your Windows CGI program to make even a slight change in the program's GGI output, presents itself because the Windows CGI program is a binary executable file. This limitation can potentially grow into a major hurdle if you are developing a general-purpose CGI application and want to provide the ability to customize the format and contents of the responses generated by your application.

To overcome the preceding two limitations, there are two approaches you can follow:

🎺 Use the Server-Side Includes (SSI) feature of your Web server.

🎺 Use template files with your CGI program.

As explained in Chapter 2, Getting Started, the Server-Side Include is an advanced feature of your WebSite server where you can insert the output of a CGI program in your regular HTML document using special server directives. For example, if you want to display the statistics of a particular guest book in the Multi-Guestbook application using the SSI approach, you can create an SSI type HTML document as shown:

```
<HTML>
<TITLE>Guest Book Count</TITLE>
<BODY>
<H3>There are currently
<!--#exec cgi="/cgi-win/book/multigb/gbcount.exe/gbdir1"-->
entries in the guest book.<BR>
The first guest book entry was added on
```

```
<!--#exec cgi="/cgi-win/book/multigb/gbfirst.exe/gbdir1"-->.<BR>
The last guest book entry was added on
<!--#exec cgi="/cgi-win/book/multigb/gblast.exe/gbdir1"-->.<BR>
</H3>
</BODY>
</HTML>
```

The GBCOUNT.EXE, GBFIRST.EXE, and GBLAST.EXE files listed in this document are three Windows CGI programs that would simply return the appropriate values for the specified guest book. Their design would be similar to the GBADD.EXE and the GBLIST.EXE programs you constructed in the previous chapter, except they would not produce any HTML codes in their output.

Although the SSI approach gives the flexibility you need to resolve the described limitations, it is not an efficient approach. As you can see from the above example, the WebSite server has to execute three Windows CGI programs to return this document. This results in three times more CGI communication overhead than having one CGI program return the complete HTML response.

Apart from the performance penalty, you also need to consider the compatibility issue in case you have to run your application on different Web servers. While most Web servers that claim to support Windows Common Gateway Interface will run a Windows CGI program as expected, they may not all incorporate the SSI capability or use mutually compatible SSI directives.

Both of these SSI-related concerns disappear when you opt for the *template file* approach, in which you design your CGI programs to produce output based on external files. Figure 14-1 illustrates how this template file approach conceptually differs from the SSI approach.

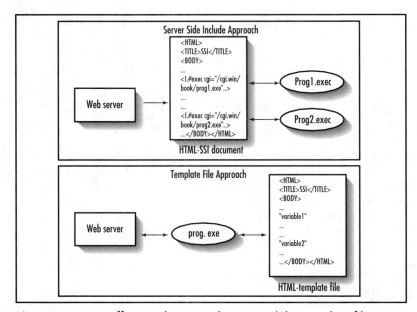

Figure 14-1 Difference between the SSI and the template file approaches

You can also include special instructions in the template files for more flexibility and design your Windows CGI program to preprocess these instructions before sending the final output to the Web server. However, this additional preprocessing step does require extra programming effort, depending on the amount of flexibility you want in your template files.

To help you with this programming effort, this book comes with a Visual Basic library module named UTILS.BAS that provides a set of powerful routines for sending data based on external template files. As an example, the following steps give a brief outline of how you can use this UTILS.BAS library in your Windows CGI program to return all the guest book statistics:

1. Create a text file with the following contents:

```
Content Type: text/html

<HTML>
<TITLE>Guest Book Count</TITLE>
<BODY>
<H2>There are currently `[R1:CountOfDateAdded]` entries in the guest book.<BR>
The first guest book entry was added on `[R1:MinOfDateAdded]`.<BR>
The last guest book entry was added on `[R1:MaxOfDateAdded]`.<BR>
</H2>
</BODY>
</HTML>
```

2. Create a Windows CGI program which opens a Recordset object based on a query that returns the desired guest book statistics in three fields named *CountOfDateAdded*, *MinOfDateAdded*, and *MaxOfDateAdded*.

3. Add code to open this text file in the read mode, and pass its file handle to the UTILS.BAS library's UTILS_ProcessFile function.

4. Send the result returned by the UTILS_ProcessFile function to the CGI output file.

The text file you create in step 1 acts as a template file. It not only describes the format of CGI response, but also contains some embedded codes (highlighted) for the desired data. The syntax of these codes is based on the coding rules supported by the UTILS.BAS library.

The UTILS_ProcessFile function essentially returns a string that represents the contents of the template file with the embedded codes substituted with their appropriate values. For instance, if the GBOOK.MDB contained 20 entries with the first and the last entry signed on 4/1/96 and 4/20/96, respectively, then the UTILS_ProcessFile function would return the following string:

```
"Content Type: text/html

<HTML>
<TITLE>Guest Book Count</TITLE>
<BODY>
```

```
<H2>There are currently 20 entries in the guest book.<BR>
The first guest book entry was added on 4/1/96.<BR>
The last guest book entry was added on 4/20/96.<BR>
</H2>
</BODY>
</HTML>"
```

The Job Listing System described in Chapter 3, Dissecting a Job Listing System, is based entirely on the concept of template files and extensively utilizes the functions in the UTILS.BAS library. In this chapter, we will examine this Web application to illustrate what you can accomplish with the UTILS.BAS library when generating CGI responses using external template files.

First, we will present the overall architecture of the Windows CGI program behind the Job Listing System and review the actual Visual Basic code that this program executes to process the template files. Then we will describe the various codes the UTILS.BAS library allows you to embed within the template files to extend their capabilities.

Finally, in the next chapter, we will go through all the important sections of this Windows CGI program to understand how it uses the template files to respond to different types of CGI requests. We assume that you have read through Chapter 4, Building a Database with Microsoft Access, which describes the structure of the JOBLIST.MDB database used by the Job Listing System.

LESSON 1: REVIEWING THE DESIGN OF THE JOB LISTING SYSTEM

The Job Listing System uses only one Windows CGI program, JOBLIST.EXE, for handling all its functions. The JOBLIST.EXE program examines the value listed in the extra logical path portion of the URL to determine which function is being requested.

The front-end design of the Job Listing System is such that for some functions the JOBLIST.EXE program is called through an HTML form by use of the POST request method, as shown in Figure 14-2.

In other cases the JOBLIST.EXE is referred through a hypertext link, as shown in Figure 14-3.

The side effect of calling the JOBLIST.EXE program through a hypertext link is that the CGI request is always made by use of the GET method, and all parameters are passed through the query string portion of a URL. For this reason, the JOBLIST.EXE program also examines the CGI request method to correctly locate the passed parameters.

Let's open the Visual Basic project associated with the JOBLIST.EXE program to observe how the program's overall design structure is implemented:

1. Launch Visual Basic and open the JOBLIST.VBP project file residing in the C:\WEBSITE\CGI-WIN\BOOK\JOBLIST\ directory.

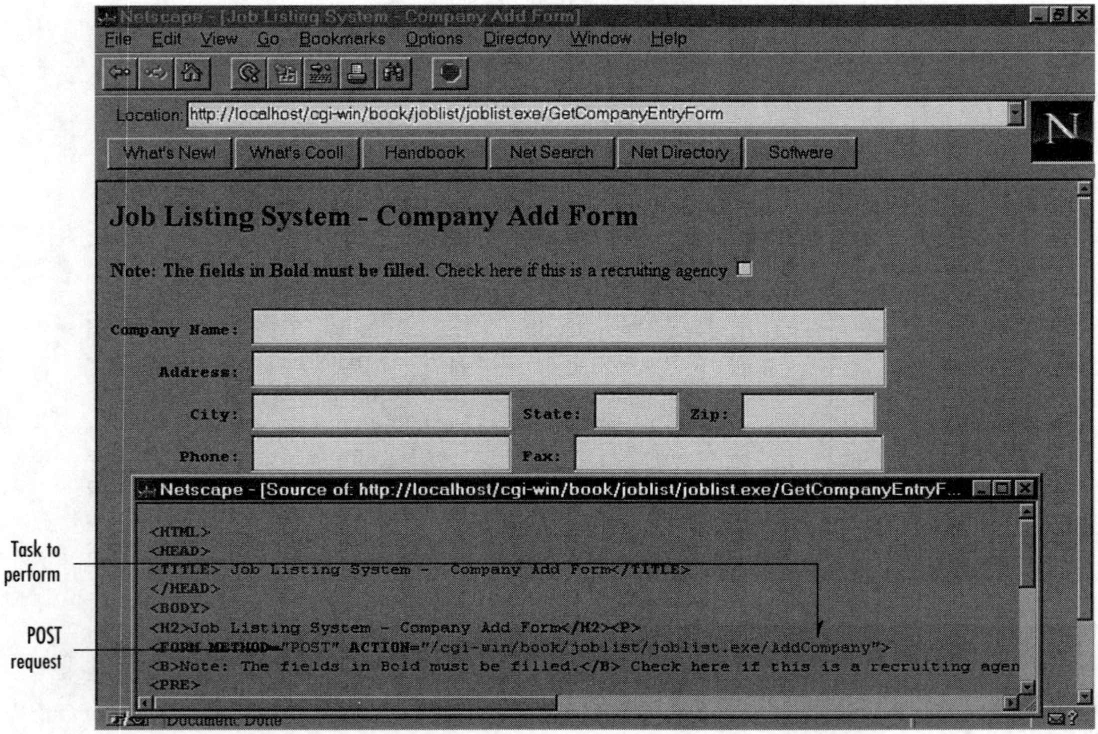

Figure 14–2 JOBLIST.EXE program being called from an HTML form

2. Select Project from VB's View menu to display the Project window, as shown in Figure 14-4.

As you can see from the figure, this project not only contains the standard CGI32.BAS library module and the application-specific JOBLIST.BAS module, but also includes the UTILS.BAS library module. Like the CGI32.BAS file, the UTILS.BAS file is designed to be shared by many programs and is thus located in the C:\WEBSITE\LIB\ directory.

3. Open the CGI_Main procedure present in the JOBLIST.BAS module to list the main control flow of the program, as shown in Figure 14-5.

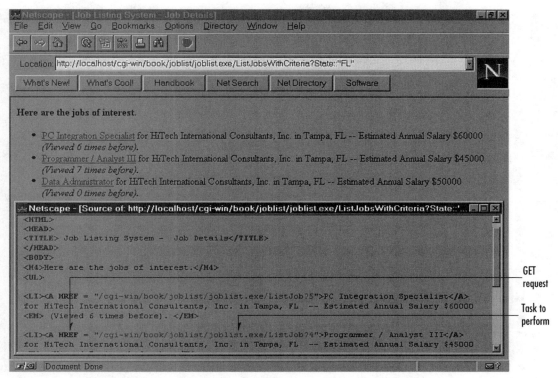

Figure 14–3 JOBLIST.EXE program being called as a hypertext reference

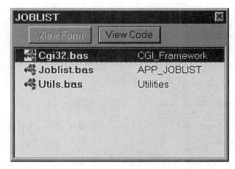

Figure 14–4 JOBLIST.VBP's Project window

```
: APP_JOBLIST                                                          _ 8 X
Object  (General)                              ▼   Proc:  CGI_Main              ▼
'
Sub CGI_Main()

  'Assign the Logical Path value to TaskSelector after removing the
  'leading "/" and converting it to uppercase.
  TaskSelector = UCase$(Mid$(CGI_LogicalPath, 2))

  'Check if any task is specified, otherwise send main menu
  If TaskSelector = "" Then
    APP_ProcessFile "NOTASK.TXT"
    Exit Sub
  End If

  ' Open the database object here since it is used by many tasks
  Set ws = Workspaces(0)
  Set db = ws.OpenDatabase(App.Path & "\JOBLIST.MDB")
  Select Case UCase$(CGI_RequestMethod) 'Examine CGI request method
    Case "GET":
      APP_DoGet            'Handle a GET request
    Case "POST":
      APP_DoPost           'Handle a POST request
    Case Else:
      APP_ProcessFile "ERR_METH.TXT" 'Send error on other types of request
  End Select

End Sub
```

Figure 14–5 CGI_Main procedure of the JOBLIST.EXE program

The CGI_Main procedure starts by assigning the TaskSelector variable to the task name specified in the CGI_LogicalPath variable. Before assigning the variable, it removes any leading "/" from the value of the CGI_LogicalPath variable and converts the remaining characters to uppercase. As an example, if the JOBLIST.EXE is called with the following CGI request:

`http://localhost/cgi-win/book/joblist.exe/ListJob?1`

then the CGI_LogicalPath and the TaskSelector variables will be assigned the values */ListJob* and *LISTJOB,* respectively. The TaskSelector variable is declared in the Declaration section of the JOBLIST.BAS module.

Next, the CGI_Main procedure examines whether the TaskSelector variable is empty. If the TaskSelector variable is empty, CGI_Main processes a template file named *NOTASK.TXT* by calling the APP_ProcessFile procedure and passing this file name as a parameter.

If the TaskSelector is not empty, then the CGI_Main procedure opens the JOBLIST.MDB database by use of the Workspace object's OpenDatabase method, as explained in Chapter 13, Utilizing an Access Database in a CGI Application. The

JOBLIST.MDB file resides in the same directory that holds the JOBLIST.EXE program, hence its path is easily determined from the value of the *App.Path* property.

After opening the JOBLIST.MDB database, the CGI_Main procedure inspects the value of the CGI_RequestMethod variable to choose between the APP_DoGet or the APP_DoPost procedure. In case the request method is something other than the GET or the POST method, it calls the APP_ProcessFile procedure to send the error message listed in the ERR_METH.TXT template file.

The APP_DoGet procedure acts as a task delegator and simply uses a large Case statement to call the appropriate procedure based on the value of the TaskSelector variable. Figure 14-6 shows the design of this procedure.

The APP_DoPost procedure is also a task delegator (see Figure 14-7), except the procedures it calls expect data from CGI requests made by use of the POST method.

Observe that both these procedures summon the APP_SendMsg procedure with slightly different arguments when they encounter a task name that they are not designed to handle. We will examine the design of the APP_SendMsg procedure in Lesson 4 of this chapter.

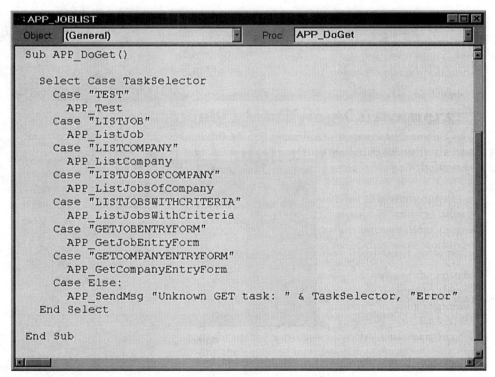

```
: APP_JOBLIST
Object: (General)                              Proc: APP_DoGet

Sub APP_DoGet()

  Select Case TaskSelector
    Case "TEST"
      APP_Test
    Case "LISTJOB"
      APP_ListJob
    Case "LISTCOMPANY"
      APP_ListCompany
    Case "LISTJOBSOFCOMPANY"
      APP_ListJobsOfCompany
    Case "LISTJOBSWITHCRITERIA"
      APP_ListJobsWithCriteria
    Case "GETJOBENTRYFORM"
      APP_GetJobEntryForm
    Case "GETCOMPANYENTRYFORM"
      APP_GetCompanyEntryForm
    Case Else:
      APP_SendMsg "Unknown GET task: " & TaskSelector, "Error"
  End Select

End Sub
```

Figure 14–6 App_DoGet procedure of the JOBLIST.EXE program

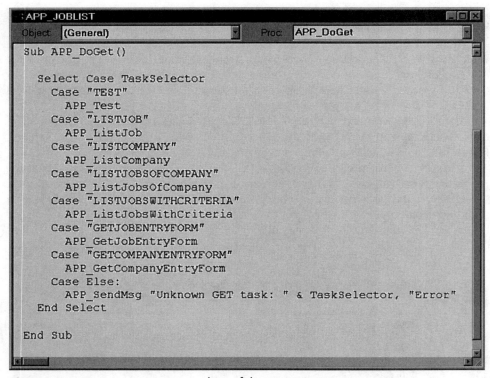

```
: APP_JOBLIST                                                    _ □ ×

Object  (General)                    ▼   Proc:  APP_DoGet              ▼

Sub APP_DoGet()

   Select Case TaskSelector
     Case "TEST"
       APP_Test
     Case "LISTJOB"
       APP_ListJob
     Case "LISTCOMPANY"
       APP_ListCompany
     Case "LISTJOBSOFCOMPANY"
       APP_ListJobsOfCompany
     Case "LISTJOBSWITHCRITERIA"
       APP_ListJobsWithCriteria
     Case "GETJOBENTRYFORM"
       APP_GetJobEntryForm
     Case "GETCOMPANYENTRYFORM"
       APP_GetCompanyEntryForm
     Case Else:
       APP_SendMsg "Unknown GET task: " & TaskSelector, "Error"
   End Select

End Sub
```

Figure 14-7 App_DoPost procedure of the JOBLIST.EXE program

LESSON 2: SENDING OUTPUT USING A TEMPLATE FILE

As described in the previous lesson, when the CGI_Main procedure finds that no task has been specified, it calls the APP_ProcessFile procedure with a parameter NOTASK.TXT and then terminates. This way, instead of hard-coding the response, the Job Listing System gives you the flexibility to provide your own custom response for this situation.

The APP_ProcessFile is a general-purpose procedure that processes a specified template file and sends the processed result to the CGI output file. The code of this procedure is as follows:

```
Public Sub APP_ProcessFile(FileName)

' Note: The variables, InpFn and ProcessResult, are declared in
'       the Declaration section of the JOBLIST.BAS module

  APP_OpenFile FileName
  ProcessResult = Utils_ProcessFile(InpFN)
  Send (ProcessResult)
  Close #InpFN

End Sub
```

414

The APP_ProcessFile procedure first calls the APP_OpenFile procedure to open the template file in the read mode. The APP_OpenFile procedure assumes that the template file resides in the directory holding the JOBLIST.EXE program and also assigns the file number of the opened file to the InpFN variable. The code of this procedure is as follows:

```
Public Sub APP_OpenFile(FileName)

  InpFN = FreeFile
  Open App.Path & FileName For Input Access Read As #InpFN

End Sub
```

After calling the APP_OpenFile procedure, the APP_ProcessFile procedure passes the file number of the opened template file to the UTILS_ProcessFile function of the UTILS.BAS library. The UTILS_ProcessFile function reads through the complete template file, taking care of all the embedded instructions during the process, and returns a string containing the processed result.

Finally, the APP_ProcessFile sends the processed result to the CGI_Output file using the Send procedure and closes the template file. Note that in Visual Basic 4.0 (32-bit version), a string can contain up to 2 billion characters, so you can process a fairly good-sized template file through the UTILS_ProcessFile function.

LESSON 3: DESIGNING AND TESTING A TEMPLATE FILE

The *template file* is a plain text file whose contents represent the data that you want to send through the CGI output. You can embed instructions in the template file that direct the UTILS_ProcessFile function to perform special processing on the designated portions of this file.

Each instruction must begin with the backquote (`) character and may end with different terminating characters based on the type of instruction. Table 14-1 summarizes the various instructions the UTILS_ProcessFile function supports. The subsequent lessons cover the syntax, purpose, and usage of these template file instructions in detail.

Table 14–1 Template file instructions supported by the UTILS_ProcessFile function

Instruction	Description
`` `[C:VariableName]` ``	Lists current value of a CGI variable
`` `[F:FieldName]` ``	Lists field value (null if absent)
`` `[V:FieldName]` ``	Lists field value (empty if absent)
`` `[Q:ParameterNumber]` ``	Lists the query string parameter
`` `Expression` ``	Lists expression result
`` `A:FieldName=Value` ``	Assigns a value to a form field
`` `?^Condition^TextIfTrue^TextIfFalse^ ``	Processes text based on the condition
`` `N@VariableName,MaxLoops,TextToProcess@ ``	Runs index-based loop
`` `[I:FilePathName]` ``	Inserts another text file

If the template file does not contain any embedded instructions, then the UTILS_ProcessFile function simply returns the contents of that file to the calling procedure. The NOTASK.TXT template file serves as a good example of this case, since it currently represents a CGI output that redirects the Web client to the main menu of the Job Listing System.

If you open the NOTASK.TXT template file residing in the C:\WEBSITE\CGI-WIN\JOBLIST\ directory through your Notepad application, you will see it only contains the following redirection header line followed by a blank line:

```
Location: /book/joblist/joblist.htm
```

To test that the JOBLIST.EXE actually returns this redirection response, specify the following URL from your Web browser while your Web server is running:

```
http://localhost/cgi-win/book/joblist/joblist.exe/
```

Your browser displays the main menu document, as shown in Figure 14-8.

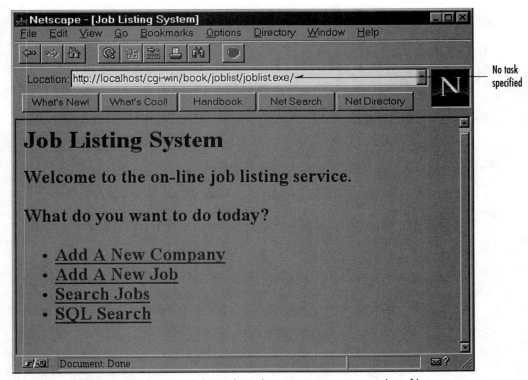

Figure 14–8 Testing the output based on the NOTASK.TXT template file

LESSON 4: LISTING PROGRAM VARIABLES IN A TEMPLATE FILE

The UTILS_ProcessFile function allows you to refer to the following types of program variables within a template file:

- CGI variables
- Form fields
- User-defined variables
- Query parameters

Referring to CGI Variables in a Template File

You can list the current value of any CGI variable within a template file using the following syntax:

`` `[C:VariableName]` ``

where *VariableName* refers to the name of the CGI variable as declared in the CGI32.BAS module without the *CGI_* prefix. For example, if you want to list the value of the CGI_Version variable in your template file, you have to insert the following code at the appropriate position within the file:

`` `[C:Version]` ``

An example of a template file that makes use of this CGI variable referencing feature is the ERR_METH.TXT file. If you look at Figure 14-5 in Lesson 1, the CGI_Main procedure processes the ERR_METH.TXT file if it encounters a request method other than GET or POST. The contents of the ERR_METH.TXT file are as follows:

```
Content-type: text/html

<HTML>
<TITLE>Request Method Error</TITLE>
<BODY>
<H2>
Unable to handle the request method: `[C:RequestMethod]`.
</H2>
</BODY>
</HTML>
```

Note: In this chapter, all template file instructions are presented in boldface for easy readability. The formatting otherwise does not have any special significance.

Referring to Form Fields in a Template File

You can refer to the value of any form field within a template file using one of the following instructions:

```
`[F:FieldName]`
`[V:FieldName]`
```

where *FieldName* refers to the name of the form field currently available to your CGI program. The only difference between these two instructions is in what value they return when a field with the specified name does not exist or contains an empty string. In particular, the `[F:FieldName]` instruction returns a Null value, whereas, the `[V:FieldName]` instruction returns an empty string ("").

As an example, if a user sends a form field named *Search Keyword* to your Windows CGI program, you can refer to the value of this field in your template file, as follows:

```
`[F:Search Keyword]`
`[V:Search Keyword]`
```

If the Search Keyword form field contains the value "Web", then both these instructions return the string "Web". However, if the Search Keyword form field is blank or unavailable (did not accompany the CGI request), then the `[F:Search Keyword]` instruction returns a Null value, whereas the `[V:Search Keyword]` instruction returns an empty string ("").

Referring to User-Defined Variables in a Template File

User-defined variables are treated as special form fields that are not passed by a Web client but are created internally by your CGI program with the UTILS_AssignField function. The syntax of this function is as follows:

```
UTILS_AssignField FieldName, FieldValue
```

where *FieldName* and *FieldValue* refer to the name and value of the form field to be created.

As an example, consider the APP_SendMsg procedure called by the APP_DoGet and the APP_DoPost procedures described earlier in the chapter. The code of the APP_SendMsg procedure is as follows:

```
Public Sub APP_SendMsg(Msg, Title)
  Utils_AssignField "Msg", Msg
  Utils_AssignField "Title", Title
  APP_ProcessFile "MESSAGE.TXT"
End Sub
```

APP_SendMsg uses the UTILS_AssignField procedure to create two new form fields named Msg and Title whose values are set based on the arguments passed to this procedure. The APP_SendMsg procedure then processes the MESSAGE.TXT file which refers to these two form fields from within the HTML text, as shown:

```
Content-type: text/html

<HTML>
<TITLE>`[F:Title]`</TITLE>
<BODY>
<H2>
`[F:Msg]`
</H2>
</BODY>
</HTML>
```

To test the APP_SendMsg procedure, enter the following URL from your Web browser while your WebSite server is running:

```
http://localhost/cgi-win/book/joblist/joblist.exe/count
```

The JOBLIST.EXE returns an error message based on the MESSAGE.TXT file, as shown in Figure 14-9.

NOTE: If the FieldName argument of the UTILS_AssignField procedure refers to an existing form field, the UTILS_AssignField procedure overwrites the previous value of that existing form field with the new value.

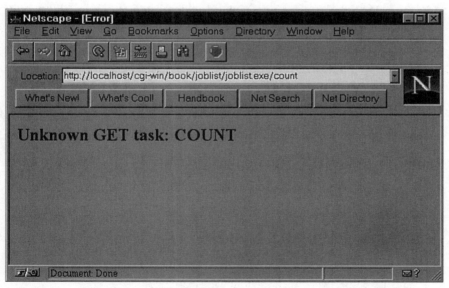

Figure 14–9 Testing the output based on the MESSAGE.TXT template file

Referring to Query String Parameters within a Text File

As mentioned before, in a GET type CGI request, parameters are passed through the query string portion of a URL. The Web server does not decode this query string; it passes it as is to a Windows CGI program through the CGI_QueryString variable. If the query string contains multiple parameters, you need a way to separate these parameters.

The UTILS.BAS library supports a scheme that uses the + character as a parameter separator. For example, if you pass the following string through the query string portion of a GET request:

`35+abc+12/12/98`

you can refer to each parameter by its parameter number in the template file using the following syntax:

`` `[Q:ParameterNumber]` ``

In the preceding example, `` `[Q:1]` `` will be replaced by 35, and `` `[Q:3]` `` will be replaced by 12/12/98 when the template file containing these codes gets processed.

> **NOTE:** As an alternative, you can also pass multiple parameters through the query string using the standard URL encoding method which lists *name=value* string pairs delimited by the & character. However, the APP_ProcessFile function currently does not support this scheme.

LESSON 5: EVALUATING EXPRESSIONS IN A TEMPLATE FILE

You can evaluate valid expressions within a template file using the following syntax:

`` `expression` ``

For example, the expression `` `1+2` `` will be substituted with the value 3 and the expression `` `"1" + "2"` `` will be substituted with the value 12 when the text file is processed. Note that the result of the string expression does not contain the double-quote characters.

Using Program Variables in an Expression

In an expression, you can refer to any of the program variables described in the previous lesson. For example, if you have two form fields named UnitPrice and Quantity containing the values 10 and 12, respectively, then the following expression:

`` `[F:UnitPrice] * [F:Quantity]` ``

will be substituted with the value 120. This expression will also evaluate to 120 (no quotes) if the UnitPrice and Quantity fields contained text strings "10" and "12", respectively. This is because UTILS_ProcessFile intelligently converts their values to a numeric data type before evaluating the expression. If, on the other hand, the field UnitPrice contained the data "$3/case", then the preceding expression would produce an error, as described in the next section.

420

> ⌦ **NOTE:** When you use program variables within an expression, you should not individually enclose them within the backquote characters. For example, the following text will not evaluate the expression, but will generate the text *10 * 12* instead:

```
`[F:UnitPrice]` * `[F:Quantity]`
```

Locating Errors in an Expression

Your expression must be based on terms that belong to compatible types. For example, the following expressions are considered invalid by the UTILS_ProcessFile function:

```
`"a" + 2`              'Trying to add a string to a number
`Hello`                'Using a string constant without quotes
`[F:UnitPrice] + 3`    'If UnitPrice field has a value: $3/case
```

In all these cases, the UTILS_ProcessFile function will substitute the expression with an HTML comment that will indicate the reason why the expression could not be evaluated. Since the error is listed as an HTML comment, the browser does not display the error. You have to view the HTML source to get to the error.

Let's experiment with a few valid and invalid expressions to see how these expressions are processed and what kind of error messages are returned. For this experiment, we will use the Test action of the Job Listing System, which returns the response based on a template file named TEST.TXT. Follow these steps:

1. Replace the existing TEST.TXT file in the C:\WEBSITE\CGI-WIN\BOOK\JOBLIST\ directory with the file named *TEST_EXP.TXT* by issuing the following commands from an MS-DOS prompt:

```
CD C:\WEBSITE\CGI-WIN\BOOK\JOBLIST\
COPY TEST.TXT TEST_BAK.TXT
COPY TEST_EXP.TXT TEST.TXT
```

The TEST.TXT file now contains the following text:

```
Content-type: text/html

<HTML>
<HEAD>
<TITLE> Job Listing System -  Testing</TITLE>
</HEAD>
<BODY>
<H1>Job Listing System - Expression Test</H1>
<PRE>
1 + 2 = `1+2`
"1" + "2" = `"1" + "2"`
```

```
"a" + 2 = `"a" + 2`
`hello`
</PRE>
</BODY>
</HTML>
```

2. Ensure that your WebSite server is running.

3. Enter the following URL from your Web browser:

`http://localhost/cgi-win/book/joblist/joblist.exe/test`

Figure 14-10 displays the response returned by the Job Listing System after processing the current TEST.TXT file.

As you can see from the figure, the first two expressions are evaluated correctly, while the result of the last two expressions does not appear on the browser's window. If you view the underlying HTML source of the response (see Figure 14-11), you will notice that the last two expressions resulted in an error, and their corresponding error messages were returned as HTML-formatted comments.

NOTE: Any expression that evaluates to a Null value (for example, `2 + Null`) is also substituted by a special HTML-formatted comment: *<!--Null-->*.

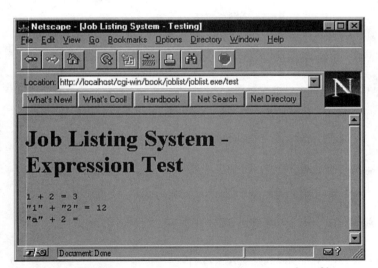

Figure 14-10 Evaluating expressions in a template file

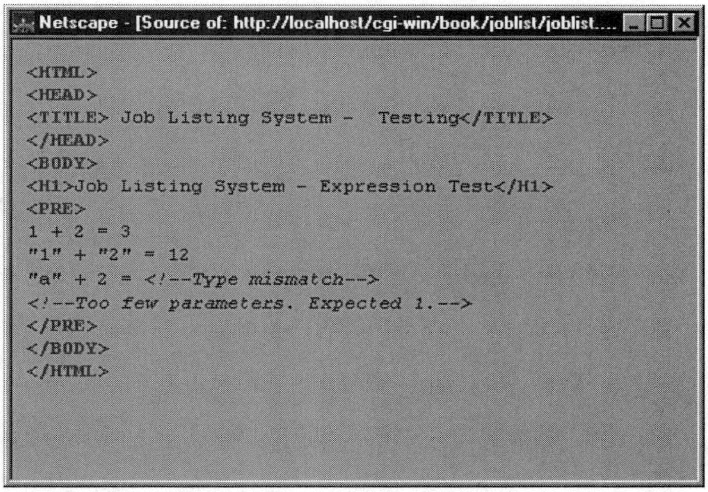

```
Netscape - [Source of: http://localhost/cgi-win/book/joblist/joblist....

<HTML>
<HEAD>
<TITLE> Job Listing System -  Testing</TITLE>
</HEAD>
<BODY>
<H1>Job Listing System - Expression Test</H1>
<PRE>
1 + 2 = 3
"1" + "2" = 12
"a" + 2 = <!--Type mismatch-->
<!--Too few parameters. Expected 1.-->
</PRE>
</BODY>
</HTML>
```

Figure 14–11 Locating errors generated during the processing of a template file

Using Built-In Functions in an Expression

You can also use built-in Visual Basic functions in an expression, as illustrated by the following examples:

```
`year(#12/20/98#)`        (results in 1998)
`day(cvdate([F:Date]))` (results in 20 if Date field="12/20/98")
`format([F:Price],"Currency")` (results in $20.00 if Price field=20)
```

Note that you should use lowercase characters to specify the function name. Also, you cannot use your own user-defined functions in an expression. The reason for this limitation is discussed further in Lesson 4, "Using Multiple Template Files to Perform the Drill-Down Search," of Chapter 15, Displaying Database Records Through Template Files.

LESSON 6: ASSIGNING VARIABLES IN A TEMPLATE FILE

As explained in Lesson 4 of this chapter, the user-defined variables are treated as special form fields which you create in your CGI program. You also have the flexibility to define new form fields from within the template file using the following syntax:

```
`A:FieldName=FieldValue`
```

where *FieldName* refers to the name of the form field, and *FieldValue* can be any valid expression. Some examples of this assignment instruction follow:

```
`A:ConversionFactor=1.25`
`A:Currency="$"`
`A:Path=[C:ExecutablePath]`
`A:TotalCost=[F:Quantity] * [F:UnitPrice]`
```

Note that there is no backquote character before the expression representing the field value. The following steps describe how you can try out this assignment instruction using the Test option of the Job Listing System:

1. Replace the existing TEST.TXT file in the C:\WEBSITE\CGI-WIN\BOOK\JOBLIST\ directory with the file named *TEST_VAR.TXT* by issuing the following commands from an MS-DOS prompt:

```
CD C:\WEBSITE\BOOK\CGI-WIN\JOBLIST\
COPY TEST_VAR.TXT TEST.TXT
```

If you display the contents of the TEST.TXT file, you will see that it now contains the following text:

```
Content-type: text/html

<HTML>
<HEAD>
<TITLE> Job Listing System -  Testing</TITLE>
</HEAD>
<BODY>
<H1>Job Listing System - Variable Test</H1>
`A:Currency="$"` `A:UnitPrice=10` `A:Quantity=12`
`A:TotalCost=[F:UnitPrice] * [F:Quantity]`
<H2>
Total cost of `[F:Quantity]` items at `[F:Currency]``[F:UnitPrice]` per ⇐
item is `[F:Currency]``[F:TotalCost]`.
</H2>
</BODY>
</HTML>
```

2. Enter the following URL from your Web browser while your WebSite server is running:

```
http://localhost/cgi-win/book/joblist/joblist.exe/test
```

Figure 14-12 displays the response returned by the Job Listing System after processing this TEST.TXT file.

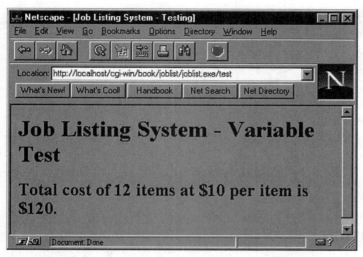

Figure 14–12 Assigning variables in a template file

LESSON 7: SPECIFYING CONDITIONS IN A TEMPLATE FILE

You can conditionally process sections of a template file based on the value of an expression. The syntax to specify such conditions is as follows:

```
`?^Condition^TextIfTrue^TextIfFalse^
```

where *Condition* is any valid expression, and *TextIfTrue* is the text that is processed if the *Condition* evaluates to a *true-type* value. The *TextIfFalse* is the text that is processed if the *Condition* evaluates to a *false-type* value. Observe that the condition instruction begins with the ` character, but ends with the ^ character. This is essential for the UTILS_ProcessFile function, which uses the ^ character to correctly determine the boundaries of condition instruction.

A condition, which can be either a string or a numeric expression, is considered to be a *false-type* if it evaluates to any of the following values:

```
"<!--Null-->", "", "0", 0, "False", "No"
```

In all other cases, the value of the condition is considered to be a *true-type*. As an example, the following template file condition will produce the text *Zero*:

```
`?^0^Zero^Non-Zero^
```

As indicated earlier, you can also embed expressions and program variables in any part of the condition instruction. For example, the following condition ensures that the rate is computed only if the quantity field is positive:

```
`?^[F:Quantity]>0^Rate is `[F:TotalCost]/[F:Quantity]`^^
```

Note that in this example, the false section of the condition instruction is empty, so no text is substituted if the quantity field is zero or negative.

Role of the Delimiter Character in a Condition Instruction

The ^ character you see in the above condition instructions acts as a delimiter character for identifying the three sections. You can also use any other character in place of the ^ character to play the role of a delimiter. For example, the following two condition instructions are equivalent:

```
`?^0^Zero^Non-Zero^
`?&0&Zero&Non-Zero&
```

When you select a delimiter character, just make sure that this character does not occur in any of the three sections of the condition instruction. Also, you cannot use the ` character in place of the ^ character.

Nesting Conditions

You can nest one condition within another condition as long as you use different delimiters with each condition instruction. The following example illustrates how you can use nested conditions to determine if the Quantity field is negative, zero, or positive:

```
`?^[F:Quantity]>0^Postive^`?&[F:TestValue]=0&Zero&Negative&^
```

Experimenting with Condition Instructions

The JOBLIST directory contains a template file named TEST_IF.TXT which includes some sample condition instructions. The contents of this file are as follows:

```
Content-type: text/html

<HTML>
<HEAD>
<TITLE> Job Listing System -  Testing</TITLE>
</HEAD>
<BODY>
<H1>Job Listing System - Condition Test</H1>
<H2>
`A:ItemPrice=0`
Item's current price: `?^[F:ItemPrice]=0^Free^$`[F:ItemPrice]`^
<BR>
`A:ItemPrice=20`
Item's current price: `?^[F:ItemPrice]=0^Free^$`[F:ItemPrice]`^
<BR>
`A:TestResult="False"`
Test result: `?&[F:TestResult]&Success&Fail&
</H2>
</BODY>
</HTML>
```

You can use the Test option of the Job Listing System as described in the previous lessons on this template file to observe how these sample condition instructions get processed. (See Figure 14-13.)

LESSON 8: CREATING LOOPS IN A TEMPLATE FILE

You can repeatedly process a section of a template file by enclosing that section within a loop instruction. The syntax of the loop instruction is as follows:

```
`N@IndexVariableName,MaxLoops,TextToProcess@
```

where *IndexVariableName* is the name of the form field that acts as the loop index, *MaxLoops* is a numeric expression that defines the maximum value of the loop index field, and *TextToProcess* is the section of the template file that is processed for each loop iteration. As an example, the following loop instruction produces the text *12345*:

```
`N@i,5,`[F:i]`@
```

In this example, the value of the index variable automatically starts at 1 and is incremented by 1 after every loop iteration. If you want the index variable to start with a value other than 1, you can preassign the index variable to one number less than the desired start value with the assignment instruction and then list the loop instruction. For example, the following set of instructions produces the text *45*:

```
`A:i=3` `N@i,5,`[F:i]`@
```

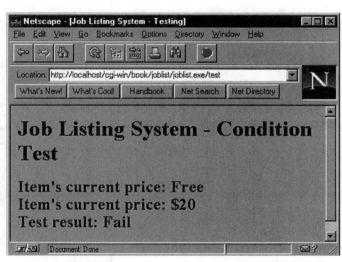

Figure 14–13 Specifying conditions in a template file

The first assignment instruction presets the value of the index variable *i* to 3 (one less than 4), causing the loop instruction to run through two loop iterations, one with i=4 and the other with i=5.

Delimiter Characters in a Loop Instruction

Just like the condition instruction, the @ delimiter character of a loop instruction can be replaced with another character, and you can create nested loops or add conditions within a loop by using different delimiter characters. Note that the commas that separate the various parameters of a loop instruction are required and cannot be substituted with another character. You can, however, add commas in the text portion of your loop instruction. For example, the following text results in *Where ID In (1,2,3,4,5,6,7,8,9)*:

```
Where ID In (`N@i,8,`[F:i]`,@9)
```

The TEST_FOR.TXT file in the JOBLIST directory contains some more examples of the loop instructions. The contents of this file are as follows:

```
Content-type: text/html

<HTML>
<HEAD>
<TITLE> Job Listing System -  Testing</TITLE>
</HEAD>
<BODY>
<H1>Job Listing System - Loop Test</H1>
`N@i,3,I will not repeat myself! @
<BR>
`A:n=10`
`N@n,15,
17 x `[F:n]` = `17 * [F:n]` <BR>
@
</BODY>
</HTML>
```

Once again, you can process this template file using the Job Listing System's Test option to see the effect of the two loop instructions listed in this file. (See Figure 14-14.)

Loop Termination Criteria

Normally, the loop is processed until the index variable exceeds the specified MaxLoops value. The only exception is when an error is generated while processing the loop, in which case the error is returned and the loop is terminated. Note that the error only terminates the current loop; the rest of the template file still gets processed.

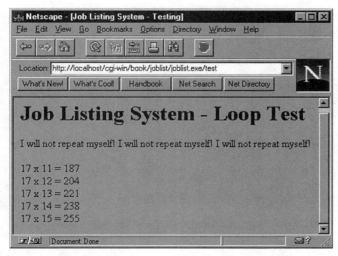

Figure 14–14 Creating loops in a template file

LESSON 9: INCLUDING THE CONTENTS OF ANOTHER FILE IN A TEMPLATE FILE

You can insert the contents of another text file in a template file using the following syntax:

`` `[I:FilePathName]` ``

where *FilePathName* refers to the absolute path and name of the file whose contents are to be inserted. An example of this instruction is as follows:

`` `[I:C:\WEBSITE\CGI-WIN\BOOK\JOBLIST\FOOTER.TXT]` ``

The inserted file is not treated as another template file, and its contents are not processed. This insert feature is provided to easily incorporate footers and headers that may be common to several template files.

The TEST_FIL.TXT file in the JOBLIST directory is a sample template file that contains one insert file instruction, as shown:

```
Content-type: text/html

<HTML>
<HEAD>
<TITLE> Job Listing System -  Testing</TITLE>
</HEAD>
<BODY>
```

continued on next page

continued from previous page

```
<H1>Job Listing System - Insert File Test</H1>
`[I:C:\WEBSITE\CGI-WIN\BOOK\JOBLIST\TEST_IF.TXT]`
</BODY>
</HTML>
```

If you process this file using the Test option of the Job Listing System, you will get the response shown in Figure 14-15.

The figure also hints at how you can use the insert file feature to output the ` character and the template file codes themselves. Alternatively, you can also output the ` character from within the template file by specifying two ` characters in sequence. For example, the text ``[F:Test]`` will result in `[F:Test]`.

REVIEW QUESTIONS

1. What are the main limitations encountered when developing a Windows CGI program using Visual Basic and the CGI32.BAS library?

2. What are the main disadvantages of the Server-Side Include approach for creating interactive Web applications?

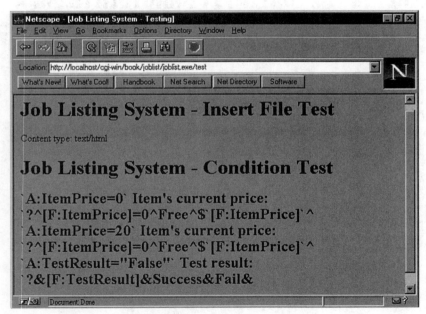

Figure 14-15 Inserting the contents of another file in a template file

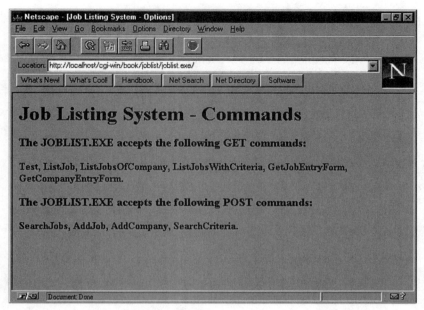

Figure 14–16 Listing the available commands of the JOBLIST.EXE program

3. What is the template file approach, and how does it differ from the Server-Side Include approach?

4. Can you mix the Server-Side Include and the template file approaches?

5. How does the UTILS.BAS library help in creating Windows CGI programs based on template files?

6. What is the format of a template file supported by the UTILS.BAS library?

7. Why does the JOBLIST.EXE program examine the CGI_RequestMethod variable?

8. How does the JOBLIST.EXE program determine which task is being requested?

9. What action does the JOBLIST.EXE program take when it encounters an unknown task?

10. What types of program variables can you access from a template file?

11. In a template file, what character is used in the beginning of every embedded variable or instruction?

12. Which procedure of the UTILS.BAS library is responsible for processing an entire template file?

13. How do you create user-defined variables in a template file?

14. What request method does a Web client use when a user clicks on a hypertext link? How are parameters passed using this method?

15. How do you evaluate expressions in a template file?

16. How do you specify a condition instruction in a template file? In what cases is a condition considered to be true?

17. How can you repeatedly process a section of a template file?

18. What are the advantages of inserting the contents of another file in a template file?

EXERCISES

1. Modify the functionality of the JOBLIST.EXE program so that it lists all the available commands as shown in Figure 14-16 when no task is specified in the requesting URL. Hint: Change the NOTASK.TXT file!

2. Change the MESSAGE.TXT template file to also include the e-mail address of the Web server administrator after the error message. Hint: List the value of the ServerAdmin CGI variable in the template file.

3. Display the response from processing the following template file on your Web browser:

```
<HTML>
<HEAD>
<TITLE> Job Listing System -  Exercise</TITLE>
</HEAD>
<BODY>
<H1>Job Listing System - Exercise</H1>
`A:Today=Date()`
`A:WeekDay=Weekday([F:Today])`
`A:Sunday=1`  `A:Saturday=6`
`?^[F:WeekDay]=[F:Sunday] OR [F:WeekDay]=[F:Saturday]^
`A:Weekend="True"`^
`A:Weekend="False"`^
<B>Today is `Format([F:Today],"Long Date")`.
`?^[F:Weekend]^
Its a weekend! Do you have any special plans?^
Another working day!^
</BODY>
</HTML>
```

15

DISPLAYING DATABASE RECORDS THROUGH TEMPLATE FILES

15

The previous chapter highlighted the advantages of incorporating the template file approach in a Web application. It introduced you to the UTILS.BAS library module provided with this book and showed how you can use the functions in this module not only to define the structure of your CGI response through an external template file, but also to perform the following operations from within the template file itself:

🎇 Assign and substitute program variables

🎇 Evaluate expressions

🎇 Define conditions

🎇 Specify index-based loops

In addition to these basic logical operations, the UTILS.BAS library also supports special instructions for listing database records directly from a template file. (See Table 15-1.) The JOBLIST.EXE program that we partially examined in the previous chapter takes full advantage of these database-specific instructions for the majority of its tasks.

Table 15–1 Database-related template file instructions

Instruction	Used To
`[Rn:*FieldName*]`	List current value of a recordset's field
`[Rn.BOF]`	List current value of a recordset's BOF property
`[Rn.EOF]`	List current value of a recordset's EOF property
`[Rn.Count]`	List number of records in a recordset
`[Rn.First]`	Make the first record the current record
`[Rn.Last]`	Make the last record the current record
`[Rn.Next]`	Make the next record the current record
`[Rn.Previous]`	Make the previous record the current record
`L@n,MaxLoops,TextToProcess@`	Recordset-based loop

LESSON 1: DISPLAYING A DATABASE RECORD FROM A TEMPLATE FILE

To display the database records from a template file, you need to follow these steps:

1. Create a Recordset object in your Windows CGI program using the method described in Chapter 13, Utilizing an Access Database in a CGI Application.

2. Set the record you want to display as the current record of that Recordset object.

3. Store this Recordset object as an element of a Recordset array named *UTILS_rsarray*.

4. Use the following syntax in your template file to list any field of the current record of that Recordset object:

```
`[Rn:FieldName]`
```

where *n* is the array position of the Recordset object being referenced and *FieldName* is the name of any field in that recordset. Note that the surrounding characters must be backquote (`) characters.

UTILS_rsarray is a global array variable declared in the UTILS.BAS module as follows:

```
Const UTILS_MAX_RECORDSETS = 5
Global UTILS_rsarray(1 To UTILS_MAX_RECORDSETS) As Recordset
```

When you specify the code `[R1:*FieldName*]` in the template file, the UTILS_ProcessFile function refers to the *n*th recordset of the UTILS_rsarray global array and substitutes this code with the value of the specified field of the current record of that recordset.

NOTE: *n* cannot be more than the value of the UTILS_MAX_RECORDSETS constant.

Example: Listing the Information of a Company Record

One function of the JOBLIST.EXE program is to return the company information when it receives a "ListCompany" task through the following GET request:

```
<A HREF="/cgi-win/book/joblist/joblist.exe/ListCompany?CompanyID>
```

As explained in the previous chapter, JOBLIST.EXE processes all the GET type CGI requests through the APP_DoGet procedure, which simply delegates the appropriate procedure to handle the requested task. For the ListCompany task, the APP_DoGet procedure calls the APP_ListCompany procedure whose code is shown in Figure 15-1.

The APP_ListCompany procedure expects a numeric CompanyID parameter in the query string portion of the requesting URL. It uses this parameter to determine which company's information it needs to return.

If the requesting URL's query string portion is empty, the APP_ListCompany procedure sends an error message; otherwise, it creates a Recordset object through a parameter query named *qryJOB_Company_AllFields*. This parameter query returns the company record for the given CompanyID as shown in Figure 15-2. Refer to Lesson 6, "Parameter Queries," in Chapter 6, Designing Advanced Queries, for a full description of parameter queries.

To accommodate the possibility that there may not be any company record with the specified CompanyID, the APP_ListCompany procedure first checks whether the parameter query returned any record, by testing the EOF property of the Recordset object. If the EOF property is true, it sends an appropriate error message; otherwise, it sends a response based on the COMPANY.TXT template file.

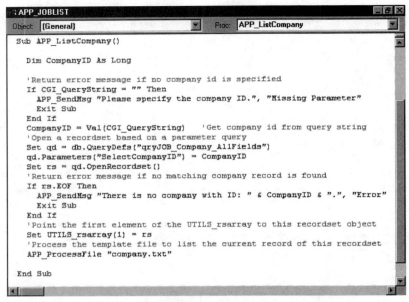

Figure 15–1 Design of the APP_ListCompany procedure

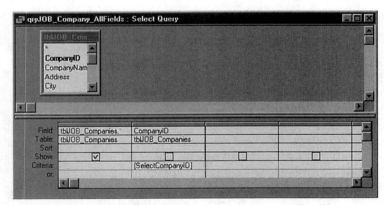

Figure 15–2 Design of the qryJOB_Company_AllFields parameter query

The COMPANY.TXT template file lists the various fields of a company record as an HTML document. The contents of this file are as follows:

```
Content Type: text/html

'A:Path=[C:ExecutablePath]'
<HTML>
<HEAD>
<TITLE> Job Listing System -  Company Details
```

```
</TITLE>
</HEAD>
<BODY>
<H2>Company Details
</H2>
<A HREF = "'[F:Path]'/GetJobEntryForm?'[R1:CompanyID]'">Add A Job For This Company</A>
<BR><B>Company ID: '[R1:CompanyId]'</B>
<BR><B>Name: '[R1:CompanyName]'</B>
<A HREF = "'[F:Path]'/ListJobsOfCompany?'[R1:CompanyID]'">List Jobs Of This Company</A>
<BR><B>Recruiter: </B>'?^[R1:Recruiter]^Yes^No^
<BR><B>Address: </B>'[R1:Address]', '[R1:City]', '[R1:State]' '[R1:Zip]'
'"<BR><B>Phone: </B>" + [R1:Phone]'
'"<BR><B>Fax: </B>" + [R1:Fax]'
'"<BR><B>Email: </B>" + [R1:Email]'
'"<BR><B>URL: </B>" + [R1:ReferenceURL]'
<P><B>Description: </B>
<PRE>'[R1:CompanyInformation]'</PRE>
</BODY>
</HTML>
```

The COMPANY.TXT file includes the template file instructions at several places in the text. To understand how these instructions get processed, let's first look at a sample response based on this template file:

1. Ensure that your WebSite server is running.

2. Specify the following URL from your Web browser:

   ```
   http://localhost/cgi-win/book/joblist/joblist.exe/ListCompany?2
   ```

   The browser displays the company information as shown in Figure 15-3.

Role of the Path Form Field

The first line of the COMPANY.TXT file defines a new form field named Path, whose value is set to the CGI_ExecutablePath variable. The Path field represents the base URL path of the JOBLIST.EXE program throughout this template file.

The main reason the template file relies on the value of the Path field instead of directly using the CGI_ExecutablePath variable is to help keep the file portable. Not all Web servers correctly report the proper URL path in the CGI_ExecutablePath variable, due either to a programming error or multiple document-mapping configurations leading to the CGI program's directory. So, if you notice that the CGI_ExecutablePath variable is not reflecting the correct path, you can just reassign the Path field with the exact URL path as follows:

```
`A:Path=/cgi-win/book/joblist/joblist.exe`
```

Construction of the Hypertext Link

The company information includes a hypertext link that allows a user to request a job entry form for that company. This link is constructed in the template file as follows:

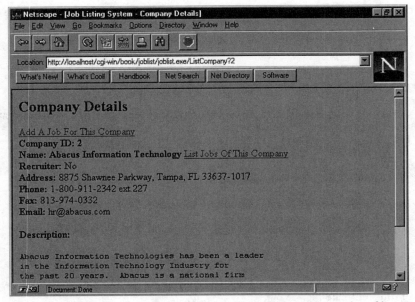

Figure 15-3 Response based on the COMPANY.TXT template file

```
<A HREF = "'[F:Path]'/GetJobEntryForm?'[R1:CompanyID]'">Add A Job For This Company</A>
```

The `[R1:CompanyID]` instruction represents the CompanyID field of the current company record and acts as a query string parameter for the URL being referenced in that hypertext link.

NOTE: This hypertext link also serves as a good example of how a Web application can include appropriate parameters in its response to maintain an interactive session with the Web user.

Listing Required and Optional Fields

The template file lists the values of all the non-Null company record's fields along with their HTML-formatted captions. Since the required fields such as CompanyID and CompanyName can never be Null, the template file codes for the required fields are simply embedded with the regular text as follows:

```
<BR><B>Company ID: '[R1:CompanyId]'</B>
<BR><B>Name: `[R1:CompanyName]`</B>
```

However, to prevent displaying the caption of an optional field that does not contain any information, a simple trick is used, where the optional field and its associated caption are concatenated by use of the + operator, as shown:

```
`"<BR><B>Phone: </B>" + [R1:Phone]`
`"<BR><B>Fax: </B>" + [R1:Fax]`
`"<BR><B>Email: </B>" + [R1:Email]`
`"<BR><B>URL: </B>" + [R1:ReferenceURL]`
```

For example, if the ReferenceURL field happens to be Null, the + operator will cause its corresponding expression to be evaluated as Null at processing time. The UTILS_ProcessFile function will then substitute that Null expression with the *<!--Null-->* HTML comment. The Web browser will not display this comment, thus achieving the net effect of hiding the optional field and its text caption.

You can see the evidence of this *nullifying effect* in Figure 15-3, where neither the Reference URL nor its caption is listed. If you examine the actual HTML source, you will see an HTML-formatted comment representing the Null value of the ReferenceURL field expression, as shown in Figure 15-4.

NOTE: When a text string is concatenated with a variable containing a Null value by use of the **+** operator, a Null value is returned. On the other hand, if the concatenation is done through the **&** operator, the text string itself is returned.

Using a Database Field in a Condition

Just as with other program variables and form fields, you can also use a record field in a condition instruction. This can be helpful when you want to provide your interpretation of a given database field. For example, the template file substitutes a more meaningful word to describe the current value of the Recruiter field through a condition instruction, as shown:

```
<BR><B>Recruiter: </B>`?^[R1:Recruiter]^Yes^No^
```

As such, the `[R1:Recruiter]` field will get substituted with either *True* or *False*.

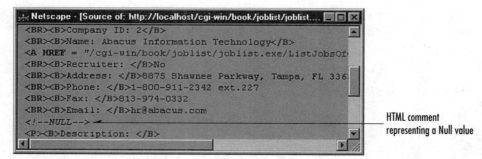

HTML comment
representing a Null value

Figure 15–4 Handling Null values in optional fields

🔑 **NOTE:** You can also hide the captions of optional fields containing a Null value by specifying a condition as follows:

```
`?^[R1:OptionalFieldName]^Field Caption: `[R1:OptionalFieldName]`^^
```

LESSON 2: NAVIGATING THROUGH RECORDS FROM A TEMPLATE FILE

In the previous lesson, you saw how to display the information from the fields of a Recordset object through a template file. When you refer to these fields, the data comes from the current record of that recordset. To list the field values of a different record, you have to first set that record as the current record.

As explained in Chapter 13, Utilizing an Access Database in a CGI Application, you can change the current record in your Windows CGI program using the move methods of the Recordset object. You can also call these move methods from within a template file as follows:

```
`[Rn.First]`
`[Rn.Last]`
`[Rn.Next]`
`[Rn.Previous]`
```

where *n* is the position of the Recordset object in the UTILS_rsarray global array.

As an example, if you want to list the first ten records of the Recordset object, you can use the move methods and a loop instruction as follows:

```
'[R1.First]'
'N@i,10,
Process Record: '[F:i]'
'[R1.Next]'
@
```

Furthermore, if you are not sure that your recordset will always contain ten records, you can test the EOF property of your Recordset object before referencing any field of the current record as shown:

```
'[R1.First]'
'N@i,10,
'?^[R1.EOF]^^Process Record: '[F:i]'^
'[R1.Next]'
@
```

For the preceding example, if the Recordset object contains only two records, the `[R1.Next]` instruction will generate an error in the third iteration, causing the loop to terminate after the third iteration. The net result will be as follows:

```
Process Record: 1

Process Record: 2


<!--No current record.-->
```

> **NOTE:** The blank lines in the preceding result are due to the newline (carriage return and line feed) characters in the text being processed through the loop. The `[R1.Next]` instruction in itself does not get substituted with any character, unless it generates an error. Generally, these extra blank lines do not affect the layout of an HTML document unless you are using the <PRE>...</PRE> HTML tag pair.

Applying the Record Count Instruction

One drawback of using the move methods with a standard loop instruction is that a *<!--No current record.-->* HTML comment is always generated when the recordset has fewer records than the specified number of loop iterations. Moreover, you also have to test the EOF property in the template file to determine if the current record has moved beyond the last record.

To overcome these shortcomings, you can specify the total record count of the recordset as the maximum limit of the loop instruction using the `[R1.Count]` instruction as shown:

```
'[R1.First]'
'N@i,[R1.Count],
Process Record: '[F:i]'
'[R1.Next]'
@
```

Note that in a loop instruction, when you use a program variable or an expression to specify a maximum limit, you do not enclose them with the backquote (`) characters. Also, the Count instruction does not change the current record of the recordset.

The preceding loop instruction on a recordset of two records produces the following result:

```
Process Record: 1

Process Record: 2
```

Using the Recordset-Based Loop Instruction

The Count feature resolves the problem of overshooting the recordset's boundaries, but you still have to issue an `` `[R1:Next]` `` instruction within the loop to move to the next record. To further simplify the process of record navigation, you can use a special recordset-based loop instruction supported by the UTILS_ProcessFile function. The syntax of this instruction is as follows:

```
`L@n,MaxLoops,TextToProcess@
```

In this instruction, *n* refers to the position of the Recordset object in the UTILS_rsarray global array, *MaxLoops* is a template file variable or expression (no surrounding `` ` `` characters), and *TextToProcess* is the portion of the template file that will be processed for each loop iteration. When you use this recordset-based loop instruction instead of a regular index-based loop instruction, the `` `[R1.Next]` `` instruction is automatically performed after each loop iteration.

The MaxLoops parameter can be a numeric expression, or it can be set to a special text value of *EOF*. The EOF value indicates that the loop should iterate until the last record of the recordset. This loop instruction also creates an implicit form field called Index_R*n* that acts as an index variable for this loop.

The following example shows how you can use this recordset-based loop instruction to navigate through all the records of your Recordset object:

```
`[R1.First]`
`L@1,EOF,
Process Record: `[F:Index_R1]`
@
```

Example: Creating the Job Entry Form

The JOBLIST.EXE program is designed to return two types of job entry forms:

- A general-purpose form that allows you to list a job for any existing company.

- A company-specific form that allows you to list a job for only a specified company.

The general-purpose form (see Figure 15-5) is returned when you specify the following URL from your Web browser:

```
http://localhost/cgi-win/book/joblist/joblist.exe/GetJobEntryForm
```

The company-specific form (see Figure 15-6) is returned when you provide the CompanyID in the query string portion of the URL, as follows:

```
http://localhost/cgi-win/book/joblist/joblist.exe/GetJobEntryForm?2
```

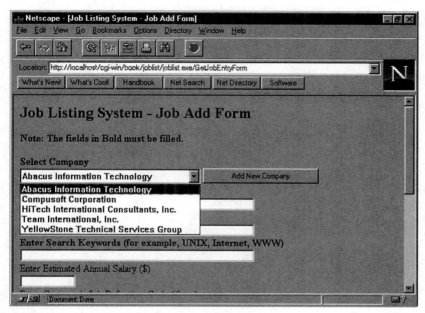

Figure 15–5 General-purpose job entry form

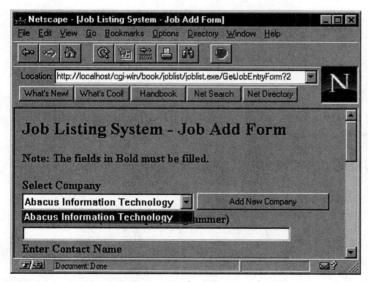

Figure 15–6 Company-specific job entry form

The only difference between the two job entry forms is the choices they provide in the Company Name selection list. The selection list in the general-purpose form lists the names of all the companies, whereas the company-specific form lists only the specified company.

Let's examine the code of the JOBLIST.EXE program to see how these two versions of the job entry form are created:

1. Launch Visual Basic and open the JOBLIST.VBP project file residing in the C:\WEBSITE\CGI-WIN\BOOK\JOBLIST\ directory.

2. Display the design of the APP_DoGet procedure.

   You will notice that the APP_DoGet procedure calls the APP_GetJobEntryForm procedure to handle the GetJobEntryForm task.

3. Display the design of the APP_ GetJobEntryForm procedure as shown in Figure 15-7.

The APP_GetJobEntryForm procedure first creates a Recordset object which represents the company records to be displayed in the job entry form. It inspects the value of the CGI_QueryString variable to determine if this recordset should contain records of all companies or just one specific company.

If the CGI_QueryString variable is empty, the procedure creates a recordset based on the qryJOB_Company_Names query, which returns the company ID and the company name of all the companies existing in the JOBLIST.MDB database. The records returned are sorted by the company name.

On the other hand, if the CGI_QueryString variable contains the CompanyID value, the APP_GetJobEntryForm procedure creates a recordset representing only that company's record. For this, it constructs an SQL statement through the code and uses that statement as the source of the recordset.

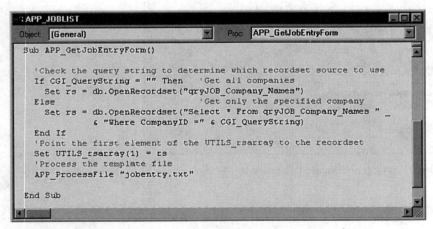

```
APP_JOBLIST
Object: [General]                    Proc: APP_GetJobEntryForm

Sub APP_GetJobEntryForm()

  'Check the query string to determine which recordset source to use
  If CGI_QueryString = "" Then    'Get all companies
    Set rs = db.OpenRecordset("qryJOB_Company_Names")
  Else                            'Get only the specified company
    Set rs = db.OpenRecordset("Select * From qryJOB_Company_Names " _
          & "Where CompanyID =" & CGI_QueryString)
  End If
  'Point the first element of the UTILS_rsarray to the recordset
  Set UTILS_rsarray(1) = rs
  'Process the template file
  APP_ProcessFile "jobentry.txt"

End Sub
```

Figure 15–7 Design of the APP_GetJobEntryForm procedure

After representing the appropriate records in the Recordset object, the APP_GetJobEntryForm procedure assigns that Recordset object to the first location of the UTILS_rsarray variable and then calls the APP_ProcessFile procedure to send the job entry form based on the JOBENTRY.TXT template file.

Understanding How the Template File Creates a Job Entry Form

The JOBENTRY.TXT template file does not have to figure out which version of the job entry form has to be generated. As far as this template file is concerned, it simply fills the Company Name selection list with all the company records in the recordset created by the APP_GetJobEntryForm procedure. The portion of the JOBENTRY.TXT template file that populates the selection list is listed next:

```
<BR><B>Select Company </B>
<BR><SELECT NAME="CompanyID">
'L@1,EOF,<OPTION VALUE='[R1:CompanyId]'>'[R1:CompanyName]'
@
</SELECT>
```

As you can see, a simple recordset-based loop instruction does the trick. Also note that the Value attribute of the selection list is set to the CompanyID field. This is to ensure that the Web browser displays the company names but passes back the CompanyID of the selected company when the user submits the form. The APP_AddJob procedure of the JOBLIST.EXE program uses this CompanyID value to link the submitted job with the correct company record.

LESSON 3: LISTING KEYWORD SEARCH RESULTS THROUGH A TEMPLATE FILE

The *one-recordset* technique used for generating two versions of a job entry form through the same template file can also be applied to send results of a database search. The basic idea is to first create a recordset representing the matching records and then process only one template file to present these records.

Chapter 3, Dissecting a Job Listing System, demonstrated three types of search mechanisms supported by the Job Listing System:

- Keyword search

- Drill-down search

- A general-purpose SQL search

While the JOBLIST.EXE program easily handles the keyword search and the SQL search using the one-recordset technique, it uses a different approach for responding to a drill-down search. The next lesson explains why the drill-down search cannot be carried out using the standard one-recordset technique and describes the alternative approach used by the JOBLIST.EXE program to perform this search.

In this lesson, we examine how the JOBLIST.EXE program manages the keyword search and the SQL-based search.

Example 1: Performing the Keyword-Based Search

The Job Listing System provides a specific HTML form (see Figure 15-8) for indicating what job-related fields can be searched on through the keyword search feature.

The keyword search form is designed to send the user-entered search parameters using a POST request method and to instruct the JOBLIST.EXE program to execute the task named SearchJobs. The Form tag of this form is specified as follows:

```
<FORM METHOD=POST
ACTION="/cgi-win/book/joblist/joblist.exe/SearchJobs">
```

The keyword search form, besides providing a standard submit button labeled "Search," also furnishes various other buttons for starting a drill-down search on different fields. All these buttons act as submit buttons and have the name "Submit," but the JOBLIST.EXE program responds differently to each button.

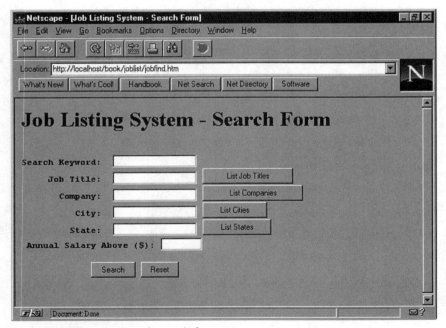

Figure 15–8 Keyword search form

Let's find out how the JOBLIST.EXE identifies which button the user clicked and what action it takes for each button:

1. Open the JOBLIST.VBP project file in Visual Basic if it is not already open.

2. Display the design of the APP_DoPost procedure, since the client submits the keyword search form using the POST method.

You will notice that the APP_DoPost procedure passes control to the APP_SearchJobs procedure to handle the SearchJobs request.

3. Display the design of the APP_SearchJobs procedure in the Code window of the JOBLIST.BAS module, as shown in Figure 15-9.

Handling Multiple Submit Buttons

The APP_SearchJobs procedure starts by inspecting the value of the form field named "Submit," which represents the submit button the user pressed to submit the request. For more information on how a Web client sends information about the clicked submit button, refer to Lesson 6, "Creating Multiple Submit Buttons," of Chapter 8, Creating HTML Forms.

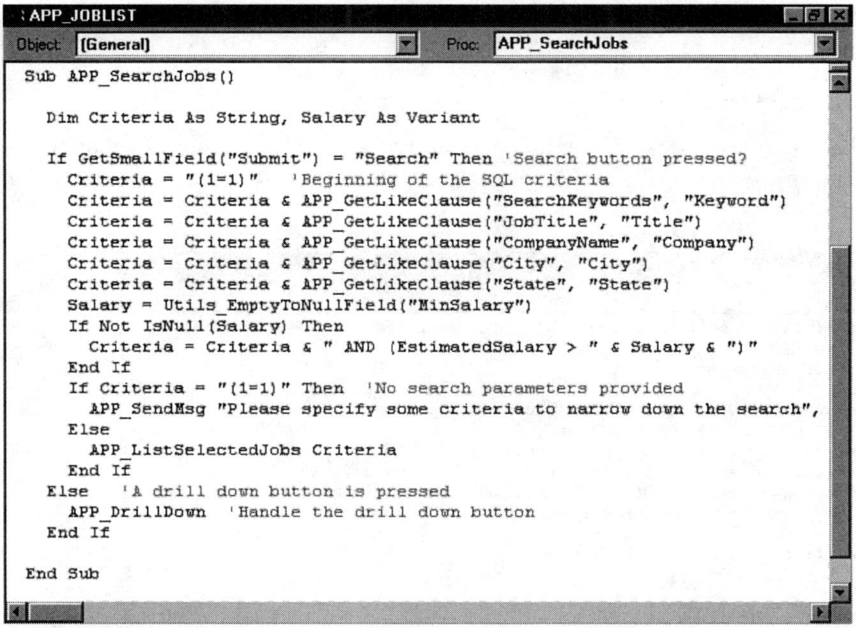

```
: APP_JOBLIST                                              _ 8 X
Object: (General)              ▼    Proc: APP_SearchJobs          ▼

  Sub APP_SearchJobs()

    Dim Criteria As String, Salary As Variant

    If GetSmallField("Submit") = "Search" Then 'Search button pressed?
      Criteria = "(1=1)"    'Beginning of the SQL criteria
      Criteria = Criteria & APP_GetLikeClause("SearchKeywords", "Keyword")
      Criteria = Criteria & APP_GetLikeClause("JobTitle", "Title")
      Criteria = Criteria & APP_GetLikeClause("CompanyName", "Company")
      Criteria = Criteria & APP_GetLikeClause("City", "City")
      Criteria = Criteria & APP_GetLikeClause("State", "State")
      Salary = Utils_EmptyToNullField("MinSalary")
      If Not IsNull(Salary) Then
        Criteria = Criteria & " AND (EstimatedSalary > " & Salary & ")"
      End If
      If Criteria = "(1=1)" Then  'No search parameters provided
        APP_SendMsg "Please specify some criteria to narrow down the search",
      Else
        APP_ListSelectedJobs Criteria
      End If
    Else   'A drill down button is pressed
      APP_DrillDown  'Handle the drill down button
    End If

  End Sub
```

Figure 15–9 Design of the APP_SearchJobs procedure

If the Submit field matches the "Search" text string, then the APP_SearchJobs procedure proceeds to construct an SQL criteria based on the values of the other search fields present on the keyword search form. In case the Submit form field has a value other than "Search," the APP_SearchJobs procedure assumes that the user has clicked one of the drill-down buttons and passes control to the APP_DrillDown procedure.

Constructing the SQL Criteria

For constructing the SQL criteria, the APP_SearchJobs procedure uses a step-by-step approach. It first initializes the Criteria variable to the "(1=1)" string. The "(1=1)" string represents a permanent True condition and is mainly used to simplify criteria construction.

Next, the APP_SearchJobs procedure appends a criteria expression for each text type search field to the Criteria variable by calling the APP_GetLikeClause function. The design of the APP_GetLikeClause procedure is shown in Figure 15-10.

The APP_GetLikeClause function takes the names of a table field and a search form field as its parameters and returns a "Like *Value*" criteria expression involving the table field and the value of the search form field. The function returns an empty string if the search form field is absent or has an empty string as its value.

As an example, if the form field named Company contained the value "Webs 'R Us" and the APP_GetLikeClause function is called as follows:

```
APP_GetLikeClause("CompanyName","Company")
```

the following string will be returned:

```
"AND (CompanyName Like '*Webs ''R Us')"
```

Note that the APP_GetLikeClause function automatically replaces the single quote in "Webs 'R Us" with two single quotes to ensure that the syntax of the criteria expression

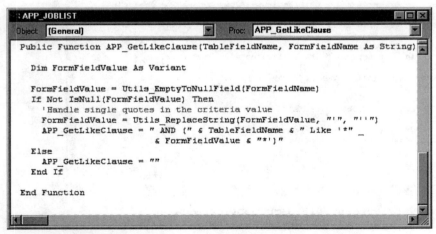

Figure 15-10 Design of the APP_GetLikeClause procedure

450

stays valid. Furthermore, this function also appends an *AND* prefix before the criteria to help the calling procedure append the current criteria expression to the existing criteria.

Now, let's get back to our discussion of the APP_SearchJobs procedure. After handling all the text type search fields, the APP_SearchJobs procedure appends a criteria expression involving the MinSalary search field to the Criteria variable if the MinSalary field has a value other than an empty string.

As its last step, the APP_SearchJobs procedure checks the final value of the Criteria to determine if the variable contains a criteria expression other than "(1=1)." If no new criteria got appended to this initial value, the procedure returns a message asking the user to specify some criteria; otherwise, it passes the Criteria variable to the APP_ListSelectedJobs procedure. Figure 15-11 shows how the APP_ListSelectedJobs procedure is constructed.

Listing Records Based on a Search Criteria

The APP_ListSelectedJobs procedure follows the same design as the APP_GetJobEntryForm procedure examined in the previous lesson. The APP_ListSelectedJobs procedure also creates one Recordset object by applying the given SQL criteria on the query named *qryJOB_SearchFields*. This query simply contains a list of job-related search fields from both the job listing table and the company table, as shown in Figure 15-12.

```
: APP_JOBLIST                                                    _ □ ×
Object [General]              ▼      Proc  APP_ListSelectedJobs          ▼

Sub APP_ListSelectedJobs(Criteria As String)

    If Criteria = "" Then
      Set rs = db.OpenRecordset("qryJOB_SearchFields")
    Else
      Set rs = db.OpenRecordset("SELECT * FROM qryJOB_SearchFields Where " _
                      + Criteria)
    End If
    If rs.EOF Then
      APP_SendMsg "No Jobs meet the search criteria. " & _
        "Please try again with another search criteria.", "No Jobs Found"
    Else
      Set UTILS_rsarray(1) = rs
      APP_ProcessFile "listjobs.txt"
    End If
End Sub
```

Figure 15–11 Design of the APP_ListSelectedJobs procedure

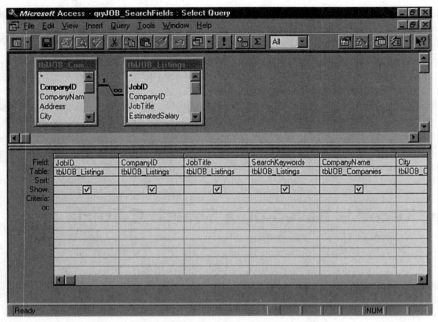

Figure 15-12 Design of the qryJOB_SearchFields query

If the qryJOB_SearchFields query returns no records, the APP_ListSelectedJobs procedure sends an appropriate message; otherwise, it sends the search results based on the
LISTJOBS.TXT template file, which also uses the recordset-based loop instruction to list
all the matching job records. The contents of the LISTJOBS.TXT template file are as
follows:

```
Content-type: text/html

'A:Path=[C:ExecutablePath]'
<HTML>
<HEAD>
<TITLE> Job Listing System -  Job Details</TITLE>
</HEAD>
<BODY>
<H4>Here are the jobs of interest.</H4>
<UL>
`L@1,EOF,
<LI><A HREF = "'[F:Path]'/ListJob?'[R1:JobID]'">'[R1:JobTitle]'</A>
for '[R1:CompanyName]' in '[R1:City]', '[R1:State]'
'" -- Estimated Annual Salary $" + ltrim(str([R1:EstimatedSalary]))'
<EM> (Viewed '[R1:ViewCounter]' times before). </EM>
@
</BODY>
</HTML>
```

Understanding How the Template File Lists the Selected Jobs

Figure 15-13 depicts the result of a sample keyword search on the word "Program" in the JobTitle field generated through the LISTJOBS.TXT template file.

As you can see from the figure, each selected job has an associated hypertext link for requesting further details on that job. The hypertext link is constructed in the template file as follows:

```
<LI><A HREF = "'[F:Path]'/ListJob?'[R1:JobID]'">'[R1:JobTitle]'</A>
```

Also note from the figure that the estimated salary is listed only for those jobs that have this information. The LISTJOBS.TXT uses the following expression to hide the text associated with the estimated salary when the EstimatedSalary field contains a Null value:

```
`" -- Estimated Annual Salary $" + ltrim(str([R1:EstimatedSalary]))`
```

This expression employs the same nullifying technique described in Lesson 1, except it has to first convert the currency type EstimatedSalary field to an equivalent string type before concatenating through the + operator.

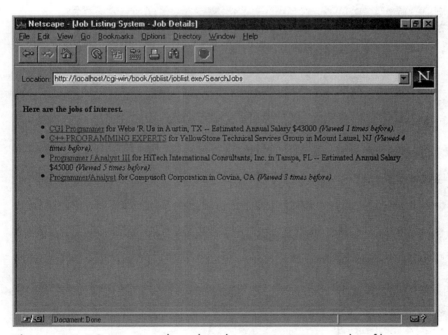

Figure 15-13 Response based on the LISTJOBS.TXT template file

Example 2: Performing an SQL Search

From the perspective of the JOBLIST.EXE program, an SQL search is just an extension of the keyword search, although the Job Listing System provides a different form (see Figure 15-14) for performing this search.

The SQL search form contains only one field, named *Criteria,* which the Web client sends to the JOBLIST.EXE program, using the POST method. The Form tag of this search form is as follows:

```
<FORM METHOD=POST
ACTION="/cgi-win/book/joblist/joblist.exe/SearchCriteria">
```

When the JOBLIST.EXE program receives the SearchCriteria request from this SQL search form, the program goes through the familiar sequence of first calling the APP_DoPost procedure, which further calls the APP_SearchCriteria procedure. Figure 15-15 displays the design of the APP_SearchCriteria procedure.

As you can see from the figure, the APP_SearchCriteria simply passes the user-specified SQL criteria to the APP_ListSelectedJobs procedure, confirming the claim that the SQL search is just a direct form of the keyword search.

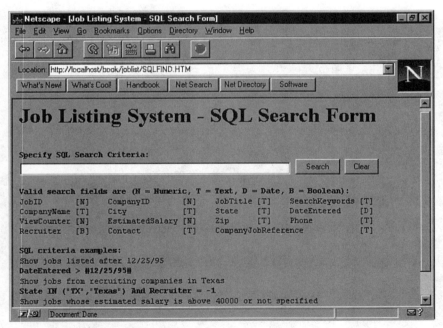

Figure 15–14 SQL search form

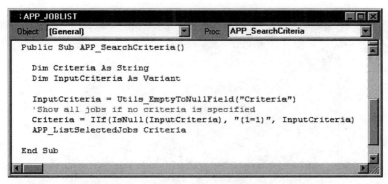

Figure 15-15 Design of the APP_SearchCriteria procedure

LESSON 4: USING MULTIPLE TEMPLATE FILES TO PERFORM THE DRILL-DOWN SEARCH

As mentioned in the previous lesson, JOBLIST.EXE uses a different approach to handle a drill-down search. This alternative approach is required to overcome the limitation that you cannot call a user-defined function from a template file. For example, the template file expression `MyFunction()` will result in an error even though you may have defined a function named MyFunction in your Windows CGI program.

Analyzing the First-Level Response of a Drill-Down Search

To understand why the drill-down search is affected by this template file limitation, let's first look at the first response generated by the JOBLIST.EXE program when you opt for the drill-down search:

1. Ensure that your WebSite server is running.

2. Request the keyword search form by specifying the following URL from your Web browser:

```
http://localhost/book/joblist/jobfind.htm
```

3. Click on the List Job Titles button.

The JOBLIST.EXE responds by presenting the list of all job titles existing in the database as shown in Figure 15-16.

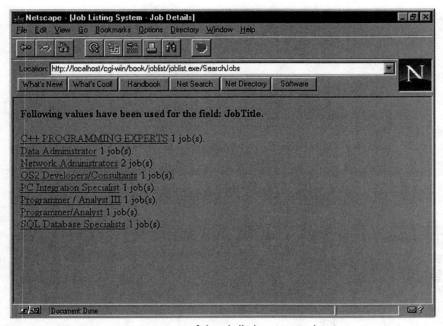

Figure 15–16 First response of the drill-down search

If you view the HTML source behind this response, you will notice that the hypertext link behind the first job title is as follows:

```
<A HREF = "/cgi-win/book/joblist/joblist.exe/ListJobsWithCriteria?JobTitle=''C++__⇐
PROGRAMMING__EXPERTS''">C++ PROGRAMMING EXPERTS</A>
```

Do not be alarmed if this hypertext link appears a little complicated. Just examine it by breaking the above HTML line into individual components of a hypertext link, as follows:

Resource being referenced: /cgi-win/book/joblist/joblist.exe
Extra Logical Path: /ListJobsWithCriteria
Query String: JobTitle::''C++__PROGRAMMING__EXPERTS''
Text being linked: C++ PROGRAMMING EXPERTS

The only strange-looking component now is the query string portion of the URL, which actually is an encoded version of the following SQL criteria:

```
JobTitle="C++ PROGRAMMING EXPERTS"
```

Encoding the Query String Parameters

The encoding is performed because you cannot directly list spaces in the query string. Also, the double quotes in the text *"C++ PROGRAMMING EXPERTS"* interfere with the double quotes enclosing the overall HREF argument. This encoding is done for each job title presented in the response by use of a special user-defined function of the UTILS.BAS library named UTILS_ConvertToQueryString.

Since this user-defined function cannot be called directly from a template file, the records have to be processed through the code itself. The difficult part is how to utilize the template file approach to dictate the format of the drill-down search response shown in Figure 15-16.

Luckily, there is a way to accomplish both objectives. The only catch is that you have to generate the response by processing not one but three template files. Let's trace through the code of the JOBLIST.EXE program and the template files associated with the drill-down search to unravel this final mystery.

Identifying the Drill-Down Field

We will start by looking at the APP_DrillDown procedure, which is called by the APP_SearchJobs procedure when it determines that the user has clicked a drill-down button. Figure 15-17 shows the design of the APP_DrillDown procedure.

The APP_DrillDown procedure checks the value of the Submit field to identify which search field the user wants to drill from. It then calls the APP_List procedure and passes the name of the table field associated with that search field to that procedure. Figure 15-18 shows the design of the APP_List procedure.

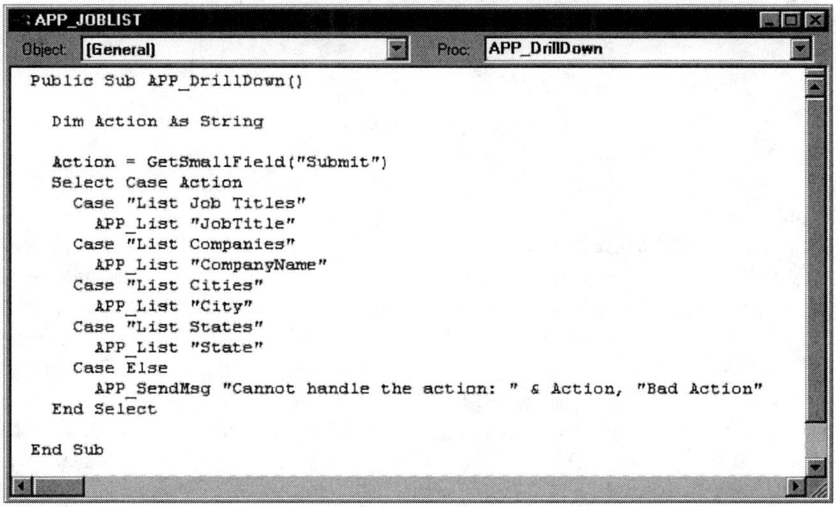

```
: APP_JOBLIST                                                    _ □ ×
Object: [General]          ▼      Proc: APP_DrillDown            ▼

 Public Sub APP_DrillDown()

   Dim Action As String

   Action = GetSmallField("Submit")
   Select Case Action
     Case "List Job Titles"
       APP_List "JobTitle"
     Case "List Companies"
       APP_List "CompanyName"
     Case "List Cities"
       APP_List "City"
     Case "List States"
       APP_List "State"
     Case Else
       APP_SendMsg "Cannot handle the action: " & Action, "Bad Action"
   End Select

 End Sub
```

Figure 15–17 Design of the APP_DrillDown procedure

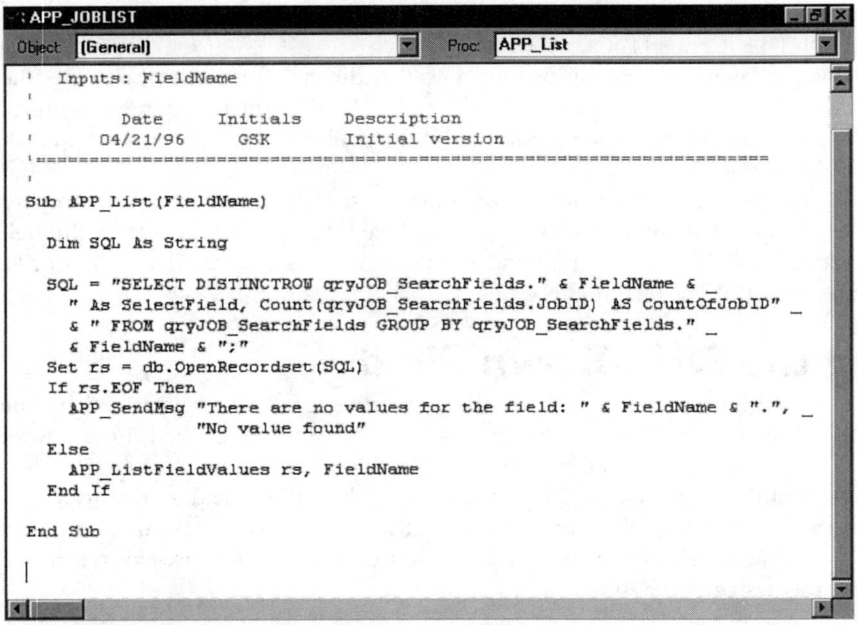

```
: APP_JOBLIST                                                    _ |8|X|

Object: [General]                    ▼   Proc: APP_List                ▼

'    Inputs: FieldName
'
'          Date      Initials    Description
'       04/21/96     GSK         Initial version
'==================================================================
'
Sub APP_List(FieldName)

  Dim SQL As String

  SQL = "SELECT DISTINCTROW qryJOB_SearchFields." & FieldName & _
     " As SelectField, Count(qryJOB_SearchFields.JobID) AS CountOfJobID" _
     & " FROM qryJOB_SearchFields GROUP BY qryJOB_SearchFields." _
     & FieldName & ";"
  Set rs = db.OpenRecordset(SQL)
  If rs.EOF Then
    APP_SendMsg "There are no values for the field: " & FieldName & ".", _
               "No value found"
  Else
    APP_ListFieldValues rs, FieldName
  End If

End Sub
```

Figure 15-18 Design of the APP_List procedure

Generating Unique Values

The APP_List procedure first constructs an SQL statement for returning unique values of the specified drill-down field. Figure 15-19 shows how this SQL statement appears in Microsoft Access' query design window when the JobTitle field is passed as the procedure's FieldName parameter.

Note that this SQL statement always generates two fields, *SelectField* and *CountOfJobID,* for all the drill-down fields. The SelectField contains the unique values of the specified drill-down field, and the CountOfJobID field indicates the number of jobs associated with each value. For more information on how unique values of a field can be produced by use of a Total type query, refer to Chapter 6, Designing Advanced Queries.

After building the SQL statement, the APP_List procedure creates a Recordset object based on that statement and passes that Recordset object and the FieldName parameter to the procedure named APP_ListFieldValues after ensuring that the recordset is not empty. Figure 15-20 shows the design of the APP_ListFieldValues procedure.

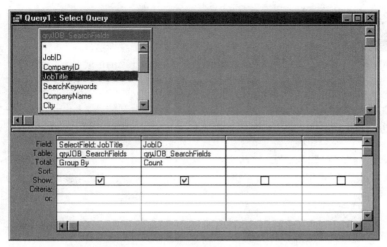

Figure 15–19 Query design of the SQL statement constructed by the APP_List procedure

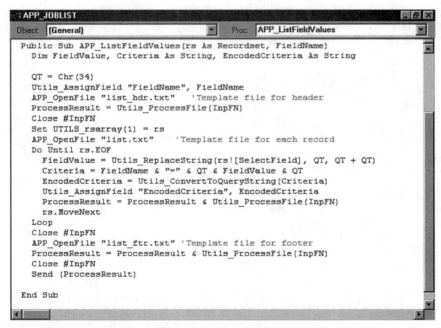

Figure 15–20 Design of the APP_ListFieldValues procedure

Presenting the First-Level Screen of the Drill-Down Search

The APP_ListFieldValues procedure handles the actual task of returning the first-level response for the drill-down search. This procedure constructs this response based on three template files: LIST_HDR.TXT, LIST.TXT, and LIST_FTR.TXT. The LIST_HDR.TXT and the LIST_FTR.TXT template files are processed only once; the LIST.TXT template file is processed for each record in the Recordset object passed to this procedure.

The Header Template File

The LIST_HDR.TXT template file contains the text that represents the header of the response. Its contents are as follows:

```
Content-type: text/html

<HTML>
<HEAD>
<TITLE> Job Listing System -  Job Details</TITLE>
</HEAD>
<BODY>
<H4>Following values have been used for the field: '[F:FieldName]'.</H4>
```

If you need to change the title or the heading of the drill-down screen, you have to modify this template file.

The Details Template File

The LIST.TXT template file contains the format for presenting the information related with each record. The APP_ListFieldValues procedure repeatedly processes this file through the following section of its code:

```
Set UTILS_rsarray(1) = rs
APP_OpenFile "list.txt"      'Template file for each record
Do Until rs.EOF
  FieldValue = Utils_ReplaceString(rs![SelectField], QT, QT + QT)
  Criteria = FieldName & "=" & QT & FieldValue & QT
  EncodedCriteria = Utils_ConvertToQueryString(Criteria)
  Utils_AssignField "EncodedCriteria", EncodedCriteria
  ProcessResult = ProcessResult & Utils_ProcessFile(InpFN)
  rs.MoveNext
Loop
```

For each record in the recordset, the APP_ListFieldValues procedure first replaces every double-quote character in the value of that record's SelectField with two double-quote characters and then constructs a valid SQL criteria of the form:

```
FieldName="FieldValue"
```

Next, the APP_ListFieldValues procedure uses the UTILS_ConvertToQueryString function of the UTILS.BAS library to encode this SQL criteria. The

UTILS_ConvertToQueryString function simply replaces all spaces with two underscore characters and all double-quotes with two single-quote characters.

After encoding the SQL criteria, the APP_ListFieldValues procedure assigns this encoded criteria to an internal form field named EncodedCriteria and then calls the APP_ProcessFile function to process the already opened LIST.TXT template file. Note that the local variable named EncodedCriteria is used just to make the code more readable.

The contents of the LIST.TXT template file are shown next:

```
'A:Path=[C:ExecutablePath]'
<A HREF = "`[F:Path]`/ListJobsWithCriteria?`[F:EncodedCriteria]`">
`[R1:SelectField]`</A>
`[R1:CountOfJobID]` job(s). <BR>
```

As you can see from these contents, the LIST.TXT template file simply refers to the current value of the EncodedCriteria form field to list the encoded SQL criteria in the hypertext link.

The Footer Template File

After processing the LIST.TXT template file for each record, the APP_ListFieldValues procedure processes the LIST_FTR.TXT template file to construct the rest of the response. The contents of the LIST_FTR.TXT template file are as shown:

```
</BODY>
</HTML>
```

Why User-Defined Functions Cannot Be Called from a Template File

The reason the UTILS_ProcessFile function cannot process a user-defined function is because your Windows CGI program is a binary executable file, and all the user-defined functions lose their identity at compile time. The built-in functions are processed by use of a special SQL-based technique which requires the presence of a database named UTILS.MDB in the C:\WEBSITE\LIB\ directory.

To find out how this SQL-based technique helps in evaluating all template file expressions, refer to the source code of the UTILS_ProcessFile and the UTILS_Eval functions listed in Appendix B, Source Code of the UTILS.BAS Library.

REVIEW QUESTIONS

1. What are the key steps required to list the value of a database record field from a template file?

2. What is the purpose of the UTILS_rsarray variable?

3. How is the template file code `[R1:FieldName]` processed?

4. What is the advantage of using a Path form field instead of referring directly to the CGI_ExecutablePath variable to specify the URL path of the JOBLIST.EXE program in a template file?

5. How does the COMPANY.TXT template file hide the captions of the optional fields that do not contain any information?

6. What instructions are available to navigate through the records of a recordset from a template file?

7. How can you list the total number of records in the recordset from a template file?

8. What is the advantage of using the recordset-based loop instruction over an index-based loop instruction for processing all records of a recordset?

9. How is the JOBLIST.EXE program able to create two versions of the job entry form using only one template file?

10. How are keyword search and the SQL search similar from the perspective of the JOBLIST.EXE program?

11. How does the APP_SearchJobs procedure determine if a user is requesting a keyword search or a drill-down search?

12. Why can't the JOBLIST.EXE program use the one-recordset technique to present the first-level response of a drill-down search?

13. How does the JOBLIST.EXE program overcome the limitation of not being able to evaluate a user-defined function from a template file?

14. How is the JOBLIST.EXE program able to incorporate the template-file approach to respond to the drill-down search?

EXERCISES

1. Review the design of the APP_ListJob procedure to determine how the JOBLIST.EXE program returns the information of a particular job.

2. Outline the steps the JOBLIST.EXE program takes to add a submitted job to the database.

3. Modify the JOBLIST.EXE program so that it returns the keyword search form for the following URL request:

```
http://localhost/cgi-win/book/joblist/joblist.exe/GetSearchForm
```

4. The version of the JOBLIST.EXE program described here is very weak on catching errors. For example, it does not check if the company ID specified for listing the company information is actually a valid number and not a text string. Add the necessary code in this program to improve its error-handling capability.

5. Currently, the response displaying the selected jobs (see Figure 15-13) does not indicate how the jobs were selected. Modify the JOBLIST.EXE program and the appropriate template file to list the SQL criteria used by the program to select the jobs.

6. Trace the design of the APP_ListJobsWithCriteria procedure to determine how it uses the UTILS_ConvertFromQueryString function to decode the encoded criteria, and present the second level of the drill-down search.

16

CREATING AN ON-LINE BOOKSTORE

16

There is a natural tendency among creative Web designers to spice up their Web sites with something different and possibly unique. While a site's uniqueness does provide its visitors a breath of freshness, it does not guarantee automatic popularity of that Web site. After you visit several sites on the World Wide Web, you notice that besides the novelty, there are many other key features that distinguish the popular sites from the ordinary ones.

Of course, one primary feature that attracts Web users is the information itself. If your Web site contains useful and up-to-date information, it is very likely that interested users will visit your site at least once to find out what your site has to offer. The trick, however, is ensuring return visits from those users.

While maintaining current and accurate information is certainly a step in the right direction, a lot depends on how you provide your information, and how easily and quickly users can assess the scope of your Web site. For instance, if your home page still shows the same information that it displayed a month ago, it can easily give occasional visitors a stale impression of your site. Furthermore, if it takes a user several minutes just to retrieve your site's home page, or if a user usually has to travel many nested links to find specific information, you may eventually lose that user as one of your frequent visitors.

Think of it this way. From a Web user's perspective, the distance between your site and your competitor's site is sometimes just a mouse-click, and it is your goal to provide all the neat and handy features on your Web site that will keep most users steered in your direction.

In this chapter we will analyze four factors that can have a significant effect on the overall appeal and usability of a Web site. If you are planning to run a CGI-based Web application on your Web site, then you should carefully assess these factors while developing the CGI application.

As a practical example, we will describe the implementation of a sample CGI-based bookstore application and how we consider these four factors to define the objectives of this application. Considering the scale of this project, it is not feasible to follow our usual step-by-step lesson-based approach to illustrate the construction of this application. Instead, we will focus on the final results of our implementation, highlighting the design and the code we used to meet the objectives of this application.

Disclaimer: For this bookstore application, we have used Waite Group Press (the publishers of this book) as our model. However, this application is only an example and not the actual Waite Group Press bookstore. Their real Web site is located at *http://www.waite.com/waite*.

FACTORS THAT AFFECT HOW YOU DESIGN YOUR WEB APPLICATION

So far, the sample Web applications we have discussed in this book have been mainly designed to serve as a good practical implementation of the ideas and techniques introduced in the previous chapters. However, for a Web application to meet the expectations and the limitations of the "real world," you need to weigh that application in terms of the following four factors:

- Speed
- Layout
- Change
- Searchability

Speed

Speed reflects how quickly Web users can retrieve the information from your Web application. It is not hard to notice that responding via a Windows CGI application takes significantly more time than sending a static file directly from the Web server, due to the additional communication overhead. You can compensate for this CGI speed barrier to some extent by opting for faster server hardware, but you will benefit the most when you strike a reasonable balance between using both static and dynamic pages in your project.

As an example, a Web site's home page is generally the most frequently visited page, and it is best if you keep it as a static file. Only if you want to provide custom responses as soon as users connect to your Web site should you consider serving the home page from the back-end of your CGI application.

The speed factor also affects how much information you should provide in your response. Remember that the majority of users surfing the Web are connected through relatively slow dial-up modems. Although these users may have learned to be patient surfers, they do appreciate Web sites that respect their bandwidth limitations and do not overload them with too much information at once.

Many Web sites, in their effort to stay bandwidth-friendly, present the requested information in several small pages while allowing the users to easily navigate between the pages. For example, when you perform a keyword search on Yahoo! (*http://www.yahoo.com*), it initially lists only a small portion of the search result. For the next set of matching entries, it provides a link at the bottom of its response as shown in Figure 16-1.

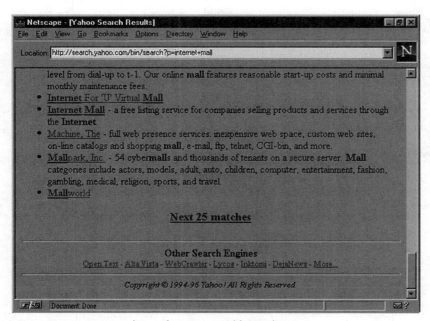

Figure 16–1 Search results presented by Yahoo!

Layout

Layout governs the overall appeal of a Web application, from the organization to the visual effects the application uses to present the information. Part of the layout is to ensure that you make judicious use of the physical page space. Pages that appear either short and overcrowded or long and skimpy tend to lose their effectiveness.

If you have to provide lengthy documents, supply an index on the top of the page. Alternatively, you can break your page into a first-level overview page and multiple second-level pages. However, try not to go too deep in the level hierarchy.

Microsoft's Web site (*http://www.microsoft.com*) provides a good example of an attractive home page as shown in Figure 16-2. It uses the HTML's Table feature to present the information in the form of a magazine layout.

Yahoo!, on the other hand, approaches its home page layout from the speed perspective. As shown in Figure 16-3, its home page is concise and embellishes itself with only a few small icons.

Change

Change ensures that your Web site remains a repeated target among Web users. Whether you periodically update your site's contents or modify your Web application's front-end, change is a highly desirable attribute. But use caution if you plan to reorganize the way your Web application presents the information. Regular visitors to your site who are used to the old way may not immediately appreciate your site's new look.

Figure 16-2 Microsoft's home page

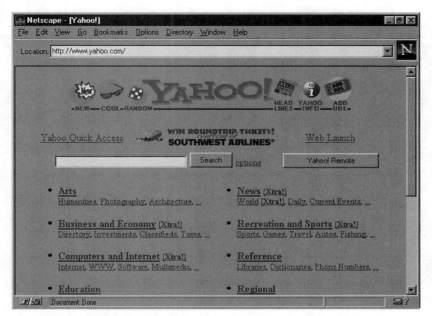

Figure 16–3 Yahoo!'s home page

When it comes to announcing the change, most users are more interested in finding what new information is available through your site than in how you changed its appearance or the technical aspects behind its operation. Be aware that "new" is a relative term. Frequent visitors may expect something new each day, while occasional visitors may want to cycle through the sequence of events that have occurred in the past month.

Most sites list their very recent events directly on their home pages (for example, Microsoft's home page in Figure 16-2) while providing a history of their past events through a "What's New" link. However, if your site does not generate new events on a regular basis, you can still keep it lively by periodically highlighting different portions of your site's contents through your home page.

One last caution on this change issue. If you are aware that other sites have established direct links to certain sections of your site, make sure that your local site changes do not affect the integrity of those links.

Searchability

No matter what type of information you present through your Web application, providing an appropriate search facility is a high-ranking feature on most Web users' wish lists. The two main attributes associated with a search feature are its flexibility and its efficiency.

The flexibility is defined by what fields users can search on and in how many ways they can specify a search criteria. If you look back at the keyword search feature of the Job Listing System (see Lesson 3, "Listing Keyword Search Results Through a Template File," in Chapter 15, Displaying Database Records Through Template Files), you will notice that although the system does allow you to search in various job-related fields, it is not entirely flexible in how it searches these fields.

For example, if you specify keywords in two or more fields, it always performs a logical *AND* operation and finds only those jobs that contain matching keywords in all those fields. Any job that matches in only some of the fields is completely ignored.

Moreover, if you search for two keywords in the same field, the system will only find those jobs where these two keywords appear in that field exactly as specified. For example, searching for "Programmer Analyst" in the Job Title field will not produce a job whose job title is listed as "Programmer/Analyst."

The inflexibility of the Job Listing System in handling multiple search keywords for one field occurs because it uses the "Like*pattern*" criteria for searching any text field. As mentioned in Chapter 5, Building Microsoft Access Queries, this pattern-matching criteria is also inefficient, since Access cannot take advantage of any field indexes when searching based on this type of criteria.

A better search utility is one that both provides the *AND/OR* capability on multiple keywords and employs some kind of word indexing to speed up the searches. Chapter 17, Enhancing the On-Line Bookstore, discusses the implementation of this type of keyword search feature in complete detail.

OBJECTIVES OF OUR ON-LINE BOOKSTORE

Based on the four factors discussed earlier, we defined the following objectives for our on-line bookstore Web application.

The Home Page

The home page should be concise, attractive, and act as a guide to all the features of the on-line bookstore. For speed's sake, it should be stored as a static file. However, to prevent the page from getting stale, it should contain a "Catch Of The Day" category that lists a different book every day.

What's New and What's Hot Options

The on-line bookstore should present a "What's New" option, which allows regular visitors to quickly locate any new books that have been published by the Waite Group Press. The "What's Hot" option should present the most frequently looked at books. In either case, the system should list the book title, authors, and the editorial of each book presented to the user.

Book-Browsing Options

The on-line bookstore should provide two ways to browse through the book titles: alphabetical and by subject. The alphabetical index should list the book titles alphabetically, and the subject index should present the book titles organized under different subject categories.

Book-Search Facility

The on-line bookstore should incorporate a keyword-search facility that allows users to locate books by searching for one or more keywords in either the title, editorial, or the author name field. The keywords could be present anywhere in the specified field for a match to occur.

Furthermore, the users should have the option to specify whether they want to find books that match all keywords (for a narrow search) or any keyword (for a broad search). The presentation of the search result should follow the pattern of the What's New and the What's Hot options.

Drill-Down Feature

All books and authors listed through the methods just mentioned should have an associated hypertext link that allows the users to view further details on a particular book or author. When presenting the author information, the system should also display all the books written by that author and published by the Waite Group Press.

THE PROJECT SETUP

Just like all the Web applications we have studied so far, our on-line bookstore also is laid out under two main directories: a document directory named C:\WEBSITE\ HTDOCS\BOOK\BOOKSTOR\ and a CGI-WIN directory named C:\WEBSITE\CGI-WIN\BOOK\BOOKSTOR\.

The document directory contains the static home page file INDEX.HTM, while the CGI-WIN directory contains the BOOKSTOR.EXE Windows CGI program, its associated project and template files, and a Microsoft Access database named BOOKSTOR.MDB.

The BOOKSTOR.MDB database stores all the book-related data except for the following information items:

- Cover page image
- Table of contents
- Book index

The cover page image of each book is stored as a GIF file in the COVERPG subdirectory of the document directory. The table of contents and the book's index, which are regular HTML files, are stored respectively in the TOC and the INDEX subdirectories of the document directory. All icons and other image files used by this bookstore application are stored under the IMAGES subdirectory of the document directory.

THE HOME PAGE DESIGN

Figure 16-4 shows our on-line bookstore's home page, which was a net result of several experimentation and alteration cycles.

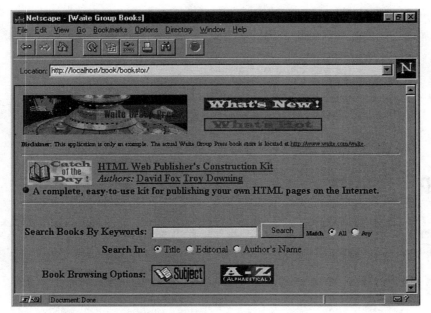

Figure 16-4 Home page of our on-line bookstore

You can display this home page on your browser by following these steps:

1. Start your Web server.

2. Request the following URL from your Web browser:

```
http://localhost/book/bookstor/
```

As you can see from Figure 16-4, this home page contains three main sections, which are separated by horizontal bars. The top section shows the Waite Group Press logo and two icons labeled "What's New" and "What's Hot." The middle section highlights a book under the "Catch Of The Day" category. The bottom section provides the interface for the keyword-search facility and the two book-browsing options.

While designing this home page, our target was to fit most of its layout within a 640x480 screen space. So we chose small icons and used HTML tables for horizontal and vertical alignment. In addition, we specified the WIDTH and the HEIGHT attributes of all images so that the Web browsers could reserve the necessary page space for the images and thus quickly display the text before actually retrieving the images.

At this point, you can open the INDEX.HTM file residing in the C:\WEBSITE\HTDOCS\BOOK\BOOKSTOR\ directory to view the HTML source of this home page.

The Top Section

The top section, which can also be called the logo section, is created by the following HTML code:

```
<IMG SRC="/book/bookstor/images/about.gif" WIDTH=257 HEIGHT=64 ALT="Welcome To Waite Group⇐
Press." ALIGN=Left>
<TABLE CELLSPACING=0 CELLPADDING=3>
<TR><TD></TD><TD></TD>
<TD>
<A HREF="/cgi-win/book/bookstor/bookstor.exe/new">
<IMG SRC="/book/bookstor/images/new.gif" WIDTH=181 HEIGHT=17 ALT="What's New"></A>
</TD></TR>
<TR><TD></TD><TD></TD>
<TD><A HREF="/cgi-win/book/bookstor/bookstor.exe/hot">
<IMG SRC="/book/bookstor/images/hot.gif" WIDTH=181 HEIGHT=17  ALT="What's Hot"></A>
</TD></TR>
</TABLE>
```

Note that the Waite Group Press logo image is not part of the HTML table. Only the What's New and the What's Hot icons are being aligned through the table rows. This was one easy way we were able to center these two icons with respect to the logo image.

The What's New and the What's Hot icons have attached links that both point to the BOOKSTOR.EXE Windows CGI program but specify a different task selector in the extra logical path portion of their URL.

The Middle Section

The middle section displays the Catch Of The Day icon and lists the title, the authors, and a catchy tag line of a randomly selected book from the book database. Later on in this chapter, we will describe how we automated the process of daily updating this section. The HTML code for this section is as listed:

```
<IMG ALIGN=Left SRC="/book/bookstor/images/catch2.gif" WIDTH=100 HEIGHT=39 ALT="Catch ⇐
of the Day" HSPACE=10>
<B><A HREF="/cgi-win/book/bookstor/bookstor.exe/showbook?1-57169-018-2">HTML Web ⇐
Publisher's Construction Kit</A></B><BR>
<I>Authors:</I><B>
<A HREF="/cgi-win/book/bookstor/bookstor.exe/ShowAuthor?20">David Fox</A>
<A HREF="/cgi-win/book/bookstor/bookstor.exe/ShowAuthor?21">Troy Downing</A>
</B>
<BR Clear=Both>
<IMG SRC="/book/bookstor/images/blueball.gif">
<B>A complete, easy-to-use kit for publishing your own HTML pages on the Internet.</B>
<HR>
```

In the preceding code, the links associated with the book title and each author request the BOOKSTOR.EXE program. The difference is that the title link sends the "ShowBook" instruction (using the extra logical path) with the book's ISBN (International Standard Book Number) as the parameter (through the query string), while each author's link sends the "ShowAuthor" instruction with their respective AuthorIDs to the BOOK-STOR.EXE program. In the next chapter, we will cover how BOOKSTOR.EXE handles the "ShowBook" and the "ShowAuthor" instructions.

The Bottom Section

This last section provides a keyword search interface and presents image icons for the two book-browsing options. The search interface not only permits users to enter one or more keywords in the input text box, but also lets them select the type and the target of the keyword search. In the next chapter, we will describe the functionality and the implementation of this search interface. The book-browsing options are discussed at the end of this chapter.

The HTML code for the bottom section is as listed:

```
<FORM METHOD="POST" ACTION="/cgi-win/book/bookstor/bookstor.exe/Search">
<TABLE>
<TR>
<TD Align=Right>
<B>Search Books By Keywords:</B></TD>
<TD>
<INPUT NAME="SearchKeywords" SIZE=20 MAXLENGTH=30>
<INPUT NAME="Submit" TYPE="SUBMIT" VALUE="Search">
<FONT SIZE=-2><B>Match</B>
<INPUT NAME="SearchType" TYPE="Radio" VALUE="AND" CHECKED>All
<INPUT NAME="SearchType" TYPE="Radio" VALUE="OR">Any
</FONT>
</TD></TR>
<TR>
<TD Align=Right><B>Search In:</B></TD>
<TD>
<INPUT NAME="SearchWhere" TYPE="Radio" VALUE="Title" CHECKED>Title
<INPUT NAME="SearchWhere" TYPE="Radio" VALUE="Editorial">Editorial
<INPUT NAME="SearchWhere" TYPE="Radio" VALUE="Author">Author's Name
</TD></TR>
</FORM>
<TR></TR><TR></TR><TR></TR>
<TR>
<TD Align=Right><B>Book Browsing Options:</B></TD>
<TD>
<A HREF="/cgi-win/book/bookstor/bookstor.exe/subject">
<IMG ALIGN=MIDDLE SRC="/book/bookstor/images/subject2.gif" WIDTH=80 HEIGHT=27 ⇐
ALT="Subject"></A>
<A HREF="/cgi-win/book/bookstor/bookstor.exe/alpha">
<IMG ALIGN=MIDDLE SRC="/book/bookstor/images/atoz.gif" WIDTH=80 HEIGHT=27 ⇐
ALT="Alphabetical" HSPACE=20></A>
</TD></TR>
</TABLE>
```

THE DATABASE STRUCTURE

The BOOKSTOR.MDB database contains all the information about the Waite Group Press books and their corresponding authors. It is a normalized database, and related information is stored in separate tables. See Lesson 5, "Normalizing Tables," of Chapter 4, Building a Database with Microsoft Access, for a discussion on database normalization.

The Book Table

The tblBK_Books table holds most of the book data in the BOOKSTOR.MDB database. We chose the ISBN of each book as this table's primary key since this number uniquely identifies each book. To view the design of this table:

1. Launch Microsoft Access and open the BOOKSTOR.MDB database file residing in the C:\WEBSITE\CGI-WIN\BOOK\BOOKSTOR\ directory.

2. Select the Table tab of the database container.

You will see many tables listed in this container as shown in Figure 16-5.

3. Highlight the table named *tblBK_Books* from the database container, and then click on the Design button.

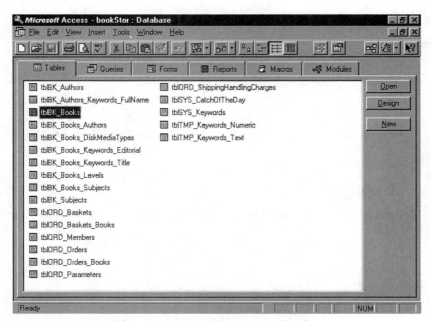

Figure 16–5 Tables in the BOOKSTOR.MDB database

Table 16-1 lists the name, the data type, and a brief description of each field contained in the tblBK_Books table.

Table 16-1 Design of tblBK_Books table

Field Name	Data Type	Description
ISBN (Primary Key)	Text (13)	ISBN of the book (unique to every book)
Title	Text (255)	Title of the book
FirstLetterInTitle	Text (1)	First letter of the book title (for alphabetical index)
PublicationDate	Date/Time	Publication date (also used by the What's New query)
Pages	Integer	Number of pages in the book
Price	Currency	U.S. price of the book
DiskMediaTypeID	Byte	Diskette, CD (see tblBK_Books_DiskMediaTypes)
NumDiskMedia	Byte	Number of disk media
MinLevel	Byte	Minimum readership level (see tblBK_Books_Levels)
MaxLevel	Byte	Maximum readership level (see tblBK_Books_Levels)
Editorial	Memo	Editorial of the book
KeyFeatures	Memo	Highlights of the book
Platform	Text (255)	Platform assumed by the book
Size	Text (5)	Physical size of the book (usually 7"x9")
TagLine	Memo	Tag line (also used for the Catch Of The Day feature)
CoverPageImageFileName	Text (50)	File name of the cover page image
TOCFileName	Text (50)	File name containing the table of contents
IndexFileName	Text (50)	File name containing the book's index
ViewCounter	Long	How many times this book has been viewed
DateLastViewed	Date/Time	Last time any user viewed this book
KeywordIndexed	Yes/No	Whether this book has been indexed for keyword search

The Lookup Tables

As part of the normalization process, the tblBK_Books table stores only a numeric ID for each of the following book-related data items:

- Disk media type (DiskMediaTypeID)

- Minimum readership level (MinLevel)

- Maximum readership level (MaxLevel)

The descriptions associated with the IDs used for these items are stored in two lookup tables named tblBK_Books_DiskMediaTypes and tblBK_Books_Levels, which both contain the following two fields:

🔩 ID (Byte)

🔩 Description (Text: 50)

The DiskMediaTypeID field is linked to the tblBK_Books_DiskMediaTypes lookup table, whereas the MinLevel and the MaxLevel fields are both linked to the tblBK_Books_Levels lookup table. Figure 16-6 depicts the one-to-many relationship existing between these lookup tables and the tblBK_Books table.

🔩 **NOTE:** Both lookup tables have only the Cascade Update option set for the referential integrity in this relationship. This way if you change an ID of a record in either lookup table, Access will automatically update the linked field in all the related book records with the new value. The Cascade Delete option is not checked, to prevent a lookup record from getting accidentally deleted while it is being used by one or more related book records. See Lesson 6, "Establishing Table Relationship and Referential Integrity," of Chapter 4, Building a Database with Microsoft Access, for a complete explanation of referential integrity and how to view the current referential integrity settings of the tables participating in a relationship.

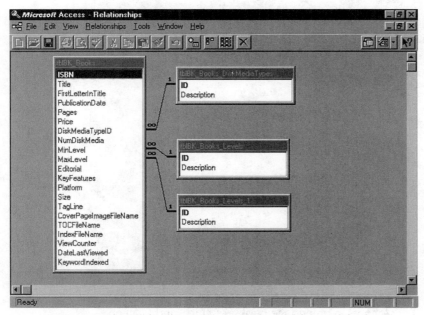

Figure 16–6 Relationship between the lookup tables and the book table

The Author Table

Observe that the tblBK_Books table does not contain any information about the authors. Again this is due to the normalization factor. It is easy to see that the books and the authors have a many-to-many relationship, since one book can have many authors, and one or more of those authors can be associated with other books.

The many-to-many situation is generally handled by use of the concept of a *junction table,* which essentially holds the primary key of the two tables participating in the many-to-many relationship. In our case, while the books are stored in the tblBK_Books table, the authors are stored in a separate table named tblBK_Authors. The tblBK_Books_Authors table acts as their junction table, as shown in Figure 16-7.

Tables 16-2 and 16-3 list the fields of the tblBK_Authors table and the tblBK_Books_Authors table, respectively.

Table 16–2 Design of tblBK_Authors table

Field Name	Data Type	Description
AuthorID	Integer	Primary Key
FullName	Text (255)	Author's full name
Bibliography	Memo	Author's bibliography
KeywordIndexed	Yes/No	Whether the full name has been indexed for keyword search

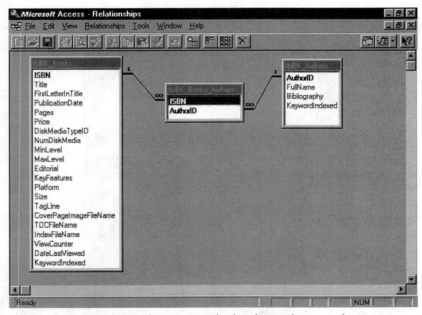

Figure 16–7 Relationship among the books, authors, and junction tables

480

Table 16-3 Design of tblBK_Books_Authors table

Field Name	Data Type	Description
ISBN (Primary Key)	Text (13)	ISBN of the book
AuthorID (Primary Key)	Integer	ID of the author associated with this book

As Table 16-2 indicates, the tblBK_Authors database table essentially holds the full name and the bibliography of each author. Since none of these fields were good candidates for the primary key, we created an integer field named AuthorID to act as this table's primary key. We refrained from using an AutoNumber type field as the AuthorID for the following reasons:

We wanted to ensure that the values for the AuthorID field followed a proper numeric sequence (1,2,3…). As shown in Lesson 4, "Manipulating Existing Records," of Chapter 4, Building a Database with Microsoft Access, if you accidentally skip a sequence number in an AutoNumber type field, there is no easy way to reenter that number, since Access does not allow you to modify the value in this field.

The AutoNumber field requires 4 bytes of storage space, and in our case an integer was sufficient to represent all the authors.

The Subject Table

The BOOKSTOR.MDB also contains a subject table, tblBK_Subjects, that holds all the different subject categories used to classify the books. Like the author table, this subject table also has a many-to-many relationship with the books table and uses the junction table named tblBK_Books_Subjects to establish that relationship. Structurally, the subject table contains just a numeric ID (primary key) and a text Description field.

THE VISUAL BASIC PROJECT DESIGN

The Visual Basic project of the BOOKSTOR.EXE Windows CGI program is stored as BOOKSTOR.VBP file in the C:\WEBSITE\CGI-WIN\BOOK\BOOKSTOR\ directory. This project contains the CGI32.BAS module, the UTILS.BAS module, and the application-specific BOOKSTOR.BAS module. The design of the CGI_Main procedure (in BOOK-STOR.BAS) is as follows:

```
Sub CGI_Main()

  Dim DatabaseFilePath

  TaskSelector = UCase$(Mid$(CGI_LogicalPath, 2)) 'Get task name
  APP_ReadPaths  'Read paths from an external template file
  DatabaseFilePath = Utils_EmptyToNullField("DatabaseFilePath")
  Set ws = Workspaces(0)
```

continued on next page

continued from previous page

```
    Set db = ws.OpenDatabase(DatabaseFilePath) 'Open BOOKSTOR.MDB
    APP_CheckHomePage 'Check if home page needs to be recreated
    Select Case UCase$(CGI_RequestMethod)
      Case "GET":
        APP_DoGet   'Handle a GET type request
      Case "POST":
        APP_DoPost 'Handle a POST type request
      Case Else:
        APP_ProcessFile "ERR_METH.TXT"
    End Select

End Sub
```

The overall logic flow in this CGI_Main procedure follows the design of the JOBLIST.EXE program we studied in the previous two chapters, except for one small difference. The logical and the physical paths used in this program are not hard-coded, but read from an external template file, PATHS.TXT, residing in the BOOKSTOR.EXE program's directory. These paths are then stored as internal form fields.

The APP_ReadPath procedure, which actually handles the task of reading the PATHS.TXT template file, is designed as follows:

```
Public Sub APP_ReadPaths()

  APP_OpenFile "PATHS.TXT"
  ProcessResult = Utils_ProcessFile(InpFN)
  Close #InpFN

End Sub
```

The PATHS.TXT template file essentially uses the Assignment template file instruction for assigning paths to different form fields. Its contents are as listed:

```
`A:Path=[C:ExecutablePath]`
`A:DocumentPath="/book/bookstor"`
`A:ImagePath="/book/bookstor/images"`
`A:CoverPagePath="/book/bookstor/coverpg"`
`A:IndexPath="/book/bookstor/bookindx"`
`A:TOCPath="/book/bookstor/toc"`
`A:HomePagePath="C:\WEBSITE\HTDOCS\BOOK\BOOKSTOR\INDEX.HTM"`
`A:DatabaseFilePath="C:\WEBSITE\CGI-WIN\BOOK\BOOKSTOR\BOOKSTOR.MDB"`
```

NOTE: The APP_OpenFile procedure, the UTILS_ProcessFile procedure, and the template file Assignment instruction were discussed in Chapter 14, Processing Template Files with a CGI Application.

THE CATCH OF THE DAY AUTOMATION

While the Catch Of The Day feature is a neat way of keeping the home page alive, it can be an annoyance if someone has to manually update the INDEX.HTM file every day to list a different book in this section. So why not have the BOOKSTOR.EXE program perform this task as well? The only problem then is that someone will have to run the BOOK-STOR.EXE program daily to create a new home page.

The way we overcame this hindrance is by making the BOOKSTOR.EXE program check whether a new home page needs to be generated every time it gets executed. Since most of the links on the home page point to the BOOKSTOR.EXE program, the first Web user who requests this program each day also creates a new home page file.

The Catch Of The Day Database Table

For the BOOKSTOR.EXE program to quickly determine whether a new home page needs to be generated, we created a table named tblSYS_CatchOfTheDay in the BOOK-STOR.MDB database to store the ISBN of the book that was randomly chosen as the catch of the day for all the past dates. The tblSYS_CatchOfTheDay table contains the following two fields:

- Date (Primary Key, Date/Time type field)

- ISBN (ID of the book that is the Catch Of The Day for the given date)

Next, we designed a query named qrySYS_CatchOfTheDay that always returns the record from the tblSYS_CatchOfTheDay table associated with the current date. The design of this query is shown in Figure 16-8.

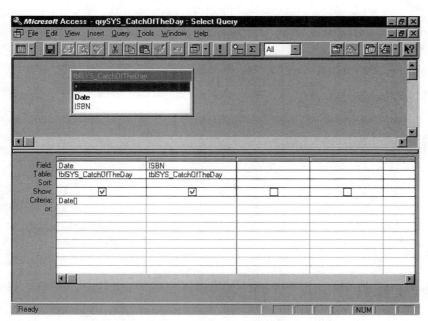

Figure 16–8 Design of the qrySYS_CatchOfTheDay query

The idea is that if this query does not return any record, we can assume that no home page has been generated for the current date and use this test to generate a new home page.

Automatically Creating a New Home Page File

If you look back at the design of the CGI_Main procedure, you will notice that it always calls the APP_CheckHomePage procedure before passing control to either the APP_DoGet or the APP_DoPost procedures. The code of the APP_CheckHomePage procedure is as listed:

```
Public Sub APP_CheckHomePage()

    Dim rsCatchOfTheDay As Recordset

    'Test if new home page needs to be generated
    Set rsCatchOfTheDay = db.OpenRecordset("qrySYS_CatchOfTheDay")
    If Not rsCatchOfTheDay.EOF Then Exit Sub 'Page already generated
    'Generate new page
    'First select a random book
    Set rsBooks = db.OpenRecordset("tblBK_BOOKS")
    If rsBooks.EOF Then 'Book table is empty
      rsBooks.Close
      Exit Sub
    End If
    APP_SelectRandomRecord rsBooks
    'Then select the book's authors
    APP_GetAuthorsOfABook rsBooks![ISBN]
    'Then create a home page using the INDEX.TXT template file
    APP_CreateHomePageFile
    'Finally, update the catch of the day table to indicate that
    'that the home page has been generated for the current date
    rsCatchOfTheDay.AddNew
    rsCatchOfTheDay![ISBN] = rsBooks![ISBN]
    rsCatchOfTheDay![Date] = Date
    rsCatchOfTheDay.Update
    'Close recordsets so that other procedures can reuse the variables
    rsBooks.Close
    rsAuthors.Close

End Sub
```

NOTE: All the variables such as rsBooks and rsAuthors that are not explicitly declared within any procedure are declared in the Declaration section of the BOOKSTOR.BAS module.

The following steps describe how the APP_CheckHomePage procedure works.

Step 1: Check If Home Page Needs to Be Created

The APP_CheckHomePage procedure first creates a recordset based on the qrySYS_CatchOfTheDay query and then checks the EOF property of that recordset to see if the query returned any record. If the EOF property is false, indicating a catch of the day record already exists for the current date, then this procedure does nothing and simply exits.

Step 2: Select a Random Book and Its Authors

If no catch of the day record exists for the current date, then this procedure opens a recordset named rsBooks based on the book table. If the rsBooks recordset is not empty, the APP_CheckHomePage procedure passes this recordset to the APP_SelectRandomRecord procedure, which sets the current record of this recordset to a random record as shown:

```
Public Sub APP_SelectRandomRecord(rs As Recordset)

  rs.MoveLast
  Randomize
  rs.MoveFirst
  rs.Move Int(rs.RecordCount * Rnd)

End Sub
```

After selecting a random book record, the APP_CheckHomePage procedure calls the APP_GetAuthorsOfABook procedure to select the authors of this book in another recordset named rsAuthors. The design of the APP_GetAuthorsOfABook procedure, which essentially uses a parameter query named *qryBK_Authors_OfABook* to select the authors (see Figure 16-9), is as listed:

```
Public Sub APP_GetAuthorsOfABook(ISBN)

  Set qd = db.QueryDefs("qryBK_Authors_OfABook")
  qd.Parameters![Specify ISBN] = ISBN
  Set rsAuthors = qd.OpenRecordset()

End Sub
```

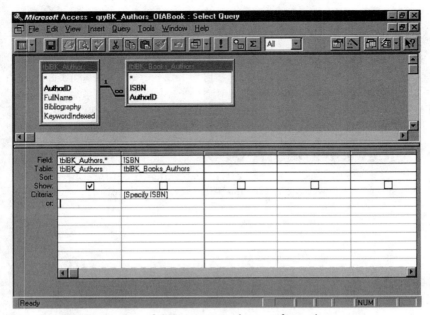

Figure 16–9 Design of the qryBK_Authors_OfABook query

Step 3: Create the Home Page File

Once the rsBooks and the rsAuthors recordset objects represent the appropriate book and author records, the APP_CheckHomePage procedure calls the APP_CreateHomePageFile procedure listed next to create a new home page:

```
Public Sub APP_CreateHomePageFile()

  Dim HomePageFilePath As String
  Dim OutFN As Integer

  Set UTILS_rsarray(1) = rsBooks
  Set UTILS_rsarray(2) = rsAuthors
  HomePageFilePath = Utils_EmptyToNullField("HomePagePath")
  OutFN = FreeFile
  Open HomePageFilePath For Output Access Write As #OutFN
  APP_OpenFile "INDEX.TXT"
  ProcessResult = Utils_ProcessFile(InpFN)
  Close #InpFN
  Print #OutFN, ProcessResult
  Close #OutFN

End Sub
```

The APP_CreateHomePageFile procedure first assigns the rsBooks and rsAuthors recordsets to the UTILS_rsarray global recordset array. It then opens the home page file indicated by the HomePagePath form field in the Write mode, and finally outputs the result of the processed INDEX.TXT template file to that home page file. See Chapter 15, Displaying Database Records Through Template Files, for the role of the UTILS_rsarray recordset array in passing recordsets to a template file.

The contents of the INDEX.TXT template file are similar to the INDEX.HTM file we looked at earlier, except it contains embedded instructions to list the book and the author records based on the information in the rsBooks and the rsAuthors Recordset objects as shown:

```
<HR>
<IMG ALIGN=Left SRC="'[F:ImagePath]'/catch2.gif" Width=100 HEIGHT=39 ALT="Catch of the ⇐
Day"  HSPACE=10>
<B><A HREF="'[F:Path]'/showbook?'[R1:ISBN]''[V:QS2]'">'[R1:Title]'</A> </B><BR>
<I>'?^[R2.Count]=1^Author:^Authors:^</I><B>
'L@2,EOF,<A HREF="'[F:Path]'/ShowAuthor?'[R2:AuthorID]''[V:QS2]'">'[R2:FullName]'
</A>
@
</B>
<BR Clear=Both>
'?^[R1:TagLine]^<IMG SRC="'[F:ImagePath]'/blueball.gif">
<B>'[R1:TagLine]'.</B>
^^
<HR>
```

As you can see from the preceding text, the template file substitutes the values of the path-related form fields for specifying the logical paths to the images and the BOOK-STOR.EXE program. It lists the ISBN and the book title using the `[R1:ISBN]` and the `[R1:Title]` template file codes.

To display the authors, the template file first checks the record count of the rsAuthors recordset through a condition instruction to appropriately list the text "Author:" or "Authors:" as the caption. Next, it uses a recordset-based loop instruction on the rsAuthors recordset to list all the authors with their associated hypertext links. Finally, it displays the BLUEBALL.GIF image and the information from the selected book record's TagLine field only if the TagLine field is not Null.

At this point, you can view all the contents of the INDEX.TXT file residing in the C:\WEBSITE\CGI-WIN\BOOK\BOOKSTOR\ directory using your Notepad application. Do not be concerned about the `[V:QS2]` and other unknown instructions you currently see in this template file. We will cover all those instructions in the next chapter. Now, let's return to the final step of the APP_CheckHomePage procedure.

Step 4: Update the Catch Of The Day Table

After the home page file has been successfully created, the APP_CheckHomePage procedure adds a new record containing the current date and the ISBN of the selected book to tblSYS_CatchOfTheDay table. It also closes the rsBooks and the rsAuthors recordsets in case some other procedure may need to reuse them.

Testing the Automatic Creation of the Home Page

To test the automatic home page creation process of the BOOKSTOR.EXE program:

1. Open the tblSYS_CatchOfTheDay table in datasheet view from Microsoft Access, and delete all the records currently in this table.

2. Close the tblSYS_CatchOfTheDay table.

3. Start your WebSite server if it is not already running.

4. Specify the following URL to view the current home page.

```
http://localhost/book/bookstor
```

5. Specify the following URL from your Web browser:

```
http://localhost/cgi-win/book/bookstor/bookstor.exe/
```

You will see that the BOOKSTOR.EXE program returns a new home page.

6. Specify the following URL from your Web browser:

```
http://localhost/book/bookstor
```

This time you will see the new home page.

NOTE: You may need to use your browser's Reload option if your browser displays the original home page from its cache memory.

7. Call the BOOKSTOR.EXE program again by entering the following URL from your Web browser:

```
http://localhost/cgi-win/book/bookstor/bookstor.exe/
```

You will notice that the BOOKSTOR.EXE program returns the same new home page that it returned earlier.

8. Return to Microsoft Access and reopen the tblSYS_CatchOfTheDay table.

You will see one record with the current date in that table.

NOTE: If you do not see a new home page through this experiment, try running this experiment again. There is a slight chance that the new book that was randomly selected happens to be the same book listed on the old home page.

THE SUBJECT BOOK-BROWSING OPTION

As mentioned earlier, our on-line bookstore application provides two book-browsing options which can be accessed from the bottom section of the application's home page. In this section, we will cover the details of subject browsing options. The alphabetical browsing option, which is implemented similarly to the subject browsing option, is left as an exercise.

The subject icon on the home page is linked to the following URL:

```
/cgi-win/book/bookstor.exe/subject
```

When you click on this subject icon, you get a response from the BOOKSTOR.EXE program, as shown in Figure 16-10.

The response first lists an index of all the subjects and then lists the book titles that fall under each subject. This response happens to be one long page, but you can quickly go to any subject category using the subject index. Also, if you browse through this response, you will notice that the subjects are listed in descending order of their book count. The subject containing the most books is listed first, and so on. Let's look at how the BOOKSTOR.EXE program generates this response.

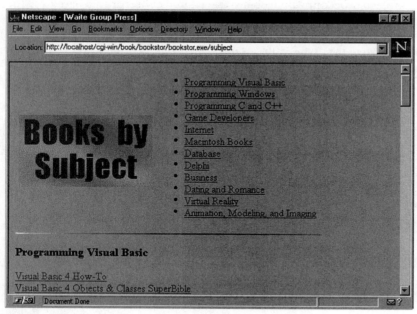

Figure 16–10 Browsing books by subject

When the BOOKSTOR.EXE program sees the text "subject" in the URL's extra logical path, it calls the APP_DoGet procedure, which further passes control to the APP_Subject procedure as listed:

```
Public Sub APP_Subject()

  Dim rsSubjects As Recordset

  'Get the list of subjects in the bookcount sort order (descending)
  Set rsSubjects = db.OpenRecordset("qryBK_Subjects")
  If rsSubjects.EOF Then
    APP_SendMsg "No subjects found.", "Subject Error"
    Exit Sub
  End If
  'Get books for each subject using the sort order of qryBK_Subjects
  Set rsBooks = db.OpenRecordset("qryBK_BOOKS_Subjects")
  'Send the response based on the SUBJECT.TXT template file
  Set UTILS_rsarray(1) = rsSubjects
  Set UTILS_rsarray(2) = rsBooks
  APP_ProcessFile "SUBJECT.TXT"

End Sub
```

The APP_Subject procedure first opens the rsSubjects recordset based on the qryBK_Subjects query, which lists the available subject categories first in the descending order of their book count and then in the descending order of their subject ID. Figure 16-11 shows the design of the qryBK_Subjects query.

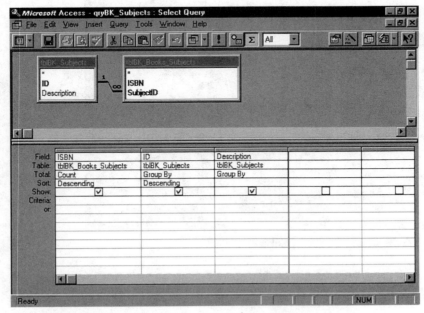

Figure 16–11 Design of the qryBK_Subjects query

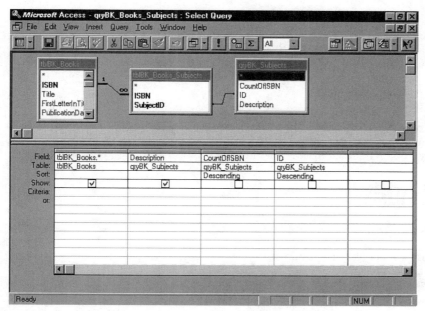

Figure 16–12 Design of the qryBK_Books_Subjects query

Next, the APP_Subject procedure opens the rsBooks recordset based on the qryBK_Books_Subjects query and then processes the SUBJECT.TXT template file. The qryBK_Books_Subjects query (see Figure 16-12) essentially lists the books with the same sort order used in qryBK_Subjects.

Having the same sort order between the qryBK_Subjects query and the qryBK_Books_Subjects query is important since the SUBJECT.TXT template file uses this assumption to list the appropriate books under each subject heading. The portion of the SUBJECT.TXT template file that is responsible for the layout of the response is as given:

```
<TABLE>
<TR><TD Align=Middle>
<IMG SRC="'[F:ImagePath]'/subject3.gif" WIDTH=209 HIEGHT=114 ALT="Books By Subject">
</TD><TD><UL>
`L@1,EOF,<LI><A HREF=#'[R1:ID]'>'[R1:Description]'</A>
@
</UL></TD></TR>
</TABLE>

<IMG SRC='[F:ImagePath]'/shade.gif><BR><BR>
'[R1.First]'
'L@1,EOF,<A NAME="'[R1:ID]'"><H3>'[R1:Description]'</H3>
'L|2,[R1:CountOfISBN],
<A HREF="'[F:Path]'/showbook?'[R2:ISBN]''[V:QS2]'">'[R2:Title]'</A><BR>
|
<BR><IMG SRC='[F:ImagePath]'/shade.gif><BR>
@
```

In the table section of this text, the template file uses a recordset loop instruction on the rsSubjects recordset to present all the subjects in one table cell as a bulleted list. In the latter section, the template file starts by resetting the current record of the rsSubjects recordset to point to the first record. It then applies two recordset loop instructions, one nested within the other, to first list the subject category and then list all the books under that category.

The limiting condition of the nested recordset loop instruction is the CountOfISBN field, which represents the book count of each category in the rsSubjects recordset. Now you can see why the sort order needs to be the same for both the qryBK_Subject and the qryBK_Books_Subjects queries in order for the books to be listed in the proper order.

REVIEW QUESTIONS

1. What is the primary feature of a Web site that attracts most Web users?

2. What aspects of a Web site can make it look pale and uninteresting?

3. What steps can you take to incorporate the speed factor when designing a Web application?

4. How can you present lengthy responses to a Web user?

5. Why is change important for a Web site?

6. How is the Job Listing System inflexible in terms of the searchability factor?

7. How do the objectives of the on-line bookstore application incorporate the four factors discussed in this chapter?

8. What book-related information is not stored in the BOOKSTOR.MDB database?

9. What HTML features does the on-line bookstore application use to make its home page concise and appealing?

10. What is the relationship between books and authors? How does the on-line bookstore application handle this relationship?

11. How are the logical and physical paths set in the BOOKSTOR.EXE program?

12. How does the BOOKSTOR.EXE program help automate the Catch Of The Day feature of the on-line bookstore?

13. Why does the sort order of the qryBK_Subjects and the qryBK_Books_Subjects queries have to be the same for the SUBJECT.TXT template file to work correctly?

EXERCISES

1. Browse through different sites on the World Wide Web, and identify what other features you can add to enhance the appeal and the usability of a Web site.

2. The BOOKSTOR.EXE program supports another feature, RecreateHomePage, as part of its function list. Find out what this function does by tracing the source code of the BOOKSTOR.EXE program.

3. Modify the on-line bookstore application so that it lists the subject categories in alphabetical order. Hint: You only need to change the appropriate queries.

4. Look into the source code of the BOOKSTOR.EXE program, and describe how the BOOKSTOR.EXE program generates the response when a user clicks on the Alphabetical Index option of the home page.

17

ENHANCING THE ON-LINE BOOKSTORE

17

In the previous chapter, we analyzed four key factors that help enhance the overall appeal and usability of a Web application. As a practical example, we introduced a Web application called the On-Line Bookstore whose objectives were defined based on these factors. In this chapter, we will continue with our discussion of this bookstore application, highlighting the following features:

🐚 The What's New and the What's Hot request options

🐚 Flexible and fast keyword search that is based on indexed words

A TOUR OF THE WHAT'S NEW AND THE WHAT'S HOT REQUEST OPTIONS

Let's start by reviewing how the On-Line Bookstore application responds to the What's New and the What's Hot icons displayed on its home page:

1. Start your Web server if it is not already running.

2. Display the home page of the bookstore application by specifying the following URL from your browser:

```
http://localhost/book/bookstor
```

3. Click on the What's New icon displayed on the top section of the home page.

The response contains a list of the five most recently published books. Each book entry contains the title, author(s), unit price, publication date, and editorial of that book as shown in Figure 17-1.

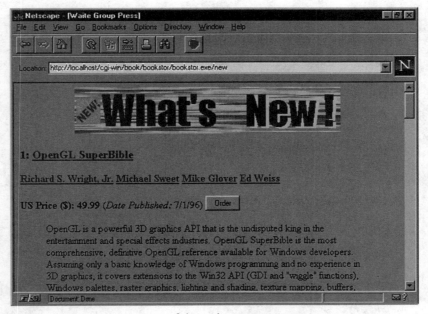

Figure 17-1 Top portion of the What's New response

The book title carries an attached link that lets you further display other information related to that book. This is part of the drill-down capability supported by the application. We will look into this capability later in the chapter.

Finally, notice that there is an Order button displayed next to each book listing. We will study its functionality in the next chapter. At this point, let's look a little further at the What's New response currently being displayed on your browser:

1. Using the scroll bars of your browser's display window, go to the end of the response.

You will see a button labeled "List Next 5 New Book(s)" as shown in Figure 17-2.

2. Click on the List Next 5 New Book(s) button

You will get a new response displaying the next five books that fall in the What's New category as shown in Figure 17-3. The bottom of this response also contains the List Next 5 New Book(s) button.

3. Display the HTML source of this response using your browser's View Source option. Go to the bottom of this source listing.

You will notice that the form containing the List Next 5 New Book(s) button requests the BOOKSTOR.EXE program with the New option passing three hidden fields as shown:

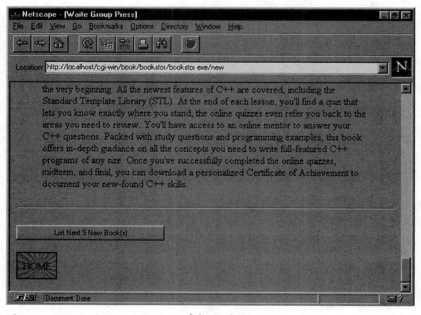

Figure 17-2 Bottom portion of the What's New response

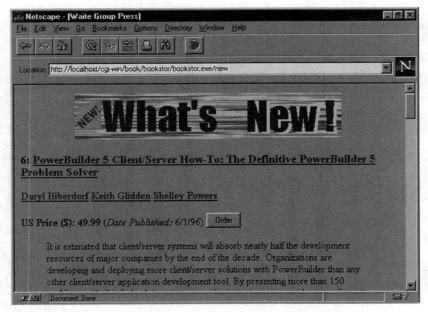

Figure 17-3 Listing the next five books in the What's New category

```
<FORM METHOD="POST" ACTION="/cgi-win/book/bookstor/bookstor.exe/new">
<INPUT TYPE="HIDDEN" NAME="BasketID" VALUE="">
<INPUT TYPE="HIDDEN" NAME="StartBookNumber" VALUE=11>
<INPUT TYPE="HIDDEN" NAME="NumBooksToShow" VALUE=5>
<INPUT NAME="Submit" TYPE="SUBMIT" VALUE="List Next 5 New Book(s)"><BR>

</FORM>
```

4. Return to your browser's display window, and click on the List Next 5 New Book(s) button.

As you probably would have guessed, this time the response contains the next five recently published books in the list and has another List Next 5 New Book(s) button. Keep clicking on this button, and you will notice that you end up cycling through all the books in the database.

The What's Hot option works the same way, except instead of displaying the books in descending order of their publication date, this option sorts the books based on the values of their ViewCounter and DateLastViewed fields. The ViewCounter and the DateLastViewed fields of a book are automatically updated when any user requests complete information about that book using the drill-down link, and thus act as a good indication of what books the users are currently interested in.

IMPLEMENTATION OF THE WHAT'S NEW FEATURE

The What's New icon on the home page is linked to the following URL path:

`/cgi-win/book/bookstor/bookstor.exe/new`

From the previous section, you saw that the List Next 5 New Book(s) button also causes the browser to request the above URL. One difference between clicking on the What's New icon from the home page and clicking on the List Next 5 New Book(s) button is the method used to send the request.

The What's New icon generates a simple GET request (with no query string parameters), while the List Next button sends a POST request. In addition, the POST request also includes two hidden fields, StartBookNumber and NumBooksToShow, that help the BOOKSTOR.EXE program determine which set of books to list in its response.

Handling Get and Post Requests for the Same Task

If you refer back to the CGI_Main procedure of the BOOKSTOR.EXE program (see the "The Visual Basic Project Design" section in the previous chapter), you will see that, by design, the BOOKSTOR.EXE program routes all the GET requests to the APP_DoGet procedure and all the POST requests to the APP_DoPost procedure.

However, when either of these procedures encounters the "New" task, they call the same procedure, APP_New, and essentially leave it to this procedure to determine how to handle the two request methods. The BOOKSTOR.EXE program takes a similar approach for all tasks that can be called by use of either request method.

The design of the APP_New procedure is as listed:

```
Public Sub APP_New()

  On Error GoTo Err_APP_New      'Set error handler
  'Get the books in descending order of their publication date
  Set rsBooks = db.OpenRecordset("qryBK_Books_WhatsNew")
  If rsBooks.EOF Then
    APP_SendMsg "No books found.", "Whats New Error"
    Exit Sub
  End If
  'Set the current record to the appropriate record in the recordset
  APP_SetRecordRange rsBooks, "StartBookNumber", "NumBooksToShow", 5
  APP_SetBasketFields 1    'Set basket related fields
  'Process the header template file
  Set UTILS_rsarray(1) = rsBooks
  APP_ProcessFile "NEW_HDR.TXT"
  'Process the template file representing the body of the response
  APP_ListSelectedBooks StartRecordNumber, EndRecordNumber, _
    "LISTBOOK.TXT"
  'Process the footer template file
  APP_ProcessFile "NEW_FTR.TXT"
Exit_APP_New:
  Exit Sub
```

```
Err_APP_New:
  If Err <> ERR_FAIL Then  'An unknown error has occurred
    APP_SendMsg Error$, "VB Error"
  End If
  Resume Exit_APP_New
End Sub
```

Explanation of the APP_New Procedure

The job of the APP_New procedure can be summarized as follows:

1. Populate the rsBooks recordset with all the book records sorted in descending order of their publication date.

2. Select the range of records to present from this rsBooks recordset.

3. Output the information of the selected books.

4. Provide a List Next button for displaying the next set of books.

Populating the Books Recordset

The APP_New procedure uses the qryBK_Books_WhatsNew database query to create the rsBooks recordset. Figure 17-4 shows the design of this query. The APP_New procedure then checks to see if the query returned any books, an extra precaution to ensure that the underlying tblBK_Books table is not empty.

Selecting which Records to List from the Books Recordset

After populating the rsBooks recordset, the APP_New procedure calls the APP_SetRecordRange procedure (see Figure 17-5) to handle the task of selecting the appropriate set of records that it has to later display. It passes the rsBooks recordset, the name of the form fields that define the record range (the hidden fields), and the default number of records to show in case these form fields are not available (for the GET request).

The APP_SetRecordRange Procedure

The APP_SetRecordRange procedure selects the records by performing the following tasks:

1. Compute and store the position of the first record to be displayed in a global variable named StartRecordNumber.

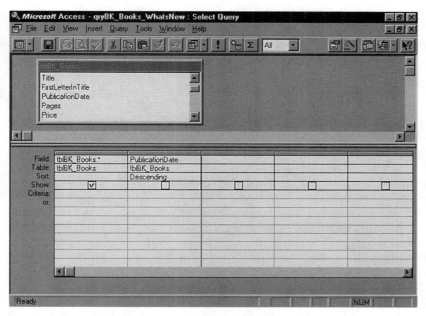

Figure 17-4 Design of the qryBK_Books_WhatsNew query

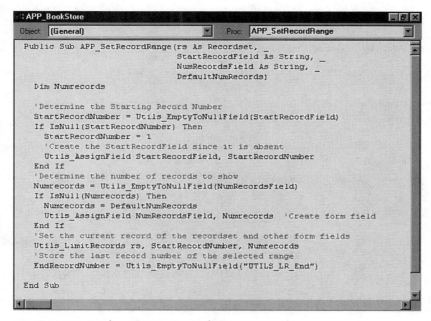

Figure 17-5 The APP_SetRecordRange procedure

2. Set the current record of the given recordset to that starting record.

3. Compute and store the position of the last record to be displayed in a global variable named EndRecordNumber. Note that the EndRecordNumber cannot always be set to StartRecordNumber + NumRecords - 1, since this may exceed the total number of records in the given recordset.

For the first task, the APP_SetRecordRange simply inspects the value of the specified StartRecordField. If this field is absent, it sets the StartRecordNumber to a default value of 1 and creates the StartRecordField so that the calling procedure can always assume the availability of the StartRecordField.

For the second task, the APP_SetRecordRange utilizes the UTILS_LimitRecords library procedure supplied in the UTILS.BAS module. The UTILS_LimitRecords procedure not only sets the current record to the specified starting record, but also creates several new form fields which indicate the expected record range for the previous, current, and the next response.

One such form field is called UTILS_LR_End, which gives the appropriate value for the position of the last record based on the position of the first record, the number of records to show, and the total number of records in the given recordset. APP_SetRecordRange uses this field to accomplish its third task.

Table 17-1 lists all the forms fields created by the UTILS_LimitRecords procedure and what values they will hold in the following instance:

- rsBooks recordset contains a total of 14 records.
- Value of the StartBookNumber form field is 6.
- Value of the NumBooksToShow form field is 5.

You can also review the design of the UTILS_LimitRecords procedure to see what formulas it applies to compute the values of the form fields listed in Table 17-1.

Table 17-1 Form fields created by the UTILS_LimitRecords procedure

Form Field Name	Value	Description
UTILS_LR_Start	6	Position of the first record in the current response
UTILS_LR_End	10	Position of the last record in the current response
UTILS_LR_Limit	5	Specified number of records for the current response
UTILS_LR_CurrentLimit	5	Actual number of records in the current response
UTILS_LR_PreviousStart	1	Position of the first record in the previous response
UTILS_LR_PreviousEnd	5	Position of the last record in the previous response
UTILS_LR_PreviousLimit	5	Actual number of records in the previous response
UTILS_LR_NextStart	11	Position of the first record in the next response
UTILS_LR_NextEnd	14	Position of the last record in the next response
UTILS_LR_NextLimit	4	Position of the last record in the next response

NOTE: If there are no more records that can be listed in the next response, the UTILS_LimitRecords procedure sets the value of the UTILS_LR_NextLimit field to 0. As you will see later in this section, the APP_New procedure uses this test in one of its template files to prevent *List Next 5 New Book(s)* from being displayed if the user reaches the last page of the What's New list.

Processing the Header Template File

After calling the APP_SetRecordRange procedure to select the records, the APP_New procedure calls the APP_SetBasketFields procedure and then processes the template file named *NEW_HDR.TXT* to generate the response header. The contents of the NEW_HDR.TXT field are as listed here:

```
Content-type: text/html

<HTML>
<HEAD>
<TITLE>Waite Group Press</TITLE>
</HEAD>
<BODY>
<CENTER>
<IMG SRC="'[F:ImagePath]'/Whatsnew.gif" WIDTH=417 HIEGHT=74 ALT="What's New">
</CENTER>
```

NOTE: The APP_SetBasketFields procedure essentially creates some additional form fields related to the on-line ordering component of this application. We explain this procedure in the next chapter. For our current discussion, you can ignore the effects of this procedure.

Listing Selected Books

To list the selected records, the APP_New procedure calls the APP_ListSelectedBooks procedure, passing it the record range and the name of the template file representing the format for listing each book record.

The APP_ListSelectedBooks procedure, which simply processes the LISTBOOK.TXT template file for the specified range of book records through a For-Next loop, is shown in Figure 17-6.

The contents of the LISTBOOK.TXT template file are as listed here:

```
<BR>
<H3>
'[F:CurrentRecordNumber]': <A HREF="'[F:Path]'/showbook?'[R1:ISBN]''[V:QS2]'">'[R1:Title]'</A>
</H3>
<B>
'L@2,EOF,<A HREF="'[F:Path]'/ShowAuthor?'[R2:AuthorID]''[V:QS2]'">'[R2:FullName]'</A>
```

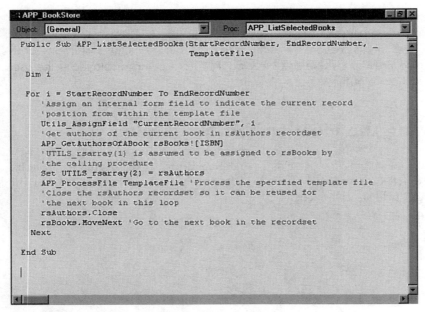

Figure 17-6 The APP_ListSelectedBooks procedure

```
</B><BR><BR>
'?^[R1:IndexFileName]^<A HREF="'[F:IndexPath]'/'[R1:IndexFileName]'">Index</A>^^
'?^[R1:TOCFileName]^<A HREF="'[F:TOCPath]'/'[R1:TOCFileName]'">Table Of Contents</A><BR>^^
'?^[R1:TagLine]^<BR><IMG SRC="'[F:ImagePath]'/blueball.gif"><B>'[R1:TagLine]'.</B>^^
<FORM METHOD="POST" ACTION="'[F:Path]'/Order">
<B>US Price ($): '[R1:Price]'</B>
(<I>Date Published: </I>'[R1:PublicationDate]')
<INPUT TYPE="Submit" Name="Submit" Value="Order">
<INPUT NAME="BasketID" Type="Hidden" Value="'[V:BasketID]'">
<INPUT TYPE="Hidden" Name="ISBN" Value="'[R1:ISBN]'">
</FORM>
<BLOCKQUOTE>
'[R1:Editorial]'
</BLOCKQUOTE>
<HR>
```

Although this template file appears long and cryptic, it is relatively simple to follow. The template file starts by listing the value of the CurrentRecordNumber form field (preset by the APP_ListSelectedBooks procedure) to indicate which book record it is presenting. Then it shows the title of the current book record and uses the recordset-based loop instruction to list the names of all the authors associated with this book.

Next, this template file uses two condition instructions to display the link for the book's index and the book's table of contents if the names of their corresponding HTML files are listed in the tblBK_Books table. Then it shows the tag line (if available), the book's price, the publication date, the Order button, and the book's editorial. The Order button is created through a form which also contains two hidden fields. We will discuss these hidden fields in the next chapter.

NOTE: The price and the publication date are listed within the <FORM>...</FORM> tag pair to display these fields and the Order button on the same line.

Providing a Link to List the Next Set of Books

After listing the selected books, the APP_New procedure completes its response by processing the NEW_FTR.TXT template file, whose contents are as shown:

```
'?^[F:UTILS_LR_NextLimit]^
<FORM METHOD="POST" ACTION="'[F:Path]''[C:LogicalPath]'">
<INPUT TYPE="HIDDEN" NAME="BasketID" VALUE="'[V:BasketID]'">
<INPUT TYPE="HIDDEN" NAME="StartBookNumber" VALUE='[F:UTILS_LR_NextStart]'>
<INPUT TYPE="HIDDEN" NAME="NumBooksToShow" VALUE='[F:UTILS_LR_NextLimit]'>

<INPUT NAME="Submit" TYPE="SUBMIT" VALUE="List Next '[F:UTILS_LR_NextLimit]' New
Book(s)"><BR>
</FORM>
^^
'?^[F:BasketID]^
<FORM METHOD="POST" ACTION="'[F:Path]'">
<INPUT TYPE="HIDDEN" NAME="BasketID" VALUE="'[F:BasketID]'">
<INPUT TYPE="SUBMIT" NAME="Button" VALUE="Review Order">
<INPUT TYPE="SUBMIT" NAME="Button" VALUE="Home">
</FORM>
^
<A HREF='[F:DocumentPath]'/><IMG SRC='[F:ImagePath]'/home.gif></A>
^
</BODY>
</HTML>
```

The NEW_FTR.TXT template file checks the value of the UTILS_LR_NextLimit field to determine if there are any more records that can be displayed in the next response. If the UTILS_LR_NextLimit field contains a nonzero value, the template file creates a form to display the "List Next xxx Book(s)" button. It then sets the values of the StartBookNumber and the NumBooksToShow hidden fields based on the computed values of the UTILS_LR_NextStart and the UTILS_LR_NextLimit form fields.

The final section of this template file that uses the condition instruction on the BasketID field is related to the on-line order processing component of this application and will be discussed in Chapter 18, Setting Up an On-Line Ordering System.

A TOUR OF THE SEARCH FEATURE

The On-Line Bookstore application supports a fast and flexible keyword search that overcomes many limitations we described for the Job Listing System's search feature in Chapter 16, Creating an On-Line Bookstore. In addition to this keyword search, this application also incorporates a simple concept-based search, which we will look at later in this section.

The Keyword Search

Let's take a quick tour of the On-Line Bookstore application's search feature to see how it works and why it is more powerful than the Job Listing System's search feature:

1. Start your Web server if it is not already running.

2. Display the home page of the bookstore application by specifying the following URL from your browser:

```
http://localhost/book/bookstor
```

3. Type the keywords *world web* in the text box labeled "Search Books By Keywords" as shown in Figure 17-7.

4. Ensure that the Match option is set to All and the Search In option is set to Title. Then, click on the Search button.

The search result lists one book, *VRML Construction Kit: Creating 3D Web Worlds,* as shown in Figure 17-8.

Notice that the title contains both the search keywords and that they do not occur in the order specified in the keyword search text box. Furthermore, the second search keyword, "world," only matches the beginning of the word "Worlds" that appears in the title.

Figure 17-7 Specifying the keywords for the keyword search

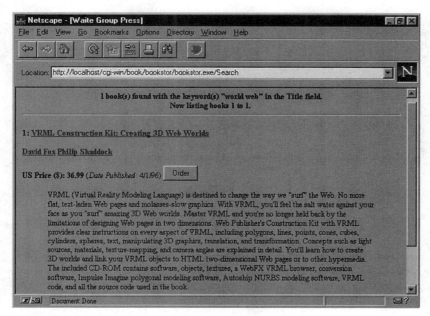

Figure 17-8 Result of the first keyword search

5. Return to the home page, and change the Match All search option to the Match Any option while keeping the same search keywords. Then click on the Search button.

    The response now contains two books that have at least one of the two specified search keywords in their title, as shown in Figure 17-9.

6. Let's change the search field this time. Once again, return to the home page, and select Editorial for the Search In option. Also, set the Match option back to All, and then click on the Search button.

    This time the response contains four books, as shown in Figure 17-10. If you browse through the response, you will notice that each listed book contains both search keywords somewhere in its editorial.

NOTE: The On-Line Bookstore application in its current state does not highlight the matched search keywords in the Editorial field. The implementation of this feature is left as an exercise.

As you can see, the On-Line Bookstore application treats each search keyword as a separate entity when searching the specified fields. Furthermore, the order of the search keywords is immaterial. The only restriction is that the keyword match is performed from the beginning of a word. For example, if you search for the word "Bible," the search utility will not find a book with the word "SuperBible" in its title.

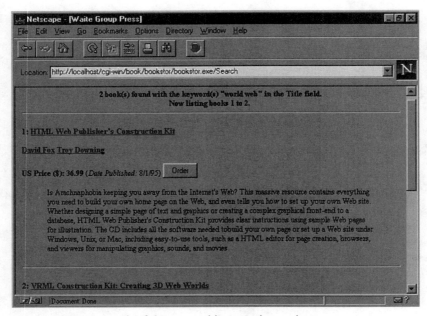

Figure 17–9 Result of the second keyword search

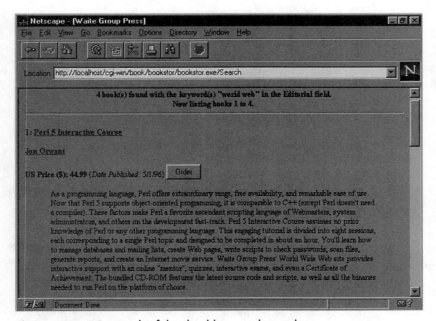

Figure 17–10 Result of the third keyword search

The "beginning-from" restriction does cause the keyword search utility to sometimes miss its mark, but as you will see later in the chapter, this restriction permits the use of indexed words, thereby facilitating speedy searches. As hinted in Exercise 5, if speed is not a critical factor, it is relatively easy to remove this restriction from the application.

The Concept Search

Although it is not too apparent, the On-Line Bookstore does support a simple concept-based search that it automatically performs when a user drills down to a particular book. To see how this concept search feature works:

1. Display the home page of the On-Line Bookstore application.

2. Type *Visual Basic* in the search keyword text box. Set the Match option to All and the Search In option to Title. Then click on the Search button.

The response contains 12 books for which both search keywords appear as part of their title, as shown in Figure 17-11.

3. Click on the first book, *Visual Basic 4 How-To*.

The response now lists all the information available for that book, including its cover page image, as shown in Figure 17-12.

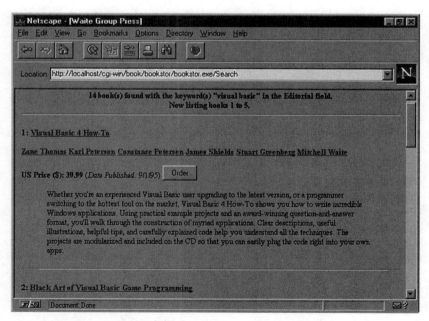

Figure 17–11 Result of the fourth keyword search

Figure 17-12 Drilling down to a specific book

4. Using the page down button or your browser window's scroll bars, go to the bottom part of this response.

You will see a section titled "Other books that may be of interest" (see Figure 17-13) listing other books whose titles have some similarity to the title of the book currently being displayed.

Note that some book titles such as *Borland Delphi How-To* do not even have the two search keywords you originally specified. However, since the book you drilled down to is a "How-To" book (indicated by its title), the drill-down feature used these two words to list other books with the words "How-To" in their title, thus giving a feeling of a concept search.

IMPLEMENTATION OF THE KEYWORD SEARCH FEATURE

To easily explain the basic idea behind the implementation of the keyword search feature, we will initially concentrate on how the application conducts the search for just the book Title field of the tblBK_Books table. Later we will show how the same ideas are applied to search the Editorial field (of tblBK_Books) and the AuthorName field (of tblBK_Authors).

The implementation of the keyword search for the Title field can essentially be broken into the following two phases:

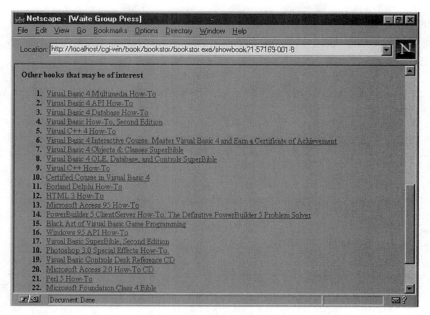

Figure 17–13 The drill-down feature listing other similar books

1. Create and store a word index of the words appearing in the Title field of each book.

2. Design queries that use this word index and the keyword search parameters to find the matching books.

Creating and Storing a Word Index for a Table Field

A book's Title field contains individual words separated by spaces, commas, or other commonly occurring delimiter characters. The task of creating a word index for the Title field involves storing these words as individual records of a new table and then establishing a link between the words of that new table and the appropriate book records.

The Keywords Table

The BOOKSTOR.MDB contains a table named *tblSYS_Keywords* which acts as that new table and holds all the unique words occurring in the Title field of all the indexed books. Think of this table as an applicationwide dictionary. At this point you can open the BOOKSTOR.MDB database in Microsoft Access and view the design of this table. You will see that the tblSYS_Keywords table contains only two fields, KeywordID and Keyword, as shown in Table 17-2.

Table 17–2 Design of the tblSYS_Keywords table

Field Name	Data Type	Comments
KeywordID	AutoNumber	Primary key
Keyword	Text (50)	Unique word

KeywordID acts as the primary key of the tblSYS_Keywords table and is defined as an AutoNumber type field. Keyword is a text field whose index property is set to True (with no duplicates). Figure 17-14 shows a portion of the tblSYS_Keywords in its datasheet view.

As you can see, each word (or even a number appearing in the Title field) is uniquely listed in the tblSYS_Keywords table and has an associated numeric KeywordID. The "Creating the Word Index" section later in the chapter describes how to populate this table. At this point, it is sufficient to say that no keyword in this table begins with a space or any other delimiter character.

The Keywords Link Table

The BOOKSTOR.MDB database contains another table, tblBK_Books_Keywords_Title, that acts as the many-to-many link between the tblSYS_Keywords table and the tblBK_Books table as shown in Figure 17-15.

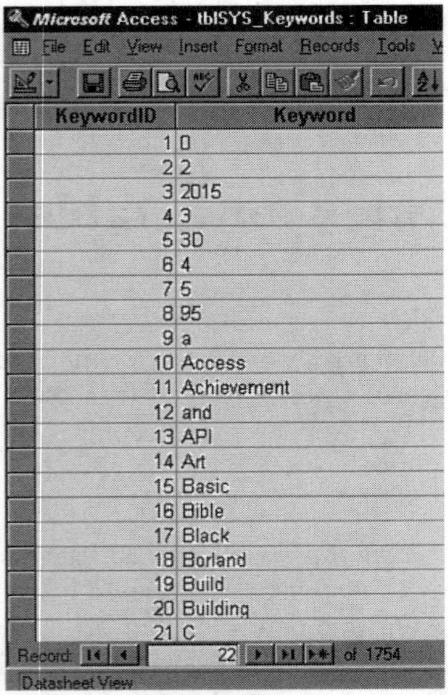

Figure 17–14 Datasheet view of the tblSYS_Keywords table

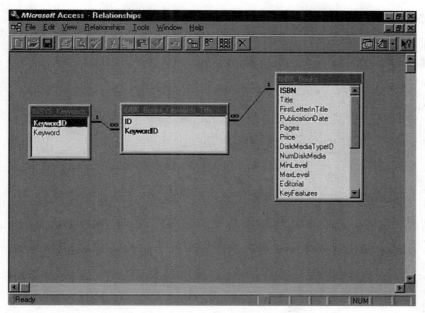

Figure 17–15 Many-to-many link between tblBK_Books and tblSYS_Keywords

The tblBK_Books_Keywords_Title table contains two fields, ISBN and KeywordID, which represent the primary keys of the two linked tables. Figure 17-16 shows a portion of the tblBK_Books_Keywords_Title table in the datasheet view. The "Creating the Word Index" section later in the chapter describes how this table is populated.

Designing Single-Keyword Search Queries

To see how the link between the tblBK_Books table and the tblSYS_Keywords table helps in efficient keyword searches, we will start by designing a search query that is based on only one search keyword:

1. Design a Microsoft Access linking query as shown in Figure 17-17.

2. Select the Run option from the Query menu to run this linking query.

Figure 17-18 shows the result of this query. As you can see, the book record appears once for each word in the book's title.

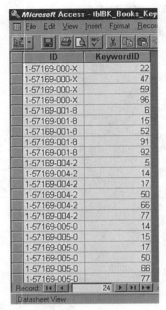

Figure 17–16
Datasheet view of the
tblBK_Books_Keywords
table

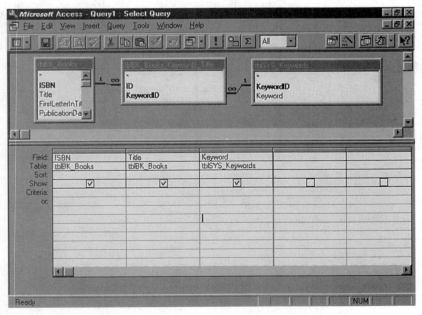

Figure 17–17 Query linking books and keywords tables

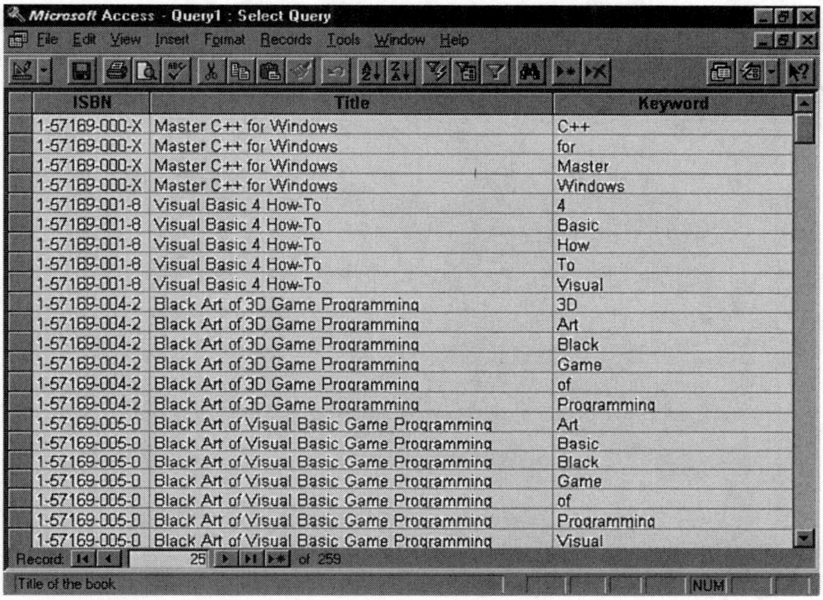

ISBN	Title	Keyword
1-57169-000-X	Master C++ for Windows	C++
1-57169-000-X	Master C++ for Windows	for
1-57169-000-X	Master C++ for Windows	Master
1-57169-000-X	Master C++ for Windows	Windows
1-57169-001-8	Visual Basic 4 How-To	4
1-57169-001-8	Visual Basic 4 How-To	Basic
1-57169-001-8	Visual Basic 4 How-To	How
1-57169-001-8	Visual Basic 4 How-To	To
1-57169-001-8	Visual Basic 4 How-To	Visual
1-57169-004-2	Black Art of 3D Game Programming	3D
1-57169-004-2	Black Art of 3D Game Programming	Art
1-57169-004-2	Black Art of 3D Game Programming	Black
1-57169-004-2	Black Art of 3D Game Programming	Game
1-57169-004-2	Black Art of 3D Game Programming	of
1-57169-004-2	Black Art of 3D Game Programming	Programming
1-57169-005-0	Black Art of Visual Basic Game Programming	Art
1-57169-005-0	Black Art of Visual Basic Game Programming	Basic
1-57169-005-0	Black Art of Visual Basic Game Programming	Black
1-57169-005-0	Black Art of Visual Basic Game Programming	Game
1-57169-005-0	Black Art of Visual Basic Game Programming	of
1-57169-005-0	Black Art of Visual Basic Game Programming	Programming
1-57169-005-0	Black Art of Visual Basic Game Programming	Visual

Figure 17–18 Result of the query linking books and keywords tables

3. Return to the design view of this query, and specify the *Like "Win*"* criteria for the Keyword field as shown in Figure 17-19.

   This criteria selects all keywords beginning with the word "Win."

4. Run the query again.

   Figure 17-20 shows the query result.

As you can see from Figure 17-20, this time the query returns only those books that have words beginning with the string "Win" in their Title field. Also, since you defined the search criteria on the Keyword field instead of the Title field, Access is able to take advantage of this field's index to quickly locate the matching keywords.

However, notice that there is one book, *Windows 95 Win32 Programming API Bible,* that appears twice in the search result. This is because its title contains two distinct words, "Windows" and "Win32," that both begin with the search string "Win." To generate one record for each matching book, you need to group the records of this query by the ISBN field as shown in Figure 17-21.

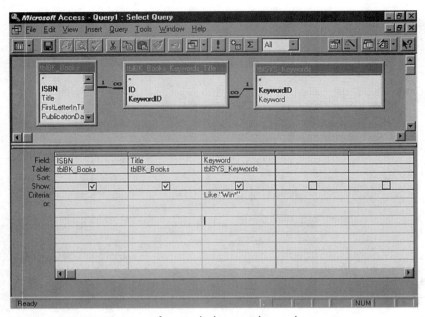

Figure 17–19 Design of a single-keyword search query

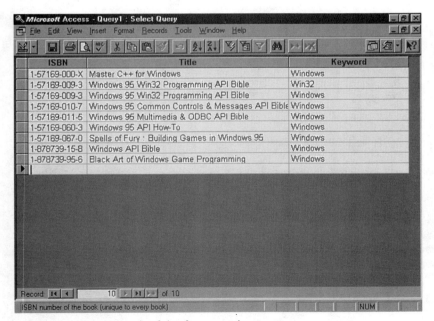

Figure 17–20 Result of the first search query

Microsoft Access - Query1 : Select Query
File Edit View Insert Query Tools Window Help
All
tblBK_Books
ISBN
Title
FirstLetterInTi
PublicationDa
tblBK_Books_Keywords_Title
ID
KeywordID
tblSYS_Keywords
KeywordID
Keyword
Field: ISBN | Title | Keyword
Table: tblBK_Books | tblBK_Books | tblSYS_Keywords
Total: Group By | Group By | Where
Sort:
Show:
Criteria: Like "Win*"
or:
Ready
NUM

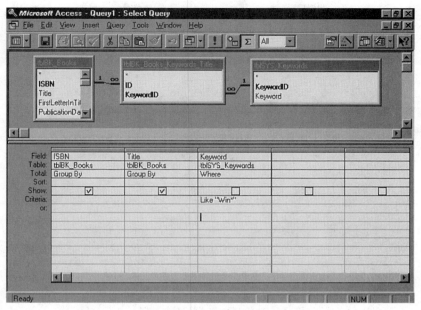

Figure 17–21 Grouping the records by the ISBN field to generate unique records

Note that the search criteria in this Group By query is listed as a precriteria (one that is applied before the records are grouped), which also causes the Show option for the keyword field to be deselected. Figure 17-22 shows the result of this grouping query.

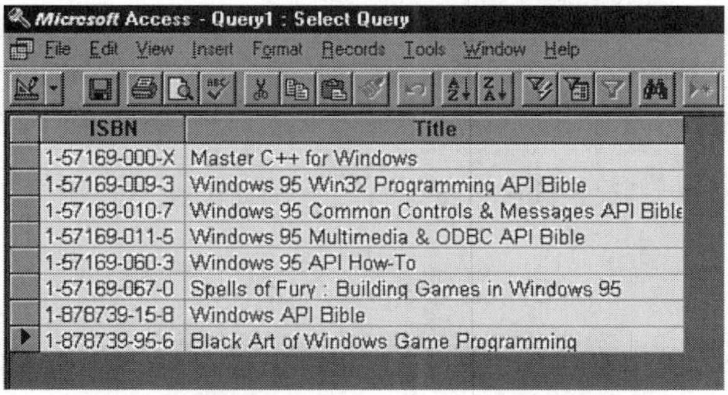

Microsoft Access - Query1 : Select Query
File Edit View Insert Format Records Tools Window Help
ISBN | Title
1-57169-000-X | Master C++ for Windows
1-57169-009-3 | Windows 95 Win32 Programming API Bible
1-57169-010-7 | Windows 95 Common Controls & Messages API Bible
1-57169-011-5 | Windows 95 Multimedia & ODBC API Bible
1-57169-060-3 | Windows 95 API How-To
1-57169-067-0 | Spells of Fury : Building Games in Windows 95
1-878739-15-8 | Windows API Bible
1-878739-95-6 | Black Art of Windows Game Programming

Figure 17–22 Result of grouping the records by the ISBN field

Designing Search Queries for Multiple Search Keywords

The one-keyword search query is simple to implement. However, when you design a search query that involves two or more search keywords, there is another factor you need to consider. How should these multiple keywords be combined? The On-Line Bookstore application gives two Match options for specifying this factor: *All* or *Any*.

The All match option signifies that only those books that have all the specified keywords in their Title field should be included in the search result. The Any option signifies that any book that has one or more specified keywords in its Title field should be included in the search result.

Clearly, the All option is useful for focused searches, while the Any option is useful for broad searches. Besides, every book selected under the All option will also be selected under the Any option.

While the Any option is relatively easy to implement in a multiple-keyword search query, the All option requires considerably more design effort. So, let's start by designing an Any multiple-keyword search query. Then we will look into what extra steps are needed for handling the All option.

Designing an Any Multiple-Keyword Search Query

To search books with Title fields containing multiple search keywords, you create a separate search criteria for each keyword and combine all these criteria using the OR logic as demonstrated in the following:

1. Create a query as shown in Figure 17-23.

2. Select the Run option from the Query menu to run this query.

Figure 17-24 shows the result produced by this query. Observe that all titles contain at least one word that begins with one of the three search keywords.

Designing an All Multiple-Keyword Search Query

The All option can be looked at as an additional filter applied to the Any search query, which ensures that only those books containing all the search keywords in their Title field are selected. To create this additional filter:

1. Add three calculated fields, InPattern1, InPattern2, and InPattern3, to the Any multiple-keyword search query with the following expressions (see Figure 17-25):

```
InPattern1: InStr([Keyword],"Win")
InPattern2: InStr([Keyword],"95")
InPattern3: InStr([Keyword],"Program")
```

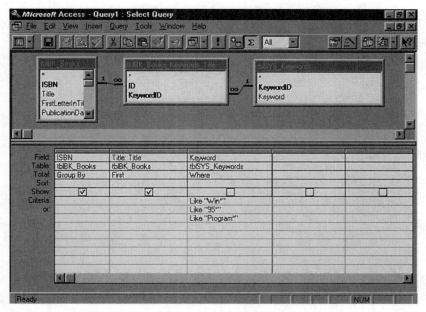

Figure 17–23 Design of the Any multiple-keyword search query

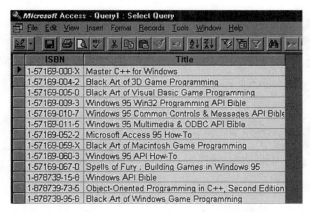

Figure 17–24 Result of the Any multiple-keyword search query

2. Select the Sum option for the Total row below each of these calculated fields.

3. On the same Criteria row, specify a *>=1* postcriteria below each calculated field. This causes a logical AND of these criteria.

4. Run the query.

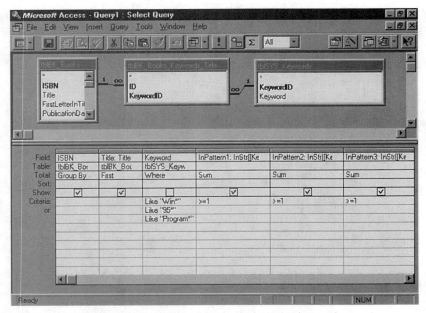

Figure 17-25 Design of the All multiple-keyword search query

Figure 17-26 shows the result of this query, which only lists one book; its title contains all three search keywords.

Let's analyze how this additional filter criteria works. The InPattern1 calculated field represents the match between the first search keyword and the Keyword field. It returns 1 if the current text in the Keyword field begins with the first search keyword; otherwise, it returns 0. The InPattern2 and the InPattern3 fields function the same way, except that they represent the second and the third search keywords, respectively.

As an example, if the current text in the Keyword field is *Windows,* then the InPattern1 field will be computed as 1 while the InPattern2 and the InPattern3 fields will be computed as 0.

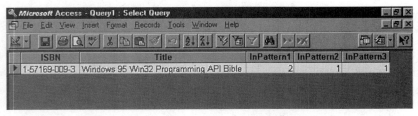

Figure 17-26 Result of the second multiple-keyword search query

When you separately sum these three calculated fields for each book record (and remove the >= *1* postcriteria), you essentially get a count of how many keywords matched each of the search keywords for that book as shown in Figure 17-27.

Now, by applying a >=*1* postcriteria for each of these match counts, you are able to filter out those books where a match occurred in all three search keywords.

NOTE: If you change the >=*1* criteria to the >=*0* criteria for each of these calculated match counts, your query turns into an Any multiple-keyword search query. We use this idea in the next section to have one search query handle both the Any and the All match option.

Search Queries Used by the On-Line Bookstore Application

Now that you have the basic idea of how multiple-keyword search queries can be designed with either the Any or the All match option, let's look at the queries that the On-Line Bookstore application uses to search the Title field. We will start with the qrySYS_Keywords_MatchingPattern query whose design is shown in Figure 17-28.

The qrySYS_Keywords_MatchingPattern Query

qrySYS_Keywords_MatchingPattern is a Parameter query that contains three parameters—Pattern1, Pattern2, and Pattern3—which represent three input search keywords. This query uses these parameter values to generate the matching keywords from the

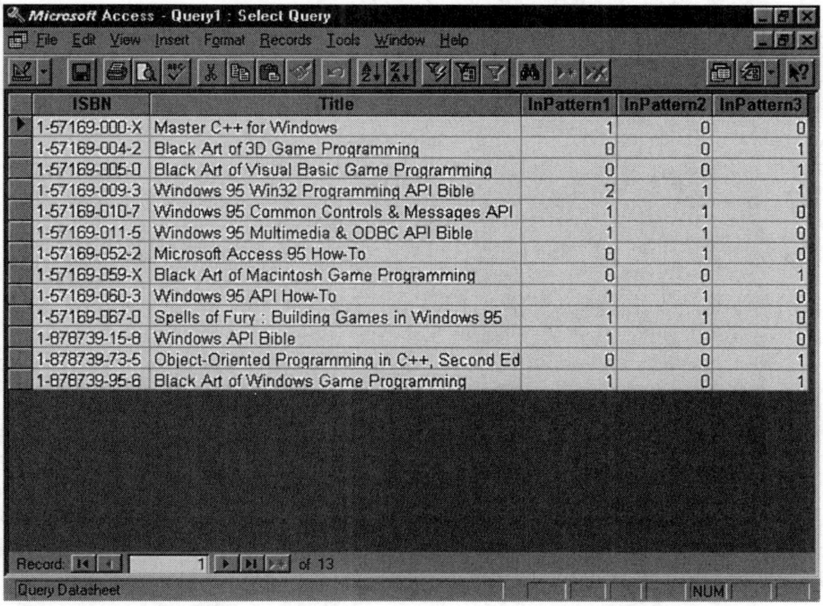

ISBN	Title	InPattern1	InPattern2	InPattern3
1-57169-000-X	Master C++ for Windows	1	0	0
1-57169-004-2	Black Art of 3D Game Programming	0	0	1
1-57169-005-0	Black Art of Visual Basic Game Programming	0	0	1
1-57169-009-3	Windows 95 Win32 Programming API Bible	2	1	1
1-57169-010-7	Windows 95 Common Controls & Messages API	1	1	0
1-57169-011-5	Windows 95 Multimedia & ODBC API Bible	1	1	0
1-57169-052-2	Microsoft Access 95 How-To	0	1	0
1-57169-059-X	Black Art of Macintosh Game Programming	0	0	1
1-57169-060-3	Windows 95 API How-To	1	1	0
1-57169-067-0	Spells of Fury : Building Games in Windows 95	1	1	0
1-878739-15-8	Windows API Bible	1	0	0
1-878739-73-5	Object-Oriented Programming in C++, Second Ed	0	0	1
1-878739-95-6	Black Art of Windows Game Programming	1	0	1

Figure 17–27 Count of keywords matching the search keywords for each book

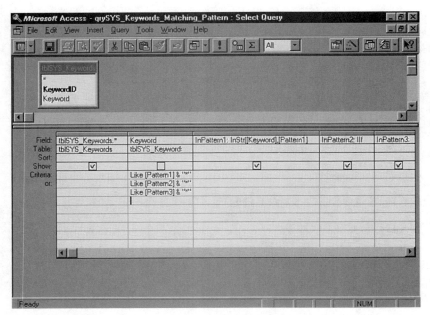

Figure 17–28 Design of the qrySYS_Keywords_MatchingPattern query

tblSYS_Keywords table. In addition, it also calculates a record level match count with respect to each search keyword using the following three calculated fields:

```
InPattern1: InStr([Keyword],[Pattern1])
InPattern2: IIf([Pattern2]=" ",1,InStr([Keyword],[Pattern2]))
InPattern3: IIf([Pattern3]=" ",1,InStr([Keyword],[Pattern3]))
```

qrySYS_Keywords_MatchingPattern is a general-purpose query designed to handle the cases where a user may specify up to three search keywords. In the case where a user specifies only one search keyword, this query assumes that Pattern1 will be set to the value of that search keyword, while Pattern2 and Pattern3 will be set to a blank space. This assumption allows this query to accomplish two objectives:

🦃 Find keywords that match only the specified number of search keywords.

🦃 Set the match counts for the unspecified keywords automatically to 1.

The first objective is achieved since no keyword in the Keyword field of the tblSYS_Keywords table begins with a space character. Thus, specifying a blank space for Pattern2 and Pattern3 (for a one-keyword search) or just Pattern3 (for a two-keyword search) essentially causes these extra parameters to be ignored when identifying the matching keywords.

In the second case, the blank space ensures that the value of InPattern2 and InPattern3 calculated fields (for a one-keyword search) or just the InPattern3 calculated field (for a two-keyword search) is set to 1 for all the selected words. As you will see in the next section, this helps prevent the unspecified keywords from interfering with the AND match option of a search query.

The qryBK_Books_Matching_Keywords_Title Query

The actual search query that handles the keyword search in the Title field is called *qryBK_Books_Matching_Keywords_Title*. Its design is shown in Figure 17-29.

NOTE: qryBK_Books_Matching_Keywords_Title also contains some other book-related fields such as PublicationDate, Price, and Editorial, which are not visible in Figure 17-29.

The design of the qryBK_Books_Matching_Keywords_Title query is similar to the design of the All search query we discussed earlier (see Figure 17-25), except for two important differences:

This query is based on the qrySYS_Matching_Keywords query which takes care of finding the matching keywords.

The post filter criteria uses another parameter, *SearchType* (0 for OR, 1 for AND), that accepts either a 0 or a 1 value.

The name of this post filter criteria parameter indicates that a 0 value for this parameter will turn this query into an Any search query, while the 1 value will turn this query into an All search query.

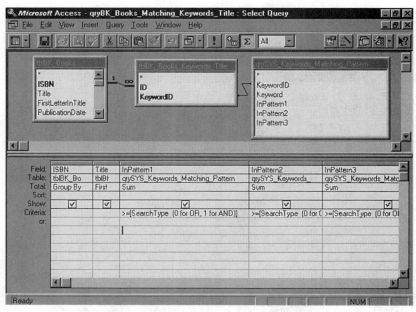

Figure 17-29 Design of the qryBK_Books_Matching_Keywords_Title query

525

You can also see how this query adapts to either one, two, or three search keywords. For example, if you specify only two search keywords through Pattern1 and Pattern2, and set Pattern3 to a blank space, the sum of InPattern3 will always be greater than or equal to 1. This makes the sum of InPattern1 and the sum of InPattern2 the only relevant values for the AND postcriteria.

NOTE: Since the qryBK_Books_Matching_Keywords_Title query is based on another Parameter query, it also inherits the parameters of that query.

Queries for Searching the Editorial and the Author Name Fields

The BOOKSTOR.MDB database contains two more queries for searching the editorial and the author name fields. They are named as follows:

📡 qryBK_Books_Matching_Keywords_Editorial

📡 qryBK_Books_Matching_Keywords_Author

Conceptually, the design of these two queries is similar to the design of the qryBK_Books_Matching_Keywords_Title query, except that they use their own keyword linking tables. Figure 17-30 shows the design of the qryBK_Books_Matching_Keywords_Editorial query.

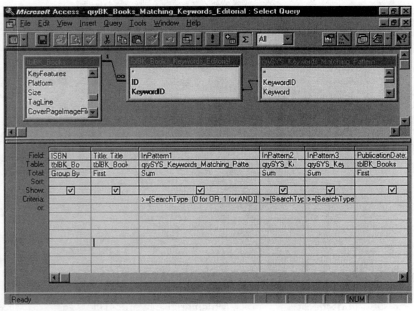

Figure 17–30 Design of the
qryBK_Books_Matching_Keywords_Editorial query

NOTE: The words in the editorial and the author name are also stored in the tblSYS_Keywords table.

Displaying the Search Results

When a user specifies the search keywords and clicks on the Search button on the application's home page, the Web browser sends the following form fields to the BOOKSTOR.EXE program:

SearchKeywords—This is a string containing the specified search keywords.

SearchType—This specifies the selected Match option. It can be either "AND" (when Match All is selected) or "OR" (when Match Any is selected).

SearchWhere—This specifies the selected search field. It can be either "Title," "Editorial," or "Author."

You can verify this conclusion by reviewing the HTML source behind the search form. See the section titled, "The Home Page Design," in Chapter 16, Creating an On-Line Bookstore.

The BOOKSTOR.EXE program handles the search task through its APP_Search procedure, which is shown in Figure 17-31.

The APP_Search procedure first verifies if the search keyword form field contains any keyword. It returns an error message for a "no keyword" situation.

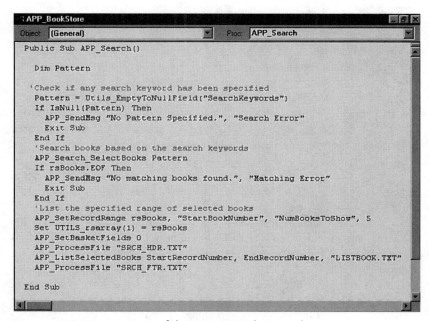

```
: APP_BookStore                                            _ 8 X
Object: (General)                    ▼    Proc: APP_Search          ▼
  Public Sub APP_Search()

    Dim Pattern

    'Check if any search keyword has been specified
    Pattern = Utils_EmptyToNullField("SearchKeywords")
    If IsNull(Pattern) Then
      APP_SendMsg "No Pattern Specified.", "Search Error"
      Exit Sub
    End If
    'Search books based on the search keywords
    APP_Search_SelectBooks Pattern
    If rsBooks.EOF Then
      APP_SendMsg "No matching books found.", "Matching Error"
      Exit Sub
    End If
    'List the specified range of selected books
    APP_SetRecordRange rsBooks, "StartBookNumber", "NumBooksToShow", 5
    Set UTILS_rsarray(1) = rsBooks
    APP_SetBasketFields 0
    APP_ProcessFile "SRCH_HDR.TXT"
    APP_ListSelectedBooks StartRecordNumber, EndRecordNumber, "LISTBOOK.TXT"
    APP_ProcessFile "SRCH_FTR.TXT"

  End Sub
```

Figure 17–31 Design of the APP_Search procedure

APP_BookOS — Object: (General) — Proc: APP_Search_SelectBooks

```
Public Sub APP_Search_SelectBooks(Pattern)
  Dim FieldToSearch, SearchType, SearchQueryName As String
  Dim Keyword1, Keyword2, Keyword3, KeywordDelimiters

  'Select the name of the search query based on the search field
  FieldToSearch = Utils_EmptyToNullField("SearchWhere")
  SearchType = UCase(Utils_EmptyToNullField("SearchType"))
  SearchQueryName = "qryBK_Books_Matching_Keywords_" & FieldToSearch
  'Open the search query and assign the query parmeters
  Set qd = db.QueryDefs(SearchQueryName)
  KeywordDelimiters = " ,.:;&-_(){}[]'""/"
  Keyword1 = UTILS_GetKeyword(Pattern, KeywordDelimiters, 1)
  Keyword2 = UTILS_GetKeyword(Pattern, KeywordDelimiters, 2)
  Keyword3 = UTILS_GetKeyword(Pattern, KeywordDelimiters, 3)
  qd![Pattern1] = Keyword1
  qd![Pattern2] = IIf(IsNull(Keyword2), " ", Keyword2)
  qd![Pattern3] = IIf(IsNull(Keyword3), " ", Keyword3)
  qd![SearchType  (0 for OR, 1 for AND)] = IIf(SearchType = "AND", 1, 0)
  'Open the recordset based on the search query
  Set rsBooks = qd.OpenRecordset()
  Utils_AssignField "Keyword1", Keyword1   'For template file use
  Utils_AssignField "Keyword2", Keyword2   'For template file use
  Utils_AssignField "Keyword3", Keyword3   'For template file use

End Sub
```

Figure 17–32 Design of the APP_Search_SelectBooks procedure

If the search keyword form field contains one or more keywords, the APP_Search procedure conducts the actual search by calling the APP_Search_SelectBooks procedure (see Figure 17-32), which populates the rsBooks recordset with all the matching book records.

Once the rsBooks recordset is appropriately populated, the APP_Search procedure follows the same route that we discussed for the APP_New procedure to list five matching records at a time. Let's examine how the APP_Search_SelectBooks procedure works.

The APP_Search_SelectBooks procedure first determines the name of the search query based on the specified search field. It then breaks the string containing the search keywords (the input parameter) into individual keywords using the UTILS_GetKeyword function of the UTILS.BAS library module. Notice that it only extracts the first three keywords from the input parameter and ignores any extra keywords.

Next, the APP_Search_SelectBooks procedure assigns the three search query parameters, Pattern1, Pattern2, and Pattern3, based on the extracted keywords. Observe that it appropriately assigns a blank space to Pattern2 and Pattern3 when there are fewer than three keywords in the input parameter.

The APP_Search_SelectBooks procedure then sets the value of the *SearchType* (0 for OR, 1 for AND) query parameter to either 0 or 1, depending on the specified Match option. Once all the query parameters have been assigned, it opens the rsBooks recordset from the search query.

Finally, the APP_Search_SelectBooks procedure assigns three new form fields representing the individual search keywords for the convenience of the template files used by the APP_Search procedure for generating the search response.

IMPLEMENTATION OF THE CONCEPT SEARCH FEATURE

The concept search feature demonstrated earlier in the chapter is also implemented by use of the link between the books and the keywords table for the Title field. When you drill-down to a specific book, the BOOKSTOR.EXE program uses the qryBK_Books_Matching_Concept_Title query shown in Figure 17-33 to list all other books that contain one or more words of the current book's title in their title.

As you can see from Figure 17-33, this query contains two copies of the tblBK_Books_Keywords_Title table linked by their KeywordID fields. The first copy is used to select the keywords for the specified book. The second copy generates a list of all the books that also contain those keywords. After that, the GroupBy command ensures that only one record for each selected book is produced.

The postcriteria prevents the specified book from being part of the list, since we only want *other* books that conceptually match the Title field of the specified book. This query also counts the number of matching keywords for each selected book and uses this count to list the closely matching books first.

CREATING THE WORD INDEX

So far we have only discussed how to use the words in the keywords table to accomplish the search functionality. Now, we will look at how this keywords table is populated and linked with the books table.

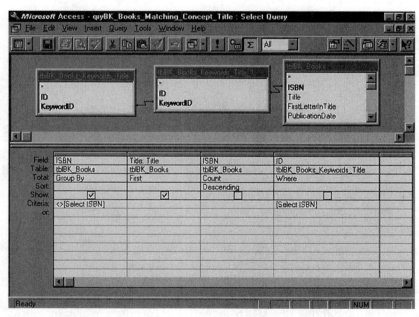

Figure 17–33 Design of the qryBK_Books_Matching_Concept_Title query

The UTILS_IndexField Procedure

The UTILS.BAS library module contains a powerful procedure named UTILS_IndexField that is designed to create a word index of a text field and store all the indexed words in the tblSYS_Keywords table. In addition, this procedure also appropriately populates the keyword link table associated with the specified field. The UTILS_IndexField procedure requires the following parameters:

- The database object where the keywords will be stored.

- The Recordset object containing the records whose text field has to be indexed.

- The name of the keyword link table associated with the text field.

- A string containing a list of delimiters that will be used to separate individual words. You do not need to specify the newline characters in this string. The UTILS_IndexField procedure automatically considers them as word separators.

In addition to the above parameters, the UTILS_IndexField makes the following assumptions:

- The specified Recordset object contains at least two fields, named ID and KeywordField.

- The specified database object contains the tblSYS_Keywords table and two temporary tables named tblTMP_Keywords_Numeric and tblTMP_Keywords_Text.

In the first assumption, the ID field represents the primary key of the records contained in the recordset, and the KeywordField field represents the text field that is to be indexed.

For the second assumption, the tblTMP_Keywords_Numeric table should contain the following fields:

- ID (Long Integer)

- Keyword (Text: 50)

while the tblTMP_Keywords_Text table should contain the following fields:

- ID (Text: 50)

- Keyword (Text: 50)

These two tables are used by the UTILS_IndexField procedure to temporarily store data during an intermediate processing step. For further details, you can open the BOOK-STOR.MDB database in Microsoft Access and look at the design of these tables.

NOTE: When creating the index, the UTILS_IndexField procedure exclusively locks the temporary tables to avoid multiuser conflict. It terminates with an error if it is unable to acquire an exclusive lock on these temporary tables. Also, this procedure appends any new words it encounters during the process of word indexing to the tblSYS_Keywords table.

Creating an Incremental Word Index

The recordset parameter of the UTILS_IndexField procedure allows you to index only a selected set of records from a given table. This is a handy option when you want to perform incremental word indexing where you index only those records that have not been previously indexed.

To track which book records have already gone through the word indexing, the On-Line Bookstore application uses a Yes/No field named KeywordIndexed present in the tblBK_Books table. It considers a book to be word-indexed if this field contains a Yes value. If you add any new books to the tblBK_Books table, make sure that this field is set to No.

After adding the new book records through Microsoft Access, you can instruct the BOOKSTOR.EXE program to create a word index of those books for both the Title and the Editorial fields by specifying the following URL from your browser:

```
http://localhost/cgi-win/book/bookstor/bookstor.exe/indexbooks
```

Procedure Used for Indexing the Title and the Editorial Fields

The BOOKSTOR.EXE program handles the "indexbooks" instruction through its APP_IndexBooks procedure, shown in Figure 17-34.

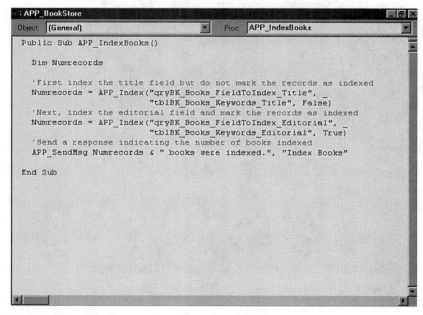

```
Object: (General)          Proc: APP_IndexBooks

Public Sub APP_IndexBooks()

    Dim Numrecords

    'First index the title field but do not mark the records as indexed
    Numrecords = APP_Index("qryBK_Books_FieldToIndex_Title", _
                          "tblBK_Books_Keywords_Title", False)
    'Next, index the editorial field and mark the records as indexed
    Numrecords = APP_Index("qryBK_Books_FieldToIndex_Editorial", _
                          "tblBK_Books_Keywords_Editorial", True)
    'Send a response indicating the number of books indexed
    APP_SendMsg Numrecords & " books were indexed.", "Index Books"


End Sub
```

Figure 17–34 The APP_IndexBooks procedure

531

The APP_IndexBooks procedure calls another procedure named APP_Index two times, first to create a word index for the Title field and then to create a word index for the Editorial field. For the Title field, it passes the following parameters to the APP_Index procedure:

🔖 qryBK_Books_FieldToIndex_Title, which contains the ISBN (alias ID) and the Title field (alias KeywordField) for all the books whose KeywordIndexed field is set to "No." Figure 17-35 shows the design of this query.

🔖 tblBK_Books_Keywords_Title, which is the keyword link table for the tblBK_Books and the tblSYS_Keywords tables.

🔖 MarkRecordsAsIndexed, which is set to False, instructing the APP_Index procedure not to automatically update the KeywordIndexed field of the selected books yet.

The Editorial field is indexed in a similar way, except that the MarkRecordsAsIndexed parameter is set to True. Figure 17-36 shows the design of the APP_Index procedure.

The APP_Index procedure first creates the recordset based on the specified query. If the query returns any records, it calls the UTILS_AppIndex procedure to generate the word index for the keyword field listed in the query result. Next, it marks the KeywordIndexed field of all the records in the recordset as Yes if the MarkRecordsAsIndexed parameter is set to True by the calling procedure. Finally, it returns a count of the records currently in the recordset as an indication of how many records were indexed.

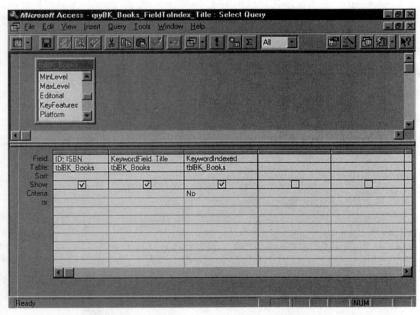

Figure 17-35 Design of the qryBK_Books_FieldToIndex_Title query

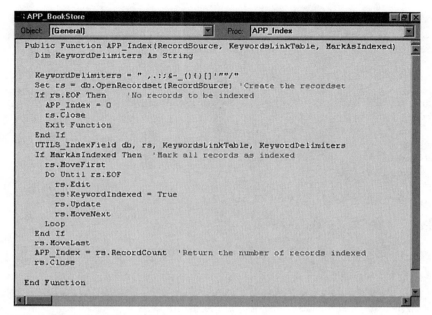

Figure 17-36 The APP_Index procedure

NOTE: The last exercise of this chapter talks about how the bookstore application supports a feature where you can add a new book and its authors using an on-line book entry form. When you add a book through this feature, the BOOKSTOR.EXE program automatically indexes the words of the three search fields associated with this book.

REVIEW QUESTIONS

1. What does the What's New feature of the On-Line Bookstore application do?

2. What does the What's Hot feature of the On-Line Bookstore application do?

3. How many books are presented at a time in response to the What's New request?

4. Why can the What's New request be sent by use of either the GET or the POST request method? What are the advantages of this flexibility?

5. How does the BOOKSTOR.EXE program determine which set of books to present when responding to the What's New request?

6. What does the UTILS_LimitRecords procedure do?

7. How is the keyword search feature of the On-Line Bookstore application more flexible than the keyword search feature of the Job Listing System application?

8. What is the one limitation of the On-Line Bookstore application's keyword search feature that may cause it to miss some books from its search? Why is this limitation enforced?

9. How does the On-Line Bookstore application perform a concept-based search?

10. What are the two phases for performing a keyword search based on indexed words?

11. How are the indexed words stored in the database?

12. How is the link established between the indexed words of the Title search field and the book records?

13. How do you design a single-keyword search query?

14. Why are the search queries grouped by the ISBN of a book?

15. How do you design a multiple-keyword search query that lets you select books with any matching keywords in their search field?

16. How do you design a multiple-keyword search query that lets you select books that contain all the matching keywords in their search field?

17. How do you create one three-keyword query that can handle both the "Any" and the "All" match options?

18. How do you create a search query that can handle a variable number of search keywords?

19. What search queries are used by the On-Line Bookstore application?

20. What does the UTILS_IndexField procedure do? What are its requirements and assumptions?

21. How does the BOOKSTOR.EXE program utilize the UTILS_IndexField procedure to create an incremental word index?

EXERCISES

1. Explore how the What's Hot option is implemented in the On-Line Bookstore application.

2. When you select the "Any" match option for the keyword search, the matching books are listed in no particular order. Change the search queries so that the books with the most matching keywords are listed first.

3. Currently, the On-Line Bookstore application only supports three keywords and ignores any extra keywords. Make the necessary changes to the APP_Search_SelectBooks procedure and the search queries to support the search of up to five keywords.

4. Enhance the keyword search feature of the bookstore application so that it highlights the keywords in the search field for the selected book records. Hint: Use the UTILS_ReplaceString function (three times) on the search field to replace each occurrence of the specified keywords with something like "<B>Keyword</B>", and then pass the result to the template file as an internally created form field.

5. Modify the qrySYS_Keywords_MatchingPattern query so that the search keywords can match any part of the word, and see how the search results change when you go through the application's search utility. Note: You may not find too much performance degradation, since the books table contains fewer than 50 records. However, if you are searching a table with a large number of records, the performance degradation is easily noticeable.

6. Although the AuthorName field is part of the tblBK_Authors table, the keyword search query for this field, qryBK_Books_Matching_Keywords_Author, makes this field appear as part of tblBK_Books and produces the same book-related fields that the Title- and the Editorial-based search queries produce. Analyze the design of the qryBK_Books_Matching_Keywords_Author query to see how this query achieves this effect.

7. You can add a new book and its associated authors and subject categories through an on-line book entry form (see Figure 17-37) by specifying the following URL:

```
http://localhost/cgi-win/book/bookstor/bookstor.exe/getbookentryform
```

8. Trace through the code of the BOOKSTOR.EXE program and the contents of the associated template files to find out how it creates this form and how it adds and indexes the submitted book entry.

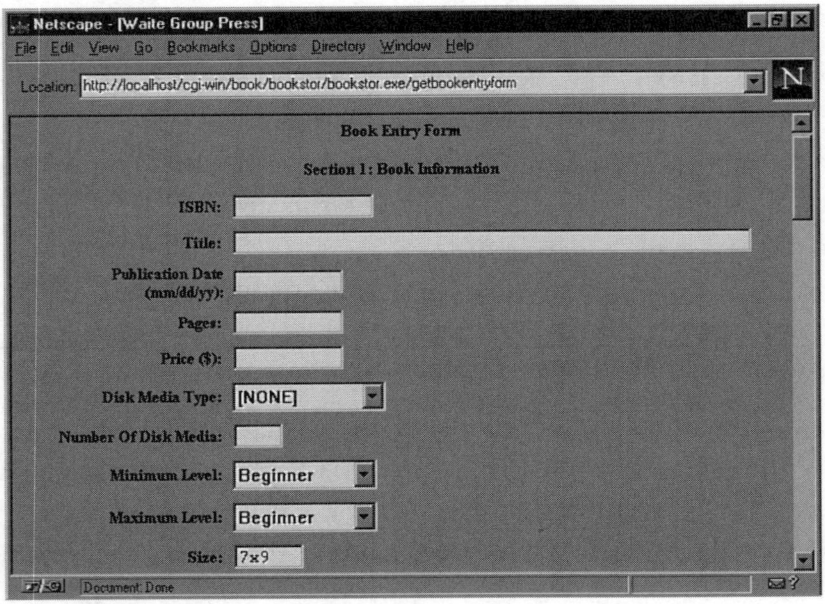

Figure 17–37 The on-line book entry form

18

SETTING UP AN ON-LINE ORDERING SYSTEM

18

Web commerce is gradually becoming a practical reality despite all the security concerns related to on-line transaction processing and electronic payments. While the support of encryption technology in the current versions of most Web clients and Web servers has played a significant role in building this momentum, a lot also has to do with the gradual acceptance of the Web as another channel for doing business.

If you browse through the Internet's virtual marketplace, you will notice that, while some Web sites involved with selling products or services simply list a phone number or an e-mail address for taking orders, others have ventured into accepting orders on-line, using one of the following approaches:

🛰 Creating an order-entry form

🛰 Simulating the concept of a shopping mall

In the first approach, a Web site simply provides an order-entry form that lists all the products and contains input fields for specifying the quantity and other attributes (such as size and color) next to each product. Web customers, after browsing through the Web site's product display, can request this electronic form and fill in the appropriate information to indicate their order.

In the second approach, a Web site allows Web shoppers to order a product while they are browsing through the product showcase. This approach mimics an on-line shopping mall, where Web shoppers can add selected items to a virtual shopping basket and then eventually pay for their basket items through an on-line checkout counter, which can perform one or more of the following functions:

🛰 Dynamically compute the applicable sales tax and shipping charges

🛰 Provide a choice of payment methods

🛰 Support a membership concept where frequent customers can identify themselves and their payment information through their personal membership or account number

The On-Line Bookstore application we have been exploring in the previous two chapters contains an on-line ordering system that is based on this shopping basket approach. In this chapter, we will look into the features of this book-ordering system and then discuss its implementation details.

NOTE: This book-ordering system is just an example. If you are interested in purchasing books published by the Waite Group Press, you can direct your Web browser to their actual Web site located at *http://www.waite.com/waite*.

LESSON 1: ORDERING BOOKS THROUGH THE ON-LINE BOOKSTORE

Anytime the On-Line Bookstore application presents one or more books to Web users, it displays an Order button next to each book. The idea is that if users find a book that appeals to them, they can simply click on the attached Order button to place that book in a virtual shopping basket. Then, if they wish, they can choose to continue with their book browsing while the system keeps track of their basket's contents.

Let's start our lesson by ordering two books through this on-line bookstore to see how closely it simulates the shopping basket metaphor:

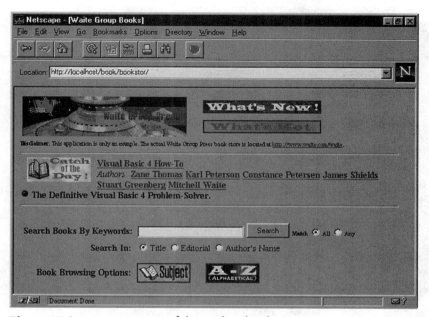

Figure 18-1 Home page of the on-line bookstore

1. Start your Web server if it is not already running.

2. Bring up the home page of the On-Line Bookstore application on your Web browser by specifying the following URL:

```
http://localhost/book/bookstor/
```

Figure 18-1 shows an instance of that home page.

3. Click on the What's New icon.

The response contains the five most recently published books selected from the BOOKSTOR.MDB database as shown in Figure 18-2.

4. Click on the Order button next to the first book.

The response now shows this first book as your current order. (See Figure 18-3.)

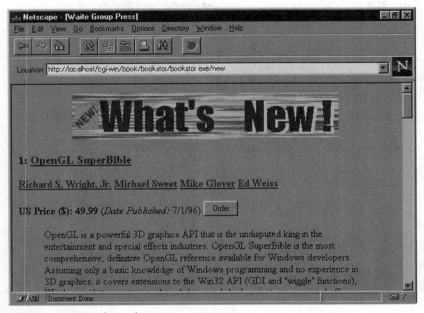

Figure 18-2 The What's New response

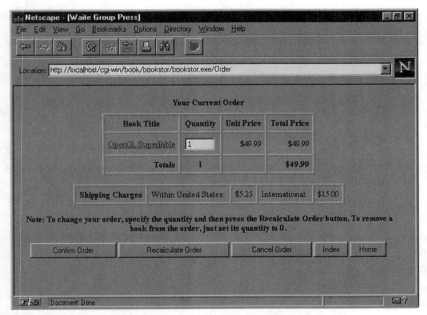

Figure 18-3 Response of ordering the first book

5. Return to the home page by clicking on the Back button of your browser twice.

You should notice no change in that home page.

6. Type *Database* in the keyword search text box, and then click on the Search button.

Your browser displays all the books which have the word "Database" in their Title field as shown in Figure 18-4.

7. Click on the Order button next to the first book listed in this search response.

You will now see two books listed in your current order, as shown in Figure 18-5. Let's examine this current order screen in more detail. As you can see from Figure 18-5, this screen first lists the title, the quantity (which defaults to 1), the unit price, and the total price for each book currently in the shopping basket. It then displays the total quantity and price of all the ordered books as well as their applicable shipping charges based on where the customer wants these books to be shipped. Finally, this screen contains buttons indicating the options you can pursue from this screen.

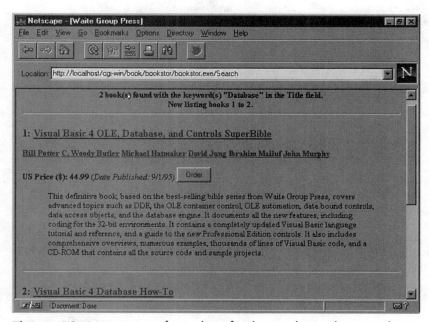

Figure 18-4 Response of searching for the word "Database" in the Title field

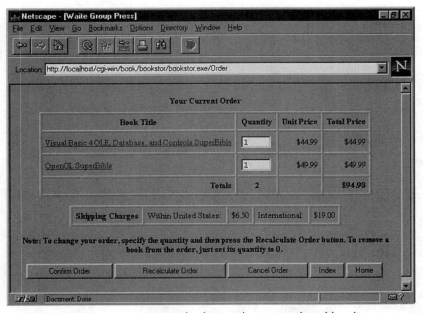

Figure 18-5 Your current order listing the two ordered books

Changing the Ordered Quantity

The current order screen shows the quantity of each ordered book in a text box field. If you want to specify a different quantity for a book, you can simply overwrite the current quantity figure displayed in the text box and then click on the Recalculate Order button as follows:

1. Change the quantity field of the first listed book to 2.

2. Click on the Recalculate Order button.

As shown in Figure 18-6, the response now shows the order totals that are based on the new quantity values. Notice that even the shipping charges are adjusted accordingly.

Removing a Book from the Current Order

The current order screen does not directly provide a delete option to remove a book from the current order. However, it does mention an indirect way in which you set the quantity of the book you want to delete to 0 and then click on the Recalculate Order button. Try removing the first book using this method. Your current order should now appear as shown previously in Figure 18-3.

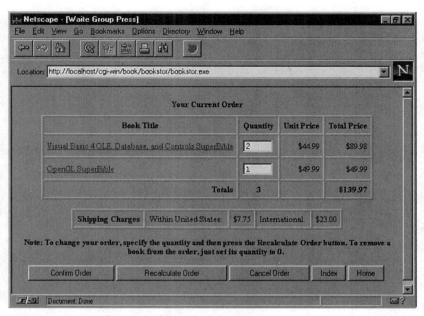

Figure 18–6 Changing the ordered quantity

Using the Home Button on the Current Order Screen

Let's say you still want to keep browsing and possibly order a couple more books. As demonstrated earlier, you can certainly use the Back button of your browser to return to any of the previous screens and continue with your shopping journey.

However, the current order screen also provides a direct link to the alphabetical index or the application's home page through its two buttons labeled "Index" and "Home." This time, let's click on the Home button displayed on the order screen.

You will see the application's home page as shown in Figure 18-7. It looks like the usual home page, except it now contains an additional icon labeled "Review Order" in its bottom section.

The presence of the Review Order icon on the home page indicates that the system is aware that you are currently going through the on-line ordering session. Furthermore, you can use this button anytime to go to the current order screen. As a matter of fact, from now on you will see a Review Order button at the bottom of every response you get from this bookstore application. The following steps illustrate this:

1. Click on the What's New icon once again from the home page your browser is currently displaying.

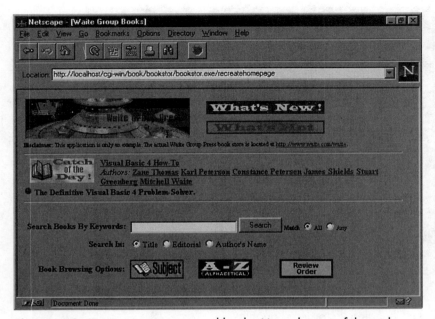

Figure 18–7 Home page returned by the Home button of the order screen

2. Go to the bottom of the What's New response using the scroll bars of your browser's display window.

As shown in Figure 18-8, the bottom portion of the What's New response now contains a Review Order button along with the List Next 5 Book(s) and the Home buttons.

Also observe that the URL listed in the browser's Location window now contains a numeric query parameter after the "new" task selector. This query parameter refers to the application assigned BasketID, whose role we will discuss later in this chapter.

Canceling Your Order

Some Web shoppers may decide that they do not want to pursue their current order. While these users can simply point their browsers to a different Web and try to forget about their current order site (just like leaving their current basket and walking out of the store), some may not feel comfortable with this approach.

To ease their concerns about a lingering order, the on-line bookstore provides a Cancel Order option on the current order screen. To see how this Cancel Order option works, use the following steps:

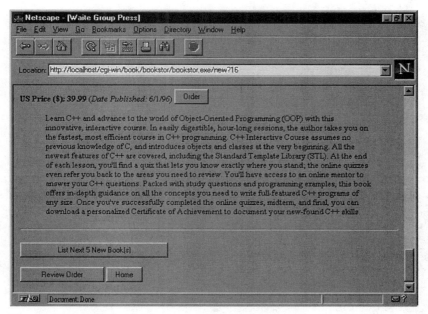

Figure 18-8 What's New response displaying a Review Order button

1. Click on the Review Order button in the bottom portion of the What's New response to bring up the current order screen.

2. Click on the Cancel Order button.

The application now returns a response indicating an empty order as shown in Figure 18-9.

LESSON 2: CHECKING OUT YOUR ORDER

In the previous section you saw how you can order one or more books and then easily cancel your order. In this section, we will explore the other side of order entry, where you decide to go through with your order. Follow these steps:

1. Bring up the home page of the on-line bookstore on your Web browser by specifying the following URL:

```
http://localhost/book/bookstor
```

Notice that the home page does not display a Review Order icon.

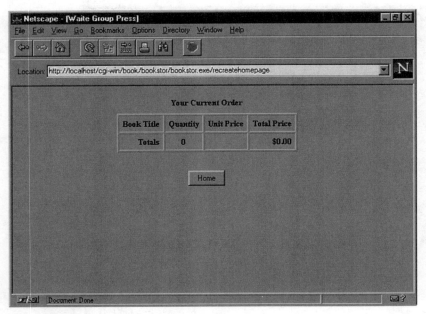

Figure 18-9 An empty order

2. Click on the Alphabetical book-browsing option in the bottom portion of the home page.

The response lists the titles of all available books in alphabetical order as shown in Figure 18-10.

3. Click on the book *Black Art of 3D Game Programming* to see more information about that book, as shown in Figure 18-11.

4. Click on the Order button listed with the book details to place this book in your current order.

5. Click on the Confirm Order button displayed on the current order screen.

You will get a response listing an order confirmation number for your current order, as shown in Figure 18-12.

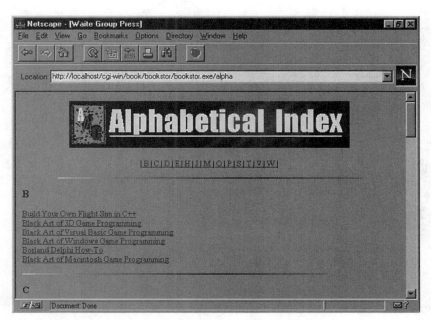

Figure 18–10 Alphabetical index of the available books

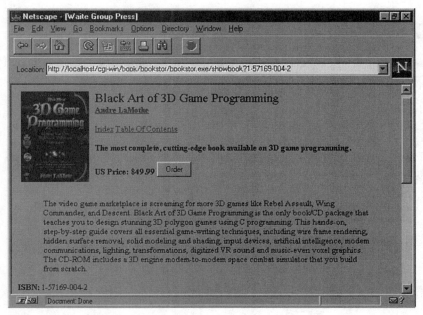

Figure 18–11 Displaying details of a book

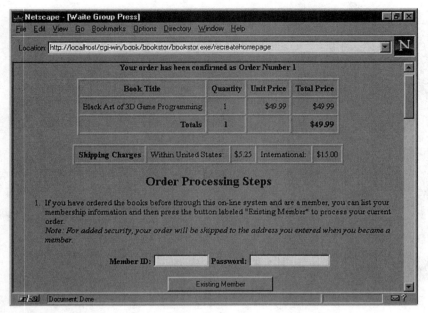

Figure 18–12 Confirming your order

Processing Order as a New Member

In addition to the order confirmation number, the response also provides instructions for processing your order. The first step gives you an option of using your Member ID and password if you are an existing member of this system. Since this is the first time you are ordering through this system, you currently cannot exercise this option. So you need to proceed to the next step, the top portion of which is displayed in Figure 18-13.

The second order-processing step contains three sections. The first section asks for your personal information, including the shipping address. Notice that the captions of the required fields are boldfaced. Fill in this section with the appropriate information, and then proceed to the second section, "Membership Option," shown in Figure 18-14.

The "Membership Option" section gives you the choice to become a permanent member of this system. All you have to do is specify a nonblank password that you can easily recall when you specify more orders in the future. Let's say for this exercise that you want to become a permanent member. Enter a good password in the Password text box.

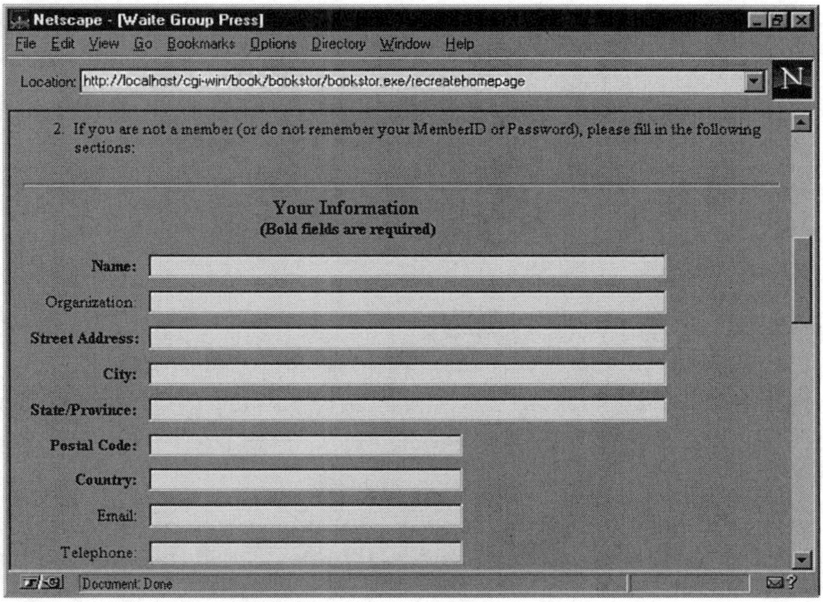

Figure 18-13 The first section of the second order-processing step

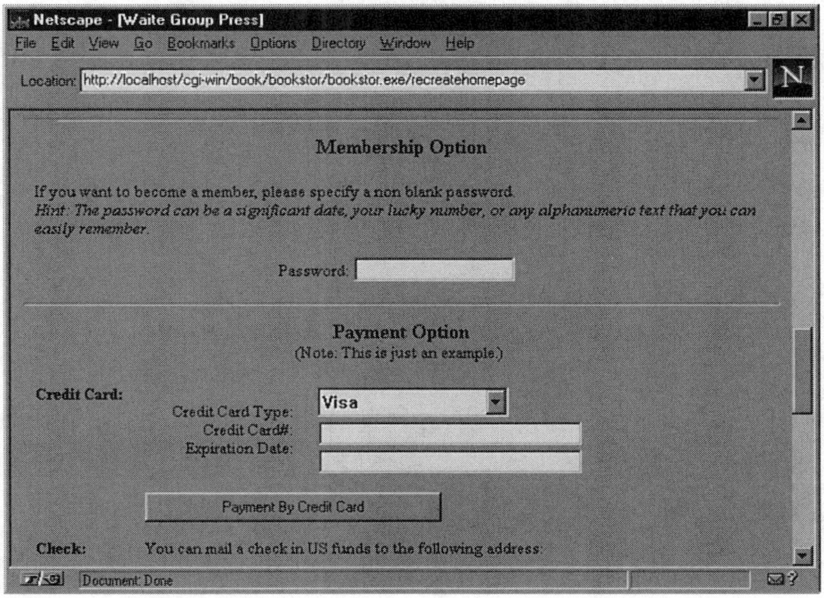

Figure 18-14 The second section of the second order-processing step

In the third and last section of this order-processing step (see Figures 18-14 and 18-15), you are asked to select a payment option from the following choices:

- Credit Card

- Check

- Fax

- Phone

- E-mail

Appropriate instructions are listed next to each choice. Let's say you want to pay by mailing a personal check. You can do that by clicking the Payment By Check button. You will get a response listing your new Member ID and repeating the instructions related to your chosen payment option as shown in Figure 18-16.

NOTE: The credit card option is not secure since the demo version of WebSite 1.1 provided with this book does not support the S-HTTP protocol, which is needed for conducting secure transactions.

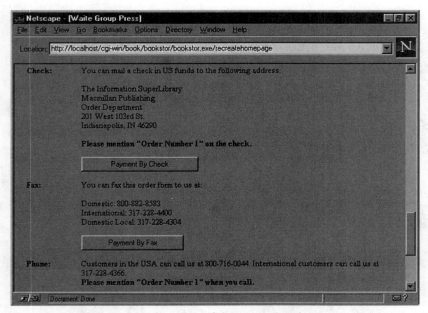

Figure 18-15 The third section of the second order-processing step

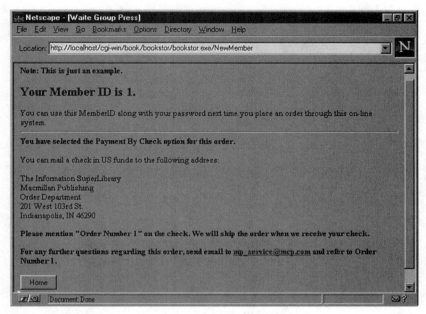

Figure 18–16 Response listing the new Member ID

Processing Order as an Existing Member

Once you are a recognized member of this on-line bookstore, you can check out your future orders by specifying only your Member ID and password as demonstrated:

1. Go to the alphabetical index, and add a book to your current order as explained in the previous section.

2. Click on the Confirm Order button from the order-entry screen.

3. Enter your Member ID and password in the first order processing step (see Figure 18-12), and then click on the Existing Member button.

You will get a response confirming your order and listing the instructions for the payment option you chose when you became a member. (See Figure 18-17.)

NOTE: If you wanted to use a different payment option for this order, you could follow the second order-processing step and apply for a second Member ID that you could use in the future for this new payment option.

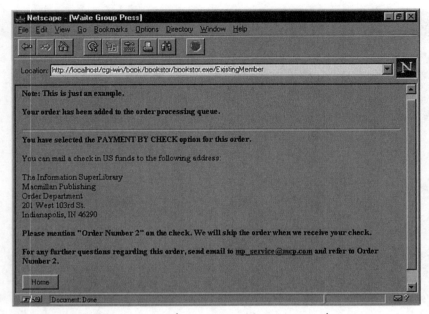

Figure 18–17 Response when using an existing Member ID

LESSON 3: TAKING A PEEK BEHIND THE SCENES

The On-Line Bookstore application is designed to activate its ordering component only when necessary. In a way, this application tries to distinguish between window shoppers and those shoppers who actually order one or more books. This distinction is primarily made to conserve database resources needed to manage and store the orders.

As shown in Lesson 1, you do not see a Review Order icon when you first display the application's home page. Also, if you review the URLs associated with the icons displayed on that home page, you will see that these URLs stay the same every time you request this home page. For example, the What's New icon is always associated with the following URL:

```
http://Your_Server_Name/cgi-win/book/bookstor/bookstor.exe/new
```

A slight change occurs when you order your first book by clicking on the Order button next to that book. The application not only stores that book as your current order, but also generates a unique number called *BasketID*, which represents the ID of the basket where your order is stored.

Once a BasketID is assigned, the application ensures that this BasketID is propagated in every future request you make to this application. This helps the system place other books you order during this shopping session in the same basket.

There is a possibility, however, that this application may not receive that BasketID in a subsequent request. One such case occurs when you use your browser's Back button to go to a page that you received prior to placing your first order and then make a request from a link on that page. The interesting part is that the application is still able to properly group your order as shown in Lesson 1.

The virtual shopping basket represented by the BasketID helps you define your order. When you check out this basket by confirming your order, the bookstore application assigns another number called the *OrderID* to that order. This OrderID serves as the actual reference to your indicated order. The customer support staff can use this OrderID as a key to locate your order in case you have any further questions.

As demonstrated in Lesson 2, the order confirmation occurs in two stages. In the first stage, you are presented with your allocated OrderID and given the available order-processing and payment options. You can choose to change or even cancel your order at this point. Only when you specify your payment method by either entering your existing membership information or by selecting one of the listed payment options does your order actually get committed.

Two things happen as a result of this order commitment:

- Your shopping basket is emptied, and your order is placed in an order-processing queue.

- You cannot access your order through this system anymore. If you want to change or cancel your order, you are instructed to communicate with the customer support staff through an e-mail, fax, or a phone call.

NOTE: The above restriction of not being able to access or change your order through this system once it has been committed is simply for additional security. It can be eliminated by requiring identity verification before the shoppers can change their order.

LESSON 4: ANALYZING THE DESIGN ISSUES RELATED TO AN ORDERING SYSTEM

There are two key issues to address when designing a shopping basket–based ordering system that allows multiple Web customers to shop simultaneously:

- Customer-basket identification
- Customer-order management

The first issue deals with ensuring that all customers get their own unique basket, which they can use as long as they plan to shop, and that there is no mix-up of these

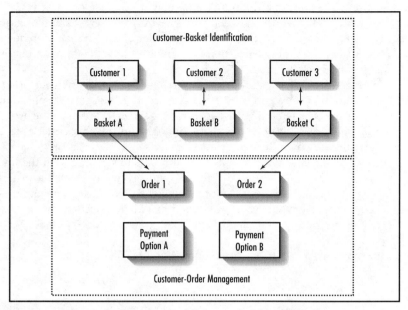

Figure 18–18 The two main issues involved in a shopping basket–based ordering system

baskets among customers. The second issue involves storing the state of each order currently being defined and then moving an order to a more secure location once the customer commits to that order. (See Figure 18-18.)

There is no one way of addressing and implementing these two issues. You can put forth as much design and programming effort as you want, depending on how sophisticated and robust you intend your application to be.

Customer-Basket Identification

Before we discuss how you can associate a basket with a customer, let's first look at some distinctions between a real store and the virtual store you want to design:

1. In a real store, you have a fixed number of baskets. In your virtual store, you can practically create an unlimited number of baskets, since in most cases a basket is nothing more than a unique tag.

2. In a real store, you deal with the customers directly. In your virtual store, the customers are hidden behind their browsers.

These distinctions play a significant role when you are trying to create a virtual store that simulates a real one. You are at an advantage when it comes to having a large number of baskets in your possession. However, you have a lot more work lined up to handle the second distinction.

The reason is simple. How do you uniquely pair up a customer with a basket when you are actually dealing with the browser and not directly with the customer? There are essentially three ways of approaching this question, depending on who is managing the baskets.

Approach 1: Customers Manage Their Own Basket

If the customers are managing their own basket, you can have them send the current basket contents with every basket update request they make to your application. You can then send the updated contents as part of your response. While this approach relieves you from storing the current contents of each basket, there are two major drawbacks with this approach:

- To maintain the current state of the basket, its contents have to be propagated for every request-response transaction that occurs between the customer's browser and your application.

- The customers have a fairly good chance of losing their order if they jump to another site and then return to your site through another page with static links (such as a home page) instead of following the most recent page returned by your application.

Approach 2: Uniquely Identifying Customers

You can overcome the drawbacks of the first approach by storing the contents of each customer's basket at your end and having the customers uniquely identify themselves when they want to update their baskets. The problem here is, how will the customers identify themselves?

One available option is to use the IP address of the machine that a customer is using to interact with your application. However, due to the dynamic IP address allocation scheme that most Internet service providers use for their dial-up Internet users, customers with a dial-up account could acquire a different IP address while they were working with your application. The bright side is that such cases do not occur often.

Since the IP addresses are not a completely reliable way of identifying the customers, why not have your customers use an identity that your application assigns to them? For instance, you can return a tag (BasketID) unique to each customer in your response and ensure that every link to your application passes that tag. However, this BasketID idea raises the same concern that we brought up for our first approach—customers may easily lose their assigned tag by not following the expected interaction sequence.

NOTE: The customer-basket identification scheme we chose for our on-line book-ordering system combines these two options. We discuss the details of our scheme in the next lesson.

Approach 3: Using Netscape Cookies

The developers of the Netscape browser recognized the concerns we raised while discussing the two previous approaches and came up with a state-maintaining scheme called *Cookies* to adequately resolve those concerns.

The idea behind the Cookies scheme is simple. If your application needs to uniquely tag a customer and have the browser pass that tag every time it sends a request to that application, it can send a "cookie" containing that tag in its response header.

The Netscape browser, on receiving that cookie header, stores the included tag in a persistent manner and passes that tag as an extra header field with every request to your application. Your application can also supply the following attributes to indicate to the browser when to send that cookie:

- The URL paths for which the cookie has to be sent

- The domain name to which the cookie has to be sent

- The time limit after which the cookie expires

The following example illustrates how your application can respond to send a cookie:

```
Content-type: text/html
Set-Cookie: NAME="AB123"; PATH-"/cgi-win/book/bookstor"
  DOMAIN-"xyz.com"; EXPIRES-"Tuesday, 27-May-97 00:00:00 GMT"

<HTML>
...
```

The Netscape browser then returns the following extra header field in its request if the specified attributes are valid for that request:

```
Cookie: NAME="AB123"
```

NOTE: If the Netscape browser holds more than one cookie that is valid for the request, it passes all those cookies using the following syntax:

```
Cookie: NAME="Cookie1"; NAME="Cookie2";
```

Cookies are no doubt the most promising approach when it comes to the consistency and reliability needed to maintain a good link between the basket and its customer. However, this feature is supported only by Netscape-compatible browsers. If you design your application based on this feature, you may still have to implement alternative techniques to handle customers using browsers that do not support this HTTP extension.

NOTE: You can refer to the following URL for the complete specifications on Netscape Cookies:

```
http://home.netscape.com/newsref/std/cookie_spec.html
```

Managing a Basket

Assuming you have selected the approach you want to follow for associating customers with their baskets, the next task is how to manage the contents of each basket. Generally, it suffices to allow customers to perform the following operations on their basket:

🍄 Add one or more quantities of an item.

🍄 Remove one or more quantities of an item.

🍄 Empty a basket.

🍄 Specify the appropriate options available for each item (such as size, color, or any other item attribute).

🍄 Compute and list the price tag associated with the basket.

These operations can be easily handled by considering each basket as an individual record of a database table (we call it the *baskets table*) which is linked to another detail table that stores the current items of each basket. This way, whenever you need another basket for a new customer, you can start by reserving the next available record from the baskets table for that customer. The next lesson covers the design of this table in detail.

One question that arises now is, how long can the customer hold a basket record? If you permanently assign that record to a customer, then there are two issues you will have to deal with. First, you probably will have to keep that record in your table forever. Second, even if you use the Cookies scheme to identify your customers, there is no guarantee that the customer will always use the same machine to visit your store.

For all practical purposes, you are better off if you delete the basket records that have not been used for a certain period. This way, you not only eliminate stale records but also recover storage space. (Lesson 6 describes how we implemented such a time-sensitive basket-holding system for our On-Line Bookstore application.)

Once the customer has defined the order and is ready to check out, you need to make a provision in your application to place the contents of a basket in an order processing queue. Again, a lot depends on how you design your implementation strategy.

One method you can follow is to add a Yes/No field to the baskets table and mark this field as Yes for every basket that results in a confirmed order. Alternatively, you can move the contents of that basket to another table that acts as the order-processing queue. Note that in either case, you still will have to take care of the following two requirements:

🍄 Request and store the customer and payment information along with the confirmed order.

🍄 Allow a customer to start another order in the same visit.

Lesson 7 shows how we fulfilled these requirements in the checkout procedure we implemented for our on-line book-ordering system.

LESSON 5: DESIGNING THE ON-LINE BOOK ORDERING SYSTEM

The ordering system of the On-Line Bookstore application associates the customers with their baskets by combining the "IP Address" and the "BasketID" ideas we discussed in the previous lesson (see Approach 2) to reduce the risk of losing an order if a customer makes a request from a page generated prior to the BasketID assignment or changes the IP address during the session. Figure 18-19 outlines this customer-basket identification process.

With this method, the only time the bookstore application can lose a customer's order is if the customer changes the IP address and uses a page with no BasketID link simultaneously during the session. This is a highly unlikely event.

For customer-order management, the bookstore application uses one table pair to store the current basket contents and another table pair to store the confirmed and paid orders. Let's look at the structure and relationship of these database tables. You can open the BOOKSTOR.MDB database in Microsoft Access at this point.

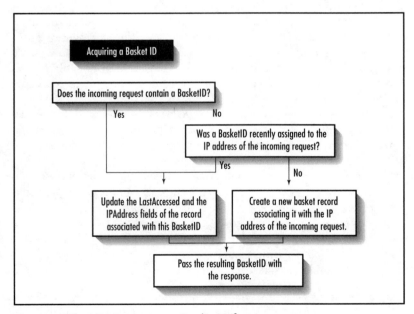

Figure 18-19 Acquiring a BasketID from a request

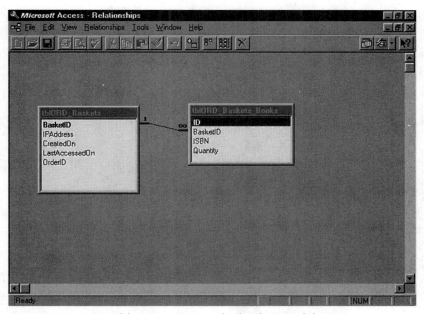

Figure 18–20 Tables representing the baskets and their contents

Tables Representing the Baskets

The tables that represent the baskets and their contents are named tblORD_Baskets and tblORD_Baskets_Books in the BOOKSTOR.MDB database. Figure 18-20 highlights the one-to-many relationship that exists between these two tables.

Each record in the tblORD_Baskets table refers to an individual basket. The primary key of this table is BasketID, which is defined as an AutoNumber field.

The IPAddress field stores the IP address of the client's machine currently associated with a basket. The date fields CreatedOn and LastAccessedOn are used to track the active life of each basket record. Finally, the OrderID field specifies a link to another table, tblORD_Orders, which is the topic of the next section.

The tblORD_Baskets_Books table stores the contents of each basket. Each record of this table represents one or more quantities of a book (represented by the ISBN field) that a customer has currently placed on order. The BasketID field in this table establishes the link with the appropriate Basket record in the tblORD_Baskets table.

Tables Representing the Confirmed Orders

As indicated earlier, the BOOKSTOR.MDB database contains another one-to-many related table pair to store confirmed orders that are ready to be processed. These tables are named tblORD_Orders and tblORD_Orders_Books. As shown in Figure 18-21, the tblORD_Orders table is linked to the tblORD_Baskets table. We will discuss the purpose of this link in the next lesson.

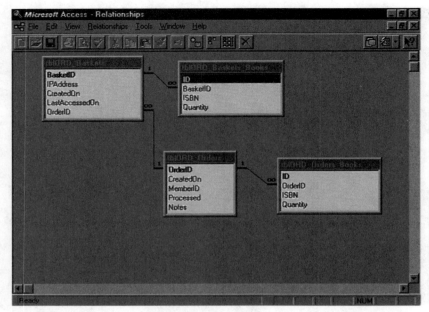

Figure 18–21 Relationship between tables representing baskets and confirmed orders

Each record of the tblORD_Orders table points to a separate order whose contents are stored in one or more records of the tblORD_Orders_Books table. The CreatedOn (Date/Time type), Processed (Yes/No type), and Notes (Memo type) fields presented in the tblORD_Orders table are defined to allow the order-processing staff to track the status of each order.

The MemberID field of the tblORD_Orders table establishes a link to another table named tblORD_Members, which stores all the customer and payment information as shown in Figure 18-22. In addition, the tblORD_Members table also stores an optional Password field, which is used to secure the identity of the existing members.

Table Representing the Ordering System Parameters

The BOOKSTOR.MDB database contains one additional table named tblORD_Parameters whose fields represent the configurable parameters related to the On-Line Bookstore application's ordering component. Figure 18-23 displays the design of the tblORD_Parameters table. We will discuss the purpose of these parameters later in the next lesson.

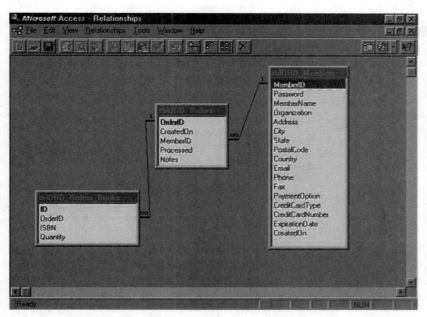

Figure 18–22 Relationship between the tblORD_Members and the tblORD_Orders tables

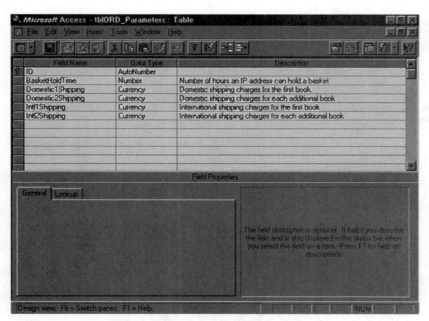

Figure 18–23 Design of the tblORD_Parameters table

LESSON 6: TRACING THE STEPS FOR ORDERING A BOOK

As shown in Lesson 1, the bookstore application allows you to order a book by clicking on the Order button displayed next to that book. Each book's Order button is initially constructed as follows:

```
<FORM METHOD="POST" ACTION="/cgi-win/book/bookstor/bookstor.exe/Order">
<B>US Price ($): 49.99</B>
(<I>Date Published: </I>7/1/96)
<INPUT TYPE="Submit" Name="Submit" Value="Order">
<INPUT NAME="BasketID" Type="Hidden" Value="">
<INPUT TYPE="Hidden" Name="ISBMN" Value="Books_ISBN_Number">
</FORM>
```

The preceding form calls the BOOKSTOR.EXE program with the task named "Order," passing two hidden fields, BasketID and ISBN, with the request. The BasketID field is empty, since no basket has yet been assigned to the customer. The ISBN field identifies the book with which this Order button is associated.

Let's trace the steps followed by the BOOKSTOR.EXE program when you click on the Order button to submit this form. At this point you can load the BOOKSTOR.VBP project in Visual Basic and display the CGI_Main procedure in the Code window.

If you go through the CGI_Main procedure, you will see that, for this request, it calls the APP_DoPost procedure, which further passes control to the APP_Order procedure shown in Figure 18-24.

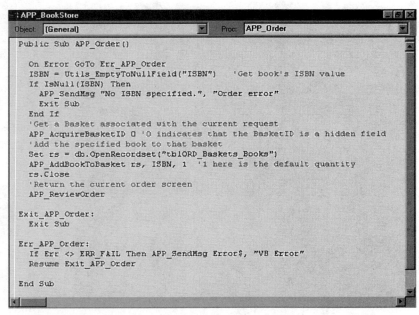

Figure 18-24 The APP_Order procedure

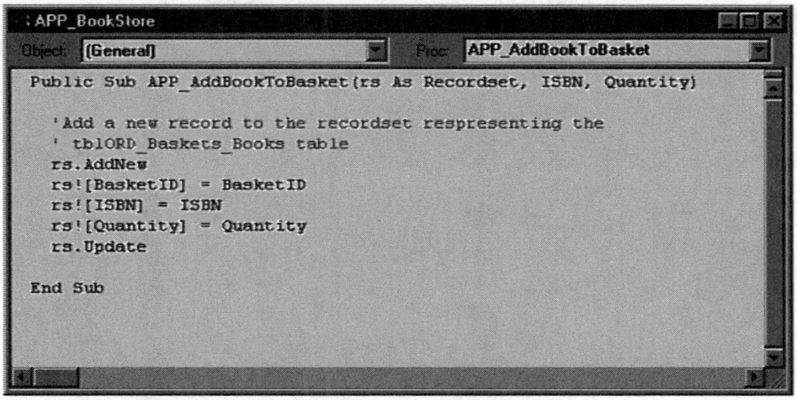

Figure 18–25 The APP_AddBookToBasket procedure

The APP_Order Procedure

The APP_Order procedure first retrieves the ISBN value of the book being ordered from the hidden ISBN field associated with the Order button. Next, it calls the APP_AcquireBasketID procedure (described later) to identify a basket record for the current request and then calls the APP_AddBookToBasket procedure shown in Figure 18-25 to add the specified book to the identified basket.

As its final step, the APP_Order procedure calls the APP_ReviewOrder procedure (also described later) to return a response showing the current order of the requesting customer. Note that there is no specific mention of a BasketID in the APP_Order procedure. This is because the BasketID is declared as a global variable which is shared by all order-related procedures in the BOOKSTOR.EXE program.

The APP_AcquireBasketID Procedure

The APP_AcquireBasketID procedure is a general-purpose procedure whose only goal is to procure an appropriate basket record from the tblORD_Baskets table and associate it with the incoming request. This procedure, shown in Figure 18-26, essentially follows the basket procurement method outlined in Figure 18-19.

Methods Used to Propagate the BasketID with Each Request

The APP_AcquireBasketID procedure accepts one parameter, QueryParameterNumber, which allows the calling procedure to indicate where to look for the BasketID value from the incoming request. The need for this parameter originates from the fact that the BasketID may appear at different places for different tasks.

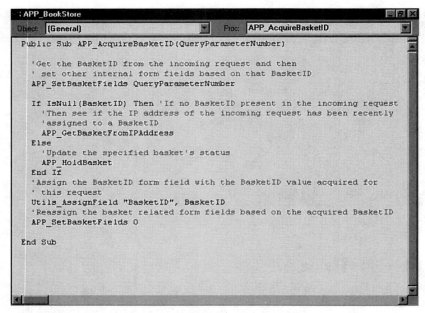

Figure 18-26 The APP_AcquireBasketID procedure

For tasks requested through a form using a POST request method, the BasketID is passed via a hidden field, as you have already seen in the case of the Order button. However, for tasks that are normally requested by use of a GET method, the BasketID can be passed as either the first or the second parameter in the query string portion of the requesting URL.

As an example, if a customer has acquired a BasketID value of 12 as a result of ordering a book and that customer then subsequently requests the home page by clicking the Home button on the review order screen (see Figure 18-7), the What's New icon will have a link pointing to the following URL:

`/cgi-win/book/bookstor/bookstor.exe?12`

On the other hand, the title of the book listed as the Catch Of The Day will have a link pointing to the following URL:

`/cgi-win/book/bookstor/bookstor.exe?Books_ISBN_Value+12`

Now that we know the three ways the On-Line Bookstore application can propagate the assigned BasketID with a request, let's continue with our explanation of the APP_AcquireBasketID procedure.

The APP_SetBasketFields Procedure

As its first step, the APP_AcquireBasketID procedure calls the APP_SetBasketFields procedure shown in Figure 18-27.

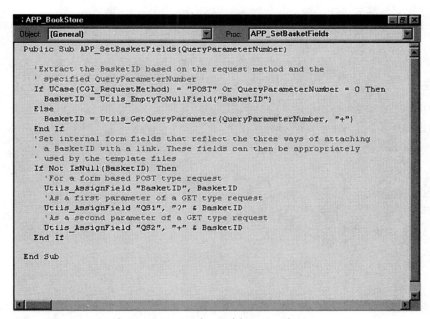

Figure 18-27 The APP_SetBasketFields procedure

APP_SetBasketFields performs two functions:

It extracts the BasketID from the incoming request, based on the specified QueryParameterNumber.

It sets three internal form fields that are mainly used by the template files to appropriately attach the BasketID parameter with each hypertext link.

After calling the APP_SetBasketFields procedure, the APP_AcquireBasketID procedure tests if any BasketID value actually got extracted. This test is performed to consider the possibility that the incoming request may not contain the expected BasketID parameter if the user does not follow the expected request-response sequence.

In such a case, the APP_AcquireBasketID procedure tries to identify the BasketID from the client's machine's IP address by calling the APP_GetBasketFromIPAddress procedure shown in Figure 18-28.

In the case where the incoming request does bring in the BasketID, the APP_AcquireBasketID procedure calls the APP_HoldBasket procedure to ensure the validity of that BasketID. We will look into the APP_HoldBasket procedure after we examine the APP_GetBasketFromIPAddress procedure. At this point, we would like to mention that the end result of both the APP_GetBasketFromIPAddress and the APP_HoldBasket procedures is a valid BasketID, whether it came with the request or was freshly generated by the system.

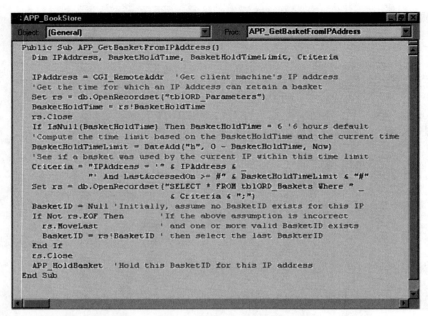

```
: APP_BookStore                                                    _ □ X
Object  [General]                  ▼   Proc  APP_GetBasketFromIPAddress  ▼

Public Sub APP_GetBasketFromIPAddress()
  Dim IPAddress, BasketHoldTime, BasketHoldTimeLimit, Criteria

  IPAddress = CGI_RemoteAddr  'Get client machine's IP address
  'Get the time for which an IP Address can retain a basket
  Set rs = db.OpenRecordset("tblORD_Parameters")
  BasketHoldTime = rs!BasketHoldTime
  rs.Close
  If IsNull(BasketHoldTime) Then BasketHoldTime = 6 '6 hours default
  'Compute the time limit based on the BasketHoldTime and the current time
  BasketHoldTimeLimit = DateAdd("h", 0 - BasketHoldTime, Now)
  'See if a basket was used by the current IP within this time limit
  Criteria = "IPAddress = '" & IPAddress & _
             "' And LastAccessedOn >= #" & BasketHoldTimeLimit & "#"
  Set rs = db.OpenRecordset("SELECT * FROM tblORD_Baskets Where " _
                            & Criteria & ";")
  BasketID = Null 'Initially, assume no BasketID exists for this IP
  If Not rs.EOF Then        'If the above assumption is incorrect
    rs.MoveLast             ' and one or more valid BasketID exists
    BasketID = rs!BasketID  ' then select the last BaskterID
  End If
  rs.Close
  APP_HoldBasket  'Hold this BasketID for this IP address
End Sub
```

Figure 18-28 The APP_GetBasketFromIPAddress procedure

As its final step, the APP_AcquireBasketID procedure assigns (or reassigns as the situation demands) the BasketID form field to the current value of the BasketID variable. Then it calls APP_SetBasketFields again to essentially synchronize the other basket-related form fields based on that value.

The APP_GetBasketFromIPAddress Procedure

The APP_GetBasketFromIPAddress procedure is designed to locate the most recent BasketID that has been previously assigned to the client machine's IP address. The definition of "recent" depends upon the value of the BasketHoldTime field present in the tblORD_Parameters table.

Whether or not the APP_GetBasketFromIPAddress procedure is able to locate a BasketID, this procedure lets the APP_HoldBasket procedure make the ultimate decision to ensure that a valid BasketID is associated with the current request. Figure 18-29 shows the design of the APP_HoldBasket procedure.

The APP_HoldBasket Procedure

The APP_HoldBasket procedure first checks if the BasketID variable currently has a non-Null value in which it tries to locate the record in the tblORD_Baskets table associated with that BasketID value. If a record is found, then the APP_HoldBasket procedure updates the LastAccessedOn field of that basket so that the basket stays "active."

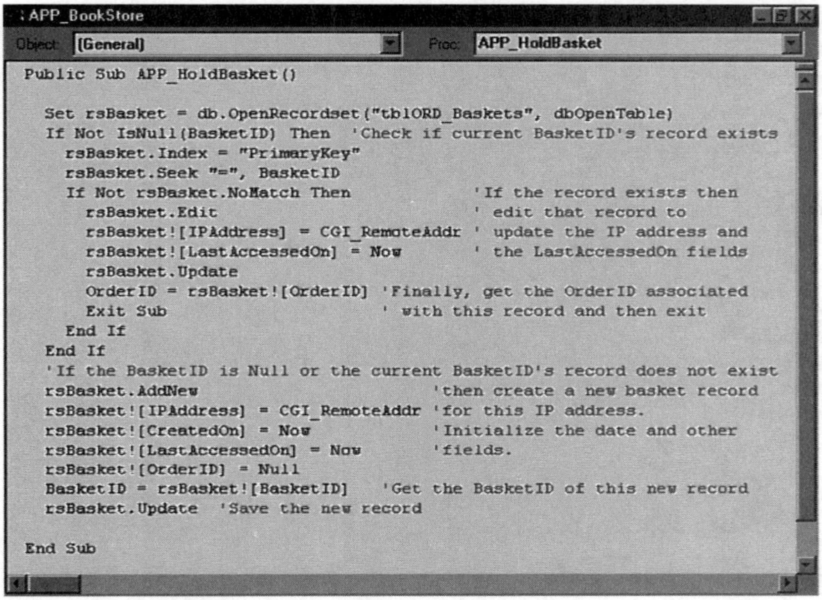

```
: APP_BookStore                                                    _ □ ✕
Object: [General]                ▼    Proc: APP_HoldBasket          ▼

Public Sub APP_HoldBasket()

   Set rsBasket = db.OpenRecordset("tblORD_Baskets", dbOpenTable)
   If Not IsNull(BasketID) Then  'Check if current BasketID's record exists
     rsBasket.Index = "PrimaryKey"
     rsBasket.Seek "=", BasketID
     If Not rsBasket.NoMatch Then              'If the record exists then
       rsBasket.Edit                           ' edit that record to
       rsBasket![IPAddress] = CGI_RemoteAddr  ' update the IP address and
       rsBasket![LastAccessedOn] = Now         ' the LastAccessedOn fields
       rsBasket.Update
       OrderID = rsBasket![OrderID]  'Finally, get the OrderID associated
       Exit Sub                       ' with this record and then exit
     End If
   End If
   'If the BasketID is Null or the current BasketID's record does not exist
   rsBasket.AddNew                             'then create a new basket record
   rsBasket![IPAddress] = CGI_RemoteAddr 'for this IP address.
   rsBasket![CreatedOn] = Now             'Initialize the date and other
   rsBasket![LastAccessedOn] = Now        'fields.
   rsBasket![OrderID] = Null
   BasketID = rsBasket![BasketID]    'Get the BasketID of this new record
   rsBasket.Update  'Save the new record

End Sub
```

Figure 18-29 The APP_HoldBasket procedure

In addition to updating the LastAccessedOn field, the APP_HoldBasket procedure also assigns the current IP of the incoming request to that basket record. This helps synchronize the IP address with the basket if a customer had to change the IP address during the current session with this application. Note that this synchronization works only if the customer sends a request from a link that contains the BasketID as its parameter.

In the case where the current BasketID value is Null or its record does not exist in the tblORD_Baskets table (perhaps as a result of deleting the old basket records), the APP_HoldBasket procedure just creates a new basket record and makes its BasketID the current value of the BasketID variable.

NOTE: The APP_HoldBasket procedure also stores the value of the OrderID field associated with the current basket record in the global OrderID variable.

The APP_ReviewOrder Procedure

The APP_ReviewOrder procedure is another general-purpose procedure that is used to return the current order screen shown in Figure 18-5. (See Lesson 1.) Figure 18-30 shows the design of this procedure.

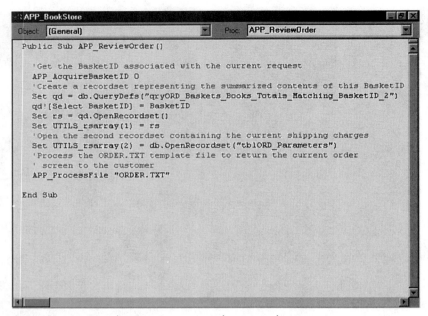

Figure 18-30 The APP_ReviewOrder procedure

The APP_ReviewOrder procedure first ensures that a valid BasketID has been associated with the current request (which some calling procedures such as APP_Orders may already have done) and then opens a recordset based on the *qryORD_Baskets_Books_Totals_Matching_BasketID_2* query. This query essentially produces a summary of the current contents of the specified BasketID (one record per book), as shown in Figure 18-31.

Next, the APP_ReviewOrder procedure opens another recordset representing the tblORD_Parameters table to pass on the current shipping rates to the ORDER.TXT template file, which is responsible for generating the current order screen. At this point, you can open the ORDER.TXT through your Notepad application to review and analyze its composition.

LESSON 7: REVIEWING HOW THE BOOK ORDERING SYSTEM CONFIRMS AN ORDER

When a customer confirms an order by clicking on the Confirm Order button on the current order screen, the BOOKSTOR.EXE program handles that request by calling the APP_ConfirmOrder procedure shown in Figure 18-32.

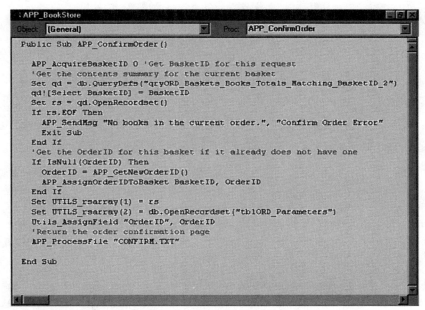

Figure 18–31 The *qryORD_Baskets_Books_Totals_Matching_BasketID_2* query in datasheet view

```
: APP_BookStore

Object: [General]                              Proc: APP_ConfirmOrder

  Public Sub APP_ConfirmOrder()

    APP_AcquireBasketID 0 'Get BasketID for this request
    'Get the contents summary for the current basket
    Set qd = db.QueryDefs("qryORD_Baskets_Books_Totals_Matching_BasketID_2")
    qd![Select BasketID] = BasketID
    Set rs = qd.OpenRecordset()
    If rs.EOF Then
      APP_SendMsg "No books in the current order.", "Confirm Order Error"
      Exit Sub
    End If
    'Get the OrderID for this basket if it already does not have one
    If IsNull(OrderID) Then
      OrderID = APP_GetNewOrderID()
      APP_AssignOrderIDToBasket BasketID, OrderID
    End If
    Set UTILS_rsarray(1) = rs
    Set UTILS_rsarray(2) = db.OpenRecordset("tblORD_Parameters")
    Utils_AssignField "OrderID", OrderID
    'Return the order confirmation page
    APP_ProcessFile "CONFIRM.TXT"

  End Sub
```

Figure 18–32 The APP_ConfirmOrder procedure

The APP_ConfirmOrder procedure first gets the BasketID associated with this request and then retrieves the contents of that basket by creating a recordset based on the summary query we discussed in the previous lesson.

There is a possibility that the customer may have previously tried to confirm an order but then decided not to go through the second phase of the confirmation at that time. In such a case, the APP_ConfirmOrder procedure tries to use the previously assigned order confirmation number (OrderID) for the current confirmation request by checking if an OrderID is already stored with the basket record.

If the basket record does not contain any previously assigned OrderID (indicated by a Null value in the OrderID variable), the APP_ConfirmOrder procedure calls the APP_GetNewOrderID procedure shown in Figure 18-33 to create a new record in the tblORD_Orders table.

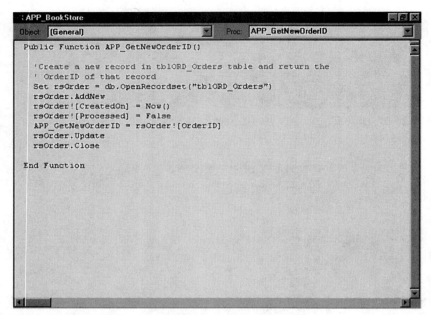

Figure 18–33 The APP_GetNewOrderID procedure

After the APP_GetNewOrderID procedure returns the new OrderID, the APP_ConfirmOrder procedure then calls the APP_AssignOrderIDToBasket procedure shown in Figure 18-34 to associate this new OrderID with the current basket record in case the customer does not go through with the order confirmation this time but may later choose this option.

As the final step, the APP_ConfirmOrder procedure sets the necessary recordsets in the UTILS_rsarray global array and generates the order confirmation response shown in Figure 18-12 based on the CONFIRM.TXT template file. At this point, you can open this template file in the Notepad application to review its composition.

LESSON 8: REVIEWING HOW THE BOOK ORDERING SYSTEM ACCEPTS PAYMENTS

The order confirmation phase we discussed in the previous lesson only assigns an OrderID for a BasketID and lists the various payment options. It does not add the contents of that basket to the order-processing queue represented by the tblORD_Orders_Books table.

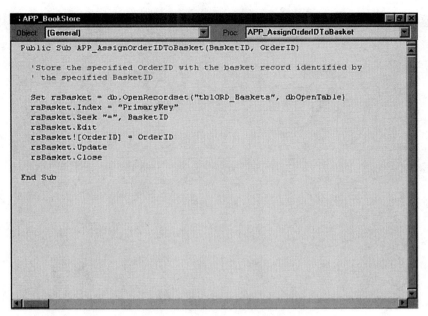

Figure 18-34 The APP_AssignOrderIDToBasket procedure

The reason for preallocating an OrderID before an order is ready to be processed is because we had to list the OrderID in order to describe the instructions for paying by check and other payment options. As you saw in Lesson 2, the order confirmation screen gives you two ways of specifying the type of payment:

By using your existing membership information

By becoming a new member

Here we will review how the bookstore application processes orders for the existing members. The analysis of how this application processes new members is left as an exercise.

Processing Orders for Existing Members

For the existing members, the order confirmation screen provides a small form asking for their MemberID and password. (See Figure 18-12.) When a customer clicks on the Existing Member button to submit that form, BOOKSTOR.EXE handles that request through its APP_ProcessOrderForExistingMember procedure shown in Figure 18-35.

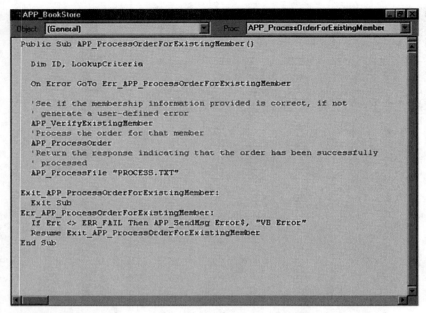

Figure 18–35 The APP_ProcessOrderForExistingMember procedure

The APP_ProcessOrderForExistingMember procedure first verifies the validity of the specified membership information by calling the APP_VerifyExistingMember procedure shown in Figure 18-36.

Once the APP_VerifyExistingMember procedure gives its blessings (by not signaling an error), the APP_ProcessOrderForExistingMember procedure calls the APP_ProcessOrder procedure shown in Figure 18-37 to move the basket contents to the order-processing queue.

The APP_ProcessOrder procedure first ensures that the current BasketID has an associated OrderID (assigned at the time of confirming the order) and then calls the APP_AssignMemberToOrder procedure shown in Figure 18-38 to attach the customer and payment information (stored in the tblORD_Members table) with the current order.

Next, the APP_ProcessOrder procedure moves the tblBK_Baskets_Books table's records associated with the current BasketID to the tblBK_Orders_Books table. It accomplishes this task in two steps. First, it copies the appropriate records from the tblBK_Baskets_Books table to the tblBK_Orders_Books table by calling the APP_CopyBooksFromBasketToOrder procedure shown in Figure 18-39.

```
; APP_BookStore                                                    _ @ X
Object: [General]                    ▼    Proc: APP_VerifyExistingMember      ▼

Public Sub APP_VerifyExistingMember()

  MemberID = Utils_EmptyToNullField("MemberID") 'Get the specified MemberID
  Password = Utils_EmptyToNullField("Password") 'and password information
  If IsNull(MemberID) Or IsNull(Password) Then
    APP_SendMsg "Please specify a Member ID and Password", "Process Order"
    Error ERR_FAIL
  End If
  Set qd = db.QueryDefs("qryORD_Members_Matching_MemberID")
  qd![Specify Member ID] = MemberID
  Set rs = qd.OpenRecordset()
  qd.Close
  If rs.EOF Then  'Invalid MemberID
    APP_SendMsg "The specified Member ID does not exist.", "Process Order"
    Error ERR_FAIL
  End If
  If rs![Password] <> Password Then  'Incorrect password
    APP_SendMsg "The MemberID and Password combination is incorrect.", _
               "Process Order"
    Error ERR_FAIL
  End If
  Button = rs![PaymentOption]           'Save the member's payment info in a
  Utils_AssignField "Button", Button ' form field for template file use
  rs.Close
End Sub
```

Figure 18–36 The APP_VerifyExistingMember procedure

```
; APP_BookStore                                                    _ @ X
Object: [General]                    ▼    Proc: APP_ProcessOrder            ▼

Public Sub APP_ProcessOrder()

  APP_AcquireBasketID 0      'Get the BasketID for the current request
  'Ensure basket has been assigned an OrderID at the time of confirming
  ' the order
  If IsNull(OrderID) Then
    APP_SendMsg "No Order ID has been assigned to the basket.", "Process Ord
    Error ERR_FAIL
  End If
  'Attach the MemberID of the customer with the current order record
  APP_AssignMemberToOrder
  'Move books from tblORD_Baskets_Books to tblORD_Orders_Books
  APP_CopyBooksFromBasketToOrder    'First copy data to second table
  APP_RemoveBooksFromBasket         'Then delete data from the first table

  'Set the OrderID of this basket to Null so that a new order number is
  ' assigned if the customer confirms another order using the same basket
  APP_AssignOrderIDToBasket BasketID, Null
  'Return the response indicating that the order has been successfully
  ' processed
  APP_ProcessFile "PROCESS.TXT"


End Sub
```

Figure 18–37 The APP_ProcessOrder procedure

```
APP_BookStore                                                    _ 回 X
Object: (General)                    ▼    Proc:  APP_AssignMemberToOrder    ▼

Public Sub APP_AssignMemberToOrder()

  'Locate the Order record
  Set rs = db.OpenRecordset("tblORD_Orders", dbOpenTable)
  rs.Index = "PrimaryKey"
  rs.Seek "=", OrderID
  If rs.NoMatch Then
    APP_SendMsg "Order ID: " & OrderID & " not found.", "Invalid Order ID"
    Error ERR_FAIL
  End If
  If Not IsNull(rs![MemberID]) Then
    APP_SendMsg "This order has already been submitted to the order " & _
                "processing queue.", "Member ID already assigned"
    Error ERR_FAIL
  End If
  'Store the MemberID link
  rs.Edit
  rs![MemberID] = MemberID
  rs.Update

End Sub
```

Figure 18-38 The APP_AssignMemberToOrder procedure

```
APP_BookStore                                                    _ 回 X
Object: (General)                    ▼    Proc:  APP_CopyBooksFromBasketToOrder   ▼

Public Sub APP_CopyBooksFromBasketToOrder()

  'Get a summary of the basket contents
  Set qd = db.QueryDefs("qryORD_Baskets_Books_Totals_Matching_BasketID_2")
  qd![Select BasketID] = BasketID
  Set rs = qd.OpenRecordset()
  'Add the summarized records to the tblORD_Orders_Books table
  Set rsBooks = db.OpenRecordset("tblORD_Orders_Books")
  Do Until rs.EOF
    rsBooks.AddNew
    rsBooks![OrderID] = OrderID
    rsBooks![ISBN] = rs![ISBN]
    rsBooks![Quantity] = rs![SumOfQuantity]
    rsBooks.Update
    rs.MoveNext
  Loop

End Sub
```

Figure 18-39 The APP_CopyBooksFromBasketToOrder procedure

Then, the APP_ProcessOrder procedure deletes those records from the tblBK_Baskets_Books table by calling the APP_RemoveBooksFromBasket procedure shown in Figure 18-40.

After moving the basket contents to the order-processing queue (which also empties the basket), the APP_ProcessOrder procedure resets the OrderID field of that basket record to Null. This ensures that a new order confirmation number is created if a customer decides to continue shopping using the current basket and eventually to place another order.

As its last step, the APP_ProcessOrder procedure sends the notification shown in Figure 18-17 by processing the PROCESS.TXT template file, which you can open in your Notepad application to review its contents.

REVIEW QUESTIONS

1. What are the two common approaches Web sites use for accepting on-line orders? Identify the main differences between these two approaches.

2. List the desired features of an on-line checkout counter.

3. What is the difference between using the Home button on the order-entry screen and requesting the home page by specifying its URL from the browser's location window?

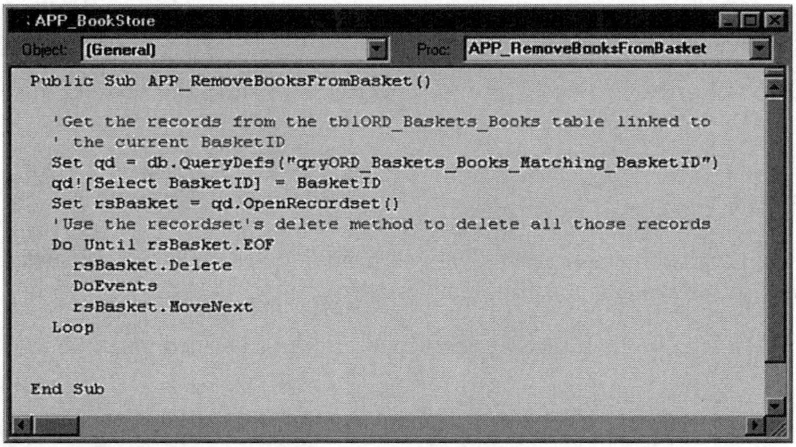

Figure 18–40 The APP_RemoveBooksFromBasket procedure

4. What is the difference between processing an order as a new member versus processing an order as an existing member?

5. Does the bookstore application allow you to cancel an order after you have confirmed it?

6. What does the On-Line Bookstore application do behind the scenes when you commit an order by specifying a payment option?

7. List the two key issues involved with designing a shopping basket–based on-line ordering system.

8. Identify the main distinctions between the operation of a real store and a Web-based virtual store.

9. What are the different approaches that you can follow to establish the association between the customers and their baskets?

10. Why can't an IP address be considered a reliable way of identifying a customer?

11. What is the Netscape Cookies scheme, and how does it help solve the customer identification problem?

12. What basic operations does an ordering system need to provide to help customers manage their baskets?

13. How does the On-Line Bookstore application resolve the customer-basket identification issue? When can its resolution method lose an existing order?

14. Which tables does the bookstore application utilize to store the baskets, their contents, and the confirmed orders? How are these tables related?

15. How does the bookstore application store the customer and payment information for a confirmed order?

16. How does the bookstore application store and handle the configurable parameters such as domestic and international shipping rates?

17. In how many ways can the bookstore application pass the assigned BasketID in its response?

18. What does the BOOKSTOR.EXE program do when you order your first book through the bookstore application's ordering system?

19. How does the BOOKSTOR.EXE program generate the current order screen?

20. How does the BOOKSTOR.EXE program handle orders for existing members?

EXERCISES

1. Do some window shopping on the World Wide Web and identify what types of on-line ordering systems are being used to run several virtual stores.

2. Analyze how the On-Line Bookstore application handles the following situations:

   - Ordering the same book by clicking on the Order button twice

   - Canceling the order that is in the process of being confirmed

   - Ordering another book after already confirming and paying for an order during the same session

3. Describe the steps the BOOKSTOR.EXE program takes for the following events:

   - Canceling an order

   - Recalculating an order

   - Paying for an order as a new member

4. Currently, the On-Line Bookstore application allows only one payment option to be stored for an existing member. Enhance this application so that a customer can use the same MemberID for specifying different payment options for different orders.

5. Modify the bookstore application so that it also allows a quantity-based discount for an order—for example, 5 percent off of the total price if the order includes five or more books. Both the quantity and the discount must be configurable parameters.

6. Extend the bookstore application so that the customer support staff and the order processing staff can easily locate and modify a confirmed order.

7. Modify the bookstore application so that it first tries to use Netscape's Cookies scheme to identify a customer and falls back on its current BasketID identification method only if the customer's browser does not support the Cookies scheme.

A
ORGANIZATION OF
FILES ON THE CD

The Web Database Construction Kit CD-ROM includes an evaluation version of WebSite Web server, Internet Explorer 3.0, Alibaba Web server, HotDog HTML editor, Webmania HTML editor, and WebForms HTML form generator. The CD-ROM also contains all the examples, sample Web applications, and the CGI utilities discussed in the book. A directory tree of the contents of the CD is shown in Table A-1. The installation instructions for the WebSite server are listed in Chapter 2, Getting Started. For the features and the installation details of the other three shareware packages, please refer to the on-line documentation provided in their respective directories on the CD.

Table A-1 CD-ROM index

Directory Tree	Contents	Related Chapters
+-CGIAPPS	Sample Web applications and book examples	All
| +-CGI-WIN	Back-end programs of the sample Web applications	All
| | +-BOOK		
| | | +-BOOKSTOR	Files related to the bookstore application	16,17, 18
| | | +-CGIOUT	Program files for the CGIOUT utility	10
| | | +-FORMAPPS	Program files for the FORMINP utility	8
| | | +-GUESTBK	Files related to the GuestBook application	2
| | | +-JOBLIST	Files related to the System Web-based Job Listing	3, 14, 15
| | | +-NEWAPP	Template files for creating a Windows-CGI program	11

continued on next page

continued from previous page

Directory Tree	Contents	Related Chapters
| | |+-SURVEY	Files related to the survey application	2
|+-HTDOCS	Book examples and front-end files of the Web applications	All
| |+-BOOK		
| | |+-BOOKSTOR	Files related to the bookstore application	16,17, 18
| | |+-CHAP2	Chapter 2 examples	2
| | |+-CHAP4	Chapter 4 examples	4
| | |+-CHAP5	Chapter 5 examples	5
| | |+-CHAP6	Chapter 6 examples	6
| | |+-CHAP7	Chapter 7 examples	7
| | |+-CHAP8	Chapter 8 examples	8
| | |+-CHAP9	Chapter 9 examples	9
| | |+-CHAP11	Chapter 11 examples	11
| | |+-CHAP12	Chapter 12 examples	12
| | |+-CHAP13	Chapter 13 examples	13
| | |+-GUESTBK	Files related to the GuestBook application	2
| | |+-JOBLIST	Files related to the Web-based Job Listing System	3, 14, 15
| | |+-SURVEY	Files related to the Survey application	2
+-EXPLORER	Internet Explorer 3.0	C
+-LIB	Library files for creating a Windows CGI program	12, 14
+-SHARWARE	Shareware version of popular Web servers and utilities	
|+-ALIBABA	Alibaba Web server (evaluation version)	
|+-HOTDOG	HotDog HTML Editor	
|+-WEBFORMS	Shareware HTML form creation utility	
|+-WEBMANIA	Shareware HTML editor utility	
|+-WEBSITE	WebSite 1.1e (evaluation version)	2

OTHER SITES OF INTEREST

Table A-2 lists the URLs and a brief description of several Web sites on the Internet with tools, utilities, and information that you may find valuable when constructing your Web applications.

Table A–2 Other sites of interest

URL (http://)	Description
www.nkn.net/nkn/resources/cgiprog.htm	A list of CGI programs on the Web
www.lifecom.com/osicgi0.htm	CGI applications for Windows NT Web servers
home.sol.no/jgaa/cgi-bin.htm	A command-line send-mail utility (freeware)
www.program.com/resources/devweb.html	Information for Web developers
www.innovision1.com/msadp/	MS Access developer's page
www.apexsc.com/vb/	Visual Basic developer's page
super.sonic.net/ann/delphi/cgicomp/	Delphi components and utilities for Win-CGI
www.prplus.com/vb4cgi/	Using STDIN-STDOUT with VB4.0 for CGI
www2.ncsu.edu/bae/people/faculty/walker/hotlist/isindex.html	Information on searchable databases
gdbdoc.gdb.org/letovsky/general/dbgw.html	Web-database gateways

B

SOURCE CODE OF THE UTILS.BAS LIBRARY

The UTILS.BAS file located in the \LIB directory of the accompanying CD-ROM is a Visual Basic library that includes several functions and procedures to help you design powerful Web applications quickly and efficiently. Chapter 14, Processing Template Files with a CGI Application, describes how to add this library to your Visual Basic project and the purpose of its frequently used routines. The subsequent chapters demonstrate how you can easily incorporate many other neat features in your Web applications using this library.

This appendix lists the documented source code of this library. We encourage you to read through this documentation and make any necessary enhancements to suit your needs.

```
'===================================================================
'     Name: UTILS.BAS
'  Purpose: Library of utility functions for creating
'           Windows CGI programs
'    Notes: This library assumes that CGI32.BAS library is also
'           loaded with the project.
'
'     Date      Initials    Description
'   07/18/96      GSK       Author of this library
'
'===================================================================


'-------------------------------------------------------------------
'                    DECLARATION SECTION
'-------------------------------------------------------------------

Attribute VB_Name = "Utilities"
Option Explicit
```

continued on next page

continued from previous page

```
'_____
'The following declarations are mainly associated with
'the template file (TF) processing portion of this library
'_____

Const UTILS_MAX_RECORDSETS = 5   'Max# of recordsets a TF can use
Global UTILS_rsarray(1 To UTILS_MAX_RECORDSETS) As Recordset

'This library uses a database called UTILS.MDB whose path
'is specified through the following constant. The UTILS.MDB
'should be on the same disk drive on which the CGI program
'resides.

Const UTILS_DB_PATH = "\WEBSITE\LIB\UTILS.MDB"

Global UTILS_Error As Integer    'For returning error codes

Dim UTILS_db As Database         'Database object for UTILS.MDB

'=============================================================
' Sub UTILS_AddKeywordsToTempTable(rsSource As Recordset, KeywordDelimiters, rsDest As ⇐
Recordset)
'
' Purpose: Creates a record in the given temp table (rsDest) for each
' keyword in the description field of the current record of the
' source recordset (rsSource).
'
' Inputs
' _____
' rsSource: A recordset containing an ID field and a text field named
'           KeywordField.
' KeywordDelimiters: String containing the set of delimiter characters
' rsDest: Recordset represting the temp table, which must have two
'           fields named ID and Keyword.
'
' Usage
' _____
' See: UTILS_IndexField procedure
'
' Notes
' _____
' - The data type of the ID field of the rsSource recordset must be
'   compatible with the ID field of the rsDest recordset.
' - The newline characters are automatically added to the set of
'   delimiter characters
'
' Example:
' Inputs:
'   Current record of rsSource:
'     ID: 123
'     KeywordField: "Create Web-based applications using Windows-CGI."
'   KeywordDelimiters: ",.:;'""""!#$[]{}()+-_"
```

```
' Results:
'   The following 7 new records added to the rsDest table:
'      ID         Keyword
'      ----       -------
'      123        Create
'      123        Web
'      123        based
'      123        applications
'      123        using
'      123        Windows
'      123        CGI
'===================================================================
'
Sub UTILS_AddKeywordsToTempTable(rsSource As Recordset, KeywordDelimiters, rsDest As ⇐
Recordset)

  Dim Ch As String
  Dim KeyWord As String
  Dim length As Long
  Dim Start As Long
  Dim i As Long
  Dim Description
  Dim Delimiters


  On Error Resume Next
  'Add newline characters to delimiters
  Delimiters = KeywordDelimiters & Chr(13) & Chr(10)
  'Remove leading and trailing spaces from the keyword field
  Description = Trim(rsSource![KeywordField])
  length = Len(Description)
  'Separate Description into individual keywords and
  'add them to the temp table
  If length = 0 Then Exit Sub
  Start = 1
  For i = 1 To length
    Ch = Mid(Description, i, 1)
    If InStr(Delimiters, Ch) > 0 Then
      KeyWord = Trim(Mid(Description, Start, i - Start))
      If KeyWord <> "" And Not IsNull(KeyWord) Then
        rsDest.AddNew
        rsDest![ID] = rsSource![ID]
        rsDest![KeyWord] = KeyWord
        rsDest.Update
      End If
      Start = i + 1
    End If
  Next
  'Handle the last keyword
  If Start < i Then
    KeyWord = Trim(Mid(Description, Start, i - Start))
    If KeyWord <> "" And Not IsNull(KeyWord) Then
      rsDest.AddNew
```

continued on next page

continued from previous page

```
        rsDest![ID] = rsSource![ID]
        rsDest![KeyWord] = KeyWord
        rsDest.Update
      End If
    End If

End Sub

'===================================================================
' Sub UTILS_IndexField(db As Database, rsSource As Recordset, KeywordsLinkTable, ⇐
Delimiters)
'
' Purpose: Creates a word-index of the Description field of a given
' recordset
'
' Inputs
' ------
' db: Database where the word-index will be stored
' rsSource: Recordset whose field has to be indexed
' KeywordsLinkTable: Table that holds the link between the each record of
'   the source recordset and the words of the tblKeywords table
' Delimiters: String containing the set of delimiter characters
'
'
' Notes
' -----
' - The db database must contain the following three tables:
'   1. tblSYS_Keywords: Table that will hold the word-dictionary
'        KeywordID: AutoNumber (Primary Key)
'          Keyword: Text (50) (Indexed, No Duplicates)
'
'   2. tblTMP_Keywords_Text: Table that will temporararily hold the
'      link between the source table that has a Text type primary key
'      and the words to be indexed
'            ID: Text (50) \
'      Keyword: Text (50) / They both form the primary key
'
'   3. tblTMP_Keywords_Numeric: Table that will temporararily hold the
'      link between the source table that has a Number type primary key
'      and the words to be indexed
'            ID: Number (long) \
'      Keyword: Text (50)      / They both form the primary key
'
'- This procedure automatically determines which temp table to use
'  and locks it while the words are being indexed
'
'- This procedure quits with an error if it is unable to lock the
'  temp table
'
'- This procedure automatically appends any new keywords to the
'  tblSYS_Keywords table. It does delete any existing keywords
'
```

```
'- This procedure does not delete any existing records in the
'  keywords link table
'
' Example
' -------
' Inputs:
'   Let's say rsSource has the following two records
'       ID          Description
'       ----        -------
'       123         "Create Web-based applications using Windows-CGI"
'       124         "Learn How To Create Windows 95 Applications"
'
'   Let's say the keywords link table is named tblLNK_Keywords and is
'   currently empty.
'
'   Let's say tblSYS_Keywords contains the following records:
'   KeywordID       Keyword
'   ---------       -------
'       1           and
'       2           applications
'       3           based
'
'   Finally, let's say Delimiters = ",.:;'""!#$[]{}()+-_"
'
'Results:
'   After this procedure is done executing:
'   tblSYS_Keywords will have the following records:
'
'   KeywordID       Keyword
'   ---------       -------
'       1           and
'       2           applications
'       3           based
'       4           Create
'       5           Web
'       6           using
'       7           Windows
'       8           CGI
'       9           Learn
'      10           how
'      11           to
'      12           95
'
' Note: The order of the ID's may be different
'
' tblLNK_Keywords (the link table) will have the following records:
'         ID        KeywordID
'   ---------       ---------
'       123             4
'       123             5
'       123             3
'       123             2
```

continued on next page

589

continued from previous page

```
'         123          6
'         123          7
'         123          8
'         124          9
'         124         10
'         124         11
'         124          4
'         124          7
'         124         12
'         124          2
'================================================================
'
Public Sub UTILS_IndexField(db As Database, rsSource As Recordset, KeywordsLinkTable, ⇐
Delimiters)

  Dim TempKeywordTable
  Dim ErrValue As Integer
  Dim rsTemp As Recordset
  Dim i, SQL

  If rsSource.EOF Then Exit Sub
  'Determine which temp table to use based on the data type of the ID field
  Select Case rsSource![ID].type
    Case dbText
      TempKeywordTable = "tblTMP_Keywords_Text"
    Case dbByte, dbInteger, dbLong
      TempKeywordTable = "tblTMP_Keywords_Numeric"
  End Select
  'Try to lock the temp table
  On Error Resume Next
  For i = 1 To 15000
    Set rsTemp = db.OpenRecordset(TempKeywordTable, dbOpenDynaset, dbDenyWrite)
    If Err = 0 Then Exit For
    DoEvents
  Next
  ErrValue = Err
  If ErrValue <> 0 Then  'Cannot lock
    On Error GoTo 0
    Error ErrValue        'Return with error
  End If
  Do Until rsTemp.EOF    'Delete any exisiting records from the temp table
    rsTemp.Delete
    DoEvents
    rsTemp.MoveNext
  Loop
  'Add keywords to the temp table from each record of the source recordset
  Do Until rsSource.EOF
    UTILS_AddKeywordsToTempTable rsSource, Delimiters, rsTemp
    DoEvents
    rsSource.MoveNext
  Loop
```

```
    rsTemp.Close
    On Error GoTo 0
    'Insert new keywords into tblSYS_Keywords
    SQL = "INSERT INTO tblSYS_Keywords ( Keyword ) " & _
          "SELECT DISTINCT " & TempKeywordTable & ".Keyword " & _
          "FROM " & TempKeywordTable & " LEFT JOIN tblSYS_Keywords " & _
          "ON " & TempKeywordTable & ".Keyword = tblSYS_Keywords.Keyword " & _
          "WHERE (((tblSYS_Keywords.Keyword) Is Null));"
    db.Execute SQL, dbFailOnError

    'Add keywords and id combinations to the destination table
    SQL = "INSERT INTO " & KeywordsLinkTable & " ( ID, KeywordID ) " & _
          "SELECT DISTINCT " & TempKeywordTable & ".ID, " & _
          "tblSYS_Keywords.KeywordID FROM " & TempKeywordTable & _
          " LEFT JOIN tblSYS_Keywords ON " & TempKeywordTable & _
          ".Keyword = tblSYS_Keywords.Keyword;"
    db.Execute SQL

End Sub

'==================================================================
' Function Utils_GetParameter(ParameterString, ParameterNumber, Delimiter)
'
' Purpose: Gets the Nth parameter value from the given Parameter
'          string.
'
' Inputs
' ------
' ParameterString: String from which the parameter has to be extracted
' ParameterNumber: Tells which parameter to extract
' Delimiter: Character used to separate the parameters
'
' Example
' -------
' Utils_GetParameter("This+is+a+string",2,"+") returns "is".
'
' Notes
' -----
' Returns Null if ParameterString is empty or if no matching
' parameter is found.
'
'==================================================================
'
Function Utils_GetParameter(ParameterString, ParameterNumber, Delimiter)

    Dim EndPos
    Dim Start
    Dim i

    If ParameterString = "" Then
      Utils_GetParameter = Null
```

continued on next page

continued from previous page

```
    Exit Function
  End If
  Start = 1
  For i = 2 To ParameterNumber
    Start = InStr(Start, ParameterString, Delimiter) + 1
    If Start = 1 Then
      Start = 0
      Exit For
    End If
  Next
  If Start = 0 Then
    Utils_GetParameter = Null
    Exit Function
  End If
  EndPos = InStr(Start, ParameterString, Delimiter)
  If EndPos = 0 Then
    Utils_GetParameter = Mid(ParameterString, Start)
  Else
    Utils_GetParameter = Mid(ParameterString, Start, EndPos - Start)
  End If

End Function


'==================================================================
' Function Utils_EmptyToNullField(FieldName As String) As Variant
'
' Purpose: Returns the value of a form field if it is not empty,
'          otherwise, returns null if field is empty or absent
'
' Inputs
' ------
' FieldName: Field whose value is to be returned.
'
' Notes
' -----
' Uses the GetSmallField function of the CGI32.BAS module
'
'==================================================================
'
Function Utils_EmptyToNullField(FieldName As String) As Variant
  Dim value

  On Error Resume Next
  value = Trim(GetSmallField(FieldName))
  If value = "" Or Err <> 0 Then
    Utils_EmptyToNullField = Null
  Else
    Utils_EmptyToNullField = value
```

```
  End If

End Function



'====================================================================
' Function Utils_ConvertFromQueryString(StringValue As String)
'
' Purpose: Decodes a string encoded using this library's
'          Utils_ConvertToQueryString function and returns.
'          that decoded value
' Inputs
' ------
' StringValue: String to be converted
'
' Example
' -------
' Utils_GetParameter("Decoded__String") returns "Decoded String".
'
' Notes
' -----
' Used for passing data through the Query String portion of a URL
'
'====================================================================
'
Function Utils_ConvertFromQueryString(StringValue As String)

  Dim ConvertedString As String

  'Convert Spaces to Underscores
  ConvertedString = Utils_ReplaceString(StringValue, "__", " ")
  ConvertedString = Utils_ReplaceString(ConvertedString, "''", """")
  Utils_ConvertFromQueryString = ConvertedString

End Function



'====================================================================
' Function Utils_ConvertToQueryString(StringValue As String)
'
' Purpose: Encodes a string so that it can be passed as a query
'          string parameter in a URL.
' Inputs
' ------
' StringValue: String to be converted
'
' Example
' -------
' Utils_GetParameter("Decoded String") returns "Decoded__String".
'
```

continued on next page

593

continued from previous page

```
' Notes
' -----
' - This encoding method is NOT the same as the standard URL encoding
' - It uses two characters to encode a special character
' - Currently it only encodes the ' ' and '"' characters.
'   You can other special characters to this list
'
'==================================================================

Function Utils_ConvertToQueryString(StringValue As String)
  Dim ConvertedString As String

  'Convert Spaces to Underscores
  ConvertedString = Utils_ReplaceString(StringValue, " ", "__")
  ConvertedString = Utils_ReplaceString(ConvertedString, """", "''")
  Utils_ConvertToQueryString = ConvertedString

End Function




'==================================================================
' Function Utils_ReplaceString(SourceString, A, B)
'
' Purpose: Replaces SubString A with Substring B in SourceString
'
' Inputs
' ------
' SourceString: String where replacements will occur
' A: Substring to replace
' B: Substring to replace with

' Example
' -------
' Utils_ReplaceString("abcdab", "ab","c") returns "ccdc".
'
' Notes
' -----
' - All occurenced of A are replaced with B
' - A and B do not have to be of the same length
'
'==================================================================
'
Function Utils_ReplaceString(SourceString, A, B)

  Dim i As Integer
  Dim NumCharsToReplace As Integer
  Dim NumCharsReplacedBy As Integer
  Dim Result As String
  Dim StringToReplace As String
  Dim Replacement As String

  Result = CStr(SourceString)
```

```
  StringToReplace = CStr(A)
  Replacement = CStr(B)
  NumCharsToReplace = Len(StringToReplace)
  NumCharsReplacedBy = Len(Replacement)
  i = InStr(1, Result, StringToReplace)
  Do While i <> 0
    Result = Mid(Result, 1, i - 1) & Replacement + Mid(Result, i + NumCharsToReplace)
    i = i + NumCharsReplacedBy
    i = InStr(i, Result, StringToReplace)
  Loop
  Utils_ReplaceString = Result

End Function



'====================================================================
' Function Utils_ProcessFile(ByVal InputFileNum As Integer) As Variant
'
' Purpose: Processes a template file and returns the processed
'          output.
'
' Inputs
' ------
' InputFileNum: File number representing the template file
'
' Notes
' -----
'
' - The template file must be opened in read mode before
'   calling this function.
' - The template file is always processed from the beginning.
'   If you do not want this feature then comment out the Seek
'   statement in this function.
' - If any error occurs while reading a file then returns the
'   an HTML formatted comment listing the error message. Also
'   sets the UTILS_Error variable to the appropriate error code.
' - The processing method is described in the UTILS_ProcessString
'   function.
'
'====================================================================
'
Public Function Utils_ProcessFile(ByVal InputFileNum As Integer) As Variant

  Const INPUT_PAST_EOF = 62

  Dim Char As String
  Dim OutputChars As String
  Dim TokenChars As String
  Dim TokenResult As Variant
  Dim NumCharsRead As Variant
  Dim ErrValue As Integer
  Dim ErrString As String
```

continued on next page

continued from previous page

```
   Dim Result As String
   Dim TokenOutput As String
   Dim RecordsetNumber As Integer
   Dim MaxLoops As Variant
   Dim LoopCount As Variant

   On Error GoTo Err_Utils_ProcessFile

   UTILS_Error = 0
   Result = ""
   Seek #InputFileNum, 1
   TokenChars = Utils_InputUpto(InputFileNum, Chr(0), 0, Char, NumCharsRead)
   Result = Result + Utils_ProcessString(TokenChars, "`")

Exit_Utils_ProcessFile:
   On Error Resume Next
   If UTILS_Error <> 0 Then
     Result = Result & ErrString
   End If
   Utils_ProcessFile = Result

Err_Utils_ProcessFile:
   UTILS_Error = Err
   ErrString = "<!--Utils_ProcessFile: " & Error$ & " -->"
   Resume Exit_Utils_ProcessFile
End Function

'==================================================================
' Function Utils_InputUpto(ByVal FileNum As Integer, Delimiters As String, MaxCharacters As
Long, MatchedDelimiter As String, NumCharsRead As Variant) As Variant
'
'
' Purpose: Reads a file until it finds one of the given
'          delimiters or if it reads specified number of
'          characters or if it reaches the end of file.
'          Returns the read portion as a string.
'
' Inputs
' ------
' FileNum: File number representing the input file
' Delimiters: String containing all the delimiter characters
' MaxCharacters: Maximum number of characters to be read
'
' Outputs
' -------
' MatchedDelimiter: Delimiter that was found when reading
'                   the file
' NumCharsRead: Number of characters that were actually read
'
' Notes
' -----
'
```

```
' - To read the entire text file, specify Chr(0) as the delimiter.
'
'====================================================================
'
Public Function Utils_InputUpto(ByVal FileNum As Integer, Delimiters As String,
MaxCharacters As Long, MatchedDelimiter As String, NumCharsRead As Variant) As Variant
   Dim Char As String
   Dim Done
   Dim Result As Variant

   NumCharsRead = 0
   Result = ""
   MatchedDelimiter = ""
   Done = EOF(FileNum)
   Do While Not Done
     Char = Input(1, #FileNum)
     NumCharsRead = NumCharsRead + 1
     If InStr(Delimiters, Char) > 0 Then
       MatchedDelimiter = Char
       Done = True
     Else
       Result = Result + Char
     End If
     If EOF(FileNum) Then Done = True
     If NumCharsRead = MaxCharacters Then Done = True
   Loop
   Utils_InputUpto = Result
End Function


'====================================================================
' Function Utils_Eval(TokenCharsToEval)
'
' Purpose: Processes a token string representing a valid expresion.
'          The token string can include embedded variables/codes,
'          which are replaced with their current values before
'          computing the resulting espression.
'          Returns the processed string.
'
'          Some embedded codes actually represent an action
'          and an empty string is returned for those codes.
'
' Inputs
' _____
' TokenCharsToEval: String to process
'
' Examples
' _____
' - Utils_Eval("1+2") returns 3
' - Utils_Eval("Search date = " & [F:SearchDate]) returns
'   "Search Date = 4/18/96" if there exists a form field named
'   SearchDate that currently has the value: "4/18/96". Note
```

continued on next page

continued from previous page

```
'      that an embedded code/variable must be enclosed within
'      square brackets.
'
' Notes
' _____
' - If an error occurs while evaluating the expression, then an
'   HTML formatted comment listing the error message is returned.
' - This function uses the UTILS.MDB and an SQL statement to
'   evaluate the expression. Currently, no other easy alternative
'   seems to be available for this purpose.
'
' SYNTAX OF EMBEDDED CODES
' ------------------------
' All embedded codes are enclosed within square brackets and contain
' an instruction, a separator(: or .), and a parameter.
' Here are the types of things you can do through embedded codes:
'
' 1. Access form fields
'      Syntax: [F:fieldname] or [V:fieldname] where fieldname refers to
'              a form field
'      Examples: [F:SearchDate], [V:SearchDate]
'      Notes: The only difference between "F" and "V" instructions is
'             in what they return when the specified field
'             does not exist or contains an empty string as its value.
'             "F" returns a Null whereas "V" returns an empty string ("").
'
' 2. Access fields of a recordset
'      Syntax: [Rn:fieldname] where n is the recordset number and
'              fieldname refers to the name of a field in that
'              recordset.
'      Example: [R1:JobID]
'      Notes: The recordset is assumed to be listed as the
'             nth element of the global array named UTILS_rsarray.
'
' 3. Change the current record of a recordset
'      Syntax: [Rn.movemethod] where n is the recordset number and
'              the movemethod can be: Next, Previous, First, or Last.
'      Example:[R1.Next] to go to the next record of the first
'              recordset in the UTILS_rsarray array.
'
' 4. Count the records in a recordset
'      Syntax: [Rn.Count] where n is the recordset number.
'      Example: [R1.Count]
'
' 5. Access the value of a CGI variable
'      Syntax: [C:variablename] where variablename refers to the name
'              of the CGI variable as declared in the CGI32.BAS library
'              without the "CGI_" prefix.
'      Example: [C:ServerName] returns the value of CGI_ServerName
'
' 6. Access a query string parameter
'      Syntax: [Q:parameternumber] where parameternumber refers to the
'              position of the parameter in the query string
```

```
'       Example: [Q:2] returns 15 if CGI_QueryString contains "4+15+test"
'       Notes: The "+" character is assumed to be the parameter
'              separator character.
'
' 7. Return the contents of a file name
'       Syntax: [I:absolutefilepath] where absolutefilepath refers to the
'               absolute path of file whose contents are to be returned.
'       Example: [I:C:\WEBSITE\HTDOCS\TEST\TEST.HTM]
'       Notes: This code must be used by itself. It cannot be part of an
'              expression.
'              For example, "A" & [I:C:\WEBSITE\HTDOCS\TEST\TEST.HTM] will
'              just return the contents of the TEST.HTM file.
'==================================================================
'
Public Function Utils_Eval(TokenCharsToEval)

  Dim TokenChars, TokenLength
  Dim Start, i, BeginMatchPos, EndMatchPos
  Dim Variable, VariableType, RecordsetNumber
  Dim FieldName As String, FieldValue
  Dim rs As Recordset
  Dim QuoteChar As String
  Dim FieldType As Integer
  Dim SQL As String
  Dim qd As QueryDef

  On Error GoTo Err_Utils_Eval

  TokenChars = Trim(TokenCharsToEval)
  TokenLength = Len(TokenChars)
  If TokenLength = 0 Then
    Utils_Eval = ""
    Exit Function
  End If
  Start = 1
  Do While True
    QuoteChar = ""
    BeginMatchPos = InStr(Start, TokenChars, "[")
    If BeginMatchPos <> 0 Then
      EndMatchPos = InStr(BeginMatchPos, TokenChars, "]")
      If EndMatchPos = 0 Then EndMatchPos = TokenLength
      Variable = Mid(TokenChars, BeginMatchPos, EndMatchPos - BeginMatchPos + 1)
      VariableType = Mid(Variable, 2, 1)
      Select Case VariableType
        Case "R"   'eg. R1:FieldName
          Eval_RecordsetField Variable, FieldValue, QuoteChar
        Case "F", "C", "Q", "V"   'eg. F:FieldName, C:CGIVariableName, Q:ParameterNumber, ⇐
V:FieldName
          Eval_VariableField VariableType, Variable, FieldValue, QuoteChar
        Case "I" 'eg: I:FilePath
          Eval_IncludeFile Variable, FieldValue
```

continued on next page

continued from previous page

```
          Utils_Eval = FieldValue
          Exit Function
        Case Else
          Utils_Eval = "Cannot handle variable: " & Variable
          Exit Function
      End Select
      If Variable = TokenChars Then
        Utils_Eval = IIf(IsNull(FieldValue), "<!--Null-->", FieldValue)
        Exit Function
      End If
      If IsNull(FieldValue) Then
        FieldValue = "Null"
        QuoteChar = ""
      Else
        If QuoteChar = """" Then
          FieldValue = Utils_ReplaceString(FieldValue, QuoteChar, QuoteChar + QuoteChar)
        End If
        FieldValue = QuoteChar & FieldValue & QuoteChar
      End If
      TokenChars = Utils_ReplaceString(TokenChars, Variable, FieldValue)
      Start = BeginMatchPos
    Else
      'Go ahead and eval
      Utils_OpenDatabase
      SQL = "SELECT " & TokenChars & " As Result FROM DummyTable;"
      Set rs = UTILS_db.OpenRecordset(SQL)
      Utils_Eval = IIf(IsNull(rs!Result), "<!--NULL-->", rs!Result)
      rs.Close
      Exit Do
    End If
  Loop

Exit_Utils_Eval:
  Exit Function

Err_Utils_Eval:
  Utils_Eval = "<!--" & Error$ & "-->"
  UTILS_Error = True
  Resume Exit_Utils_Eval
End Function

'================================================================
' Function Utils_GetCGIVariable(VariableName)
'
' Purpose: Returns the value of the specified CGI variable name
'
' Inputs
' ------
' VariableName: Name of the CGI variable
'
```

```
'================================================================
'
Public Function Utils_GetCGIVariable(VariableName)

   Select Case VariableName
     Case "ServerSoftware"
       Utils_GetCGIVariable = CGI_ServerSoftware
     Case "ServerName"
       Utils_GetCGIVariable = CGI_ServerName
     Case "ServerPort"
       Utils_GetCGIVariable = CGI_ServerPort
     Case "RequestProtocol"
       Utils_GetCGIVariable = CGI_RequestProtocol
     Case "ServerAdmin"
       Utils_GetCGIVariable = CGI_ServerAdmin
     Case "Version"
       Utils_GetCGIVariable = CGI_Version
     Case "RequestMethod"
       Utils_GetCGIVariable = CGI_RequestMethod
     Case "RequestKeepAlive"
       Utils_GetCGIVariable = CGI_RequestKeepAlive
     Case "LogicalPath"
       Utils_GetCGIVariable = CGI_LogicalPath
     Case "PhysicalPath"
       Utils_GetCGIVariable = CGI_PhysicalPath
     Case "ExecutablePath"
       Utils_GetCGIVariable = CGI_ExecutablePath
     Case "QueryString"
       Utils_GetCGIVariable = CGI_QueryString
     Case "RequestRange"
       Utils_GetCGIVariable = CGI_RequestRange
     Case "Referer"
       Utils_GetCGIVariable = CGI_Referer
     Case "From"
       Utils_GetCGIVariable = CGI_From
     Case "UserAgent"
       Utils_GetCGIVariable = CGI_UserAgent
     Case "RemoteHost"
       Utils_GetCGIVariable = CGI_RemoteHost
     Case "RemoteAddr"
       Utils_GetCGIVariable = CGI_RemoteAddr
     Case "AuthUser"
       Utils_GetCGIVariable = CGI_AuthUser
     Case "AuthPass"
       Utils_GetCGIVariable = CGI_AuthPass
     Case "AuthType"
       Utils_GetCGIVariable = CGI_AuthType
     Case "AuthRealm"
       Utils_GetCGIVariable = CGI_AuthRealm
     Case "ContentType"
       Utils_GetCGIVariable = CGI_ContentType
```

continued on next page

continued from previous page

```
      Case "ContentLength"
        Utils_GetCGIVariable = CGI_ContentLength
      Case Else
        Utils_GetCGIVariable = "<!-- Unknown CGI Variable Name: " & VariableName & " -->"
    End Select

End Function

'================================================================
' Sub Utils_OpenDatabase()
'
' Purpose: Opens the UTILS.MDB database if it is not already open
'
'================================================================
'
Public Sub Utils_OpenDatabase()

  Dim i

  On Error Resume Next
  i = UTILS_db.name
  If Err <> 0 Then
    Set UTILS_db = Workspaces(0).OpenDatabase(Left(App.Path, 2) & UTILS_DB_PATH)
  End If

End Sub

'================================================================
' Function Utils_ProcessString(InputString As String, Delimiter As String)
'
' Purpose: Processes a string based on the embedded instructions and
'          returns the processed result. The embedded instructions
'          allow if/then conditions, loops, and variable assignments.
'          You can also evaluate expressions supported by the
'          UTILS_Eval function.
'
' Inputs
' ------
' InputString: String to process
' Delimiter : The character that represents the beginning of
'             an embedded instruction (normally "`" is used)
'
' Examples
' --------
' - Utils_ProcessString("Your IP is: `[C:RemoteAddr]`","`") returns
'   "Your IP is 127.0.0.1" if the CGI request was made from localhost.
' - Utils_ProcessString("`1+2` and `3+4` makes `1+2+3+4`","`")
'   returns "3 and 7 makes 10".
' - Utils_ProcessString("If `?^"0"^Non-zero^Zero^","`") returns
'    "If Zero". See below for the syntax of the if instruction.
'
' Notes
```

```
'  _____
'  - All embedded instructions must start with the delimiter
'    character.
'  - All characters that are not parameters of any embedded
'    instruction are returned as is. So if the input string does
'    not contain any embedded instructions then it will be returned as is.
'
'  - See also the documentation of UTILS_Eval function.
'
' SYNTAX OF EMBEDDED INSTRUCTIONS
' -------------------------------
' All embedded instructions must start with the delimiter character.
'
' Here are the types of things you can do through embedded
' instructions:
'
' 1. Process expressions
'     Syntax: `expression`
'             where expression is a string that can be processed
'             by this module's UTILS_Eval function. See the
'             documention of UTILS_Eval function for more details.
'     Example: `[F:SearchDate]` returns the current value of the
'             SearchDate form field.
'
' 2. Assign variables as form fields
'     Syntax: `A:variablename=expression` where variablename refers
'             the name of the variable and expression represents a
'             valid string that can be processed by the UTILS_Eval
'             function.
'     Example: `A:Path=[C:ExecutablePath]` creates a form field
'              named Path if it does not already exists and
'              assigns Path to the value of the CGI_ExecutablePath
'              variable.
'       Notes: You can reassign a variable to different
'              expressions any number of times in the input string.
'
' 3. Process only selected section of a string based on a condition
'     Syntax: `?^condition^truesubstring^falsesubstring^ where
'             condition is an expression that is considered false if it
'             evaluates to "<!--Null-->", "", "0", 0, "False", or "No",
'             otherwise the condition is considered true.
'             If condition is true then truesubstring is processed else
'             falsesubstring is processed.
'     Example: `?^[F:Test]^Non-zero^Zero^ returns "Zero" if the
'             form field Test evaluates to one of the false
'             conditions, otherwise it returns "Non-zero".
'       Notes: You can create nested if conditions by using
'             different separator characters. For example, the
'             following returns the string "Positive":
'             `?^1>=0^ `?*1>0*Positive*Zero* ^Negative^
'                      |_____|
```

continued on next page

continued from previous page

```
'                        (Nested If using * as seperator char)
'
' 4. Process loops based on a recordset.
'     Syntax: `L|n,maxloops,stringtoprocess|
'             where n is the recordset number, maxloops is a an
'             expression that indicates the number of iterations to
'             perform, and stringtoprocess is the string which will
'             be processed during each iteration.
'   Example1: `L|1,3,<B>Rec#: </B>`[R1:ID]`|  returns
'             "<B>Rec# ID: </B>1<B>Rec# ID: </B>2<B>Rec# ID: </B>3"
'             if the first three records of recordset 1 have an ID
'             field with values 1, 2, and 3 respectively.
'   Example2: `L|1,EOF,<B>Rec#: </B>`[R1:ID]`| will process
'             the string for all records of recordset 1.
'     Notes: - Normally MaxLoops must evaluate to a numeric expression.
'              The only exception is the value EOF, which means, loop
'              till the end of the recordset.
'            - The recordset must be listed in the nth element of the
'              UTILS_rsarray aray.
'            - After every iteraration, the current record is set
'              to the next record in the recordset.
'            - In the string, you can refer to form field named
'              Index_Rn for determining the iteration number.
'              For example: `L|1,3,Index = `[F:Index_R1]` | will return
'              "Index = 1 Index = 2 Index = 3 "
'            - You can use different separator characters to
'              create nested loops.
'
' 4. Process loops using an index variable to simulate For/Next loops
'     Syntax: `N|variablename,maxloops,stringtoprocess|
'             where variablename is the name of the index variable
'             (stored as a form field), maxloops is a numeric
'             expression that indicates the number of iterations to
'             perform, and stringtoprocess is the string which will
'             be processed during each iteration.
'    Example: `N|i,1+2,i = `[F:i]` |  returns
'             "i = 1 i = 2 i = 3"
'     Notes: - You can preassign the value of the index variable to a
'              starting value other than 1 using the assignment
'              instruction as shown in the following example:
'              "`A:i=5``N|i,7,i = `[F:i]` |" will return
'              "i = 5 i = 6 i = 7"
'            - You can use different separator characters to
'              create nested loops.
'
'
'====================================================================
'
Public Function Utils_ProcessString(InputString As String, Delimiter As String)

    Dim StringToProcess As String
    Dim Char As String
    Dim FirstChar As String
```

```
Dim OutputChars As String
Dim TokenChars As String
Dim TokenResult As Variant
Dim NumCharsRead As Variant
Dim ErrValue As Integer
Dim ErrString As String
Dim Result As String
Dim ProcessChars As String
Dim DelimiterChar As String

On Error GoTo Err_Utils_ProcessString

Result = ""
StringToProcess = InputString
UTILS_Error = 0
Do While StringToProcess <> ""
  Char = ""
  OutputChars = ""
  OutputChars = Utils_ScanUpto(StringToProcess, Delimiter, 0, Char, NumCharsRead)
  StringToProcess = Mid(StringToProcess, NumCharsRead + 1)
  If StringToProcess <> "" Then
    FirstChar = Left(StringToProcess, 1)
    DelimiterChar = Mid(StringToProcess, 2, 1)
    ProcessChars = Utils_ScanUpto(Mid(StringToProcess, 3), DelimiterChar, 0, Char, ⇐
NumCharsRead)
    Select Case FirstChar
      Case Delimiter
        OutputChars = OutputChars + Delimiter
        StringToProcess = Mid(StringToProcess, 2)
      Case "." 'Exit
        StringToProcess = ""
      Case "A" 'Handle assignment
        ProcessString_Assign StringToProcess, NumCharsRead, Delimiter
      Case "?" 'Handle if/then statement
        ProcessString_Condition StringToProcess, NumCharsRead, Delimiter, DelimiterChar
      Case "L" 'Handle recordset based loops
        ProcessString_LoopRecordset ProcessChars, StringToProcess, NumCharsRead, ⇐
Delimiter
      Case "N" 'Handle index based loops
        ProcessString_LoopIndex ProcessChars, StringToProcess, NumCharsRead, Delimiter
      Case Else    'Handle direct expression
        TokenChars = Utils_ScanUpto(StringToProcess, Delimiter, 0, Char, NumCharsRead)
        StringToProcess = Mid(StringToProcess, NumCharsRead + 1)
        TokenResult = Utils_Eval(TokenChars)
        OutputChars = OutputChars & TokenResult
    End Select
  End If
  Result = Result + OutputChars
Loop

Exit_Utils_ProcessString:
  On Error Resume Next
```

continued on next page

605

continued from previous page

```
  If ErrValue <> 0 Then
    Result = Result + OutputChars + " --" & ErrString & "-- " + "<PRE>" + StringToProcess ⇐
+ "</PRE>"
  End If
  Utils_ProcessString = Result
  Exit Function

Err_Utils_ProcessString:
  ErrValue = Err
  ErrString = Error$
  Resume Exit_Utils_ProcessString

End Function

'=================================================================
' Function Utils_ScanUpto(InputString As String, Delimiters As String, MaxCharacters As ⇐
Long, MatchedDelimiter As String, NumCharsRead As Variant)
'
' Purpose: Returns the leftmost portion of a string upto a matching
'          delimiter character or upto a specified number of
'          characters, whichever happens first.
'
' Inputs
' ------
' InputString: String to scan
' DelimiterChars: List of delimiter characters to match
' MaxCharacters: Maximum number of characters to return
'
' Outputs
' -------
' MatchedDelimiter: Delimiter that was matched
' NumCharsRead: Number of characters returned
'
' Example
' -------
' Utils_ScanUpto("This is a test"," .",0,MatchChar,NumChars) returns
'   "This" with MatchChar = " " and NumChars = 4.
'
' Notes
' -----
'
' - Setting MaxCharacters to 0 does not impose any max character limit
'
'=================================================================
'
Public Function Utils_ScanUpto(InputString As String, Delimiters As String, MaxCharacters ⇐
As Long, MatchedDelimiter As String, NumCharsRead As Variant)

  Dim Char As String
  Dim i, FoundPos
```

```
  NumCharsRead = 0
  MatchedDelimiter = ""
  For i = 1 To Len(Delimiters)
    Char = Mid(Delimiters, i, 1)
    FoundPos = InStr(InputString, Char)
    If FoundPos > 0 Then
      MatchedDelimiter = Char
      If MaxCharacters > 0 And FoundPos > MaxCharacters Then FoundPos = MaxCharacters + 1
      NumCharsRead = FoundPos
      Utils_ScanUpto = Left$(InputString, FoundPos - 1)
      Exit Function
    End If
  Next
  MatchedDelimiter = ""
  FoundPos = Len(InputString)
  If MaxCharacters > 0 And FoundPos > MaxCharacters Then FoundPos = MaxCharacters
  NumCharsRead = FoundPos
  Utils_ScanUpto = Left$(InputString, FoundPos)

End Function

'===================================================================
' Function Utils_DLookup(db As Database, FieldExpression, RecordSource, Criteria,
PickRecord)
'
' Purpose: Looks up a value from a database record source.
'
' Inputs
' ------
' db: Database object representing an open database
' FieldExpression: The expression or the field name whose value
'                    is to be returned
' Recordsource: Name of the table or query that acts as the
'                  source of the records
' Criteria: A valid SQL criteria to filter the records from the
'            Recordsource
' PickRecord: Which record to look up from in case multiple matching
'              records are found. Options are: "First", "Last", and
'              "Random".
'
' Examples
' --------
' Utils_DLookup(db,"JobID","tblJB_JOBS","JobState = 'FL'", "First")
'    returns the JobID of the first job in table tblJB_JOBS whose
'    JobState field has a value of "FL".
' Utils_DLookup(db,"Trim([CompanyName])","tblJB_Companies", "", "Random")
'    returns a random company name from table tblJB_Companies after
'    applying the trim function.
'
' Notes
' -----
' - Works similar to the DLookup function provided in Access.
```

continued on next page

607

continued from previous page

```
'
'====================================================================
'
Public Function Utils_DLookup(db As Database, FieldExpression, RecordSource, Criteria,
PickRecord)

'PickRecord = "First", "Last", "Random"

   Dim SQL
   Dim CriteriaClause
   Dim rs As Recordset
   Dim RecordNumber, i

   Utils_OpenDatabase
   CriteriaClause = ""
   If Criteria <> "" Then CriteriaClause = " WHERE " & Criteria
   SQL = "Select " & FieldExpression & " As LookupValue FROM " & RecordSource & ⇐
CriteriaClause & ";"
   Set rs = db.OpenRecordset(SQL)
   If rs.EOF Then
      Utils_DLookup = Null
   Else
      Select Case PickRecord
         Case "First"
         Case "Last"
            rs.MoveLast
         Case "Random"
            rs.MoveLast
            Randomize
            RecordNumber = Int(rs.RecordCount * Rnd)      ' Generate random value between 0 and ⇐
RecordCount - 1.
            rs.MoveFirst
            For i = 1 To RecordNumber
               rs.MoveNext
            Next
      End Select
      Utils_DLookup = rs!LookupValue
   End If
   rs.Close

End Function

'====================================================================
' Function Utils_GetQueryParameter(ParameterNumber, Delimiter)
'
' Purpose: Returns the specified query parameter from the CGI query
'          string.
'
' Inputs
' ------
' ParameterNumber: Which position of the parameter to be extracted
' Delimiter: The character that separates the parameters
'
```

```
'==================================================================
'
Public Function Utils_GetQueryParameter(ParameterNumber, Delimiter)
  Utils_GetQueryParameter = Utils_GetParameter(CGI_QueryString, ParameterNumber, Delimiter)
End Function

'==================================================================
' Sub Utils_AddField(FieldName, FieldValue)
'
' Purpose: Adds a fieldname/fieldvalue tuple to the list of
'          form fields.
'
' Inputs
' ------
' FieldName: The name of the field to add
' FieldValue: Value of the field name
'
' Notes
' -----
' - Does not check for duplicate fields
'
'==================================================================
'
Public Sub Utils_AddField(FieldName, FieldValue)
  CGI_FormTuples(CGI_NumFormTuples).key = FieldName
  CGI_FormTuples(CGI_NumFormTuples).value = FieldValue
  CGI_NumFormTuples = CGI_NumFormTuples + 1
End Sub

'==================================================================
' Function Utils_Min(Value1, Value2)
' Purpose: Returns the minimum of two values
'
' Inputs
' ------
' Value1: First value (Variant)
' Value2: Second Value (Variant)
'
' Notes
' -----
' - Assumes values to be of the same types
'
'==================================================================
'
Public Function Utils_Min(Value1, Value2)
  If Value1 < Value2 Then
    Utils_Min = Value1
  Else
    Utils_Min = Value2
  End If
End Function

'==================================================================
```

continued on next page

continued from previous page

```
' Function Utils_Max(Value1, Value2)
'
' Purpose: Returns the maximum of two values
'
' Inputs
' ------
' Value1: First value (Variant)
' Value2: Second Value (Variant)
'
' Notes
' -----
' - Assumes values to be of the same types
'
'===================================================================
'
Public Function Utils_Max(Value1, Value2)

   If Value1 > Value2 Then
     Utils_Max = Value1
   Else
     Utils_Max = Value2
   End If

End Function

'===================================================================
' Private Sub Eval_RecordsetField(Variable, FieldValue, QuoteChar)
'
' Purpose: Sub procedure of UTILS_Eval function for evaluating
'          a recordset based code.
' Inputs
' ------
' Variable: The code to evaluate
'
' Outputs
' FieldValue: Current Value of the variable
' QuoteChar: " for text type variable, # for date type, and none for numeric
'
' Notes
' -----
' - Assumes values to be of the same types
'
'===================================================================
'
Private Sub Eval_RecordsetField(Variable, FieldValue, QuoteChar)
   Dim FieldName As String
   Dim Operation
   Dim RecordsetNumber
   Dim CurrentBM As String
   Dim FieldType
   Dim FieldNumber As Integer

   RecordsetNumber = Mid(Variable, 3, 1)
```

```
    Operation = Mid(Variable, 4, 1)
    FieldName = Mid(Variable, 5, Len(Variable) - 5)
    Select Case Operation
      Case "."
        FieldValue = ""
        Select Case FieldName
          Case "Next"
            UTILS_rsarray(RecordsetNumber).MoveNext
          Case "Previous"
            UTILS_rsarray(RecordsetNumber).MovePrevious
          Case "First"
            UTILS_rsarray(RecordsetNumber).MoveFirst
          Case "Last"
            UTILS_rsarray(RecordsetNumber).MoveLast
          Case "Count"
            FieldValue = UTILS_rsarray(RecordsetNumber).RecordCount
            If FieldValue > 0 And Not UTILS_rsarray(RecordsetNumber).EOF Then
              CurrentBM = UTILS_rsarray(RecordsetNumber).Bookmark
              UTILS_rsarray(RecordsetNumber).MoveLast
              FieldValue = UTILS_rsarray(RecordsetNumber).RecordCount
              UTILS_rsarray(RecordsetNumber).Bookmark = CurrentBM
            End If
          Case "EOF"
            FieldValue = UTILS_rsarray(RecordsetNumber).EOF
          Case "BOF"
            FieldValue = UTILS_rsarray(RecordsetNumber).BOF
        End Select
      Case Else
        If Operation = "/" Then
          FieldNumber = Utils_EmptyToNullField(FieldName)
          FieldType = UTILS_rsarray(RecordsetNumber)(FieldNumber).type
          FieldValue = UTILS_rsarray(RecordsetNumber)(FieldNumber)
        Else
          FieldType = UTILS_rsarray(RecordsetNumber)(FieldName).type
          FieldValue = UTILS_rsarray(RecordsetNumber)(FieldName)
        End If
        Select Case FieldType
          Case dbDate
            QuoteChar = "#"
          Case dbText, dbMemo
            QuoteChar = """"
        End Select
    End Select
End Sub

'====================================================================
' Private Sub Eval_VariableField(VariableType, Variable, FieldValue, QuoteChar)
'
' Purpose: Sub procedure of UTILS_Eval function for evaluating
'          a variable based code.
' Inputs
' ------
```

continued on next page

continued from previous page

```
' VariableType: The type of variable to evaluate: F,C,Q, or V
' Variable: The code to evaluate
'
' Outputs
' FieldValue: Current Value of the variable
' QuoteChar: " for text type variable, # for date type, and none for numeric
'
' Notes
' -----
' - Assumes values to be of the same types
'
'==================================================================
'
Private Sub Eval_VariableField(VariableType, Variable, FieldValue, QuoteChar)
  Dim FieldName As String
  Dim Operation
  Dim RecordsetNumber
  Dim CurrentBM As String
  Dim FieldType

  FieldName = Mid(Variable, 4, Len(Variable) - 4)
  Select Case VariableType
    Case "F", "V"
      FieldValue = Utils_EmptyToNullField(FieldName)
    Case "C"
      FieldValue = Utils_GetCGIVariable(FieldName)
    Case "Q"
      FieldValue = Utils_GetQueryParameter(Val(FieldName), "+")
  End Select
  If VariableType = "V" And IsNull(FieldValue) Then
    FieldValue = ""
  End If
  QuoteChar = """"
  If IsNumeric(FieldValue) Then
    QuoteChar = ""
  Else
    If IsDate(FieldValue) Then QuoteChar = "#"
  End If

End Sub

'==================================================================
' Private Sub Eval_IncludeFile(Variable, FieldValue)
'
' Purpose: Sub procedure of UTILS_Eval function for including the
'          contents of an external file
' Inputs
' ------
' Variable: The path and name of the file to be included
'
' Outputs
' FieldValue: The contents of the specified file
'
```

```
'=====================================================================
'
Private Sub Eval_IncludeFile(Variable, FieldValue)

   Dim FilePath As String
   Dim FN As Integer
   Dim MatchedDelimiter As String
   Dim NumCharsRead

   FilePath = Mid(Variable, 4, Len(Variable) - 4)
   FN = FreeFile
   Open FilePath For Input Access Read As #FN
   FieldValue = Utils_InputUpto(FN, Chr(0), 0, MatchedDelimiter, NumCharsRead)
   Close #FN

End Sub

'=====================================================================
' Function Utils_AcquireField(FieldName As String, QueryParameterNumber)
'
' Purpose: Returns the value of a given field based on the request
'          method CGI variable.
'
' Inputs
' ------
' FieldName: Name of the field whose value has to be returned
' QueryParameterNumber: Postion of the field in the query string for
'                        a get type request
'
' Notes
' -----
' - This procedure comes in handy when you sometimes pass a parameter
'   in the query string portion of a GET request or as a form field in
'   a POST request.
'
' - If the Request Method is POST then this procedure simply returns the
'   value of the specified form field.
'
' - If the Request Method is GET then this procedure does two things:
'        o returns the decoded value of the query string parameter whose
'          position is specified by the QueryParameterNumber
'        o Assigns the returned value to a form field with the specified
'          FieldName
'
' This procedure also creates another form field named [FieldName]_Coded,
' that contains the returned value in the encoded form.
'
' The encoding and decoding is done using the Utils_ConvertToQueryString
' and Utils_ConvertFromQueryString functions.
'
'=====================================================================
```

continued on next page

continued from previous page

```
'
Public Function Utils_AcquireField(FieldName As String, QueryParameterNumber)

   Dim FieldValue
   Dim CodedFieldValue

   CGI_RequestMethod = UCase$(CGI_RequestMethod)
   If CGI_RequestMethod = "POST" Then
     FieldValue = Utils_EmptyToNullField(FieldName)
     If IsNull(FieldValue) Then
       Utils_AssignField FieldName & "_Coded", ""
     Else
       Utils_AssignField FieldName & "_Coded", Utils_ConvertToQueryString(CStr(FieldValue))
     End If
   Else
     CodedFieldValue = Utils_GetQueryParameter(QueryParameterNumber, "+")
     If Not IsNull(CodedFieldValue) Then
       FieldValue = Utils_ConvertFromQueryString(CStr(CodedFieldValue))
       Utils_AssignField FieldName, FieldValue
       Utils_AssignField FieldName & "_Coded", CodedFieldValue
     Else
       Utils_AssignField FieldName, ""
       Utils_AssignField FieldName & "_Coded", ""
       FieldValue = Null
     End If
   End If
   Utils_AcquireField = FieldValue

End Function

'===================================================================
' Sub Utils_AssignField(FieldName, value)
'
' Purpose: Assigns the given value to a form field with the specified
'          FieldName
' Inputs
' ------
' FieldName: Name of the form field
' value: Value to be assigned
'
' Notes:
' ------
' If the field with the given Field name does not exist, then this
' procedure creates a new field with that name.
'
'===================================================================
Public Sub Utils_AssignField(FieldName, value)

    Dim i As Integer
    Dim FieldValue

    FieldValue = value
    If IsNull(FieldValue) Then FieldValue = ""
```

```
    For i = 0 To (CGI_NumFormTuples - 1)
        If CGI_FormTuples(i).key = FieldName Then
          CGI_FormTuples(i).value = FieldValue
          Exit Sub
        End If
    Next i
    Utils_AddField FieldName, FieldValue

End Sub


'====================================================================
' Function Utils_GetShortFormField(FieldName As String) As Variant
'
' Purpose: Returns a value of a form field without any conversion
'
' Inputs
' _____
' FieldName: Name of the form field
'
'====================================================================
Public Function Utils_GetShortFormField(FieldName As String) As Variant

    Dim i As Integer

    For i = 0 To (CGI_NumFormTuples - 1)
        If CGI_FormTuples(i).key = FieldName Then
            Utils_GetShortFormField = CGI_FormTuples(i).value
            Exit Function          ' ** DONE **
        End If
    Next i
    Utils_GetShortFormField = Null

End Function

'====================================================================
' Sub Utils_LimitRecords(rs As Recordset, Start, Limit)
'
' Purpose: Sets the record at the Start position as the current record
'          of the given recordset. Also, computes several form fields
'          based on the number of records in the recordset and the
'          specified Start and Limit parameters.
'
' Inputs
' _____
' rs: The Recordset object
' Start:Position of the record that has to be set as the current record
' Limit: Maximum number of records to be returned from the current
'        recordset
'
' Notes:
' _____
```

continued on next page

615

continued from previous page

```
' This procedure is useful when you want to return the selected records
' of the recordset in a sequence of multiple pages. For example, the first
' 10 records in the first page, the next 10 records in the second page,
' and so on.
'
' The way you achieve this sequence effect with this procedure is as
' follows:
'    1. When you send the first page as your CGI response, give a link
'       to return the second page. That link should contain two
'       parameters: 11 and 10.
'
'    2. When the user clicks this link, regenerate the recordset with all
'       the records and pass that recordset to this procedure with the
'       Start paramter set to 11 and the Limit parameter set to 10.
'
'    3. This procedure will automatically set the current record of your
'       recordset to the record at position 11. Additionally, it will
'       set the following internal form fields to help you create the
'       link for the next page (assuming the recordset contains 26 records):
'           FieldName                 Value
'           ---------                 -----
'           UTILS_LR_Start              11
'           UTILS_LR_End                20
'           UTILS_LR_Limit              10
'           UTILS_LR_CurrentLimit       10
'           UTILS_LR_PreviousStart       1
'           UTILS_LR_PreviousEnd        10
'           UTILS_LR_PreviousLimit      10
'           UTILS_LR_NextStart          21
'           UTILS_LR_NextEnd            26
'           UTILS_LR_NextLimit           6
'
'    4. You can use the values of the UTILS_LR_Start and UTILS_LR_End
'       fields to output records 11 to 20 using a For loop. You can
'       use the values of the UTILS_LR_NextStart and UTILS_LR_NextLimit
'       fields to set up a link for requesting the next page. You can
'       use the values of the UTILS_LR_PreviousStart and
'       UTILS_LR_PreviousLimit fields to set up a link for requesting the
'       previous page.
'
'===================================================================
Public Sub Utils_LimitRecords(rs As Recordset, Start, Limit)

    Const DEFAULT_RECORD_LIMIT = 10
    Dim StartRecord As Long
    Dim RecordLimit As Long
    Dim EndRecord As Long
    Dim NextRecordLimit As Long

    If rs.RecordCount = 0 Then Exit Sub
    StartRecord = 1
    RecordLimit = DEFAULT_RECORD_LIMIT
```

```
If Not IsNull(Start) Then StartRecord = Start
If Not IsNull(Limit) Then RecordLimit = Limit
rs.MoveLast
EndRecord = Utils_Min(StartRecord + RecordLimit - 1, rs.RecordCount)
rs.MoveFirst
rs.Move StartRecord - 1

Utils_AddField "UTILS_LR_Start", StartRecord
Utils_AddField "UTILS_LR_End", EndRecord
Utils_AddField "UTILS_LR_Limit", RecordLimit
Utils_AddField "UTILS_LR_CurrentLimit", EndRecord - StartRecord + 1

Utils_AddField "UTILS_LR_PreviousStart", Utils_Min(StartRecord - RecordLimit, 0)
Utils_AddField "UTILS_LR_PreviousEnd", Utils_Min(StartRecord - 1, 0)
Utils_AddField "UTILS_LR_PreviousLimit", Utils_Min(StartRecord - 1, RecordLimit)

Utils_AddField "UTILS_LR_NextStart", Utils_Min(EndRecord + 1, rs.RecordCount)
Utils_AddField "UTILS_LR_NextEnd", Utils_Min(EndRecord + RecordLimit, rs.RecordCount)
Utils_AddField "UTILS_LR_NextLimit", Utils_Min(rs.RecordCount - EndRecord, RecordLimit)

End Sub

'===================================================================
' Private Sub ProcessString_LoopRecordset(ProcessChars, StringToProcess, NumCharsRead, ⇐
Delimiter)
'
' Purpose: Sub procedure of UTILS_ProccessString procedure for
'          processing a recordset-based loop instruction
'
' Inputs
' ------
' ProcessChars: Characters forming the loop instruction (up to the ending
'               delimiter character)
' StringToProcess: String left to be processed (the loop portion + the
'                  rest of the text in the template file)
' NumCharsRead: Length of ProcessChars
' Delimiter: The "`" character
'
' Outputs
' -------
' StringToProcess
'
' An example showing how the input parameters are related:
' StringToProcess:= "R@1,EOF,ABCDEF@GHIJKL"
' ProcessChars:= "1,EOF,ABCDEF@"
' NumCharsRead:= 13 or Len(ProcessChars)
' Delimiter:= "`"
'
' Result StringToProcess after the procedure gets done
' If another loop iteration is left, then
'     StringToProcess:= "ABCDEF`R@1,EOF,ABCDEF@GHIJKL"
```

continued on next page

continued from previous page

```
' If this was the last loop iteration, then
'    StringToProcess:= "ABCDEFGHIJKL"
'
' Notes:
' This procedure uses internal form fields to maintain the state
' of the loop between iterations
'
'==================================================================
'
Private Sub ProcessString_LoopRecordset(ProcessChars, StringToProcess, NumCharsRead, ⇐
Delimiter)

  Dim RecordsetNumber As Variant
  Dim MaxLoops As Variant
  Dim i As Variant
  Dim TokenChars As String
  Dim FieldName As String
  Dim FieldNameMax As String
  Dim Char As String
  Dim CharsRead As Long

  TokenChars = ProcessChars
  'Get the recordset number used for this loop
  RecordsetNumber = CInt(Utils_ScanUpto(TokenChars, ",", 0, Char, CharsRead))
  'Get the loop termination limit
  TokenChars = Mid(TokenChars, CharsRead + 1)
  MaxLoops = Utils_ScanUpto(TokenChars, ",", 0, Char, CharsRead)
  'Get the text to iterate on
  TokenChars = Mid(TokenChars, CharsRead + 1)
  'Determine the internal form field used by this loop
  FieldName = "Index_R" & RecordsetNumber
  'The following field holds the loop termination limit
  FieldNameMax = FieldName & "_Max"
  'Get the current value of loop index form field
  i = Utils_EmptyToNullField(FieldName)
  If IsNull(i) Then 'Loop has just started (1st iteration)
    'Determine loop termination limit from the input string
    i = 1
    If MaxLoops = "EOF" Then
      MaxLoops = 2147483647
    Else
      MaxLoops = Utils_Eval(MaxLoops)
    End If
    'Assign loop termination limit to a form field. The future
    'iterations will refer to this field to determine the loop limit
    Utils_AssignField FieldNameMax, MaxLoops
  Else 'This is not the first iteration of this loop
    i = i + 1
    UTILS_rsarray(RecordsetNumber).MoveNext   'Move to the next record
    'Get loop termination limit from the form field
    MaxLoops = CLng(Utils_EmptyToNullField(FieldNameMax))
  End If
  'Store the current value of the loop index into the form field for
```

```
'future reference
Utils_AssignField FieldName, i
If Not UTILS_rsarray(RecordsetNumber).EOF And i <= MaxLoops Then
  'Loop has still more iterations to go
  StringToProcess = TokenChars & Delimiter & StringToProcess
Else
  'This was the last iteration
  StringToProcess = Mid(StringToProcess, NumCharsRead + 3)
  'Make the loop index form field empty so that another
  'recordset-based loop instruction can work properly
  Utils_AssignField FieldName, ""
End If

End Sub

'===================================================================
' Private Sub ProcessString_LoopIndex(ProcessChars, StringToProcess, NumCharsRead, ⇐
Delimiter)
'
' Purpose: Sub procedure of UTILS_ProccessString procedure for
'          processing an index-based loop instruction
'
' Inputs
' ------
' ProcessChars: Characters forming the loop instruction (upto the ending
'               delimiter character)
' StringToProcess: String left to be processed (the loop portion + the
'                  rest of the text in the template file)
' NumCharsRead: Length of ProcessChars
' Delimiter: The "`" character
'
' Outputs
' -------
' StringToProcess
'
' An example showing how the input parameters are related:
' StringToProcess:= "N@i,5,ABCDEF@GHIJKL"
' ProcessChars:= "i,5,ABCDEF@"
' NumCharsRead:= 11 or Len(ProcessChars)
' Delimiter:= "`"
'
' Result StringToProcess after the procedure gets done
' If another loop iteration is left, then
'     StringToProcess:= "ABCDEF`N@i,5,ABCDEF@GHIJKL"
' If this was the last loop iteration, then
'     StringToProcess:= "ABCDEFGHIJKL"
'
'===================================================================
'
Private Sub ProcessString_LoopIndex(ProcessChars, StringToProcess, NumCharsRead, Delimiter)

  Dim MaxLoops As Variant
```

continued on next page

continued from previous page

```
    Dim i As Variant
    Dim TokenChars As String
    Dim FieldName As String
    Dim FieldNameMax As String
    Dim Char As String
    Dim CharsRead As Long
    Dim PreviousMaxLoops As Variant

    TokenChars = ProcessChars
    'Get the name of the loop index field
    FieldName = Utils_ScanUpto(TokenChars, ",", O, Char, CharsRead)
    'Get loop termination limit
    TokenChars = Mid(TokenChars, CharsRead + 1)
    MaxLoops = Utils_ScanUpto(TokenChars, ",", O, Char, CharsRead)
    'Get the text to iterate on
    TokenChars = Mid(TokenChars, CharsRead + 1)
    'Determine the name of the form field that may hold the
    'loop termination limit
    FieldNameMax = FieldName & "_Max"
    'Get current value of the loop index field to determine which
    'iteration is being processed
    i = Utils_EmptyToNullField(FieldName)
    'Check if any loop termination limit has already been set by the
    'previous iteration
    PreviousMaxLoops = Utils_EmptyToNullField(FieldNameMax)
    If IsNull(PreviousMaxLoops) Then 'This is the first iteration
      MaxLoops = Utils_Eval(MaxLoops)  'Evaluate loop termination limit
      'Assign this limit to the form field for future reference
      Utils_AssignField FieldNameMax, MaxLoops
    Else 'This is not the first iteration
      'Get the termination limit from the form field
      MaxLoops = PreviousMaxLoops
    End If
    'Set or increment the loop index
    If IsNull(i) Then
      i = 1
    Else
      i = i + 1
    End If
    'Assign current index value to the loop index field
    Utils_AssignField FieldName, i
    MaxLoops = CLng(MaxLoops)
    If UTILS_Error = O And i <= MaxLoops Then 'Not the last iteration
      StringToProcess = TokenChars & Delimiter & StringToProcess
    Else 'Last iteration
      StringToProcess = Mid(StringToProcess, NumCharsRead + 3)
      Utils_AssignField FieldName, ""
      UTILS_Error = O
    End If

End Sub
```

```
'===================================================================
' Sub ProcessString_Condition(StringToProcess As String, NumCharsRead, Delimiter,
DelimiterChar As String)
'
' Purpose: Sub procedure of UTILS_ProcessString function for
'          processing a condition
'
' Inputs
' ------
' DelimiterChar: Delimiter character used for the condition, generally (^)
'
' Inputs and Outputs
' ------------------
' StringToProcess: Text left to be processed
' NumCharsRead: Number of characters read till the next occurrence of
'               the delimiter char
' Delimiter: The main delimiter character (`)
'
' Notes
' -----
' - Condition is considered false if it evaluates to "<!--Null-->","",
'   "0","False", or "No", otherwise it is considered true
'
'===================================================================
'
Public Sub ProcessString_Condition(StringToProcess As String, NumCharsRead, Delimiter, ⇐
DelimiterChar As String)

   Dim TokenChars As String
   Dim Condition As String
   Dim TrueExpression As String
   Dim FalseExpression As String
   Dim ConditionResult As String
   Dim Char As String
   Dim StoreError As Variant

   StringToProcess = Mid(StringToProcess, 3)
   Condition = Utils_ScanUpto(StringToProcess, DelimiterChar, 0, Char, NumCharsRead)
   StringToProcess = Mid(StringToProcess, NumCharsRead + 1)
   TrueExpression = Utils_ScanUpto(StringToProcess, DelimiterChar, 0, Char, NumCharsRead)
   StringToProcess = Mid(StringToProcess, NumCharsRead + 1)
   FalseExpression = Utils_ScanUpto(StringToProcess, DelimiterChar, 0, Char, NumCharsRead)
   StringToProcess = Mid(StringToProcess, NumCharsRead + 1)
   StoreError = UTILS_Error
   UTILS_Error = 0
   ConditionResult = CStr(Utils_Eval(Condition))
   If UTILS_Error <> 0 Then
      StringToProcess = ConditionResult & StringToProcess
   Else
      UTILS_Error = StoreError
      Select Case ConditionResult
        Case "<!--Null-->", "", "0", "False", "No"
           StringToProcess = FalseExpression & StringToProcess
```

continued on next page

continued from previous page

```
      Case Else
         StringToProcess = TrueExpression & StringToProcess
   End Select
End If

End Sub

'===================================================================
' Sub ProcessString_Assign(StringToProcess As String, NumCharsRead, Delimiter As String)
'
' Purpose: Sub procedure of UTILS_ProcessString function for
'          processing an assignment instruction
'
' Inputs and Outputs
' ------------------
' StringToProcess: Text left to be processed
' NumCharsRead: Number of characters read till the next occurrence of
'               the delimiter char
' Delimiter: The main delimiter character (`)
'===================================================================
'
Public Sub ProcessString_Assign(StringToProcess As String, NumCharsRead, Delimiter As ⇐
String)

   Dim Char As String
   Dim TokenChars As String
   Dim TokenResult As Variant
   Dim FieldName As String

   'Get the name of the form field to assign
   TokenChars = Utils_ScanUpto(StringToProcess, "=", 0, Char, NumCharsRead)
   FieldName = Mid(TokenChars, 3)
   'Read the expression whose result has to be assigned to this field
   StringToProcess = Mid(StringToProcess, NumCharsRead + 1)
   TokenChars = Utils_ScanUpto(StringToProcess, Delimiter, 0, Char, NumCharsRead)
   'Remove this assignment statement from the StringToProcess variable
   StringToProcess = Mid(StringToProcess, NumCharsRead + 1)
   'Evaluate the expression
   TokenResult = Utils_Eval(TokenChars)
   'Store the expression result in the specified field name
   Utils_AssignField FieldName, TokenResult

End Sub

'===================================================================
' Function UTILS_GetKeyword(KeywordString, KeywordDelimiters, KeywordNumber)
'
' Purpose: Returns the specified keyword from the KeywordString based on
' specified set of keyword deimiters
'
' Inputs
' ------
' KeywordString: String containing a list of keywords
```

```
' KeywordDelimiters: String containing the set of delimiter characters
' KeywordNumber: The position of the kwyword being sought
'
' Example:
' UTILS_GetKeyword(" Word1 Word2 Word3"," .;:",2) returns Word2
' UTILS_GetKeyword(" Word1 Word2 Word3"," .;:",4) returns Null
'
' Notes:
' Returns Null if no keyword found for the specified position
'
'====================================================================
'
Public Function UTILS_GetKeyword(KeywordString, KeywordDelimiters, KeywordNumber)
  Dim Ch As String
  Dim KeyWord As String
  Dim length As Long
  Dim Start As Long
  Dim i As Long
  Dim Description
  Dim Delimiters
  Dim CurrentKeywordNumber

  CurrentKeywordNumber = 0
  UTILS_GetKeyword = Null
  Delimiters = KeywordDelimiters & Chr(13) & Chr(10)
  Description = Trim(KeywordString)
  length = Len(Description)
  If length = 0 Then Exit Function
  Start = 1
  For i = 1 To length
    Ch = Mid(Description, i, 1)
    If InStr(Delimiters, Ch) > 0 Then
      KeyWord = Trim(Mid(Description, Start, i - Start))
      If KeyWord <> "" And Not IsNull(KeyWord) Then
        CurrentKeywordNumber = CurrentKeywordNumber + 1
        If CurrentKeywordNumber = KeywordNumber Then
          UTILS_GetKeyword = KeyWord
          Exit Function
        End If
      End If
      Start = i + 1
    End If
  Next
  If Start < i Then
    KeyWord = Trim(Mid(Description, Start, i - Start))
    If KeyWord <> "" And Not IsNull(KeyWord) Then
        CurrentKeywordNumber = CurrentKeywordNumber + 1
        If CurrentKeywordNumber = KeywordNumber Then
          UTILS_GetKeyword = KeyWord
          Exit Function
        End If
    End If
  End If

End Function
```

C

INTERNET EXPLORER 3.0: A FIELD GUIDE

A new day dawned. The sun reached its fingers over the digital outback. The mighty Navigators (*Netscapus navigatorus*)—a species that reproduced like rabbits, and ran nearly as fast—covered the landscape. Yonder, on a cliff that seemed to be beyond the horizon, a trembling new creature looked out over the Internet jungle. This strange new creature, calling itself the Explorer (*Microsoftus interneticus explorus*), sniffed around, considering whether it should enter the fragile ecosystem. Netscape gators gnashed their teeth, but the Explorers were not daunted. Explorer was a formidable beast. It became a part of the jungle and thrived. And even though it began as a mere pup, it evolved, and it evolved and it evolved.

Now the jungle is rife with two intelligent species.

What follows is a guide to domesticating Internet Explorer. You will learn how to care for your Explorer, and even how to teach it tricks. Before long, you shall find truth behind the old axiom that the Explorer is man's (and woman's) best friend.

INTRODUCING EXPLORER TO YOUR ECOSYSTEM

Whether you're running Windows NT or Windows 95, installing Explorer is easy. Explorer's own installation program makes setup a breeze, and you only need to select one file on the CD-ROM (called MSIE30M.EXE) to launch this installer. Make sure the CD-ROM included with this book is in the CD-ROM drive; then, depending upon your system, follow the directions below for either Windows 95 or Windows NT.

Windows 95 Installation

1. Click on the Start button in the lower-left corner of your screen.

2. Click on the Run... option in the Start menu. A dialog box similar to the one shown in Figure C-1 appears.

3. Using the Run dialog box, type in a pathname and specify the location of the Explorer installation program. MSIE30M.EXE is in the CD's \Explorer directory, so if your CD-ROM drive is designated as D:, you'd type

    `d:\explorer\msie30m.exe`

NOTE: If your CD-ROM drive has a different designation letter, type in the appropriate drive designation letter in place of D:.

4. After typing the proper pathname, click the *OK* button to start the Explorer's installation program. Depending upon your system, it may take a moment to load.

5. Once the installation program loads, follow the on-screen prompts to set up Explorer on your computer.

Windows NT Installation

1. Click on *File* in the main menu bar at the top of your screen.

2. Click on the Run... option in the *File* menu. A dialog box similar to the one shown in Figure C-2 appears.

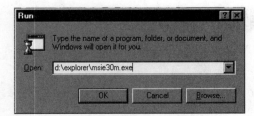

Figure C-1 The Windows 95 Run dialog box

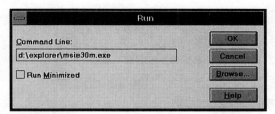

Figure C–2 The Windows NT Run dialog box

3. Using the Run dialog box, type in a pathname and specify the location of the Explorer installation program. MSIE30M.EXE is in the CD's \Explorer directory, so if your CD-ROM drive is designated as D:, you'd type:

```
d:\explorer\msie30m.exe
```

NOTE: If your CD-ROM drive has a different designation letter, type in the appropriate drive designation letter in place of D:.

4. After typing the proper pathname, click the *OK* button to start the Explorer's installation program. Depending upon your system, it may take a moment to load.

5. Once the installation program loads, follow the on-screen prompts to set up Explorer on your computer.

Once you've run the installation, you'll need to restart your system. You can then click on the Internet icon on your desktop. If you've already selected an Internet provider with Windows dial-up networking, you'll be connected. If not, you'll be walked through the dial-in process. You'll need to enter the phone number of your Internet provider, your modem type, and other related information. Ultimately, you'll be taken to Microsoft's home page, where you can register your Explorer and find out about its latest features.

NOTE: The Explorer is a constantly evolving animal. For the latest updates, plug-ins, and versions, be sure to regularly check out Microsoft's neck of the woods at *http://www.microsoft.com/ie/*.

Explorer Components

Explorer is more than a plain-Jane Web browser. As you work through the installation, you'll be able to choose a variety of components. You can select the following add-ons:

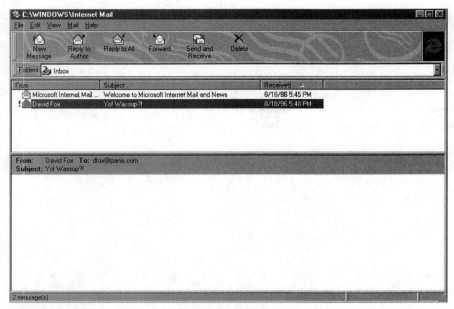

Figure C-3 The Internet Mail main window

Internet Mail—This is a comprehensive e-mail package. Using simple icons, you can write and read your mail off-line, and then log on quickly to send and receive your latest batch of correspondence. See Figure C-3.

Internet News—This is a window that lets you browse through thousands of news-groups, read through the threads, and post your own messages. The News system is very easy to use. You can easily keep track of your favorite topics and automatically update with the latest news.

ActiveMovie—This feature of Explorer lets you watch all sorts of video clips—MPEG, AVI, and QuickTime formats. It even supports a special streaming version of video that downloads movies as you watch them, letting you view video with little delay. The ActiveMovie system also lets you listen to all the popular formats of audio files—AU, WAV, MIDI, MPEG, and AIFF. This makes it easy to add background sound to Web pages.

VRML Support—This feature is a separate module that lets you download and coast through Virtual Reality Modeling Language worlds. This allows you to explore true 3D landscapes and objects.

🦔 NetMeeting—This is a full-featured package that lets you hold entire meetings over the Internet. You can chat with one person—or with dozens. If you have a microphone, you can use the Internet phone feature to hold voice conversations with other people. You can share applications—for example, you and a client can edit the same word processing document together. A whiteboard feature lets you draw on a "digital blackboard" that can be updated live across the Internet.

🦔 HTML Layout Control—This tool lets Web page publishers create spiffy versions of HTML pages, the way professional designers would lay out a magazine page or a newspaper. Designers can choose exactly where to place elements within a Web page. You can make objects transparent and layer objects over each other, which helps make a Web page eye-catching yet uncluttered.

THE NATURE OF THE BEAST

Internet Explorer features very up-to-date HTML. It supports HTML 3.2, including the following:

🦔 Frames—These break up the Web page window into several areas. For example, you can keep an unchanging row of navigation controls along the top of the page while constantly updating the bottom. You can use *borderless frames,* which split up the page without making it seem split. A special type of frame known as the *floating frame* lets you view one Web page within another.

🦔 Cascading Style Sheets—These allow your Web sites to have the same general look and feel.

🦔 Tables—You can create or view all sorts of fancy tables, with or without graphics, borders, and columns.

🦔 Embedded Objects—Internet Explorer can handle Java applets, ActiveX controls, and even Netscape plug-ins. These objects are discussed later in the "Symbiotic Partners" section of this appendix.

🦔 Fonts—Explorer supports many fonts, allowing Web pages to have a variety of exciting designs.

From the get-go, Internet Explorer has included a few special bells and whistles. For example, it's easy to create and view marquees across Web pages. This lets you scroll a long, attention-drawing message, similar to a tickertape, that puts a great deal of information in a very small space.

TRAINING THE EXPLORER

By its very nature, the Explorer is a friendly beast. You can access the full range of the Explorer's talents by pushing its buttons. These buttons, which appear in the toolbar at the top of the screen as depicted in Figure C-4, are as follows:

Back—Use this to return to the Web page you've just come from. This will help you retrace your steps as you take Explorer through the Internet maze.

Forward—Use this after you've used the Back button to jump forward again to the page from which you came.

Stop—If a Web page is taking too long to load, press this button. Any text and graphics will immediately stop downloading.

Refresh—If your Web page is missing some graphics or if you've previously stopped its loading using the Stop button, you can reload it using Refresh.

Home—This takes you to your preset home page. By default, this is Microsoft's main Web page, but you can set your home to any you'd like. See the "Taming the Beast" section.

Search—This takes you to a special page that allows you to search for a Web page using a number of cool search engines. See the "Hunting Skills" section.

Favorites—This button lets you access a list of your favorite Web sites. See the "Favorite Haunts" section.

Print—This allows you to print out the current Web page, allowing you to keep a perfect hard copy of it.

Font—Find yourself squinting at a Web page? Just click here to zoom in. The font size will grow several degrees. Too big now? Click a few more times, and the size will shrink once again.

Mail—This will launch the Internet Mail program, which allows you to send and receive e-mail and to access newsgroups.

PLAYING FETCH

Your Explorer is a devoted friend. It can scamper anywhere within the Internet, bringing back exactly what you desire.

If you know where you want to go, just type the URL into Explorer's Address box at the top of the screen. If you like, you can omit the *http://* prefix. The Web page will be loaded up. You can also search for a page or load up a previously saved page.

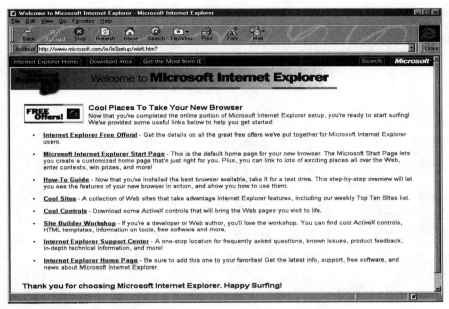

Figure C-4 A cosmetic look at Explorer

You can now click on any *hyperlink*—an underlined or colored word or picture—to zoom to that associated Web page or Internet resource. Some hyperlinked graphics may not be obvious. Explorer will tell you when you are positioned over a valid hyperlink because the cursor will change into a pointing finger. Continue following these links as long as you like. It's not uncommon to start researching knitting needles and end up reading about porcupines.

NOTE: If you're an aspiring Web page writer, you might want to take a peek at the HTML source code to see how that page was created. Just select View, Source.

HUNTING SKILLS

If you want to find Web pages dealing with a specific category, the Explorer makes it easy to find them. Click the Search button. The Search screen will appear, as in Figure C-5. You can search for more than Web pages. With Explorer, it's easy to find:

 Phone numbers, zip codes, and addresses.

 Information on a number of topics—health, home, education, consumer affairs, finance, weather, sports, travel, and so on.

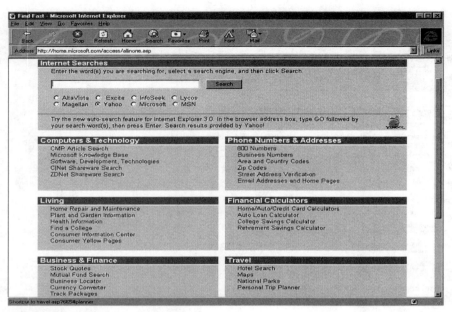

Figure C-5 The search screen

 References—maps, a dictionary, a thesaurus, quotations, and an encyclopedia.

On-line books, newspapers, and magazines.

TIP: You can also quickly hunt for any idea, word, or category. Simply type GO in the Address box at the top of the screen, followed by the word or phrase you want to search for.

FAVORITE HAUNTS

It's easy to keep track of the Web pages you visit most. When you want to save a page for future reference, simply click the Favorites button or choose the Favorites menu item. Select the Add To Favorite option. The current Web page will now be added to the list of favorites, which appears each time you click on the Favorites button or menu.

After a while, your list of favorites will get long and cluttered. It's simple to keep track of huge lists of favorites—just put them into separate folders. Organize your Favorites, as shown in Figure C-6, by selecting Favorites, Organize Favorites.

To create a new folder, click on the New Folder icon (the folder with the little glint on it) at the top of the window. Now drag and drop your Web page bookmarks into the appropriate folders. You can also move, rename, or delete a folder by selecting it and using the corresponding buttons at the bottom of the screen.

 TIP: You can even include or attach a favorite Web document within an e-mail message, the way you would attach any other file.

NOTE: On Windows systems, the Favorites list is actually a folder within your Windows directory. This reflects a Microsoft trend—treating the entire World Wide Web as just another folder to explore on your desktop. Eventually, you'll be able to drag and drop documents across the Internet as easily as you would within your own hard drive.

MEMORY

Internet Explorer keeps track of every Web page you visit. This is kept in a vast history list. You can view the entire history list, in chronological order, by clicking the View History button. Just click on any page you'd like to revisit.

NOTE: The history list is cleared every 20 days—you can set this value within the Navigation properties sheets.

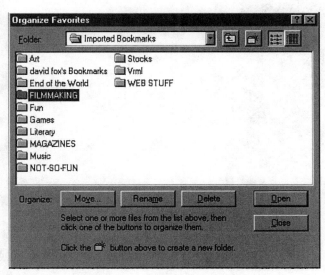

Figure C–6 Organizing the Favorites list

TAMING THE BEAST

Now that you and your Explorer are getting acquainted, why not tame it so that it acts and looks exactly like you want? Select View, Options and pick a tab at the top of the window to customize the following properties:

General—The General properties sheet is illustrated in Figure C-7. Since multimedia content (such as sounds, movies, and graphics) takes longer to load in Web pages, you can choose to not load certain media types. You can also easily customize the color of the text and hyperlinks. Finally, you can decide how little or how much information appears in your toolbar.

NOTE: You can change the size and position of your toolbar simply by clicking on its borders and dragging it to a desired location.

Connection—You can adjust your connections settings, as shown in Figure C-8, by clicking on this tab. This lets you choose your Internet provider. If you're connecting to the Internet through a network firewall, you can also set your proxy server information here.

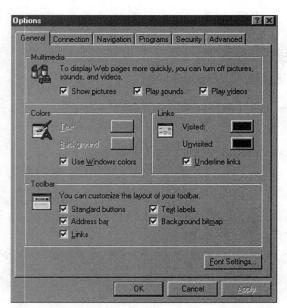

Figure C–7 The General properties sheet

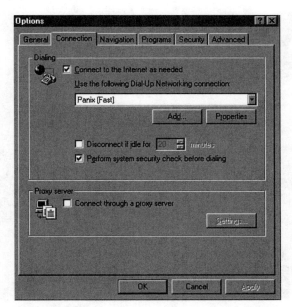

Figure C–8 The Connection properties sheet

> Navigation—You can customize which page you'd like to use as your starting home page. Just enter its URL in the Address box here.

> Programs—This allows you to set which programs you'd like to use for e-mail and for Usenet news. By default, you can use Microsoft's Internet Mail and Internet News, which are included with Explorer. You can also tell Explorer how to handle various types of files by selecting the File Types button. It allows you to designate which program or plug-in should be launched whenever Explorer comes across various unfamiliar file formats.

> Security—You are able to customize how securely documents will be handled by Explorer. If you want to keep your computer extremely safe, you may tell Explorer not to download possible security risks such as ActiveX controls, Java applets, or other plug-ins. Another nice feature is a Content Advisor. Click on Settings; the Content Advisor window will appear as in Figure C-9. You may now decide which Web pages to skip based on Adult Language, Nudity, Sex, or Violence. Many questionable Web pages are written with certain tags so that the pages can be weeded out by people who don't want to see them. This is a great option to use if your kids surf the Internet, or if your prurient sensibilities are easily offended. To turn ratings on, click on the Enable Ratings button. You can also lock this window with a password.

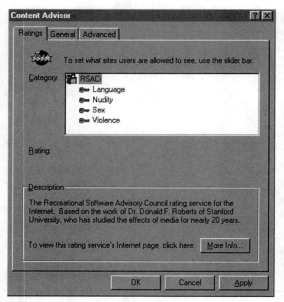

Figure C–9 The Content Advisor window

Advanced—This properties sheet lets you customize when Internet Explorer will issue warnings. This is useful if you deal with sensitive information and want to know which Web pages are secure and which are not. You can also set a number of other advanced Java and Security options here.

SYMBIOTIC PARTNERS

Explorer includes many of the latest Web technologies. These make your Web pages sing, dance, and even act as entire applications. The line between what a computer can do in general and what a computer can do over the Internet is thinning.

ActiveX

Microsoft's proprietary ActiveX technology lets you drop *controls* into your Web pages. Controls are software components such as specialized buttons, input forms, graphics viewers, sound players, and so on.

When you load a page with an ActiveX control, Explorer will check if you already have that control on your system. If not, you'll be asked whether you'd like to download it. You'll be told whether the control has been authenticated by Microsoft. If the control is secure, it'll automatically be downloaded and installed for you. The resulting Web page may look more like a software program than a Web page. Don't be surprised to find all new types of buttons, such as the up and down arrow controls in Figure C-10.

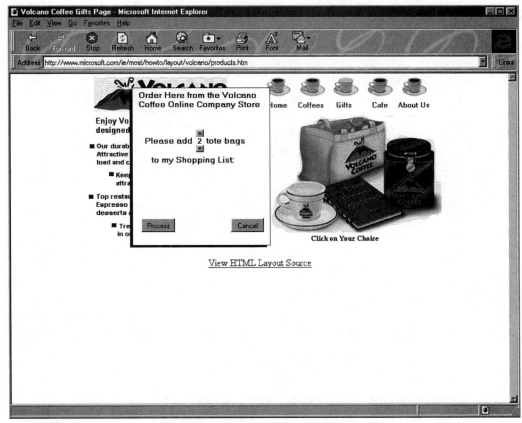

Figure C-10 Loading a page with an ActiveX control

Scripts

Internet Explorer allows Web page writers to add different types of scripts right into the source code of the Web page itself. This means you can get instantaneous feedback and control of the Web browser, ActiveX controls, Java applets, and other plug-ins. This makes interactivity fast and easy. Internet Explorer supports Visual Basic, Scripting Edition and JavaScript languages.

Java

Finally, Explorer fully supports the popular Java language. Java is a programming language that lets you write full applications that run directly within your Web browser. Java is great for writing games, graphics demonstrations, databases, spreadsheets, and much more.

Total Mastery

Now that you are fully in control of Explorer, you can learn, work, and have fun using it with the greatest of ease. Wandering through the Internet faster than ever, you are ready to investigate new paths of adventure with your trusty, obedient Explorer guiding you every step of the way.

INDEX

B

N

Q

Books have a substantial influence on the destruction of the forests of the Earth. For example, it takes 17 trees to produce one ton of paper. A first printing of 30,000 copies of a typical 480-page book consumes 108,000 pounds of paper, which will require 918 trees!

Waite Group Press™ is against the clear-cutting of forests and supports reforestation of the Pacific Northwest of the United States and Canada, where most of this paper comes from. As a publisher with several hundred thousand books sold each year, we feel an obligation to give back to the planet. We will therefore support organizations that seek to preserve the forests of planet Earth.

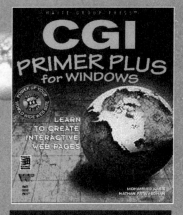

This is a legal agreement between you, the end user and purchaser, and The Waite Group®, Inc., and the authors of the programs contained in the disk. By opening the sealed disk package, you are agreeing to be bound by the terms of this Agreement. If you do not agree with the terms of this Agreement, promptly return the unopened disk package and the accompanying items (including the related book and other written material) to the place you obtained them for a refund.

SOFTWARE LICENSE

1.   The Waite Group, Inc. grants you the right to use one copy of the enclosed software programs (the programs) on a single computer system (whether a single CPU, part of a licensed network, or a terminal connected to a single CPU). Each concurrent user of the program must have exclusive use of the related Waite Group, Inc. written materials.

2.   The program, including the copyrights in each program, is owned by the respective author and the copyright in the entire work is owned by The Waite Group, Inc. and they are therefore protected under the copyright laws of the United States and other nations, under international treaties. You may make only one copy of the disk containing the programs exclusively for backup or archival purposes, or you may transfer the programs to one hard disk drive, using the original for backup or archival purposes. You may make no other copies of the programs, and you may make no copies of all or any part of the related Waite Group, Inc. written materials.

3.   You may not rent or lease the programs, but you may transfer ownership of the programs and related written materials (including any and all updates and earlier versions) if you keep no copies of either, and if you make sure the transferee agrees to the terms of this license.

4.   You may not decompile, reverse engineer, disassemble, copy, create a derivative work, or otherwise use the programs except as stated in this Agreement.

GOVERNING LAW

This Agreement is governed by the laws of the State of California.

LIMITED WARRANTY

The following warranties shall be effective for 90 days from the date of purchase: (i) The Waite Group, Inc. warrants the enclosed disk to be free of defects in materials and workmanship under normal use; and (ii) The Waite Group, Inc. warrants that the programs, unless modified by the purchaser, will substantially perform the functions described in the documentation provided by The Waite Group, Inc. when operated on the designated hardware and operating system. The Waite Group, Inc. does not warrant that the programs will meet purchaser's requirements or that operation of a program will be uninterrupted or error-free. The program warranty does not cover any program that has been altered or changed in any way by anyone other than The Waite Group, Inc. The Waite Group, Inc. is not responsible for problems caused by changes in the operating characteristics of computer hardware or computer operating systems that are made after the release of the programs, nor for problems in the interaction of the programs with each other or other software.

THESE WARRANTIES ARE EXCLUSIVE AND IN LIEU OF ALL OTHER WARRANTIES OF MERCHANTABILITY OR FITNESS FOR A PARTICULAR PURPOSE OR OF ANY OTHER WARRANTY, WHETHER EXPRESS OR IMPLIED.

EXCLUSIVE REMEDY

The Waite Group, Inc. will replace any defective disk without charge if the defective disk is returned to The Waite Group, Inc. within 90 days from date of purchase.

This is Purchaser's sole and exclusive remedy for any breach of warranty or claim for contract, tort, or damages.

LIMITATION OF LIABILITY

THE WAITE GROUP, INC. AND THE AUTHORS OF THE PROGRAMS SHALL NOT IN ANY CASE BE LIABLE FOR SPECIAL, INCIDENTAL, CONSEQUENTIAL, INDIRECT, OR OTHER SIMILAR DAMAGES ARISING FROM ANY BREACH OF THESE WARRANTIES EVEN IF THE WAITE GROUP, INC. OR ITS AGENT HAS BEEN ADVISED OF THE POSSIBILITY OF SUCH DAMAGES.

THE LIABILITY FOR DAMAGES OF THE WAITE GROUP, INC. AND THE AUTHORS OF THE PROGRAMS UNDER THIS AGREEMENT SHALL IN NO EVENT EXCEED THE PURCHASE PRICE PAID.

COMPLETE AGREEMENT

This Agreement constitutes the complete agreement between The Waite Group, Inc. and the authors of the programs, and you, the purchaser.

Some states do not allow the exclusion or limitation of implied warranties or liability for incidental or consequential damages, so the above exclusions or limitations may not apply to you. This limited warranty gives you specific legal rights; you may have others, which vary from state to state.

SATISFACTION REPORT CARD

Please fill out this card if you wish to know of future updates to
Web Database Construction Kit or to receive our catalog.

t Name: _____   Last Name: _____

Street Address: _____

City: _____   State: _____   Zip: _____

E-mail Address _____

Daytime Telephone: (___) _____

Date product was acquired: Month _____ Day _____ Year _____   Your Occupation: _____

Overall, how would you rate *Web Database Construction Kit*?

☐ Excellent   ☐ Very Good   ☐ Good
☐ Fair   ☐ Below Average ☐ Poor

What did you like MOST about this book? _____
_____
_____

What did you like LEAST about this book? _____
_____
_____

Please describe any problems you may have encountered with installing or using the disk: _____
_____

How did you use this book (problem-solver, tutorial, reference...)?
_____

What is your level of computer expertise?

☐ New   ☐ Dabbler   ☐ Hacker
☐ Power User   ☐ Programmer   ☐ Experienced Professional

What computer languages are you familiar with? _____
_____

Please describe your computer hardware:

Computer _____   Hard disk _____
5.25" disk drives _____   3.5" disk drives _____
Video card _____   Monitor _____
Printer _____   Peripherals _____
Sound Board _____   CD ROM _____

Where did you buy this book?

☐ Bookstore (name): _____
☐ Discount store (name): _____
☐ Computer store (name): _____
☐ Catalog (name): _____
☐ Direct from WGP   ☐ Other _____

What price did you pay for this book? _____

What influenced your purchase of this book?

☐ Recommendation   ☐ Advertisement
☐ Magazine review   ☐ Store display
☐ Mailing   ☐ Book's format
☐ Reputation of Waite Group Press   ☐ Other

How many computer books do you buy each year? _____

How many other Waite Group books do you own? _____

What is your favorite Waite Group book? _____
_____

Is there any program or subject you would like to see Waite Group Press cover in a similar approach? _____
_____

Additional comments? _____
_____
_____

Please send to: Waite Group Press
                        200 Tamal Plaza
                        Corte Madera, CA 94925

☐ **Check here for a free Waite Group catalog**

BEFORE YOU OPEN THE DISK OR CD-ROM PACKAGE ON THE FACING PAGE, CAREFULLY READ THE LICENSE AGREEMENT.

Opening this package indicates that you agree to abide by the license agreement found in the back of this book. If you do not agree with it, promptly return the unopened disk package (including the related book) to the place you obtained them for a refund.